Bismarck and the
Creation of the
Second Reich

Bismarck and the Creation of the Second Reich

Friedrich Darmstaedter
with a new introduction by Eda Sagarra

Transaction Publishers
New Brunswick (U.S.A.) and London (U.K.)

Library of Congress Catalog Number: 2008017406

ISBN: 978-1-4128-0783-8
Printed in the United States of America

Library of Congress Cataloging-in-Publication Data

Darmstaedter, Friedrich, b. 1883.
   Bismarck and the creation of the Second Reich / Friedrich Darmstaedter.
      p. cm.
   First published: London : Methuen, 1948.
   Includes bibliographical references and index.
   ISBN 978-1-4128-0783-8 (alk. paper)
   1. Bismarck, Otto, Fürst von, 1815-1898. 2. Political culture--Germany--History--19th century. I. Title.

DD218.D27 2008
943.08'3092--dc22
                                                            2008017406

BISMARCK
AS PRUSSIAN PRIME MINISTER, 1870

TO

MRS. MARGIT KOHON

CONTENTS

ILLUSTRATIONS

*Photographs supplied by
University Library, Cambridge*

INTRODUCTION TO THE TRANSACTION EDITION

Friedrich Darmstaedter, whose study of Bismarck appeared just sixty years ago, was not a historian but a lawyer by training and profession. He had been a lecturer in Heidelberg, then as now one of Germany's leading universities, before going into exile from Hitler's Third Reich. His short monograph covered Bismarck's early years and career up to a defining moment in German history: 1871. As in the case of Erich Eyck before him, the author of the three-volume critical *Bismarck. Life and Work* (1941–44),[1] which was written and published during the war years in Zurich, Darmstaedter's study was the product of reflection in exile. In one sense, namely in the systematic character of his challenge to the cult of the founding father of modern Germany, Erich Eyck had broken new ground in Bismarck biography. Like Darmstaedter a lawyer, Eyck wrote as a disappointed liberal, for whom Bismarck destroyed the Germany that might-have-been, a Germany in the tradition of Western European liberalism. To his contemporaries among German historians, notably the influential Hans Rothfels, author of more than a dozen publications on Bismarck, among them an edition of his speeches and letters, the particular merit of Eyck's work lay in its being the first full-length biography of Bismarck the man and his career. However, Eyck's vision of this "other Germany" was, in Rothfels' view, simply utopian.[2] In the English-speaking world of the 1950s and 1960s, Eyck's intimate knowledge and understanding of the primary sources and of constitutional and administrative matters, together with his critical stance, gave his study the status of a standard work. Published in English in an abbreviated edition in 1950, Eyck's *Bismarck and the German Empire*[3] shaped judgement of the German Chancellor in North America and Britain long before the de-mythologizing of Bismarck by younger German historians took off in the late 1960s. The importance of Eyck's *Life* in addressing the issue of continuity in German history, and in the historiography of German nationalism, of the Second Empire and its founder, Otto von Bismarck, remains uncontested. Its author's ideological stance has, however, inevitably dated his work.

Bismarck and the Creation of the Second Reich, while more modest in length[4] and scope, formed part of, and was an early contribution to, the debate on the person of Bismarck and his responsibility for subsequent events which has endured for almost half a century. In his short introduction Darmstaedter declares that he only encountered Eyck's work when he was "well advanced" in the writing of his own (xii). While broadly in agreement with Eyck's position, he stresses that his work was specifically directed at "a restricted section of the reading public, the English-speaking world," and that its perspective was quite specifically that of Germany's collapse in 1945, which post-dated Eyck's final volume by a year. Part of the context of Darmstaedter's work was the publication, just one year after the collapse of Hitler's thousand-year Reich, of an epoch-making book-long essay: *The German Catastrophe* by the German historian of ideas, Friedrich Meinecke, in which he held modern German history to account.[5] Thus in choosing the German term "Reich" rather than "Empire" for his title, Darmstaedter was clearly making a polemical point. His is a political biography, with little or no reference to those areas which feature so prominently in Bismarck biographies and studies of subsequent generations, namely society, the economy, and culture. He draws, as Eyck had done in greater detail, on the substantial body of official documents of the Bismarck years, the bulk of which were published after the fall of the German Empire in 1918, as part of the Weimar Republic's legacy to the nation,[6] and on Bismarck's own inimitable voice in his speeches and correspondence.[7] One of its merits for students today is the author's use of older Bismarck biographies and the reminiscences of contemporaries, which are often forgotten in the voluminous mass of modern and contemporary Bismarck studies. Darmstaedter's factual tone and fluent style makes the distant world of European politics and diplomacy, which dominated much of the history writing of his time, easily accessible to the modern reader. However, the ideological message informing the text is clearly evident, programmatically, not to say polemically, set out in the words of his *Introduction* (xii):

> Does not the collapse of his work fifty-five years after he left the stage compel us to doubt his right to be called 'the greatest man of the age'?

And in occasionally emotive language he describes what is left of that much-vaunted legacy as "pitiable political plants which at present grow on the soil of what was once was Bismarck's Reich...artificial flowers, for they are not the expression of political strength but of political impotence" (x). At the heart of his argument lies the alleged relationship between Bismarck's "creation" and subsequent cataclysmic events which, with no doubt unconscious irony, he describes in biological metaphors:

> The question with which we are mainly concerned is whether in Bismarck's creation of the Reich the essential germs of the disintegration which took place in 1945 were not only simply latent, but can be clearly discerned....

In the Third Reich, he goes on to declare:

> life in the state was not only likened to the struggle for survival in the animal world, but the individuals composing the state were actually made to accept this struggle as an ethical ideal.

Though we find the seed of all this in Bismarck's work, the Second Reich, it is in the Third Reich that we find the devilish distortion that was its fruit.

One of National Socialism's many victims among her academics and legal professionals, Darmstaedter focuses on the figure of Bismarck rather than "his times."[8] The appearance of his monograph coincided with the centenary of the failed Revolution of 1848,[9] the celebration of which marked the beginning of a long process of reflection on the consequences of that failure for the subsequent development of Germany in the era of nationalism and imperialism. Darmstaedter ascribes to the Chancellor a major role in the "death of liberal Germany," prompting Rothfels' somewhat impatient stricture that many of the liberal and democratic "heroes" of Bismarck's day, such as Waldeck, had nursed rather more expansionist aspirations than the Prussian prime minister. Rothfels, who himself had been expelled in 1934 from his chair of history at Königsberg by the National Socialists, went on to quote at length the reviewer of *Bismarck and the Creation of the Second Reich* in the *London Times*, who questioned the notion of making Bismarck solely responsible for all the destructive forces subsequently released in Germany.[10] Today's reader could argue that the historical interest of Darmstaedter's work lies precisely in recapturing the atmosphere of the immediate postwar years, when historical debate was informed by tensions and fears about the stability of Germany and Europe, on the very eve of the founding of what has proved one of postwar Europe's most successful creations: the Federal Republic of Germany. Moreover, when we encounter, more particularly towards the end of the book, numerous references to Bismarck as "dictator,"[11] a position no-one would accept today, we are in fact witnessing the anger of those German intellectuals whose homeland had been destroyed by the Third Reich and who sought one explanation in the notion of Bismarck's "culpability."

After Eyck and Darmstaedter, the person of Bismarck dominated the historiography of mid- and later nineteenth-century Germany for many years to come. In Germany, the tradition of *"Männer machen Geschichte"* died hard, namely that history, in the words of Thomas Carlyle in his much-quoted *On Heroes, Hero Worship and the Heroic in History* (1841), is the history of great men.[12] While a conservative historian such as Arnold Oskar Meyer, writing his posthumously published *Bismarck. The Man and the Statesman* during the Third Reich, could subscribe to the cult of Bismarck as Germany's greatest statesman and nation-builder, pointing to the contrast with the current masters of German destiny,[13] those German historians who wrote on the subject in the context of the collapse of "Bismarck's Reich" continued to see his particular achievement as *"Reichsgründer,"* or founding father of the German nation state. Among the most distinguished of these was Gerhard Ritter in his magisterial, multi-volume *Staatskunst und Kriegshandwerk: Das Problem*

des 'Militarismus' in Deutschland,[14] which devoted a substantial section
to addressing the relationship of politics and the military in the years
of Bismarck's administration.[15] From the earliest years of the young
Federal Republic of Germany the topic of Bismarck and his political
legacy played a central role in her historians' agenda. Four months after
its foundation, namely in September 1949, they met as a professional
body in Munich and immediately afterwards at the international historical
conference at a former seat of the Holy Roman Empire at Speyer. Their
discussions centred on the issue of reaching an objective assessment of
what Ritter called "the Bismarck problem."[16] The internationalization of
the German debate thus occurred very early; Rothfels, for example, and
the biographer of Heinrich von Treitschke, Andreas Dorpalen,[17] published
position papers in the influential English-language journal, the *Review of
Politics*. The ideological thrust of some Bismarck research in the 1950s
gradually gave place to a more dispassionate tone in a number of studies by British and American political and diplomatic historians, among
them Werner E. Mosse, *The European Powers and the German Question,
1848–1871* and William N. Medlicott, *Bismarck, Gladstone and the
Concert of Europe*.[18] In Germany, the authoritative voice on Bismarck's
foreign policy was Andreas Hillgruber.[19] Two years after the appearance
of what would constitute the first volume of Hajo Holborn's pioneering
A History of Germany from the Reformation to 1945, a synthesis of the
nineteenth-century record was offered by the Oxford historian Agatha
Ramm in her *Germany 1789–1919. A Political History*,[20] which despite
its dry tone and focus on elitist politics remains a source of precise and
often recondite information, not least on the principalities which made
up Germany and the Empire. The complex constitutional issues of unification had been addressed in the monumental study of Otto Becker:
Bismarcks Ringen um Deutschlands Gestaltung.[21]

Meanwhile, attention was being directed in a series of influential books
on very different topics by (mainly) German refugees to the United States
from Hitler's Third Reich. Fritz Stern's brief monograph: *The Politics
of Cultural Despair* [22]—the context of which had been provided by Leonhard Krieger in his longitudinal study of 1957: *The German Idea of
Freedom*[23]—stimulated an extended debate into the pessimistic temper
of Bismarck's later years. Subsequent scholarly enquiry yielded a large
body of work on areas as diverse as the character of German nationalism[24] and its organizations in the Second Empire, popular philosophers
such as Treitschke and Paul de Lagarde, popular political culture and its
institutional articulation, the origins and nature of anti-Semitism in the
Second Empire, and, as an enduring achievement of the historiography
of Germany in the last third of the twentieth century, German-Jewish
history.[25] A second major focus of debate on Bismarckian Germany
received powerful impetus from Hans Rosenberg's *The Great Depression* of 1967.[26] The comparative studies by Gerschenkron and Landes[27]

highlighted the role of Germany's industrial revolution in creating the context for the "little German" (*"kleindeutsch"*) or Prussian solution to German unification. Rosenberg established economics and the politics of industrialization as central to an assessment of Bismarck's years as imperial chancellor, thus linking up with the debate addressed by Stern. If today historians speak of the years 1873 to 1896 rather as a period of extended stagnation rather than "great depression," nonetheless the impact of Rosenberg's research into the impact of business cycles on historical structures, processes, and mentalities, has been far-reaching. The related area of Germany's superior exploitation of military technology in her wars of unification, notably against France in 1870/71, had been the subject of the now classical study by the British military historian and editor of the Gladstone diaries, Michael Howard: *The Franco-Prussian War: the German invasion of France, 1870–1871.*[28]

By the early 1970s, the first of a number of authoritative state-of-research reports on Bismarck historiography could make its appearance. In 1971, Lothar Gall, a future biographer of Bismarck and future editor of Germany's leading historical journal, the *Historische Zeitschrift*, published a collection of essays on Bismarck dating from the years 1947 to 1966, prefaced by his own succinct introduction.[29] The volume includes contributions from leading German and English-speaking historians from often conflicting perspectives, as well one each by the founding president of the Republic, Theodor Heuss, and Henry A. Kissinger. Gall's *Das Problem der Bismarckforschung in der Geschichtsschreibung nach 1945* is of further interest in having appeared in what would prove to be an influential series, the *Neue Wissenschaftliche Bibliothek* or New Scholarly Library, covering, together with literature, the four social science disciplines of economics, psychology, sociology, and history. Easily identifiable by their bright yellow covers, the robustly bound paperbacks were much used by students. The sociology editor was Jürgen Habermas, and for history Hans-Ulrich Wehler of the new polyuniversity of Bielefeld, a name as yet relatively little known outside Germany.

Within a couple of years this would change radically. In 1969 Wehler had published his *Bismarck und der Imperialismus*, arguing that the Chancellor had used the imperial idea to deflect opposition at home, and in 1970 his *Krisenherde des Zweiten Reichs, 1871–1918. Studien zur deutschen Sozial- und Verfassungsgeschichte* (Crisis points of the Second Empire 1870–1918. Studies in the social and constitutional history of Germany).[30] This last was described by the reviewer in the *Journal of Modern History* as "the most interesting book on Imperial Germany since Fischer's *Griff nach der Weltmacht*" (on German responsibility for the outbreak of war in 1914). The author, Konrad H. Jarausch went on to suggest in accurate characterization of the "phenomenon Wehler" with his penchant for "bibliomaniacal footnotes," "has left no taboo untouched in order to write a counter-history which raises immensely stimulating issues."[31] But it was Wehler's brief, brilliant and thoroughly controversial *The Second German Empire, 1871–1918*,[32] a structuralist analysis of the socio-economic context of imperial politics, which made his name both at home and abroad among student and academic readers alike. Meanwhile his earlier ground-breaking edited volume *Moderne Deutsche Sozialgeschichte* (1966) was going into a number of editions; it helped to set the research agenda in the field of nineteenth-century German social history for years to come. It was followed a generation later by his magisterial three-volume *Gesellschaftsgeschichte* (Social History), dense, incisively written, and hugely informative.[33] Wehler's thesis of Germany's *Sonderweg*, elaborated with gusto in academic debate and in the German quality press, of her uniquely individual path to nationhood and her failure to match economic with political and social modernization in the manner of other European states, purported to offer some explanation for Germany's succumbing to right-wing dictatorship in 1933. Wehler was only one, if the one with the highest profile, of what became known in the following years as the "Critical School" of German historians. Their work proved immensely attractive to the newly politicized generation of (the students' revolt of) 1968, engendering more than a decade of intense controversy. As democrats they and their students felt an affiliation with one group of Bismarck's most notable "victims," the Socialist party and its supporters, and the labor movement more generally.[34] A major critical voice from North America was that of Otto Pflanze, author of *Bismarck and the Development of modern Germany. The Period of Unification 1815–71* (1963), in his research report of 1982.[35] Here he challenged a number of theses of the Critical School with regard to Bismarck's ruling technique as one of deliberate fostering of negative consensus. Among these were the concept of Bismarck's alleged "Bonapartism," the use of plebiscitary democracy à la Louis Bonaparte, his politics of "negative integration," [36] "social imperialism,"[37] and the notion of 1878/79 as a "Second Founding of the Reich,"[38] when the Chancellor dropped the National Liberals as parliamentary political partners, abandoned Prussia's traditional free trade policy in favour of protectionism and proscribed the Socialist Party.

Undoubtedly the most important feature of these extended debates was to promote a body of research into the Second German Empire which has substantially changed our understanding of the "Bismarck era." Indeed, a casualty of sophisticated historical enquiry, including the major Bielefeld research project into the German middle classes,[39] has been, not simply the *Sonderweg* thesis, in Richard J. Evans' witty rhetorical question,[40] but the very concept of a unique "Bismarck era." Besides Evans, other younger British historians proved to be among the most incisive critics of the *Sonderweg* thesis, polemically formulated in *Peculiarities of German History* [41] by David Blackbourn and Geoff Eley, historian of the German Right and of popular culture.[42] Blackbourn, now teaching at

Yale, and Evans as Regius Professor of History at Cambridge, England, leading authorities in the field of modern German history, have helped re-orientate the historical assessment of Bismarck by setting him in an inclusive socio-cultural context of regional, confessional, grassroots and "subjective" historiography. Evans' undoubtedly mischievous but also accurate observation in his review of the third volume of Wehler's *Social History*, that "this is basically the history of the male half of German society in the period under question,"[43] could apply to the work of almost two generations of postwar historians of Bismarck's Germany. One of Evans's own earliest works (1976) had been on women's social history in the late nineteenth- and early twentieth-century Germany, including particular reference to prostitution.[44] Subsequent publications dealt with criminality, proletarian life, the history of epidemics and public health in Bismarck's and Wilhelmine Germany, always from the perspective of both genders.[45] Stimulated meanwhile by the impact of the New Women's Movement in Germany of the 1970s, a great deal of work was done and continues to be done by gender historians and literary and cultural historians[46] to counter the traditional exclusion or marginalization of women. This is evident today in the general histories, both major monographs and textbooks, which now adopt the perspective of both genders as a matter of course and in social and regional studies. One of the earliest general studies was Ute Frevert's *Women in German History* of 1986, which she followed by studies of male values in Imperial Germany: *Men of Honour: A Social and Cultural History of the Duel* and *A Nation in Barracks: Modern Germany, Conscription and Civil Society*.[47]

David Blackbourn made his name through work in another field neglected by his fellow German historians, namely Catholic Germany, neglected despite the established body of research by Catholic historians in the pre-and postwar years.[48] Following his study of the operation and compass of the Catholic Centre Party in Württemberg of 1980, Blackbourn exemplified Goethe's thesis of the superior merits of proceeding from the particular to the general. *Marpingen: Apparitions of the Virgin Mary in Bismarck's Germany,*[49] is not just regional, Kulturkampf, Catholic, and social history (of one of the poorest parts of Bismarck's Germany, the Saarland). It provides a vivid and detailed account of the actual working of the institutions and policies of Bismarck's Reich in the 1870s from the dual perspective of their objects and the authors.

But this is to anticipate events. Resting on the earlier debates and on the foundations of extensive primary research on both sides of the Atlantic, the "long" decade[50] 1980 to 1990 saw major and ambitious developments in Bismarck research, not only in the interpretation of the historical personality of Bismarck in new full-length biographies, but, for the first time in almost two generations, a series of "grand narratives" of Germany's nineteenth century history. German students of Bismarck and his times have not enjoyed what has always formed a key source of understanding for students of Victorian England, namely the tradition of the great political biography, such as Morley's *Life of Gladstone* (1903) or Gwendolen Cecil's four-volume biography of her father, Lord Salisbury (1921-23). And not only prime ministers, but virtually all the major and very many of the minor figures of British history have attracted their biographers, both in their lifetime and thereafter. Many British politicians, even ministers of the Crown, as products of great English public schools such as Winchester and Eton, which saw education in the ancient classics as the school of life and politics, wrote major political biographies of "life and times."[51] True, some leading figures of German liberalism (with their interest in and aspirations for forms of British constitutionalism) had had their biographers, among them Hermann Oncken (Rudolf von Bennigsen, 1910) and Wilhelm Mommsen (Johannes Miquel, 1928). However, the many biographies of Bismarck published in his life time and in the following decades were generally, like his own notorious memoirs, *Gedanken und Erinnerungen (Reflections and Memories* [1901-1919]), rather more about myth-making than writing political biography in the grand manner.

It was not until the Bismarck years had been exposed to intensive scrutiny by new generations of historians over the space of a quarter of a century that major political biographies of its chief protagonist made their appearance. Despite seminal contributions to the reassessment of Germany in the nineteenth century and to the debate on the issue of the so-called "Bismarck era" from Great Britain and elsewhere, the most important achievements of the last decades in the field of political biography have come from German and American historians. Alan (A. J. P.) Taylor had made his name as a historian of Germany in his *The Struggle for Mastery in Europe*[52] and his short Bismarck biography of 1955 proved immensely popular, not least as a paperback at a price students could afford. *Bismarck, the Man and the Statesman* was extremely fluently written by a first-class media communicator, but in the Lytton Strachey[53] tradition of pandering to prejudice, in this case to the Germanophobia endemic in certain circles in Britain. Lothar Gall's single volume: *Bismarck. Der weiße Revolutionär* (1980, *Bismarck: The White Revolutionary*, 1986), and Otto Pflanze in his three-volume: *Bismarck and the Development of Germany* (1990) (German translation 1997),[54] thus represent landmark achievements in the later twentieth-century historiography of modern Germany. Gall's portrait had been preceded in 1977 by Fritz Stern's double biography with the evocative title: *Gold and Iron: Bismarck, Bleichröder and the Building of the German Empire.*[55] His study of the relationship between Bismarck and his banker Bleichröder, the only orthodox Jew to receive a patent of nobility in the Second Empire, threw new light (among much else besides) on how Bismarck financed his political career and his lifestyle. Stern's study, like Margaret Anderson's biography of the leader of the Catholic Centre Party, published in 1981,[56] showed how it was possible to combine important scholarly research[57] with books one could read in an armchair. Mid-way between Gall and Pflanze, the "Nestor" of East German nineteenth-century historians, Ernst Engelberg, published his Bismarck biography under the title of: *Bismarck's Origins and Foundation of the Empire (Bismarcks Ursprünge und Reichsgründung*.[58] Although Engelberg had access to archives not then always accessible to Western scholars, its contribution lies principally in Bismarck's early years, namely the history of his mother's family, the Menckens, and his friendship from student days with the American historian John Lothrop Motley. Pflanze's magisterial study is in three volumes, the first of which had appeared in 1963 and was reissued in 1990 with updated bibliography. It represents truly half a lifetime's work, and succeeds in combining close reading of the sources, dispassionate judgment with modern political biographical writing in its most sophisticated form. It is also illustrated by a rich selection from contemporary material, including the treasury of German satirical political cartoons which flourished throughout Bismarck's public career and whose artists delighted to feature him. Pflanze's work succeeds in being both great biography and a comprehensive history of nineteenth-century Germany.

The appearance of the Bismarck biographies of the 1980s and early 1990s, emerging from the vigorous debates characteristic of the Critical School of German historians, coincided with the publication of a number of major histories of the period, both in German and in English. While the editors and authors of other general histories, such as the Oxford *History of Britain*, had continued to see the recording of "the history of a people" as a self-evident task, and one which would engage the expertise of each new generation of historians, West German historians had been either reluctant to attempt to write "national" history from the perspective of the day.[59] In East Germany things were radically different. Official policy after the foundation of the new state in October 1949 had, by contrast, demanded an immediate engagement with the re-interpretation of Germany's nineteenth- and twentieth-century history on Marxist-Leninist lines. Bismarck's persecution of the German Socialist Party and their leaders' spirited challenge to his authority featured prominently in such accounts. In the German Democratic Republic, particular attention was paid to the rewriting of school and university textbooks in terms of the new orthodoxy. While active repression of dissident voices among the community of East German historians continued, as indeed of intellectuals generally, the coherence of research and educational policy in this regard had the effect over time of making citizens of the German Democratic Republic comfortable with their own identity as East Germans, in a way not generally true of the Federal Republic.

The first step had been taken by the American Hajo Holborn in his much-cited A *History of Germany*, a rare single-authored history covering the entire modern period.[60] His successors for nineteenth-century Germany, Craig, Sheehan, Wehler, Nipperdey, Mommsen[61] and Blackbourn, built on an immense mass of historical research, much of it in areas which had been virtually or totally ignored by older German historiography.[62] The new histories were informed by the internationalization of the discipline, again in contrast with the powerful and long-enduring tradition of "national" history-writing prevalent up to the mid-years of the Federal Republic. While in the view of a number of older Germans in the post-war decades, and of many younger Germans in the changed climate of post-unification Germany (1989/90-), such an approach burdened a whole nation with generational guilt, it also had the considerable merit of making (West) Germans as a nation open to their past in a manner few nations have achieved.[63] For it is useful for later generations of students to appreciate that in postwar Germany, historical research, including (particularly) research into the nineteenth and twentieth centuries, and the ample state funding of the training of younger historians abroad and of international collaborative projects, operated with a significant degree of design as a form of "restitution" on the part of the west German state.[64]

The title of Gordon A. Craig's masterly *Germany, 1866–1945* (1978)[65] was programmatic in the sense that it departed from the notion of 1871 as the apogee of Germany's national history, establishing instead the year 1866 as the key date for nineteenth-century German and Central European history. In that year, Austria's defeat by Prussia in the so-called Six Weeks' War led to her expulsion, as part of the future Reich Chancellor's grand strategy, from the Germany she had either ruled or had had a central involvement in for almost a millennium. In 1965, Craig had published his vivid account of a single day (3 July 1866), showing how accident as much as design had determined the outcome of the critical battle of Königgrätz and Prussia's fortune.[66] Seen in the *longue durée* of Central European history, 1866 was thus seen as a seminal date, upsetting for almost a century the balance between north and south. Craig's younger colleague, James J. Sheehan, the authoritative voice on German liberalism,[67] would bring the account from the age of Enlightenment to 1866 in his *German History 1770–1866* of 1989.[68] Here as in his earlier work, Sheehan departed from the perspective of German history as viewed "from Berlin" and culminating in Bismarckian unification. Sheehan, as Theodor Hamerow had done in *The Social Foundations of German Unification, 1858–1871*,[69] and Eda Sagarra in *A Social History of Germany 1648–1914*,[70] gave prominence to the regional and societal dimensions of Germany's history, which would become a self-evident dimension of subsequent general works by both English-speaking and German historians. From the perspective of a German looking back from the early twenty-first century on the historiography of her or his country, the year 1984 could be called a landmark date. This was when Thomas

Nipperdey, professor of history at the University of Munich, published what would become the first volume of his three-volume history: *German History 1800-1866*, with the sub-title: *Middle-Class World and Powerful State. German History 1866-1918*, two volumes, followed in 1990 and 1992, the first dealing with the world of work and the citizen, the second with power versus democracy, politics and the state. Even a superficial perusal of the history section of a German university library provides evidence from the well-thumbed volumes of Nipperdey's history what a powerful impact it has had on student readers. His approach is reminiscent of that of the seminal essay of Victorian scholarship, G. M. Young's *Victorian England. Portrait of an Age* of 1936.[71] In the first two volumes of his history of nineteenth-century Germany, Nipperdey prefaces and contextualizes his treatment of the political history of Imperial Germany in the third. He provides detailed chapters on such varied aspects of her history as demography, daily life and mentalities in rural and urban settings, the economy, the social classes, sciences, the arts. Unusually–impressively!–in the case of a German historian, *Deutsche Geschichte* has no footnotes. Only the final section of his account of the development of the German state between 1866 and 1890 bears the title: "The Bismarck era" (3, 359-470). Modern judgement thus no longer subscribes to the notion of "Bismarckian Germany." Accordingly, Blackbourn devotes some five pages to his treatment of Bismarck in his *Long Nineteenth Century* and Berghahn in *Imperial Germany* just under eight. The changing focus of historiography of Germany in the nineteenth century over the last decades from the history of high politics to that of the history of the German people has impacted on many areas. Thus for example Bismarck's treatment of the Reichstag, traditionally described in terms of his relations with the politicians, is now more often seen "from below." Today voter behaviour, electoral issues and the organization of politics at grassroots level has been the subject of particular scrutiny,[72] which, incidentally, as in accounts of the behaviour of Polish voters in the late 1880s and 1890s, offers new insight into the complex reasons for Bismarck's discriminatory policies against the Catholic and Polish minorities. Generally, the extensive empirical studies and syntheses of issues of central concern to ordinary people as well as policymakers, such as demography, (em/imm/)migration, housing, public health, crime, justice, youth and social policy, generational conflict, high and mass culture, together with their many regional variations, have greatly enriched our understanding of what it was to be a citizen of the Reich in the Bismarck years and thereafter. The net effect—though this is not always made explicit to the reader—is to recreate the perception typical of by no means all, but of a very great many of Bismarck's contemporaries, that their Empire was a good place to be.[73]

In looking back, then, on the "phenomenon Bismarck" half a century or more after Darmstaedter's biography, we might remind ourselves of what constituted an endless source of admiration for discriminating contemporaries of Bismarck: his command of the written and spoken word. "He speaks as Heinrich Heine writes,"[74] Prime Minister Disraeli reported back to Queen Victoria from the Congress of Berlin in 1878. The novelist Theodor Fontane (1819–98), one of Germany's most subtle writers and towards the end of Bismarck's administration and in the years after 1890 one of his most incisive critics, commented in a letter on "the sheer brilliance of his imagery when he speaks." "Not even Shakespeare," he goes on, "can match the simplicity and immediacy of his language."[75] Fontane attended the Reichstag almost daily to hear the Chancellor speak; when he returned home in July 1898, following news of Bismarck's death, Fontane, according to his daughter Martha, sat at home in his armchair and wept. Yet he could describe his contemporary in private correspondence as an infuriating mixture of "genius, saviour of the nation and sentimental traitor," of "superman and fox, founder of the German nation and stable-tax evader...of hero and cry-baby, who wouldn't hurt a fly."[76] Fontane did not live to enjoy Bismarck's memoirs, the first volumes of which appeared three years after both had died in 1898. Mendacious they might be, but Bismarck's *Gedanken und Erinnerungen* constitute one of the great literary documents of the age. The authentic voice of one of Germany's most accomplished rhetoricians, schooled in the language and imagery of Martin Luther and the ancient classics, is still to be heard in his speeches and in his letters, in the latter particularly those of his early and middle years.

"In the beginning was Bismarck."[77] The intensive, at times almost obsessive debate among historians, German and non-German alike, about the figure of Bismarck extended for almost half a century after the collapse of the Third Reich. From the time of his first appearance on the national stage as a daredevil opponent of the 1848 revolution,[78] the "Junker, smelling of blood," as his subsequent king and emperor, Wilhelm I, would call him, was a controversial figure. In every sense, including his physical stature, sheer bulk, and gargantuan appetite for food and drink, Bismarck conformed to Cassius' judgement of Caesar in Shakespeare's *Julius Caesar*, as "striding the world like a Colossus." But of course the post-1945 historical reassessment of Bismarck and his contribution to the formation of Germany in the second half of the nineteenth century was at least as much about the reordering of the German polity after the cataclysm of the Third Reich, as it was about the Imperial Chancellor and founder of the Second Empire. As one of very many such contributions to the topic in the post-war period and in the early years of Konrad Adenauer's chancellorship of the Federal Republic, Darmstaedter's work made abundantly evident the context in which he was writing. That Adenauer, who was born in 1876, a Rhinelander and deeply anti-Prussian, a democrat who, though favoring a thoroughly paternalistic style of governance, had scant sympathy for Bismarck or his legacy, is nicely illustrated in the anecdote told of his meeting with Prime Minister Winston Churchill. Aware of Adenauer's anti-British prejudices since his days as mayor of Cologne during the 1945-49 British occupation, Churchill allegedly addressed Adenauer as "the greatest German chancellor since Bismarck." "Is that supposed to be a compliment?" was the dry response. [79]

Modern historical judgment of Bismarck in his age may perhaps be summarized in two observations. The first is by Lothar Gall, that Bismarck,

> despite his decisive impact, both in a positive and in a negative sense, on the shaping of the German Empire, was certainly not the all-determining figure, as which some have liked to portray him. [80]

The second comes from the epilogue of the first volume of Thomas Nipperdey's *German History*, where in his attractive personal style he declares that

> for all the controversial debates about our relationship to our past and its 'overcoming', we all of us [Germans], nearly half a century after 1945, accept as thoroughly obsolete the notion that the imperial era was but the precursor of National Socialism and Hitler. [81]

As a kind of anticipatory codicil to Nipperdey and as an explanation for the fascination of Otto von Bismarck continues to exercise over a century after his death, the last word should belong to one of the many non-German historians who have contributed to our understanding of the man and his times, namely that:

> the Empire created by Bismarck remains a source of enduring importance for the ongoing German quest for self-definition. [82]

Eda Sagarra

Notes

1. The first edition having been largely destroyed by fire, the second, edited and with an introduction by Rothfels, appeared after the author's death (Stuttgart: Köhler, 1949).
2. Rothfels, "Probleme einer Bismarck-Biographie" (first published in 1947 in the *Review of Politics*) in Gall, 90f (note 16 below).
3. London: Allen & Unwin 1950. The 3rd ed. appeared in 1968.
4. In a ratio of approximately 1:4.
5. The English translation appeared in 1950 (Cambridge MA: Harvard University Press). Meinecke had been the teacher of some of America's leading historians of Germany, before they came to the United States as exiles from Hitler's Germany. Among them were Felix Gilbert, Hajo Holborn, and Hans Rosenberg

xxii   *Bismarck and the Creation of the Second Reich*

who rewarded him with their loyalty and concern, sending him CARE packets in the immediate postwar years when Germans were suffering from hunger and malnutrition.

6.   E.g. Documents on Prussian Foreign Policy (*Die Auswärtige Politik Preußens 1858–1871. Diplomatische Aktenstücke*, Berlin: Historische Kommission, 1930 et seq.), 12 vols.

7.   The Collected Works (*Bismarck. Die gesammelten Werke*) (Berlin: Otto Stolberg, 1924–35), ed. Hermann von Petersdorff, 15 vols.

8.   A central issue of the major histories of nineteenth-century Germany and the Bismarck biographies published between the late 1970s and early 1990s has been to challenge the idea of describing the period from the 1860s to 1890 in Germany as "the age of Bismarck."

9.   The excellent brief study by Wolfram Siemann, *Die deutsche Revolution von 1848/1849* (Frankfurt a.M.: Suhrkamp, 1985) (English translation 1996), is the best introduction to the subject.

10.   Rothfels, p. 90 (note 2).

11.   Examples include "the dictator in the guise of bureaucrat" (333), "twenty years or so of Bismarck's dictatorship which followed 1871" (398), or Bismarck's "dictatorial position in the new Reich" (concluding paragraph of book, 407).

12.   The full sentence from his public lectures of 1841, published in the same year in essay form, reads: "As I take it, Universal History, the history of what man has accomplished in this world, is at bottom the History of great men who have worked here."

13.   *Bismarck. Der Mensch und der Staatsmann* (Stuttgart: Köhler, 1949).

14.   Munich: R. Oldenbourg, 1954–68 (*The sword and the sceptre. The problem of militarism in Germany*, 4 vols., 1972–3).

15.   The Scottish-American historian Gordon A. Craig published his classical longitudinal study: *The Politics of the Prussian Army, 1640–1945* in 1955 (New York, Oxford: Oxford University Press). Critical analysis of the role of the army in German politics and society became a focus of interest in Germany in the 1970s: see Manfred Messerschmidt, *Militär und Politik in der Bismarckzeit und im wilhelminischen Deutschland* (Darmstadt: Wissenschaftliche Buchgesellschaft, 1975) (Erträge der Forschung 43); also Martin Kitchen's useful introduction: *A Military History of Germany from the Eighteenth Century to the Present Day* (London: Weidenfeld & Nicolson, 1975).

16.   "Das Problem Bismarck," re-published in Lothar Gall (ed.), *Probleme der Bismarckforschung* (Cologne: Kiepenheuer & Witsch, 1971) (Neue Wissenschaftliche Bibliothek), 119–137. See his polemical assertion (here 120): "The history of the academic biographies of Bismarck can be described as one long disaster."

17.   Rothfels in vol. 9 (1947), 362–382 and Dorpalen as: "The German historians and Bismarck," 15 (1953), 53–67, both reproduced in Gall.

18.   New York: Cambridge University Press, 1958 and London: English Universities Press, 1965.

19.   *Bismarcks Außenpolitik* (Freiburg i. B.: Rombach, 1972).

20.   London: Methuen 1967. On Holborn see below.

21.   Berlin: Quelle & Meyer, 1958.

22. See in this context the study by the Oxford historian, Peter J. Pulzer (also a refugee from the Third Reich): *The Rise of Political Anti-Semitism in Germany and Austria* (Oxford: Oxford University Press, 1963).

23. Princeton, NJ: Princeton University Press, 1957.

24. The literature on German nationalism in the nineteenth century is immense. See in particular: Heinrich A. Winkler (ed.), *Nationalismus.*(Königstein/ Taunus: Athenäum, 1978); also Hagen Schulze, *The Course of German Nationalism. From Frederick the Great to Bismarck, 1763–1867* (Cambridge: Cambridge University Press, 1991); John Breuilly, *The Formation of the First German Nation State, 1870–1871* (Basingstoke: Macmillan 1996); and H. W. Smith, *German Nationalism and Religious Conflict* (Princeton NJ: Princeton University Press., 1998). For some illuminating reflections on how post-1989 Germany has impacted on contemporary views of the Empire, see also Ronald Speirs and John Breuilly (eds), *Germany's Two Unifications. Anticipations, Experiences, Responses* (Basingstoke: Palgrave Macmillan, 2005). Pflanze's treatment of Bismarck and German nationalism in Book 5, chapter 4 of his Bismarck biography (see below) is authoritative.

25. For bibliography see Michael Meyer ed., *German-Jewish History in Modern Times*, vol. 3: *Integration in Dispute 1871–1918* (New York: Columbia University Press, 2003).

26. *Große Depression und Bismarckzeit: Wirtschaftsablauf, Gesellschaft und Politik in Mitteleuropa* (Berlin: de Gruyter, 1967).

27. Alexander Gerschenkron, *Bread and Democracy* (New York: Columbia University Press, 1966); David S. Landes, *The unbound Prometheus: technology, growth and economic development in Western Europe from 1740 to the present* (Cambridge: Cambridge University Press, 1969). A British historian, W. O. Henderson, had been publishing since the 1930s on the economic context of German unification. Though narrow in focus, his work was well informed and widely read. See: *The State and the Industrial Revolution in Prussia 1740–1860* (Liverpool: Liverpool University Press, 1958) (U.S. edition 1959).

28. London: Methuen, 1961. For a recent acclaimed study, see Geoffrey Wawra, *The Franco-Prussian War. The German Conquest of France in 1870–1871* (Cambridge, New York, Melbourne: Cambridge University Press, 2003).

29. *Einleitung*, 9-24.

30. The first appeared in Cologne: Kiepenheuer & Witsch, the second in Göttingen: Vandenhoeck und Ruprecht.

31. *Historische Zeitschrift* 48 (1970), 728 and 731.

32. Göttingen: Vandenhoeck & Ruprecht, 1973; English translation 1985.

33. Munich: C.H. Beck 1987–1995.

34. See i.a. *The Social Democrats in Imperial Germany. A Study in Working Class Isolation and National Integration* (Totowa, NJ: Bedminster, 1963) by the Columbia sociologist Günther Roth, Hans-Ulrich Wehler, *Sozialdemokratie und Nationalstaat* (Göttingen: Vandenhoeck and Ruprecht, 1970), and for the later period: Dieter Groh, *Negative Integration und revolutionärer Attentismus. Die deutsche Sozialdemokratie am Vorabend des Ersten Weltkriegs* (Frankfurt a.M.: Ullstein, 1973).

35. *Historische Zeitschrift* 234 (1982), 561–599.

36. Note 34 above.

37. Note 30 above.
38. See the influential collection of essays ed. by Helmut Böhme: *Probleme der Reichsgründung 1848–1879* (Cologne: Kiepenheuer & Witsch, 1969) (Neue Wissenschaftliche Bibliothek) and bibliography.
39. The comparative approach was an important dimension of Jürgen Kocka (ed. with Ute Frevert), *Bürgertum im 19. Jahrhundert. Deutschland im europäischen Vergleich*, 3 vols. (Munich: dtv, 1988).
40. "Whatever became of the German *Sonderweg?*" in ibid., *Rereading German history. From unification to reunification 1800–1996* (London: Routledge, 1997).
41. Oxford: Oxford University Press, 1984. Interestingly, the German translation is rendered as "Myths" (1986).
42. E.g. G. E. (ed.), *Society, Culture and the State 1870–1930* (Ann Arbor: Michigan University Press, 1996).
43. *Rereading German history*, p. 19.
44. *The Feminist Movement in Germany, 1894–1933* (London: Sage, 1976).
45. As an example see Volker R. Berghahn, *Imperial Germany, 1871–1918. Economy, Society, Culture and Politics* (New York, Oxford: Berg 1994).
46. The very substantial body of work on German women by cultural and social historians of literature is still not always sufficiently integrated into mainstream historiography.
47. English translations: Oxford: Berg, 1989; Cambridge: Polity, 1995; Oxford, New York, Berne: Berg, 2004.
48. This is not the case for English-speaking historians, such as G. G. Windell, *The Catholics and German Unity 1866–1871* (Minneapolis: University of Minnesota Press, 1956), M. L. Anderson in *Ludwig Windthorst* (note 56 below) or Jonathan Sperber, *Popular Catholicism in Nineteenth-Century Germany* (Princeton NJ: Princeton University Press., 1984). Cf. also David Blackbourn, *Populists and Patricians. Essays in Modern Germany* (London: Allen & Unwin, 1987).
49. Oxford: Clarendon Press, 1993; the second edition of 1995 carries a new subtitle: *Rationalism, Religion and the Rise of Modern Germany*. There is now a very substantial body of work on Bismarck and the Kulturkampf. For a good summary of the political dimensions see Wolfgang J. Mommsen in his history: *Das Ringen um den deutschen Nationalstaat* (Vol. 7/1 of *Propyläen Geschichte*) (Berlin: Propyläen, 1993). See also the extended treatment of the churches and religion in Nipperdey (1990), 428–530 and on the political aspects (1992), 337–51, 364–81 and 541–54.
50. Overlapping at each end of the decade, by analogy with David Blackbourn's *History of Germany, 1780–1918: The Long Nineteenth Century* (London: Fontana, 1997).
51. Roy Jenkins, former prime minister and subsequently European Union Commissioner, has been among the most prolific in the present time. See particularly his *Gladstone* (London: Fontana Papermac, 1995).
52. Oxford: Clarendon Press, 1952.
53. Author of *Eminent Victorians* (London: Chatto & Windus, 1929).
54. Princeton N.J.: Princeton University Press., 1990. Pflanze dedicated his work to Hajo Holborn.
55. Berkeley: California University Press, 1977.
56. *Ludwig Windthorst. A Political Biography* (Oxford: Oxford University Press).

57. I.e., the banking system and German-Jewish studies and the history of Catholic Germany, particularism, and party politics, respectively.
58. Berlin: Akademie Verlag 1985. See also Joachim Streisand's contribution from an East German perspective to the debate on 1878/79: "Bismarck und die deutsche Einigungsbewegung des 19. Jahrhunderts in der westdeutschen Geschichtsschreibung," in Böhme (note 38), 384–401, and Dorpalen: *German Historians of Marxist Perspective. The East German Approach* (London: I.B. Tauris, 1985). On Bismarck historiography see 231f.
59. This is not to dispute the significance of the solid multi-volume and regularly re-conceptualized Gebhardt: *Handbuch der deutschen Geschichte*, which first appeared in 1891. The tenth edition (Stuttgart: Klett, 2001-), which has Kocka as one of its editors, breaks with the traditional chronicle-type treatment and takes a much more analytical approach.
60. London: Eyre & Spottiswoode, 1965-69. Vol. 3 covered the period 1840–1945.
61. See note 49 above.
62. An outstanding exception is Franz Schnabel's *Deutsche Geschichte im 19. Jahrhundert*. (Freiburg i. Br.: Herder, 1948–51), 4 vols., covering the years from 1815 to 1848 only. Initially overlooked by his contemporaries—Schnabel had been removed from his Karlsruhe chair by the National Socialists—his work proved to be a powerful influence on a number of later prominent social and cultural historians. In particular, Schnabel's treatment of religion and the church in vol. 4 has continued to be widely cited.
63. By contrast, for example with Austria, which at official level only began in any systematic way to address its relationship to the Third Reich following the half-centenary commemoration of the 1938 *Anschluss*, Hitler's march into Austria. And this despite the vigour and experimental focus precisely on Austrian Nazism and its manifestations which characterized Austria's extraordinarily vibrant modern literature from the late 1950s and the early 1960s forward, by writers such as Ingeborg Bachmann, Thomas Bernhard, Peter Handke, Elfriede Jelinek, and the German-Austrian Max (=W.E.) Sebald.
64. In East Germany this was very far from being the case. The East German state was formed as the German Democratic Republic in October 1949 from the former Soviet zone of occupation, following the unification of the three western zones of occupation (American, British and French) on 23 May 1949.
65. Oxford: Clarendon Press.
66. London: Weidenfeld & Nicolson. A seminal study on the impact of Bismarck on Austrian history is provided by Heinrch Lütz, *Österreich-Ungarn und die deutsche Reichsgründung. Europäische Entscheidungen* (Frankfurt .M., Berlin, Vienna: Propyläen, 1979).
67. *German Liberalism in the Nineteenth Century* (Chicago: Chicago University Press, 1978).
68. Oxford: Clarendon, 1989.
69. 2 vols., Princeton NJ: Princeton University Press, 1969–72.
70. London: Methuen, 1977, re-issued with a new introduction by the author in 2003 by Transaction Publishers (New Brunswick, NJ and London).
71. London: Oxford University Press. Strangely, this brilliant portrait of the politics, institutions, society, culture and above all changing mentalities of each generation over an entire age by a scion of the Trevelyan family, is never mentioned in German bibliographies.

72. E.g. Larry E. Jones and James N. Retallack (eds), *Elections, Mass Politics and Social Change in Imperial Germany. New Perspectives* (Cambridge: Cambridge University Press, 1992 and Jonathan Sperber, *The Kaiser's Voters. Electors and Elections in Imperial Germany* (Cambridge: Cambridge University Press, 1997)

73. In this, despite common perceptions that it was otherwise, Germans in the age of Wilhelm I and Wilhelm II were not so very different from the citizens of the British Empire in the last days of Queen Victoria's reign.

74. One of Germany's greatest poets and her finest political satirist (1797–1856).

75. 8 January 1891 to Paul Heyse. *Werke, Schriften, Briefe*, Section 4, *Briefe* IV (Darmstadt: Wissenschaftliche Buchgesellschaft, 1982), 86.

76. 19 January 1891 and 1 April 1895 (Bismarck's 80th birthday) in ibid., 326 and 440. For those unfamiliar with his fiction, letters and autobiographical writings, Fontane, almost an exact contemporary of Bismarck, provides a sure-footed guide to the history of their times. See Gordon A. Craig: *Theodor Fontane: Literature and History in Nineteenth-Century Germany* (Oxford: Oxford University Press, 1999) also: Eda Sagarra, *Germany in the Nineteenth Century. History and Literature* (New York: Peter Lang, 2001).

77. To adapt, as is appropriate, Thomas Nipperdey's opening remark of the first volume of his history: "Am Anfang war Napoleon" to the political self-understanding of generations of Germans between the foundation of the Second German Empire and the Adenauer era (1949–1963)

78. As Darmstaedter (78f.) reminds us, he responded to the crisis for the Prussian monarchy with a characteristically histrionic gesture of assembling and arming the peasants on his estate, prior to advancing on Berlin to succour his king.

79. See Gordon A. Craig's overview, *From Bismarck to Adenauer. Studies in German Statecraft* (Oxford: Oxford University Press, 1958).

80. In his introduction to *Otto von Bismarck und die Parteien* (Otto-von-Bismarck Stiftung Wissenschaftliche Reihe, vol. 3), (Paderborn, Munich, Vienna, Zurich: Ferdinand Schöningh, 2001), xi.

81. Nipperdey (1990), 837.

82. Evans (note 40), 45.

INTRODUCTION

When in 1885 Charles Lowe published his *Prince Bismarck, an Historical Biography*, he might well introduce his hero to the English-speaking world as ' the greatest man of the age '. He could do this because in the life of his hero he could see at the same time the ' Political History of Modern Germany '. Those who share Lowe's view that the life of Bismarck is identical with the political history of what then was modern Germany must revise his judgement on Bismarck as ' the greatest man of the age '. This revision is necessary, not so much because a great quantity of new material for investigation has reached the public since that utterance was made, but rather because the course of history itself has thrown a new light on Bismarck. To-day, seventy-four years after the creation of United Germany, fifty-five years after its creator laid down his tools, history has completely destroyed his work. This destruction has been performed so thoroughly that the very materials which Bismarck found ready to piece together for his work no longer exist but are smashed beyond recognition. ' For an hour the whole Universe seems wrapt in smoke and flame,' says Carlyle in *The Hero as King*, ' but only for an hour. It goes out : the Universe with its old mountains and streams, its stars above and kind soil beneath, is still there.'

Bismarck's ' greatness ' lay in the greatness of what he created, the German Reich of 1871. This Reich is simply the product of his genius, and in it his genius took complete and adequate shape. Let us remember that for decades, nay, in some way for centuries, political chaos reigned over a wide area of central Europe. It was a chaos which it seemed impossible to reduce to order and which threatened to obscure every region of political life. Let us then consider that in less than a decade this chaos was brought to an end and in its place a homogeneous state began to arise. The structure of this state seemed not only to leave no room for opposing political forces, which exhausted each other to the point of annihilation, but rather to make ready a roof under which these forces might rally, support each other and gain strength through each other. In this way a single, harmonious political force, secure in itself and bestowing security, would be created. That centrifugal forces were not yet dead was to be shown in the subsequent years, but the well-disposed observer might see in their existence a possible means of testing the strength of unity rather than a danger to it.

When in 1918 Sir Charles Grant Robertson's excellent biography of Bismarck appeared, certain not inconsiderable cracks and fissures could be seen in the structure of Bismarck's Reich.   But still it was standing ; it was still possible to credit it with the power of resistance rather than to fear it might collapse because of the damage it was suffering ; it was still possible to admire it as the embodiment of the genius of the ' greatest man of the age '.

To-day there no longer exists that united political force which we had admired in the great work of Bismarck, and even the several political forces out of which and in whose place it had been built are extinct.   Instead there reigns in Germany a political force which has not developed in the country itself but which is imposed upon it from outside.   The pitiable political plants which at present grow on the soil of what was once Bismarck's Reich are but artificial flowers, for they are not the expression of political strength but of political impotence.

No one will ever deny the overpowering character of Bismarck's personality, but does not the collapse of his work fifty-five years after he left the stage compel us to doubt his right to be called ' the greatest man of the age ' ?   Does it not subtract from the greatness of his work and put in doubt his creative power in the judgement of history ?   If his work was merely the means by which he achieved a career for himself, a charge which not even Bismarck's worst enemies have ever brought against him, his position remains unchanged. Purely personal success could not have made him a great historical figure.   Yet, the task which he had set himself was indeed an objective one : the solution of the question of German unity in the sense of Prussia.   Thus the value of Bismarck's work could not be measured by the life of an individual, but only by that of a whole nation.   Now what within the life of a nation are fifty-five years ? Are they more than ' an hour ' or ' but only an hour ' ?   If from the viewpoint of history we describe the solution of the question of the political existence of a people which after only twenty-five years shows cracks and fissures and which after fifty-five years proves to be altogether inadequate, as a work ' only for an hour ' then we cannot help doubting the historical greatness of the work and also of the man who created it.   Let us for a moment try to imagine what would have been Bismarck's reaction had he known that the Reich which he founded would be changed in its most essential elements in the lifetime of his children, and be crushed to dust in that of his grandchildren.

This reflection cannot be refuted by maintaining that the collapse of 1945 was not a *propter hoc* but a *post hoc* of the foundation of 1871, for this difference does not exist in respect of historical facts that occur within one nation.   Nor can the *propter hoc* be replaced by a ' despite *hoc* ' by pointing to the National Socialist episode as the proper cause. For the solution of a political question of decisive greatness in history implies not only the removal of existing opposing forces and defence against the enemy from without, but also protection from the poisonous germs within. In our case these have to include both William II's clumsy war game and the resulting National Socialist experiment. Nor can it reasonably be said that Bismarck's solution was good, but the people bad, for the goodness of a political solution depends upon whether it is suited to the people for which it is destined. Finally, the sentence *in magnis voluisse sat est* is true least of all in politics; Bismarck himself would never have accepted it if used against him, and even less had it been asserted in his favour. At his time success was the only touchstone in politics, and if to-day morality is as often a topic of discussion as it is rarely a principle of action in politics, even then it is not cited for its own value but rather as a means of making success permanent.

The question with which we are mainly concerned is whether in Bismarck's creation of the Reich the essential germs of the disintegration which took place in 1945 were not only dimly latent, but can be clearly discerned. As regards Bismarck's solution of the problem of German unity this question must be asked now in particular and it must be directed especially to the English-speaking world, since it is that world that will have a decisive word to say in the impending attempt to solve the German political question, and therefore it is bound to decide what must be its attitude towards Bismarck and his work. However, the point from which our inquiry must start is the creation of the Second Reich, and not the administration of the Reich after its creation because only there do the essential features of the man and the work lie before us clear and undimmed.

Of these features there are three which the following analysis aims at placing in the foreground.

Bismarck was a man possessing a self-assertiveness and a self-righteousness which were exceptional even among his Prussian comrades. Strengthened by his peculiar religious conceptions these characteristics were not modified by service to the state, but rather deepened and intensified by it. In this service he knew of no collaborators but only subordinates, and whoever did not share his views was an enemy of the state. Without acknowledging any restriction or restraint he claimed for himself the decision as to the choice of means in politics. He utterly rejected any political development in his state which sprang from the nation and not from the government, i.e., from himself; the Reich had to be centred, not around the nation but around his own person: he controlled the nation, not vice versa.

In his psychological approach to the capture of power in the state Bismarck started with the experience of the state as a community of human beings in union with each other and with their leader. He did not, however, secure and strengthen this bond of unity directly, but by pointing to a common foe against whom it was necessary to close ranks and prepare military forces of one's own. Thus he transformed the power of the state from an association of human beings into a potential war machine, and his own relation to it from the sense of a feeling of community into indulgence in power.

The community from which Bismarck started when he formed his conception of the state was first the family and clan, then the landlord caste and finally the people. These communities found their unifying force in the King, who as their patriarchal head enjoyed divine honours as ruler by the grace of God. The existence of the state was justified as the framework within which these communities existed, and it had thus a biological as well as a religious content. This idea of the state as a supreme moral command of religion was too powerful a driving force to be dropped in favour of the rational view of the state as a potential war machine. Bismarck indeed reconciled the two concepts by a clever use of the idea of the 'people in arms', an idea which had originated in German history as a means of defence, but which now was changed into one of aggression. As a means of defence this idea may only be an application of the doctrine of the 'struggle for survival'. In order to become a means of aggression it had to be changed into a moral precept commanded by religion, and indeed into the supreme precept. Thereby life in the state was not only likened to the struggle for survival in the animal world, but the individuals composing the state were actually made to accept this struggle as an ethical ideal.

Though we find the seed of all this in Bismarck's work, the Second Reich, it is in the Third Reich that we find the devilish distortion that was its fruit.[1]

---

[1] The author did not know of the monumental work on Bismarck by Erich Eyck until he was well advanced in the elaboration of the present volume, and did not actually see Eyck's book until his own was being prepared for publication. Thus, insofar as the author's views coincide with those of Eyck this coincidence may corroborate the standpoints taken ; while where the present author expresses a different opinion this does not mean conscious opposition to Eyck. This volume does not aim at competing with Eyck's work yet may perhaps coexist with it, for it addresses only a restricted section of the reading public, the English-speaking world, and looks on its subject from the angle of Germany's collapse in 1945 which could not be taken into account by Eyck.

CHAPTER I

Family and Descent

At the beginning of the fifteenth century the Hohenzollerns settled in the state of Brandenburg as its sovereigns. They had come here from their south-German home, where they originally occupied a castle in Suabia from which they derived their name. Through thrift, skilful buying and profitable marriages, but above all through their cleverness in choosing the right side in the politics of the German Empire, they had acquired great possessions and attained to a political position of high honour, leading at the end of the twelfth century to their being rewarded with the lordship (Burggrafschaft) of Nuremberg. The administration of this important imperial residence brought them into frequent contact with the head of the Reich and with the highest political activity in Germany. It was no light task which Count (Burggraf) Friedrich von Hohenzollern undertook when he accepted the lordship of Brandenburg. Of this he was well aware, for he had already been for some time active in the service of the Empire in this state, but it belonged to the tradition of his house not to shrink from a difficult and dangerous enterprise if it promised advantage and gain.

Brandenburg at that time comprised less than 10,000 square miles and less than 100,000 inhabitants, but its lord was in virtue of his position charged with the high office of Imperial Elector (Kurfürst), i.e., he had, together with six other German princes, the right to elect the King of the Roman Empire, then to be crowned Emperor by the Pope. The Brandenburg state was then in a quite anarchic condition politically and economically. Its sovereign dynasty had repeatedly changed in the previous century. Its rulers, coming from the south of the Empire, could not feel comfortable in a country where the climate was so harsh, the land so barren, and raw materials so lacking. Its inhabitants, who had wrenched the territory from the Wendish Slavs a few centuries before and had recently been obliged to defend it against the attacks of the Poles and the Lithuanians, were a hard and rough race, quite different from the inhabitants of the south of the Empire, who, being milder and more willing to adapt themselves, lived on undisputed territory in safety and comfort. So it came about that many of the previous rulers had not even taken up residence in the land they governed, and had no interest in its welfare. In constant need of money, they had sacrificed important sovereign rights, estates, and revenues, pledging some to private individuals and cities, and throwing away others for a small price. The nobility had no concern for the sovereign, paid no taxes, neglected their properties, and lived on highway robbery. The few towns, consequently, were unable to prosper and did not develop. They had to look after their own security against foreign and internal foes, and to this end formed alliances among themselves and with foreign towns. The peasants were without rights, vegetated at the lowest cultural level, and laboured under the greatest poverty. The last ruler, Siegmund, of the family of the counts of Luxemburg, was at the same time King of Hungary and had claims on the kingdom of Poland. He pawned his whole earldom of Brandenburg in order to provide means for his military expeditions against those who disputed his kingdoms. On his election as German King he sent to Brandenburg as his deputy Friedrich von Hohenzollern who belonged to his entourage. The conditions which the latter found there did not prevent him from allowing his royal master to reward him some years later with the lordship of the country and the dignity of Imperial Elector. The new deputy was the right man for the job. Patience, resolution, and unscrupulousness in his choice of means were the qualities which brought him gradually to his goal. He made use of the rich revenues which were placed at his disposal by the Empire or accrued from his own fortune in order to redeem what his predecessors had pawned. He sought and found an understanding with the independent cities, but his main object was to gain mastery over the recalcitrant nobility. He first tried to do this peaceably by recognizing both privileges which had been legally won and those which had been usurped by unilateral action. But this led to an armistice, not to a peace. Part of the nobility evidently regarded the will towards understanding displayed by the deputy and subsequent ruler as a weakness and thought that they could use this to secure and extend their own special interests. So there ensued a regular war between the new ruler and his nobility. The troops whom the former introduced had been brought by him from his south-German home. They had to fight against the Brandenburg nobility, sometimes in pitched battle, sometimes in siege warfare, and suffered thereby considerable casualties. But they came out victors, not least because the southerners were already familiar with mobile heavy guns, while the northerners only used stationary ones. So the forts of the nobles were reduced and finally the leader of the rebellion was taken prisoner.

The new ruler of Brandenburg would certainly not have mastered the recalcitrant nobles so quickly if some families had not kept the agreement which had been reached. Among these are mentioned the Bismarcks. The Bismarcks had not belonged to the native Brandenburg landed aristocracy from their first appearance in history; their genealogy does not record the family as among the original nobility. About 1300 a bearer of the name is mentioned as master of the guild of clothiers at Stendal, a town in Brandenburg. But quite a long time before the Hohenzollerns, this ' Suabian family ', had come to Brandenburg, the Bismarcks had entered the circle of the landed nobility. The son of that guild master, Claus von Bismarck, from having been a town patrician became a nobleman in the country. He was given an important border castle of the ' Alt-Mark ' (the oldest part of Brandenburg) as a fief and was able to leave this to his children and grandchildren. He also played a part in the political life of his homeland and witnessed the passing of the sovereignty to the house of Luxemburg. On their arrival he withdrew from public life and entered into open opposition to the economic misgovernment which had now set in. That his grand-children unreservedly supported the new ruling family of the Hohenzollerns was certainly due to the hope that the latter would bring better times not only to the country, but also to the Bismarcks. In fact, however, they had to show their devotion to this ruling family through a sacrifice of no mean order. Their ancestral estate in the ' Alt-Mark ' aroused the greed of the then heir to the throne, who staked his power to induce the Bismarcks to exchange it for estates in parts of the country which had been acquired later. This was an exchange which was not only very unfavourable financially, but had the additional disadvantage of sundering the Bismarcks from the particularly proud and highly honoured society of the noblemen of the Alt-Mark. The Elbe now separated them from their old home, on which they always looked as their real mother-soil, although they quickly enough entered into close personal relations with those of their own rank in their new environment and intermarried with them.

Among the possessions acquired at that time were the castle and estate of Schönhausen, in which Otto Eduard Leopold von Bismarck was born on 1st April 1815, 250 years from the time when it first came into the possession of the family. The name of this estate was often added as a suffix to the family name by him and his successors. A year after Otto's birth the family took a further step away from their ancestral home in the ' Alt-Mark '. Through the decease of a relative they had inherited properties in Pomerania to the right of the Oder and they moved to their new estate, Kniephof. Since the beginning of the eighteenth century the property of the family had fairly considerably increased. Some of the heads of the family had then resolved to spend their life on their estates and to make the care and increase of their possessions their aim. So not only was the estate of Schönhausen rounded off, but also fine estates in other parts of the country were added to it. Some went to different branches of the family through the inheritance being split up, but some became united in one hand through other branches dying out. Otto von Bismarck's immediate ancestors had devoted themselves to the military profession either in their youth or during their whole life. His great-grandfather, a commander of the dragoons, had distinguished himself in the first Silesian War and fell at the hands of the enemy. His grandfather was wounded in the Seven Years' War as cavalry captain of the cuirassiers and then carried on business in Schönhausen. He had also scholarly interests, and spent many hours in the enjoyment of works of contemporary literature and music. His youngest son, Ferdinand, the father of Otto, had given up military service in the cavalry when quite young in order to help his father, who had just been left a lonely widower, in the management of the estate of Schönhausen, which he then inherited from him. So the relation of personal service to the King and the love of his home and his own soil provided the background of his life. In the summer of 1806, long after the death of his father, he married at the age of thirty-five a much younger woman, Wilhelmine Menken.

The Menkens originated in a quite different social circle from the Bismarcks. That they did not belong to the nobility is a fact which we must not overlook in considering an age when in Germany, and especially in Prussia, the division between nobility and bourgeoisie was still so firmly maintained ; when it was considered so essential for a nobleman not to marry beneath him, and when purity of one's genealogical tree was not only highly significant in social intercourse but also the condition of the attainment of many positions of honour and financial profit. The Menkens, however, belonged not to the aristocracy of birth, but to the aristocracy of mind. For more than a century they had in unbroken sequence and in several branches of the family held chairs at German universities and made a name for themselves in the field of learning. The father of Wilhelmine was intended by his parents for a chair at the university of Helmstedt but strove for a place in a wider sphere, more connected with practical life. In the service of the Prussian state he acquired a high position involving a personal relation to the King. He had witnessed the revolutionary happenings in the neighbouring France with attentive eyes and heartfelt sympathy. He was a representative of the better type of that bureaucracy which stamped out the diversity of the different Germanic peoples united under the Prussian sceptre and produced the uniform Prussian type. He died early when his daughter was only a child, but his memory and the tradition of his views remained active in her.

The influence of bourgeoisie, intellectual aristocracy, and humanism entered the Bismarck family with Wilhelmine Menken, thus blending with an atmosphere in which so far only Prussianism, loyalty to the King, military service, and the love of home in the narrowest sense had prevailed. The atmosphere of the town associated itself with the devotion to the land, the adherence to cultural values with the simplicity of instinctive man, a bureaucratic sense of duty with the stubbornness of a Prussian noble family. The robust health and bodily strength of the man was enhanced by contrast with the delicate constitution and the bodily sensitiveness of the woman. However, in the way in which these different elements were here combined, they constituted a contrast rather than a con-flict. The goodwill was present to enable them to fit together in peace and harmony. While the realist Ferdinand von Bismarck was faced, through this union, with the task of adapting himself by widen-ing and diversifying his mental horizon, his wife, on the contrary, was brought down to solid earth and took to thinking in a more concrete fashion. Both of them through their relation to each other were led to cultivate their own character and also to understand and respect each other.

These mental changes took place in a harmonious and prosperous environment. We see at first a well-tended, spacious house, not marked by oppressive splendour, but by the greatest warmth and comfort. This house was built about 1700 by an ancestor of good taste and is a distinguished example of the baroque style. The interior was both homely and adapted to extensive entertaining. The furniture was ponderous and had for the most part long been in the possession of the family. To this were added the family portraits on the walls, which depicted the men in the uniforms of Prussian cavalry regiments, named with pride as having been tested in many wars ; the ladies bore the names of neighbouring nobility : so that both were evidence that the family had grown up with the momentous history and the rise to power of their fatherland and had done so not only as passive recipients but as fellow-creators. That was what Schönhausen was like. Kniephof was more modest : an old-fashioned building, but not less comfortable and equally con-nected with the tradition of the caste and the state. To both houses there belonged great parks in which nature and art were blended in harmonious unity. Clipped hedges, ornamental bushes, flower-beds, and well-tended avenues were succeeded by meadows, clusters of mighty oaks, little streams and lakes. Here the grown-up members of the family moved about as lords on their own land, and by their side went only the guests they had invited. The children had their ground on which to play with comrades of their own choosing. Near by the manor stood the church of the village, in which the family attended service on Sunday. The pew of honour occupied by them, the memorial stones to their dead all round the walls, the mode in which the worshippers looked up at the squire and in which the pastor turned to them in his sermon must have strengthened in them the feeling that they were deeply rooted in the soil and stood as lords over their fellow-men. To this was added the position of the squire, first as lord over his inherited serfs, then as provider of work for his household and for many of the villagers, then as a person charged with magisterial and police functions, and lastly his position as private adviser and confidant to his dependents. As such he enjoyed throughout his domain the position of the head of a family, and many who occupied this position took their duties of advising and providing care very seriously. All the members of the seigneurial family had a share in the honour paid by young and old.

With the neighbouring members of the same class they were connected by bonds of blood and friendship. This group represented the governing class of the country, a close circle socially, fully conscious that everybody else whom they met was of lower rank and had a longing to come into relation with them. At the same time these squires were by virtue of birth and of their possessions placed among the rulers of the realm, so that in many questions they had the power to decide what was to be done, and without their approval nothing could be planned and carried out. Above this group of nobles stood the King, exalted over them, but yet one of them. Their own social circle included the King and the royal house. These noblemen, and nobody else, were the court. On the occasion of their more or less frequent visits to Berlin they became personally acquainted with the royal family and with their fellow-squires from all over the land, thus preserving unity and class-comradeship among them. On the maintenance of this social structure the welfare of the whole accordingly depended. Men were therefore willing to render unconditional obedience to the sovereign, and they proved this not only in the way they filled the offices in court and state which were open only to people of their rank, but above all through their service as commanders of companies, battalions, and regiments in the army, these positions also being reserved for the nobility. Nevertheless they were also conscious that they provided the real decisive guarantee of the preservation of the royal power and that this was dependent on them. So they regarded their own presence as primarily a continuation and maintenance of the well-proven past. Care for their own future as individuals did not play the decisive part in this circle ; it was not so much that they expected of the future great good fortune as that they were convinced that so long as the state remained and they stood fast in their own ranks, their future would be secured. On the other hand, the dangers of war to life and property were inseparable elements in their existence. These were not regarded as extraordinary menaces but gave to the structure of their life its particular colouring. But war provided also the opportunity to gain distinctions which they strongly desired, it provided the most legitimate means of social advancement and of the increase of family estates.

Ferdinand von Bismarck and his wife with their three surviving children, Otto, the five-years-older Bernhard and the much-younger Malvine, felt quite at home in this secure and well-established social system. That their inner life was richer and more animated than was the case with most of their fellows only meant that they could more consciously enjoy and appreciate the security and harmony of their environment. The deficiency in the genealogy of the wife had apparently hindered their rise in the social scale but little and if perhaps it was sometimes felt as a disturbing influence it did not affect their prevailing harmony more than superficially.

The first important outer event in their married life was the occupation of their home by the French after the battles of Jena and Auerstädt. French troops were billeted in Schönhausen and displayed a vivid and irritating consciousness of the victory they had won, for a hole in a door of one of the drawing-rooms is attributed to the bayonet of a vehement officer who pursued the young mistress of the house. The young lady is said to have been compelled for some time to reside away from Schönhausen. Damage done to the lime-tree which was a special feature of the estate is supposed to have occurred through vandalism of the French. The memory of these events lived on in the family ; they were again and again revived in conversation and they made a permanent impression on the children. It was not only the love of one's soil and the idea of its sacredness and inviolability which was implanted in the descendants. There was also a substantial dose of exaggerated contempt for the aggressors, ' the hereditary foes, the eternal, tireless, destructive enemies ', as Baron vom Stein called them in 1815, who were declared to be worthless and were yet secretly admired, combined with the desire to avenge their ' crimes '.

In the years following the marriage of the parents there occurred the abolition of hereditary serfdom, of forced labour, and of similar restrictions on the Prussian peasantry, together with the granting of permission to the nobility to sell their land outside their class and a general weakening of the cast-iron walls between the classes. These changes were effected by the Stein-Hardenberg reforms. But the significance of them for the social position of the noble landowners was not at once fully realized by them, since the common fate of the fatherland absorbed their attention. Some years later there gathered the armies which were to restore to Prussia her freedom. A group of selected volunteers was for a time billeted in Schönhausen, mostly students and middle-class town people. They took the oath in the church there, were drilled in the neighbourhood, and helped in enlisting and training recruits. Everywhere they were greeted with love and admiration by the neighbouring landlords and their retinues. For they saw in them only the future liberators of their fatherland from the oppression of the foreign enemy and had no idea that with them there had appeared a class of people whose liberal and national demands would revolutionize the inner political life of Prussia, based as it was on devotion to the royal power as well as the social structure which was based on the superiority of the nobility. For to the state of the Prussian nobles they opposed their will towards the national state as a spiritual community. Their national self-consciousness did not arise from the consciousness of being a factor in the political structure, but rather from the fact that the German thinkers and poets preceding them became conscious of and expressed a distinctive spirit common to them all. From these thinkers the future liberators of the fatherland had learned that it is the spirit expressed in their culture which differentiates one people from another; that the *Kulturstaat* is the adequate expression of a national entity. They believed in the superiority and genius of the Germans because they alone had remained 'idealists' and alone were capable of putting into practice the postulates of idealism. This idealism meant not only the readiness to sacrifice oneself for the state, but to live in accordance with the postulates of the one, divine Reason. Their ideal was 'a realm of true justice founded upon the equality of all human beings'. 'The remarkable feature in the German national character', their admired thinker, Fichte, says, ' is that they are able to exist without the state and beyond the state in their purely spiritual culture. Among Germans the state is to grow out of the development of individual liberty.'

The experience of watching the volunteers gathered to restore to Prussia her freedom from foreign oppression left a permanent mark in the family memory and was imprinted on the receptive mind of the children. Here at first it left roots as strong as those implanted by the crimes of the ' hereditary ' French foe.

CHAPTER II

School Years

Otto spent only the first year of his life in Schönhausen. The years in which he came to self-consciousness were spent in the simpler and more modest Kniephof. Here the house was for the boy merely a place of shelter in the midst of surrounding nature. The farms, gardens, fields, and woods which were the real seat of his life, determined his mode of living even within the house. Sport, his chief interest in youth, led him far afield, while comfort within the house only served as a means of rest. With his parents too the main interest lay out of doors. Their task was now no longer to preserve and hand on an estate of great value, but to restore to a tolerable degree of prosperity one which had been neglected and reduced to poverty. This may have been partly due to losses incurred through the hostile occupation and the subsequent events of the war, but also to the effect of the social reforms. Otto's parents had to work like colonists, and thus became somewhat used to the life of colonists. Above all, this meant for the delicate mother a thorough change in her style of life. The land had ceased to be a mere place in which to live quietly and had become a task and a problem to which she devoted herself with much zeal and not without success. But neither parent was completely subjugated to this activity. The yearly winter visit to Berlin and the summer visit of the mother to a spa, sometimes in the company of her husband and children, prevented them from being so.

For Otto and his brother Bernhard life in Kniephof meant an important factor in their education owing to their close connexion with nature. As with every child who has grown up in the country, his senses were awakened to all natural processes, the state of the fields in different seasons, the uses of woods and streams, the habits and needs of cattle. But his interest was no less aroused in the beauties of the landscape with its variety of hill and dale, its vast fields and sequestered glades, its product of natural and cultivated flowers, with the song and beautiful garment of the birds, as well as with the peculiarities and habits of the animals the father hunted. The customs and practices of the boys modelled themselves on what nature provided in carefree enjoyment and demanded in resolution and adaptability. The reference to the family tradition and its connexion with the history of the fatherland were less important at Kniephof than at Schönhausen. Except for a few visits to the Schönhausen estate, this tradition was brought home to the boys

9

much more by the presence of their parents and the stories they told them than by anything else. But his two parents impressed Otto with it in very different ways. The not very gifted though very good-hearted and strictly conservative father, a big eater and big drinker as were many of his ancestors, full of health and strength, was a man whose very presence inspired the boy. He in his own person was for Otto the family of the Bismarcks. The whole line of ancestors, knights with clattering armour, bewigged cavaliers of the Thirty Years' War, and finally the pig-tailed cavalrymen of Frederick the Great were vividly linked in the boy's imagination with his father. The delicate mother, very gifted and proud of her knowledge, possessed of restless ambition and a progressive mind, represented for the boy not exactly the past, which would have attracted him, but the future, and not a future which bestowed gifts, but one which demanded services. The father attracted him by his self-possessed demeanour, the ease and dignity of his movements, his reserved friendliness in conversation. He was sought out by his son as confidant and adviser, his judgement and his decision determined every issue. The mother taught, criticized, and stimulated him. She expected of him knowledge and refinement. She was occupied with thoughts of his future position in life and this idea determined her efforts to influence her son. The nature of his father appealed to his emotional side, with him the son felt secure and at ease ; the intellectual gifts of the mother were respected, but at the same time they kept him at a distance and even frightened him. Neither parent lacked religion completely. The father's was more in accord with the traditional sentimental illiberal piety of the Junkers. The mother was inclined to religious *Schwärmerei* which stood in striking contradiction to her cold intelligence.

The boy felt the contrast between his parents long before he was conscious of it. It is equally true that his decision was taken long before reflection could determine it. He was a Bismarck and wanted only to be a Bismarck. Already in externals he represented the robust build of his clan and showed little of the delicate graceful constitution of his mother. Temperamentally he was anything rather than a cool man of reason, although in the later course of his life what he had inherited from his mother was to prove stronger than his reaction against her. But in the resulting conflict a balancing and pacifying influence was exercised by the exuberant will to life of the ' terribly healthy ' youth which would not admit of brooding or of doubts. There helped also the daily renewed joy which flowed from contact with nature, and of a nature with which he felt really at one, through his origin and his anticipation of future possession, ' a home in which he had grown up so as to be one with it by birth, memory, and love '.

This natural and little fettered life was to come to an end early through the decision of the mother. Before he was seven years old, Otto was removed from his home and together with his elder brother was sent to Berlin to school. He was to be educated at the Plamann School which had been developed in accordance with the then novel requirements of a system intended to bring teachers and pupils in close personal contact. It stood at a high intellectual and cultural level, was based on humanism, and so was quite in accord with the wishes of the mother which were derived from the views that her father had handed down to her. Its teachers followed the trend of liberalism set up by the liberators of Prussia from the oppression of the foreign enemy. They held that the youths entrusted to their care ought to be educated in the belief that the Germans alone had remained ' idealists ' and were capable of putting into practice the postulates of idealism. Otto entered the small circle of full boarders who were to be brought up in a close communal system subject to a strict discipline and a spartan regimen. Religious worship, physical training, an open-air life, gardening on a plot of their own, played an important part. But to one who like Bismarck was used to freedom and self-willed selection of friends this kind of community, this regimentation and supervision must have seemed like life in prison. He knew how to get on with his fellow-scholars, his school work was satisfactory throughout, over-haste and superficiality were occasionally blamed in him, though he was rather indifferent to his teachers' opinion about him. Yet the Bismarck in him was opposed to the ideals which characterized the school atmosphere. Also he suffered because he often could not spend his holidays at home, owing to his mother's delicate health.

At the age of twelve Otto was removed from the Plamann School, and for the next five years he was at a Grammar School (Gymnasium) in Berlin. The study of classical antiquity and of its ideals was regarded as a very serious task in the ' Grey Convent ' where Otto at Easter, 1832, passed his leaving examination. But his achievements in classics did not exceed the average. He was interested in modern languages, of which he learned French and English, and in history. But it cannot be said that he had any affinity to the class of the learned. His school friendships were limited to a small circle of sons of family friends. Of intimate relations with teachers we hardly know anything.

At the beginning of the education in the Grammar School the two brothers Bismarck lived in a house which their parents had rented some time before for their own winter sojourn in Berlin. In the absence of the parents they had a household of their own, run by a housekeeper who had been for long in the family service, and with a resident tutor to supervise them. When Bernhard, three

years before Otto, started attending the university, the latter was
boarded with a teacher who looked after him well, and who praised
highly his domesticity and unexacting ways.   Here also he began to
read on his own, thus laying the foundation of the comprehensive
knowledge which he held fast in a reliable memory.   There was,
however, only a slight connexion between this knowledge and what
he had learnt at school.   Modern history and literature, especially
French and English, occupied him.   But his attitude towards what
he read was rather that of being interested than that of being fas-
cinated, that is, he read chiefly for information and entertainment.
Bismarck liked Schiller, admired Goethe, enjoyed Chamisso, Uhland,
and Heine ; but none of these aroused passion or enthusiasm in
him, only cool assent and readiness to absorb what they said.   Still
Bismarck never quite belied his humanistic education and gladly
quoted classical literature.   He was receptive to aesthetic impressions, and despite his denials of this he had a true understanding for
classical music.   But it was not here that he reached the high peaks
of his inner life ; he took aesthetic experience when it was offered
him and found in it relaxation, but he hardly looked for it on his
own accord.   Intellectual and artistic work and creation as an end
in itself he respected, but it was quite foreign to his nature.   Intellectual formulation and creation meant for him only an instrument
of expression for the practical will and practical action in which he
saw his own lifework.   As such he employed it with complete
competence.   But even his brilliant letters and speeches or his
masterly *Reflections and Reminiscences* he would never have regarded
as artistic creations nor would he have accepted such an estimate of
them.   In accordance with this attitude towards intellectual and
artistic creation Bismarck was bound to reject the conception that
the work of the German thinkers and poets should differentiate
the German people from others and shape the *Kulturstaat* as the
adequate form of a national entity.

The personal contact with the social world in which Bismarck
had been born was continued and extended in Berlin and in his
holiday visits to the country.   This was less the case as regards the
time when he was at the Plamann School when even in his hours
of leisure Otto was supervised and strictly limited in his movements.
At that time he often spent his free hours at an uncle's who, as a
discharged officer of high rank, had a landed estate near Berlin.
More extended were the social relations which he enjoyed through
living with his parents during the Berlin winter.   The Prussian
nobility had lost some of their political power and economic advantages through the Stein-Hardenberg reforms, the rise of the
bourgeoisie in the Wars of Liberation, and the intellectual and
social preparation for these.   The middle classes now set themselves

BISMARCK
AT THE AGE OF 11 YEARS, 1826

Painting by Franz Krüger

to develop a self-consciousness of their own. But they lacked the political and social influence necessary to give a secure basis to this change. Apart from the Rhineland, which had been recently added to the Prussian state, the Prussian towns were not very numerous, rich, or populous. Berlin with slightly more than 200,000 inhabitants had rather the appearance of a country town. The prosperity of the inhabitants was still in process of being gradually built up. Sumptuous entertaining would not have been in keeping with economic circumstances. The social and private life of the burghers was centred on the cultivation of intellectual goods. The nobility, on the other hand, had managed to replace the power which they had lost by securing what privileges they still had and by maintaining their inner cohesion and their personal relationship to the ruling house. Many reforms in the interest of the peasantry were held up. The new provincial and district councils, as well as rural administration, were now the basis of the aristocratic power. The increased personal contact with the bourgeoisie in public and social life was regarded and used by the nobles rather as a means of emphasizing and displaying their position of privilege than as a surrender of this. The partly bourgeois ministerial bureaucracy, in spite of any liberal inclinations of their own, took their stand on the side of the King and the nobility.

This state of affairs, characterized by sharply marked contrasts and by the interplay of progress and reaction, human equality, and class distinction, was brought to the consciousness of the wide-awake boy Bismarck through the influence of his immediate social environment. The ground was indeed already prepared through his two lines of inheritance. The experience of this played an important part in his youthful development, certainly not less significant than that played by what he learned through school and private reading. Bismarck stated later in his *Reflections and Reminiscences* that he left the Grammar School 'if not as a republican, yet with the conviction of the reasonableness of being one'. This conviction may well have been casually aroused through observing particular political and social evils in his environment. The youth was sufficiently clearsighted not to overlook such things, and sincere enough to admit them to himself. But it is certain that this conviction influenced his political will just as superficially as the humanism and liberalism then prevailing among scholars influenced his intellectual attitude.

Those in Bismarck's immediate environment could indeed not ignore the nationalist German tendency with its liberal and constitutional flavour, anticipated by the volunteers billeted in Schönhausen when they were mustered to fight against the oppression of the foreign enemy. It was tolerated by his mother and cultivated at the Plamann School. But this ' republicanism ' was thoroughly contrary to Otto's temper. Here there ruled with ever-increasing power the inborn, congenial, highly personal devotion of the aristocrat to the Hohenzollern monarchy, as due in an authoritarian state. There was present in the background something like an ' imperial German consciousness ' (*kaiserlich deutsche Gesinnung*). But it was directed, not towards an institution, but towards a predominant ruling personality, and not to one of the political present, but of the German past, the time when there was still a German Emperor, the time before the Thirty Years' War. For the present it demanded for the imperial house in Austria, as the venerable symbol of this past and the friend of the Hohenzollerns, only a due respect. The young Prussian Bismarck had not yet heard anything either of a political present or of a political future for Germany. And yet it was a period in which German literature and philosophy stood at their zenith and served many patriotic men as a basis and stimulus for the political revival of a Germany which had already revived culturally. Bismarck's political ideals were embodied in the conceptions of order and authority. These he saw to be best realized in the Prussian state. Consequently he pictured to himself a political development on this basis, not beside, still less against, but through Prussia. He felt now not only willing to subordinate himself to this order and authority, but also called to take his share in the responsibility for it.

An event at this time which seemed intended to be a turning point in Bismarck's inner life evidently passed him by without leaving much impression. That was his confirmation just before his sixteenth birthday, by the great theologian Friedrich Schleiermacher. The latter was one of those German thinkers who prepared the path for the national ideas of the *Kulturstaat* on German soil. He was a man whose very presence, owing to his unmistakable earnestness and sincerity, should have made a strong impression on a receptive young mind. And yet Bismarck passed him by unawares. From his parents he could not obtain any decisive stimulus and help towards the religious life. However, in the circles in which Bismarck grew up, discussions of the problems of religion, if not real religious devotion, were of common occurrence. Perhaps it was not always original inner need which made these men turn to religion, but various stimuli of another kind. There was the idea of the union between throne and altar which was very vivid here. It was their aim not only to use religion as a firm bond to maintain obedience among the peasantry to king and state, but also to give them as perfect as possible an example of this attitude. Also the life of the landowner who had many hours of leisurely solitude in his often remote country house was well adapted to stimulate religious ideas and meditations, even if the experience of growth, bloom, harvest, and decay in nature did not inspire him to it. Finally, the close connexion of life in this class with the occurrence of war and its incalculable dangers for health and life provided occasion enough to look away from the ever-obvious dependence of the present life on uncontrollable conditions to the unconditioned object of religion.

No doubt, Bismarck, even long after his childhood, was unconsciously influenced by this atmosphere with its tendencies to religion. For up to his sixteenth year he still said his prayers before going to bed. But increasing knowledge and reflection had not furthered but hindered what was left of the religious side in his nature. For he consciously abandoned prayer as in contradiction with the nature of God who knew everything and was not liable to be influenced by men. This was the time in which the rationalist attitude to religion of Ludwig Feuerbach first influenced the religious outlook of Germans. Religious teaching and confirmation had not checked but rather hastened this decay of religious belief in Bismarck. ' After a course of religious teaching which I attended only irregularly and did not understand, I had at the time of my confirmation by Schleiermacher no belief except a bare deism which did not long remain without an admixture of pantheism,' he reports.

CHAPTER III

Student Days

It had been due to the influence of his mother that Otto received his first education in the unaristocratic Grammar School and not in the cadet corps which were really designed to educate the young Prussian nobility. Now it was again the mother who opposed the proposal that Otto should, after finishing his course at the Grammar School, take up the profession of cavalry officer traditional to his class and his family. Strange to say, on this occasion the mother had the son on her side. So the family abandoned the project of a military career. Now it would have certainly agreed with the wishes of the father if Otto had devoted himself to their estates, but the mother was evidently thinking of a career corresponding to that of her own father, for instance a high post in the diplomatic or administrative services. No doubt the son had the least precise idea of his professional future. He had the vague but firm feeling that the whole world was open to one of his descent, vitality, and talents. He now displayed ever-increasing self-assurance and confidence. That is shown by the letters of the last years in which he begins to develop a style of his own. The features of an aristocratic, keen-sighted, self-possessed young gentleman with a touch of sovereign irony appeared ever more clearly. The following extracts from letters are characteristic. Speaking of his (then about ten years old) sister he says : ' Little Malvine begins to look as if she had quite a personality of her own.' He himself was living ' like a god in France ' ; on his neighbour's estate he ' diverts himself for a few hours with the pretty Mrs. X '. He is plunged into the water with his horse as the mare was ' so obliging as quite unexpectedly to give me a pleasant bath'. When in the country there was anxiety about a cholera epidemic, he says : ' We are already making plans to fortify Kniephof.'

In these words there speaks a man who knows the present to be his own, who lets the future take care of itself, and for whom the inherited basis of a nobleman's estate is the best conceivable starting-point for every venture into the future. The paths of approach to everything that society had to offer in the way of activity and success in politics, service of the state, and private life were ready paved for him. It was hardly possible to miss them, he had only to utilize and to increase the advantages which were originally at his disposal.

These were the reflections which led the son to comply with the wishes of his mother that he should pursue a university course.

16

Now it was a question of choosing the university. Berlin was naturally the first that would occur to their thoughts. This still youthful university was the most distinguished representative of the intellectual life of the new humanism which was now re-awakening in German-speaking lands. It also represented the uprising of a nationalistic German and liberal movement, though with a strong admixture of conservative Prussianism. The mother was not only much influenced by those tendencies, but also calculated that Berlin would be the place where from the beginning the personal relations could be established which would prepare the way for her son's future career. The son thought little of all this; it is the youthful love of freedom and pleasure which is indicated by his proposal to choose Bonn, the cheerful, life-loving town on the Rhine, or Geneva, situated on the lake renowned in song and at the foot of the most awe-inspiring part of the Alps.

That they eventually decided on Göttingen was no mere compromise. It was on the contrary the place which could satisfy the different desires involved. Göttingen was then for the young Prussian a foreign town. Moreover, it was frequented by non-Germans, especially English and Americans. It thus meant an extension of the horizon for a young Junker from the east of the Elbe. It was a markedly aristocratic university, the very place to find useful friends. Life in Göttingen, marked by its freedom and unrestrained individualism, provided a young man with all that German student life could offer in the way of social attractions. Göttingen, moreover, had the best, universally recognized reputation in those subjects in which Bismarck was most concerned to obtain instruction and education, namely political science and history. This reputation dated in particular from the second half of the preceding century. There was still living and working at Göttingen a man who belonged to this period, the historian and political theorist Arnold Heeren, who owed his fame to encyclopaedic works on politics and history that he had written a long time before. Now an old man, anti-democratic and anti-revolutionary, he saw in the German Confederation, founded in June 8, 1815, by the Vienna Congress, loosely combining thirty-nine sovereign states and represented by the German Diet sitting in Frankfort on Main, the rebirth of the German nation. By his side there worked in the same field Ch. Dahlmann, one of the recognized leaders of the nationalist liberal movement of the bourgeoisie, striving after a genuine unity of the people, a man who was a model to many Germans, not only through his intellectual qualities, but above all through his manly courage and integrity. He was a genuine fellow in spirit of those fighters in the wars of 1813–15 ' against the oppression of the foreign enemy '.

Placed amid these possibilities of education and enjoyments of student life, Otto von Bismarck as a freshman displays a quite touching picture of embarrassment. We have the impression of a young man who stands helpless before the learning provided by the university and who at the same time is pressed by exhortations from his parents to devote all his energies to acquiring it. After a short time he was attending a great number of lectures on the most different subjects : Jurisprudence, Philosophy, Political Theory, Mathematics, etc. The unskilled way in which he selected the lectures he should attend shows that the student had no advice or guidance from anybody and also no desire to be guided by his teachers. The teacher who attracted Bismarck most was Arnold Heeren. If one takes as the object of university education not only an increase of knowledge but the training of the mind and forming of the will, there was nothing to be got from Heeren. The teacher in Göttingen at the time who had something to offer in this respect, Dahlmann, did not, however, come into contact with Bismarck. The latter did not find his way to the distinguished man, and probably did not even look for it. At any rate, he never mentions him. This is not merely a chance accident. It was not in Bismarck's nature to seek out somebody but rather to hold himself back and let others approach him. The cause of this was originally certainly not any conscious policy, but rather an aristocratic laziness and a tendency to wait and see. This is not contradicted by the fact that in a few decisive situations he knew very well how to take the initiative in personal matters, go to another, open his heart, and win him for himself by throwing his own personality fully into play. But in the lecture-rooms of Göttingen University he was not concerned to do that. The attitude of the academic student who looked up in wonder to the superior mind of his teacher, then very much in vogue in the German universities, was quite foreign to his nature. The aim of his studies at the university was very sober and prosaic. He wanted to acquire a definite quantum of knowledge which could be of use for his further career.

But it was only quite at the beginning that the greater or even a considerable part of Bismarck's student days at Göttingen were spent in the premises of the university. The real student life soon acquired the upper hand with him. In the German universities of the time this life had its principal seat in the student fraternities. In those years the latter fell into two sharply distinguished groups : the German Burschenschaft and the Landsmannschaften or ' Corps '. The former was definitely political in its tendencies. It cultivated the ideals of the great middle-class movement of the period, namely, national unity and political freedom as set up by the youthful fighters in the wars against the oppression of the foreign enemy. However, it represented German national feeling in as loud, peremptory, and striking a form as possible.   In their behaviour its members stressed originality and disregarded any code of polite conduct.   With the ' Corps ' the political interest took second place.   They aimed above all, as already the name Landsmannschaft indicates, at the strengthening of social ties between students coming from the same district. This task was the more important in that the liberty to change your university was highly valued and the distance of the university from their home was rather an attraction than a drawback to German students.   In their behaviour the Corps were somewhat more reserved and formal than the Burschenschaft.   Socially, both kinds of corporation were mainly recruited from the circles of the petite bourgeoisie.   Common to both was also the inclination to copious drinking, chiefly of beer, which was regarded as a kind of sport. Another kind of sport common to both was duelling, which left scars on the face that were highly prized as honourable proofs of valour. Both kinds of club were viewed with suspicion by those in power. The university authorities feared indiscipline and were motived by a paternal benevolence ;   the police directed their measures rather against the Burschenschaft and were rendered suspicious and hostile by political considerations.

The fraternities were always set on the acquisition of new members among the students and acted therein in a very aggressive manner.   A man with the physique of the young Bismarck was bound to strike them and to appear as a particularly desirable accession.   He was tall and very slender, yet powerfully built, with rough-hewn features and somewhat bristling fair hair, intelligent and clear eyes, and a firm chin.   His demeanour was secure and self-possessed, indeed presumptuous and challenging.   It was customary among the Göttingen students to distinguish oneself by striking clothes, to smoke over-long pipes, and to take big dogs about with one.   Soon this custom appealed to the wild spirits of Bismarck, he sought to outbid it.   He enjoyed wearing in public a bright garment, similar to a dressing-gown, reaching to the ground, a striking cap designed by himself, the high boots of a cuirassier, and an enormous walking-strick.   He was accompanied by a white bulldog, and he did not forget to smoke a pipe reaching almost to the ground, though the students were forbidden to smoke in the street.   Then the Burschenschaft approached the young student.   At first he let himself be wooed by them, but he soon felt repelled by their uncouth manners and the radicalism of their political views akin to those which had repelled him already when a schoolboy.   Then he came into touch with one of the ' Corps ', the Hanovera, in that he challenged some of its members who had loudly ridiculed his get-up. From being an antagonist he quickly became a member, although he did not come from Hanover.

Bismarck tasted richly of the fraternity student life. He fought a particularly large number of duels by way of sport. He also fought for the honour of the Prussian King and challenged a foreigner who made fun of the ' German Michel '. He was, as the true son of his father, given to the pleasures of the table, and in drinking bouts he was one of the most eager and efficient participants. He also took part in, or actually led, many students' rags. In his corps he occupied a series of posts of honour and often came into conflict with the university authorities for breaking the regulations. He was therefore regarded as a pattern of conduct by the German ' corps students ', who in later Germany played a very important rôle socially and politically. On the popular fancy he left a deep and permanent impression as a smart and dashing student. In reality, Bismarck never wholly surrendered himself to the corps life. He never subscribed to its ' ideals ' and hardly made a single lasting friendship with members of his corps. He played with this kind of life rather than devoted himself to it. It did not mean to him much more than a way of sowing his wild oats and of asserting himself among his fellow-students. His irregular and none too frequent letters home from Göttingen often spoke of corps affairs in the supercilious tone which corresponds to this attitude.

Bismarck's social life as a student was not limited to his corps, nor did it culminate in this. In Göttingen, this ' university of princes and counts ', there was a large circle of aristocratic students, especially from north Germany and the Baltic States, and it was natural for Bismarck to cultivate his connexion with them. Here he moved in the circle to which he belonged by descent and to which he felt akin in mode of life and disposition. He is hardly likely to have opposed the supercilious mockery of the corps prevailing here ; rather would he join in it. Bismarck also seems to have visited family gatherings. But he chiefly moved in a circle which stood quite apart from this whole world. There was among the Göttingen students of his time a specially considerable group of Americans and Englishmen who were attracted by the reputation of Göttingen for learning. Here they studied zealously, and participated in student life almost only as wondering and amused onlookers. Bismarck, aided by his knowledge of foreign languages, came into contact with them. Here a different side of his nature was developed, his interest in poetry, belles-lettres, and music. Above all his historical and social views and his political wishes and aims are likely to have been deepened and clarified having encountered the quite different outlook of a free and progressive world. They seem, however, to have confirmed him in his reactionary attitude rather than rendered him susceptible to liberal German tendencies. Distinguished among these foreigners was the American, John L. Motley, later known as a great historian and statesman who had a lifelong friendship with Bismarck. A few years later Motley published a novel, one character in which was none other than the Bismarck of Göttingen. In him are depicted particular characteristics of Bismarck which could have hardly been ascertained by the writer without an intimate knowledge of his hero. It is significant enough that Bismarck expressed himself most openly just where he felt himself safest owing to the fact that he was separated by a great distance in character, and national and social environment.

After three terms his life at Göttingen came to an end. It is not known whether the initiative came from Bismarck himself or from his parents, in which case it would no doubt be his mother's work. Anyhow, Bismarck did not find it very hard to leave Göttingen. His relations with the corps had become unsatisfactory and his own position with the university authorities progressively more difficult; he himself had the unconfessed feeling that Göttingen had not much more to offer him and might end by endangering his development. For the conclusion of his studies Berlin was selected, and Bismarck was a member of this university till the spring of 1835. His relations at Berlin to the university professors were perhaps even more loose than they had been at Göttingen. He had now come to the decision to take a law examination, but in order to prepare for this he did not take the way provided by the university lectures which called for intellectual penetration and real mastery of detail, but the easier one provided by a crammer who handed the candidate the subject-matter ready prepared for examination purposes. So in the spring of 1835, when he was just twenty, he passed the final examination in jurisprudence satisfactorily. Apart from preparation for this, an occupation which did not take up very much time, Bismarck was mainly engrossed in the activities natural to a well-to-do aristocrat with intellectual interests and sociable inclinations. His closest Göttingen friends had meanwhile also moved to Berlin. These were J. L. Motley and the count Alexander Keyserling. The latter was at once a nobleman and a scientist, deeply concerned with religious and philosophical problems, and a practising musician of talent and taste, and it was in this latter respect that he was the giver and Bismarck the receiver. To the more reserved Keyserling, the fresh and vivacious conversation of the American provided a welcome supplement. Motley was immensely interested in German literature and thought, and he felt the need to communicate to his German friend his knowledge and his discoveries in this field as well as to receive his criticisms and suggestions. But besides Goethe, also Shakespeare and Byron obtained what was due to them, and Bismarck especially relished the biting irony of the latter. Motley, who resembled Bismarck in his indestructible vitality and love of life, often kept him half the night discussing these subjects. They emptied many a bottle of wine together, and Motley also understood when his friend in matters of love followed his natural instincts without many scruples. Bismarck was interested in actresses, and in the evening at the opera behaved as rudely as possible in the front seats. He again acquired a wardrobe which attracted notice by its extravagance. To a friend at Göttingen he speaks with scornful arrogance about aristocratic society. Of a member of his own class he says, ' He was lacking in everything that beseemed a man, but in nothing that beseemed a royal chamberlain, except that he had no padlock in front of his mouth.'

But this excursion in Bohemian ways was only a temporary diversion ; he remained conscious that he must seek his permanent abode in the aristocratic circles from which he sprang. In the families of his relatives he liked to be received as a guest, was ready for a little love-making, but did not let himself be caught. ' In the evenings I have tea in some worthy family circle and talk about the weather and look as if I was not by any means saying all I knew.' At that time Bismarck even let himself be introduced at court. At a court ball he met the man with whom twenty-five years later his life work would lead him into the closest association, the second son of the King then reigning, Prince William of Prussia, later King and Emperor William I. On that occasion the Prince, who was nearly twenty years older than Bismarck, had nothing to say to the tall young man except the remark : ' Does the minister of justice nowadays pick his recruits according to the measurements required for guardsmen ? '

Despite all his social activities Bismarck was not spared those occasional moods of loneliness and sense of abandonment which hardly any highly gifted young man escapes. These moods aroused in him a desire which was otherwise foreign to his nature, for someone on whom to depend. He wrote to the above-mentioned Göttingen friend : ' In my loneliness I think very much of my old friends who are still unreplaced, and your report showing how vividly the members of the Hanovera Corps still remember me made an unusually profound impression on me.' In such hours also a deeply buried religious sense was to some extent excited in Bismarck. A hint by Keyserling of discussions on ' inner piety ' gives an indication of this. But such moods went as they came and left few and superficial traces.

After having passed his examination Bismarck worked at the Berlin city court as junior civil servant. He there entered an atmosphere of pettifogging detail and philistine provincialism. This applied both to the matters dealt with and to the personal characteristics of the magistrates who dealt with them. Nor did he fail to notice the lack of seriousness and conscientiousness with which even important matters were handled. That Bismarck did not feel at home here followed as a matter of course. The aristocrat of his class revolted from the beginning against the coercion and the levelling tendency of the bureaucracy, especially of the small fry among them. An anecdote, which, though not well authenticated, is at least an appropriate invention, illustrates Bismarck's relation to this profession. He was present at a trial in order to write minutes. The accused was behaving in an aggressive manner. Bismarck shouted at him : ' Sir, behave yourself, or I shall throw you out of the room.' Thereupon the presiding magistrate made it clear that throwing out of the room was his business. When the accused still did not yield his point, Bismarck now thundered : ' Sir, behave yourself, or I shall have you thrown out by the lord justice.'

So up to the present Bismarck's life provided no basis or stimulus for the choice of a future career. He even from time to time flirted with the idea of returning to Kniephof to manage the estate. ' I will wear leather trousers, allow myself to be laughed at at the Stettin wool market, and when I am called Baron, I will good-naturedly stroke my moustache and sell 2 thalers cheaper. I shall take a wife, have children, and ruin the morals of my peasants through the excessive manufacture of brandy.' But those were at that time only passing moods. The idea also occurred to him of becoming officer in a distinguished Berlin regiment. This project was now actually favoured by his mother, since her son ' seems to have no inclination at all for study'. But most attractive seemed the diplomatic career, perhaps more to the mother than to the son or even to the father. In the winter of 1835–6, serious steps towards this career were in fact taken. In preparing for it, it was customary to work for some time in a department of the home administration, and this in turn necessitated a new examination (*Regierungsreferendar*). After nine months' work at the Berlin city court, Bismarck took leave in order to prepare for this test.

CHAPTER IV

Civil Servant

Bismarck's change of employment brought with it a number of alterations in his external circumstances. First, a change of place was involved. He was not to be a government employee in Berlin but in Aachen and so in the very Rhine Province whose charming university, Bonn, had four years before so attracted him. The Rhine Province, except for some small parts, had come into the possession of Prussia only by the decision of the Vienna Congress of 1815. Before, it had consisted of about a hundred autonomous states, subject only to the Empire. An important part, e.g., the districts of Cologne and Trier, were subject to clerical rule. The country was extraordinarily beautiful, especially the valley of the Rhine proper ; it boasted a great number of cultural and historical monuments, reaching back to Roman times. Historically it had no direct cultural or political connexion with the old Prussian territories. It was incorporated with these without the consent of its inhabitants on the ground of the arguments of the conference table. In contrast to Old Prussia its population was more than two-thirds Catholic and very convinced and militant in its catholicism. While Old Prussia was purely agrarian, the Rhineland belonged to the parts of Germany which were industrially most developed. In agriculture, small landholdings were very common, especially in the important wine districts. There was here a great wealth of minerals, which were almost totally lacking in Old Prussia. The population was incomparably more prosperous than that of those older parts. Also in their manner of life the Rhinelanders were radically distinct from the Prussians. Like the south Germans, to whom they were akin, they were attracted by the French way of living and strongly and immediately stirred by the French Revolution. They were gifted, easily moved, credulous, amiable, and receptive to new men and new ideas. Their political sympathies then were liberal and constitutional, bourgeois in character and leaning towards the ' equality of all human beings '. The idea of the *Kulturstaat* as the ' adequate expression of a national entity ' was firmly rooted here. Not very persevering nor reliable, they stood in critical opposition to the hard, rude, and arrogant Prussian nature, with its tendency towards bureaucracy and militarism.

That the Prussian authorities were here confronted with tasks and difficulties which they were spared at home is clear. For an active and alert man this was bound to make work there particularly

24

attractive. In Berlin, account had been taken of the peculiar position in that there were appointed to the key posts men who through natural gifts, knowledge of the world and striking demeanour seemed particularly qualified to meet the special demands. Thus the president of the provincial administration at Aachen, Count Adolf von Arnim-Boitzenburg, was one of the richest and most distinguished of the Prussian noble landowners. Clever and amiable, but proud and self-possessed, he at the age of thirty-three had already obtained this eminent and highly responsible post.

What induced Bismarck to apply to him for a post suitable for a successful candidate in the civil service examination is not entirely clear. The personality of his prospective superior may have attracted him. It was also said that the preparatory service for an aspiring diplomat could be discharged more conveniently and quickly in the Rhine Province than in Old Prussia. But we should be ignoring an essential side of Bismarck's nature if we were to deny that association with quite novel conditions and the happy and easy life of the Rhineland attracted him. One might also well expect him to be interested in the peculiar nature of the task of the ruler in a land which had psychologically still to be won over, and was economically rapidly advancing.

Firstly, however, the candidate had to present two dissertations which constituted the first part of the examination for admission to the government service. Of the two months which Bismarck devoted to this, he spent a large part in Schönhausen. Of his manner of life there he gives to the friend at Göttingen, who has already been mentioned as correspondent, the following charming account :

For a good four weeks I have been here in an old haunted castle with pointed arches and walls four feet thick, about thirty rooms, of which two are furnished, magnificent tapestries, the colour of which is only to be recognized in a few rags, rats galore, chimneys in which the wind howls, in short ' in my old ancestral castle '. Nearby there is a fine old church ; my bedroom has a view on the graveyard. On the other side of the castle there is one of those old gardens with clipped hedges of yews and fine old limes. In this decayed environment your friend is fed and attended by a dried-up old housekeeper, the playmate and nurse of my sixty-five-year-old father. I prepare for the examination, listen to the nightingales, shoot at targets, read Voltaire and Spinoza's *Ethics* from the castle library, which is pretty rich in pig skin. The peasants say : ' Our poor young master, whatever ails him ? ' I only sleep six hours and find great pleasure in study.

Again we find the overbearing personality looking round about in sovereign fashion, a character with sharp contours and clear in relief.

The product of this study, the two dissertations, deal with

' Economies in State Administration ' and ' The Nature and Admissibility of the Oath '. The first work is little more than an extract from the work of a contemporary French economist. It shows no originality in thought, even in the conception of the nature and task of the state. It regards the state as an instrument for the advantage of the individual, a view which the later Bismarck would have rejected most emphatically. The second dissertation testifies a little more promise and originality. Here also it is based on a recently published book as source, but the dependence is less slavish, and there are signs of more extensive reading. In particular the *Ethics* of Spinoza, a reference to which has already been quoted, has exercised an influence not only in details but even in the general religious attitude. There are found in it further some thoughts of the author's own, e.g., the hostile position taken up towards everything catholic and the interpretation of the biblical prohibition of the oath. Characteristic of both works is the extraordinary reserve which he displayed in omitting to express his personal belief where one would expect him to do so, as regards both his attitude to the Prussian state and the question of God and immortality. It was still more remarkable that both works were based on the rationalism and liberalism of the times, points of view which were so alien to Bismarck. Was it a lack of inner maturity or a conscious arrogance which prevented the twenty-one-year-old man from expressing in the two theses anything of his own nature ? At any rate, they did not mean more to him than what appeared on the surface, namely, a piece of intellectual merchandise ordered and delivered for a purely practical object. His relation to the state showed itself, as with many of his circle, not as an immediate one, but as mediated through the personal feudal relationship with the royal head of the state.

In Aachen Count Arnim showed an uncommon personal interest in his new assistant. He seems to have found pleasure in Bismarck's self-confident manliness. Bismarck was, however, not so confident in himself as not to be flattered by the complimentary attitude of the president. ' Already in the summer I had to regard it as a mark of distinction that I was the only one to whom he gave a tête-à-tête talk about mistakes committed. He is always very well informed, but quite free from prejudice.' Care was also taken to see that Bismarck had the opportunity of studying the different departments of government : Government Estates, Forestry, Home Affairs, Military Affairs, Municipal Self-Government ; thus gaining a working knowledge of them all. This was all the more important for him, because his efforts at a diplomatic career did not attain the success he had expected. There was dominant in the Prussian Ministry for Foreign Affairs at the time a peculiar prejudice against the capacities of their own countrymen for diplomatic work. This prejudice included even the nobility. As a result of the tradition of the seventeenth and eighteenth centuries and the views of Frederick the Great, the opinion had developed that they had not sufficient mental adaptability and social *savoir-vivre* for this service. It was common, therefore, to prefer Frenchmen, who had for different reasons settled in Prussia in considerable numbers, and Poles, who lived in the territory annexed by Prussia. So the young civil servant Bismarck was given to understand that he should finish his training in internal administration in the regular fashion, before he sought admission to the diplomatic corps. No doubt the ambitious mother, who already saw her handsome tall son standing before her, resplendent in diplomatic uniform, suffered very much from this decision. The son, on the other hand, seems to have accepted it with relative indifference. He said coolly when breaking the news : ' I took the hints to heart, and resolved to comply with them for the time being.'

We naturally look now for expressions of opinion by the future statesman about the particular problems with which the government of the Prussian Rhineland was faced owing to the recency of its acquisition. We look in vain for such an expression. Certainly Bismarck at this time tried to do ' what was expected of him and more '. For the president, Arnim, he ' undertook the making of terribly comprehensive reports, which he went through privately with me, which I appreciated very much '. Bismarck was allowed to borrow books from Arnim's own library ' which is much better equipped than the government library '. These he studied ' with redoubled energy '. The order of the president : ' Herr von Bismarck is to be permanently employed in the departments, so that as soon as possible he shall attain full maturity in the work,' he regarded as a sure sign of special interest and a spur to industry. But apart from the narrow circle of interests of a pure official we do not discover any concern and interest in the wider political problems connected with his work. In his contemporary correspondence there is not a word about these. Moreover, even in the *Reflections and Reminiscences*, we look in vain for any indication of insight into the unusual social and political situation of the Rhineland of those days. He only says casually about the Aachen days that the personnel employed was not always as good as it might have been, that the business of the government offices was too much concerned with petty details and was not taken sufficiently in earnest.

Yet, just in these years, in addition to the questions connected with the acquisition of the new territory, a special issue of great political significance pre-occupied, and indeed very much excited, the Rhineland. It was further a question which must have affected Bismarck personally. There was, namely, a dispute between church and state, between the Prussian government and the leaders of the Catholic Church in the Rhineland. The subject of dispute was the treatment of mixed marriages. On the side of the church was a particularly well-known and highly honoured man, the Archbishop of Cologne, Cl. A. von Droste Vischering. In the course of the dispute the unusual step was taken of arresting him, and this aroused a veritable storm. Bismarck was not indeed employed in the government of the district where this dispute took place, but he had gained knowledge of such ecclesiastical questions in his own district, and the president under whom he worked had, in addition to his ordinary functions, undertaken to mediate between the Berlin government and Archbishop Droste. Yet about the effects of these events we do not hear a single word from Bismarck. At a time when as an individual he had already given clear signs in word and deed of an original personality of his own, and when his views on catholicism were well developed, he was still as a member of the political, ecclesiastical, and social community quite unawakened, and simply acquiesced in the situation in which his rank had placed him. Thus he was actually and consciously interested only in the questions which concerned his immediate circle. The relation between church and state, which was to play so decisive a part in the development of his personality, did not yet directly affect him.

Apart from his professional work, it was social life which increasingly attracted Bismarck and took up his time. Aachen was not only part of the charming life-loving Rhine Province. It also, as a world famous and much visited spa, had a special characteristic social life of a vivacious and amusing type. The house of the president was one of the centres of fashion in the town, and around it were grouped just the kind of people with whom Bismarck wished to become acquainted without his having to trouble to seek them out. Here he came in touch with the local upper bourgeoisie, not as the official called to a political task, but as the spirited and overbearing member of the conquerors' caste. He was proud of the professed indignation of the inhabitants of Aachen at the ' arrogance and lack of culture of the Pomeranian nobles '. He enjoyed ' irritating them by appearing in the theatre in public every week sleeping stretched out on three chairs '. Here again as before his particular social interest was directed towards foreigners, who were numerous in Aachen, and among these above all Frenchmen and Englishmen. His capacity to express himself in their languages was strengthened considerably by association with them. This was indeed the only point where his life there connected with his plans for a future diplomatic career. He came into particularly close connexion with the family of the Duke of Cleveland, which led to his being strongly attracted by a young lady belonging to that circle. An engagement was imminent when the family left Aachen and the relation ended suddenly. There followed a period of particularly wild living involving heavy losses in the public casino, a great number of short-lived love-affairs and frequent pleasure trips, either for the purpose of hunting or in the company of visitors departing from the spa. Then came an illness which brought with it many hours of reflection and serious reading. Above all, he took up Spinoza again. He felt regretful for his previous mode of life and his gambling losses.

All this was naturally not favourable to his work. Complaints arose about his lack of zeal. His parents were alarmed by the news of his illness, rendered uneasy by demands for payment of the debts he had incurred, and disturbed by reports about their light-hearted son. Then followed another serious love-affair with an English lady. In July 1837 Bismarck took a fortnight's leave from his office and travelled to the south together with this lady and her family. After two months he wrote from Berne, apologizing for having over-stayed his leave. He gave as excuse that his sick father wanted his company and expressed the intention of applying for removal to a government post in Old Prussia. But he continued his travels and only arrived at Kniephof at the beginning of November. Here he found an unhappy state of affairs. His father was indeed in good health, but his mother was suffering from a disease from which she never recovered, and the management of the Pomeranian estates left much to be desired. The income derived from them was diminishing, while the illness of the mother and the mode of life of the son made increased demands on their resources. He now took steps to bring about his removal to the provincial government in Potsdam in order to be nearer home while times were bad. Count Arnim agreed, whilst screening the petitioner in an exemplary manner, without, however, being able to prevent certain mistakes on the part of his subordinates which gave Bismarck away when he applied for the new post. The latter's expressions of annoyance at this show that the recollection of his offences against the regulations in no wise oppressed him. In an official letter he declared that 'he by no means intended to render the government an account of his personal relations'. His good father did his part to help him in that he facilitated a suitable settlement of the private affairs of his son. Herewith ended Bismarck's time at Aachen, no doubt the least disciplined, one of the most picturesque, and also the emptiest part of his life.

There followed the winter 1837–8, which he spent working under the provincial government in Potsdam, then an insignificant and unattractive town. The civil servants there displayed a narrow but well-meaning correctness in their daily work. For the rest of the time they lived in the manner of a restricted aristocratic circle where everybody knew everybody else and everybody watched everybody else. In addition, Bismarck resumed social life at court in the neighbouring Berlin. For the young man Potsdam was a harsh and colourless place in contrast to the rich and free life of Aachen. There followed in the spring of 1838 a step which meant a considerable further limitation and regimentation of his life, namely his entry into a battalion of troops garrisoning Potsdam in order to fulfil the legally prescribed regular period of military service. The later protagonist of the military way of life and of military power undertook this without any active interest or inner enthusiasm.

The news of financial difficulties and worries played an increasing part in his father's letters. But still more disquieting was the news of the health of his mother. Her disease had shown itself incurable and made it necessary to remove her to a hospital in Berlin. The son spent what leisure his Potsdam duties left him by his mother's sick-bed. For the first time he told her that he was tired of his work in the government office and revealed his desire to devote himself to the administration of the family estates, asking for her help in carrying out this project. It was then decided that the father should settle at Schönhausen and the two sons, Bernhard and Otto, should jointly receive the Pomeranian estates together with Kniephof. The two brothers had always been on good terms with each other and it was understood that they would together conduct the management of their lands. In September Bismarck was in accordance with his wishes transferred from Potsdam to a different battalion stationed at Greifswald in his Pomeranian homeland. There he was first given leave for a time, so that he could look about in his new environment even during his period of military service. This he did with great seriousness. The old spirited and undisciplined Bismarck was not, however, buried. We hear from Greifswald, a small university town, of rags and escapades, which remind us vividly of the Göttingen days. But he steadily continued to pursue the road to the new profession on which he had now entered. When leave from the government service was refused he formally resigned in September 1839. His mother, who had died in the preceding January, had through her advice and sympathy thus helped in a decision, which meant a clear victory in Otto's mind of Bismarck the landowner over Menken the bureaucrat.

Bismarck was not induced to take this step by considerations of principle. He does not show any signs of having asked himself the general questions what his attitude to the state should be, what were the political duties of a citizen and whether opposition to the state was ever permissible. The ' poor opinion of our bureaucracy ' with which Bismarck left Aachen was based, not only on his experience there, but also on the aristocratic attitude which he had already brought with him to Aachen. It was the instinct to satisfy the needs and wishes of his own personality, a kind of subtle instinct of self-preservation, which prompted him to act in the way he did. He felt that he required for his proper expansion and development a wider field and a larger variety of opportunities than state service gave. He required a living connexion with his native soil and active work on the land of his ancestral home. The decision to give up his post in the civil service was obviously not the product of political liberalism, but of a highly personal will to independence. It was the decision of Bismarck the individual and not of Bismarck as a social being. The words: ' I will play the tune which I think good, or else none at all', was the motto which expressed it.

CHAPTER V

Bismarck as Landowner

The new position which Bismarck took up was a responsible and distinguished one. In Easter, 1839, at the age of twenty-four, he, together with his elder brother, Bernhard, took over the management of the three Bismarck estates in Pomerania ; Kniephof, Külz, and Jarchelin. The two brothers chose as their residence the largest of the three, Kniephof, the abode of six important years of Otto's childhood. Here there was not, as at Schönhausen, a village close to the manor or independent peasants, besides the employees of the estate ; the buildings were all part of the manorial property. Apart from the manor and its annexes, including stables, store-houses, a distillery, a smithy, &c., there were 11 houses shared by the forty to fifty families of workers on the estate. The cash payment to the workers was small, payment in kind played a greater rôle ; besides house and heating, most of them had a plot· of ploughed land, a garden, pasture for cattle and poultry, a share in corn, free medical treatment, and a scanty provision for old age. This dependence on their landlord was increased by the legal privileges of the latter in the domain of police, jurisdiction, and church affairs. The government official to whom Bismarck was directly responsible was the Landrat in the neighbouring little town of Naugard. The nomination for this office was submitted to the King by the noble landowners, who always proposed one of themselves. He was helped in the work of administration by an advisory committee, the Kreistag, which was made up from the same social class. It was a matter of course that the brothers Bismarck should belong to the Kreistag, and it was the wish of the family, though one fulfilled only a few years later, that Bernhard should become Landrat and Otto his deputy.

The main object of the two brothers, however, was to improve the economic position and agricultural status of the property and increase the income derived from it. In this work the initiative was decidedly with the younger brother. Otto was in the years of this administration anything but an amateur landlord. He tried hard to master both the technical and the financial questions involved. He became an expert in land values and in the possibilities of cultivation and exploitation, and this not only in regard to his own land, but in regard to that of all the neighbours within a wide radius. He studied market conditions for his produce and his agricultural implements, not only practically at the local market, but also

32

theoretically in relation to the general market. He also interested himself in the economic position of the farmers and agricultural labourers in general. Beyond that he was full of interest in the everyday questions arising in connexion with the practice of agriculture: the weather, the condition of the crops, the health of the cattle and poultry, loans and insurance, the condition of the buildings and equipment. Finally, he concerned himself also with book-keeping, making the entries and drawing up the balance sheet himself. He participated in the activities of agricultural associations and was considered for a decoration on account of his work as a landowner. He also paid attention to beautifying his domain. He extended and improved the park, and even thought of building a new manor. He did not indeed escape from financial difficulties. He often had to borrow moderate sums, and he always complained heatedly about the burden of taxation and public expenses. But still his efforts considerably increased the value of the property he farmed. He himself valued the increase a few years later at 25 per cent.

Through this manner of life the sentiment of union with nature, which had already been awakened in his childhood, became a still more pronounced and well established part of his character. He turned his attention to the movements of game and took care of the waters for fishing. He became acquainted with the life of the cattle and their requirements in regard to food, breeding, and veterinary treatment. At the same time he acquired a deeper sense for the beauty of colour and form in nature, for the wealth and variety of light effects, for the order and bounty displayed in the sequence of the seasons. He was greatly impressed by the intervention of natural forces in this order, sometimes miraculously promoting, sometimes terribly destroying, in the presence of which man feels his helplessness and can only devise sorry schemes of succour. He was captivated by the mystery of life in its germination and decay, which arouses ever new wonder and remains a still unsolved problem, but one which almost inevitably strikes us as the revelation of an inconceivably mighty, all-wise, and all-powerful will.

But Bismarck also had his full share of the specific attractions and pleasures of life as a wealthy landowner : the life on his own land which gave him enough room to spread himself in all directions, the enjoyment of the unlimited abundance of air, light, and warmth, blocked or shared by no neighbouring buildings, and the absence of meddlesome neighbours. All contributed towards making his position a privileged one, though he took it for granted as his due. A house of this style was an exception among the Germans who generally live closely crowded together, ten, fifteen, twenty, and even more proletarian families under one roof, while four, six, or more well-to-do middle-class families occupy different flats in the same house.   Bismarck also experienced the benefits of a natural and simple mode of economic life, in which the connexion between producer and consumer is hardly interrupted so far from being distorted by a host of intermediaries, many objects of daily use and consumption figuring not as merchandise but as one's own products.   To that was added the unlimited abundance of personal service in all the situations of daily life, not as an unproductive luxury but as everywhere forming part of the process of production.   Further, there was the aristocratic pleasure of travelling on horseback or in a carriage, and the nobleman's enjoyment of hunting and fishing.   All this was crowned by the impressive unity of the conduct of life, which was not divided between a private and a professional existence.   The professional work was based on the wishes and activities of the private householder and was nothing but man's original mode of life from the time he ceased to be a nomad.

It is true that this professional work was subject to external pressure, seasons, climate, and weather conditions.   But this pressure was not coercion by another man but by objective facts.   That was of special significance for Bismarck ' whose ambition was directed rather not to be commanded than himself to command '.   Bismarck had never been an early riser and did not become one in the country. He liked to work and read till late into the night, and he kept this habit even during his farming days.   Physical exertions and long hours of work did not impair his bodily power in these years, and were only felt as beneficial exercise.   The fact that he came into contact with the market, sold his products there, and purchased goods for purposes of business and life, gave superficial colouring to his profession, but did not constitute its main point.   He had no need of the market to find labour and, on the whole, his business transactions took the form of trade with friends in a neighbourly spirit and on an equal footing.   Where a trader by profession did intervene, the transaction usually took place on a basis of personal acquaintance, where the foibles and wishes of the parties to the transaction were considered rather than one's own profit.   On the other hand, to get the better of the Jewish trader through his superior position in life, through the sheer physical impressiveness of his person, as well as through stinging sarcasms, was one of the pleasures which Bismarck by no means failed to enjoy.

In the manor in Kniephof family life was lacking.   The brothers understood each other very well as regards ordinary human relations and business matters.   However, the slow, quiet, and intellectually mediocre Bernhard was not made to be a stimulating companion for his very differently constituted brother.   This lack became even more obvious when Bernhard in the summer of 1841 left the estate as Landrat of the district. But this lack of family life only led to social life flourishing all the more at and around Kniephof. It was a social life which involved lavish giving of entertainment and hospitality among the owners of the great Pomeranian estates, but exclusively limited to these landowners and their kindred. Opportunities were provided for it in occasional visits and special festivities, in dinners and week-end parties. In practically every one of these manors there was a whole row of rooms for invited and also for unexpected guests. Hunts, food, and drink played a decisive part. These big and powerfully built men, whose work and pastimes were mostly physical and carried out in the keen open air, with a touch of brine from the neighbouring sea, were ever ready for sumptuous feeding and strong drink. Their larders were always full, and there was usually also a well-stocked wine-cellar. It was considered due to the honour of the house to be ready with the best, and the guests were anxious to do justice to what was prepared for them. Perhaps the drinking bouts at the meetings of the landowners' clubs, the Kreistag, and the market days went to greater excess. There, any restraint due to the presence of ladies disappeared, and gambling frequently raised the spirits and with these the thirst. Not less enjoyment was to be found in the officers' messes of the neighbouring garrisons, which Bismarck frequented, sometimes as a guest, sometimes on the occasion of military exercises, which he attended from 1841 on in his capacity of officer in the Landwehr. Here, youth was at the helm and everyone felt quite at home. During one of these exercises Bismarck carried out a feat of heroism when, at the risk of his own life, he saved that of his orderly who had fallen into a swollen river, a deed which brought him official recognition. Bismarck took the full share of the eating, drinking, gambling, and cursing of the Junker. He was anything but a spoilsport. His performances in the way of carousing were unsurpassed, his hospitality was boundless ; the reputation of his wine-cellar was especially good. His inclination to joking and ragging had hardly abated since his student days. He had always a pistol ready and he liked to let it off in order to wake his guests, to frighten them, or to remind them of an appointment.

While Bismarck was so much in demand and admired and taken as a pattern in the society of his gentlemen friends, the world of ladies were not equally unanimous in accepting him. Certainly, he was a wealthy bachelor, the Bismarcks were among the best families, he himself had achieved success in the management of his estates and fitted well into their circles with his tall, imposing presence. So it was only too natural that many mothers should have their eyes on him and that many daughters should dream of him as their future husband. But there were shocking stories about his life and doings at Kniephof. These did not concern only hunts and drinking bouts, but also told of visits from women who did not belong to the right circle, and who appeared and disappeared equally secretly. He was also accused of fickleness on account of the frequent changes in his life plans. It was felt, too, that there was something uncanny about him. It is true, he was generally polite and tactful, but at times he gave vent to expressions which left people nonplussed and sounded almost like mockery. That it was not only in bodily size that he surpassed his neighbours was fully realized, but not always to his advantage.

This ambiguous position expressed itself in an unfortunate love-affair. Bismarck's affections were directed towards a young lady of his class, whose mother owned a fine property in the neighbourhood. The daughter returned his affection, but the mother demanded a period for reflection. Bismarck rather suffered under these cir-cumstances and after several months had elapsed, there followed a move which showed a new side of his nature. The mother re-ceived a letter signed by Bismarck's father. This appeared at once tactful and naïve. It depicted the mental distress of his son, as speaking from the anxious heart of a true father and urged a short-ening of the probationary period. This letter cannot have been composed by Ferdinand von Bismarck, since in style and mental content it lies quite beyond his capacity. It is the work of Otto and is the first expression of the diplomat Bismarck, now acting in a highly personal matter. It is the first occasion on which we find him aiming at his goal in a roundabout fashion oblivious of truth. It was not to lead him to the desired goal. The mother remained firm in her opposition.

Not all the personal relations which Bismarck formed in Kniephof were of the kind which found their high point in hunts and carouses. The foundation was laid for a number of valuable personal ties during his residence there. One of the most noteworthy personal-ities with whom he came into contact was Ernst von Bülow Cummerow, the owner of a neighbouring estate, his senior by several decades. He was a man of great public spirit, far-reaching practical schemes, and unremitting energy. In speech and writing he opposed the bureaucratization of the Prussian state and defended a caste system on principle, but urged that while the landowning nobles must have a decisive function in it, the rest of the people should also actively participate, a kind of liberal conservatism. He was also interested in foreign affairs, wanted a unified Germany through Prussian intervention and under Prussian leadership, and desired a greater unity in Europe, especially the restraint of the Power which he regarded as the chief disturber of the peace, France. Bülow was also active in practical social reform. In particular he founded a private land-bank, and took a leading part in the activities of the landowners' societies.

A question which specially interested in a practical way both men and their whole social circle was that of the patriarchal rights of jurisdiction of the landlords over their dependents. Since the freeing of the serfs through the Stein-Hardenberg reforms of thirty years before, the task had involved particular difficulties for the landlords in consequence of the increased self-confidence of those subject to the jurisdiction. But its significance as an honorary right told against its abolition. Bülow had worked out a compromise proposal, according to which the jurisdiction should be effected through boards of magistrates, as was the case with the state courts. These boards should retain the character of patriarchal justice, and besides the courts there should be single magistrates to retain the connexion with the individual landed proprietors. Before submitting his proposal to the ministry of justice, he showed the draft to Bismarck and several other of his friends, and won their agreement and signatures. It was therefore through Bülow that Bismarck first came into contact with the problems of state and society in their fundamentals. He did so through a man who was quite similar to himself in his attitude to life, in his professional activity, and especially in his exalted position in society.

Besides Bülow, we find among the friends and counsellors of 'Bismarck the likewise much older Adolf von Thadden-Treglaff, the zealous protagonist of a theocratic and patriarchal type of political thought. These views of his were theoretically represented by the teacher of jurisprudence, Ernst Julius Stahl, since 1840 professor at Berlin university, particularly in his chief work *Philosophy of Law on an Historical Basis*. Thadden was not so brilliant or many-sided as Bülow, but a man of considerable moral fervour and humanity. For him, the legal right of the authorities sprang from the divine will and must be used by the ruler in the way in which a great landowner should use his estate in relation to his dependents. The position of the landlord was to be regarded as that of a small monarch according to the will of God, and his power to be wielded in that spirit. Besides these two men we may mention Bismarck's earliest and most devoted friend of his own age, his neighbour Moritz von Blanckenburg, not because he had very much to offer him intellectually, but because he brought to him a disposition which could see nothing but good in his friend. In face of accusations brought against the latter's mode of life he declared in anger: 'Bismarck lives more respectably than anybody in the neighbourhood.'

Bismarck's first attempt at a literary production on a public question occurred at the time when he was in contact with these men. This was an article for a newspaper of the beginning of 1843, but it was never printed. It was intended as a reply to a letter to the editor, which objected to the hunting with hounds of the Pomeranian barons on the score that it damaged the land. Now Bismarck did not write as one whose mind was much enlightened by the theories of Bülow and Thadden. He still speaks presumptuously of himself as one of those 'whose revolting privilege of having the particle " von " prefixed to his name conceals from mourning Germany the rising sun of civic and social equality '.

Another stimulus for Bismarck was provided by journeys of entertainment and instruction. He undertook his first big journey of this kind in the summer of 1842, soon after the unfortunate love-affair, indeed it was no doubt occasioned by the latter. It took him in particular to England and Scotland, then to France and Switzerland. He visited Edinburgh, York, Manchester, and London, and travelled everywhere with eyes open. English agriculture interested him no less than the factories of Manchester. He got a view of parliamentary life, visited works of art, and also came into touch with military society. He gives attractive pictures of the peculiarities of daily life in England. The journey aroused in him the desire for more extensive travels and he spoke of a visit to Egypt and Syria. As a matter of fact, however, he only managed smaller journeys, for instance a visit to Paris, apparently a year later, and two years afterwards one to the neighbourhood of the North Sea, where he freely indulged in nautical sports.

This already indicates that Bismarck had not, or at least not permanently, found the complete satisfaction for which he had hoped in living and working on the land. Besides days and weeks of the most energetic professional work and unrestrained social enjoyment, we find hours in which he felt existence as a Junker intolerable. He speaks of ' that disease of idleness, from which I have suffered for long '. He bitterly exclaims : ' I am carried without an effort of will on the stream of life with no pilot save the inclination of the moment, and it is a matter of fair indifference to me on what shore it brings me to shipwreck.' In such an hour the desire may easily have been aroused in him once more to try the career of state service. Five years after his resignation he applied to the president of the province of Brandenburg for re-admission to the civil service, as ' my circumstances no longer require my presence in the country estate '. This request was granted. Bismarck punctually joined the service, but after hardly a fortnight he took leave owing to ' illness in the family ' and never returned to his post. Some months later he sought for the post of Landrat of the district in which Schönhausen lay. However, he was not elected. Later on he took the place of his brother for several months in directing the business of the Landrat in Naugard. But when he came to the end of the period he wrote: 'To-morrow I expect Bernhard back, and am glad to be free of the Landrat business.'

But his discontent sprang not only or chiefly from the nature of his professional work. He described his feelings later thus picturesquely: 'What a depression masters me when the door of my room yawns in front of me and there stands opposite me dumb furniture in the silent rooms bored like myself.' In this inner void the sympathy of his young sister Malvine was a bright spot. She lived with their father at Schönhausen, which Bismarck frequently visited, and she spent a winter with him at Kniephof, where she came to know her future husband, Oskar von Arnim, a friend of her brother. To her Bismarck poured out his heart, confiding his lack of satisfaction in his profession, his misfortune in love, his discontent with life. There was a correspondence between them, carried on in a charming conversational style, which shows an ability to see the humorous angle even in very serious matters. The daughter had inherited intelligence and farsightedness from her mother, but was of a warmer and happier temperament.

Another source of inner enrichment for the Bismarck of the Kniephof days was a varied, serious, and well-chosen course of reading. He cultivated his interest in history, also Shakespeare and Byron were taken up again. The dramatic power and the directness of Shakespeare's view of history, the melancholy and the inner disharmony of Byron he experienced as a part of his own self. He copied down poems of Byron's and kept the copies in his writing-case. He read English novels by Bulwer-Lytton and Dickens, French novels by Georges Sand and de Vigny, the German classics and contemporary political poems by writers like Freiligrath and Herwegh. He took part in a reading circle in the home of his friend Adolf von Thadden, where among other writers, Shakespeare and the German romantics from Brentano to Jean Paul were read. There he again heard good music, not only classical composers, but also Mendelssohn and Liszt. But his striving and doubting took him further afield. Besides Spinoza, he now took up also Hobbes, 'the materialistic atheist'. He turned to Hegel, though indeed only to lay him aside as 'not understood'. However, he then directed his attention to the Hegelians in philosophy of religion, who were at that time in the very bloom of their success, to D. F. Strauss' *Life of Jesus*, L. Feuerbach's *Essence of Christianity*, B. Bauer's *Critique of the Gospels*. These writings did not leave his thought and feeling quite unaffected. From his journey to the North Sea we have the account of a storm in the open sea. 'Several ladies fainted, others wept, and the silence in the men's cabin was broken by the loud prayers of a Bremen merchant who until then had seemed to me to have set more store by his clothes than by his God. . . .

The prayers of the Bremen gentleman saved us this time.' Here we have before us the rationalist and sceptical Bismarck, the same person who at the age of sixteen had abandoned prayer as contrary to reason.

CHAPTER VI

His Engagement

The spring of 1845 brought with it a particularly sudden and violent flooding of the Elbe. The dykes broke and the park in Schönhausen was inundated. After the water had receded, his old father told Bismarck that six of his finest lime-trees had been victims of the flood. 'The lime-trees have passed away, I soon shall also pass away,' he is reported to have said. He did not survive the end of the year. This meant an important change in the life of his now thirty-year-old son Otto. The two brothers discussed the division of their inheritance and agreed that Otto should take possession of Schönhausen besides keeping a part of the Pomeranian lands. Otto thereupon decided to remove his place of residence to Schönhausen once more, thus changing himself from a Pomeranian back to an inhabitant of the Marches. At the end of 1846 he let Kniephof. The new possession created a larger and more impressive outer framework for his life, but also gave him new responsibilities. His father had not been a particularly clever and far-seeing landlord. The financial position of the estate was not favourable, there had been bad harvests shortly before and they continued after Bismarck's arrival. He had now to deal, not only with dependent employees, but also with self-willed peasants, and was therefore less at liberty in his decisions. However, he did not allow himself to be thereby frightened off from carrying out the task he had undertaken.

Still he had by no means given up the idea of public activity. On the contrary, this project was pursued with real earnestness after his removal to Schönhausen. It was not now inspired merely by occasional moods of depression and discontent, but as an object desired for its own sake. But the public activity had to conform to Bismarck's desire that things should come his way of their own accord. This tendency had now been increased through his sojourn of many years' duration on the land, and had acquired something of the real peasant's cautiousness. He could and would no longer look on that activity as a leap from one sphere of duties to another, but had to connect it with the task of managing his estates handed down to him and let it grow out of the latter as its extension. In a letter written at this time he expresses the conviction ' that true pleasure in a public office is only to be expected where one works in a circle of which one has a full view and remains in individual contact '.

From this standpoint there presented itself to him one official function almost as a matter of course, and as if of its own accord. This was the inspection of the Elbe dyke (Deichhauptmannschaft). This dyke played a decisive part in the whole economic system of the valley of the Elbe along the Marches, and so also for Schönhausen. The Elbe was a source of the fertility of this region, but at the same time a danger for its products. In summer the water flowed comfortably along in the manifold windings of its course; in spring, however, the stream could be dangerous and harmful, not following its normal course but bursting its banks. At the points where danger threatened, adequate protection could be provided only by a dyke. This dyke required conscientious and expert supervision. Already before he inherited Schönhausen Bismarck had arrived at the conviction that the office of the inspector of the dyke, which was held as a part-time post by one of the neighbouring landlords, was not properly discharged. He addressed a petition to the government office responsible, depicted the existing bad conditions, not sparing the present holder of the office, and made proposals for improvement. That he himself was seeking the post was of course not mentioned, but neither was the idea suppressed.

This first intervention by Bismarck on his own initiative in public affairs already displays an important characteristic of his public activities in general, namely, the close connexion between objective and personal aims and motives. No doubt the management of the dyke was not efficient, and the surrounding properties were thereby endangered or unprofitably burdened. But Bismarck did not come forward as a mere representative of the interests of others, subordinating his personal interest to these. He speaks just as much on his own behalf as on behalf of others and is not afraid of intervening expressly for his own advantage. His move in the public interest is also combined with a personal attack on those who seem to be guilty of previous neglect. In this he spares neither the governing bodies nor the individuals responsible for inspection. The attacks on the persons concerned are throughout sharp and emphatic, while the proposals for improvement are equally well weighed and objectively justified. Bismarck never tried to camouflage or conceal the attack behind its objective aim. If, in his efforts for the cause, it transpired that the man who called attention to the grievance was also the very man called to better it, we still do not have the impression of a concealed place-hunter, but of a man who is convinced that he can and will serve the public cause.

It was not enough in the matter of the Elbe dyke to direct a single petition to the government office before Bismarck was offered the post of inspector of the dyke two years later. How he conceived the fulfilment of this task is described by him graphically in a private letter :

The Elbe has risen 2 feet overnight. It is now 7 a.m., snow has been falling gently for an hour. The country is covered by mist. Outside there is nothing to hear but the light clatter of the ice floating on the water, a welcome message that the thaw will keep on. The men at the dyke all look so sleepy, as they have had the worst turn of night duty, from 12 to 6. They are relieved four times in 24 hours, but I am never.

If Bismarck's concern with the Elbe dyke preceded his inheritance of Schönhausen, the latter was followed in the same year by his election as deputy for a member of council of the province in which Schönhausen lay. He thus came in loose contact with the only parliamentary representation which Prussia owned at that time, one of the eight provincial councils charged only with the business of the provinces and not topped by a common parliament of the whole kingdom. He approached this assembly as one of the elected representatives of the landed nobility. At the same time, however, began Bismarck's participation in another matter of public concern. This was the question of the right of the landlord to jurisdiction, the patriarchal jurisdiction. This question had already been discussed at Kniephof with his friend Bülow-Cummerow. Bismarck had at that time accepted his friend's view. Now, at Schönhausen, he heard of another proposed solution, likewise handed in to the ministry. This proposal had been drawn up by an expert in law, the president of the court of appeal in Magdeburg, Ludwig von Gerlach. In his view of the state and of religion Gerlach was a spiritual relation of Adolf von Thadden, his brother-in-law. He was a man of strong Protestant conviction, resolved in his defence of the patriarchal class state. Gerlach's proposal, too, envisaged a combination of a system of boards with one of individual judges, but it laid a stronger emphasis on the individual judges, so that the landowning patron, closely combined with these, came more into prominence. Bismarck now took a hand in the controversy with a written exposition, directed to Gerlach, in which he went beyond the standpoint of the latter. Patriarchal judges should, according to Bismarck, ' essentially and exclusively be officials of the caste of landowners, of noblemen ', the ' lack in corporate spirit and in the aristocratic mode of life in our corn-growing nobility ' must be removed. Bismarck thus defended with great distinctness and emphasis a caste system against state officialdom. As landowning Junker he speaks against the hated and despised bureaucracy. The decision of the ministry went against Gerlach's proposal and thereby also in essence against the standpoint of Bismarck.

Now for the first time Bismarck was practically concerned in a public affair in which he was called upon to express his views on the nature of the state. It is here the patriarchal caste and the bureaucratic-absolutist view of the state which come into opposition to each other. Though the earlier Kniephof newspaper article of the beginning of 1843 did not defend a theory, in particular not the theory of Bülow and Thadden, the attitude adopted there was here retained. Yet there are still differences between his present and his earlier attitude. It is no longer a question of the personal conduct of life which is now at stake, but one concerning a decisive factor in the social position of the whole class that had to be newly regulated. The attitude of a Junker attached to his caste had thus taken a still firmer hold of Bismarck. The views he now expressed had no longer the earlier presumptuous, challenging form, but were throughout restrained and dignified.

It was not by chance that it was just at Schönhausen that the connexion between the goals at which he aimed and the conditions of his social existence presented itself to Bismarck's consciousness with a deeper significance. The decisive reason was the change in his external circumstances. As Bismarck had said in a letter to a Göttingen student friend in the days when he was an examination candidate, he had returned 'to his father's ancestral castle', this time, however, not as a guest and for a temporary visit, but to take permanent possession as its lord. What his father had formerly meant to him—the embodiment of the clan of the Bismarcks, the last link in the chain of knights, cavaliers, wearers of wigs, pigtailed horsemen—he had now himself become. He was the actual representative of the will and mind embodied in this clan, he was the life of the tradition working in this family. From being a Pomeranian owner of land he had become a baron of the Marches. He reports of his personal retinue that 'many of them had already served for two generations in Schönhausen and that their fathers have held the same post under my grandfather and father'. 'I cannot deny', he says, 'that I am somewhat proud of this triumph of the conservative principle for many long years in the house in which my ancestors for hundreds of years were born, lived, and died in the same rooms.'

That the present representative of this race could not remain a bachelor, but had to continue the family through his descendants was no less obvious than that he had to maintain a household and hospitality in keeping with the castle. This provided Bismarck with the external inducement to marriage and to marriage with one of his caste. But the inner motives which led him to this step came from quite a different source and had much deeper roots in his nature. To expound them we must digress from the Schönhausen period and return to Kniephof. We last saw Bismarck at

Kniephof as rationalist and doubter, as a man who had experienced loneliness amid society and abandonment amid the bustle of life. He had spent there 'many hours of comfortless depression with the thought that the existence of myself and other men is futile and fruitless, perhaps nothing but a random whim of creation'. Bismarck was much too healthy and full of vitality to succumb to such doubts and be overcome by them. His readings of sceptical works had taught him to be ironical with himself and his own doubts. But he had also too serious a disposition simply to shut his eyes to them.

In February 1843, that is a considerable time before his removal to Schönhausen, on the occasion of a visit from Kniephof to his friend Adolf von Thadden in Treglaff, Bismarck had a discussion on religious matters with Frau von Thadden and her daughter, Marie, the fiancée of Moritz von Blanckenburg. Of course, he knew that he was in the company of markedly religious people, but he did not conceal from them his negative attitude in relation to belief in God and the way in which he had reached that position. He spoke of this, so it seemed to the ladies, not in a superficial and light-hearted fashion, but as one innerly moved and with an open ear for their comments. They had the impression that Bismarck would either never visit them again or do so very quickly. Bismarck did the latter. It was the world of pietism with which he thus came into touch. The founder of the movement in the seventeenth century, P. J. Spener, had impressed on his adherents the importance of prayer, both by the individual and by a closely united group, and of the Bible reading and discussion of the Bible in small circles as a means of strengthening belief. He had insisted that in Christianity the inner experience was not enough, but that practical action was still more required. The movement spread into Prussia and found especially in Pomerania a circle of adherents among the landlords. Meditation on the Bible fitted well into the pattern of life of those among them who lived in the more isolated and remote places. Bible studies in small circles were partly forced on them by the life on landed estates, which tended very much to seclusion, and partly desired by them on account of their aristocratic exclusiveness. The doctrine of good works turned their attention to their poverty-stricken dependents as a command of mercy as well as of utility. The pietist circle of the family of Thadden included also the family of Bismarck's friend, Moritz von Blanckenburg, Ludwig von Gerlach in Magdeburg, a family von Puttkamer in Reinfeld in Pomerania, and many others.

Bismarck treated his new friends with great respect as persons. 'I saw', he explained later, 'that the members of this circle in their external activity were almost complete patterns of what I wished to be. That confidence and peace reigned in their hearts was not surprising to me, for I had never doubted that these accompanied faith.' But he was honest and upright enough to add in regard to himself : ' Faith cannot be given or taken ; and I thought that I must wait submissively to find whether it would come to me.' This was not the view of the pietist friends who were concerned with Bismarck's belief. The first to take charge of him was his restless, zealous friend, Moritz von Blanckenburg. He tried in a number of letters to win him with his warm personal friendship' and the overflowing religious fervour of one who had himself only just been converted. He was convinced that he could make Bismarck change his views, the latter being ' a man of such a clear and self-confident mind ' and one who ' sees and admits his wretchedness '. But Bismarck refused to commit himself to belief in a personal God without being really gripped by the belief. ' Oh Otto, Otto,' replied his friend, ' every word in your letter is true ; this is just how you would speak of God, whom you do not know.' But these appeals tended rather to close the doors of Bismarck's mind than to open them. He eventually broke off the correspondence, thinking that he saw at work in the other cheap pity and spiritual pride. Blanckenburg, for the time being, abandoned the contest. Not less well-meaning but more restrained were the attempts of Blanckenburg's fiancée and subsequent wife, Marie von Thadden, to win over their friend to the side of religion. She, a person of much more strength of will and independence of thought than her husband, was deeply moved ' at seeing a man who suffered so much under the chill of unbelief as did Otto von Bismarck. I have been made really sad by the experience that it is impossible for one person to help another.' On one occasion she was rendered anxious by ' the dangerous smoothness with which this great, interesting man of the world repels arguments ' ; on another occasion she was delighted that ' the great Otto gave himself with such a familiarity and charm that my eyes brimmed over '. She felt like calling to him : ' Otto, Otto, do start a fresh life, tear yourself away from your wild ways ! ' She did not, indeed, bring herself to make this appeal, but she discussed it very openly and thoroughly with her friends, above all with Johanna von Puttkamer, the daughter of the landlord of Reinfeld. So she paved the way for the relation which was to be for Bismarck the most important of his life. Certainly Marie was not quite unbiassed in speaking about Bismarck's religious· struggles, but saw him as illuminated by the light thrown on him through her missionary aspirations, and perhaps not only by these. Bismarck's own remarks emphasize more the human than the religious side of this friendship : ' I soon felt at home in that circle, and experienced a well-being which I had not before enjoyed, a family life which included me, almost a home.' That the Bismarck of Kniephof, about whose private life there had been such wild rumours, should be accepted thus without reservation in this circle so firmly rooted in their faith and so exclusive to outsiders, without his belonging to them or accepting their religion, is a proof of the irresistible power of his personality.

The Blanckenburg-Thadden marriage was concluded under no auspicious star. At the marriage festival in October 1844 at which Bismarck with Johanna von Puttkamer belonged to the bridal retinue, a serious fire broke out when a firework was being let off. The wedding guests helped to put it out and Bismarck distinguished himself specially in this. In the following winter, the last which he spent in Pomerania, he was a frequent guest of the young couple at their small modest manor of Cardemin near Treglaff. We also find Johanna von Puttkamer here as guest. In the summer of 1846 arrangements were made for a holiday stay in the Harz Mountains with a larger circle which included the Thaddens as well as Johanna. Johanna was at that time twenty-two years old. Her appearance was distinguished by heavy black plaits and sparkling brown eyes, but for the rest she was more attractive than beautiful and was altogether lacking in youthful charm. Physically she was delicate. In social intercourse she was mostly tart and reserved. Yet, among friends she could be open and affable, nay, even merry and witty. Above all, she was unaffected and upright and incapable of any but genuine emotion. Her friends boasted that she possessed ' a temper singularly adapted to give happiness, a warm, deep, strong, undefiled power of love '. Inspired by a genuine inner piety, she was yet not so actively involved in the pietist character of her surroundings as was her friend Marie. She had some musical talent and played the piano fairly well. She was not a very ' brilliant match ' for a man like Bismarck, either in her personality or in her possessions, nor did she promise to be a particularly easy companion for him in life. She might very well be qualified worthily to manage a household suitable to his present rank in Schönhausen, but Bismarck could neither expect from her an understanding for the extravagances of his Kniephof household nor count on her being able to move freely and naturally in a more distinguished and more elegant social milieu.

The fortnight or so in the Harz Mountains was full of variety and delight. The days were spent in long walks and in visits to places of historical interest, in the evenings there were gay dinners, stimulating discussions about religious, artistic, and literary questions, walks in the moonlight and musical performances. The nine of them, mostly young people united by a harmonious bond of friendship, behaved in this lovely country with greater freedom and less reserve than they did in their usual environment. They gave themselves over entirely to the holiday mood, were always ready to joke and laugh, to prepare for each other little pleasures and surprises and to share in each other's enjoyment. At the end of the holiday, they spent a few days together in Berlin and supplemented the pleasures of the country with the excitements of the town, society, theatres, concerts. For Bismarck the journey meant more than a pleasure trip, it brought him to the point of making up his mind to sue for the hand of Johanna von Puttkamer. In the course of the journey there took place between them conversations about religion and marriage in general, but they did not lead up to a formal proposal.

After this journey the Blanckenburg couple resumed their religious correspondence with Bismarck. In its course Bismarck dispatched a short letter in Latin to Blanckenburg at the beginning of September 1846, which had no religious content but revealed his intention to press his suit for the hand of Fräulein von Puttkamer, obviously with the purpose of contacting her parents indirectly. But before further steps were taken in this direction, an event of grave consequence occurred in the family of Blanckenburg. A severe epidemic spread through Pomerania. At the beginning of October Frau von Thadden, and at the beginning of November, Marie von Blanckenburg herself, after a marriage of hardly two years, succumbed to the disease. Concerning the impression of the tragedy on Bismarck, the young widower reported to Johanna von Puttkamer: 'My dear friend Otto said, this is the first heart lost to me of which I really know that it felt warmly for me. Now I believe in immortality, otherwise the world has not been made by God.' A few weeks later, on the 14th of December, Johanna met Bismarck at the estate of the parents of Blanckenburg.

Bismarck made allusion to the death of Marie von Blanckenburg when at the end of December 1846 he wrote the most important letter of his life so far to Herr von Puttkamer in Reinfeld, suing for the hand of his daughter Johanna. The letter expresses throughout a spirit of religious devotion. Bismarck declares that what Marie von Blanckenburg could not achieve in her life, she had achieved in her death, his 'conversion' to belief in a personal God. He depicts to the father of his beloved his religious life as a child, the time of his irreligion, and finally his relation to the couples Thadden and Blanckenburg and their circle. He goes on:

By the advice of others, as well as by my own inclinations I was led to read the Bible more consistently. That which was stirring in me came to life, when I received the news of the mortal illness of our dead friend in Cardemin. Then the first fervid prayer, unaccompanied by doubt about the rationality of praying, burst out of my heart. God did not answer the prayer I then uttered ; but he did not reject it, for I have not lost the capacity to pray, and feel, if not peace, yet confidence and courage to live, such as I had lost.

He does not make any protestations about his feelings or any promises for the future. ' My only surety for the weal of your daughter lies in my prayer for the blessing of the Lord.' The lengthy letter closes with the words : ' I am of course ready to give you accurate and upright information about everything that you wish to know, but I think I have said what is most important .' So this time we have anything but a diplomatical suitor's letter. It expresses the needs of his heart, and it ignores the financial and social aspects of marriage traditional in his class and time. Moreover, it presupposes the same disinterestedness in his future father-in-law.

On the occasion of a visit of Bismarck to Reinfeld on the 12th January next, there followed his formal betrothal to Johanna von Puttkamer.

CHAPTER VII

From Engagement to Marriage

The two persons who were to be Bismarck's parents-in-law could well be compared to his own parents. The father-in-law, Heinrich von Puttkamer, a man twenty-five years older than Bismarck himself, showed the same warmth, openness, loyalty as did Ferdinand von Bismarck. Like him he irradiated health and good humour, but intellectually he stood on a higher level. He had studied law and worked in the government service. He had fought in the Wars of Liberation as officer. At the age of twenty-seven he had chosen as his profession the management of an estate. Religious experience stood at the centre of his being, his faith was deeply felt and a matter of the heart rather than of outward expression. His wife, Luitgarde von Glasenapp, was far more active and vivacious than he, also, like Bismarck's mother, intellectually more alive and critical. With all her warmth of heart, she was influenced by the desire to make her presence felt. Not so healthy as her husband, she was also not so well balanced innerly as he. The piety, too, of the wife was less reserved than that of the man. She had an active pietistic trait and was not without the capacity for seeing the weaknesses of her fellows.

In one thing, however, the two were completely of one mind, in their love for their only child, Johanna, who returned this love without reserve. The bond which united these three people was one of the greatest strength. Care for the daughter was always in the foreground of the parents' thoughts. The wish to see her happy and contented surpassed all other desires ; but they were convinced that nobody was so qualified for giving her this happiness and content as themselves. The daughter, too, felt thoroughly at her ease under the care of her parents and was very much dependent on them inwardly and outwardly. In her thoughts and feelings she was firmly rooted in the atmosphere of her father's house. Her father was ' horrified ' by the thought that his daughter should marry, and especially that she should marry this man, ' of whom he had heard much evil and little good '. But the daughter opposed him and proved ' an extremely warm and eloquent defender of Bismarck's '. In this she was supported by their common friend Adolf von Thadden who, following the recent death of his wife and daughter, had spent Christmas with the Puttkamers in Reinfeld, increasing through his presence the significance of this merciful and happy season. Bismarck's strongest asset, however, was his own personality. He did not enter on the delicate visit to Reinfeld altogether without hesitation, and when he arrived there the matter was in no wise yet decided in his favour. At any rate, there were still ' far-reaching negotiations ' to go through. But, before these had begun, he at once lovingly embraced his would-be fiancée before the eyes of her parents, to their ' speechless amazement ', with the result that the negotiations were omitted and ' within five minutes everything was all right '.

Now Bismarck was in a position very rapidly to gain a footing in the Puttkamer family. He tells his brother Bernhard that his father-in-law ' drank champagne with me and played waltzes to which I danced with his daughter ', and that the mother had taken the ' bearded heretic to her excellent heart '. But Bismarck was also deeply impressed by the love and openness with which he was received. With real enthusiasm he wrote a few weeks later to a friend in a responsible government post: ' I look forward with glad hope to a union which could not have been concluded without manifold miraculous dispositions of providence and in the blessings of which I may entertain all the greater confidence in that its basis lies purely in our inner nature and will not change.' He does not speak in such lofty tones in a somewhat earlier letter to his brother. It is true, he knows how to praise his fiancée's ' rare intelligence and rare nobility of mind ', but he also appraises her in a lighter fashion as ' very lovable and *facile à vivre*, as I have never known a woman to be '. Finally, however, he finds a sentence which can only be regarded as an anticlimax to the former grandiloquence : ' In short, I am very satisfied with the whole affair, and I hope you are too. Moreover, I love pietism in women,' he added frivolously.

He knew what a part religion had played in bringing about the decision in his favour and that his fiancée ' would have given me the go-by if God had not taken compassion on me and had at least let me look through the keyhole of the door of admission to his mercy '. But he surprisingly reported to his fiancée what one of his friends had replied to his remark about reading the Bible : ' Well, in Reinfeld I should speak like that too in your place. But that you should believe that you can pull the leg of your oldest friends, that is ridiculous.' And he set, side by side with this, a similar remark of his brother-in-law, Oscar von Arnim, about his ' turning pious ' almost as if to support it. What was there in Bismarck's mind when he wrote these words three weeks after the engagement ? One would like to see in them the stamp of real sincerity. But had not he also to consider the possibility of these words causing offence or anxiety to Johanna ? Or was he so sure of himself and of her that this thought did not enter into his mind ?

Later on we shall come across the many cases of disconcerting frankness through which in political combat he brought his friends into confusion and overthrew his enemies. Is there anywhere in some corner of Bismarck's inner nature a common root for these two different manifestations of frankness ? It is worth noting that he says nothing to his fiancée about his reply to those remarks and as indication of his own attitude to them lets fall only this ambiguous comment on Arnim's words : ' Some very clever people have curious views of the world.' Speaking of the comparative lack of religion in his parents, Bismarck tells his fiancée the story of a Frisian chief who, standing before the baptismal font, asked the priest ' whether his unbelieving ancestors were in hell because of their unbelief ' and ' on receiving an affirmative answer refused to be baptized, for where his father was he would also be '. Had he put to himself the question how it would affect his fiancée when he added : ' I am only speaking historically, without applying it to myself ' ?

On the other side there exist numerous expressions of opinion on religious and moral questions, just in the earlier letters of the fiancé, some of them in a tone of strong self-accusation. He speaks at great length about his own reading in the Bible and in biblical commentaries. In the course of a few lines he cites no less than fifteen texts and refers to ' an endless number of others '. He accuses himself of ' heartless selfishness ' because in a letter to Moritz von Blanckenburg ' he has mocked his grief by the picture of his own happiness '. He even criticizes his own sorrow over the death of Marie von Blanckenburg : ' My first grief was of the passionate selfish kind one feels for one's own loss.' Then he added : ' For Marie, for her own sake, I do not feel sorrow, for I know she is in good hands.' He also has doubts about the genuineness and force of his practical love of his neighbours :

This winter, [he says] I have taken somewhat more trouble about helping the poor of the neighbourhood and found distress such that one could hardly have worse. When I think how a single thaler [3 sh.] helps such a hungry family for weeks ; it seems to me almost like a theft from the poor who are hungry and cold if I spend thirty on the journey,

i.e., to visit his fiancée. The question gives him no peace, he returns to it in the same letter : ' It is a very ticklish question, how far I can consider myself justified in spending on my pleasures what God has given me in trust, as long as there are people in my neighbourhood who are sick with want and cold and whose beds and clothes are in pawn.' He is so deeply occupied with this problem that a week later he turns to it again. He had refused alms to a woman who asked him for them, because she had been guilty of a theft. ' That was really very uncharitable of me,' he complained. 'I will inquire into her circumstances with greater care and not try to take on the office of God as judge.'

We cannot dismiss these utterances of Bismarck without further ado as mere concessions to the religious feelings of his fiancée. At any rate, he fought against the tendency to insincerity. He had already spoken to his father-in-law about 'the suspicion I feel that I could unconsciously be insincere towards you and towards myself'. He had this at heart also in his relation to his fiancée, she also must not 'doubt his honesty'. In any case, within the sphere of religion properly speaking he maintains his own different point of view undisguised. A few weeks after the engagement he writes to her:

Why do you usually have so little confidence in your belief and wrap it so carefully in the cottonwool of seclusion, so that it should not be chilled by any breath of air from the outside world? Many earnest, upright, humble seekers yet believe that they can find truth somewhere else or in a different form.

Three weeks later he repeats this rejection of the belief 'which permits the believer to separate himself from his earthly brothers'. With that is combined the further admission 'that even I have so far not been able to accept everything that is written in the bible'. All this constitutes no surprise for someone who remembers the words of the letter containing his proposal of marriage. The will to be sincere and humble seems to be a ruling factor now as then, combined with the will of the 'seeker', who 'has not yet found peace'.

What is involved in Bismarck's conversion to religion is a reflection of the attitude which since the days of St. Paul has characterized every earnest christian conversion; the state of self-righteousness is to be overcome by the longing to be in safe keeping through the grace of God. But faith in God is for Bismarck ever more, not the belief that 'the grace of God will not let my soul go adrift after having once touched it', rather is it a pledge of active work. 'I pray really fervently to God that he will give me the power to do my duty,' he exclaims. He avers that for a man—as well as for a whole people—distinguished by particular gifts and talents or entrusted with a high office, by means of which he can affect the course of history, there is no greater danger than self-righteousness and vainglory. He therefore continues to force himself 'to surrender humbly to the will of God who does not need my co-operation and sets the limits to my powers'. Then it is certain 'that the grace of God will not suffer me to be deprived of the staff of a humble faith amid the dangers and perplexities of my profession'. He has no doubt that he has been chosen by God for his office and that this is founded on a divine calling. 'God has placed me here and bids me take my task seriously.' ' I am God's soldier ', he declares, ' and where he sends me, there I must go, and I have faith that he sends me where I should go and shapes my life in accordance with his plan.' When Bismarck was a politician the practical consequence of this sense of obligation towards God and of being called by God was to intensify his readiness to throw his whole personality into what he did, but not to limit his choice of means and measures in his behaviour towards his fellow-men. He knew, as an adoring biographer expressed with great reticence, that ' politics is a dirty business ', that ' politics is unthinkable without violence and trickery ', and that the politician ' has to take on himself the responsibility for bloody tears '. But he resigned himself to these facts. In this blindness of his in relation to the religious commands regarding the use of honourable means lies a characteristic of Bismarck's religious outlook, its moral weakness and its practical strength. He had and kept a good conscience whatever he did. What God demanded of him was, according to his convictions, that he should utilize all his power and capacities to carry out the task entrusted to him. ' I am really thankful to God,' he cried out, ' that he has thought me worthy to render considerable service to the good cause.' However, that the full exercise of one's own power should lead to success is not only a matter for the man who acts, but also a gift of divine providence ; so ' if I did not believe in a divine order, I should not have taken on the task of meddling with the intricacies of diplomacy '. Yet this principle served him even more to disguise his real intentions. In one of the gravest hours of his official life, when it was a question of the King deciding between peace and the war prepared by Bismarck, the latter told the King that he did not wish ' to press him, but would leave it in confidence to God to guide the heart of your Majesty for the welfare of the fatherland and I shall rather pray than advise '.

Of the mutual personal relations of Bismarck and Johanna before their marriage we have a great number of testimonies in the letters exchanged by them. Bismarck's letters are full of the most tender feeling and sincere reverence, full of concern for the happiness and health of his fiancée. At the same time he tries cautiously to educate and teach her, giving entire freedom to her will and yet setting before her the full power of his personality. The letters give a colourful and vivacious account of daily trifles and are animated throughout by a humour sometimes warm and sometimes sharp. So they are a delicate mixture of spontaneous unreflective monologue and of appeals, confidences, confessions, exhortations addressed to his fiancée. They are the most direct, uncalculated outbursts of the human heart and at the same time gems of literature, both when descriptive of events and when expressive of thoughts. In them there speaks forth a knowledge of the loftiest and noblest human tendencies and of the inner personal life of his fiancée, such as would be denied to any clever rationalistic reflection and could be attained only by the intuition of the genius. In an unbroken series they depict the development of a man who from the rôle of a seeking and desiring lover grows ever more securely into that of the watchful and protecting husband, and who, in his relation to the woman, knows how to establish an ever more perfect harmony between joy at her charms, happiness in the development of her mind, sympathy with her delicate health, and help for her progress towards her future life work.

Johanna, through her inherent nature and the fact that she had so far been brought up in the uniformity of a rather narrow environment, was not used to expressing her inner life in speech, and even less so in writing. Now she was overwhelmed by a plenitude of emotional experiences and so was herself at first uneasy and inhibited. She, herself sensitive, easily felt injured and was always concerned not to hurt or bore her fiancé. Her future prospects rejoiced her, but also to some extent oppressed her. Would she be qualified for her new task ? Would her health last ? Would her external attractions be sufficient ? She took refuge in invalidism ; she found herself lacking in beauty and looking old beyond her age. She was in doubt about Bismarck's and her own love. Tears, not only of joy, but also of wistfulness and despondency flowed freely. But she fought her way through her inhibitions and doubts. She gave herself to her fiancé more and more openly and freely, and her anxieties disappeared as she communicated them. Her belief in his genuineness and reliability increased. Resistance to the fascination of his personality fell away. She became conscious and sure of the working on him of her own woman's nature and gave to him all the strength and depth of her woman's feelings. Still a month after her betrothal we hear from her : ' How endlessly I talked—I believe I am ill. I need only a little push to make me shed tears in abundance. And you do not want me to be like that. You deserved a better letter from your beloved. Have patience with me and wait for the spring and your care.' And she speaks still more despondently in another letter of about the same time : ' I expect all the love, all the loyalty of your heart. If I am mistaken—what then ? Mistrust is the most terrible, the bitterest torment there can be.' A month later, however, she told how she collected a letter from her fiancé at the post office :

When I saw the dear long letters, I seized this dear pledge of your affection in some haste, broke open the seal and did not trouble myself about the few passers-by with their questioning looks. Let them wonder,

I was and am so fully occupied with you, and your warm beloved love delights me so much that I must come and see you, if only for a moment.

Love kindled imagination and grew beyond the banality of her Pomeranian environment into a realm of vision in which she took her place side by side with Bismarck in power of literary expression.

I read to-day of a kind of sea bird [she wrote a few weeks later, in the beginning of May] who fly in their sleep, who hover up and down over the waves. If they touch the water with their wings, they wake up, but they do not let themselves be disturbed by the chill, yet go on flying in their sleep, on and on over the white foam under the blue sky. Whether this is a mere fancy or really true, I find it extraordinarily attractive, intoxicatingly beautiful, and would like to be such a bird.

A short time afterwards, however, there came a nervous breakdown, which was obviously due to bodily conditions. There followed complaints about all possible physical ills, combined with expressions of deep despondency which went so far as to give rise to the wish that the wedding intended for July should be postponed till September.

Bismarck shared with her all these emotions and journeys of the spirit. Once he came as a teacher to her: 'I love you as you are and as you think it well to be. Having said this, which expresses the most sincerely felt and the unembroidered truth, I beg you to occupy yourself a little with French, not much, but somewhat, by reading French works which interest you. If you get bored, drop it.' But also the note of moral warning is not lacking. 'If you do not wish to be an unmerciful judge over me, you should really trust me till you should find by experience that I deserve not to be trusted. But if you love me you should forgive me up to seventy times seven, even if I have really sinned against you.' Humour plays its part too: 'Now a black cat is playing with my heart in the sunshine as though it were a ball of wool, and I enjoy the game.' Surprisingly expert observations on literature culminate in the remark: 'Exaltation founded on serenity gives the concept of majesty, a majesty which is faintly radiated by man only in a few rarely privileged moments.' By way of encouragement he says to her: 'Never be fainthearted towards me. And if something in yourself depresses you, think that everything of that kind is to be found in me a thousand times over.' Finally, however, he gives himself in strong words to his fiancée, to the woman's nature in her:

That fragrant breath from the unfathomable inner depths of the mind, that is neither poetry, nor love, nor religion, but which, wherever it breathes, fortifies, elevates, and makes more receptive all three, is what I experience when I am with you: I cannot think of a word for it at the moment.

Bismarck repeatedly complained that the offices of 'fiancé and inspector of dykes are almost incompatible ', and she also finds that ' to be an inspector of dykes is really the most horrible occupation there is '. But not only did Bismarck devote himself to this office with his whole energy and ambition ; he also undertook and carried out with zeal other public functions which hindered him from being with Johanna. She, however, spent almost the whole period of her engagement in Reinfeld with her parents. So it came about that during this whole time the two of them saw very little of each other. Bismarck, indeed, repeatedly prepared for visits to Reinfeld without carrying them out. In February he was ' itching all over to fly to her to-day ', but he did not act accordingly, and at the very end 'of the month he remarked, ' when I am to see you is dependent on how the position of the Elbewater develops '. Similarly in June he writes to Johanna : ' I have been in Kniephof ; I had covered half the way to your house, but could not cover the other half.' This is the same man who ten years before had not hesitated on account of a love-affair to ask for quite a long leave from his official functions at Aachen and not only to devote this period to the then object of his affections, but in violation of his duty as a civil servant to prolong of his own accord his absence by several weeks. Now, however, his professional work ranked with him not only side by side with the desire of his heart, but apparently even before it. Indeed, the two were combined ; through his love he took his professional duties more, in fact, very seriously, and by doing so tried to convey to her the seriousness of his affection.

Thus, besides religion and their personal relationship, there was a third increasingly important topic treated in the letters of Bismarck, namely these professional activities. They are depicted with vivid colour and imbued with a warm breath of life. The figure that makes the strongest and most immediate impression is undoubtedly the inspector of dykes, whose

tattered flag in the storms and rain of the night fluttered along the fringe of the unruly waters, myself mounted on a brown horse which expressed its terror in earsplitting snorts, heard above the thundering. din of the battle between the ice-floes when they threw up their mighty ruins splintering in the whirlpool.

So the gigantic figure stood upright, sharply silhouetted in the clear night sky, watching intently the Elbe bank. On another occasion we see him in quick buoyant movement : ' Half an hour later Miss Breeze was galloping with me along the Elbe, clearly proud to bear one betrothed to you, for never before did she strike the ground so contemptuously with her hoofs.'

Extraordinarily vivid are also the descriptions of the business

negotiations which he had to carry out. Here there appears, besides
the thane, the diplomat, who in the choice of his means is just as
calculating and just as little squeamish as when he once tried to
win a bride by a deceitful letter. Pretended excitement and rage,
threats clothed in persuasion, playing his business partners off
against each other are all used now by him without scruple and
clearly with success. He told Johanna that a ' certain accomplish-
ment ' in the art of deceiving was ' very desirable ' and was indeed
not seldom required in the interests of good manners. As magistrate he brought about ' an agreement between 41 insolent peasants,
each of whom felt a bitter hate against the other 40 '. While his

predecessor had let this matter drag on for four years, after four hours'
work in which I mingled flattering friendliness and rude coarseness,
sometimes getting really angry, I brought them together. The moment
when I again mounted my carriage with their signatures in my pocket was
one of the few happy ones for which I have to thank my official position
so far.

An element of melancholy is contained in another transaction.
This was concerned with the letting of Kniephof which, since the
death of Ferdinand von Bismarck, had ceased to be a family residence. The prospective tenant had brought with him ' an assistant
known to the whole country as the most objectionable and spiteful
delighter in law-suits '. He worked against an agreement with all
means at his disposal.

Towards evening when all the carriages were ready waiting, I thought
of the happy expedient of being so rude to the assistant, without actually
giving him cause for a libel action, that he left the room at once and went
away. Then I came to an agreement with my tenant in five minutes.

However, this agreement meant good-bye to Kniephof. ' I
thought sadly how the rooms in which I played as a child would
be inhabited by strangers, how all my flower-beds and parks would
become overgrown and go to ruin, how the white bridges and benches
would fall to pieces.' And then there speaks, besides the man,
the baron : ' It is the first time since Kniephof has been in the
possession of our family that it is inhabited by strangers.' Nor
was this the only way in which he showed that he was a baron.
He accepted an invitation to dinner in the house of a rich burgher
because the host had forced him to come ' at the point of a gun '.
The dinner was ' as I had anticipated, very boring, all kinds of fat
grocers' wives, three liberal members of parliament who at once
tried to ingratiate themselves with me '. A certain untitled caller
he found ' intolerable ' : ' I made a face like a prison door and
did not say a word, but he sat for nearly two hours and told me
home-made stories.'

To Bismarck's minor business affairs were added business demands of a more far-reaching importance. He began to take a part in state affairs on a wider scale, having in the first place to carry further the work he had done in connexion with the reform of patriarchal jurisdiction. He had to settle 'a piece of business with the minister of justice, which will make necessary a stay of some days in Berlin', as he informed Johanna. 'Besides this I have some fairly extensive pieces of writing to produce with which I have been entrusted by the representatives of several districts of the province and I have been chosen their representative in Berlin in this affair.' He had to 'bring forward important matters in the Kreistag', and he must not 'fail to appear in the assembly where the whole knighthood of the Province is present'. Another meeting took place at the castle Erxleben, and afforded Bismarck the opportunity of giving his fiancée an attractive description of 'towers, spiral staircases of stone, gabled roofs, bow-windows, and battlements'.

Bismarck had obtained his introduction to parliamentary life when he was elected as deputy to the member for Schönhausen in one of the provincial councils. It was a parliament on a very small scale and with very modest functions which first gave Bismarck his place. Introduced in 1823 as a late fruit of the Stein-Hardenberg reforms, the provincial councils included a majority of the owners of manors, practically all noblemen, and a minority of representatives of the owners of town property, besides a small number of representatives of farmers and landowners not of noble birth. They thus made up a body which was rather a class organization than a parliament. Their activity was limited, since they could only give advice, not make a final decision, and were concerned with affairs of the provinces not of the whole country and with questions of merely technical administrative interest without involving political principles. But the struggle for a parliament of the whole state, an assembly of truly parliamentary character and with truly parliamentary functions, went on. When, on the 3rd of February 1847, this struggle attained its provisional goal through the formation of the 'United Parliament' (Vereinigte Landtag), i.e., through the convocation of the members of the provincial councils in a single assembly, this seemed at the time of no practical significance for Bismarck, as only the ordinary members of these councils were summoned and not their deputies.

But at the beginning of May Bismarck told Johanna of an event which was bound to be of the greatest importance for the future pattern of his life. Not without repeated apologies for having upset their plans for meeting, he told her that he had after all been called to the newly constituted United Parliament in Berlin and that he had accepted, mentioning how he, although 'quite new in the province' and but recently elected, was, contrary to the traditional custom, designated first and not last of the six deputies. The ordinary representative, who had fallen ill, 'resigned specially so that I should be his successor'. Bismarck clearly admitted the pride he felt at this distinction and added : 'I cannot decline the invitation without decidedly insulting the assembly and destroying any of my prospects for the future which depends on the backing of my class.'

On July 28th, 1847, Bismarck was married to Johanna von Putt-kamer 'under the wooden roof' of a simple village church. Shortly afterwards they went on their honeymoon. Johanna was quite over-whelmed by the idea of a trip across the Alps : 'But Otto, is it possible ? Salzburg, Tyrol !' This holiday journey lasted almost two months and took them through Salzkammergut and south Tyrol to Venice, upper Italy, Switzerland and the Rhine Valley. By now Bismarck had already laid the foundations of his reputation as parliamentary politician.

CHAPTER VIII

Bismarck as Member of Parliament

What was at the back of this United Parliament in Berlin of which Bismarck was now a member ? It was a creation of the man who at that time had already sat on the Prussian throne for seven years, Frederick William IV. This king, an easily excitable and very self-willed man, the ' romantic on the throne ', had a far-flung imagination, but was incapable of facing facts or of taking them into account. He had plenty of ability but was completely unfit to take a deliberate decision. He had many varied intellectual and artistic interests, but was without any sure judgement. It was impossible to be on intimate terms with the King, yet he was capable of placing trust in some and was without any petty touchiness. This Hohenzollern was in no wise cowardly, but the least military among his family. He was always ready to be stimulated and to receive suggestions, but equally ready to let them drop, being a man of sudden inspirations and sudden changes of opinion. His overstrong consciousness of his position and personality did not withstand any serious test. His incapacity for ' vigorous decisions ' was contrasted, as Bismarck emphasized, with his gift of expressing his thoughts ' in an eloquent, and indeed poetical manner, which could rarely be criticized on the score of language '. He was well aware of this gift and much enjoyed making use of it.

The King shared with his father and predecessor, Frederick William III, a strong Prussianism and a deep aversion to the liberal and constitutional aspirations of the bourgeoisie, which was just entering on the road to social and political power. In this culturally and politically active bourgeoisie he saw ' the representative of the revolution '. Frederick William III had, on the 22nd of May 1815, issued a decree promising the establishment of ' representation of the people ' in Prussia. From now on, father and son did everything to postpone the fulfilment of this promise and to pretend that the provincial councils, authorized in 1823, already fulfilled it.

In other respects father and son were very different. Frederick William III's rule had embodied a bureaucratic state government, for he himself was a bureaucrat, pedantic, with the disposition of a subordinate, lacking élan. Certainly, the intellectually free type, exemplified in Bismarck's grandfather Menken, had not entirely died out, and produced much useful work in this bureaucracy. But on the whole the civil service of Frederick William III was aptly described by Bismarck when he said that ' the old pigtail was

61

general ', but the physical was supplemented by an 'intellectual pigtail'. Frederick William IV, on the other hand, had the conception of a government based on autocracy and the castes, which we have already seen theoretically defended by Fr. J. Stahl and championed in action by Bismarck's friends Bülow-Cummerow, Thadden-Treglaff and Ludwig von Gerlach, and to which Bismarck now inclined clearly and consciously in increasing measure. In this conception he felt himself keenly related to Frederick William IV: ' I had the feeling that the King is on the right road ', he declared already at the beginning of his parliamentary activities. The King's politics, according to Bismarck's approving words, found its religious basis, ' in the idea that the King, and the King alone, knows the will of God better than anybody else, rules according to this will, and therefore demands trustful obedience, without discussing his ends with his subjects or even informing the latter of them '.

From the brain of this man there sprang the idea of the United Parliament in Berlin. On his accession to the throne, when reminded of his father's still unfulfilled promise of ' representation of the people ', he replied : ' My father, while keeping far away from the prevailing ideas of universal suffrage, entered upon a road based on the course of historical development and adapted to the natural genius of the German people, that of provincial and local organization in accordance with the hierarchy of the castes.' Still Frederick William IV had in the first seven years of his reign never altogether let drop the idea of a single parliament for his whole kingdom and constantly discussed it with his advisers. The solution of the question in the sense of an aristocratic caste system suited him, but he showed occasional inclinations to liberal experiments. However, his brother, Prince William of Prussia, who as head of the Prussian cabinet had something important to say on the subject, opposed every innovation or at least introduced as many reservations as possible. The ' Memoirs ' of Leopold von Gerlach, the brother of Ludwig von Gerlach, one of the most influential advisers of Frederick William IV, remark on such a liberal whim : ' We must build in the interest of the King, even without him.'

When, finally, on the 3rd of February 1847, there appeared the long-awaited law concerning the ' Summoning of a United Parliament ', it decreed that this parliament was not to meet periodically, but ' as often as the needs of the state required either new loans or the introduction of new or the increase of existing taxes '. The functions of the United Parliament should consist, firstly, in being ' an advisory body in legislation ', similar to the provincial councils, secondly, in ' co-operating in arrangements regarding interest and repayment of state debts ', and, finally, in ' the right of petition in internal, not merely provincial, affairs '. So the King's attitude ' of keeping far away from the idea ' of a ' representation of the people ' was throughout maintained. The written constitution which was expected at the same time did not materialize, and, to add obscurity to inadequacy, a ' United Committee of the Councils ' was introduced. This was made up by uniting the committees of the different provincial councils, which committees had long been in existence and had represented these councils between sessions. Each committee was about a quarter of the size of a provincial council. The United Committee had the same powers as the United Parliament itself and was to be its ' periodically summoned representative ', whereas the right to be periodically summoned, which was a particular object of popular demand, was denied to the parliament. So the committee made superfluous the parliament which it represented.

In view of these defects and obscurities of the representative system it can hardly have been a recommendation for the liberal and national bourgeoisie that the King instituted besides the house of representatives also an Upper House (Herrenkurie) of which the royal Princes and a large number of the high nobility were to be members. The King, however, congratulated himself on this creation of his with the words : ' An assembly of lords, a chamber of peers, unparalleled in history.' But it was not enough for him to deny the constitutional liberal party the fulfilment of all their wishes and hopes. When the King opened the United Parliament on the 11th of April 1847 with a solemn speech from the throne, he again warned the deputies emphatically against thinking ' themselves representatives of the people in the modern style. You have been summoned to defend rights, the rights of your class and at the same time the rights of the throne ; to express opinions is not your business.' Alluding to their disappointed ,hopes for a written constitution he said : ' No piece of paper shall come as a second providence between God in heaven and this land.' No wonder that this attitude aroused a sharp opposition, not only among the liberal bourgeoisie who had their headquarters in the Rhineland, but also deep within the circle of noble landowners of the East. Even a man so favourably disposed to the monarchy as Bülow-Cummerow thought it advisable to warn the King against such ' half-measures '.

Bismarck, on the other hand, had no doubt that his place was with the throne and indeed without any condition or limitation. However, he still had no chance to express openly his approval of the King's speech from the throne, for, still being a deputy member only, he was not summoned to the opening ceremony and was thus unable to comment on the King's speech in parliament. His indignation against the address made by the parliament in reply to the King with its insistence on a written constitution and constitutional rights had to remain unspoken. The four weeks which elapsed before he was himself summoned to parliament were very unpleasant for him.   His friends reminded him of his capacity for such activities. 'It seems to me that for a man of your energy and ambition a splendid field of parliamentary activity is opening.'   He, too, was well aware that his development in the last years led up to such a career, and that it was in this direction that the deployment of his faculties lay.   When he wrote to Johanna shortly before the meeting of the United Parliament: 'The country and the King certainly lose by my absence one of their best representatives and lose, more-over, a pillar of the throne in parliament, but our love is a winner thereby,' this humorous turn was not free from an appreciable tinge of bitterness.   Ten days after he had accepted the invitation to attend he excused himself to Johanna by saying that his refusal would have 'offended his peers'.   He told her frankly and openly: 'It was my earnest desire to be a member of parliament', and he added: 'Regard the excuses which seemed to you somewhat farfetched as a natural expression of courtesy.'

But in fact we have here in Bismarck's mind not only a contest between mere personal ambition and the voice of the heart.   He really was inspired by the conviction that his presence in parlia-ment was indispensable for the cause of the King.

The debates in parliament [he wrote shortly before taking part in them himself] are assuming a course which will disturb every well-disposed person.   The best of intentions, the legally most correct actions on the part of the government are misunderstood and distorted out of sheer party spirit.   The government, though completely in the right, is always in the minority.

Consequently 'it may be a matter of a single vote, and it would be bad if that was the vote of an absentee'.   But when referring to the Opposition, Bismarck speaks still more from his heart: 'It is extra-ordinary how persistent the speakers are in rising in view of their feeble capacities and with what shameless self-satisfaction they dare to force their empty phrases on so great an assembly.'   Yet the leader of the liberal Opposition was by no means a bloodless theorizer who dealt in abstractions, but on the contrary a very self-confident aristocrat, proud of his ties with his native soil, the baron Georg von Vincke, an owner of large estates in Westphalia.   He was four years older than Bismarck and had been Landrat of his district for ten years.   He was acclaimed by competent opinion as 'the greatest Prussian parliamentary speaker' of his time.   As formerly in the struggle for the office of inspector of dykes, now too in Bismarck's mind, zest for his objective goal, personal contempt for his opponent, and selfish ambition kindle each other into a blazing flame.   This time it is not a case of emotion artificially excited to gain his ends as we have sometimes seen it happen with the business affairs in Schönhausen. Here it is the real thing, we see the whole man thrown into the struggle. 'We are looking forward with the greatest excitement to dealing with real political questions,' he said after the preliminary sessions, ' the matter has taken hold of me more than I thought. So you can understand that I am in a continual state of tension which hardly allows me to eat or sleep.' That in this excitement personal animus against his opponents played a decisive rôle is a circumstance which Bismarck never concealed from himself or from others. Concerning his attitude at that time in party warfare, he said that ' it demanded equally loyalty to one's friends and distrust or enmity towards one's opponents '. ' The conviction that his opponent in everything that he undertakes is at best limited, but probably also malicious and devoid of conscience ' was at that time ' vivid and sincere '. ' In these days we really regarded each other as either fools or knaves,' he later on declared complacently. This attitude could, in Bismarck's view, by no means be condemned on religious grounds, since it meant that the man, who thought himself under the command of God, threw all his strength into the fray. ' I was ready to give my enemy food, but as for giving him my blessing—that would be a very external affair, if I did it at all.'

It goes without saying that a man of such a temperament thirsting for expression would not remain silent for long in parliament and that this expression would not take place without his dealing the Opposition a blow in the face. Nine days only after he took his seat, the new member made his maiden speech. A member of the liberal Opposition, referring to the desire for a written constitution, declared that it was not national hatred that had been the driving force in the people in the anti-napoleonic war of 1813 ; it had been the inner understanding between ruler and people, and it was now their holiest duty to re-establish this harmony. Bismarck rose at once in opposition to a claim which in fact had never been made, namely, that

the movement of 1813 had needed any other motive besides the disgrace of seeing foreigners in command of our country. In my opinion it is doing ill service to the national honour to assume that the maltreatment and humiliation which the Prussians suffered at the hands of a foreign tyrant was not sufficient to make their blood boil and to deaden all other feelings in comparison to the hatred of alien rule.

This view had been put before Bismarck in the house of his fathers from earliest childhood and had been always vivid in him. But now it led him to flog his parliamentary opponents :

A person who asks that the parrying of blows which he had himself received should be regarded as a meritorious service to a third party, calling for reward, admits that he is lacking in every feeling of honour. As if we had defended ourselves in order to be able to say to the King, 'We have reconquered your Majesty's land, what will you give us for this?'

This sounds emphatic enough, but it may be that we are already dealing with a version re-edited for publication. Bismarck from the beginning attached the greatest importance to the revision of his parliamentary speeches and often told Johanna how busy he was doing this. Perhaps the original words were still more emphatic. At any rate Bismarck reported to his fiancée: 'I applied to 1813 the principle that anyone [the Prussian people] who had been flogged by somebody else [the French] for so long till he resisted, cannot claim any merit in the eyes of a third party [our King] for having done this.'

It was natural that the aggressive words of 'the young man' who 'arrogated judgement on a time through which he had not lived himself', should be received with 'repeated and loud murmurs'. This was reported by him with self-satisfaction to Johanna as an 'unheard-of storm of opposition'. But it did not hinder him from using the reference to himself as 'a young man' as the occasion to ask for permission to speak again. When he appeared for a second time on the speaker's platform, he was greeted with a 'loud din', so that for a time he could not utter a word. He reacted to this excitement with a quite unusual procedure, which the later Bismarck repeatedly described with much gusto. While cries of '*Pfui!*' rang all round him, the thirty-two-year-old politician turned his back to the tumultuous assembly, took a newspaper out of his pocket and read it quietly till the storm had blown over. Then he led up to the trenchant climax of his speech. He could 'not deny that he was not yet alive in 1813', but his 'former diffidence in viewing that time was lessened by the statement put forward to-day that the yoke against which the Prussians then revolted was not the work of foreigners but was due to the weakness of their own people'. This was a challenge not only to this parliament and German parliamentarism as a whole but also to German liberalism and democracy, and to their spiritual and philosophical foundation.

This episode made Bismarck a well-known man. From now on he obtained 'some influence' in parliament on the 'deputies of the so-called court party and the other ultra-conservatives', as he himself characterized his political friends. 'When the other side were guilty of some insolent word, men often looked to see whether from my seat there would not rise a warrior on the side of truth.' A fortnight later he spoke again, on the relation between crown and parliament, this time at greater length and with some reference to fundamental questions. He emphasized that the Prussian monarch who 'by the

Grace of God is in possession of a practically unlimited royal power had given voluntarily to the people a part of his rightful privileges '. He demanded for the King ' time to come to a decision ' about the granting of a constitution and refused to ' pull up and cast away the flower of trust as a weed which prevents us from seeing the bare legal ground in its full nakedness '. When in the following month the authorization of a loan for railways was discussed, he expressly and unambiguously described the conduct of the Opposition, who wished by refusing the authorization of the loan to force the government to make constitutional concessions, as ' blackmail '.

Bismarck's state of mind during this period became more and more tense and excited. Again and again he told Johanna of the ' political passion which has seized control of me beyond what I had expected '. ' In parliament, I get angry every day and cannot even express my anger.' When he had been in parliament hardly three weeks, he says that ' the rattling machinery of political life becomes every day more obnoxious to my ears '. While thus he seemed to lose interest in the struggle for its objective aim, his personal hostility to his opponents increased in bitterness, reaching the level of sheer hate. ' From morning till evening I am full of gall at the lying, slanderous dishonesty of the Opposition.' He speaks about the ' commonplace, trimmed-up phrases of the Rhenish wine-merchants' politics ', of the ' shameless ' conduct of the Opposition who ' make everything a party matter '. He refers to one of his fellow-Junkers, a liberal, as a ' champion in the boundless nonsense of his Jacobin ideas '. Of himself he admits : ' Party rage fills my head,' he rejoices that his friends have given him the name of ' Vinckecatcher ' (Vincke is an old-German word for finch). He is proud of ' the power to bite which I have displayed on several occasions '.

So he resolved after some hesitation to come forward in parliament on an issue where there was hardly any question of fighting for an objectively valuable end, but plenty of scope for the bitterest personal quarrels, namely, the question of the Jews. The man who as landlord had rejoiced in injuring Jewish merchants by his sharp tongue, who in the stage-coach had moved away from his neighbour because the latter was ' the direct descendant of Abraham ', who in a discussion with his friend Gerlach about the religious beliefs of the Jews mockingly decided the issue by saying : ' I do not ask them, I just tell by their faces,' this man now made of his personal aversion a demand based on religion. In supporting this demand he who recently felt himself called to be ' champion and pillar of the throne ' now passes to the attack, although he is here ' not in agreement with the government '. That the royal decree under discussion, aiming at improving the conditions of the Jews, failed to win the approval of the liberals is not to be wondered at, since it did not give in any way equal political rights to the Jews, and in particular excluded them from all appointments in the civil service. It is, however, difficult to understand Bismarck when he allows himself too readily to be enticed into battle ' by the sentimental waddle ' of the ' tedious babblers about humanity ', and in urging the rejection of the decree based his argument on the conception of the Christian state. He espoused the cause of religious principles against ' the vague and changeable concepts of humanity '. In his speech he gave vent to the fear that the decree might lead to a disappearance of the defences against movements like communism. But perhaps Bismarck's mocking expression of sympathy with the ' medieval prejudices of the mob ' takes on a far more earnest significance than he himself suspected. It may be that his utilization of Christian ideas in this context was in conformity with the desires of many of his pietist friends. We cannot, however, avoid the impression that for Bismarck the theory of the Christian state is here rather the cloak than the body of his contribution.

A little while before he had said to Johanna half, but only half, joking : ' One holds fast to principles only so long as they have not been put to the test.' In fact, the speaker does not long feel well at ease in this restricting garment of principles. He throws it off, and before us there stands the aristocratic baron.

> If I think of myself facing a Jew as representative of the Holy Majesty of the King whom I must obey, I am bound to admit that I should feel myself deeply abashed and depressed ; that the joy and the upright feeling of honour with which I now strive to discharge my duties to the state would forsake me.

Remaining in the realm of personal feelings, he continues in a fury :

> I know a region in the country where every article of furniture from the bed to the fire tongs belongs to the Jews, where the cow in the shed belongs to them too, and the peasant pays for every single article his daily rent, where the corn on the fields and in the barn belongs also to the Jews and the Jew sells to the peasant corn for bread, seed, and fodder measure by measure. Of a similar usury by Christians I have never heard.

This is undoubtedly personal aversion to the Jews carried to its highest point ; Bismarck, however, declared : ' I am no enemy of the Jews, and if they should turn out to be my enemies, I forgive them ; under certain circumstances I even love them.' But this declaration of love none of the would-be objects of this love can ever have taken seriously ; the bitter irony is not to be overlooked. If, further, Bismarck leaves the question of the desirability of settling Russian Jews in Prussia to the judgement of those ' who have had the good fortune to come to know Russian Jews *en masse* ', we shall ask in vain for the ' circumstances ' which could ever change such an aversion into love. In the debate on the question Bismarck expressly denies that his policy was motivated by any theory.

The nobility of the present day [he declares], are willing to renounce their hereditary rights without a murmur if the interests of their fatherland are at stake. But that we should do this merely because theorizers about the abstract notion of citizenship and envious supporters of French equalitarianism pelt us with the phrases of 1789, that no one can demand.

Nor did Bismarck forget to deal a blow at his parliamentary opponents. To those ' who seek for their ideals beyond the Vosges ', he exclaims, ' the proud sense of national honour does not so readily turn itself to search abroad for patterns of conduct worthy of imitation and admiration as is the custom here '.

But Bismarck advances a step further still in his personal attitude to the struggle. While in these days he was the aggressor against the Jews, he talked himself with great skill into the rôle of the attacked, so as to justify and at the same time increase and exaggerate his anger. Already in the speech we have mentioned he had hypothetically spoken of the possibility that the Jews might be his enemies. The same evening, however, he wrote to Johanna : ' This morning it was the Jews again. I made a long speech against their emancipation, and expressed myself very bitterly. I am not going to walk through the Königsstrasse in the evening for fear the Jews might kill me.' No doubt it was a joke, but what an absurd attitude of mind to kindle one's own will to aggression by imagining oneself to be the person attacked ! The trait of Bismarck's character which made him fly into a rage when he encountered personal opposition in pursuing his objective aims appears here with special distinctness and emphasis. It is just as if the furies had seized him by the hair and carried him off. The man who is now revelling in bitterness and hate is the same who at the same time in respect of his fiancée showed himself the tenderest, most attentive and most conscientious of lovers !

This speech of Bismarck, by the way, remained without any influence on the decision concerning the emancipation of the Jews. His friend Moritz von Blanckenburg of course approved without reservation of his attitude and took the view that ' he had rendered the most decided service to the King and to Christ '. But he did not gain this whole-hearted approval from those whose ' champion and pillar of the throne ' he strove to be, namely the King and his entourage. He himself was always ready to enter into relations with the court. At the end of May he told Johanna that he had taken part in a regatta on ' the great blue basin of the Havel ', in the centre of which there stood the royal boat. Four weeks later he spoke of a reception of conservative deputies in Potsdam. ' The day before yesterday we were with our friend the King and I was very much in favour with those high up.' But the favour shown him seems to have come mainly from the royal Princes, in particular Prince William, to whom he had already been introduced as a junior civil servant; the Prince now as presumptive heir of his brother, the childless King, bore the title of Prince of Prussia. Johanna called Bismarck ' pampered pet of princes '. On the other hand, his friendship with the King seems to have been very one-sided. In reality, as he reports in his *Reflections and Reminiscences*, he was noticeably avoided at court festivities, not only by the liberal-minded wife of the Prince of Prussia, Princess Augusta, but also by the King himself. They would not speak with him on these occasions, and in welcoming guests at receptions always stopped short of him. This treatment was by no means a matter of indifference to Bismarck; he reports that during his honeymoon he was recognized by the King at the theatre in Venice and invited to his table. From the conversation which then took place and from the request of the King to call again in Berlin he concludes with evident relief and satisfaction that, if ' the King at the time of the meetings of parliament avoided speaking to me in public, it was not that he thereby intended to express a criticism of my political attitude, but only that he did not wish at the time to show his approval to others '. Bismarck is very glad to see that he ' stands high in the favour of Their most Gracious Majesties '.

CHAPTER IX

The Revolution of 1848

In his *Reflections and Reminiscences* Bismarck surprises us by the following remark concerning the beginning of his parliamentary activity : ' The unlimited authority of the old Prussian royal power neither was nor is the last word for me. Ever since 1847 I have been in favour of striving to secure the possibility of public criticism of the government in parliament.' Actually this activity was more in keeping with the views of the man who wrote to his King : ' What I owe to the grace of your Majesty has as its basis and indestructible core my position as a vassal of Brandenburg and as Prussian officer of your Majesty, and for this reason any amount of popularity would be worthless unless your Majesty found satisfaction in me.' This element of feeling in Bismarck's attitude to the state and its head was further enhanced by his marriage.

The family had always played an important part in Bismarck's relation to the state, up to now as a tradition, representing a centuries-old association with the royal house, expressing union with the soil of the fatherland, and giving him membership in a privileged class intended to preserve the state. Now the family appears as something that is to be built up for the future ; with the prospect of descendants it became for Bismarck quite decidedly a subject of duty. He felt under an obligation to secure and improve its economic status and to strengthen and elevate its social position. With Bismarck the feelings of the lover were very soon intermingled with the consciousness of being the head of a house and *pater familias* and with the awareness of an extraordinarily extended sphere of obligations and responsibilities. He expressed this to his wife four years after his marriage, on the occasion of a visit to Wiesbaden. Alluding to the excursion he had made to this spa in his wild Aachen days he called it ' the site of earlier folly, where the champagne of twenty-two-year-old youth futilely effervesced and left behind stale desires ' ; and he continued to say :

How much is small to me now, which then seemed great, how much is worthy of honour now, which I then mocked. I cannot now understand how I endured life in those times. Had I to live now as I did then without God, without you, without the children, I really do not know why I should not cast away this life like a dirty shirt.

Marriage was for Bismarck not predominantly a personal relationship between two people, it was rather a social institution, on the basis of which man—and this means for Bismarck the male partner —stands in society endowed with a new dignity, as one who now represents a family, as the preserver of the past and the builder of the future of the state itself. We have already seen how Bismarck had come near to accepting the patriarchal idea of the state maintained by Ludwig and Leopold von Gerlach and their political friends. This idea derives the state genetically from the family, or thinks of the state in terms of the analogy of the family, and values it accordingly. Now, as a married man, he sees in his family, his house, a germinal cell of the state, of such a kind that everything that would serve and help this constituent part must necessarily serve and help the whole organism. But he was no less unquestionably convinced that the germinal cell of his house was entitled to make unrestricted use for its own purposes of the greater organism, the state. He takes it as obvious that the state and his own activity for it and in it is destined to give his wife a materially secure and comfortable life and a pleasant position in society and his children particularly good opportunities of development and prospects for the future. His desire was that they, as sons and daughters of their father, should be privileged in life and marked out from others. There is hardly a decision or a measure taken by the mighty statesman in which hate and the desire to persecute his opponents does not play a part; but there is also hardly one in which the head of the household and the father of the family does not manifest himself.

At the beginning of October 1847, the young couple, after two months' honeymoon, took up residence in the stately castle of Schönhausen. As children of the land they were both responsive to the beauties of nature and had enjoyed in amplest measure the scenes visited in their journey. Johanna, having rarely moved beyond the immediate neighbourhood of her home, took an almost childlike delight in the new and surprising impressions she now received. Bismarck greatly enjoyed the lively response of his wife to these impressions. He himself was a more deliberate and trained sightseer, in a period in which journeys for pleasure and study were beginning to provide a prominent means of instruction and recreation for wider circles of the cultured classes in Germany. The way in which Bismarck travelled and the manner in which he received and conveyed impressions was a pattern and stimulus for many of his followers in enjoyment. The people to whom Goethe's 'Italian Journey' seemed like a fairy tale which they could never hope to realize would find Bismarck's impressions of his journeys as calling for imitation and emulation. Vivid descriptions of landscapes, towns, peoples, episodes in the journey, and personalities met, stand in the foreground, historical associations are limited more or less to the recent past. Works of art play a less prominent rôle, and there is not very much in the way of literary reminiscences. Personally, the Bismarcks found themselves very comfortable everywhere, since they met many fellow-travellers of the aristocratic class, with whom personal contact was welcome and easy. Particular ways of making the journeys more pleasant and attractive were naturally communicated from one to the other.

This first journey of the Bismarck couple provided an inexhaustible stock of memories for the enrichment of their married life. In conversations and letters they again and again exchanged reminiscences of these days of travel. When they had occasion to revisit a place the memory of the experience of that time was quite especially vivid. ' I lived quite in '47 as I passed through the Prater', he wrote five years later from Vienna. In 1865, when staying at Ischl, he remembered the place ' where we were together 18 years ago ', and, in 1866, on the way to the Austrian battlefront, he thought of the time when they had travelled that way ' 19 years ago '. The honeymoon concluded with the festive entry into the ancestral home, which for this purpose seemed to have tried to convert itself by means of fireworks and lightning effects into the goal of a journey in fairyland. But now there ensued for the married couple the everyday life of a landed estate. This meant for the wife a habit dear to her heart ; for the husband, owing to the presence of his beloved companion, freedom ' from the deluge of self-neglect and lovelessness ' and from hours of ' depression ' in which ' the doors of the room yawned ' and ' there stood opposite me dumb furniture in the silent rooms bored like myself '. Full of zeal he turned his attention to the management of his estate and the business of assisting in the government of the district. His activity as inspector of dykes called him ; he again had sometimes to act as the Landrat, sometimes to work as his assistant. Social intercourse with the neighbouring noble landowners was taken up again in increasing measure. There was a general desire to meet the young bride of the widely known owner of Schönhausen. This social life was not limited to friends and neighbours, Johanna's parents were also received as guests, as well as Bismarck's sister Malvine with her husband and the lonely Adolf von Thadden. Also there was hunting, and the pleasure in a good drink had not abated. So the young husband came to be still more rooted in his native soil. But this soil could not monopolize him exclusively.

With the conclusion of the session of the ' United Parliament ' at the end of June Bismarck had lost his place on the orator's platform before the whole Prussian people. The privilege of meeting regularly, which parliament had so hotly desired, was denied it, so there was at present no question of it being recalled. The ' United Committee ' began to function, commencing their activity in the following January. Bismarck, however, did not belong to this body as member, but only as deputy for another member. Consequently he had to seek a new way of expression. Even before the conclusion of the session of the United Parliament, some of the members of the Right, among them Bismarck himself, came together in order to found a daily newspaper representing the interests of their caste and of the monarch. The plan encountered difficulties. In the first place it was not very easy for them to provide the necessary funds. Then there were also differences of opinion in regard to questions of principle. The two brothers von Gerlach wanted the paper to base itself on religious principles, with possibly an inclination towards pietism. Bismarck himself, in agreement with the majority of the prospective patrons, decided in favour of ' religious neutrality '. The negotiations dragged on till January 1848 and a visit of Bismarck to Berlin in the first days of this month also failed to lead to any result at the time. So Bismarck for the present had to be content with other means of furthering his political and class interests. Thus there opened up for the married couple a life of pleasurable business and busy pleasures, just sufficiently punctuated with small jars and difficulties to prevent monotony and boredom. Such a life seemed to be their lot for the whole foreseeable future.

But the Bismarcks of that period were not destined to enjoy the beginning of their married happiness without disturbance or check. The father, Ferdinand von Bismarck, had in the autumn of 1806, a few months after his wedding, to face the French occupation of Schönhausen and to miss the company of his young wife. ' The storm, too, which burst on Schönhausen within six months of Otto von Bismarck's wedding had its origin on the other side of the Rhine, in France, but this time it was not called War but Revolution. On the 24th of February 1848, unexpected by Opposition and government alike, the Revolution broke out in Paris at a moment when only a change in the Cabinet was anticipated. The seventy-four-year-old King abdicated ; France became a republic again and a provisional republican government was established.

When these events became known in Germany, Frederick William IV was startled, but not horrified. He wrote a somewhat depressed letter to Queen Victoria of England about the instability of European thrones, which could only be saved by unity, by the combining of forces against revolution, but would then be saved ' with certainty '. The associates of Bismarck also hardly considered at first the possibility that the revolutionary movement might spread into Prussia. Their first thought was of war. They believed that they could defend the monarchical principle on the battlefield. Moritz von Blanckenburg, ' both reverend and cheeky, like a real Pomeranian ', quoting a party-friend, wrote to Bismarck : ' There must be and ought to be war. His Majesty on earth owes this to His Majesty in Heaven.' Bismarck himself also thought of the possibility of war, coolly measuring it, but without enthusiasm. In wide circles of the middle class, however, the conviction gained the upper hand that now the moment had come to realize the idea of their forefathers of ' a realm of true justice founded on the equality of all human beings ' and that it would now have to become evident that ' among Germans the state is to grow out of the development of individual liberty '. The first sign that the revolution was spreading across the Rhine was a middle-class meeting at Mannheim on the 27th of February 1848, in which the chairman put forward the well-known liberal demands for the freedom of the Press, trial by jury, permission to carry arms and the summoning of a German parliament. When this became known the first feeling which arose in Bismarck was one of personal hate against the supporters of the movement; a hate formerly directed against his liberal school teachers, the radicalism of the Burschenschaft at Göttingen, and the liberals in the United Parliament. ' I have a real bloodthirsty malice against the dogs at Mannheim who, appealing to the French bayonets in support, make the maddest demands.' King Frederick William IV now thought he could anticipate an extension of the movement to Prussia by granting to the United Parliament the right to regular sessions which they had so hotly demanded. This he did on the 6th of March 1848. A few days afterwards he promised a revision of the press laws and actually summoned the Prussian parliament for the 27th of April. At the same time the attempt was made in south Germany to arouse in the masses themselves the long-suppressed and now stormily manifested desire to open a regular way to political rights and political activity. On the 5th of March there was held in Heidelberg a meeting of distinguished German politicians who put forward the demand for the immediate summons of a German parliament in order to decide the future constitution of unified Germany. Rather less than a week afterwards a committee of this assembly called together the ' Pre-Parliament ' in order to determine the composition and summons of this ' German National Assembly ' at Frankfort on Main. On the 31st of March the ' Pre-Parliament ' met to fulfil its task.

It was however too late to prevent the revolution. This led at first to a cheap and bloodless, but almost decisive success in Vienna. The man who had become the personal symbol of the autocracy which was to be overthrown, the political leader of Austria, Clemens von Metternich, after some disturbances in the streets, handed in his resignation on the 13th of March, and it was accepted a few days later. Then the modest political concessions made by the King of Prussia definitely proved inadequate. On the 15th and

16th of March there occurred in Berlin bloody riots, in which it came to the erection of barricades and to the use of weapons, and to shooting on the part of the police and the military. Now the King was at a loss what to do. The autocratic consciousness of his divine right called a halt to any surrender which went beyond the concessions he had already made. But the brutal fact that blood had been shed opened up prospects which the King could only view with fear and horror. These were brought more vividly to his consciousness by the bad news from Vienna, by a deputation from the Rhineland, notorious for its liberalism, and by other alarming tidings. Meanwhile his advisers and especially—so it was popularly rumoured—his brother, Prince William, warned him against any concession. After a sleepless night the simple desire for self-preservation prevailed in the wavering, insincere man over the fanciful dream of his divine right. At noon on the 18th of March the 'beloved Berliners' were surprised by a decree of the King introducing at once the freedom of the Press, summoning parliament for the 2nd instead of the 27th of April, promising to grant a written constitution to Prussia and to promote the union and constitution of Germany as a whole.

The resulting thanksgiving of the 'beloved Berliners' in front of the royal palace was misunderstood by the military who were not used to an immediate contact between King and people nor to a belief in the 'flower of confidence' so highly appraised by Bismarck. Heavy shooting resulted in front of the palace and then in the town, in the course of which there were killed 230 men on the popular side and some 20 officers and soldiers. Now, despite the opposition of his brother, the autocrat descended almost at one stroke from vicegerent under God to people's King. The self-willed Prussian was almost completely replaced by the protagonist of German unity. The royal decree of the 18th of March was followed on the 19th by a manifesto of the King, appointing a liberal Cabinet, at first under the presidency of Bismarck's former Aachen chief, the count Adolf von Arnim-Boitzenburg, an advocate of moderate reforms. Ten days later, immediately before the opening of the second United Parliament, he was succeeded by Ludolf Campenhausen, a Rhinelander well known as a liberal. The military were withdrawn from the capital to Potsdam, and the citizens allowed to carry arms and to form a civic guard. Prince William left Berlin for a visit to England. The immediate contact between King and people was continued in a series of singular scenes. On the 21st of March the King rode slowly through the excited city, frequently halting and conducting meaningless conversations with the crowd. Instead of the colours of black and white, which symbolized the autocratic Prussian monarchy, he wore on his arm a broad band of black, red, gold, the symbol of the union of Germany in a republic, afterwards adopted by the Weimar Republic. He then paid his reverence in deep humility before the bodies and afterwards before the coffins of the victims of the revolution. A few days later, on the 25th of March, he left Berlin, and took up residence in the castle in Potsdam. Several months subsequent to these events, the King gave to his confidants an account of those days. It was intended to be spread among 'well-disposed men', and maintained that he 'would indeed keep unbroken his promises, the justifiable as well as the foolish ones, without the least equivocation, but he would consistently maintain the rights of the crown'.

Meanwhile Bismarck, who had not been in Berlin since his visit in connexion with the newspaper affair, remained in peace and comfort in his Schönhausen, devoting himself to his daily occupations. The earliest first-hand report of the events in Berlin he received through some ladies who had fled from the capital. The next news came to him from peasants of Schönhausen. They brought a warning which they had received from other quarters, bidding them to display the black, red, gold flag on the church-tower. The first step thereupon taken Bismarck describes as follows : ' I asked the peasants whether they wished to defend themselves. They answered with a unanimous and emphatic "Aye".' There must after all be something compelling in democratic institutions, if the extreme reactionary Bismarck, when he set out to destroy democracy and republic, had to use as his weapon of warfare the old democratic institution of a popular vote. On his own ground, where he ruled as autocrat, he did not proceed in the fashion which he admired in-Frederick William IV ; he did not demand 'trustful obedience, without discussing his ends with his subjects or even informing the latter of them'. There must, moreover, be something obviously right contained in this institution of a popular vote, if the mighty statesman without hesitation reaffirmed the rightness of this method, as he did forty years later in his *Reflections and Reminiscences*.

The remaining measures of Bismarck, on the other hand, corresponded entirely to the attitude of the Prussian baron in his castle. He ordered the black and white flag to be hoisted on the tower and took in hand the military mobilization of the village, mustering in all seventy usable hunting rifles, sent for ammunition and drove with his wife to the neighbouring villages in order also to mobilize these against revolution and democracy.

Not less characteristic was Bismarck's attitude when the event in Berlin of 18th March became better known to him. No word of sympathy or even mention was called forth by the fate of the 230 victims in the civil population, thus making all the more conspicuous his references to the few military casualties. Their death is described as 'murder' and his feeling about them as 'bitter anger' (*Verbitterung*). When, one and a half years later, he stood by the graves of the civilian victims he wrote to his wife: 'I could not even forgive the dead. My heart swells up with poison when I see what they have made of my fatherland, these murderers, at whose graves the Berliners still practise idolatry.' Also in his family circle he turned himself against 'weak compassion'; 'the rebels remain murderers and liars'. His view of the conduct of the King, his 'most gracious, all-highest Lord', is at once formulated as the preconceived opinion that the King was not 'free', but found himself 'in the power of the rebels'.

In accordance with this view, Bismarck sets himself as task 'the freeing of the King'. Nothing can make more clear to us Bismarck, the man of will, in his strength as well as in his limitations, than this resolve and the attempt to carry it out. In doing so, he had soon to learn what it means to belong to a class against whose leading position popular opinion had turned. In Potsdam, where he first went and which was after all in the hands of the royal troops, one of the members of his caste refused to be seen talking to him in the street. When he made the bold leap to the city of Berlin, which was still protected by the civic guard, the proud baron made up his mind to adopt a very humiliating disguise; he had his beard shaved off, he donned a soft felt hat which cast a shadow on his face, and fastened to the hat something that he shamefacedly called a 'piebald cockade', that is presumably a cockade with the republican colours 'black, red, gold'. The frock coat which he wore under his overcoat on account of the intended call on his 'all-highest Majesty' must sometimes have been visible. This strange attire seems to have rather attracted than avoided the attention of passersby. Now this mode of appearance was not to be regarded as a sign of cowardice or concern for his own safety; of this Bismarck had in fact little, and he had to assure his young wife when writing from Berlin: 'I will not tempt God to guard me in dangers which I have no calling to seek.' But what must strike us as extraordinary is that we are always noticing how little inclined Bismarck is to reject disguise, deceit, fraud, as a means of his policy.

On the whole, Bismarck's enterprise to 'free the King' failed. At Potsdam he offered the general in command the help of his mobilized peasants, if he would march back to Berlin. 'Do not send us any peasants, we have enough soldiers,' the general replied.—'So you are going to fetch the King out of Berlin,' Bismarck rejoined.—'There would be no difficulty about that,' was the opinion of the general, 'but without orders I can take no steps.' Then Bismarck tried to find Prince William of Prussia, who would have been the person best qualified to help and also one likely to need some help himself. He had an audience with the Prince's wife, Princess Augusta, and made further efforts on his behalf. But Bismarck was too late, since the Prince had already left Berlin for England. To reach the King in person through the civic guard which watched him proved impossible, and a letter sent to him by messenger remained unanswered. Bismarck appears to have attended the humiliating scene in which the King paid reverence to the coffins of the revolutionary victims as spectator among the crowds. Soon afterwards he seems to have left Berlin without having achieved his object and returned to Schönhausen. But a few days later we find him again in Potsdam. On the occasion of this visit he witnessed the arrival of the King from Berlin, and in the Potsdam palace into which Bismarck had made his way he heard the words of the King to his officers : ' I have never been more free and more safe than when guarded by my citizens.' The ' murmur of the men and the thud of scabbards, a sound such as a King of Prussia has never heard and, it is hoped, never will hear again amid his own officers' produced in Bismarck a ' feeling as if of bodily pain ', and the words of the King could not shake his preconceived opinion about the latter's lack of freedom when in the power of the rebels.

It is understandable that influential men in Prussia could not all share Bismarck's view of the King's lack of freedom. A number of earnest, thoroughly patriotic Prussians, though members of the political Left, were soon agreed in the conviction that the King had shown himself in March to be incapable and unworthy of his position of ruler and that it was therefore justifiable to agitate for his abdication, to pass over Prince William of Prussia and to appoint his liberal wife regent for their young son. It was intended to let this move take the form of a resolution of the parliament which was to assemble on the 22nd of April. This was in fact an idea of the most far-reaching significance, which could have given the greatest stimulus to parliamentary life in Germany and could have been of the greatest value for the parliamentary education of the German people. It was advocated above all by the leader of the Left, Georg von Vincke. However, its supporters were concerned also to win members of the Right for the idea. Vincke himself undertook to bring over Bismarck to their side by means of a personal interview. As a result of this Bismarck imparted to Vincke his answer : ' I should reply to a request of this kind by a request for legal proceedings on the charge of high treason.' Bismarck tried to repress the idea that the King's ride through Berlin on the 21st of March had been a piece of ' undignified pageantry ' and that the King's ' effeminacy, under the pressure of unqualified, perhaps treasonable, advisers, urged by the tears of women ' was to blame for the political situation which had gone wrong. If for a moment he assumed the attitude of a *frondeur*, a few friendly words of the King were sufficient to ' overcome him ' and ' completely to disarm and win ' him.

In Parliament Bismarck's view found a somewhat strange expression on the occasion of a vote on the address of thanks to the King for the introduction of two bills in preparation of the promised constitution : a liberal electoral bill for the Prussian parliament to draw up the constitution and a bill laying down various liberal principles for the promised new constitution itself. Bismarck, together with Adolf von Thadden, were the only members who, in opposition to all the rest, gave their votes against the address. For Bismarck, who was already in bad enough repute with the revolutionaries, this was undoubtedly a deed which required some courage in the still very disorderly Berlin, although a civic guard of ten thousand men had been marched up to protect the assembly. As a justification of his vote, Bismarck declared before parliament : ' I cannot give thanks and rejoice for what I must regard as at least a course of error.' The given political situation he could only ' accept under the force of circumstances '. Further he· says in his *Reflections and Reminiscences* : ' I wanted to say more, but was rendered incapable of speech by my inner excitement and fell into a fit of weeping which compelled me to leave the platform.' To his wife, however, he wrote that the only significance of the speech was ' that I was determined not to be reckoned in the class of a few bribable bureaucrats, who with contemptible shamelessness turn their coat according to the wind '.

This second United Parliament lasted only nine days. Bismarck spoke on three more occasions during this period, to inquire about the attitude of the government in the Danish and Polish questions, respectively, and thirdly to oppose the grant of a credit to the liberal minister of commerce, the Rhinelander Hansemann, whose claims to ' justice and prudence ' he denied. He used the opportunity to complain about the undue favour shown the big towns and industry by this credit at the expense of the petty bourgeoisie and of agriculture. On the 10th of April, with the conclusion of the session, Bismarck's second period in parliament came to a sudden end, even more quickly than his first. At the time there was no more scope for a merely advisory assembly based on the principles of the absolutist class system which was regarded as overthrown.

Bismarck made no very energetic effort to secure a seat either in the Prussian ' constituent parliament ' of the 22nd of May or in the German ' National Assembly ' at Frankfurt on Main, whose opening had been fixed for the 18th of May by the ' Pre-Parliament '. He watched from Schönhausen the beginning of the real German parliamentary life in Berlin and Frankfurt. This parliamentarism was the opponent whom he was determined to fight and conquer. He spoke of the ' Frankfurt game of carnival night ' or ' fools' game ' ; in view of his position in party politics he thought he could reckon on this ' game of shadows ' having only a short duration ; he believed that it therefore did not pay him to take part in it even as a member of the Opposition and thereby indirectly to recognize it. After his vote against the address of thanks at the beginning of April it was not indeed in his power even to try to turn his coat according to the wind ' with contemptible shamelessness '. He could hardly have obtained enough votes to elect him and in any case he would have had an impossible position in either of these two parliaments.

The period in the summer of 1848, when he was away from parliament, was spent by Bismarck—at the expense of forgoing many of the amenities of the family life on which he had just started —in fighting against the new parliamentarism from outside. He did this through the direct canvassing of the neighbouring members of his caste and the ordinary people of the district, but especially through the founding of societies intended to defend their common political and professional interests, the Preussenvereine. Bismarck also took part in the so-called ' Junker-Parliament ' of August 1848, a conference of the conservative electors, and spoke here against the land tax. To enable him to influence wider circles, two means were available which he utilized fully. One was the Press. Bismarck was in those days a zealous and successful journalist. Some of his numerous articles were concerned with the disadvantageous position of the country people as compared with the town people in regard to taxation and the alleged ' artificially fostered anger against the landed aristocracy '. Above all the newspaper which had been planned for the conclusion of the previous year now actually appeared. It had, however, the strongly Christian emphasis which Leopold and Ludwig von Gerlach had formerly demanded. These two were founders, and J. Stahl, the theorist of the Christian idea of the state, one of the earliest promoters of the *Neue Preussische Zeitung*, ordinarily called *Kreuzzeitung*, which appeared for the first time on the 16th of June. Its editing was undertaken by the very clever Christian-Socialist agitator Hermann Wagener, and Bismarck was for years one of its outstanding contributors. Both men were opposed to politics ' lapsing into bureaucratic absolutism or being swallowed up by vulgar constitutionalism '.

The other, not less important, means for fighting the new parliamentarism was presented for Bismarck by his personal relations to the King. The latter had not forgotten the invitation which he had extended to Bismarck when they met at Venice the previous September, and Bismarck had had the opportunity to make himself pleasurably remembered in the meantime. The unanswered letter to the King in March expressing his devotion had reached the monarch in due course and is said to have been kept by the latter on his desk for the whole summer as a ' precious token of unchanging Prussian loyalty '. The King continued to stay at his Potsdam palace during this summer and watched from there the proceedings in Berlin within and around the Prussian Constituent Parliament. During this time he discussed with his ministers, quarrelled with them, gave way to them, tried to win them to his side, asked them to give an account of their actions, complained of them, pretended to go some way with them, and still maintained complete obscurity as regards his real aims.   On the 14th of June 1848 a crowd stormed the Berlin arsenal, which was mainly used for the preservation of relics of former wars and was for the true Prussian a kind of national sanctuary.   The civic guard posted to defend it offered no resistance. A few weapons were stolen, a few relics defiled.   A week later the King dismissed the president of the Cabinet, Camphausen, and replaced him by Hansemann, formerly minister of commerce, also a liberal Rhinelander, but one possessed of greater energy.   He, to-gether with Auerswald, had now the task of forming a Cabinet.

It was now that Bismarck paid his first visit to the Potsdam palace.   He tells how the King expressed doubts about his legal rights in face of the proceedings of parliament which were felt by him as an usurpation.   In view of the government's equivocal position between a constitution still in force and a parliament en-trusted with the formation of a new one, Bismarck gave the King the very characteristic assurance that it was only necessary for the sovereign to have strong faith in his rights ; that he was master in the land and possessed the power to re-establish the order which was being threatened.   The storming of the arsenal Bismarck pointed out as an adequate occasion for ordering the military to march back to Berlin.   The King was not any too easy to persuade. But Bismarck did not fail to back the plea with his eloquence.   He tried to convey to the King the idea which became ever clearer in his own mind that the alternative for the dynasty was either to prove its ' vitality ' or to have to ' face the barricades ', and that the ' pivot ' on which his policy had so far turned was not even a real threat of street fighting, but only the ' fear ' of one.   He now expressly declared himself in favour of ' placing in the foreground the strong military forces available rather than theoretically dis-cussing paragraphs in the constitution '.   Here we find Bismarck using for the first time the expressions *Realpolitik* and ' political relations of power ', based on the ' serried ranks of our troops ', in opposition to the ' gospels of speakers ' on the parliamentary platform and ' the faith which they arouse in the masses '.   Yet in these alternatives, does there not lurk a quite distinct criticism of Bis-marck's against the conduct of ' his all-highest Majesty ' ?   How was

it that in spite of this criticism Bismarck clung fast to the legend
that the King was not free in face of the forces behind the barricade ?
It is strange to find him writing to his wife a few months later in an
admonishing tone : ' Do not speak disparagingly of the King. We
are both at fault in this matter and ought to speak of him as we do
of our parents, even if he errs and fails, for we have sworn faith and
homage to his flesh and blood.'

In bringing his influence to bear on the King Bismarck soon
found capable allies. Prince William of Prussia had returned from
England at the beginning of June. One of the first to greet him on
Prussian soil was Bismarck. With satisfaction he noted the words
of the Prince : ' I know that you have worked for me and shall not
forget it.' Equally important allies against the new parliamentarism
Bismarck found in the members of the ' court camarilla ' surrounding
the King, at that time the most influential body in bringing about
government decisions. At its head stood the Adjutant General,
Leopold von Gerlach, whom Bismarck had long known well, and
whom he described as ' a distinguished and selfless character and a
true servant of the King ', but as ' slow in thought and decision '.
Bismarck's most useful ally, however, proved to be the Constituent
Parliament itself, the ' parliament of labourers ' as it was contemptuously called in these circles. Its activities made it easy for the
court clique to represent to the King that its draft of a constitution
of the 26th of July was far too liberal for Prussia, and that the
requirement that the Cabinet had to obey the request of the Chamber
was a violation of rights. But the Chamber went further still. It
suppressed the title of ' King by the Grace of God ', it voted for the
abolition of nobility, of orders and of titles. When Vienna was
occupied by the Austrian Imperial troops and the radical politician
Robert Blum was courtmartialled, the Chamber demanded the
intervention of the Prussian government to defend the freedom of the
Viennese people. Nothing could be more contrary to the conservative patriarchal inclinations of the King than such a proceeding.

At first the object of the court clique was to put in power a
Cabinet which should be ready to carry out the wishes of the King
and his advisers without taking too much heed of the constitution.
At the beginning of November there was indeed formed a Cabinet
under Count Brandenburg which was prepared for anything. Its
president said to Bismarck : ' I have undertaken the task, but am
unacquainted with questions of state and can do nothing more than
put my head into the noose.' Otto von Manteuffel, a reactionary
bureaucrat, belonging to the antiliberal wing of that bureaucracy
so hated by Bismarck, became minister of the interior. Bismarck
was entrusted with the task of winning him over. He did this by
means of a conversation lasting ' from nine to midnight '. It was

also said in Berlin that a wing adjutant of the King had made the
streets unsafe with a revolver in his hand threatening everyone with
death who refused to accept a post in the Cabinet. Hardly had the
Cabinet taken office when the troops were ordered to return to Berlin.
They entered the city on the 10th of November, without encountering
the least resistance. The civic guard broke up and a state of siege
was proclaimed in the capital. The Constituent Parliament was
removed on the 27th November to a small place outside Berlin and a
week later was altogether dissolved. On the 5th of December the
King forced on the people a constitution which, while retaining the
secret, universal, and equal suffrage, at the same time restored the
two-chamber system so congenial to the King with his beloved Upper
House (Herrenkurie).

Bismarck was not, as he might well have hoped, one of the
new ministers. The King is said to have written on the margin of a
note proposing him : ' Red reactionary, still smells of blood, to be
used later.' In fact, Bismarck was not altogether satisfied with the
concrete results of the change in politics. Though he was now
convinced that the ' spectre had wholly disappeared ', yet he would
have wished that ' when a constitution was enforced, its basic formula
should have been amended more definitely in the monarchical
sense '. He was, however, still more dissatisfied with the bloodless
manner in which the change had taken place. He blamed the
government because the Constituent Parliament had not been dissolved at once, but at first only removed to another place. Yet most
of all he blamed the military leaders, because they had allowed the
civic guard to dissolve voluntarily. For ' if there had been the least
fighting Berlin would have been taken not as the result of a capitulation, but by force, and the political position of the government
would have been quite different '. This thought went very deep
with Bismarck. In his letters to his wife he always returns to it.
On the day of the military occupation he is in doubt ' whether there
will be blows '. A few days later he says : ' Berlin is in a state of
siege, but still no shots fired.' A little later we find : ' That it
should pass off without firing, I can hardly believe.' Finally :
' The troops are burning in their hearts for scenes of violence, the
passive resistance of the democrats seems to me only a convenient
expression for what one could have otherwise called fear.' Yet the
events did pass off without the hoped for violence.

Bismarck decided to stand for the parliament based on the
enforced constitution. Once more he fell into a condition of great
agitation as he said : ' Through all this digging up of quarrels I have
been brought into a state of feverish excitement.' He was elected
under the slogans : ' Fight the Revolution ' and ' Re-establish the
old Bond of Trust between Crown and People '. In his election

platform dictated by ' the acceptance of the force of circumstances ' are to be found such ambiguities as ' Recognition of the Constitution —Defence against Anarchy ', ' Equality before the Law—no Abolition of the Nobility ', but also unambiguous demands, such as ' No Diminution of the Standing Army ' and ' Strict Press and Club Laws '.

CHAPTER X

The Way to Olmütz

We mentioned two interpellations of Bismarck during his second period as member of parliament in April 1848. One related to the Polish, one to the Danish question. With these two interpellations he entered the domain to which he had felt himself called in his youth, with his bent for diplomatic activity, and the domain in which he was soon to achieve the great triumphs of his life : foreign affairs.

We shall first deal with the interpellation on the Polish question with its bearing on the relations with Russia. The Poles living under Prussian rule had not forgotten, even in the nineteenth century, the time of political independence. Their memory was kept alive by the fact that their blood-brothers in the neighbouring Russia from 1815 to 1832 enjoyed considerable political freedom and a constitution of the type approved in the West. This constitution was, however, abolished and replaced by direct government by Russia after the sanguinary suppression of a revolt by the violent and reactionary Tsar Nicolas I. In the Prussian part of Poland, in 1846, the preparations for a political rising were detected and suppressed, and the leaders were sentenced and imprisoned, some of them in Berlin. In the days of March 1848, these were liberated by the rebellious mob and their pardon was secured from the King. They took an energetic part in the disturbances in the Prussian capital and caused the revolutionary movement to spread to Prussian Poland itself. A deputation from this province appeared in Berlin and, shortly after the worst disturbances, they were promised by the government ' a national reorganization of the grand-duchy of Posen '.

Bismarck opposed this promise in parliament. He noted it as remarkable ' how the inhabitants of Berlin in the good-natured simplicity of their enthusiasm for everything foreign could ever imagine that the Poles could be anything else but our enemies '. In his interpellation he called this concession by the government nothing less than the beginning of the ' re-establishment of a Polish kingdom with the boundaries of 1772 '. One of his subordinates later said, ' although the partitions of Poland had taken place a hundred years ago, Bismarck was the first to appreciate their full significance '. However, Bismarck's speech in support of his interpellation was soon interrupted by the assembly and the responsible minister. He then published the content of his intended speech in a newspaper article, which is of interest as the first public announcement of what he wished done in foreign affairs. He ironically referred to ' the liberation of the Poles condemned for high treason ' as ' one of the triumphs of the March struggle in Berlin and indeed one of the most important '. With gross exaggeration he declared, concerning the events in Prussian Poland, that ' the men liberated have brought on the German inhabitants of a Prussian province plunder and murder with the massacre and barbarous mutilation of women and children '. He, Bismarck, would have found it ' intelligible if the first élan of German strength and unity had vented itself in demanding that France should surrender Alsace and in hoisting the German flag on the tower of Strasbourg cathedral '. His article is not quite in accord with historical fact, when he refers to the land won through the partitions of Poland as something ' that German weapons had won in the course of centuries '. ' But how ', was Bismarck's final appeal, ' can a German for the sake of lachrymose sympathy and unpractical theories be carried away by the desire to create for his fatherland on her very borders an unremitting foe, who is bound to be greedy for conquest at our cost.'

Still more important at the moment was the Danish question. The two duchies of Schleswig and Holstein were united with the kingdom of Denmark under a joint monarch, the three being bound together by an indivisible legal union. Holstein belonged to the German Confederation ; Schleswig was of importance for the latter as inseparable from Holstein. So the two duchies, in view of their relations one with another, with the kingdom of Denmark and the German Confederation, in which Holstein was represented by the King of Denmark, gave rise to a legal problem full of almost insoluble difficulties. The national liberal popular movement of the first half of the nineteenth century had concerned itself with this problem, but had laid stress on the political rather than on the legal point of view. It was one of its essential nationalist demands that the two duchies should remain ' for ever undivided ', should be separated from the ruling Danish King and should be put under the House of Augustenburg, on the ground that the latter were descended from a younger branch of the Danish royal family. This would mean that both of them became members of the German Confederation in their own right and that the Danish King would have nothing more to do with this Confederation. Naturally, the dynastic interests of the German petty Princes were on the side of the claims of the Danish royal family.

On the 8th of July 1846 an ' Open Letter ' of the then ruling King of Denmark, Christian VIII, sought to cut this tangled knot of political and legal difficulties with a single stroke by demanding that the two duchies should be legally separated, Schleswig being completely incorporated in Denmark and the conditions of the personal union with Holstein being more precisely fixed. The Estates in Schleswig and Holstein protested at this, and the liberal and national movement of the German middle class took up their cause. Now even the legitimist tendency of the German petty Princes could not come to the help of the Danish King, since the latter himself was now engaged in violating legitimate rights. So the organ representing the interests of the Princes, the German Federal Diet in Frankfurt on Main, now mustered up courage for a hesitating countermove and, on the 17th of September 1846, issued a warning to the King of Denmark, calling on him to observe existing rights and laws. Availing himself of the revolutionary disturbances in Europe at the beginning of 1848, the son and successor of Christian VIII, Frederick VII, gave legal form to the idea of the ' Open letter ' on the 22nd of March 1848. The two duchies were declared to be legally separated, and Schleswig was declared completely incorporated in the Kingdom. Two days later both duchies seceded from Denmark and formed a provisional government of their own which, as one of its first measures, asked the German Confederation to admit also Schleswig. The liberal and national movement of Germany, whose self-confidence had been greatly intensified by the events in Vienna, Berlin and other towns, intervened passionately in the public debate on the question of the two duchies both in parliament and in the Press. They regarded it as bound up with the constitutional reform and the national unification of Germany which they sought.

Frederick William IV of Prussia, who at that time was still sitting in his palace in Berlin, separated from his army and protected by the Berlin civic guard, was the geographically nearest ruler to take up the cause of the duchies. He had, moreover, just promised, openly and formally, that he would take steps in the matters of the German constitution and of German unity. The King, who had mostly opposed the liberal and constitutional aspirations of the German movement and had only now under the severest pressure and very much against his will made them a few concessions, was not by any means equally averse to the idea of a united German nation. His romantic dreams made him see this question in a medieval setting constructed in brilliant but deceitful colours. What Bismarck called ' the phrases speaking of the German mission of Prussia and of moral conquests ' in Germany were capable even of competing with the King's strong sentiments for Prussia and showed themselves at times stronger than the latter.

The King's adviser in these matters was the former officer and later diplomat, Joseph Maria von Radowitz. He came from a

Hungarian family and was a Roman Catholic in faith. Radowitz's catholicism was in conformity with the High Church tendency of the King, his foreign descent tempted the King's fancy. He had a breath of the spirit of that *Kulturstaat* which had animated the fighters in 1813-15. This liberal inclination appeared to the King as a justification of his own political change of front in March 1848. In their romantic preference for the Middle Ages they seemed to agree. But it was just these qualities which made the Prussian Junkers hate and despise Radowitz in the extreme. How did this Roman Catholic interloper manage to force himself between them and their King and influence the latter in opposition to their tradition and their interests ? Bismarck called Radowitz ' the clever costumier for the medieval phantasies of the King '. He expressed the suspicion that Radowitz used his influence ' in the interests of Roman Catholicism in order to prevent Protestant Prussia from seeing its good opportunities ', and even described him as ' a catholicizing opponent of Prussia '. Consequently Bismarck, as he reports to his wife at the end of August 1849, repeatedly attacked Radowitz in the *Kreuzzeitung* with such vehemence that finally Gerlach himself had to write an article for the sake of reconciliation.

In 1847 Radowitz drafted for the King a memoir concerning the reorganization of the German Confederation. This went so far as to demand that, if Austria refused to co-operate in the reforms, Prussia should carry them out alone. A little before he had published a pamphlet about the Schleswig-Holstein question, called ' Who is to be heir in Schleswig ? ' At the beginning of 1848 the King had sent him to Vienna in order to take practical steps towards the reform of the Confederation in conjunction with Metternich. But the revolution and the resignation of Metternich prevented him from taking the intended measures.

Now the state of the Danish question provided Radowitz with an immediate opportunity to work for his ideals. It was not difficult to persuade the hard-pressed and deserted King to intervene on behalf of the inhabitants of Schleswig and Holstein and the Duke of Augustenburg, towards whom he was favourably disposed. For this was in complete accord with the King's desire to win again the affection of his ' beloved Berliners ' by an action which served the cause of unification, without making any considerable concessions to those who supported a liberal constitution such as would impair the power given him by the Grace of God. In a declaration of the 24th of March 1848, Frederick William IV recognized the right of the duchies and promised to protect it. Prussian troops were sent to the border in order to fulfil this promise of protection, and the German North Sea States were called upon to help.

On the day before Bismarck's interpellation the first Prussian troops crossed the border of the duchies. Bismarck did not leave it in doubt that he was opposed to this venture. He evidently saw in it a move towards an alliance between ' Dynasty and barricade ' and somewhat of a surrender to the latter. Or, as he later said, he fought to 'prevent ' the Schleswig-Holsteiners from securing their supposed or real rights against the sovereign by revolutionary violence '. In his speech, however, he referred to the increasing harm done to trade in the Baltic by political complications and spoke quite generally about the disturbing ' Phaeton-like flight ' of Prussian foreign policy. The government in their reply described the dispatch of troops as carrying out the resolution of the Bundestag passed on the 17th of September 1846, which gave Denmark no ground for war and would not affect trade in the Baltic. Denmark, however, at once declared war, and in the course of the military operations, which extended over the whole summer, the Baltic trade was after all adversely affected, thus leading to diplomatic intervention by England and Russia. But in this further development Bismarck was reduced to using the *Kreuzzeitung* as a means of pressing his views. From May 1849 on there appeared a great number of articles by his pen, especially on conditions in France and England.

The concern of the Prussian King and his government with the nationalistic interests of the Germans was not limited to the Schleswig-Holstein question. After the reverse which the Austrian monarchy had suffered through the resignation of Metternich, Prussia seemed called to take the lead in the German question, just as Radowitz had wished and sought. Frederick William IV had addressed his proclamation of the 19th of March not only ' to my People ' but also ' to the German nation '. On the occasion of his ride through Berlin on the 21st of March, he had told the crowd that he ' felt himself called to save German freedom and unity '. These had to be ' guarded by German faith on the basis of a genuine parliamentary German constitution '. On the same day the King received an impressive deputation of statesmen and politicians from southern and central Germany, who in agreement with the governments of Saxony, Württemberg, and Baden, offered him the Prussian leadership of Germany. But a few days later the King's feverish enthusiasm for the mission of Prussia as the leader of Germany had fallen back to a normal temperature. After he had left Berlin and retired behind the protection of his troops at Potsdam, a declaration was made in the name of Prussia to the Federal Diet in Frankfurt regarding the German National Assembly. It said, that the King was ready to send representatives to the impending assembly, but that, in opposition to the suffrage law worked out by the ' Pre-Parliament ', he had decided to let the deputies representing Prussia be appointed by the extremely reactionary Provincial Councils.

However, he cancelled this decision four days later and ordered elections according to the universal, equal, and secret ballot stipulated by the ' Pre-Parliament '. He was now glad to see that his confidant Radowitz was among those elected.

The original tendency prevailing in Germany to bring about the constitution of the new German Reich by an agreement between the Frankfurt National Assembly and the governments of the separate states was overcome by the former's decision to give Germany a constitution by its own power. However, this development towards the ' sovereignty of the people ' was counterbalanced by the fact that at the end of June 1848 a regent of the future Reich was elected who came from the innermost circle of the traditional dynasties, the Archduke Johann of Austria. This was a clear renunciation of the barricades, but also an equally clear condemnation of the vacillating policy of Frederick William IV. The latter had shortly before referred to the Austrian emperor as ' the honoured head of the German nation '. Now he retorted by refusing to allow the Prussian troops to wear the German colours and to partake in a parade in honour of the regent. The King's attitude of opposition was still further increased, when Prussia, who on behalf of the duchies of Schleswig and Holstein had after all crossed swords with Denmark and driven the Danish armies back, now under the pressure of England and Russia concluded an armistice with the defeated state at Malmö in August. This was generally interpreted as the prelude to the surrender of Schleswig and Holstein to the Danes. In the excitement which arose among the liberals at Frankfurt in consequence of this event, two Prussian deputies of the parliamentary Right, personally closely associated with the Prussian King, were barbarously murdered. The tension between the King and the Frankfurt National Assembly increased still further when the former reverted to the reactionary Cabinet headed by Brandenburg-Manteuffel and enforced a constitution on Prussia. On the 12th of December 1848 the King wrote to a confidant telling him of his reluctance to put himself at the head of the constitutional system produced in Frankfurt :

> The crown which the Saxon Ottos, the Hohenstaufens, the Hapsburgs have worn, a Hohenzollern can of course also wear. But the crown which you have in mind dishonours its wearer in the extreme with its stink of the revolution of 1848. Should a legitimate King, and a King of Prussia at that, allow himself to receive such an imaginary hoop, baked of filth and clay ?

These words showed that Bismarck's misgivings at ' the phrase about the German mission of Prussia ' had prevailed over the efforts of the ' catholicizing opponent of Prussia ', Radowitz.

In the speech from the throne at the opening of the new Prussian Parliament on the 26th of February 1849, the King declared, concerning the German Reich which was to be built up in the Frankfurt National Assembly, that he would not proceed further in this question without the agreement of all the German sovereigns, words which led Bismarck to exclaim in joy : ' Everything will then remain as it was, for Austria and the others will not have anything to do with this Frankfurting.'   So when the Frankfurt Assembly on the 28th of March 1849 elected the Prussian King to be German Emperor they were ill-advised.   Their preference can only be explained by the fact that since November 1848 the tide of reaction in Austria under Prince Felix von Schwarzenberg had raged with even greater fury than in Prussia.   The views of the advisers to the King were in conflict with each other.   That Radowitz was in favour of acceptance is obvious. Yet even so one-sided a Prussian as Prince William supported acceptance with reservations.   Most remarkable of all, Bismarck joined in signing a petition in favour of acceptance.   But the opposite view gained the upper hand.   To the commission of the Frankfurt Assembly, which came to Berlin a few days later in order to offer him his new dignity, the King declared that he must decline this offer with thanks, so long as ' the free agreement of the crowned heads of the Princes of Germany ' was not obtained. ·

In explanation of this, Bismarck, forty years later, after he had himself introduced universal suffrage, ascribed the King's action to the ' revolutionary, or at least parliamentary, origin of the offer '— a curious combination of adjectives. As ground for his ' satisfaction at the time with the refusal ', Bismarck himself named his opposition to a parliamentary system his ' instinctive mistrust of the development of affairs since the barricades of 1848 and the parliamentary consequences of this development ', and his Prussianism, his ' sensitive regard for the prestige of the Prussian crown and its wearer '.   He thus referred with remarkable frankness to the two motives which jointly determined his decisions.   To his opponents of that time, ' the leading men in Parliament and the Press ', he attributed the ' programme : everything must be ruined '.   He expressed the conviction that under Frederick William IV ' a continuation and strengthening of the institutions of the kingdom, such as later took place under the Emperor William (i.e., through Bismarck himself), was hardly to have been expected '.   Prussia at that time was ' not ripe to take over the leadership of Germany in war and peace '.   But what he dreamed of as a solution of the German question is perhaps even more interesting.   It was ' a close alliance of Prussia and Austria ', as ' the first condition of the unity and freedom of Germany ', a view which he had imbued in the house of his parents from childhood.

The refusal of the German imperial crown by the Prussian King brought about a renewed outburst of revolutionary activity, especially in Saxony and south Germany. Prussian troops were sent into the field against it, and they rendered speedy and thorough service, especially in the south, under the leadership of Prince William of Prussia, thus bringing him the title of 'grapeshot-prince'. At the same time revolutionary disturbances broke out in Hungary, which induced the Austrian Emperor to avail himself of the military help of Tsar Nicolas I against his own subjects. The Frankfurt Assembly now lost the justification for its existence and drew its last breath in the middle of June.

The dispute about the Frankfurt constitution also brought to an abrupt end the Prussian Parliament and with it Bismarck's third parliamentary period. Bismarck maintained also in this parliament, in which the Left was easily predominant, his extreme and defiant attitude against his political opponents. When on the mention of the anniversary of the revolution a member of the Left spoke of the 'will of the people', he retorted : 'No expression has been more misused in recent years than the word " people ". Everyone has understood thereby just what suited his own purpose. Generally they mean a random mob of individuals whom they have succeeded in winning for their views.' 'The true Prussian people', he added with a hardly concealed threat, 'has in recent times shown a great deal of patience with those who call themselves " friends of the people ".' In the debate on a proposed amnesty for political offences he defended against parliament the view that pardon was 'a right of the crown' and that the very essence of this right ' consists in its free and voluntary exercise '. He formulated his fundamental view, which had now very little to do with the seemingly conciliatory attitude of the election platform of six weeks before : 'The struggle of principles which has this year shaken Europe to its foundation is one that permits of no mediation. The one side bases its right nominally on the will of the people, really on the club-law of the barricades. The other is based on the sovereign by God's grace set in power by God.' And again, uttering a threat : 'The decision concerning these principles is not to be reached by parliamentary debates : sooner or later God, who directs the battles, must throw the iron dice of decision.' To the objection that the constitutional principle united the power of the people with the power of the crown, Bismarck retorted : 'I have pointed to an antithesis, the antithesis between legal right and revolution.' 'How can one place on a par a rightful sovereign and a treasonable faction ? ' he asked at the same time in his family circle, as a man whose youthful political ideals were embodied in the conceptions of order and authority.

Now there came the day of decision for the parliament, the 21st of April, when the Left proposed that Prussia should accept the Frankfurt constitution *in toto*, i.e., including the election of the Prussian King as Emperor of Germany, a dignity just declined by the King. Bismarck forgot the signature which a few weeks before he had appended to the petition in favour of the acceptance of the imperial crown, and opposed the motion with all the bitterness and scorn of which he was capable :

The Prussian constitution of the 5th of December [i.e., that enforced by the King himself] leaves the government hardly the barely necessary minimum of those rights without which no government can be carried on at all. Meanwhile the Frankfurt constitution has drawn still deeper from the well of wisdom of those theorizers who have learnt nothing and forgotten much since the time of the 'Contrat Social'—those theorizers whose castles in the air have cost us in the six months of last summer more blood, gold, and tears than a thirty-three-year-long absolutism. The crown of Frankfurt may glitter very brightly, but the gold, which lends truth to its glitter, has first to be won by melting down the Prussian crown, and I have no confidence that the recasting will succeed with this constitution.

Bismarck's opposition was naturally without any result, except that his opponents bestowed the epithet upon him of 'Most Humble of All Humble Subjects'. As a matter of fact, the Frankfurt constitution was accepted as a whole by the Prussian parliament. In addition, the Chamber resolved that the state of siege, proclaimed by the King in Berlin on the 10th of November, should be raised. Thereupon the King dissolved parliament on the 27th of April 1849. Thus ended after two months Bismarck's third parliamentary period. He had accompanied it by particularly energetic work with the *Kreuzzeitung*. The editor, Hermann Wagener, reports in his *Memoirs* on the journalistic activity of this foe of the 'leading men in the Press' :

During the parliamentary session there was hardly one issue of the *Kreuzzeitung* which did not contain a longer or shorter article of Herr von Bismarck. In addition to this a not inconsiderable proportion of the political jokes, and by no means the worst of them, stand to his credit.

But the cessation of parliament left Bismarck only a short time to enjoy ' playing *pater familias* ' in Schönhausen. For the King was not content with getting rid of the former Parliament, he also got rid of the franchise, by which it had been elected, and ordered new elections. A royal decree of the 30th of May 1849 replaced the universal, secret, equal franchise of the constitution of the 5th of December 1848 by a franchise based on the three-class system with public voting. Bismarck decided to stand for the elections fixed

for the 27th of July 1849. But in his former constituency he was
told : 'We are conservative, very much so, but not Bismarckian.'
From a peasant he had to hear that when his name was mentioned,
'it was as if they received some old-Prussian strokes of the lash'.
And yet 'I am the kindest man in the world towards common
people,' he added in telling this to his wife. All the same he was
eventually re-elected, but he complained to his wife very much of
'the pitiful canvassing, where one never has to fight against political
convictions but against the most miserable personal vanities and
intrigues', he who, a little while before, had spoken so ironically
about 'holding fast to principles'. What he did not mention to his
wife was that during the excitement of the election people had gone
so far as physically to attack him.

But Bismarck had to endure another disappointment at this time.
He had to see that after all the 'German mission of Prussia' meant
more for the King than a mere 'phrase'. The rejection of the
'Frankfurt crown' did not signify for the King a rejection of the
idea of the German Reich as such. It only meant that he furthered
this idea in a direction more suited to himself. Radowitz proposed
to him that the Reich should be created by the voluntary association
of the Princes under the presidency of Prussia with a Reich parliament, but that this should be included in a wider confederation
comprising also Austria. The King thereupon invited the German
rulers to come to Berlin to discuss this proposal. But the Prussian
scheme had already an opponent who had the resolution and the
capacity to hinder it wherever it gained a footing. This was the
Austrian chancellor, Prince Felix von Schwarzenberg, a man just
as determined in his Austrian sentiments as he was clever and
unscrupulous in his choice of means for carrying them out. So
Prussia's invitation was accepted only by Hanover and Saxony.
Thanks to the efforts of Radowitz, under pressure and with reservations, there was concluded on the 26th of May the so-called
'Three Kings' Union' between these two states and Prussia. It
was for the period of a year and intended 'for the purpose of preserving the external and internal security of Germany and the
immunity of the members of this union from injury'. In order to
bring about agreement between the rulers on a common constitution
of the future Reich, Prussia was to summon a Reich parliament.
Thus the German Confederation of 1815 was replaced by the
Three Kings' Union and thereby *de facto* abolished for those who
signed the new agreement. In the course of the next months a
certain number of the smaller states joined the Union. Quite a
considerable assembly of former representatives of the Frankfurt
parliament also expressed their approval of it at Gotha, forming the
so-called 'Gotha-Group', which based its policy on the principles

of the Union. The larger states, on the other hand, mostly sided with Austria.

The Prussian three-class parliament assembled on the 7th of August. Two weeks later Radowitz reported to the Chamber on the Three Kings' Union in a speech which was described by a competent authority as 'his greatest oratorical performance, by which the hope for the success of the work seemed to be everywhere revived'. Bismarck reported on it in the *Kreuzzeitung* with vicious irony :

He [i.e., Radowitz] uttered every word clearly and precisely without stammering or correcting himself, and he never said too much or too little to give the impression he desired. His oratorical victory was complete. The professional orators looked at the platform with unconcealed jealousy, the gentlemen from Frankfurt gazed round triumphantly as if they wanted to say 'See, we all talk like that there.' Emotion was general, without our being able to indicate in the printed speech exactly the place where each one wept. Among the delicately built souls few kept their eyes dry. A high official of the Finance Ministry had a budget of tears running down his reddened cheek. One of the most central pillars of the Prussian government made unusual facial contortions in his efforts to suppress his emotion. At the conclusion of the speech the applause reached the height of a pyramid.

In the sitting of the 6th of September Bismarck declared himself expressly against the Three Kings' Union. Yet he did not wish on this account to oppose the Prussian Cabinet, inasmuch as 'he recognized and honoured in it the supporters against democracy of a civilized society and a civilized state'. He maintained that 'the much abused German Confederation' might be recognized as 'the last means of holding together German unity'; nor did this seem to him at all undesirable, for the Prussian position of power had been strengthened through this Confederation. And now he bursts out :

What has survived the revolution was the maligned arch-Prussiandom, the devotion of the Prussian population to the hereditary dynasty, the old Prussian virtues of honour, loyalty, obedience, and courage which animate the army. This army is not inspired by the German flag. It is content to be called Prussian and is proud of the name. The Prussian people do not want to see their Prussian kingdom dissolved in the rotten fermentation of South German indiscipline. Their loyalty is not based on a paper presidency of the Reich. We all wish the Prussian eagle to spread his wings from the Memel to the Donnersberg as guardian and ruler. I hope to God that we shall long remain Prussians after this scrap of paper [i.e., the Three Kings' Union] has been forgotten like a faded autumn leaf.

It was what he called its 'connexion with revolution and liberal constitutionalism' that made the Three Kings' Union detestable to Bismarck. The Union gave away 'the conquests of the Prussian sword with generous hand ' to ' a phantom which, under the invented name of " spirit of the times " or " public opinion " deafens the reason of the Princes with clamour '. ' Public opinion ' becomes for Bismarck from now on in ever-increasing measure ' a clamour of unreason ', and therewith a danger to the ' power of the dynasty to live '. Still it was public opinion which drove the rigid Prussian Bismarck to emphasize more strongly his inclination towards the representative of the Austrian imperial idea, the reactionary extremist Schwarzenberg. These words were doubtless meant to be a warning to Frederick William IV to turn away from Radowitz and back to Austria. It was now the hope of Bismarck, just as it had been when the King refused the crown ' baked of filth and clay ', that Prussia and Austria, once united, would be in a position by themselves to make an end of German liberalism and democracy. For there was already to be discerned the threat of intervention in German affairs by the bitterest enemy of all revolutionary tendencies, Tsar Nicolas I, of whom a German statesman has said : ' For years the German courts were trained in the fear of God and of Tsar Nicolas.' To his wife Bismarck mentioned in this connexion as the greatest danger ' that conservative armies (i.e., the Prussian and the Austrian), who love and honour each other, will cut each other's throats '. In the *Kreuzzeitung* he exclaims : ' Austria and Prussia must become united ' in order to ' rescue Germany from the hands of the revolution or of her foes lusting for booty '.

The new Prussian Parliament had to concern itself not only with the constitution of the ' Three Kings' Union ' but also with the new Prussian one, since it had the right to confirm the enforced constitution. Bismarck took part also in the debates on this subject, but he missed the stimulus of personal opposition. ' The battle with the gangs of democrats in the preceding parliament ', he said in his family circle, ' after all gave more amusement than we have now with these watery constitutional opponents, who cover their poison with the sugar of patriotic pretences.' To the ' amphibious creatures of the Chamber ' he opposes ' the men with the nature of soldiers who have warm Prussian blood in their bodies '. One of the most important questions in connexion with the new constitution concerned the right of parliament to refuse taxes. While this was logically a necessary corollary of the right to impose taxes and as such widely admitted in the western European states, it was the object of the Prussian reactionaries, especially of Bismarck, to deprive parliament of this right of refusal. He replied to the advocates of this right who had pointed out as examples various foreign constitutions, foremost the French and the English, by opposing the intention to clothe ' our healthy body with the Nessus garment of French political theory '. But above all he cried out :

References to England are our misfortune. Give us everything English which we have not got, give us the English fear of God, and the English reverence for the law, give us the general conditions governing English landed property, give us English wealth and English public spirit, but above all, an English Lower House, then I shall say that you can also rule us in English fashion.

This is the same Bismarck who later said of himself : ' In regard to foreign countries I have throughout my life only had sympathy for England and its inhabitants, but the people will not let themselves be loved by us.' Anyhow, the question whether the devotion of the Prussian population to the hereditary dynasty might not provide an adequate basis for institutions on the English line was one on which Bismarck did not touch. The 'recently so praised flower of confidence' he was not going to 'tear up as a weed', but neither would he plant it in the soil fitted for it by advocating a parliamentary system on the basis of which it might develop. On the contrary, he defended what he called ' equal rights of the crown and the two houses of parliament ' and deduced from this thesis that the right to refuse taxes ' destroyed the independence of the crown for the sake of a majority in the Chamber '. Again and again he emphasized his rejection of the practice of imitating foreign institutions. Thus on the occasion of the debate on civil marriage he spoke of Prussians who were ashamed of being Prussians ' as long as we have no civil marriage, since foreign customs have always a certain air of distinction for us '. At the same time, however, Bismarck succeeded in representing the Prussian nobility as champions of the political freedom of parliament. For ' true freedom, political independence, without which freedom could not exist in Prussia' were quite essentially the work of this nobility, and 'in the most recent times we must not undervalue the service of this class in suppressing anarchy and saving Prussia from the most disgraceful of tyrannies '. This ' true freedom ' was the contrary of the individual liberty of German idealism and at the same time the very tyranny against which its adherents had summoned true justice founded upon the equality of all human beings.

On the 26th of January 1850 parliament had completed its work on the enforced Prussian constitution. Almost all its decisions had gone against the convictions and against the vote of Bismarck. He must also have felt it as a blow when the King on the 31st of January 1850 ratified and, a week later, took the oath to observe this constitution, thus giving it a duration which outlived not only himself but also Bismarck.

There followed now for Bismarck no prospect of a return to Schönhausen, but rather a parliamentary task whereby he was to be confronted directly with the problem of the national unity of

Germany. Prussia had concluded a treaty with Austria on the 30th of September 1849 concerning the German question, the so-called 'Interim', which presupposed the continuance of the Act of the 8th of June 1815 constituting the German Confederation. She had thereby given Austria a means to secure the continuance of this Confederation in so far as she was concerned. But as the 'Three Kings' Union', which had been concluded just four months before, meant the *de facto* abolition of the Act of 1815, Prussia had thus struck a blow against the Union, an 'ambiguous attitude' in the words of Bismarck. When in spite of this Prussia summoned the Reich Parliament provided in the 'Three Kings' Union' at Erfurt with a view to creating the united German Reich and writs were issued for elections for this purpose, Hanover and Saxony took the opportunity to break away from the Union. They refused to hold the elections which had been prescribed and thus again won the goodwill of Austria. Their example was followed by Kur-Hesse, which state had only joined the Union after them. Consequently the Reich Parliament, opened at Erfurt by Radowitz as personal representative of the Prussian King, had only the presence of a few deputies from the petty states and several members of the Gotha-Group to give it the prestige of a German, as opposed to a merely Prussian, institution.

This provided his fifth parliamentary period for Bismarck who was one of the Prussian deputies. How he would interpret the task thus set him of co-operating in the creation of the German Reich could not be in any doubt in view of his previous public and private assertions. In addition, he had expressly made his opinions known in his electoral platform. This called for firm opposition to the efforts of the democratic party and for a definite decision in a truly conservative sense. He urged the realization as far as possible of the idea of the federal state, but insisted that 'the strength or the honour of Prussia must not be menaced by a one-sided carrying-out of the idea of German unity'. So attempts which the King made through the prime minister, Count Brandenburg, together with the minister of the interior, Manteuffel, to win Bismarck's support for the government policy, remained without success.

Once more Bismarck's parliamentary activity lasted only for a few weeks. The assembly was completely under the spell of Radowitz's eloquence and was therefore ready to accept his proposals as a whole. Bismarck, in view of the prevailing mood of the assembly, had to confine himself to 'small combats to relieve somewhat his gall'. He made a particularly malicious attack by proposing to substitute for the expression 'German Reich' that of 'German Union', on the ground that otherwise one would make the whole scheme 'ridiculous'. He dilated at length on this with great self-satisfaction, saying that he was afraid ' that the impression of hilarity could be increased further if of the states now allied through the Union some more would burst the net or tie of German brotherly love, and if consequently the constitutional machine, run by the steam of Frankfurt, which had not yet cooled off, in spite of the greatest efforts did not succeed in bursting the valve of opposition by the Princes '. On another occasion he turned against the colours ' black, red, gold ', which he himself had worn two years before to escape the mob, now the ' colours of riot and the barricades ', with the words : ' If you do not make more concessions to the Prussian spirit you will find in it a Bucephalus who will cast the unskilled Sunday rider on to the sand, together with his black red gold harness.' Bismarck even drew up an Opposition scheme which, Prussian and monarchical in tone, was intended to serve as a particularly effective weapon against the projected constitution.

But all this was of no help to Bismarck and those who shared his views. The proposal drawn up by Radowitz was accepted as a whole in the middle of April 1850. Thereby the Erfurt Reich Parliament had done its duty, but now it was the responsibility of the Prussian government to put German Unity into practice. This was easier said than done. For in the meantime the efforts of the Austrian Chancellor, Prince Schwarzenberg, had succeeded in taking the last wind out of the sails of Prussia's movement towards unity. Using the weapon placed at her disposal by the treaty of the 30th of September 1849, the ' Interim ', Austria summoned again to Frankfurt the Federal Diet set up by the Act of Confederation of 1815, a few weeks after the first meeting of the Erfurt Reich Parliament. That Prussia could not accept this invitation after the conclusion of the ' Three Kings' Union ' was obvious. But she had to see to her disappointment that some of the states connected with her at Erfurt had no such scruples.

The opposition between Prussia and Austria was, however, to become even sharper in the course of the summer of 1850. The still unsolved question of Schleswig-Holstein was one disturbing factor. Following the expiry of the armistice concluded at Malmö in August 1848, Prussia, in July 1850, after various vicissitudes, surrendered Schleswig-Holstein to the Danes. Austria, going a step further, a month later joined in an agreement on this question in London with the European Powers, England, Russia, and France. This treaty recognized Denmark, including the two duchies, as a single state with a single monarch and put her under the guarantee of these powers. This step was not rendered more tolerable for the German national movement and for the German petty Princes by the fact that the rights of the German Confederation in regard to Holstein and the indivisibility of the latter from Schleswig were formally retained. The position of Prussia was now especially awkward and isolated ; for on the one hand Austria was annoyed that she had not joined in the London agreement (or rather joined in it one and a half years later, in May 1852) ; on the other hand, the dissatisfaction of the German nationalists and of the petty Princes centred itself on the fact that they had expected from Prussia the liberation of Schleswig and Holstein.

The immediate occasion which brought the differences between Prussia and Austria to a head was provided by occurrences in Kur-Hesse. Here the particularly reactionary sovereign had begun to put aside once more the constitution which he had accepted under the pressure of the revolution and in particular to abolish the parliament's right to grant taxes. Since his secession from the ' Three Kings' Union ' the Prince had enjoyed the special goodwill of Austria and could reckon on her support when in the middle of September 1850 he asked the newly summoned Frankfurt Federal Diet for Federal help to force his unwilling subjects to pay taxes. Prussia, mindful of her ' German Mission ' under the influence of Radowitz, supported the cause of the Hessian parliament and the Hessian people. At the same time Radowitz was nominated member of the Prussian Cabinet. This led to a stiffening of the policy of the ' Three Kings' Union ' in Prussia, thus increasing her sympathy with the German constitutional movement and her opposition to Austria. Manteuffel as well as Gerlach considered resigning their posts because they were in favour of an understanding with Austria. Bismarck himself, extremely annoyed by the increasing influence of the ' great deceiver ', Radowitz, strove to avoid the worst. ' Politics be hanged,' he wrote to his wife. But now the Russian Tsar intervened vigorously in the dispute after having formerly only attempted to mediate. He made it clear to Prussia that Austria was defending the cause of legitimacy and that Prussia was aiming at revolutionary goals both in the German and in the Hessian question. Thereupon the prime minister, Count Brandenburg, ventured to advise the abandonment of the Hessian parliament and the toleration of the Federal Execution in Kur-Hesse. Radowitz scented the forthcoming opposition ; the clique round Gerlach and Bismarck felt the wind in their sails.

Bismarck spent part of the summer on the North Sea coast. In autumn we find him in Schönhausen, while his wife paid a visit to her parents in Reinfeld. The official Prussian politics he had followed the whole summer with scorn and misgivings. He publicly described it as ' a mongrel product of cowardly government and tame revolution '. But it seems that he did not think it advisable to oppose Radowitz in the presence of the King. He confined himself to exposing his views in the *Kreuzzeitung*. An invitation to the royal

hunt at Letzlingen, where he hoped he could express personally to
the King his objections against the Erfurt policy, was cancelled, a
bitter disappointment for Bismarck's craving for political influence.
However, matters seemed to be taking the course which he desired
even without his help. Count Brandenburg took more energetic
steps and caused a conciliatory note to be despatched to Vienna on
the 2nd of November. The success of this measure exceeded all
Bismarck's expectations, for it was the occasion which led to the
resignation of Radowitz. ' I rode on my chair round the table for
joy,' wrote Bismarck to H. Wagener in this connexion, 'and many a
bottle of champagne has been drunk to the health of Radowitz. For
the first time I feel grateful to him and wish him a happy journey
without any grudge.' This is the man who expressed himself concerning another of his political opponents, the radical Robert Blum,
who was sentenced to death in Vienna : ' When I have an enemy in
my power I must destroy him,' and about one of his closest friends
on the occasion of the latter's engagement, ' he is intolerably happy ',
and even ' insultingly happy '.

But Bismarck's side had not yet defeated the adversaries of
Austria. On the 6th of November Count Brandenburg died
suddenly after an illness lasting three days, it is said, as a martyr to
the excessively exacting duties of his post on account of which he
had now actually ' put his head into the noose '. And even before
he had passed away, the Cabinet had, under the pressure of Prince
William of Prussia, ordered mobilization against Austria and summoned parliament for the end of November. The Prussian troops
advanced towards Kur-Hesse, and on the 8th of November some
shots were exchanged between the Prussian and the Austrian out-
posts. A few days afterwards, Schwarzenberg sent an ultimatum
to Prussia demanding the evacuation of Kur-Hesse.

Bismarck reports how he visited the minister of war in Berlin
with the mobilization order sent to him as officer in the Landwehr
and the invitation to parliament sent to him as deputy in his pocket
in order to find out which of these had priority. He personally was
of the opinion that ' the Hessian affair had not sufficient interest for
Prussia, and especially for our party for it to be worth while to
sacrifice men, and soldiers at that '—an expression in which the two
points of emphasis call for special attention. What then could be
more agreeable to him than to hear from the minister of war, ' a
dashing old soldier, of whose moral and physical courage I am certain '
that ' we must at present avoid a breach as far as possible. We have
no adequate forces to stem the Austrians.' He gladly ignored the
point that the minister himself was not free from blame for the
inadequacy of the preparations for war, since this was grist to his mill.
He now renounced the military service which was otherwise so highly

valued by him. It served him much better to use as cloak his position as deputy in the parliament which he despised in his heart. So he prepared not only himself but also his party for the sitting of the end of November by striving to influence them in favour of a peaceful understanding with Austria.

The ultimatum of Schwarzenberg had not failed in its effects on the successor of Count Brandenburg, namely the former minister of the interior, Manteuffel. The Prussian troops evacuated Kur-Hesse, and Manteuffel, under the pressure of Russia and against ' Gotha [i.e., the liberals of the so-called " Gotha-Group "], bureaucracy and court ', on the 15th of November induced the remaining members of the ' Three Kings' Union ' to decree its dissolution. He thus placed himself in the sheerest opposition to Prussia's obligation to put into force the draft of a constitution accepted at Erfurt. With this in his hand Manteuffel then hastened to Olmütz, there to meet the omnipotent Austrian chancellor, Schwarzenberg. On the 29th and 30th of November there were drawn up the famous ' Minutes of Olmütz ' which settled the Danish question in accord with the demands of Austria, referred the constitutional quarrel of Kur-Hesse to a conference to be called at Dresden and ordered the disarming of the mobilized troops. This was the first step in the complete surrender of Prussia to the will of Austria.

That was bad enough, especially for Frederick William IV, who could not so easily tear himself away from the dreams and hopes of his adviser Radowitz and who had but recently solemnly declared himself in their favour in his speech at the opening of the Prussian parliament.

I have called up [he said] the full military power of the country. We do not seek war, but we demand an organization of the common father-land which would be better adapted to our present position in Germany and Europe. We will remain strongly armed with weapons in our hands till we are certain of the recognition of our rights.

So Olmütz meant for Bismarck and his clique not only a victory over the hated Radowitz but also over the King himself. Bismarck could not suppress his pleasure at the latter victory, although Olmütz indeed meant the exposure of the King in the eyes of Austria and of his own people. Bismarck had therefore no light task when on the 3rd of December he made his speech in the Chamber to express his views on the general political situation. But he carried out his task with consummate skill. The call to arms of the King he separated from its context in the actual situation and mentioned as worthy of general approval the fact that ' the Prussian people have always risen in unison on the summons of the King of Prussia '. As opponents of his own policy he mentioned no names and he referred to the defeated Radowitz only as member of 'the narrower circle in whose hands the reins lie in the last resort'. But he gave full vent to his boundless scorn and contempt against this circle : ' I have here found nothing great but personal ambition, nothing great but suspicion, nothing great but party hatred.' He declares concerning the Erfurt policy of German unity : ' It is a singular unity which requires us to shoot down and stab our German countrymen in the south ', those countrymen who were shortly before referred to as the ' rotten fermentation of indiscipline '. The intervention on behalf of the Hessian parliament is for him ' playing the game of Don Quixote for insulted parliamentary celebrities '. The decisive point is in his opinion ' that Prussia should keep herself free from any shameful alliance with democracy '. It is now no longer Russia against whose intervention in German affairs he issues warnings, but France who had emerged from the revolution of 1848 as a republic, and whose revolutionary president, Louis Napoléon, would use this opportunity to become emperor by means of a plebiscite and thereby to support the idea of democracy. ' The only sound foundation of a great state ', Bismarck exclaims, ' is the state's egoism, and not romantic ideals.' But one must in fact describe as a ' romantic ' self-deception Bismarck's own view of what Olmütz implied, namely that from now on ' in Germany nothing should happen without the agreement of Prussia ' and that ' what Prussia and Austria after common independent consideration hold to be rational and politically right should be carried out in common by the two protecting powers of Germany with equal rights '.

How this ' independent consideration ' and these ' equal rights ' would look like in the ' free ' conference in Dresden could not be in doubt after the ' Olmütz Minutes ' and least of all to so clever a politician as Bismarck. In fact this conference ended with the final renunciation by Prussia of any independent Reich policy, with her agreement to the revival of the Federal Act of 1815 desired by Austria and the renewed dispatch of a Prussian plenipotentiary to the Federal Diet which sat at Frankfurt under the despotic presidency of Austria. It is true, Austria made certain concessions as well, withdrawing her demands for a further strengthening of her position of power inside Germany. However, she did not do this in favour of Prussia nor under her influence, but only because the other European powers, Russia, England and above all France, now becoming very active in foreign affairs under her president, Louis Napoleon, would not allow a really strong central Power to arise in the heart of Europe, since they looked on this as ' a threat to the European balance of power '. In view of this combination of forces, Schwarzenberg actually brought himself to conclude a secret defensive alliance with Prussia on the 16th of May 1851. Bismarck gave as cause for the undeniable political defeat of Prussia at Dresden that she had sought by ' a display of German-mindedness ' to attain ' successes which could only be won by fighting, or by preparedness for fighting '. Yet he had only just expressed himself publicly for a peaceful understanding with Austria.

During the remainder of the session, which lasted till May 1851, the first Prussian three-class parliament concerned itself mainly with internal and economic problems, Bismarck having an eager part in the discussions. This gave him the opportunity of again taking a stand against the right of parliament to refuse taxes which he had already denounced the year before as ' destroying the independence of the crown '. He now supported the proposal that the financial arrangements of the budget for the previous year should, in accordance with the Prussian constitution, be prolonged without further ado till the new budget came into force. Nor did he let the opportunity slip of forcibly expressing his aversion to the bureaucracy, which he now declared to be *in toto* an ' ally of the revolution '. Already in the previous summer he had in the *Kreuzzeitung* described the bureaucracy as a ' cancerous sore ' and spoken of the ' wormeaten bureaucracy '. He then had written to H. Wagener : ' The bureaucracy is cancerous in head and limb, only its stomach is healthy.' Now he said in parliament : ' I have never loved bureaucracy, rather do I regard it as the individual bearer of the revolutionary principle in general .' On the other hand, he did not fail to take the opportunity of the military budget to sing a paean on the national significance of the officer corps, and to call upon the Prussian people to render to it their debt of thanks. In his peroration he again impressed the Chamber with his own self-assurance as Junker : ' For our part we shall yet bring honour and distinction to the name of junkerdom.' The Junker Bismarck did not know that he was on the point of himself joining the class of hated and despised bureaucrats, if only as a bureaucratically disguised Junker.

All through 1849 and 1850 Bismarck stood in the centre of parliamentary and court life, was concerned in every intrigue, and even let himself be wooed by the extreme democratic opposition who sought him as ally against the moderate liberals of the Gotha-Group.

CHAPTER XI

Ambassador to the Federal Diet

Bismarck describes in excessively dramatic fashion how about the end of April 1851 he was to his surprise offered a post in the Prussian bureaucracy, for the time being as a councillor to the embassy to the Frankfurt Federal Diet with a view to becoming ambassador himself. But in fact he had already hinted in letters to his wife at the impending offer several days before.

After I had simply replied with ' Yes ' [he said later on] to the sudden question of the minister von Manteuffel whether I would accept the post of ambassador, the King summoned me before him and said : ' You have a great deal of courage that you are thus prepared to accept a quite new post without hesitation.' I answered : ' The courage is altogether on the part of your Majesty in that you offer me such a post. I have the courage to obey if your Majesty has the courage to command.'

The already familiar picture of ' vassal of Brandenburg and Prussian officer of his Majesty ' is by these words brought before our eyes with particular vividness. According to other reports he even went a step further in displaying his mastery of the situation. With all the disconcerting frankness at his command, which he could so skilfully use as a political weapon, he is said to have explained to the King : ' The relation of Manteuffel to the conservative party cannot possibly remain as it is at present. In public he disavows us on every occasion. If he advocates my appointment as an ambassador he will compromise himself so much in the eyes of the liberals that he cannot draw back.' This reference to the antagonism between the bureaucracy, which was more or less flirting with the liberal opposition, and the Junker party, unconditionally bound up with the patriarchal monarch, is said to have been received by the King with a delighted chuckle.

To his wife Bismarck admitted that he did not really feel so secure as he seemed to be outwardly. ' This sudden social exaltation frightens me,' he said, and again : ' I am still quite overcome by the suddenness with which the wheel of life has carried me off.' Finally when, just before he became full ambassador, his predecessor had temporarily gone away, Bismarck said with emphasis : ' Then I am for the first time in my life an independent representative of Prussia.' What this might mean for him is shown by what he had said two months before in the parliamentary debate about the German Federal Diet; ' I challenge you to name any period of

106

history since the times of the Hohenstaufen in which Germany enjoyed greater respect abroad and a higher degree of political unity than she enjoyed during the time in which the Federal Diet controlled the external relations of Germany.'

Bismarck's appointment was certainly due to a personal decision of the King himself, in recognition of the devotion of the 'Most Humble of All Humble Subjects'; at the same time it was an appreciation of the talents of the 'red reactionary' which made him appear to the King as qualified, if not for cabinet office, at any rate for a post abroad. But the appointment also denoted a turning-point in Prussian policy. It signified the return to the Prussian principles of patriarchal rule in internal affairs which had prevailed before the 1848 revolution. Yet the appointment of the man who was destined to establish Prussian supremacy in Germany was meant to stress Prussia's abandonment of an independent policy in the German question, and the recognition of Austria's omnipotence in Germany. At the same time this change implied the return to power of the 'court camarilla' whose head, Leopold von Gerlach, declared : 'Bismarck's appointment is altogether my work.' Bismarck himself remarked to his wife : 'My nomination to some such post would of itself be a public pledge that the government had really and wholly renounced the revolution.'

Ever since its foundation the German Federal Diet in Frankfurt had constituted the centre of reaction in Germany. Under this banner the Diet was recalled after the interruption due to the German revolution. Its core was constituted now as before by Austria. Round her gathered the smaller states, while Prussia, suspected of an inclination to liberalism, democracy, and revolution, was kept at a distance and treated with distrust and arrogance. Bismarck's policy of siding with Austria as an indispensable ally in the struggle against liberalism and democracy was of course known in Frankfurt and strengthened his personal position there. Still he had to realize that the opinion concerning the state which he repre-sented would reflect on the personal valuation of himself as well as vice versa. Now that Bismarck had reached a focal position in political life, his mind was almost inevitably turned to the fact that personal self-assertion may become a means to be 'utilized in order to carry out the political task entrusted to him'. So he would naturally strive to replace what was lacking in his state as to power and reputation by throwing his personal weight into the scales, and would mercilessly use it to oppose and humiliate the exponent of any counter move in the Diet. We saw Bismarck's exaggerated self-assurance already in the judgements of the youth hardly above school age at Kniephof, in the demeanour of the young landowner in regard to his candidature for the inspectorship of dykes, in the behaviour of the new member of parliament on his first appearance before the Prussian Chamber, and on many other occasions. Now that this self-assertion was of use to the state and was demanded by the latter, any scruples about its presence completely disappeared. The religious duty, too, ' to resign oneself in humility to the will of God ', could not provide a counter-motive, since self-assertion now was the very backbone of those activities which became more than ever a fundamental religious demand. The conception of himself as ' independent representative of Prussia ' made Bismarck combine with—real or apparent—' loyalty and homage sworn to the royal flesh and blood ' an ever sharper indirect or even direct criticism of royal measures. He actually managed to join to this loyalty open or veiled disobedience of royal commands. The monarchy, as the central institution of the state, and the state itself as a power, became for him increasingly separated from the person of the individual King, and a quite distinct conception as the real guarantee of ' order and authority ' to which he had already pointed in his youth. Nevertheless, he did not become a bureaucrat who receives his self-assurance from the state, but remained an aristocratic Junker who himself contributes it to the state.

The first reports of Bismarck from Frankfurt to his superior, von Manteuffel, the bureaucrat who now stood between the romantic patriarchal monarch, Frederick William IV, and the realistic patriarchal monarchist, Otto von Bismarck, are, on account of ' the lull in federal business up to the present ', chiefly concerned with personal matters. The most interesting item is the report on his Austrian colleagues, headed by Count Thun, the ambassador of Austria and as such presiding representative in the Federal Diet.

> He shows [Bismarck says] in his external appearance something of a blustering nature. Underneath this outward attitude, Count Thun conceals an unusual degree of cleverness and calculation which, as soon as politics is concerned, is displayed with great presence of mind from behind the mask of harmless bonhomie. I regard him as an opponent who is dangerous to everyone who trusts him honourably. We must never expect the Austrian statesmen of the Schwarzenberg school to make legal right the basis of their politics just because it is legal right. Their view seems to me rather that of a gambler who has an eye for the chances and for this purpose takes as cloak the bold and contemptuous carelessness of an elegant cavalier.

All the little misdemeanours of Thun are conscientiously reported, his negligent dress at committee meetings, his failure to return calls, and the way in which he unnecessarily kept visitors waiting, his bad manners in not offering them a seat in the reception-room and in not standing up when they entered the room. Regarding Thun and his two councillors, Bismarck writes about the same time to Leopold von Gerlach : ' All three are devoid of any qualities which arouse confidence. Cautious insincerity is the most noteworthy characteristic displayed by them in their intercourse with us.'

In this light were now revealed to Bismarck the men with whom, according to his recent speeches in the Prussian Chamber, Prussia had to find and carry out ' the rational and politically right ' course, instead of entering into the ' shameful alliance with democracy '. He himself, already two weeks after he had entered on office, wrote to his wife :

> These diplomats with their pettifogging which pretends to be important are already much more ridiculous to me than was the member of the second chamber with all his sense of his dignity. Not even the most malicious doubter of a democrat would believe what charlatanism is hidden in this diplomacy.

This supercilious criticism did not, however, save Bismarck from himself wading about with delight in this swamp of pettifogging. In November 1851 he reported to the minister von Manteuffel that the celebrated actress, Henriette Sontag, ' is to be found in every salon ; she has beautified herself since she left Berlin. The coppery colour of her complexion has almost disappeared.' It is equally charming to read from the reports of Bismarck to Manteuffel how he mockingly tells his superior, the man who had been defeated at Olmütz and Dresden, about the way the victors conducted their campaigns against him, bringing their motto of ' *avilir, puis démolir* ' to the notice of one who had felt the fruits of this motto so keenly in his own person. Bismarck himself, soon after the beginning of his activity at Frankfurt, found that he was unable to suppress the consciousness that ' many of the leading factors in terms of which his Erfurt politics had reckoned did not exist ', in particular that Austria was not the sincere and vigorous ally which he had hoped for and needed in the fight against liberalism and democracy.

However, after a short while, Bismarck was naturally not without practical political work to do in Frankfurt. This work was of a fundamentally ambiguous character. It had something to do both with home as well as with foreign policy. For the German Confederation carried with it in virtue both of its origin and its later development seeds of the German national unity, the German unitary state ; or, at any rate, it had the function of serving as a substitute for this. On the other hand, the Confederation was nothing but a contract under international law which left to the federated states sovereign independence and set them side by side as autonomous subjects internationally. It might now be questionable whether the main aim of the politicians of the Confederation was the deepening and strengthening of its unity, thus treating it as a single state, or the settling of disputes as between different states, by compromise or concealed war or even open economic warfare. It was certainly a fact that in Frankfurt under the occasional protection of the cloak of the German will to unity there was going on a real struggle for the particular interests of the separate states. It may, indeed, have happened that many a Frankfurt diplomat failed to distinguish between real and feigned intentions both in himself and in his fellow-diplomats. For Bismarck this ambiguity constituted the ground on which his extraordinary capacities as a diplomat and a statesman developed and realized themselves. This fundamental ambiguity led up to Prussia's ambivalent relation to Austria, whom she regarded as an ally against liberalism and democracy, and at the same time as an opponent of Prussia's ' state-egoism as of a power fully entitled to be the protective power of Germany '. The weaker Bismarck's confidence in Austria as an ally became, the more was he bound to see in her the opponent in the political struggle for superiority and the more was he bound to substitute for attempts to win her by persuasion the display of power and force as a means of intimidation.

In fact Bismarck, the official representative of Manteuffel's policy of compliance with Austria, began very soon after entering on office to conduct a secret guerrilla warfare against her. As was usual with him he roused himself to do so by looking upon himself and the state represented by him as victims of aggression, anticipating from the other side nothing but a ' secret delight in preparing obstacles for us '. He had soon as much control over all the methods and tricks of diplomatic intrigue as if he had worked at them for years or had been born for them. He now availed himself of the practical experience which he had acquired in working for the *Kreuzzeitung* for making use of and manipulating the Press with a skill of which any one of the ' leading men of the Press ', whom he so hated, might well have been envious. Public opinion which he had so despised as a ' clamour of unreason ' now became something of which he was willing to take very much account, working on it with all means at his disposal. He learned as well as any diplomatist how to organize and to employ secret agents and how to guard against and keep an eye on foreign spies. He was aware that his correspondence, official as well as private, was opened and copied, and learned how to attain knowledge of the correspondence of others. Bismarck from the very beginning was the exact opposite of the ' caricatured pigtail diplomats ', as he called the representatives of the petty states. In June he advised the minister against the suggested recall of the Prussian representative in Karlsruhe : ' Through replacing him by a new personality we shall lose ground to Austria.' In connexion with a discussion with a journalist friendly to Prussia he reports very unfavourably to his superior about Schwarzenberg's domestic policy. For, Bismarck says, ' if the man carries out his system we ourselves shall live to see the practical proof of how little he deserves the name of a 'conservative'. A little later there occurred, as Bismarck reports, a struggle between himself and Count Thun about cigar-smoking in the sittings of the Federal Military Commission. Bismarck not only arrogated the right of smoking, hitherto reserved for the president, but ' actually asked the presiding representative for a light, conduct which was regarded by the latter and the others present with astonishment and dissatisfaction '.

Bismarck was convinced that this concealed guerrilla warfare was being waged by both sides, and that ' Austrians agitated in Berlin against my appointment because my " black-white " [Prussian] is not " yellow " [Austrian] enough for them '. So he was all the more glad that in reporting to Berlin he was not confined to the official channels. Manteuffel was regarded as quite fixed in his attitude towards Austria. Consequently Bismarck was almost reserved in the utterances addressed to him. He was proud of his reports to him, ' which read as well and neatly as leading articles, and if Manteuffel after he has read them can say what is in them he can do more than I can ', although he explains a little later to Prince William of Prussia that ' complete frankness reigns ' between Manteuffel and himself. Of his written communications the most sincere and relevant were addressed not to Manteuffel but to Leopold von Gerlach, the royal adjutant general, by whose aid the King could be made immediately accessible to his suggestions. This circumvention of his superior, the foreign minister and prime minister, by Bismarck, the ambassador, a manœuvre carried out with the agreement of the King and of his immediate entourage, characterizes the conditions prevailing in the Berlin governing circles. In consequence of the weakness, indecision, and fickleness of the King, there was a complete lack of unity in the conduct of affairs, and the King, Prince William, the Cabinet, the camarilla, and similar cliques were all at cross purposes with each other, pushed each other aside, and trumped each other's cards. ' In the morning we receive ', relates a diplomat to the editor Wagener, ' a dispatch from the foreign office, in the afternoon we receive one from the adjutant general, and in the evening one from his Majesty himself, and they frequently contradict each other.' Yet a still more revealing light is thrown on Bismarck himself when we contemplate how he makes use of these conditions at the Berlin court in order to increase the effect of his political efforts, and was acting on the assumption that he was entitled to use any means for his own political ends.

Simply from the point of view of his professional duties, the circumvention of his superior minister was a serious breach of regulations
on the part of Bismarck, who was so very fond of speaking of the
'strictness of his concepts of subordination and duty of service'.
He, however, avoided the consequences of his action by means of
that open-hearted bluff which he sometimes displayed in that he
gave his superior occasional reports of his correspondence with
Gerlach.

In this correspondence, Bismarck speaks about Austria and the
Federal Diet without mincing words. Yet, he had said : ' I came
to Frankfurt as a good friend of Austria ', had considered Austria's
'unity with Prussia' as more important than anything else and
the Diet as ' the last means of holding together Germany '. But
now he refers to the Diet thus : ' That we shall be able to reform
Germany with this gang of people, I do not believe. The common
peril of 1848 is forgotten, and the mutual envy and touchiness
will hardly allow of decisive and agreed action on the part of the
Confederation.' He points out already that he regards abandonment of the policy of compliance with Austria as the right course
to follow ' in view of the much greater probability that Austria
has need of us than that we have need of Austria '. Indeed, he now
indicates that it would be useful for Prussia to take the initiative in
what he calls the ' German material question ', thus showing his
readiness to accept the slogan of the ' German mission of Prussia '.
But he only admits it as a means of attacking Austria and in regard
to ' minor matters, such as unification of measures, weights, and
money, and similar tripe '. He did not ' rate the importance of
these very high and did think them difficult to carry out, yet one
ought to show good will and make a little puff in honour of the
piece of work '.

Bismarck was able also to open for himself the direct way of
approach to the King and was willing to use it without hesitation.
' The King not only asked ', he tells us, ' for my opinion regarding
the questions of internal and external policy, but also entrusted me
from time to time with the task of working out proposals.' He lost
no opportunity of appearing personally in Berlin and calling wherever
he hoped for success. In order to keep up his extensive contacts
with Berlin he also thought it important that he should be re-elected
member of the parliament there, a wish which was fulfilled in
October 1851. But, meanwhile, here, too, he had to find out that
' the intrigues in the Chamber are beyond all measure trite and
unworthy '. Again and again we hear of audiences with the King ;
he himself says that he travelled from Frankfurt to Berlin and back
like the ' pendulum of a clock '. He also fostered his relations with
Prince William, the heir apparent, who since the end of 1848 had

resided in Coblenz and so was particularly accessible from Frankfurt.

While Bismarck was thus sailing in the midst of intrigues and diplomatic tricks, he himself and his position were the object of such intrigues. In the first instance he had been given only the expectation of the post of ambassador in Frankfurt. Now the final appointment was at stake. The first question to be asked was what attitude the former holder of the post, a general, would take to the change. He had indeed after a short period of collaboration praised Bismarck's ' outstanding qualities of intellect and character ' and recommended him for the diplomatic profession as ' an ornament of Prussian Junkerdom ' and ' the pride of the well-disposed '. But now he postponed his resignation of the post again and again. Remarkable was the attitude of Prince William who in the meantime had apparently forgotten the ' never-to-be-forgotten ' services of Bismarck on account of the latter's preference for Austria in the days of Erfurt and Olmütz. He objected to the appointment to this high post of ' a second lieutenant in the Landwehr '. Bismarck in turn was later to complain that the Prince ' unfortunately did not deserve the title of " grape-shot Prince " ', which had been given him. Some weeks after making his objection, however, the Prince said that he preferred Bismarck to his predecessor as being a more capable and a stronger man. Yet there were still reports that an official of the Berlin Foreign Office was being considered for the Frankfurt post. It does credit to the objectivity of Manteuffel that he supported Bismarck's appointment. The post was finally given to him in the middle of July, but he was informed of that only a month later. On the 27th of August there followed his formal induction into the post which he was to hold for eight years.

This appointment also led to a big change in Bismarck's family life. Since Bismarck had moved from Schönhausen to Berlin in March 1848 in order to ' liberate ' his King, he had been forced by political circumstances constantly to change his place of residence, and life in his family circle, ' the quiet happiness of a home life filled with love ', was restricted to a few weeks or months at a time. Meanwhile the family had increased through the birth in 1848 of a daughter, Mary. There followed in 1849 a boy, Herbert, and, three years later, a second boy, William. Of the birth of the daughter Bismarck reports : ' The whole day long I am alternating between political plans at my desk and the apron of a nurse by the sick-bed.' Again and again we find in his letters to his wife bitter complaints about the intolerableness of constantly removing. After one of his short visits the ' *aqua fortis* of tears ' was actually running ' down on to his beard '. ' It was,' he wrote, ' I believe, the first time since the days of my school holidays that a parting has cost me tears.' He asked for news : 'Only write me a couple of lines to tell me that you are alive and whether you are well or ill, but don't hurt your eyes and do not write with artificial light.' There was no lack of attempts at the beginning of this forced separation to arrange a common household. We learn of such an attempt in March 1849, when it was intended to take a flat in Berlin together with Bismarck's sister and his brother-in-law, von Arnim-Kröchlendorff, and of another in the autumn of that year. On this occasion Bismarck reported to his wife about a whole series of houses in Berlin which he had in view and sent her sketches. He actually rented one of them, but they lived in it together for only a short time. Even Bismarck's visits to Schönhausen did not always lead to a re-union of the pair, since the wife often spent the time of her husband's absence with her parents in Reinfeld.

Bismarck's letters to his wife were full of a sincere devotion. Every little attention or gift on her part is noted with the very deepest gratitude ; he is at her disposal for help in every matter of concern, however remote from his ordinary interests ; he seeks to save her from everything disturbing and to remove every care from her path. He shares with her the worries connected with the servants and takes on the task of engaging new ones. He suffers with her in her toothache and advises her how to treat it. He gives her detailed instructions about travelling. For her birthday he promised to be ' peaceable and humble, not only in feeling but also in action '. Everywhere in Bismarck's letters to his wife we find descriptions of nature vividly visualized and admirably expressed. Thus he writes on an evening in Schönhausen : ' The trees were standing so still and high beside me, the air was full of lime-blossom, in the garden a quail was calling and the partridges were clucking and behind, over Arneberg, lay the last pale red hem of the sunset.' Or take an autumnal picture in Berlin : ' The beautiful great maple had already tinted its leaves a dark red ; the limes, black alders and other backboneless creatures strew the path with their yellow rustling leaves, and the round cupolas of the chestnut trees exhibit all the shades of an autumnal play of colour.' Again and again he displays his mastery in describing experiences of travel, a heath-cock chase in the Thuringian Forest in pouring rain, an excursion with jolly company in a hay-cart drawn by four horses in the friendly Odenwald near Frankfurt, a holiday visit lasting several days in order to take part in the fashionable life at Baden-Baden, a voyage down the Rhine to Rüdesheim famous for its wine, above all a call on the once omnipotent Prince Clemens Metternich, now very old and living away from the world on his magnificently situated castle, Johannesberg, on the Rhine, who ' talked without stopping about the politics of 1788–1848 in a very charming and genial way '.

Belief in God keeps its place in Bismarck's correspondence with his wife. 'God knows His sign,' he wrote, 'think of the great good which he has done us, and the great evil from which he has spared us.' He assures his wife that he persisted in daily prayer ; yet he makes this admission to her : 'Pray for me that I remain true to God ; here I get so worldly and so angry, when you are not with me.' On another occasion when, on account of an inevitable postponement of a meeting with her, he had given vent to an unjustified outburst of anger, he writes : 'In the evening I begged God to forgive my impetuosity and surrendered myself to his will.' What Bismarck has to say to his wife about his own professional activities now sounds somewhat more remote. He even apologizes to her for speaking about politics, taking in account that she is not interested in it. But while absent he shows all the more interest in his children at home. The anxious father is glad that 'the little one has not got quinsy but only whooping cough, which is not so dangerous as the former'. He is concerned about the competence of the nurse, considers from all points of view the question of having the children vaccinated and is full of sympathy about 'the restlessness of the youngster at night'. After consulting a specialist in the capital he gives precise directions how to make weaning more tolerable for the baby. When his little daughter is in danger of catching scarlet fever he gives advice and help and sends a medicine which could not so easily be obtained in the country. All this happened in a time of the most strenuous and exciting political enterprises and decisions.

In spite of the obvious significance which marriage and family life had for Bismarck, he no doubt is not too serious when he describes his imminent appointment to the diplomatic service as 'attractive less for my own sake than for that of the cause to which we are devoted, for I must renounce for a long time the hope of living quietly with you and the children as I did in our first winter'. 'I feel as if we were emigrating to America,' he added later at the prospect of the removal to Frankfurt. When his wife complains about having to face another 'long parting', he gives her an enticing and detailed description of the pleasant social life which was awaiting her in the new residence, and of the large income, the wealthy manner of life, and the amenities of living there. He also describes fully certain social arrangements, and after an invitation from Baron Rothschild, 'quite the petty Jew-dealer', he cannot refrain from mockingly imitating the baron's way of speaking and reporting : 'There were many hundred weights of silverware, golden forks, and spoons', in order pointedly to add: 'May God give us our daily bread.'

Already two months after his arrival in Frankfurt Bismarck writes to his wife : ' I am now beginning to look about for a house here where my darling can give dinners and balls and be terribly fine.' Immediately after his final appointment he speaks of having looked at ' half a dozen dwelling-places ', and makes detailed proposals about the appointment of his numerous household staff, about the articles of furniture to be moved from Schönhausen, and about the removal of his wife planned for the end of September, with a knowledge of the situation and an interest as great as if nothing else existed for him. A week later, in spite of being overburdened with professional work, he reports the renting of a house ' 1200 paces from the gate, a beautiful garden, a villa, elegant and gay with flowers '. He then gives a ground plan of this, describing the single rooms. He expresses the intention of looking for the furniture in Schönhausen himself, which will cost him ' probably three nights in the train '. For the journey of his wife from Reinfeld to Frankfurt he gives precise directions, but adds ' you do quite as you like '.

At the beginning of October, Frau von Bismarck arrived in Frankfurt with her children. She was soon very much at her ease in the house prepared by Bismarck and gave her husband the home life for which he had longed so much. Bismarck wrote soon after her arrival to General von Gerlach : ' It is to me a rare pleasure to sit for a quarter of an hour with my wife and with a father's satisfaction to listen to the din of the most good-for-nothing children in the world ' ; this is to him the ' most pleasant part of the day ', as he told his mother-in-law. His friend of student days, Motley, who visited Bismarck in Frankfurt twenty years after their common university period in Göttingen and Berlin, reports about his home life : ' Here there are young and old, grandparents and children and dogs all at once ; eating, drinking, smoking, piano playing and pistol-firing (in the garden) all going on at the same time.' Thus in his home in Frankfurt his family life sometimes rendered his professional activity repellent to him, as before in the days of his life as landowner, but of course these fits were even less serious and lasting than before : ' Just as there hovers before the traveller the vision of a warm quiet place by the fire, so there hovers before me, through all the good and bad weather of politics, the vision of an independent family life in the country.' But while Frau von Bismarck shared with her husband the feeling for home life, she was without his pleasure in elegant society. ' Yesterday there was a soirée,' she wrote to a friend, ' but I again could not find a sensible word to say to anybody. I know that they are all kind enough to gossip about me, so why should I really go through the labour of showing them a love which will not be returned ? ' She thinks wistfully of the Reinfeld society where ' one lives joyfully every day, and we love each other without bounds '. So we can well

JOHANNA VON BISMARCK
née VON PUTTKAMER

understand that on the occasion of a reception which the Prussian King held near Frankfurt she felt herself put in the background and slighted in her 'Pomeranian backlands loyalty' by the behaviour of the royal family, and Bismarck thought himself driven to take steps which were almost official.

The man who in his natural family ties to wife, children, parents, and other relatives was full of love, patience and readiness to make sacrifices, who was always prepared to listen to his personal friends and to appreciate their merits, who accepted without reserve the community of the Prussian Junkers as one big family, was as a statesman in Frankfurt full of aggressiveness, hatred, and contempt in his political relations.

All this time, the secret guerrilla warfare which Bismarck waged with Austria and her satellites continued. As a 'turning-point' in the increasing intensity of this warfare, Bismarck later mentioned his reading of a dispatch by Schwarzenberg in which the latter 'depicted the events at Olmütz as if it had depended on him whether Prussia should be "humiliated" or generously pardoned'. But Bismarck's struggle did not remain secret long. Soon to this kind of warfare was added open conflict, which Bismarck called 'the defensive against Austria'. There were not lacking occasions for this, and Bismarck was not the man to miss such opportunities, but rather to conjure them up. At first only minor issues were at stake. There was the episode of the minutes of the Diet. The decision about these was effected by a committee in which Prussia was not represented. Bismarck had already experienced in Berlin what use one can make of a parliamentary episode by means of publicity, and what significance therefore belongs to the decision about its publication. He objected to the way in which the committee was composed. Further, he defended Prussia against the Austrian attempt to establish a Federal Press Law, for this would curtail the independence of his state. In taking this line he declared that he was demanding this freedom not out of liberal opinions but in the interests of Prussia's power. Moreover, he attacked the right of the presiding Power independently to determine the order of procedure, this being a handle for increasing her influence; the strict authoritarian defended a constitutional limitation of the presidential authority. Moreover, Bismarck was trying to push another step forward in relation to the method of voting in the Diet. He had in view the lasting opposition between Austria and Prussia, and he certainly could not count on the other members of the Confederation for a favourable attitude towards Prussia. So the majority principle in these divisions meant the danger of Prussia being permanently put in a minority. Therefore Bismarck was a protagonist of the extension of unanimity rule in matters curtailing the

power of the single states. Already on the occasion of the dispute
about the publication of the minutes he had made a sounding in
this direction. In agreement with Manteuffel he threatened that he
would meet the rejection of the proposal regarding the composition
of the committee with passive resistance, 'a greater reserve in our
political collaboration with the states federated with us', and was
soon able to report in Berlin the full success of his action.

A somewhat more fundamental question of dispute was provided
by the German Navy. In 1848 the Frankfurt National Assembly
had, in connexion with the war against Denmark, ordered the
establishment of a small German North Sea Fleet. This served
primarily the interests of Prussia in protecting her coast against
Denmark, and consequently she regularly paid her contribution for
maintaining the fleet, while Austria and the inland German states
showed their lack of interest by not paying their portion of the
costs. After the quarrel with Denmark had been settled by the
Conference in London, nobody was interested in the continued
existence of this fleet, but all the states concerned wanted to be freed
from the debts which they had incurred or with which they were
threatened in connexion with it. Bismarck took a lively interest in
this matter. At the end of July he wrote to his wife : ' I have
now to read endless figures about German steam-corvettes and
gunboats which rot in Bremerhaven and eat up gold.' At the end
of October he declared in the Federal Diet that Prussia also would
not go on paying, and recommended the distribution or sale of the
ships. He suspected Austria of wanting to get hold of the ships
without having to pay for them and thus as presiding Power winning
control of North Sea affairs by means of a fleet. So Prussia on her
part entered into negotiations with Hanover with a view to taking
over the fleet jointly.

Bismarck used this opportunity again to suggest cautiously to
Manteuffel that it was impossible to continue collaboration with
Austria. But he had not yet given up the idea that Austria might
be of some use as an ally against liberalism and democracy. So in
a memoir to the minister he added that ' the insecurity of the
present situation in relation to the revolutionary movement ' required
' a postponement of the questions of dispute which inevitably exist
between the two states '. Austria, he contended, was suggesting to
the small states that Prussia was bound, in view of her geographical
position, to try to bring the neighbouring Princes into a ' relation
of dependence of some kind to her ; Austria was therefore flattering
the particularism, especially of the south German sovereigns '. To
Gerlach Bismarck openly described Austria as ' mendacious ' and
' double-tongued ' ; and, influenced by the aversion which he had
already shown earlier to ' south German lack of discipline ', he

remarked generalizing : ' The south German children of nature are very spoilt.' He now again had an opportunity of making use of the lever at his disposal for preventing Prussia from being put in a minority in the Federal Diet. The latter had resolved on raising a loan from the Rothschild Bank for the fleet, and Bismarck saw in this a means by which Austria sought to appropriate the fleet to herself. Consequently, Prussia made a direct protest to the bank against the payment of the loan. Count Thun rightly interpreted this step as a ' mockery of the decisions of the Diet '. But in spite of the latter's violent excitement, Bismarck did not yield. He demanded of Austria either that she should pay in cash her contributions to the fleet or else allow the sale of the ships, since Prussia's negotiations in order to secure a joint ownership of the fleet had failed. He again threatened passive resistance in the event of being put in a minority. If an impending division did not result more in accord with ' justice ', he wrote to Gerlach, then he was going to make a *coup d'état*, i.e., ' disappear from Frankfurt without appointing a deputy '. On this occasion victory was on the side of Bismarck. The sale of the first German war fleet was resolved by the Federal Diet in April 1852 and the ships were accordingly sold by public auction.

In the Schleswig-Holstein question Bismarck had personally an extraordinarily difficult and delicate task. Through the agreement concluded at the London Conference of May 1852 the Great Powers not only guaranteed the continuance of the joint Denmark state including the duchies of Schleswig and Holstein, but also made provision in case of the death without heirs of the present ruler, Frederick VII. In that emergency the related house of Sonderburg was to succeed. Bismarck had now the task of persuading the Duke of Augustenburg, whose cause Prussia had formerly favoured, but then abandoned following the withdrawal of her forces from Denmark, to renounce his claim to the two duchies. Bismarck as a mediator was to offer him as compensation a repayment of part of his fortune from the King of Denmark. We have already seen Bismarck as a landowning Junker active in business of a similar kind, and we have noted how he brought about agreement in peasants' disputes by ' mingling flattering friendliness and rude coarseness '. Now what was at stake was a throne ; but the method adopted by Bismarck remained the same. With a skill and insight which a professional go-between would envy, by means of concealed threats and exaggerations of what he had to offer, directed towards both parties, on the 30th of December 1852 he brought about an agreement which at first, at any rate, satisfied them both.

But it would be inexact to say that Bismarck, apart from occasional tasks like the above, regarded it as his function in the German

Federal Diet to oppose Austria and her supporters merely in a negative way. Looking at the German Confederation at Frankfurt from Berlin he had regarded German unity as something merely foreign and external, in relation to which Prussia should adopt a purely negative attitude, being ready to defend herself against it. The view which he at that time expressed that 'in Germany nothing ought to happen without the agreement of Prussia' only meant an extension beyond the Prussian frontier of the defence against the principles of democracy and liberalism. But now that Bismarck himself sat in Frankfurt at the centre of the unifying tendencies there inevitably occurred to him another aspect of Prussia's relation to German unity, namely the positive aspect, signifying a possibility of extending Prussia's power and establishing Prussia's will within it. He decided to serve this purpose by winning allies for his state in this camp. External circumstances soon gave him the chance of working in this direction as Prussian state official. An opportunity was presented by the development of the German Customs Union. This development enabled him to intensify his hostile attitude towards Austria by actively propagating the German desire for unity and so to strengthen Prussia's 'initiative in the German material questions'. Thus Bismarck took as his chief concern at Frankfurt the work for German unity not as an end in itself, but as a Prussian weapon against her competitor Austria.

The Federal Diet was in these days not the only link which held together the German states. There was a second link of far less impressive aspect externally but considerable practical significance, the German Customs Union, which had as its end the unified management of fiscal affairs in the Confederated States. Capably carried on since 1819 by the Prussian bureaucracy of ill fame, this Union had as a Prusso-German Customs Union considerably increased its extent and significance. In 1842 further states joined it, and it was renewed for twelve years. The admission of Austria was always opposed by Prussia. The ground given by Bismarck for this refusal was purely economic, namely, that, owing to the fact that Austria was less industrialized, the kind of exports and imports required by her was different from those required by the other German states. In fact, however, power politics no doubt always played an important part. Austria continually pressed for admission, particularly since the renewal of the German Confederation after the revolution of 1848. For Schwarzenberg this was a matter of political prestige in the sense of his policy as tested by the Olmütz episode. His minister of commerce desired it as a stimulus for the development of the Austrian economic system and the financiers hoped from it an improvement in the bad condition of the state's treasury. But the admission of Austria was also furthered and favoured on the part of the south German states. On the other hand, these states were offended because Prussia in September 1851 had promised admission to Hanover and Oldenburg, which were still outside, by means of an agreement which was at first kept secret. This proceeding on the part of Prussia was condemned as a usurpation of rights. Thereupon Prussia, on the 11th of November 1851, gave notice that she would leave the Customs· Union on the expiry of the treaty, i.e., on the 1st of January 1854, and at the same time invited the old members to a conference at Berlin on the 1st of April 1852 in order to engage in negotiations about its renewal with the inclusion of Hanover and Oldenburg.

There followed at once a counterstroke by Austria. The latter had in 1850, under the guidance of her very competent minister of commerce, abolished all customs duties between her separate provinces and thereby became the largest free-trade area within the Confederation. Now she herself invited to a conference in Vienna on the 1st of January 1852 the states which had been invited to Berlin for the following April. The subject of this conference was to be the complete ' fiscal unification ' between Austria and the rest of Germany, perhaps excluding Prussia. The competition herewith conjured up between Austria and Prussia and the struggle to win to their side and lure away from their opponent the other states in this question of the Customs Union was at the beginning fought out to no small extent in Frankfurt. Here, the two rival states had both strengthened their delegations since the end of 1851 by the appointment of men with expert knowledge of tariffs. With their help the small states were now canvassed. This winning and retaining of the support of adherents in the struggle with a third power was an occupation both congenial to Bismarck's tastes and suited to his capacities in handling men. It was his task to thwart the Vienna ' fiscal unification ' and to prepare the smaller states for the new Customs Union to be proposed in Berlin. He tried to influence the Press of these states ; he had pamphlets distributed ; he formed relations with influential financiers friendly to Prussia ; and he secured the presentation of petitions in the parliaments of the smaller states. He worked up in himself a belief in an impending second Olmütz, an Olmütz which was now quite divested of the halo lent by sympathy with Austria. He now no longer concealed, even from Manteuffel, his sharp opposition to Austria, and gave the following harsh answer to Count Thun :

A Prussia which, as he [Thun] expressed himself, would ' renounce the heritage of Frederick the Great ' in order to devote herself to her true providential mission as Imperial Arch-Chamberlain is not to be found in Europe. Before I advise my government to adopt such a policy, I should rather be obliged to seek a decision with the sword.

That the Vienna conference in January did not come to a resolution, as Austria had wished, Bismarck could ascribe to his own activity at Frankfurt. The Berlin conference had just assembled when the death of Schwarzenberg at the beginning of April brought about a vital change in the situation. Gerlach expressed the view that the new Austrian foreign minister, Count Buol, would not be easier to deal with than his predecessor had been. But Bismarck seems already to have been convinced that Buol lacked the energy and ruthlessness of Schwarzenberg. He therefore believed that his policy of opposition adopted at Frankfurt would from now on attain a greater success, and that the economic unity of the Customs Union would develop more and more into a unified political front directed against Austria, the connexion between the member states at the same time growing into a political alliance. We may regard it as a recognition of this attitude on the part of the fickle Prussian King when he summoned Bismarck to Potsdam at the end of May 1852 and offered him the place of the sick Prussian ambassador in Vienna, first as his deputy and later as his successor. A very personal letter to the Emperor, written in the King's own hand and reproduced by Bismarck in his *Reflections and Reminiscences*, designated the latter as belonging to a ' knightly family which has continued in our Marches longer than my own House ' and appraises his qualities of ' free knightly obedience and unrelenting opposition to the revolution '. In Frankfurt he had ' with keen and clear sight prevented what the smaller states, for ever flirting with the idea of a Rhine League, with delight call the difference between Austria and Prussia '. This obviously meant that Bismarck had depicted these states as a wedge to force Austria and Prussia apart and had claimed the merit of having ' always acted correctly towards Austria in their presence '. Finally, the letter says concerning Bismarck's diplomatic mission in Vienna that he is in a position to explain the King's ' conception and treatment of the Customs Union affair '.

Herewith the main rôle in the affair of the Customs Union was transferred from the Frankfurt Federal Diet and the Berlin conference to the person of Bismarck himself on his way to Vienna. He had now the opportunity of reviewing the situation in the heart of the hostile camp and of crowning his Frankfurt policy by manœuvring his opponents into a recognition of the united front to be formed by Prussia in the matter of the Customs Union. Bismarck, remembering Schwarzenberg's rudeness to Manteuffel in Olmütz and Dresden, was gratified about his personal reception at the Austrian court, where he found that ' externally I was received with more honour than I could expect '. At the time, however, the Emperor was not himself in Vienna, but had temporarily moved his quarters to Hungary, and Bismarck intended after his audience with the new foreign minister, Buol, to go on at once to Budapest. But Buol objected to this because, as Bismarck reported to Berlin, he ' did not wish that I should come into relation with the Emperor without him being present or having prepared the way '. The Austrian minister ' still felt himself but little familiar with the business ', and therefore showed nervousness ' both in making decisions and in watching over the intercourse of others with the Emperor '. So Bismarck had to spend a fortnight in Vienna before he could obtain an audience with the Emperor. These weeks he employed in pursuing his business transactions and reconnoitring the enemies' forces and their movements. But the Prussian policy with which Bismarck had expressly identified himself : no admission of Austria to the Customs Union, first the conclusion of a new Union, then only a trade agreement with Austria, found no response in those quarters. Even before his audience with the Emperor Bismarck had been driven to the conviction that his mission would be ' without success '. In these days he wrote to his wife in exasperation : ' I find myself superfluous here. The people here either feel no need to come to an agreement with us, or suppose that we are in a greater need of an agreement than they. This will be a bad setback for relations between us.' Bismarck was obviously enraged because his opponents in Vienna were concerned with the defence of their own interests and refused to surrender themselves to his ' irresistible ' art of persuasion.

At the only audience that Bismarck had with the Emperor—in the absence of Buol—he had to learn that, while the monarch wished for friendly relations between the two sovereigns and states, he was completely on the side of his minister in the matter of the Customs Union. To this audience we also owe an attractive picture of the young Emperor, Francis Joseph. In a letter to Gerlach, Bismarck said : ' The young ruler of this country has made a very agreeable impression on me : the fire of a twenty-year-old, coupled with the dignity and decision of ripe age, beautiful eyes, particularly when animated, and a winningly frank expression, especially when he smiles.' This was the man whose life and work Bismarck a few years later set himself to wreck. There followed a few days of festivity in Budapest and its neighbourhood, of which Bismarck sent his wife charming and colourful descriptions. He depicts the view from his room in the Imperial Palace in Pest far into the endless Hungarian plains. He gives an account of a popular feast in front of the court in the mountains near Pest. Next to him on one side there sat ' the white-haired archbishop of Gran in black silk gown with a red hood, on the other side a very elegant cavalry general, the Prince of Liechtenstein '. There followed a lonely journey over the boundless steppes in a low haycart with three galloping native horses and an escort of Uhlans.

After his return to Vienna Bismarck had his farewell meeting with Buol, where the failure of his Vienna mission—and thereby of a good part of his former political activity in Frankfurt—was emphatically underlined by the words of Buol: ' Austria must make a political question of her exclusion from the Customs Union, and must break it rather than admit that it can be secured without her.' In Vienna it was clearly seen then that the question of the Customs Union involved a challenge by the political might of Prussia, and it was resolved to take up the challenge in this sense. For the rest, those in the Austrian capital showed that they had no further need for Bismarck. Buol let him know that Count Thun was reproaching him bitterly for keeping Bismarck away from Frankfurt. Therewith this interlude had come to an end, and Bismarck for ever lost his desire for the Vienna post. When the King later on referred to it again, he replied that the ' aversion of the Austrian court ' to him forbade him from going there voluntarily. That this personal experience was not quite without influence on Bismarck's future political attitude towards Austria is likely considering the way in which objective and personal motives combined to intensify each other in his politics.

After his return to Frankfurt, Bismarck made every effort to influence the negotiations at Berlin about the Customs Union in such a way as to lead to a political combination of the smaller states against Austria under the leadership of Prussia. At the Berlin conference meanwhile the attitude of Austria had had its effect on the south German states. In September they held a conference at Munich and there agreed on a reserved attitude towards Prussia. In November, even Hanover began to hesitate as to whether she should adhere to the treaty of the previous September. Also foreign politics outside Germany made Prussia more inclined to an understanding. So she gave in, and in opposition to the views advocated by Bismarck, without waiting for the renewal of the Customs Union treaty, she concluded a commercial treaty with Austria, under conditions much more favourable to the latter than had originally been anticipated (19th February 1853). This treaty even envisaged a ' fiscal unification ' with Austria after a six years' trial of the commercial treaty. Only two months later Prussia succeeded in renewing the Customs Union with the smaller states. The ' bad setback ' prophesied by Bismarck thus actually took place ; but it was not Austria, at least from Bismarck's standpoint of power politics, but Prussia which suffered. Prussia had now, in spite of Bismarck's activities in Frankfurt and Vienna, again moved towards the ' Olmütz dirt '.

Thus Bismarck's intervention in Vienna in the politics of the Customs Union had failed. In his relation to his superior, Manteuffel, the latent tension gave place to an ' alienation ', as Bismarck puts it, and even to open opposition. As so often in Bismarck's relations, personal causes of friction and objective differences of opinion go hand in hand. Bismarck relates that he had expressed in private in Vienna the intention of ' seeing the world ' as ambassador for ten years, then being minister for another ten years, then thinking over his experiences on his estate. This utterance was reported to Manteuffel in such a way as to make it seem ' that I was working to bring about his downfall '. In this form his words had attracted the attention of wider circles and in particular had come to the ears of the King and of Gerlach. Bismarck made every effort to take the edge off the rumour. The King could be convinced without difficulty. Manteuffel himself replied to Bismarck's detailed defence with characteristic objectivity : ' I have never believed in this silly gossip.' To Gerlach, however, who had apparently taken the words at their face value, Bismarck is very explicit, insisting that he would not wish to change positions with Manteuffel : ' My life here in Frankfurt is like paradise. This mixture of Junkerdom, parliament, and idle quarrels in the Federal Diet pleases me.' The diplomat Bismarck thus knew how to sweep away with a gesture of superior indifference the misfortune that had befallen him in regard to the circumstances of the Customs Union and his personal relation to his superior.

However, hardly three months before this affair Bismarck had proved that as parliamentarian he was just as passionate and unrestrained as in 1847. At the special request of the King he had made repeated use of his membership to the Landtag, which had fallen to him in October 1851. He spoke less frequently than in former sessions, but when he did speak he displayed his old temperament. Again he ' hurled the sharpest of his wordy arrows against the great cities as carriers of the poison of revolution '. Another of his speeches was concerned with the defence of a few items in the military budget against his former opponent, Georg von Vincke. The battle of the two fighting cocks quickly descended on personalities, and Vincke, referring to the episode in the Military Commission of the Federal Diet, let fall the remark that he withdrew the description of Bismarck as ' distinguished diplomat ', since ' all that I know of his diplomatic achievements is limited to his lighted cigar '. This attack, involving the misuse of a remark dropped in conversation, constituted for Bismarck the occasion for a challenge to a duel with pistols. He reported to his mother-in-law that it was agreed to reduce the number of shots from three to one and that both duellists had missed.

God forgive me for my grave sin [he added] in that I did not recognize his grace, but I cannot deny that when I looked through the smoke and saw my opponent still standing, I was prevented from joining in the general jubilation by a feeling of dissatisfaction. The reduction of the number of shots to be fired was distasteful to me, and I should have gladly continued the fight.

This episode was practically the end of Bismarck's activities as deputy. In the subsequent proceedings in the Chamber he kept himself in the background even more than before. On the termination of the session of the Second Chamber he did not stand again in the new election in the autumn of 1852 and in the autumn of 1854 he was called to the Prussian First Chamber, which the King, making use of Bismarck's influence on the conservative party, had converted into a 'House of Lords', exclusively appointed by the King. But Bismarck never spoke there.

At the court and in parliament Bismarck, in the spring of 1852, encountered a new party group, called Bethmann-Hollweg's after its leader, or *Wochenblatt* party after its newspaper. 'The Bethmann-Hollweg faction of climbers', they were later called by Bismarck, who was in opposition to them, not only on principle, but much more personally. The members of the party were nearly as much aristocratic Prussian diehards as were Manteuffel and Bismarck themselves, but they had a touch of liberalism and German nationalism, though in not so large a measure as that which Radowitz had defended. In particular, they did not subscribe to the policy of absolute submission to the will of Austria in the fashion of Manteuffel. Consequently they sometimes won the ear of the King. Above all, Prince William, who could not overcome the memory of Olmütz, was to a considerable extent drawn to them. The organ of the party, the *Preussische Wochenblatt*, was financed by the members of the party, some of whom were very wealthy. Bethmann-Hollweg, a renowned jurist, was no doubt in earnest with his political convictions; he was a sincere follower of the noble-minded original defenders of the German *Kulturstaat*; but some of the most influential members opposed Manteuffel on personal grounds, either because they had not been allowed the position in politics which they thought their due, or because they hoped that the fall of Manteuffel would at once give them such a position. One of the most gifted of these was Count Robert von der Goltz. In these circles it was naturally known, not only what an independent attitude Bismarck had assumed towards Austria, but also how difficult his relations were with Manteuffel. The *Wochenblatt* party therefore sought contact with Bismarck; the latter, to whom their relation to the heir of the throne was not unknown, showed himself more accommodating than might have been expected towards these

' climbers '. Now Goltz took the lead and invited Bismarck to co-operate in overthrowing Manteuffel. That Bismarck as much as listened to this invitation is not easily reconciled with his ' strict concept of the duty of service '. Yet he rejected it, giving as his reason that he ' had accepted the post in Frankfurt with the full confidence of Manteuffel, and that I should not regard it as honourable to use my relation to the King to bring about the overthrow of Manteuffel, as long as the latter does not force me to break with him ', an answer which obviously was not intended to burn the bridges, especially the bridge connecting him with Prince William.

What dominated Bismarck at that time were the antitheses: Prussia *v.* Austria, dynasty *v.* democracy. He was in favour of the Confederation having power in trifling matters (' tripe '), but hostile to it when he scented an attack on the independence of Prussia. When the Confederation issued general regulations against the misuse of the Press, his only concern was, as a biographer puts it, ' that his Prussia should not come under Austrian tutelage '. When general measures for the supervision and restriction of the clubs were debated, he advised his government to accept the law in the Diet, but ' not to publish it in Prussia '. When it was a question of the Confederation helping the smaller states ' to do away with their revolutionary ' constitutions, Bismarck was, in the case of Lippe-Detmold, concerned mainly with giving ' a turn to the matter which permits the confidential mediation of Prussia '. He allows himself to be personally approached by the King of Hanover as an expert in the question ' how the constitution of 1848 could be revised with the help of the decisions of the Confederation '. The inveterate foe of the Jews advocates emancipation of the Jews in Frankfurt ' as decisively as I have opposed it and will oppose it in Prussia '. In the Frankfurt case he could not support a measure against them because the measure was the work ' only of decided and in some cases passionate opponents of Prussia '. When means for the repair and improvement of the federal fortresses at Ulm and Rastatt were under discussion, Bismarck thus explained his ground for opposing these proposals to Gerlach : ' I regard it in the interests of Germany as a matter much more important than this building of defences that Austria should at least learn to deal with us as we are entitled to demand.' When in a dispute with the Grand-Duke of Hesse-Darmstadt the latter made a demand that Prussia ' should place herself decisively on the soil of German politics ', Bismarck replied : ' I have again observed here that everyone understands under the name " German politics " what he demands for his own advantage from his fellow-members of the Confederation.' Bismarck, however, did not hate and despise only the south German governments, but also the south German men. ' I have never seen ', he contemptuously wrote in April 1853 to Gerlach, 'two men fighting in all the two years I have been here. This cowardice does not prevent the people, who are completely devoid of all inner Christianity and all respect for authority, from sympathizing with the Revolution.' The saying of an Austrian politician of this time : ' Where the specifically Prussian attitude begins, there ends the German sense of moral right ', seems indeed not far removed from the truth.

CHAPTER XII

The Crimean War

The French Revolution of the 24th of February 1848 had unchained the revolutionary March movement in Germany. To the subsequent counter-revolutionary development in Germany there corresponded a similar counter-revolutionary development in France, connected with the name of Louis Napoléon Bonaparte. On the 4th of November 1848 the republican constitution of France was completed, and on the 20th of December Louis Napoléon was elected president with an overwhelming majority by an universal plebiscite. On the same day he took the oath to observe the constitution, but from the first moment he used the great powers possessed by the president to fight parliament to the uttermost. Exactly three years after his election, on the 2nd of December 1851, when Bismarck had just spent half a year in Frankfurt as ambassador, Louis Napoléon broke his oath, dissolved parliament, and suspended the constitution. He secured by a plebiscite, first of the army, then of the whole population, dictatorial powers as president for ten years with the right to issue a new constitution at his own pleasure. By this means he was to become, with the help of a strongly centralized bureaucracy, ' the beneficial driving force of the whole social order ', and on the 2nd of December 1852 he adopted, again after a plebiscite, the title of ' Emperor of the French ', as Napoléon III.

With Napoléon III there appeared a personality on the European political stage who was to be of decisive importance for the further development of Bismarck and for the direction and ends of his political activity. Seven years older than Bismarck, the Frenchman was in mind and character not such a self-assured and elemental person. Together with a marked gentleness and readiness to help others we find in his boyhood signs of hardness and stubborn self-will, so that his mother called him ' a soft yet stubborn fellow '. Compared with Bismarck's imposing and attractive appearance he seemed almost comical with his overheavy body and his short legs, a deficiency of which he was well aware and that influenced the way in which he appeared in public. Also, in his early years he was regarded as clumsy and ungifted. Consequently he was not undisposed to increase the effectiveness of his personality by theatrical display, while Bismarck to achieve his purposes worked himself up to fits of disconcerting frankness. He was no less a lover of his homeland than was the Prussian, yet his love had not the unconditional and natural character of Bismarck's. A close connexion with his country was for Napoléon rather the end than the basis of his will, since he was of Italian stock, had till his fortieth year mostly lived abroad, and had been *putschist* and political prisoner almost all the time he had lived in France. Intellectual interests and practical will did not, as with Bismarck, form with him a compact unity. Mental development became for him an end in itself; practical activity was sometimes preceded by excessively long or irrelevant deliberations, or was actually suppressed by these, so that he was often called a 'dreamer' or 'maker of projects'. He represented a remarkable combination of indecision and obstinacy. Although personally brave, he was not, like Bismarck, the sort of man to take pleasure in the excitements of battle. His relations to women were irregular. They wore him out rather than strengthened him. The personal rather than the social aspect of marriage was predominant with him, which is the reverse of what we find in Bismarck.

Napoléon's political activity was not so much the product of mere expediency as was that of Bismarck ; he indulged somewhat in those 'romantic ideals' to which Bismarck so scornfully opposed 'the state's egoism of a great state'. Before taking up power Napoléon had disclosed his views in a few publications, particularly in the *Idées napoléoniennes* which had appeared ten years before, basing them on definite principles described as carrying on the Bonaparte tradition. They were summed up under the heading 'great interests of civilization', and stood in a remarkable position between that which the German thinkers and poets aimed at as *Kulturstaat* and the practical political ends which Bismarck championed on grounds both of inclination and tradition. Napoléon too defended the legitimate rights of a dynasty, namely that of Bonaparte, and he defended them his whole life long with all his power and even with a kind of faith. Yet he alleged that these rights were not ultimate but were founded on the political will of the people. He was 'Emperor of the French by the Grace of God and the National Will'. He was the prototype of the 'modern democratic national Caesar'. So his aim from the beginning was to see as unity or to form as unity what Bismarck saw in the sharpest opposition, 'the life force of the dynasty' and 'democracy, the will of the people', which for Bismarck was 'in truth the club-law of the barricade'. The democratic and liberal element, the roots of which in the political development of Germany Bismarck had come to see in the *Kulturstaat* so distasteful to him, he saw in the France of Napoléon III as part of the body politic. For Napoléon the unity found its practical expression in his election by an overwhelming majority in a general popular vote. The people, on the other hand, should willingly allow themselves to be managed and guided by the modern Caesar. He, on his part, directed his efforts towards preserving and increasing their favour, without having to grant them any active share in his government. Napoléon regarded as the chief bearers of the national will the proletariat (alienating it from socialism), the army and the clergy. He constructed railways, roads and towns and cultivated land, in order to win the proletariat; he aimed at glory for the army and at an understanding with the pope for the clergy. To an administration supported by the people he sought to unite a strong authoritative type of rule, successful in foreign policy, serving both as ends in themselves and means to each other. As long as Napoléon could keep parliament compliant, maintain prosperity, and gain diplomatic successes, he was the arbiter of Europe. As 'surgeon accoucheur to the ideas of the nineteenth century' (R. Morier) he fought for nationality against autocracy, strove for the adoption of international conferences as a means of avoiding war, and announced as his final aim the '*sainte alliance des peuples*'.

For Bismarck, Napoléon III was the representative of the French spirit, 'the hereditary foe, the eternal, tireless, destructive enemy', which he had from childhood hated and despised. Napoléon was for him also the holder of a political power with which he had to reckon, because it was capable of endangering Prussia, but which was not to be rejected as a possible supporter. Napoléon, as time went on, became for Bismarck the representative of a manner of government which overlapped his own view of the nature of public power and with which he had therefore to reckon. Already in his speech in parliament on the 3rd of December 1850, Bismarck had referred to the danger threatening from the revolutionary president of France. Now, at the end of December 1851, he expressed in a letter to Gerlach his conviction that Napoléon's *coup d'état* would bring the 'dictatorial wielding of the iron sceptre', without which the French people could not be ruled. At this time he was thoroughly opposed to adopting this kind of government for Prussia. Here it is 'primarily embodied in the liberalizing bureaucracy', which he had earlier described as the 'individual bearer of the revolutionary principle'. Passing on to foreign policy, Bismarck declared, 'as Prussian I cannot rejoice' about the *coup d'état*, 'because I now see recovering an enemy who was sick, with the incidental consequence that a frivolous and lying friend, Austria, acquires an increasing insolence from this event. I do not believe that Bonaparte desires war, since war would separate him from his army'. However, Bismarck repeats somebody else's opinion that Louis Napoléon 'does not rank so high in the scale for political judgement that one could expect him always to do what is to his advantage'. Yet Louis Napoléon was preparing to adopt the title of Emperor in the following year with the aid of the slogan: '*L'empire, c'est la paix.*' In another letter to Gerlach Bismarck further develops his anxieties about the international situation. He expected that Austria would 'at some time or other utilize the menace which a friendship between the Bonapartism of Vienna and the Bonapartism of Paris would carry with it in order to put a stop to the mischief occasioned by Prussian rivalry in Germany', a tendency which the semi-official Press of Vienna was showing 'with insolent clarity'. We can see here how in foreign politics, even in his early days at Frankfurt, Bismarck takes a more constructive line than he did with his purely negative attitude in the Berlin interpellations about Poland and Denmark.

In fact, under the influence of bureaucracy, there was to be felt in the Austrian governing circles, an inclination in favour of Louis Napoléon. This was expressed by Schwarzenberg in a memorandum of the 29th December 1851. It described Napoléon as the best mainstay of order in France and counted it to his credit that he had renounced the parliamentary form of government and was thereby helping the monarchical ideal to victory. What on the 2nd of December 1851 at first aroused people's attention was not so much the person or the system of the wielder of power, but rather the fact that he had come into power by means of a *coup d'état*. In a number of smaller German states the governments strongly approved of 'Bonapartism', for this meant to them a support of their desire forcibly to revise in a reactionary sense the constitutions given in 1848. Even in Prussia there were to be found influential persons who greeted the Napoléonic breach of the constitution as the signal for a reactionary revision of the constitution of the 5th of December 1848, going beyond the amendments of 30th May 1849 and of 31st January 1850. This attitude was found not only in the 'court camarilla' surrounding Gerlach, but also inside Manteuffel's Cabinet, and it was conveyed to Bismarck at Frankfurt under the guise of precautions against a threatening revolution. Bismarck had not so long ago been of the opinion that this constitution left 'hardly the barely necessary minimum of those rights without which no government can be carried on at all'. But now, in a report to Manteuffel, he expresses himself quite decisively against a *coup d'état* in Prussia :

Revolts in France or Germany without the participation of the French army [which Bismarck held to be pro-Bonapartist] can only serve the cause of reaction [Bismarck's own side] and would appear to me rather to be desired than to be dreaded. At the peril of being regarded by your Excellency as a constitutional renegade [Bismarck continued], I beg to remark that I do not regard as desirable, let alone necessary, a forcible coup to put aside the constitution. The constitution has, owing to the manner in which it has been developed and interpreted in the last two years, ceased to hamper government. I suppose [he added mockingly] that the alleged spirit of the constitutional system carries with it no obligations for the government.

SAMPLES OF BISMARCK'S HANDWRITING
AT THE AGES OF 30, 45 and 80 RESPECTIVELY

In fact, there was no danger of detecting this ' spirit ' anywhere in Prussian government circles. For example, the government in the summer of 1852 stopped the execution of the liberal law of 1850 concerning municipal self-government in the villages, a law which had put a final end to Bismarck's fight for the right of patriarchal jurisdiction.

What Bismarck had said to Manteuffel shows a decided change in his political tactics in the fight against the main enemies, liberalism and democracy. In this, in addition to the former weapons, aggression and violent threats, others are now recommended : deceit and trickery through the misuse of parliamentary forms against the parliamentary cause. Bismarck's change of outlook was no doubt due to the Frankfurt atmosphere, and to his practical acquaintance with Bonapartism.

While Napoléon III, as representative of a new mode of government, thus was the object of theoretical considerations for Bismarck, Napoléon, as holder of a political power, became for him very soon a practical factor in political action. Bismarck's first contact with him concerned a matter of subordinate importance, the diplomatic recognition of the French imperial regime. At the turn of the year 1852–3, Bismarck, in consequence of a change in the representation of Austria, acted for some time as presiding representative in the Federal Diet. When the states represented in this body had to discuss the recognition of the French Emperor, Bismarck thus had quite a decisive part to take. Common action by the two great Powers, Austria and Prussia, was intended, and they were called upon to represent the whole Confederation in this matter. Bismarck was against any ' overhaste ' which might be interpreted as ' exaggerated anxiety '. But Bavaria and other medium states felt that they were thereby being put in the background and, in order to affirm their sovereignty and because of ' their need to see their relations with the Emperor of the French soon regulated ', they ignored the proceedings of the Great Powers. Thereupon, some of the smaller south German states independently extended their recognition to the French Emperor in somewhat more emphatic form, while the other negotiations were still pending. Bismarck was infuriated against these ' Rhineleaguers '. Now, when he himself had to come forward in the name of the combined forces of the Confederation, he forgot that he had recently acknowledged the idea of German unity only in ' trifling matters '. He very angrily declared that in this way ' there is exhibited deplorably the looseness of the bonds with which in times of peril the German Confederation links together these small states '.

During the celebrations connected with the diplomatic recognition of the new French Empire, at which Bismarck was the central figure, there appeared the first rumours concerning the intended marriage of Napoléon with the Countess Montijo, who was of a rank much lower than that recognized by international custom as suitable for royal marriages. The *Kreuzzeitung* allowed itself a few sorties about this ' declaration of war (i.e., against sacred international customs) in the form of a card announcing a betrothal '. This ' provocation ' by the newspaper, regarded abroad as semi-official, aroused Bismarck to express himself to Manteuffel in a way which shows not only how much his relations to his former favourite paper had relaxed, but also how intensely considerations of foreign politics had taken possession of him. ' I am as far as anyone ', he said, ' from sympathizing with the idea of a French alliance ', but we must not openly give to our opposition to France the stamp of irrevocability '. Austria might ' misuse the situation ' and compel us ' to seek and to buy an alliance ' with herself instead of it being her ' affair to gain and keep our·support. I am convinced that it would be a great misfortune for Prussia if her government entered into an alliance with France. But we must not cut ourselves off from the possibility of choosing this as the lesser of two evils.' The idea of placing Prussia at the fulcrum which should give her the power to decide the balance in a possible conflict between France and Austria now became one of the main features in Bismarck's foreign policy.

The accession of Napoléon did not remain without consequences in the complications of European politics. In fact, Bismarck's doubts as to Napoléon's desire for war were justified, though the Emperor of the French was not so much in earnest with his watchword ' *L'empire, c'est la paix* ', as he was with his desire to keep and strengthen his position. But he well knew that the means most suited for this end, success in foreign policy, were not available without the risk of war. Already at the end of 1852 he began an active policy against Turkey and indirectly against Russia and her interests in Turkey. The Russian Tsar, Nicolas I, the sanguinary suppressor of the constitutional movement in Poland and of the Hungarian efforts for freedom, had in the autumn of 1850 put himself on the side of Austria against Prussia and branded the action of the latter in the German and the Hessian questions as revolutionary. For him the seizure of power by Napoléon meant revolution, and Schwarzenberg's memoir on it had ' disgusted ' him. Napoléon was not unaware that he had in the Tsar an enemy whom he could not hope to win over. His opposition to Nicolas on the Turkish question concerned the protection of the interests of the Christian religion and was therefore by no means a bad start. The dispute had to do with the keys to the holy places in Bethlehem, which the Turkish Sultan had promised first to France, then to the Greek clergy under the protection of Russia. A slight pressure on the part of France was sufficient to induce the Sultan to keep his first promise. This was at Christmas, 1852. Thereupon the Tsar mobilized some troops and spoke to the English ambassador about the 'sick man' who 'should not slip away from us before all necessary arrangements were made'. But England held back and left the first step to France. Yet when the latter's concentration of her fleet in the Aegean Sea failed to hamper the Russian mobilization, England decided on a joint diplomatic step with France and others in the Russo-Turkish dispute in August 1853, the so-called Vienna Note. Both this and a Franco-English naval demonstration in the Dardanelles in favour of Turkey remained without result. There followed the Turkish declaration of war in October 1853, an Anglo-French alliance with Turkey, and the French and English declarations of war on Russia in March 1854. This common military action with England had for the strengthening of Napoléon's European position a significance which went far beyond the particular occasion, lending him a halo of English respectability.

The tension between these three European Great Powers as the clouds of war gathered could not but affect the two remaining, Austria and Prussia. Austria had a common frontier not only with Russia but also with Turkey; she was therefore interested immediately in the 'necessary arrangements' concerning the legacy of the 'sick man', or rather concerning the measures to prevent the disease from ending in death. For such an event was bound to place Austria in an almost insoluble dilemma between the danger of constriction by a much extended Russian frontier and the guilt of violating her obligations of gratitude to Nicolas for his help in the recent dangers from Hungary and Prussia. Thus in the spring of 1853 Austria had already taken up her position in the political events leading up to war. In May a letter from Francis Joseph begging Russia to postpone action, was badly received by Nicolas, who had counted on the unreserved gratitude of Austria. From this time onwards the friendship between Russia and Austria began to weaken. Still in agreement with Napoléon, the favourable relations with whom had continued after Schwarzenberg's death, though with occasional lapses, the Austrians made fresh efforts to prevent war. In the intervention in August 1853, which led to the Vienna Note, Austria as well as Prussia took part. At the same time Austria tried to make her policy more impressive and effective by involving the German Confederation in it.

The Prussian attitude towards the Balkan dispute might well have been even more reserved than the Austrian, since Prussia was without any immediate interest in this affair. In fact, however, political inclinations in Berlin were divided. It was once again clear that, in consequence of the indecisiveness and fickleness of the King, unity of policy was completely lacking. Bonapartists were no longer to be found in government circles, after the proposal made under the influence of the Napoléonic *coup d'état* to bring about a compulsory change of the constitution had come to nothing. But the opponents of Napoléon differed in their attitude. At the extreme wing, now as before, there stood the *Kreuzzeitung*. This paper continued to express its opposition in so venomous a fashion that Bismarck once more took up a stand against it, and even Manteuffel had the paper occasionally ' rectified ' and also confiscated. The aversion of the King towards Napoléon was, though subject to oscillations, very outspoken. ' His Majesty has suddenly become very anti-Napoléon,' wrote Manteuffel once during the period to Bismark. In other respects the King sympathized with Austria and did not wish to spoil relations with Russia, although the latter's ' breach of right ', i.e., of the European peace, angered him. But he hated still more England's alliance with France and Turkey, ' incest with revolution and heathendom '. So he decided in favour of neutrality in the impending war. The influential clique of the *Wochenblatt* party were inclined towards an England allied to France, were opposed to Austria, and saw the time ripe for inflicting retribution on Russia for her anti-Prussian intervention in the days of Olmütz. This view was also championed by Prince William of Prussia, who, by the way, was opposed to Napoléon as a parvenu, and by his liberal wife, Princess Augusta, now more than ever prejudiced against Russia. Of the influential people surrounding the King, the Queen and Leopold von Gerlach in particular were pro-Russian. Manteuffel continued to hold to his compliant policy towards Austria. He was obviously under the influence of Bismarck when he occasionally formulated his policy thus : ' We must not allow ourselves to be taken in tow by Austria and Russia, but let us be sought for, and also found.' This sufficed for Gerlach to call him a Bonapartist.

Bismarck maintained his attitude of mistrust against Austria, but through the change brought about by the appearance of Napoléon this attitude, formerly confined to German questions, came more and more to be connected with European affairs. At the beginning of July 1853 he wrote to Gerlach : ' In relation to Austria I cannot keep myself from suspicion. I am convinced that she is proceeding in no straightforward fashion towards us. She will use us as she needs, without giving anything in return, and then cast us aside.' A fortnight before offering mediation in common with Austria and others by means of the Vienna Note, he wrote officially to Manteuffel : ' I fear that we in the Balkan question are again giving to Austria our fullest, most honourable help, without having the least thanks in return.' Bismarck's positive proposal in the matter was to take position at the point of the balance between France and

Austria in such a way as the international situation at the moment demanded.

An alliance with France, indeed [he wrote to Gerlach], we cannot conclude without being guilty of a certain degree of baseness. But if we can bring Russia to do it, then the mad policy of Vienna might force us to make the third in this monstrous league before Austria did so. Very honourable people have sometimes preferred to escape through a sewer rather than get a thrashing.

As a précis of his exposition he gave the following : ' We must not ourselves be trapped by phrases about " German politics ", which always tell against us, never for us ', and must ' boldly proclaim a specifically Prussian policy '.

In aiming at this goal of his European policy, Bismarck was confined to giving advice. The act of mediation through the Vienna Note was already a first indication that his advice to take up a position of balance was being ignored, since this action implied Prussian interference in the conflict. As regards the second goal of his policy, namely the acquisition of allies within the Confederation, Bismarck's powers went beyond mere advice, since he was ambassador to the Federal Diet. This search for allies now took a new turn in view of possible tension between the France of Napoléon and Austria, a tension hoped for and fanned by Bismarck. ' I knew nothing ', wrote Bismarck about this time to Gerlach, ' that would be better suited to hinder the Rhine-League policy [i.e., the inclination of the smaller German states towards Napoléon] than the thought that Prussia might be brought some time by this policy to come to an understanding with France.' ' Armed neutrality,' he said in a report to Manteuffel about the Balkan complications, ' if possible in combination with other German states, would be a policy corresponding to our interests and a worthy attitude which would give a new élan to our influence in Germany outside Austria.'

Two factors seemed to favour Bismarck's activities among the smaller members of the Confederation, one personal, and one objective. At the beginning of 1853, Herr von Prokesch-Osten arrived in Frankfurt as successor of Count Thun. Bismarck at once made up his mind to be on even worse terms with him, if possible, and to judge him even more adversely than his predecessor Thun. But, what is even more important in this connexion, Bismarck hoped for a similarly unfavourable attitude in the other members of the Federal Diet. Immediately after the appointment of Prokesch, and before he had come into personal contact with him, Bismarck reported officially to Berlin : ' I believe that personal conflicts between the new presiding representative and his colleagues are not to be avoided.' Naturally the conflicts did not fail to occur, least of all with the colleague immediately concerned, Bismarck himself. As early as the end of May he told Manteuffel,

that the ease and facility with which Prokesch makes false, and disputes true, statements exceeds even my high expectations, and finds its completion in the cold-blooded way in which he lets the subject drop as soon as the falsehood is revealed. Where necessary, he covers such a retreat with an outburst of moral indignation or with an attack which is often very personal.

Finally, so Bismarck reports, it came to such a point that he told Prokesch on the occasion of such a charge : ' You have no right to speak to me in this way, and I shall in no wise allow it to happen ' ! It is in fact difficult to believe that these disputes were confined to private encounters between the two men.

Of much greater importance was the objective factor which favoured Bismarck's attempts to win the smaller states. This was the growth of the catholic ultramontane movement within the territory of the Confederation. Bismarck defended the view that this movement supported the Roman Catholic power, Austria, in her opposition to Prussia and to the other Protestant members of the Confederation, and that therefore ' the Protestant governments had to strive to act more in common than before in their policy towards the Roman Church '. Since the time when Bismarck, as a junior government employee in the Rhineland, had let the struggle about the Archbishop Cl. A. von Droste Vischering of Cologne pass by with indifference, he had mainly owing to his clash with Radowitz changed his opinion about the political significance of the Catholic Church for the power of Prussia. In 1851, he learned that a leading south German ultramontane had pronounced the intention : ' We desire to encompass the old Protestant centre in Prussia with a net of Catholic clubs, to secure these fetters by numberless convents and thereby to crush Protestantism and make the Hohenzollerns harmless.' At the end of 1852 Bismarck wrote to Manteuffel : ' The desire for conquest in the Catholic camp will in the long run leave us no alternative to open battle with them.' The immediate occasion for battle was provided by a dispute about the limitations of the powers of the state which had been demanded by the Archbishop of Freiburg in Breisgau. In this struggle the cause of the state was represented by the Grand-Duke of Baden and with him the Duke of Nassau, and the cause of the church by the Bishop von Ketteler of Mainz. Now Bismarck sought, and therefore found, behind the whole affair the desire of Austria to strengthen her political power by a union with the church. ' The partisanship of Austria against Baden rose to such a pitch as to take on the character of a threat,' he reported at the beginning of 1854 to Manteuffel. He spoke of ' ultramontane machinations and the agitation of Austria on their behalf' in different south German states, especially in Nassau. For him personally this conflict was rendered sharper by the fact that he found no help in the High Church inclinations of the King, and had an outspoken opponent even in his friend Gerlach. In bitterness he wrote about the latter to Manteuffel, saying that he could not understand, ' how someone who is undoubtedly inspired by a lofty patriotism can emancipate himself to such an extent from any Prussian way of looking at things '. To Gerlach he defined the connexion between these events and his own struggle in Frankfurt thus : ' In the meetings of the Federal Diet to be a Catholic and to be an enemy of Prussia means the same thing, whether they paint their hatred against us black-yellow [the Austrian colours], French, or democratic.'

Bismarck therefore, with his characteristic tendency to exaggerate the aggressiveness of his adversaries, saw an alliance between the two catholic Powers, Austria and France, as the aim of the ultramontane movement within the Confederation. So his work at the Federal Diet was connected immediately with his efforts in foreign politics to make Prussia the beneficiary in a possible dispute between France and Austria. Thereby his purpose of winning allies among the Protestant members of the Confederation for a settlement of the issues with Austria acquired a more far-reaching significance. As in earlier days this policy had as its basis the economic interests of the members of the Customs Union, so now in its new form it had as its basis the religious controversies among the members of the Confederation. In regard to the new plan for winning allies, Bismarck could not approach directly either Gerlach or the King, so he decided to turn this time to Manteuffel, though even to him he had to express himself with the greatest caution. ' The Prussian government', so he proposes to the latter, should ' provisionally open a correspondence with the other Protestant governments with the object of supplying current mutual information about their relations with Rome ; if in this way a link between all those concerned is once established, this can be used as the basis of further steps '—without saying which steps he had in mind. Even if at the time, he adds, the circumstances of some Protestant members of the Confederation ' put great difficulties in the way of the plan for an allround understanding ', yet the plan goes at least ' quite in the direction in which alone we may expect a healthy development of the internal affairs of Germany, namely by bringing about through voluntary and revocable agreements some understandings founded on actual needs and serving for purposes for which the Confederation is not adequate '. Bismarck hoped that even ' the governments now opposed to it ' would let themselves be won in time, and concludes with the words : ' It should be urgently recommended that the plan itself be established as a goal of our policy to be reached in time and kept unwaveringly in view.'

Meanwhile, the attempt of Austria to make more effective her intervention in the Balkan question through involving the German Confederation began to make itself felt. Prokesch came forward in the Federal Diet with the wish that the question should be debated in a full session. Bismarck opposed this. As an effective means of agitation against the Austrian attempt he insinuated that any warlike move of Austria might involve complications in which her allies, the smaller confederate states, would have to share without having any interest of their own at stake. But Bismarck knew how cautious he had to be in these proceedings, in relation not only to Austria, but also to influential circles in Berlin. Consequently he had now, even more than in regard to the question of the Customs Union and of ultramontane policy, to discuss the winning of allies, not in an open campaign, but in the twilight of semi-secret discussions at the seats of the individual governments, where much could be ventured which would have to avoid the full daylight of the Federal Diet. So in the plenary session of November 1853 Bismarck declared : ' Prussia will continue further to utilize the freedom of decision which she has reserved up to the present, in order to devote all her powers in union with her allies to secure the peace.' To his minister he reported that he wished thereby to prevent Austria ' making the affair look as if she were the managing director of the common firm " Austria and Prussia " and had spoken in this capacity '.

However, Bismarck's policy within the Confederation underwent a change owing to the development of the foreign situation. The declaration of war by France on Russia of March 1854 threw its shadow in advance. Bismarck knew that in Vienna the advocates of a breach with Russia and, if possible, of joint action with France and England were more and more gaining the upper hand. At the turn of 1853–4 various proposals of Russia to reach an understanding were rejected by Austria, and in February 1854 it was decided to draft an ultimatum, demanding from Russia the evacuation of certain occupied Turkish territories near the Austrian frontier. The international dispute of Austria in which Bismarck wanted Prussia to intervene was thus no longer directed against France, but against Russia. Of course, Bismarck was at once ready to connect his own aims with this reversal. He had no interest in the France of Napoléon III as such, but desired to keep her out of the combinations effected by Prussia in her foreign policy. Bismarck had twice before been brought into connexion with Russian politics, though only indirectly, once through his interpellation on the Polish question as member of the Prussian parliament, and secondly through his inclination to the side of Austria, then supported by Russia, in the matter of the Olmütz Minutes. On both occasions it had been made apparent that there was a—quite natural—agreement between Bismarck's wishes and the efforts of Tsar Nicolas I, both being inclined to side with authoritative monarchy against liberalism and democracy. The letter to Gerlach in July 1853 shows that at that time too a combination between Prussia and Russia was much more in accord with Bismarck's wishes than was such a combination with France. It must therefore have seemed to him even more desirable to pursue an anti-Austrian policy in a dispute between Austria and Russia than it did in a dispute between Austria and France.

Circumstances at first seemed to favour Bismarck. In February 1854, when the decision had been made in Vienna to send an ultimatum to Russia, he reported to Berlin the visit of the Russian diplomatic representative to Frankfurt which gave him the impression that ' they will be content if we do not let ourselves be moved by the other side to hostile demonstrations against Russia '. He declared in support of this : ' I do not see what could drive us to do this. We could not direct our efforts against Russia without making ourselves in the same measure dependent on Austria and losing ground in Germany.' Again and again at this time Bismarck issued a warning against ' in any way deliberately increasing the gulf between us and Russia ' and urged the government not to follow the line of Austria in committing herself, but to use the action of Austria for the purpose of what he cautiously described to Berlin as ' a demarcation more favourable for Prussia between the two Powers in Germany '. As the fruit of his soundings in the courts of the smaller states he let Berlin know that their first interest was peace and that they feared that the action of Austria would bring on ' the danger of a war ' and the ' misuse of the strength of Germany for a war not necessary in itself '. A ' sounding ' of a less earnest character in connexion with the imminent Crimean War was communicated by Bismarck to Gerlach about the same time.

> I was just at the club when the news of the recall of the Russian ambassador from Paris arrived [he wrote], and I considered whom I could best frighten thereby. My eye fell on Rothschild. He turned as white as chalk when I gave him the news to read. His first remark was ' If only I had known it this morning ', his second ' Will you do a little business with me to-morrow ? ' I declined his offer in a friendly way, thanking him, and left him to his agitated reflections.

While Bismarck inside and outside the Confederation sought for allies for Prussia in her position as fulcrum in the balance regarding the Balkan disturbances, events were coming to pass in Berlin which were to bring all his Frankfurt plans and enterprises to nothing.

This counter-stroke was the work of the man whom Bismarck had lately made the confidant in his plans, von Manteuffel. A few weeks after the decision to draft an ultimatum against Russia, the Emperor Francis Joseph received in Vienna a letter from Frederick William IV, in which the latter spontaneously offered him an alliance in support of Austria's position in the Balkan question, thus giving him the very thing which Prokesch had worked so hard to obtain against Bismarck in the Federal Diet. Negotiations followed immediately, in the course of which Austria asked for an offensive and defensive alliance but was eventually contented with the renewal of the secret defensive alliance concluded at Dresden on the 16th of May 1851, to join which all the remaining German states were to be invited. Prussia thereby pledged herself to intervene with her diplomatic power on behalf of Austria if Russia should not accept the ultimatum which was to be sent to the Russian government. The conclusion of the treaty followed on the 20th of April 1854, three weeks after the declaration of war on Russia by England and France. To the mind of Frederick William IV, as Bismarck thought, this treaty presented itself as winning Austria for a policy friendly to Russia, and removing her further from the Western Powers. The more clearsighted Leopold von Gerlach, speaking from his russophil attitude, said that the conclusion of the treaty, 'which Manteuffel has brought about, can mean nothing but a lost battle'.

Bismarck, left in uncertainty, but warned by hints from a third party, anticipated evil. Shortly before the conclusion of the agreement with Austria he wrote to Gerlach : ' I am forced to assume that we are letting ourselves be persuaded by Austria to become, together with her, the first members of a new Rhine League, out of cowardice letting ourselves be drawn into action against Russia.' Then ' we shall have once more destroyed the faith of the German Governments in us. If we really break with Russia, then it will only cost the French a friendly word to Russia and all the German Governments will fall into her lap, and we shall be the dupes.' So Bismarck sees in the approaching agreement between Prussia and Austria not only the collapse of his efforts to secure allies within Germany and an independent position for Prussia in foreign affairs, but also the prospect of Prussia being excluded from a Franco-Russian combination. However, some comforting words from Gerlach about the supposed content of the imminent treaty stimulated anew his faculty for devising combinations in foreign politics. He even thought of resuming, at least for a time, his Olmütz attitude, reversing his entire Frankfurt policy. It was the idea of a combination of Prussia, Austria, and the smaller German states as the fulcrum in the European balance, the idea of action together with Austria which ten years later he was again to make a political reality. He expressed pleasure to Gerlach at the thought that 'hand in hand with Austria we can challenge our century'.

But when the news of the treaty with Austria leaked through this prospect was to become very doubtful. Even on the days immediately after its conclusion, Bismarck knew nothing about the content of the treaty and complained to Gerlach that he would only hear of it through the newspapers, 'a summary way of giving their instructions to royal ambassadors'. When he did come to know it he was naturally disappointed. But he received with approval the suggestion of Gerlach 'that in the treaty everything is made dependent on mutual understanding'. He understood Gerlach's reference to the King, who 'now that he had used the help of a servant to make a fool of himself, holds fast to this servant and treats his reasonable friends badly'. Bismarck is very careful in what he says about the treaty to his superior, Manteuffel, with whose help the King had 'made a fool of himself'. He congratulates him on its conclusion and designates it in respect of its content almost in Gerlach's sense as 'an agreement to make an agreement'. He says that it is 'the interpretation' which will be decisive and expresses the wish that Prussia should 'avoid by all means warlike proceedings against Russia' and that the 'Prusso-Austro-German combination of states' will be available as a 'real brake against the premature zeal for war of Austria'. Gerlach he informs that he has 'put a good countenance on' towards the minister, and is more outspoken than towards the latter in insisting on 'an interpretation quite decisively in our sense'.

Bismarck was, however, in no wise inclined to resign himself to the treaty of the 20th of April 1854 and to its interpretation by Manteuffel. Behind the back of the minister he succeeded with the help of Gerlach in arranging an interview with the King. This gave occasion to a 'piqued letter' from Manteuffel who complained that he 'had not heard of the interview before'. Bismarck's object was to win the King by verbal representations for an 'interpretation quite decisively in our sense'. In a letter addressed shortly before to Prince William is to be found the justification which Bismarck gave for this enterprise. In the well-feigned style of the honest man he informs the Prince that his 'programme' is the 'unreserved support of the decisions of His Majesty'. But in the guise of the 'intentions of the All-Highest as far as they have come to my knowledge' there appear now Bismarck's own special intentions, namely 'the adoption in union with the Vienna Cabinet and the German Confederation of as independent a position as possible'.

It was soon seen that Bismarck's assumptions about the 'intentions of the All-Highest' were indeed hasty and incorrect. The talks between him and the King took place between the 12th and

15th of May. Bismarck reports that he proposed to the King 'to raise Prussian policy from its secondary and unworthy position and take up an attitude which would have won us the sympathy and the leadership of the German states who wished to remain with us and through us in independent neutrality'. He made proposals to the King about Prussian manœuvres and troop movements which looked much more like an attempt to change the treaty than an attempt to interpret it. But the King still remained faithful to Manteuffel and his subservient policy towards Austria. He said to Bismarck: 'My dear, that is all very nice, but it is too expensive for me. Such coups de force a man of Napoléon's kind can well make, but not I.' In Vienna Frederick William's feebleness was known and there was no thought, as Gerlach had hoped, of 'making everything dependent on mutual understanding'. Bismarck's idea of an 'agreement to make an agreement' remained unheeded. On the contrary, the Vienna government, six weeks after the conclusion of the defensive alliance, without first communicating their intentions to Prussia or to the other German states, had the ultimatum, demanding the evacuation of the territories near her frontier, delivered to Russia. The Prussian King, however, accepted an invitation from the Emperor Francis Joseph to Teschen, and a week after the despatch of the ultimatum he not only signified to the Emperor his agreement with it, but pledged himself to send a telegram in its support to Petersburg and to act conjointly with Austria in winning to their side the governments of the other German states. These governments had already come part of the way to meet Bismarck's demand in a letter to Gerlach: 'Accession to the treaty [i.e., that of the 20th of April 1854] must be negotiated between the courts, otherwise there will be dirty linen to wash in the Federal Diet'. They had of their own accord separated the negotiations on the question of joining in this treaty from the Federal Diet and had started them at Bamberg. The object of discussion there was just the ultimatum to Russia on the draft of which Austria had decided. But they were anticipated by Austria, when she despatched it to Russia, and by the King of Prussia, when he declared his agreement with it. Again Bismarck was disavowed. This time the refusal was particularly painful for him, for he had expressly declared before the Federal Diet that Prussia ought to 'devote her powers for making peace secure', by which it was understood in general that he wished her to oppose the intervention of Austria in the Balkan crisis. Bismarck, who at this time wrote to Manteuffel about the 'pampered egoism of Austria who has for centuries only too often succeeded in smuggling in her own dynastic interest in the guise of the interests of Germany', now had seen his attempts in support of the dynastic interests of Prussia fail badly for the third time.

Even forty years later Bismarck complained bitterly about the treatment which he had received from the Berlin government :

In Frankfurt, when at the time of the Crimean War the members of the Confederation other than Austria demanded that Prussia should stand for their interests against the violent action of Austria in combination with the Western Powers, I was unable as representative of the Prussian policy to escape the experience of shame and embitterment when I saw how in face of the demands of Austria we sacrificed any policy of our own, abandoned point after point, and, depressed by a sense of inferiority, sought protection in the wake of Austria.

This shame and embitterment felt by Bismarck can well be understood. It is less easy to see why Bismarck co-operated in these efforts to ' seek protection in the wake of Austria ' which were so obnoxious to him, and why after he had failed to carry through his own policy he had no qualms about acting as the representative of a policy which was most profoundly ópposed to his conviction. We do not hear that he made the least attempt to resign his post or even that he ever considered such a move at all.

But it was not as if the only alternative for Bismarck was to withdraw from his post to the independent family life on the land, so often lauded by him. He himself speaks repeatedly of the possibility offered to him of fixing the goals of Prussia's foreign pòlicy as cabinet minister. He, however, did not take the opportunity. He stooped so far as to allow the King whenever the latter had just fallen out with Manteuffel, to ' let him come ever more frequently to Berlin ' as a means of ' intimidating ' Manteuffel, and that he was ever more ' used by the King as a counter in the game against Manteuffel '. For instance he had to make alternative drafts to official letters. Once he was even asked to compose a speech from the throne. It also occurred that an alternative draft of Bismarck was communicated to the German governments as an official document in opposition to the minister in charge, an event which filled Bismarck not with misgivings but with pride. He announces in a mocking air óf assumed indifference that he ' thereby fell externally into the class of those climbers who were striving to bring about the fall of Manteuffel '. But he said emphatically that ' a post as cabinet minister lay at this time altogether outside my wishes '.

Bismarck, moreover, had no hesitation about openly stating the reasons for his unwillingness to take office : ' I was convinced that I could not obtain a position as cabinèt minister that was tolerable for me in relation to the King.' In confessing his motives he goes a step further : ' I myself avoided a responsible position under this lord as far as I could and kept reconciling him with Manteuffel whom I visited in the country for this purpose.' A corresponding offer by Manteuffel to become a colleague of his in the Cabinet was refused by Bismarck in such a fashion as to lead Manteuffel to exclaim: 'He just laughed at me.' If the 'intolerableness' of a ministerial position had been due to an objective or patriotic Prussian point of view, Bismarck would certainly not have continued to work under Manteuffel's leadership, which he regarded as so damaging to Prussian interests, and still less would he have striven to secure the latter's continuance in office. At any rate, he ought to have attempted to make a success of a post as responsible minister. Thus this post was 'intolerable' to him exclusively on account of personal reasons, especially the interests of his personal career. While we must not blame the average official too much if he does not altogether ignore such considerations in making his decisions, it is hard indeed to understand how a man of the type of Bismarck and with so 'strong a sense of subordination and duty' as he said he had, should not be prepared to do anything to avoid having to work against his political and patriotic convictions. Yet Bismarck preferred to be ambassador on behalf of Manteuffel's policy of subservient compliance with Austria and to keep a clenched fist in his pocket, confiding to Gerlach his sharp opposition to the official foreign policy.

The active foreign policy of Austria continued at high pressure after the success in Teschen against Prussia. On the 14th of June the Austrian foreign minister, Buol, concluded an agreement with Turkey about the occupation by Austria of the territories to be evacuated by Russia. At the beginning of July Buol declared that the reply of Russia, half agreeing to the demands of the ultimatum, was inadequate, and asked for the mobilization of Prussian contingents, for which the Prussians in fact thereupon took preparatory measures. Now Russia gave way altogether and the governments of the German states, who now no longer regarded the Austro-Prussian treaty as carrying with it a danger of war, conformed to the wishes of Austria and joined in the treaty. But on the 10th of August there followed a further ultimatum from Austria to Russia. The latter was required on the termination of her military occupation to surrender also her political influence in the Turkish territory formerly occupied by her. This second ultimatum was made particularly offensive to Russia because it was synchronized with similar demands by her military opponents, France and England. Prussia was not taken into her confidence by Austria, but despite this the Prussian King, after being informed of the ultimatum, pressed in Petersburg for its acceptance on the advice of Manteuffel.

Bismarck wrote furiously to Gerlach: 'This is the way in which we have to be treated if someone wants to make a really impudent demand on us.' To Manteuffel he reported the remark of the representative of one of the confederated states that 'he sees the time approaching when the German states will again start a race to conclude separate agreements with France, as Austria has given the first example '. The general attitude of the confederated governments he described to Manteuffel a few days later as that of the ' policy of the Rhine League ': ' If Prussia cannot restrain Austria from war we shall go with Austria and France, as long as their two ways run together, but we shall go with France as soon as she separates herself from Austria.' To the second ultimatum of Austria Russia sent a reply, in form negative, but in fact compliant. At the same time the news of Russian military reverses reached Vienna, and Austria thereupon asked Prussia and the other confederated governments to extend the obligation to armed support which they had undertaken on the 20th of April to cover also this ultimatum. The latter were inclined to give in. Bismarck wrote to Gerlach : ' The only way of taming this *miles gloriosus* [i.e., Austria] is for Prussia to adopt a powerful and menacing attitude towards Austria. Fear and fear again is the only thing that has effect in the government residences from Munich to Bückeburg '. Only ' viciousness and determination ' should guide the Prussian attitude. From Karlsruhe the Prussian representative at the court of Baden wrote : ' Nobody is afraid of us. Our policy since 1848 has done all it can to prevent that.' But Berlin held fast to Manteuffel's policy of compliance with Austria. After half-concessions on the part of Austria regarding a cautious policy towards Russia an agreement was concluded in accordance with the former's wish for the extension of military help to back the new ultimatum. In a letter to Gerlach which expresses embitterment at this weakness, Bismarck says at the end : ' I do not write that sort of dirge to Manteuffel. It cannot help and only makes him vexed.' Austria, however, drew the ultimate conclusion from Prussia's compliance, making an agreement with the Western Powers on the 2nd of December 1854 without informing her. In this it was stipulated that the terms of peace drafted by France and England together with Austria in Vienna should be communicated by these three Powers to Russia, and that they should take joint military action against Russia if she had not accepted the terms by the 31st of December 1854. Only on the 16th of December was this agreement submitted to Prussia with a view to her joining in it.

This then was the reality in which ended the idea of the Prusso-Austro-German combination of states as fulcrum in the European balance, by means of which Prussia was to go ' hand in hand with Austria to challenge our century '. The King confronted the request for participation in the agreement with the Western Powers without knowing what to do. Manteuffel's policy had now brought him to a position in which he seemed certain to be involved in war-like complications, in complete opposition to his wish, expressed at the beginning, to maintain neutrality. For the time he decided on an evasive answer. This gave Bismarck an occasion to praise his superior Manteuffel : ' It warms the cockles of my heart ', he wrote to him, ' to see your Excellency treat the question of our joining the alliance with cool dignity.' He was consequently asked by the minister to express his opinion officially about the question before the final decision had to be made. Bismarck supported the view that without ' vague fears of so-called isolation and of war against the three contracting parties of the 2nd of December we should defend our position as Great Power if necessary against everyone by the most desperate means and efforts '. In fact, the Prussian government rejected the request that they should join in the agreement, and a few weeks later Bismarck was able to persuade the confederated governments to follow the Prussian example.

That this policy alienated Prussia not only from Austria but also from England and in particular from France, without giving her fresh support from a Russia pursued by military misfortune, Bismarck was well aware. But he was also to experience it in his own person, for people already realized abroad that his countermoves were a factor in determining Prussian policy. Buol complained to Manteuffel that Bismarck had ' given his activity the character of hostility towards Austria ', and the French ambassador in Berlin, whom Manteuffel was supposed by Bismarck to have used in order ' to convert him to a Western European policy ', remarked to Bismarck : ' La politique que vous faites va vous conduire à Jéna ', and received from him the reply : ' Pourquoi pas à Leipzig ou à Rossbach ? ', a reply which caused much indignation. With satisfaction Bismarck mentioned the ' praise ' which the King gave him for having made the ' right answer '.

The terms communicated to Russia by the three Powers led neither to peace, nor to military intervention on the part of Austria, but rather to a state of tension between her and the victorious Western Powers. ' Now it was Austria who felt herself isolated and looked for the way back to Prussia and the confederated governments. But Bismarck had by now lost his former inclination to a Prusso-Austro-German combination. His original idea of the fulcrum position for Prussia alone appears again, but now less emphatically. ' The only means of furthering our policy in Germany lies in Austria being convinced that we will let her go to disaster if she continues in her former course. Then she will finally know how to find the way to our door.' Also the plan of winning allies within Germany seemed to him no longer so urgent : ' All voices in Munich and Stuttgart are unanimous in condemning Buol,' he reported to Berlin after a visit to the courts in these towns, ' in Stuttgart as in Munich people are for the moment good Prussians.' But, he adds by way of reservation : 'An eternal unity is not to be achieved with them.' In fact, Bismarck was soon to become aware that also with the favour of the Berlin government for his proposals in foreign policy no 'eternal unity' was to be achieved. In February 1856 the joint peace negotiations with Russia began in Paris without Prussia participating. Prussia was only invited after they had been almost concluded. This time the conduct of Manteuffel no longer 'warmed the cockles of Bismarck's heart', as the former followed the call of Austria and her allies with his old compliance, as if that was just what he had been waiting for. 'How dignified and independent would have been our position', Bismarck exclaimed in indignation, 'if we had not forced ourselves into the Paris Congress in so humiliating a fashion'.

The peace of Paris on the 30th of March 1856, signed on behalf of Russia by the Tsar Alexander II, the successor of Nicolas I who had died a year earlier, now constituted for Bismarck the appropriate occasion for summing up his previous activities in the Federal Diet and his views on European complications. This he did in a memoir to Manteuffel, the content of which he, feigning detachment, described as 'conjectural politics which still belongs to the realm of dreams'. At the centre he put, as already in the letter to Gerlach of July 1853, the combination of Russia and France, but with the accent shifted to the latter, since Napoléon, now at the height of his power, 'has the choice of alliances at his command'. Franco-Russian alliance had to be viewed with care. The inclination of the smaller German states to the Rhine-League policy could not be met by a counterweight within the Confederation. 'The inner rottenness' of the Confederation had been laid bare by the policy of Austria. A Prusso-Austrian alliance was impossible on account of 'mutual political mistrust and military and political jealousy', since Austria was capable of 'any perfidy' against Prussia. Bismarck did not wish 'to bring about the decision between us and Austria', but declared that 'it was not in our power to avoid it'. He told his pro-Austrian superior : 'In not too long a time we shall have to fight for our existence against Austria.' For the present he only declares it 'desirable to show a little more inexpensive friendship towards Napoléon, and to reject every attempt to fasten us gratuitously in the tow of others' (i.e., Austria). Apart from this the supporter of 'inexpensive friendship' now declares himself as an opponent of the 'flagrant ingratitude' of which Russia had accused Austria. He found it 'not only not handsome treatment but not wise treatment'. The former 'pro-Austrian in Berlin' who had now turned to a 'cossack on the Spree who smells of Russian leather', at the same time discloses the place in his heart which had been won by the parvenu Napoléon. So he was able eventually to carry out the attack on Austria not as a merely frontal assault, as he had intended in his early days in the Federal Diet, but rather as a kind of encirclement, backed or tolerated by the whole of Europe.

CHAPTER XIII

The Change of Government in Prussia

Ever since the beginning of his activity at Frankfurt, Bismarck's views on foreign politics had continued to approximate to those of Prince William, in so far as they concerned the handling of the Austrian question raised by the episodes of Erfurt, Olmütz, and Dresden. Like the Prince he now regarded the continuation of the previous policy as incompatible with Prussian interests. The closer contact politically and personally between them found a striking manifestation in a memoir of September 1853 addressed by Bismarck to the Prince. The document indeed cautiously abstains from dealing with any problems of foreign policy, though as regards the problems of internal affairs, which are mentioned, such as the question of municipal self-government, it is very thorough and revealing. For there still remained differences of opinion between these two men about foreign affairs. These concerned in particular the relation of Prussia to the Western Powers and to Russia. About this time the wife of Prince William, Princess Augusta of Sachsen-Weimar, became in increasing measure a factor in Bismarck's thoughts and efforts in foreign affairs. This Princess had spent her youth at the liberal, broad-minded court of her parents, in immediate contact with Goethe and many other poets and thinkers of German idealism. The idea of the *Kulturstaat* as the adequate expression of a national entity and of its foundation on the development of individual liberty constituted the intellectual atmosphere in which she had grown up. Consequently these circles were rather open to the influence of Western European civilization. This was enough to repel Bismarck. He remarked viciously about the Weimar court that ' it was not free from the delusion that a Frenchman, and above all an Englishman, through his nationality and birth, is a more distinguished human being than a German '. Yet he himself in his youth had always sought the society of Englishmen and Americans, and as parliamentarian had spoken of his ' sympathy ' for the English and his disappointment that they ' would not let themselves be loved by us '.

Princess Augusta was of a harsh and ambitious nature. She unwearyingly strove to increase her husband's predilection for England and to alienate him as far as possible from Russia. Bismarck asserts : ' At breakfast the Princess gives her husband a lecture, bringing forward in her support letters and articles in newspapers.' He indeed goes so far as to say that these have ' sometimes been edited for the purpose '. He does not conceal the fact that he has ' occasionally hinted to the Prince that certain letters had been fabricated or amended by Herr von Schleinitz at the instigation of the Princess '. The man referred to was in the service of the Foreign Office. He was a friend of the Prince and Princess and at that time lived in Coblenz in their retinue. Bismarck admits also that these remarks brought him a very sharp reprimand, and in this connexion boasts of the chivalry of the Prince, without considering whether the recklessness of his own action against the Princess was reconcilable with his duty as ' feudal vassal of Brandenburg '. The Prince and Princess were connected with the *Wochenblatt* party, in whose circles at the height of the Crimean War, according to Bismarck, a document was distributed and welcomed which demanded a territorial partition of Russia, while the Prince at this time described Bismarck's predilection for Russia in a private letter as the ' politics of a schoolboy '.

On this issue Bismarck reports a very violent scene with the Prince. The account is very characteristic of Bismarck, whether it is historically true or not. The Prince is said to have asked Bismarck to support a policy which will ' force Russia to make peace ', and in this way ' rescue her as our friend even against her will '. Bismarck gave as his answer that Prussian interests were against a breach with Russia. Whether from ' fear of France ', or as a ' service of love ' towards Austria and England, Prussia must not ' take on the rôle of an Indian vassal Prince '. Bismarck ˙then continues, to quote his actual words : ' My expression wounded the Prince's feelings. With a face red with anger he interrupted me with the words : " There is here no talk at all of vassals and fear." ' We are here for a moment startled to find Bismarck himself admitting that he had made such a daring reply to the successor to the throne. But Bismarck at once reassures the reader : the Prince ' did not break off the interview ; anybody who has once won his confidence and stands in his favour could speak to him very freely from his heart and even become violent '. We encounter again here in Bismarck the carefully observed expression of his feelings, calculated and devised with a view to its effect on the person to whom he was speaking. He regarded the Prince as a decided supporter of the military attitude, and an aristocratic opponent of all democratic government ; he also was convinced that the Prince's Prussianism would never leave him room to understand ' the phrases about the German mission of Prussia and about moral conquests ' in the sense of Frederick William IV. Already as far back as 1848 the Prince had written to Gerlach : ' I knew, and dreamt of, an independent Prussia only, as a Great Power within the European system of states ', and a year later to a friend : ' Who wants to rule Germany, must first conquer her for himself.' This was also the main purport of a memoir of the 19th of March 1850, directed by the Prince to the King. It culminated in the sentence : ' The historical development of Prussia indicates that she is called some time to stand at the head of Germany.' In this the writer relies on ' the star of Prussia, her army and her right '. So since Olmütz, the relation between the two brothers, the King and the heir apparent, was not without friction. Bismarck describes the ' attitude to each other of the courts of Sans-Souci [the seat of the King] and Coblenz [the seat of the Prince] ' as ' a concealed opposition '. Under the influence of fresh political developments this was capable of becoming an open opposition. In connexion with the conclusion of the treaty of alliance of the 20th of April 1854 between Prussia and Austria, Bismarck had the opportunity of intervening in such an open clash as mediator. The Prince, who saw in Prussia's attitude towards Austria a continuation of the hated policy of Olmutz, left Berlin, where he had been visiting, and travelled to south Germany, an action which was regarded as a hidden protest. He is even said to have thought of an open protest in the name of the army. That Bismarck should be given the task of following him on his journey and inducing him to be more compliant shows what confidence he enjoyed at court. But this time he missed the occasion of proving his tested capacity as mediator, for the Prince took a step towards reconciliation on his own initiative. Yet, when half a year later the accession of Prussia to the treaty of the 2nd of December 1854 between Austria and the Western Powers was under consideration, the opposition between the two brothers flared up again, and this time Bismarck was, in fact, able to bring about a reconciliation.

In these years, Bismarck came also nearer to the Prince's political attitude to the Western Powers, though more markedly so in the case of France than in the case of England. Whether it was that Bismarck now thought it possible to bring himself to that ' pitch of baseness ' which was necessary for ' an alliance with France ', or that in view of the present constellation of power in Europe the baseness required no longer seemed so great, Bismarck thought it now the time to approach Napoléon personally, at least with ' acts of friendship which cost nothing '. In the summer of 1855, he made use of an invitation to Paris to visit the Great Exhibition there in order personally to contact the people who ruled the Western Powers. It is remarkable how the courtier in Bismarck no less than the statesman is interested in this visit, as he had also shown himself much concerned in Frankfurt about the treatment of his wife at court. He gives in his *Reflections and Reminiscences* a thorough description of the Paris court customs at a court festivity, and is extraordinarily pleased to find ' that service at court and the education and manners of the court society with us (in Prussia) are of a higher standard than in Paris '. On this occasion he was presented to the English Queen and the Prince Consort, apparently merely as a ceremonial affair which led to no conversation worth mentioning. Bismarck only says that the royal pair had seen in him ' a remarkable but unsympathetic personality ', and that he thought he found in Prince Albert ' a touch of ironical superiority '. He ascribed this to the fact that for the Prince he was ' a reactionary party-man who put himself on the side of Russia in order to carry out an absolutist Junker-policy '.

Very different was the interview at that time with the Emperor Napoléon. The latter was now, ' after the death of Nicolas I " the Emperor " *sans phrase* in Europe '. He was soon to acquire for the Prussian Bismarck a still more immediate significance as sponsor of national unity in Italy, as supporter of Polish nationalism, and as uninvited co-agent in the production of German national unification. The conversation between the two statesmen was concerned with external, and probably also with internal, politics. Bismarck concluded that the Emperor looked on Prussia with goodwill in his plans for the future of Europe. He relates that Napoléon had ' at that time in several conversations let him know in general terms his wish and his purpose for a Franco-Prussian relation of intimacy '. ' Both these neighbouring states ', the Emperor had said, ' which on account of their culture and their institutions stand at the peak of civilization are dependent on one another.' Bismarck added that Napoléon ' had been much more lenient to us for our sins against the politics of Western Europe than had been England and Austria '. About his discussions with the Emperor on internal politics Bismarck tells us nothing. There is no doubt that he saw through ' the secret of the Bonapartist method of government ' on the spot, and so came to know ' how easily a monarchical government can exploit liberal national ideas and parliamentary institutions, in order to strengthen its own power '. It could not escape his observation ' with what a sure hand the Third Napoléon utilized the *coup d'état* ' and how easy it must be ' for a strong nature with a little political skill to make use of the principle of majority rule for the benefit of the government '. When he saw in France how one could outvote the liberals in the towns with the help of the conservative country people, and what successes could be attained through the influence of, for example, priests on the voting, the question of universal suffrage may have lost some of its horrors. That problems of this kind were discussed at this or at a later meeting is more than probable. At any rate, Napoléon, a few years later, had ' let a proposal be made in Berlin for healing the inner sickness (of Prussia) by means of universal suffrage'. He also, when this was introduced in the North German Confederacy in 1866, expressed officially his pleasure, saying that 'henceforward the two countries would obey the same political system'.

Bismarck was well aware that his personal rapprochement with Napoléon was suspected in Berlin as Bonapartism. From this point of view it is of interest how he represented his new friend to the King. He described him, according to his own account, as an 'intelligent and amiable man', but one who is 'not so clever as the world estimates him to be'. Against the view that Napoléon was 'a kind of *génie du mal* who is always only thinking how he can cause trouble in the world', Bismarck puts forward the view that the 'Emperor is glad if he can enjoy something good in peace, his understanding is over-valued at the expense of his heart. He has an uncommonly large fund of thankfulness for every service rendered him.' The King referred with irony to Bismarck's view that Napoléon's 'heart was better than his head'. There is no doubt at all that these words do not express fully Bismarck's view on Napoléon. We may assume that Bismarck in this case was particularly glad to yield to his inclination towards contemptuous judgements, since the person under review now suffered from the stigmata of being French and a revolutionary, but still had statesmanlike qualities and ideas to which Bismarck could not deny recognition. At the same time Bismarck took away by this means any practical political significance which might attach to his relations with Napoléon in the eyes of the Berlin court. But there was indeed quite an element of truth in Bismarck's judgement. Napoléon's softness of heart and readiness to help, already mentioned by his mother, which Bismarck's shrewd insight into the human heart at once discovered, were very soon to be utilized by the ironically critical King.

The Swiss canton Neuf-Châtel was at the same time a principality under the Prussian crown and was as such the only non-republican member of the Swiss Confederation. In the year 1848 the canton had, by a bloodless revolution, thrown off the hardly perceptible royal yoke. On the 3rd of September 1856 there was an attempted royalist counter-revolution, the only event in which was the arrest of the ringleaders under the charge of high treason. The King took an altogether unreasonably serious view of the matter, one of the signs of his approaching mental derangement. Not only did he feel himself responsible for the fate of his supporters at Neuf-Châtel, but he also saw in the event a matter of principle, a case of having to settle issues with the revolution. On the other hand, he could not make up his mind to accept the condition laid down for the release of his adherents, namely that he should renounce his rights over the principality. Yet to fight for them he would have had to send troops through the sovereign states of south Germany, which was bound to lead to difficulties. Then the King may have thought of Bismarck's account of Napoléon's character, and the Monarch by the Grace of God approached the Son of the Revolution in a personal letter, asking him to act as a mediator. Napoléon at once started acting in accordance with this wish, but a first note to the Swiss Confederation remained without effect. So the matter came before the Diet at Frankfurt, and Bismarck had to deal with the question of sending Prussian troops through south German territory. He had now an opportunity of proving his assertion to Gerlach that an understanding between Prussia and France hindered the policy of the Rhine League of the smaller states against Prussia. The readiness of Napoléon to help had indeed a wonderful effect. The right to march through was granted against the vote of Austria. Bismarck was very proud of this testimonial to his political keensightedness. That he had expelled Satan (the Rhine League politics of the small states) by means of Beelzebub (the Rhine League politics of Prussia) did not disquiet him. On the contrary he wrote full of satisfaction to Berlin, ascribing his success expressly ' to the opinion that our relations with France have lately become more friendly '. Nevertheless, Switzerland did not give in. It was necessary not only that Prussia should prepare for a march to the Swiss border, but further that Napoléon should renew his intervention in the form of an official warning to Switzerland before the Swiss government could be induced to release the royalist offenders and sit down with Prussia at the conference table in Paris.

At this Paris Conference in the spring of 1857 Prussia was represented by her ambassador there, but Bismarck attended as ' a holiday traveller for pleasure '. He tried to bring the exaggerated demands of the King into accord with what was attainable and so effected an agreement with Switzerland in which the King renounced his rights to the principality. At the same time Bismarck was concerned to continue and deepen his personal contacts with the French Emperor. As regards what was said about questions of internal politics, Bismarck only informed Manteuffel that the Emperor had shown much interest in the ' inner constitution ' and the ' internal condition ' of Prussia. We learn more of the discussions about foreign affairs. In particular they talked about what one might call a Prussian Rhine League policy, and indeed in such a fashion that Bismarck thought it right to tell Manteuffel nothing at all about what was said, and Gerlach only 'verbally. The Emperor came to the point of speaking about a project to extend French territory by means of a future war. This he sought essentially—apart from '*une petite rectification des frontières*'—not in an easterly direction, i.e., on the Rhine, but in a southerly direction, towards the Mediterranean. He did not think of making the latter exactly a French lake, '*mais à peu près*'. As a fruit of a coming war he anticipated a relation of intimacy and dependence between Italy and France; and now he continued, making more precise his hints of the summer of 1855: it was part of his project that Prussia should not oppose him; Prussia and France were interdependent; he regarded it as a mistake that Prussia, in 1806, had not taken the same attitude to Napoléon I as had the other German states, i.e., had not joined the Rhine League. It was desirable that Prussia should be consolidated by the addition of Hanover and Schleswig-Holstein. Above all, he wished to make sure of the neutrality of Prussia in view of the possibility that he might be involved in war with Austria on account of Italy.—This was then the other side of Napoléon's policy of defending the rights of nationality against the claims of autocracy.

Many of these suggestions could not possibly have satisfied Bismarck, whereas others indicate a perfect understanding of the latter's aims. The Emperor's adaptability appears to us, however, by comparison with Bismarck's insight into the human heart as a weak subjection to the other. At any rate, in one point Napoléon was right, namely in his belief that Bismarck wanted Prussia to be neutral in a French conflict with Austria. This policy would enable Prussia to hold the balance of power between Austria and France, and so exercise her free choice in determining her relation to these two countries. But just because there were now indications of the approaching realization of this project, caution was especially necessary in respect of Berlin. Bismarck certainly had still in mind the words of the King: 'My dear, that is all very nice, but it is too expensive for me.' Thus the King had only in part accepted Bismarck's turning to a policy of a better understanding with France; the latter could reckon on nothing but opposition from the extreme reactionary, one-sidedly Russophil camarilla around the King and their newspaper, the *Kreuzzeitung*, whose close connexion with Bismarck had ceased some time before. He again stirred up Manteuffel against the newspaper which had launched gross attacks, when the King addressed the cousin of the French Emperor, Jerome Napoléon, then on a visit to him, as the member of an 'exalted house' and as belonging to 'a great nation friendly to Prussia'.

Bismarck settled accounts with the camarilla group not least in the person of their leader, Leopold von Gerlach. The latter became more and more touchy in face of Bismarck's growing political independence. It was not enough that Bismarck begged Gerlach, 'do not regard me as a Bonapartist', and assured him that 'the man does not overpower me in the least '. Bismarck was bound to show his hand more clearly to him than to the King. The dispute between the two is of particular interest because it reveals how very much the decisive factor in Bismarck's relation to the state is constituted now as before by expediency and sentiment, and how theoretical considerations about the state continue to be indifferent to him. A very intelligent liberal politician, whose over-readiness to help was described by Bismarck as ' Jewish cheek ', was driven to make the appropriate remark : ' Bismarck sees and feels as a categorical imperative what seems to him to be useful at the time.' To a charge made by Gerlach that in his attitude to Napoléon he was ' sacrificing ' a principle, he, the champion of *Realpolitik*, said that his accuser was ' ignoring realities '.

If you mean, however, by this principle [he added] a principle to be applied to France and her legitimacy, I certainly admit, that I subordinate it completely to my specifically Prussian patriotism. France, irrespective of the person who happens to be at her head, counts for me only as a pawn, though one we cannot ignore, on the chessboard of politics, in which it is my profession to serve only my King and my country. The standard for my conduct towards foreign governments I derive only from the harmfulness or usefulness for Prussia which I ascribe to it.

Thus the only principle of which we were in a position to speak up to the present, ' the principle of the fight against the revolution ', is no longer adhered to. He expressly declares it impossible to ' carry it through in politics in such a way that it constitutes so to speak the only trump-card in the game, in which the lowest card trumps the highest of any other suit '. Consequently it seemed to him ' neither sinful nor dishonourable to enter into closer relations with the recognized sovereign of an important land, if the course of politics involves it. That this connexion is in itself something desirable I do not say, but only that to take any other chance would be a worse risk '. The Franco-Russian rapprochement, to which he again and again calls attention, meant for him yet another inducement to ' accept France's suit ', i.e.,. soon to come to an understanding with her. For in that way the danger that Prussia as the ' third party ' might subsequently have to seek admission to the alliance after it had been already concluded, would ' perhaps be averted ' or at least ' modified in its effects '.

That the man whose horizon thus expanded in proportion to the complications of European politics should lose his interest in the affairs of the Federal Diet is quite understandable. He no longer continued to carry on the search for allies among the smaller states and the attempt thus to undermine from within the German Confederation which he had formerly conducted with such zeal. ' The small states will never learn to trust us ', he wrote in June 1857 to

Manteuffel. Full of scorn he notes that the confederate Princes will not undertake anything on behalf of Prussia 'if the superior power is not on her side'. An improvement in the position of Prussia in the Confederation he expects only from 'fear', as for instance from the fear 'instilled in them by ostensible signs of our good relations with France'. In any case he now repudiates expressly the policy of 'laying our foundations in the sand of the German Confederation and quietly awaiting their collapse'. Also, in relation to what he called 'the German material questions', he is now in favour of the greatest reserve on the part of Prussia. When in the summer of 1856 the very active and energetic Prime Minister of Saxony, von Beust, to whom Bismarck cherished a special personal aversion, introduced a proposal to reform the Confederation by assimilating the constitutions of the different states with the intention of counteracting that 'looseness of the union' so deplored by Bismarck in the days when he was deputy president, Bismarck advised Berlin to meet the situation with a strict negative. He described the proposal as 'promoting the efforts to force Prussia out of the course of her natural development under the pretext of unifying Germany and to draw her on to the path pursued by the imperial Austrian state'.

When about the same time it was proposed to station an Austrian garrison in the confederate fortress of Rastatt in Baden, Bismarck opposed this on the ground 'that Austria, being supported by the Catholic sympathies of the Baden population, is in any case making her position in the land a completely dominant one'. When after prolonged discussions Austria made a compromise proposal, Bismarck thus expressed himself to Manteuffel: 'Austria can hardly have regarded us as so weak or silly as to expect our immediate assent. But she is trying to find out how far our courage and our wisdom go, and whether we cannot by browbeating, persuasion by third parties, and intimidation be made cheap for Austrian ends.'

A memoir sent in March 1858 to Prince William of Prussia, and also put at the disposal of the Prime Minister, sums up practically everything that Bismarck had learned in the course of his activities at Frankfurt about the German problem of Prussia. This 'Booklet of Herr von Bismarck' bore the title *Some Remarks on Prussia's Attitude to the Confederation*. The question raised here now sounds direct and unambiguous. It is whether and how it is possible ' to deprive Austria of her dominating influence'. 'Prussia's German mission' ceases to be a 'phrase' or a trifling matter and becomes a reality of the highest importance. For there is now for Bismarck 'nothing more German than the development of the particular interests of Prussia rightly understood' or, as he expresses it in his *Reflections and Reminiscences*: 'Let us from the Prussian standpoint look on the leadership of Prussia, or, from a national standpoint, on the unification of Germany, as the chief thing; the two ends coincide.' For this reason Prussia should 'help in a more rigid centralization of the relations between the confederate states only in so far as she can win the leadership of the Confederation '. But this leadership will not fall to her lot as long as the decisions of the Confederation 'depend only on the German Princes and their ministers '. Prussia's internal politics must be subordinated to the aim of enabling her to win again this leading position. 'The power of Prussia as a whole must not be broken by friction within.' To bring this about she need not rely onesidedly on the power of the government. For the 'security that the King of Prussia will still remain master in the land even if the trained standing army were withdrawn' is unique on the continent. Therefore the Prussian 'government may without danger allow parliament more elbow-room even in purely political questions than before '. But the presupposition of this is ' readiness to meet the government with loyalty and self-sacrifice' based on the success of the country in 'gaining an independent and respected position in foreign affairs '.

The similarity of these thoughts with the political purposes of Napoléon is striking. This applies not only to the function, though subordinate, which was to be allowed parliament in order to win it to the side of the rulers, but quite generally to the replacement of Bismarck's stubbornly defended antithesis between dynasty and ' barricade ' by a clear affirmation of some kind of synthesis between them. This synthesis as in the case of Napoléon was based on opportunism and was thus quite opposite to the scorned ' spirit of the constitutional system' and to the unity of the *Kulturstaat* founded on the postulates of idealism. The principle that foreign policy should have the primacy over internal policy was here defended by him with all emphasis, a problem the significance of which the legal shape of the German Confederation had specially impressed upon him. He hints at the belief that the powerful position of the state in external affairs constitutes an important binding link for the people by the side of the uniting force of the dynasty. The antithesis between the conquest of Germany by Prussia and the amalgamation of Prussia with Germany is effaced, but great emphasis is laid on Prussia's antagonism to her political opponent, Austria. Austria was almost entirely losing her significance as ally against liberalism and democracy now that Prussia's opposition to these was to diminish in intensity.

Bismarck's increasing interest in the general political situation in Europe finds expression also in his journeys. These journeys combine, as the one to Paris had already done, the objects of a holidaymaker with those of a politician who wants to study European politics at its different focal points, personally to learn the methods in use, and to come into immediate relation with the men at the helm. In August 1857 he visited one of these focal points, Denmark. He was received in the capital by the King, and discussed the 'Danish Question' with the entourage of the latter. He did not, however, omit to visit the museums, still less to seek enjoyment in hunting in the neighbourhood of Copenhagen. He lived, so he told his wife,

in a white castle, situated high up on a peninsula surrounded by a great lake. Through the window I look into thick ivy which allows me some glimpses through it on to the water and the hills beyond. Yesterday we stalked stags. After dinner we are going on the lake and will perhaps shoot wild duck.

The Danish visit was followed by one to Sweden. Here also he was invited to hunt. To Manteuffel he reported that 'some people at the summit of the political world of the North will be there. I shall therefore have plenty of opportunity for obtaining information.' To his wife he wrote of his stay in the country: 'High heather mingled with short grass and bog, at times impenetrably thick with birches, juniper, firs, beeches, oaks, alders, at others bare waste, only sparsely wooded, smelling of wild rosemary and resin.' In September, there followed a first visit to Russia, in the shape of a trip to Courland. But before Bismarck, in the capacity of politician and tourist, could spend a longer period in Russia, he was summoned to Berlin by important political events.

We have already seen in connexion with the Neuf-Châtel dispute how Frederick William's lack of judgement and resolution had reached an abnormal pitch. In fact his behaviour in that crisis was a sign of approaching insanity. In the summer of 1857 Frederick William had two apoplectic strokes in quick succession. The mental disturbance setting in at the beginning of October made it impossible any longer to entrust affairs of state to him. That they should now be the responsibility of Prince William of Prussia resulted as a matter of course from the latter's legal position as heir apparent. Thus there came into power a man who, on account of the influence of his wife, was suspected in some quarters of occasional fits of constitutionalism and sympathy with the Western Powers. However, he was also regarded as exclusively interested in the army, without any statesmanlike qualities, and as particularly difficult to influence and stubborn in his decisions. Naturally, besides the *Wochenblatt* party, the whole entourage of the King from his wife to the prime minister von Manteuffel, including the camarilla with General von Gerlach at its head, however much they differed in regard to other political questions, were unanimously against him.

They all were of the view that a form of appointment for the vice-gerent must be chosen which would prejudice the position of the King as little as might be and leave it possible for his authority to be restored at any time. Through a royal decree of the 23rd of October 1857 the Prince of Prussia, instead of being appointed regent, was made deputy for the King for three months only. His tenure of the office was prolonged successively for three more periods of three months each. Before the end of the last period, in the autumn of 1858, a serious attempt, so Bismarck reports, was made with the help of the Queen to obtain the signature of the King to a letter to his brother, in which he declared himself well enough to take on power again. The government was then, on the authority of the King's signature, to be carried on by members of the court.

Bismarck already opposed the decision of the 23rd of October 1857 in a letter to Gerlach, which remained unanswered. ' A long continuance of this provisional state of affairs is a misfortune for the country,' he exclaimed. He then gave an accurate description of what it was that the camarilla wished to prevent and he to bring about. ' A lively participation in affairs cannot be expected from the Prince as long as he is not sure that he is the established ruler.' From this point onwards the political co-operation of Bismarck with Leopold von Gerlach and his friendship with the two brothers drew towards their close. There was practically no more interchange of opinion by letter. According to entries in his ' Diary ', Leopold von Gerlach complains in 1860 that Bismarck has gone so far astray in his hate against Austria, that he has thereby done a great deal of harm. Ludwig himself writes, a year after the death of his brother in January 1861, concerning ' Bismarck's absolutist politics ' : ' Egoism admittedly made the supreme principle, hate of Austria, inclination to Bonapartism. With what lack of thoroughness do we handle such fundamental questions.' In fact, Bismarck had long ago done the preparatory work on the ' fundamental question ' of his career, certainly not omitting egoism, perhaps his ' supreme principle ', and had come to a decision after having, as he thought, adequately completed his preparations. The policy on which he decided was one of immediate, unreserved support of the new regent. On the news of the threatened loss of capacity in the King, Bismarck had at once hurried to Berlin and obtained an interview with Prince William four days before the 23rd of October. The account which he gives of this interview is extremely characteristic of him, both in the description of the external circumstances and that of its content. In accordance with his inclination to dramatize matters the interview appears like a kind of conspiracy. It did not take place in the palace, ' where the walls have eyes and ears ', but in the course of ' a long walk through the New Parks '. They discussed the question which had been so much ventilated in Berlin since the *coup d'état* by Napoléon and which now amounted to asking whether the Prince 'should accept the constitution as it stood or insist upon its revision before taking office'. Obviously Bismarck already felt himself to be the political adviser of the future Prussian sovereign. In the first instance he gave an answer to the legal side of the question which sounds highly sophistical. According to feudal law, 'the heir was bound by the arrangements of his father, but not by those of his brother'. But Bismarck maintained that revision was not desirable, thus continuing the policy which he had described to Manteuffel by denying that he was a 'constitutional renegade'. In doing so he was influenced by his conception of foreign politics. 'Constitutional questions should be subordinated to the political situation of the country', i.e., in relation to foreign affairs. 'A compelling need to lay hands on our constitution has not arisen at the moment; at present the question of our power in the world and our inner unity is the main one.' The interview became known to the camarilla in spite of the efforts to keep it quiet. Bismarck was asked soon afterwards by one of its members why he did not return to his post, where he was badly needed in the present emergency. Bismarck seems to have taken the question as an unjustified reprimand. He reports his categorical, if commonplace, answer: 'I am much more needed here.'

Shortly after the dispatch of the 'Booklet' to the Prince, the hour which Bismarck had awaited seemed at last to have struck. The Prince was considering the exclusion of two members of the Cabinet which he had taken over from his brother, and approached Bismarck with a view to his becoming foreign minister. He accepted at once, but the plan was not carried out. Apparently the author of the 'Booklet' did not seem to the Prince, and still less to his entourage, the right man for the job, for all his readiness to 'allow parliament more elbow-room even in purely political questions than before'. In other respects also the business relation between the two did not develop quite in accord with Bismarck's wishes. The first business that brought them together after the commencement of the vice-gerency was the question of garrisoning Rastatt. Prince William was naturally very anxious not to complicate further his difficult work as deputy by an acute conflict with Austria. So in the middle of February 1858 he directed an extremely polite letter to the Emperor of Austria, which suggested an agreement in regard to the Rastatt affair. Meanwhile Bismarck in Frankfurt maintained his intransigent attitude towards Austria. By means of a direct report to the Prince, he sought to win the latter's agreement in favour of the cause on which he himself had entered. At the end of July 1858 Bismarck forced a division in the Federal Diet about the question and sustained an annihilating defeat. Thereupon the ministers representing the two Powers, Manteuffel and Buol, took the matter immediately in hand and reached an agreement by the end of the year.

Bismarck, however, did not on this account by any means give up the fight for the favour of the Prince. Occasion for a further step was given by the news of the attempt to bring about a resumption of the King's rule in the autumn of 1858. Apparently it was hoped to win Bismarck for this enterprise. But he declined, certainly not only because ' that would be a rule by the harem '. As a logical sequel to this refusal he travelled to the Prince who was staying at Baden-Baden, and exposed the plot to him. What the Prince said in reply was as honourable as it was unpolitical. He declared : ' Then I say good-bye.' Bismarck then gave what was undoubtedly the most suitable advice, namely to summon to Baden-Baden the prime minister von Manteuffel, who had been initiated into the councils of the Berlin court clique, but who apparently also did not anticipate the impending ' government by the harem ' with unqualified approval. Manteuffel saw the real purpose of the invitation and complied with it at once. So these three men could now take the measures necessary for frustrating the Berlin plan and at the same time discuss the steps needed for changing the Prince's office of deputy into that of Regent. Manteuffel undertook to do everything in his power to bring this about, Bismarck himself hastened to Berlin so that he might attend a meeting of leading members of the conservative party which had been throughout opposed to the scheme. He there supported decisively the proposal that they should accept the regency. On the 23rd of October 1858, a year after the appointment of the Prince as deputy, the regency was in fact set up.

With his appointment as Regent the Prince's way was made free for the ' lively participation ' expected by Bismarck, i.e., in the first instance for the appointment of a Cabinet of his own choice and enjoying his own confidence. Both Bismarck and Manteuffel could rely on a place in the Cabinet on account of service rendered. It is amusing to notice how each of the two conspirators reckoned on his own share in the booty and grudged the other his. Immediately before the initiation of the regency, Bismarck wrote to his mother-in-law : ' The great question is whether Manteuffel stays [i.e., in the new Cabinet]. If he went, I think, I should change my post.' When Manteuffel a few days later ' gave him his most recent correspondence with the regent to read ', Bismarck answered him : ' It is quite clear that the Prince wants to say good-bye to you.' Manteuffel, who naturally knew the wishes and purposes of his rival very well, considered—as Bismarck himself says—this answer 'insincere, perhaps ambitious'. It was certainly the latter. But it was also true, for the list published on the 6th of November did in fact not include the name Manteuffel. But ' the change of post ', delicately hinted by Bismarck to his mother-in-law, did not follow either. The list of cabinet ministers did not include the name of Bismarck. What was even worse, it included no names at all of representatives of his party, the extreme Right. The Cabinet of the ' New Era' was drawn from the Opposition, partly the opposition constituted by the *Wochenblatt* party in the court, partly the moderate old-liberal opposition in the Chamber. In addition to its head, who served rather in an ornamental capacity, a Prince of Hohenzollern, distantly related to the royal house, the Cabinet included Bethmann-Hollweg, the leader of the *Wochenblatt* party, Count Schwerin-Putzar, leader of the Opposition in the Chamber, and, the most important personality for Bismarck, von Schleinitz, as foreign minister. He was the very man whom Bismarck a little while before had denounced to the Prince as an unscrupulous political adviser of his wife. All this made it clear that the liberal wife of the Prince had had a word to say in the formation of the Cabinet of the ' New Era '. Bismarck, with an exaggeration which is easily understood in view of his personal aversion and his own disappointment, thus described the intervention by the Princess : ' In the " New Era " Her Highness had before her a Cabinet whose founder and patron she might well consider herself.'

But things were to get even worse from the point of view of Bismarck. Even in October he had written to his mother-in-law : ' That I shall personally be affected by it (i.e., by the change of régime) against my will is not likely.' Three months later he told his wife : ' People at the court are more friendly to me than ever, quite especially the Prince, but also the Princess.' However, the distant tone of uncertainty, present even here, is clearer in a some-what earlier letter to his sister : ' For a long time I seemed pretty sure of St. Petersburg', now he hoped to remain in Frankfurt ; and in another letter to his wife, where he says that he is ' taking precautions that we should not get to Paris or St. Petersburg '. None the less, it must have been like a thunderclap to him when in a social function at court he gathered in conversation from one close to Princess Augusta that his removal from Frankfurt to St. Petersburg, which had ' already been planned several times ', would now definitely take place. The very manner in which the news was brought to him was bound to hurt him very deeply. He, who a little while before had regarded himself as the chosen adviser and even the personal friend of the Prince-Regent, had now to hear that the latter had disposed of his post over his head. Objectively, it meant that his policy at Frankfurt and in particular his attitude towards Austria, was publicly disavowed. At the same time his removal to St. Petersburg brought him to a court in relation to which the sympathy towards the Western Powers, characteristic of the ' New Era ', might mean a certain difficulty for his diplomatic work. The worst thing was that the distance to St. Petersburg forbade travelling ' like the pendulum of a clock ' such as he had carried on between Berlin and Frankfurt. This was quite evidently now not only impossible, but undesired. His influence on general politics was to be brought to an end, and he personally 'left in the cold'.

Once again departure from his post to the often praised ' independent family life on the land ' was an alternative that Bismarck came near adopting. To his sister he wrote in bitter jest : ' I shall retreat behind the guns of Schönhausen and watch how the Prussian government is conducted with the support of left-wing majorities.' But Bismarck was not the man to let himself be left in the cold without taking any further steps. The day after he had heard of his intended appointment he begged for an audience with the Prince-Regent, and without beating about the bush asked for a reversal of the decision which had been made. He had a little while before described his Frankfurt post to a friend as ' the sieve of the Danaids ', and had said to his wife : ' If only to annoy the intriguing chatterbox [the wife of his intended successor], I shall remain in Frankfurt.' But in talking to the Prince he found quite different words. He referred to the productive work which he had yet to do there, to the ' very complicated position ', the ' relations to many courts and ministers ', the ' eight years' experience which cannot be bequeathed to another '. When these arguments failed to produce any effect, Bismarck began to abuse his prospective successor, calling him a bungler and ' no man of business ' ; he, Bismarck, did not believe that the other would carry out conscientiously ' the instructions given him '. But the Prince cut short any further objections with the adroit, not quite unambiguous, remark : ' St. Petersburg has always counted as the highest post in the Prussian diplomatic service ; you should regard it as a proof of great confidence that I send you there.' Then Bismarck, evidently influenced by the experience which had taught him that he could speak to the Prince ' very freely from the heart ', proceeded to criticize the new Cabinet as a whole and its individual members. ' In the whole Cabinet there is ', so he said according to his own report, ' not a single person who is capable of statesmanship, only mediocrities, limited intellects. Without intelligent ministers '—a hint which the person to whom it was addressed could hardly misunderstand—' Your Royal Highness will in the event not find any satisfaction.' As though this was not enough, Bismarck then went on to criticize every single minister adversely. The minister of war, von Bonin, a man known for his

lofty liberal-mindedness and his connexion with the military re-
formers of the Wars of Liberation, Bismarck called a person who
'could not keep a drawer in order, let alone a ministry'. He did
not spare even the minister of foreign affairs, who was his immediate
superior and a friend of the royal pair : 'Schleinitz is a courtier, no
statesman,' he said. Nevertheless, the interview ended, if without
objective results, yet 'in a gracious manner on the side of the
Regent', and on Bismarck's side, as he later adds, 'with the feeling
of undisturbed devotion to the Prince and increased contempt for
the climbers to whose influence, supported by the Princess, he was
at the time subject'. The feelings of the Regent towards him
Bismarck did not analyse, but assumed, with his characteristic self-
confidence, to be favourable.

Bismarck was in no hurry to comply with his new appointment
which had been announced on the 29th of January 1859. He did
not leave Frankfurt till the 6th of March, and then remained till
the 23rd of March in Berlin. His journey to the 'honourable
exile' in St. Petersburg he described very vividly to his wife from
the point of view of a holiday traveller. He could go only as far as
Königsberg by train. He then journeyed by stage-coach for ninety-
six hours as far as Pskov, remaining in the vehicle by day and night,
in such deep snow that the horses were repeatedly stuck and could
not go on, over hills which were covered with glazed frost and half-
frozen rivers, in bitter winds and blizzards in the long ice-cold
nights. When, however, the coach could make progress at all,
the horses flew uphill and downhill, over bridges and across fords.
At Pskov the railway line to St. Petersburg began. His reception
in the court was very favourable, the Tsar and the Tsarina being
'extraordinarily gracious'. By the mother of the Tsar, the widow
of Nicolas I, a Prussian Princess, Bismarck was specially well received. 'The Prussians', he writes, 'are gladly seen here, if they
do not wantonly make themselves unpleasant.' 'All official relations', he adds, 'are in comparison to Frankfurt as roses after
thorns. The naughty pricks of the Federal Diet and the poison
of the president look from here like childish pranks.' Highly
favourable at first is Bismarck's opinion of the Russian minister
for foreign affairs, Prince Gortschakoff. To Schleinitz he describes
him as the focus of all external affairs, as a man of wide cultural
interests, incorruptible in money matters, with outstanding gifts,
and a hard worker. After a year of working together he wrote to a
friend : 'Business, thanks to such a charming minister as
Gortschakoff, goes without vexation.' Also in the *Reflections and
Reminiscences*, in reference to this period, he accuses him only of
'exaggerated vanity', and confirms his 'unbounded goodwill'. On
the other hand, he writes to Schleinitz : 'My German colleagues

[i.e., the representatives of the minor states] are a chronic evil.' Descriptions of customs at court and of figures in court society show Bismarck's continual lively interest in such affairs. He distinguishes ' the *grands seigneurs* from the reign of Alexander I with their European and classical culture ', the contemporaries of Nicolas I, who ' are accustomed to limit their conversation to affairs of the court, the theatre, their careers, and military experiences ', and the generation of Alexander II, who ' in their behaviour in society sometimes display bad manners and aversion to what is German and especially what is Prussian '.

' How the Austrians are looked down upon here ', Bismarck writes with much satisfaction, ' one has no idea. It is only since I have been here that I believe in war. The whole Russian policy seems to leave hardly room for any other thought but how to strike at the life of Austria.' Herewith a way was shown to Bismarck of using the period during which he was ' left in the cold ' in St. Petersburg to prepare for the settling of accounts with Austria. The often-discussed Prussian alliance with Russia and France now offered itself as a direct means of isolating Austria. The correspondence with Schleinitz furnishes indications that he raised this question at St. Petersburg and that interest was shown in his approaches, especially on the part of Prince Gortschakoff, who was favourably inclined to the Western Powers and Western ideas. But circumstances were not propitious for immediate success. For in Russian politics questions of internal affairs stood in the foreground, such as recovery from the evils which were made manifest or brought about by the Crimean War, and the preparation for the projected freeing of the serfs. Moreover, the emerging focus of a new complication affecting the whole of Europe was Italy, and she was too far removed from Russian soil and Russian interests to provide a keen stimulus for active intervention. In Berlin, on the other hand, though the authorities had become markedly more reserved in their compliance towards Austria after the departure of Manteuffel, still they were not yet ready to join combinations directed against her, as Schleinitz let Bismarck know at St. Petersburg.

Bismarck, however, was only to be taught by experience that his influence on general politics in Berlin was completely unwelcome to the leading personalities there. On the 12th of March 1859 he sent to Schleinitz a memoir of the same type as the ones earlier sent to Manteuffel. He again asserted the conviction he had expressed in March 1858 as to the purely negative significance of the Confederation for Prussia, but this time in more cautious language.

I see in our relation to the Confederation an infirmity of Prussia which we earlier or later will have to heal, *ferro et igni.* I should only wish to

see the word German instead of ' Prussian ' written on our flag if we were
bound more closely and adequately with our other fellow-countrymen than
we have been up to the present.

At about the same time Bismarck wrote to Herman Wagener, who
meanwhile had turned his back on the *Kreuzzeitung*, that ' if to-day
the Confederation were dissolved without anything else being put
in its place ', this would mean an improvement in the relation of
Prussia to her neighbours. Yet in his report to Schleinitz Bismarck
does not confine himself to quoting his Frankfurt experiences, but
is incautious enough to give advice concerning the general policy
to be pursued in ' such dangerous times as the present '. He
ventures to express the conviction that ' we shall not easily again find
circumstances so favourable as regards Austria, France, and Russia,
for an improvement of our position in Germany '. But the answer
which he received does not seem to have encouraged him to continue
this kind of correspondence ; he later writes in an astonished and
hurt tone :

I believed in the possibility of influencing decision in Berlin in my
position as ambassador in St. Petersburg, as I had done from Frankfurt,
without realizing that these efforts were bound to be quite fruitless,
because my direct reports either never reached the Regent, or only reached
him together with comments which prevented them from making any
impression.

The idea that the Regent had perhaps himself rejected the reports
on account of their content Bismarck refused to consider.

Apart from this, there were many bitter moments in Bismarck's
St. Petersburg activities, ' under this uncongenial sky ', under which
he described himself to Schleinitz as ' condemned to endure '.
' By day and by night he was dreaming of the portfolio,' says one
of his most intimate collaborators at that time. He complains
that in Russia ' conspirators spread discontent against the court
and the Tsar's house, right down to the lowest classes of the people '.
He admits that ' the immediate entourage of the Tsar is unfortunately
not free of elements which provide the worst breeding place for
such '. He expresses himself at length about the menacing condition
of the Russian state finances. He speaks of the ' severest sickness
of the Russian empire ', of the ' army of badly paid and dishonest
officials'. One has the impression that in all this, vexation at his
own unsatisfying professional task finds its outlet. He became
stiffer and stiffer in' his conviction that ' the accuracy of his reports
on the moods of the Tsar was becoming suspect ' in Berlin and that
the Prussian government had purposely sent a diplomat, formerly
military attaché in St. Petersburg, ' in order to control him '. To
his wife he described the latter as a ' false friend ' and a ' rampant

Austrian '. In a letter to Schleinitz concerning his visit he asked whether ' he had not the full confidence of the government, a suspicion which is always present if somebody on a special mission is put side by side with an ambassador '. It sounded like an echo of this mood when he, describing a war with Russia as unlikely, added the reservation ' unless liberal stupidities or dynastic blunders lead to misinterpretation '. To his wife, who only later followed him to St. Petersburg, he complained : ' There is nothing on earth but trickery and deceit, and whether fever or grapeshot removes this mask of flesh, it must fall sooner or later. Be it as God wills ; I would just as lief live in the country.' His most frequent and bitter complaints relate to the lack of work. He would ' gladly have written a political report ', he once wrote to the foreign minister, but ' there is no material for it whatever '. In a letter to his sister he says :

> I feel like an old-age pensioner, who has finished with the work of this world. Till twelve every morning I am occupied with drinking the Karlsbad waters, going walks, having breakfast, dressing myself. From then till five o'clock my office gives me just enough regular work to prevent me from feeling superfluous in the world. Dinner tastes excellent, especially what I must not eat.

Bismarck's health at this time was not very good. In a hunt in Sweden, in the summer of 1857, he had injured his shinbone and the treatment of this was first neglected and then entrusted to an un-qualified doctor whose prescriptions led to a poisoning of his whole body. In the unfavourable climate of St. Petersburg, perhaps as a further consequence of this poisoning, there developed a ' rheumatic-gastric-nervous ' complaint. In the late autumn of 1859 this led to him spending many weeks in German spas. Towards the end of the same year, on his way to St. Petersburg, Bismarck fell sick in East Prussia in the house of a friend from ' rheumatic fever with an affection of the breast muscles '. He had to spend the whole winter 1859–60 there, partly in bed and partly as a convalescent.

But Bismarck's frequent absences from his St. Petersburg post were due not only to illness. He also travelled about in Russia for his instruction and pleasure. He visited Moscow, the ' most beautiful and original town there is ', as he wrote to his wife. He acquired by means of some stray remarks the reputation of a con-noisseur of art ; as a guest he much enjoyed the imposing residences of the high Russian nobility in court and country ; he visited by special permission the palaces of the Tsar with their works of art, rarities, and curiosities ; and he missed no opportunity of hunting in the primeval forests of Russia.

To these travels must be added the political journeys of Bismarck.

His travelling to and fro ' like the pendulum of a clock ' of Frankfurt times was no more desired, his memoranda were not appreciated, but his wish to ' have some influence on the decisions in Berlin ' remained. With this end in view Bismarck spent many months of his three years at St. Petersburg in journeys. In September 1859 we find him visiting the Prince-Regent in Baden-Baden. At the end of October he was at Breslau on the occasion of the meeting of the latter with the Tsar, in March, April, and May 1860 at Berlin in order to ' put his advice at the disposal of the Prince-Regent ', in October 1860 at a meeting of the Prince-Regent with the Russian and Austrian Emperors in Warsaw, and then in their company in Berlin. There he negotiated with the prime minister concerning his taking over the ministry of foreign affairs; but once more the Prince-Regent refused his consent, this time after the meeting of the Crown Council where, following a *mise en scène* apparently ' the outcome of the will of the Princess ', Schleinitz defeated Bismarck. In July 1861 Bismarck again visited Berlin and then was at Baden-Baden with the Prince-Regent, who found his visit ' an unpleasant surprise ', and again with him at Coblenz in September. Only a month later Bismarck returned to St. Petersburg, where he was to hold his post for half a year longer, till April 1862.

CHAPTER XIV

The Struggle for the Premiership

The event in foreign affairs which brought home to Bismarck in a particularly painful way the consciousness of his office in St. Petersburg as 'leaving him in the cold' was the Italian complication, which affected the whole of Europe. For its focus was not only far distant from Russian soil and Russian interests, but equally far from Bismarck's own sphere of influence. Yet it was just the development of the Italian question which seemed from the beginning to provide once more a special opportunity for bringing nearer the realization of the plans which he had formed for raising Prussia to the rank of a Great Power. Now there was once more the question of rightly valuing the France of Napoléon ' as a pawn and indeed an inevitable one, in the chessboard of politics '. One had to avoid giving the opposition to the latter ' the stamp of irrevocability ' and to ' show Austria that it is her business to earn and keep our help '. There might also open up a fresh opportunity to attract the smaller members of the Confederation to Prussia through the knowledge that the latter could ' come to an understanding ' not only with Austria, but ' even with France '. But Bismarck had also every occasion to doubt whether this balance-of-power policy would gain any more support in Berlin than it did at the beginning of the Crimean War, or that his support of it would mean anything more than it did then.

The national unification of Italy was one of the most important imminent problems that was set the European Powers to solve. Napoléon III had entered the sphere of European politics as champion of the principle of nationality. He could not ignore Italian efforts at unification, and in his own interest had no intention of doing so. Already in the summer of 1857 he had made a hint of this to Bismarck when he spoke of Italy's greater ' intimacy with, and dependence on, France ', as a result of the next war. Against whom this war would be fought was clear from the beginning. Austria ruled over large parts of the Italian peninsula. Her loss of these territories would be inevitable if Italy was unified. Therefore, unification could not be accepted by Austria without resistance. In the summer of 1858, a year after the hint to Bismarck, Napoléon in a secret conference at Plombières with the then head of the Italian *resorgimento*, Count Camillo Cavour, prime minister under King Victor Emmanuel of Sardinia, decided on a common war against Austria and came to an agreement as regards the prizes of victory. They

172

were the acquisition by a unified Italy of the Italian territory held by Austria and the cession by Sardinia of Savoy and Nice to France. On the occasion of an immediately subsequent visit to Baden-Baden, at which he just missed Bismarck, Cavour dropped a hint to the Prince-Regent of Prussia about coming events. On the 1st of January 1859 Napoléon than gave the signal for immediate preparations for war when he told the Austrian ambassador in a solemn New Year's reception: 'I regret that the relations between our governments are not so good as formerly.'

Austria now took the necessary military measures and looked round for allies. From the England of Palmerston and Derby she might expect mediation, but not armed help ; from hostile measures on the part of Russia she could only feel secure because the latter had no direct interest in the question and was not inclined to help the revolutionary Italian movement in any way. So Austria had no resource but to ask help from Prussia and the Confederation. Thereby was fulfilled on the chessboard of European politics the situation which Bismarck with his combinations had repeatedly envisaged. Would the opportunity be grasped in Berlin and utilized in accordance with his intentions ? And what direct influence could he have on its utilization ? He was only allowed to make a very insignificant and indirect move. Among the measures which Austria first adopted in view of the threat of war with Napoléon was included a proposal in the Federal Diet for the strengthening of the federal forts which were intended to protect the Rhine and the country behind it from immediate invasion by the French. This proposal was made in February 1859, just as Bismarck was making ready to pack his belongings for his removal to St. Petersburg. But he did not fail to deal with the proposal, and this gave him the opportunity of a somewhat cheap personal triumph as well as of producing a, very temporary, disturbance of the relation between Prussia and Austria. The Austrian military attaché had induced his Prussian colleague to vote for the proposal, without first asking his superior, the ambassador Bismarck. There followed a stiff report from the latter to Berlin, and he obtained the answer that the Attaché ' might only take action in questions which affected political interests after first arriving at an understanding with the King's ambassador '. The Austrian proposal was, however, carried.

This pin-prick exhausted the weapons which Bismarck could use in order to exercise an immediate influence on the attitude of the two German Great Powers in the Italian conflict. He had now to wait inactively at St. Petersburg to see whether the solemn words which the Prince had uttered on the occasion when he took over the regency : ' Prussia must stand on a most friendly footing with all Great Powers without tying her hands prematurely by agreements ', would find their fulfilment also in relation to Austria. He had now impotently to watch how everywhere within the Confederation 'the wrath against the hereditary French enemy whose thrust would affect the security of all German lands ' was kindled and kept burning by Austria and her supporters. On the other hand, he welcomed the news that an offer by England to mediate had been rejected in Vienna on the ground that ' we need not mediators but allies ', and that on the occasion of a proposal by Russia to hold a congress at which the Italian states would be present, Count Buol is reported to have exclaimed : ' I should rather go to the gallows than to this congress.' Bismarck became uneasy when he heard of the visit to Berlin of the Archduke Albrecht, who in the event of war had in view an Austrian army for the Rhine of 250,000 men under the personal leadership of the Emperor and asked for an equal contribution from Prussia and the Confederation. For, as Bismarck reported to the Prince-Regent, this would mean a war ' which from being Austrian would become Prussian when the first cannon shot was fired on the banks of the Rhine '. He was again relieved when Austria, without awaiting assent to her request, on the 23rd of April dispatched an ultimatum to Turin demanding complete disarmament and thereby assumed in the eyes of the whole world the guilt of having broken the peace. For he was convinced that ' under the influence of his wife and of the *Wochenblatt* party the Regent was near to taking part in the war '. When on the 26th of April Prussia declared that she would confine herself to defending the territory of the Confederation but would otherwise remain neutral, the Austrian manifesto : ' Our German brothers will not let the Austrian army fight alone ' was disavowed. Bismarck saw in this a decisive step in the direction of the balance of power policy for which he contended, and wrote with much exaltation to Berlin : ' The Prince-Regent has adopted an attitude which has the undivided approval of all those who have a right to judge Prussian policy.' But this ' undivided approval ' did not last on the part of Bismarck. For as the political position of Austria became worse, he had to see how a Prussian plenipotentiary was sent to Vienna to offer intervention in order to preserve the Austrian possessions in Italy, though only on condition that Prussia should have full control over the military forces of the German Confederation. However, Austria did Bismarck the service of declining this conditional offer and asking for unconditional intervention, ' so that the demon of revolution should be securely chained and the blessing of universal quiet and order restored to Europe '. These are words which Bismarck himself might well have used at the time of Olmütz, but from which the Bismarck of the ' Booklet ', to whom Prussia's opposition to liberalism had lost some of its credit, had diverged. Also in Austria men would soon become aware that this attitude no longer was in conformity with the power of their country. She suffered reverse after reverse in the field. She had to evacuate more and more of her Italian possessions, and her subjects there rose against her rule and chased away its tools.

Now Prussia took a step which must have made Bismarck in St. Petersburg extremely uneasy. She mobilized, at first six army corps, and ten days later the whole army. She also proposed in Frankfurt the mobilization of two confederate corps. The army was to take up position on the Rhine under Prussian leadership. No doubt, under strong political guidance this would have been the course which came nearest to Bismarck's own ideas if it had been followed by a Prussian march into south Germany, the forcible uniting of the latter with Prussia, war against Austria and joint action with France. But it was just this strong hand which was lacking in the actual Berlin ministry of ' mediocrities, limited intellects '. Consequently Bismarck saw the danger that this military power would be willingly or unwillingly manœuvred into a position of alliance with Austria. He wrote warningly to the Prussian plenipotentiary at Frankfurt, who was a personal friend of the Prince-Regent : ' With the first shot on the Rhine the German war will become the main question, because it threatens Paris. Austria will get a breathing space.' She will certainly not ' use her freedom to help us to play a glorious part '. He also tried direct warnings to Berlin. He pointed out that ' the Tsar wished for friendship with Napoléon in the interests of Russia ' and that ' if France, owing to the action of the rest of Germany in taking sides on behalf of Austria, is threatened by superior force, Russia will take the weight off France '. But there was still a third possibility, of which Bismarck himself had apparently not become fully aware. It was that the Prussian mobilization, under a political control which was not sure of itself and in opposition to an abler policy on the part of Prussia's opponent, might lead Prussia into a trap. In that case Prussia, instead of being arbiter over the parties at war and the decisive factor in settling the dispute, would become the object of exasperation, misunderstanding, and even ridicule for belligerents, members of the Confederation and neutrals alike.

It was just this third possibility that was realized. No sooner had Napoléon won the decisive victory of Solferino over the Austrians than he, on receipt of the news of the Prussian mobilization, gave up the further exploitation of this success and offered the Austrian Emperor an armistice, which the latter at once accepted. In the peace treaty which followed Austria lost a large part of her Italian possessions but was allowed to keep Venice. Napoléon received Savoy and Nice, but had only partly fulfilled his promises to Cavour. The Italy of Cavour had to halt half-way in her march to unity. The Prussian army was demobilized without having struck a single blow or being able to point to any political success as the result of her intervention. From Austria there came the bitterest reproaches against Prussia. Napoléon, who had safe hold of his share of the booty, knew how to represent Prussia to the Italians as the really guilty party. The Prince-Regent William made as always an honourable but unpolitical retort : ' I bear the abuse hurled at me from all sides with great composure, because my conscience absolves me completely from all the reproaches which are made against me.' Bismarck, however, had learned from a practical example that the balance of power policy required a great measure of thorough preparation and deliberation, and that Napoléon now at any rate, had attained the ' height of political judgement ' which enabled him ' to do what is useful to him '. Although in this conflict the antagonism between him and Napoléon had only been an indirect one, still it had shown him that the latter was an opponent to be reckoned with, and that this time he had to avow himself beaten as a political thinker.

But the Italian episode was not the only political problem in relation to which Bismarck felt his stay in St. Petersburg as excluding him from the influence which he desired to exercise. The second, a matter of internal politics, was for the future of Prussia and, moreover, of Germany, of still more decisive significance. This was the struggle of Dynasty versus People, or the dynastic power policy versus the club-law of the barricade. The epoch of Prussian politics characterized by the appointment of the cabinet under Prince Hohenzollern was called the ' New Era ', because it was intended to introduce a period of liberal, or at any rate less reactionary and autocratic, control of the affairs of state. The Prince-Regent William was himself in no wise a liberal man. He did not differ much from his elder brother and predecessor in the conviction that the form of government suitable for Prussia involved the subordination of parliament to the crown and not a parliamentary régime. When looking back on the Prince's life as a whole Bismarck described as the core of his being ' his consciousness as Prussian officer and as Prussian King '. He emphasized the reliability and straightforwardness of the Prince's character, his gracious modesty, his deep sense of duty, and his great courage. He praised his inaccessibility to backdoor influence and slander. But in regard to the events of the ' New Era ' Bismarck came to waver in his belief in most of these qualities and especially ' in the lasting firmness of his Majesty against palace influences '. He explained these events by a reference to a tendency of the monarch ' through concessions to his enemies to make himself able to dispense with the support of his friends '. Among the enemies he counted not least his own enemies, the ' climbers ' of the *Wochenblatt* party. This tendency of the monarch was supplemented, in Bismarck's opinion, by that of his wife who thought that ' opponents of the monarchy could be changed into friends and supporters by liberal concessions '.

That in fact the turning to the liberalism of the ' New Era ' was for the Regent not the expression of a heartfelt need is clear from one of his private letters of this time : ' I shall not investigate whether constitutions are beneficial. But where they exist one should keep them and not falsify them by forced interpretations.' This view was still more clearly expressed in an address of the 8th of November 1858, with which the Prince-Regent opened the first sitting of the new cabinet and which gained the ear of the public. He denied that he intended to pursue a policy of reaction in church and state, but he added : ' Of a break with the past there can never never be a question.' He declared it to be his own conviction and the conviction of all his ministers that he should seek to come to an understanding with the desires of the liberals and German nationalists, but that ' the inseparable welfare of crown and land ' rests ' on healthy, strong conservative principles '. He continued : ' Above all, I warn you against the stereotyped phrase that the government must let itself be driven further and further in the direction of developing liberal ideas because these will otherwise make their way by force.'

About the time when the Prince-Regent made his cautious attempt to replace the Opposition between crown and people, which he had found prevailing by a synthesis of both extremes, Bismarck, as we know, was occupied with similar questions. He was certainly opposed to the practical plan of the Prince-Regent, not least because it involved his own rejection. But what was Bismarck's attitude to the thought on which the attempt was based ? At the time of the speech of the Prince-Regent just referred to, that is some time before Bismarck took the post in St. Petersburg, the latter had a talk with a friend of his in the Liberal Opposition, Victor von Unruh : ' So much is clear,' Bismarck remarked, ' Prussia is completely isolated. There is only one ally for Prussia, if she knows how to win and how to deal with that ally.' When Unruh asked whom he meant, Bismarck replied : ' The German people.' On seeing the look of amazement on Unruh's face, he continued : ' Well ! What else did you think ! I am the same Junker as I was ten years ago, but I should have no eyes and no understanding in my head if I did not see clearly the real state of affairs.'

Do these words really represent a break in Bismarck's attitude to liberalism and democracy ? At the time ten years before to which Bismarck referred in the words quoted, he had exclaimed that what mattered most for him was ' that Prussia should keep herself free from any shameful alliance with democracy '. If we were to accept the view that he had now given up this idea it would contradict his

own words when he said that he was still ' the same Junker '. The
Junker in him was only concerned with ' seeing clearly the real state
of affairs '.   So Bismarck's utterance was quite divorced from any
principle of political theory.   Rather is it based on a mood at the time
of his words about ' shameful alliance ', which he had expressed in
the sentence : ' After all I am the kindest man in the world towards
the common people.'   The ' understanding in his head ' which
some years before had already come to the conclusion that it was no
longer ' dishonourable ' to come to an agreement with Napoléon and
that the Prussian ' government may without danger allow parliament
more elbow-room even in purely political questions than before ',
warned him against this presumptuous ' kindness '.   It told him
that in the ' New Era ' this kindness, combined with ' old-Prussian
strokes of the lash ', was not the right sort for dealing with the
people as allies of the Prussian crown and for sending them to
death on the battlefield if occasion required.

This concept of the people had nothing to do with the people as
' expression of a distinctive common spirit ' as taught by the classical
German thinkers and poets.   On the contrary, Bismarck was influenced by the example of Napoléon III, from whom he had learned
how one might win, keep and increase the favour of the people by
granting them the universal franchise, without having to give them
any important practical share in the control of policy, if only this
policy was successful.   The result of this deliberation he had already communicated to the Prince-Regent in the ' Booklet ' of
March 1858, though only in the negative form that Prussia with the
help ' only of the German Princes and their ministers could not win
the leadership of the Confederation '.   Now if Napoléon in France
was able to win such a selfless readiness to help from the people,
how much easier would that be for the Prussian monarch !   Bismarck, in deliberating on this, unhesitatingly made use of the
attitude with which he had charged his opponents ten years before,
when he said : ' No expression has been misused in recent years
more than the word " people ".   Everybody has understood thereby
just what suited his own purpose.'   At the time of his conversation
with Unruh, Bismarck did not adopt the socio-economic concept
of people as used by Napoléon in the distinction between proletariat and; bourgeoisie, but utilized an ethnological concept.   The
people is to him the clans (*Stämme*, e.g., Prussians, Bavarians, Saxons,
&c.) which make it up.   The German clans are the born " allies " of
their dynasties.   ' German patriotism usually needs, in order to
become active and effective, the stimulus of dynastic loyalty.'   ' That
a dynasty should be indispensable as a link for holding together a
particular fraction of the nation under the name of this dynasty is
a specific peculiarity of the German people.'

The Prince-Regent, too, looked on the people not in a socio-economic way, but ethnologically as clans. But he was immersed in that ' dynastic sentimentality ' which Bismarck, as ' Brandenburg feudal vassal ', indeed needed in his politics, yet which he ridiculed as ' devilish cant about sovereignty '. At the first meeting of the new Cabinet on the 8th of November, the Regent said : ' In Germany Prussia must make moral conquests through a wise law-giving at home and through the elevation of all elements that make for good morals. The world must know that Prussia is ready everywhere to defend right.' Those were fatal words for Bismarck, who had never expected the militarist Prince-Regent to speak of ' moral conquests ', just as his unrealistic brother, Frederick William IV, had done.

Most people accepted the words of the Prince-Regent in a very different spirit from Bismarck. Within Prussia they received considerable applause from all shades of Left Wing opinion, from the party of Bethmann-Hollweg and the Old Liberals to the Radical Democrats. Their opponents of the Extreme Right felt the ground shake under them. The elections to the Prussian parliament fixed for the middle of January 1859 resulted in a complete change in the composition of the House of Deputies. This political turn meant not only a revival of the ideas of liberalism and democracy, which had been asleep since 1849, but was at the same time an expression of a shift of classes within the politically unprivileged part of the population. It now became increasingly clear that an upper middle class was developing, marked off from the lower by economic possessions, cleverness in practical matters and social superiority and based on the development of industrialism in the modern sense with its big enterprises. This class now demanded that its special economic and social significance should be recognized also in political life. They did not wish that this should be done in opposition to the government yet they desired that they should not remain a mere instrument under it, but be given a position by the side of it. This movement of a decisive socio-economic significance developed within the people and asked for political acknowledgement just at the time when the Prince-Regent and also Bismarck were thinking of the people as an ethnological entity. It was not only in Prussia, but also in the smaller states of the Confederation, that this rising upper middle class made itself noticeable in politics. Thus for the first time since the unsuccessful attempt of 1848-9 the question of reforming the Confederation began indeed to be not only a matter for ' the German Princes and their ministers ' but one for the ordinary citizens. Many of these were in favour of accepting the leadership of Prussia just because they appreciated the Prussian bureaucracy with its child, the Customs Union, and the liberal policy of the

'New Era'. The new Prussian Regent by his appointment of a liberal Cabinet and by the views he had expressed to this Cabinet seemed to show the people that he had an open ear for their constitutional wishes and a will quite ready to carry them out. Just then Austria in the preparation and the initiation of the Italian war displayed her inner weakness, and at the same time showed again that tendency to take on the 'danger of war' and to 'misuse the strength of Germany for a war not necessary in itself', which Bismarck had previously alleged against her. Thus among the 'people' the champions of a solution of the German question through the unification of Germany under Prussian leadership with the exclusion of Austria (the so-called *kleindeutsche* solution) now formed a political group ready for conflict and willing to throw in their resources. There arose in the middle of September 1859 at Frankfurt the 'Nationalverein', a union of north and south German constitutional and liberal elements and a kind of continuation and development of the 'Gotha-Group'. This body set themselves as goal a unified German nation with a constitutional Prussia as core and basis. It was pointed out that the governments of the confederate states must 'make a sacrifice' and 'transfer a part of their functions to a German Federal Power'. The Nationalverein frequently appealed to the 'nation's consciousness of right' as the basis of this claim. In its ranks side by side with the liberals among the nobility the rising upper middle class came to occupy a leading position, while the idea of acknowledging the industrial workers as a separate class was abhorred. This middle class fought for the attainment of economic ends and spoke therefore of *Realpolitik*. But also the ideal of the *Kulturstaat* as the adequate expression of a national entity grown out of the development of individual liberty maintained its validity with them. Almost simultaneously with the foundation of the Nationalverein occurred the centenary of the birth of Schiller, who of German classical poets and thinkers had been one of the most whole-hearted and devoted exponents of that ideal; this centenary provided the occasion for emphasizing idealism as the basis of their national community in the widest circles of the German people.

Now that Austria had lost a great part of her Italian possessions, she was all the more interested in preserving and strengthening the German nationality within her territory and her own position within the Confederation. To the Nationalverein she opposed the Reformverein which as against the *kleindeutsche* solution of the German question championed the *grossdeutsche* solution, involving the inclusion of Austria in the union to be founded. If the relations between Austria and Prussia had already been tense owing to the Italian war, there was now a danger that, as the two came into immediate opposition on the political battlefield of Germany, the controversy would become acute. But the rulers of both countries wished at any price to avoid an open conflict. However, a minor issue in connexion with the reform of the Confederation forced them at once to take sides. This was the constitutional quarrel in Kur-Hesse between ruler and parliament. This question was ticklish enough, for, when the dispute first broke out in 1850, it had been a quite essential factor in bringing relations between the two states to the verge of an open breach. The Prince-Regent therefore summoned some of his ministers to discuss the attitude of Prussia. In particular he asked the foreign minister, von Schleinitz, to meet him at Baden-Baden in September 1859. This was for Bismarck the first opportunity he had during his stay at St. Petersburg of meeting the Regent in person and being admitted to his discussions with his ministers. It was just the negotiations about the question of the constitution of Kur-Hesse which he had earlier characterized as ' playing the game of Don Quixote for insulted parliamentary celebrities '. Now it might give him the opportunity to show how deeply rooted his recommendation in favour of a synthesis between dynasty and parliament and of an ' alliance between the German people and Prussia ' had become in the meantime. In fact, Bismarck agreed in the course of the discussions at Baden-Baden that the Prussian plenipotentiary in the Federal Diet should hand in a memoir in support of the constitutional party in Hesse and that about this question Prussia should enter into negotiations with the Austrian government. Had then the people perhaps become for Bismarck something more than an ally for the crown to ' deal with ' ? Bismarck himself supplies the clearest answer to this question. In his last letter of all to Leopold von Gerlach he discusses his position in the question of the Hessian constitution and remarks : ' I regard it as a misinterpreted conservatism ', to oppose the constitutional party in Hesse, ' because the princely authority is on the opposite side '. And then, acknowledging his fundamental view without pretence, he declared : ' Abroad as at home I see things in doubtful cases with the eyes of my caste, the nobility, and this is not on the side ' of the ruler in the problem in dispute.

Another question regarding the reform of the Confederation was raised at Baden-Baden, and one which was highly relevant to the deep military interests of the Prince-Regent, i.e., the improvement of the Federal organization for war, which had during the Italian war shown itself very cumbrous and imperfect. In particular it was decided to propose to the Diet that the supreme command of the Confederate army should be equally shared both by Prussia and Austria. When this resolution was actually introduced Bismarck was very pleased, and wrote to his successor in Frankfurt : ' The move about the organization for war was splendid. Only go on in this way, coming forward with our proposals openly and bluntly.' But the smaller members of the Confederation had a different view since they wished for a threefold division of the command between Austria, Prussia and the rest of Germany; and so had Austria, who wished to retain the command for herself alone. Consequently the proposal of Prussia was rejected. But the Federal organization for war was in no wise the only, or even the chief, military care of the Prince-Regent with his enthusiasm for soldiering. The condition of the Prussian army concerned him far more deeply. ' Moral conquests ' were no doubt a fine thing, but not less fine was the possession of a superior army ready to strike. The Regent was convinced that Prussia did not possess such an army. Thus in the above mentioned speech of the 8th of November we find the words :

The army has created the greatness of Prussia and has won for her by fighting the opportunity for growth. In the meantime an experience of forty years has made us attentive to the fact that much that has failed to prove its value will give occasion for changes. Prussia's army must be strong and respected, so that when the hour comes it may be able to throw a heavy political weight into the balance.

When the Prince-Regent thus spoke it was not only a general principle that he had in view ; he was quite ready to give his purposes shape in concrete measures, and indeed measures of really far-reaching significance, the increase of the yearly levy by more than half, the general enforcement of the three years' service, the establishment of many more regiments of the standing army, the reduction of the Landwehr (territorials) in favour of the standing army, and connected with all this a considerable increase in the military budget. The mobilization of the Prussian army on the occasion of the Italian war had confirmed the Prince-Regent in his conviction of the army's need for reorganization. Consequently he had already begun to carry out the measures he had in view, and had only partially de-mobilized his forces in the summer of 1859. According to the expressions of public opinion when the plans for reform became known it was clear that they would encounter fierce opposition in the Chamber. The upper middle class which was dominant there was indeed quite prepared to render positive help in furthering the power and greatness of Prussia. But they had no desire to create new regiments for the sake of parades, to increase the number of arrogant lieutenants, to give their sons and their employees for military service for an extended period, and to make heavier the taxes which they already felt as a crushing burden. The suppression of the Landwehr, that product of the Wars of Liberation, was regarded as a suppression of the spirit in which the volunteers of that day stood up against the foreign enemy. The Landwehr stood for the idea that among Germans the state is to grow out of the development of individual liberty and was therewith the guarantee of democracy and liberalism within the Prussian army.

Under these circumstances the Prince-Regent was in doubt whether the minister of war in the liberal Cabinet, von Bonin, who according to Bismarck's views was not capable ' of keeping his drawer in order ', was the right man to advocate the plans for reform before the Chamber. Bonin was pre-eminently a supporter of the idea of the Landwehr in its original liberal and ideal significance. This question, too, was raised at the discussions at Baden-Baden in September 1859. At the beginning of October there was summoned to the discussions a man who had already co-operated in preparing the army reforms and who was to be of decisive significance, not only for the fate of the reforms, but for the future career of Bismarck, Lieutenant-General Albrecht von Roon. Roon, a close relative of Moritz von Blanckenburg, and through him a friend of Bismarck's of long standing, was twelve years older than the latter. He was a many-sided man and one exceptionally competent in his own subject. But he was also extremely reactionary and anti-constitutional in his politics. In a memoir of 1858 he had attacked the Landwehr particularly sharply. ' The Landwehr as a military institution is all wrong, because it is lacking in the real genuine strong soldierly spirit and is without firm discipline.' While Bonin saw in Roon the man who would ' divide the army from the country ', Roon accused Bonin of being ' rather a Liberal than a Prussian soldier ' and of regarding himself as a ' parliamentary minister '. ' Thank heaven that we have not come to that yet,' he exclaimed, ' if we had, we should have come a great deal nearer to a republic and the sovereignty of the people.' The Prince-Regent now discussed with Roon the further fate of the military reorganization. The result of these discussions was that Roon, as member of a military commission, took part in drawing up the bill, that he was appointed minister of war in December 1859 and entrusted at the beginning of the following year with the task of bringing this bill, including the authorization of credits to meet the expenditure involved, before the new House with its large liberal majority. This House had been recommended a little while before in the Speech from the Throne to ' investigate the bill without prejudice and give it their support '. When Bismarck after his stay in Pomerania in 1859–60 as an invalid came to Berlin in March, the military proposals and their fate in the Chamber constituted the principal topic for discussion in political circles. The condition of the army still depended on the laws of 1814–15. The new proposals were prejudiced from the start by the fact that the constitutional relation of the new bill to these former laws, which had been issued by the King on his own authority, was legally doubtful and that no attempt was made to clarify it.

From the beginning Bismarck stood unconditionally on the side of his friend Roon, whose purpose was to carry the bill through parliament by all means at his disposal and without any scruples connected with constitutional law.   However, in the Chamber Roon had to encounter not only the united opposition of the liberal majority headed by the stubborn Georg von Vincke, but also the half-support of his liberal colleagues.   It was a great relief for him when Bismarck used his influence in the Upper House to bring it about that the bill including the provision for credit was accepted unanimously, for in the House of Deputies Roon had to be content with an acceptance limited in time to the fiscal year of 1860.

The Prince-Regent, however, carried out the reorganization of the army, not as a provisional measure for one year, but as a final arrangement.   When he, on the death of his brother, at the beginning of January 1861, ascended the throne as William I, one of his first measures was to carry out the solemn dedication of the standards for the newly established military forces.   In his first Speech from the Throne as King, on the 14th of January 1861, he spoke of the reorganization of the army as a completed piece of work.   None the less, the Lower House agreed to accept the bill if only again for a single year, 1861, and with certain deductions from the sum demanded by the government.

The opposition between government and parliament and within the government grew more intense.   Men were already talking of the return of a situation like that of March 1848.   The tension found its expression in the foundation, soon after the end of the session in June 1861, of an extreme liberal party, the party of progress, which put forward as their platform the democratic principle of the responsibility of ministers to parliament.   On the other hand, the King decided to celebrate his accession to the throne by asking for a solemn act of feudal homage thus to emphasize the divine character of his office.   When the liberal ministers refused to give their consent to this 'feudal and reactionary measure', the King insisted all the more on its being held.   Roon utilized this controversy with the liberal ministers to convey to the King his belief that with this ministry a final settlement of the military question was not possible. With ever greater emphasis he referred the King to Bismarck as a suitable person to be made a member of the Cabinet.   But at first the King did not welcome this proposal.   However, in the summer of 1861, Bismarck received in St. Petersburg a letter from Roon, in which he said : ' Up to now I have with difficulty prevented the King from giving way [i.e., in the question of feudal homage].   But I stand alone, quite alone.   Now I ask you whether you regard the traditional act of feudal homage as an attempt against the constitution.' If not, Bismarck could be sure of office.

Schleinitz is going in any case. But it is doubtful whether you have to take over his or another portfolio. The King is suffering terribly. His closest relatives advise a dishonourable peace. God grant that he may not give way. If he does we shall steer full sail into the morass of parliamentary government.

Bismarck in reply declared his willingness on principle to join the ministry. The question of the feudal homage stimulated him to some general remarks which apparently refer to liberal criticisms, especially from the entourage of the Grand-Duke of Baden who was a son-in-law of the King:

In my opinion, the chief defect of our actual policy lay in the fact that we stand for liberalism in Prussia and for conservatism abroad, holding the rights of our own King cheap and the foreign Princes' too high. I am loyal to my King to the bitter end, but towards any other Princes I do not feel a trace of obligation in a single drop of my blood. Our foreign policy must become more independent of dynastic sympathies.

Thus Bismarck was indeed the sort of politician ' who is prepared to appear as a revolutionary in foreign affairs, so that he might be a conservative in internal affairs, and to surrender the foreign Princes in order to save the Brandenburg nobility ', to quote the words of a Prussian historian of the time.

But although Bismarck was ready to join the ministry and to approve of the feudal homage in principle, in the actual political situation he was enough of a shrewd politician to regard the dispute about the latter as a hindrance rather than a boon.

It is a pity that the breach has come just in this way. The good royalist mass of voters will not understand the dispute about the feudal homage and the democrats will misrepresent it [he writes to Roon]. It would have been better to keep your chin up in regard to the military question, break with the Chamber, dissolve it, and thereby show the nation how the King stands to the people.

In fact, however, Bismarck did not expect a breach. He hoped that the Chamber would bend before the pressure, and that, as he had said to Manteuffel ten years earlier, it had ' ceased to hamper government '. The pretended constitutionalism of Napoléon provided for this the enticing pattern. Why should the management of the Chamber which seemed to be possible in Paris not also be practicable in Berlin ? It is this point of view, much more than the distance between his residence and Berlin, as alleged by an eminent biographer, which seems to have hindered Bismarck from recognizing ' the sharpness and magnitude of the opposed tendencies leading up to a conflict in their elemental forces '.   In fact it proved, for the time being, to be a case of bending, not of breaking ; but it was not the Chamber which did the bending, it was the King.   The latter, as Bismarck says, ' entered upon an ill-masked retreat ' in as much as he, instead of the act of feudal homage which he had originally desired, contented himself with the less offensive ' solemn coronation '.   The liberal ministers expressed their satisfaction. Roon, who complained of the ' spiritlessness and weariness ' of the King, had to ' shelve the almost complete list of ministers '; the settlement of accounts with the Chamber was further postponed, and Bismarck was again disappointed in his hopes of a Cabinet post. The crisis in the ministry ended in a fashion particularly annoying for him, when in September of this year at Coblenz, whither he had accompanied the King, the foreign minister von Schleinitz was replaced by Count Bernstorff, who was a less definitely party politician than Bismarck.   Roon, however, tried to counteract ' the tendency to fall under the yoke of parliament and republicanism, the process of universal decomposition ', not by drawing up lists of Cabinet Ministers, but by striving ' to keep uncorrupted the only organ capable of resistance, the army ', so that the latter ' should not also be contaminated '.

The settlement of the issues with parliament and liberalism was put off by the yielding of the King, but not put to an end.   William I vented his anger at his deprivation of the feudal homage ceremony by putting the crown on his head in the coronation act and uttering a few powerful words to the effect that he had received it from no one but God and was only responsible to God ; the houses of parliament were only entitled to advise him.   Objectively, Bismarck was content with this action, but he was straightway to become aware that it did not involve any improvement in his own position.   For the King avoided meeting him ' from anxiety ', so Bismarck assumed, ' lest he should come to be looked on in a reactionary light through his relations with me '.   This interpretation of the situation was correct.   The words of the King were regarded as a challenge.   The answer to it was given in the election for the Chamber which took place seven weeks later.   In this the new Party of Progress with the parties allied to it nearly obtained an absolute majority, and the old liberal party not quite a third of the seats, while the conservatives were reduced to a vanishing minority.   The hostile attitude towards the government and towards the military bill—which formed the central point of the struggle—came to a head at the beginning of March, two months after the convocation of the Chamber, when the party of progress moved that the military budget should be presented ' in detail '.   The Cabinet saw in this the intention to tie its hands completely in regard to this budget and to make the carrying out of the army reorganization practically impossible. The King was deeply offended. 'The King is not to rule, they want to rule,' he wrote about this time in a private letter. But Roon saw that his hour had now definitely come. 'Ministers with a previous parliamentary history are your Majesty's ruin,' he told the King. He advised him to choose the way which leads 'with all the glory of arms to the heights which rule life'. He explained that the King of Prussia was not tied to the constitution. This was left to the free decision of the King, its fulfilment being 'dependent on further free royal decisions'. When the Chamber carried the proposal of the party of progress, the King decided to accept the resignation of the liberal Cabinet and dissolved parliament. Therewith the 'New Era' came to its end after little more than three years. With it, parliamentarism in Prussia was to be extinguished for a long time to come and the idea that among Germans the state was to grow out of the development of individual liberty received a severe blow. The King summoned a conservative Cabinet under the leadership of Prince Hohenlohe. Roon remained minister of war and Count Bernstorff foreign minister. Bismarck again found himself excluded from the list of people summoned to be ministers. That Queen Augusta and the Grand-Duke of Baden and, as was soon to be seen, the then Crown Prince, Frederick William, were his enemies, certainly had something to do with this. But that the King did not feel at home with him was no doubt the decisive factor. One of Bismarck's admirers said that the King had felt 'the sovereignty of the great man' as a danger for 'royal sovereignty'.

Once more in Bismarck personal ambition, enmity against the rivals preferred to him and the desire at last to get the centre of Prussian government into his own hands combined and fired each other so as to produce deep bitterness and depression. In the letters of this time from St. Petersburg to his sister these emotions find strong expression. 'My power to adapt myself to changed circumstances is lost. Three years ago I could still have made a useful minister. Now I think of myself as a sick circus-rider. I am as afraid of the Cabinet as of a cold bath.' In a second letter he gives the assurance that he 'looks with indifference on the question of a change of post. Princely letters', he continues, 'speak of H's resignation and of my replacing him. I do not believe that this is really intended, but I should decline if it were. I do not feel well enough for so much excitement and work.' However, when in April 1862, a few weeks after the inauguration of the Hohenlohe Ministry, his recall from St. Petersburg to Berlin took place, he was at once like a changed man, although the offer of a Cabinet post was at least very doubtful and a mere change of place to the embassy in Paris or London must have seemed more likely. For he had formed the

impression that the new Cabinet would not remain in power very long
and drew from this, consciously or unconsciously, conclusions for
his future career.   On the 12th of April he wrote from St. Petersburg to Roon in reference to the behaviour of one of the present
ministers that the latter ' with his well-known sagacity foresaw a
change and altered his own conduct accordingly ' and that he,
Bismarck, deduced from this that there would shortly be a re-
shuffling of the Cabinet.   On arriving in Berlin at the beginning of
May Bismarck was very soon in the midst of government affairs and
of conversations with Cabinet ministers.   The Prussian intervention
in the struggle for the constitution of Kur-Hesse had just led to an
understanding between Prussia and Austria about the measures to be
taken.   At the same time, however, the Elector of Kur-Hesse treated
a letter directed to him personally from the Prussian King with gross
disrespect in the presence of witnesses.   Bismarck was told of this
by Bernstorff shortly after his arrival in Berlin, and, to the horror
of the·latter, gave the following answer : ' The circumstance that the
Elector has thrown a royal letter on the table is hardly a good *casus
belli* ; but if you want war you appoint me your under-secretary, and
I promise within four weeks to deliver you a German civil war of the
best quality.'   But there was still no ministerial post for Bismarck,
although Prince Hohenlohe implored him, so he relates, ' to redeem
him from his martyrdom by instantly taking over his office '.   Thus
on the 17th of May Bismarck wrote to his wife, who had remained
behind in St. Petersburg : ' Berlin stands more in the foreground,
I do nothing for or against it.   But I shall get good and drunk
once I have my credentials for Paris in my pocket.'   Five days
later he really had these credentials in his pocket.   The situation
' so offensive to my self-respect of being at anchor in Berlin in
an hotel in the guise of a suitor ', a situation which was in such sharp
conflict with the desire he had always had to let men and things come
to him, was at last at an end.   But of getting drunk we hear nothing,
though we hear that despite his new appointment he cast glances
again over Paris back to Berlin.   ' Whether I shall go to Paris for
long ', he wrote to his wife two days after his appointment, ' that
God knows, perhaps only for months, or weeks !   It is possible that
I may be called back again before my things have arrived.   It is rather
a case of making a fugitive visit than of removing to a new place of
residence.   I am ready for everything that God may send.'

The relations between France and Prussia were not unfavourable
when on the 29th of May 1862 Bismarck arrived in Paris.   In the spring
of 1859, indeed, Napoléon had been offended with Prussia because the
mobilization of the latter had prevented him from exploiting fully
his military successes against Austria.   This was followed by a like
annoyance on the side of Prussia, when the acquisition by France of

Savoy and Nice, at the end of March 1860 according to the agreement at Plombières, was made public together with its official justification that France had thereby recovered her natural boundaries. However, the Prussian Prince-Regent after long hesitation had decided to meet Napoléon in person. The meeting took place in the middle of June 1860 in Baden-Baden in the presence of several Confederate Princes. At this meeting Napoléon explained to William, and later to the other Princes, that the annexation which had been carried out constituted ' an exceptional case in consequence of the previous agreement ' with the intention of thereby depriving it of any significance as a symptom of his future policy. At the same time the relations between Prussia and Austria were, as the result of the refusal of military help in the Italian war, still too delicate for it to be possible to place a further burden on them through an apparent understanding with France. So the Prussian Prince-Regent visited the Austrian Emperor in Teplitz at the end of July, gave him assurances about the political relations of Prussia with France and tried hard to come to an understanding about a reform in the Confederation. It was a great event for the court of Paris when at the beginning of October 1861 William I returned the Baden-Baden visit of Napoléon by a visit to Compiègne. Half a year later Prussia approached France in the matter of a commercial agreement and was favourably received. In Austria, on the other hand, where the government was never satisfied with Prussia's commercial policy, this undertaking was bound to arouse violent anger. In March 1862, a commercial treaty was concluded between France and Prussia according to the principles of free trade, including a provision to the effect that Prussia would only renew the German Customs Union agreement with those states which would join in this treaty.

So Bismarck might hope to find in Paris a friendly atmosphere, and also a continuance of the confidence which Napoléon had shown in him. On the 1st of June he reported to his wife : ' To-day I was received by the Emperor. He received me in a friendly fashion.' Bismarck no longer encountered the omnipotent ruler whom he had met five years before. Napoléon had recently decided to make real concessions to the principle of parliamentary government and these began to irk him. He had resolved on a military expedition to Mexico, which was just on the way to becoming a highly dangerous adventure. People were speaking of a serious illness in connexion with him. But Bismarck writes to his wife that the Emperor ' looks well, has put on some weight, but is not at all fat and aged, as he is represented in caricatures to be. The Empress is still one of the most beautiful women I know.' Roon was informed at the same time that the audience ' did not bring in politics, which was postponed to another day when I should be received in private '. One

of the first political remarks of Napoléon concerned the idea which
Bismarck had occasionally cherished at the time of the Crimean War,
the ' Prusso-Austro-German block of states ', as fulcrum in the
European balance.   Napoléon asserted very decisively that he would
' under no circumstances agree to the entry of Austria as a whole
into a German Confederation '.   In other respects he showed himself, as already in 1857, favourable to the desire of Prussia to expand
within the Confederation.   The main political discussion took place
three weeks later during a walk at Fontainebleau.   Again, as five
years before, the Emperor very quickly plunged *in medias res*, and
asked Bismarck whether he ' thought that the King would be inclined
to enter into an alliance with him '.   That was somewhat more than
Bismarck himself with all his support for an understanding with
France desired.   Especially at the present moment, when the outlook for France was not of the rosiest, he did not want Prussia ' to
cut off the possibility ' of an understanding with Austria, ' evil ' as
that possibility was.   Also, he knew that his King would not wish to
have anything to do with such a ' lascivious proposal of alliance '.
So Bismarck made an evasive answer, whereupon the ' idea of a
" diplomatic alliance " ' was further developed by Napoléon.   The
Emperor, who obviously disliked Bismarck's reserve, tried to bait his
interlocutor by representing himself as occupying the very place of
fulcrum in the balance which Bismarck strove to obtain for Prussia.
But he put it on too thick to persuade so astute a reader of the human
mind as Bismarck, perhaps because he really regarded Bismarck as
' not a serious man ', as he told his entourage at the time.   ' You
cannot picture to yourself ', so Bismarck reports Napoléon saying,
' what singular offers I have had from Austria a few days ago.'   The
Austrian ambassador had said to him that ' he had instructions which
went so far that he himself was frightened of them.   He had unlimited plenipotentiary powers to come to an understanding with me
in regard to any and every question at any price.'   The Emperor,
however, added that he ' had an almost superstitious aversion to
mixing himself up with the fortunes of Austria '.   The doubts which
Bismarck rightly felt about the truth of this report did not prevent
his using it as stimulus to the venom which was always present in his
mind against Austria.   Reporting to Bernstorff on this episode, he
breaks out against Austria : ' In Frankfurt I had already come to the
conviction that the politics of Vienna under certain circumstances
shrank back from no combination, that the phrase " the German
mission " is current in the Austrian Palace as long as it is used as a
bridle for us. If a Franco-Austrian coalition is not already in
existence, we owe that not to Austria but to France ', namely to
' the misgivings of Napoléon as to whether Austria is in a position to
sail with the strong wind of the time—nationality.'   What position

Napoléon in his political combinations had intended for Russia, Bismarck did not say. But he did report to Berlin his conviction that a Franco-Russian alliance was just as possible as a Franco-Austrian. Bismarck and Napoléon also discussed questions of internal politics, and Napoléon, who had just made concessions to the parliamentary principle, expressed his conviction that ' a government which furthers the patriotic parties always has in relation to the Chamber the needed measure of power and freedom '.

Of practical political business there was as good as nothing for Bismarck in the summer months. He felt deserted and aimless in the French capital. ' In the middle of great Paris I am more lonely than you are in Reinfeld, and I sit here like a rat in a deserted house,' he wrote to his wife already at the beginning of June. So the ' holiday traveller for pleasure ' in Bismarck again joined hands with the politician. At the end of June we find him in London visiting the World Exhibition. He also came to know personally Palmerston and John Russell. The former he blamed because ' his arguments are seldom of an objective character '. In regard to both he emphasized their 'complete ignorance about the state of affairs in Prussia'. He also came to know Disraeli. To the latter he is said to have expressed himself most openly. Questioned what he would do if he came into power Bismarck is reported to have amazed him by the answer : ' The first thing I shall do is to help to organize the army, with or without the assistance of the Second Chamber. Then I shall take the first opportunity to declare war on Austria, to dissolve the German Confederation, to bring into subjection the middle and smaller states, and to give Germany national unity under the leadership of Prussia.' This remark should not be hard to rank among those unexpected pieces of frankness with which Bismarck put his political friends and opponents out of countenance.

About the middle of July there followed a journey intended simply as a holiday. Strange to say Bismarck did not go to Pomerania to see his family, although he tells his wife that he ' feels it very strange that he does not hasten to her at full speed, so that after so long. a parting he may enjoy the delight of being in the midst of his family '. Nor does he think of asking his wife to join him in his intended journey to the South of France. As compensation, however, she received beautiful letters describing his travels, for instance one from the district of Bordeaux : ' Wheat vanishes and is replaced by maize ; in between there are luxuriant vines and woods of chestnut trees, castles big and small with many towers, chimney pots and bay windows, all white with high pointed slate roofs.' Writing from Bayonne he speaks of the ' apparent mixture of juniper trees, bilberry bushes, &c., which covers the ground, but reveals itself really as all sorts of foreign plants with leaves like myrtle and cyprus. The splendour with which the heather here displays its violet, purple, and blue is amazing. The whole makes a variegated carpet.' Of the Spanish border he says : ' The district is extraordinarily beautiful, green valleys and wooded heights, crowned by fantastic lines of fortifications, row behind row, gulfs of the sea with quite narrow entrances which cut deep into the land.' Bismarck's stay in Biarritz which followed these days lasted longer than he had originally anticipated. Bismarck found in ' the Orlows ' (the Russian ambassador in Brussels, Prince Orlow, and his wife) attractive company, and described the lady to his wife as ' jolly, fresh and natural '. All excursions he made ' *à trois* with the Orlows, after whose arrival my loneliness has disappeared '. He forgets for the first time to send his wife the usual congratulations on the anniversary of their wedding, calls Princess Orlow ' my excellent Kati ' and asks for forgiveness ' because he is somewhat enthusiastic about her '. Afterwards when ' this bit of romance has reached its end the longing for you and the children comes into its own again with full power ', he says with pitiless condescension to his wife concerning the end of their holiday *à deux*. He thus reminds himself again of the ' independent family life in the country ' as a ' pleasant goal in political as well as other storms '. In the hangover following this episode he writes at the end of his journey to Roon : ' My things are still at St. Petersburg, my carriages are still in Stettin, my horses near Berlin in the country, my family in Pomerania, I myself on the road.' A few days later he received from Roon a prearranged telegram calling him to Berlin. The purpose of it was that he should be once more on the spot to await developments. On the 18th of September he left Paris for Berlin. This time things really came to a head.

In the meantime the correspondence with Roon had not been broken off, so that Bismarck obtained information about political events in Berlin from a person most intimately concerned with them. To the great pleasure of Bismarck Roon was assuming a still more decisive line than he had done during the ' New Era '. In connexion with the debate on the address of the Chamber to the King following the fresh elections in May 1862 which had resulted in a yet further movement to the Left, Bismarck replied to a report of his friend : ' If these people take the sham battle over the address as a real victory and scatter themselves plundering and marauding in the legal domain of the King, the time will come for those who are marked out as the enemies to unmask their batteries and shoot straight. Your letter breathes the honourable wrath of a warrior, sharpened to greater keenness by the dust and heat of the battle. You have given an excellent answer without flattery.'

However, the relations between government and Chamber this summer at first seemed to be better than one could expect. The action of the government against the autocracy of Kur-Hesse, the conclusion of the commercial treaty with France, and the negative attitude to a recent proposal of the Saxon prime minister, von Beust, for a reform of the Confederation to include Austria and some further similar measures, had given satisfaction to the Chamber. This strengthened Bismarck in his opinion that at last the Chamber would let itself bend before pressure ; in a letter to Roon of the 15th of July Bismarck suggested that the Cabinet should indeed oppose the motions of the Chamber rejecting certain items in the military budget, ' should, however, bring about no crisis in regard to them but let the Chamber carry the debate on the budget to its end ', and that the Cabinet would thus ' manipulate ' the conflict. ' The further the matter is prolonged the lower will the Chamber sink in public respect.' When the Chamber was ripe for its decay his, Bismarck's, nomination was bound to come. Then one must ' rattle one's weapons of an. enforced constitution and *coups d'état* '. His ' old reputation of frivolous proneness to violence ' would do the rest.

But when in August the discussion about the military budget really came to its height things turned out quite differently. In the debates on the committee stage of the 22nd to 29th of August the government was ready to make a compromise on the basis of a two years' period of service and had actually obtained for that the express agreement of Roon. But the King himself rejected the compromise and held fast to the original proposal. There followed in a full session of the Chamber a bitter war of words about the military budget. On the 23rd of September, by a majority of 273 against 68 the cost of the reorganization of the army was struck out of the budget for the year 1863, and this budget was then accepted by a similar majority. Anticipating the abandonment of constitutional government, Hohenlohe, Count Bernstorff, and several other cabinet ministers at once tendered their resignations. Roon, as the senior of the remaining ministers, reported on the situation to the King. The latter had already asked his eldest son and heir, the Crown Prince Frederick William, who held a high government post at Stettin, to come to Berlin, and had proposed to him his own abdication. The Prince, however, replied that under existing circumstances he would not accept the succession. Yet in court circles the question of abdication continued to be discussed.

When Bismarck on the 20th of September arrived in Berlin he forthwith called on the Crown Prince, who, he alleged, had ' summoned ' him. This action has been suspected as a premature approach to the expected successor to the throne. The King, on hearing the report, said : ' He, too, is no good, he has already been to my son.' Bismarck himself asserts that he did not know ' that the King was thinking about abdicating '. Two days later, through the mediation of Roon, Bismarck was received by the King and asked whether he ' was ready to enter the Cabinet as minister for military reorganization '. Bismarck agreed and expressly declared his resolve ' to enter on and conduct his office even against the majority of the Chamber ' and to carry on the government ' even without a budget '. ' Then it is my duty ', Bismarck quotes the King as replying, ' to seek to continue the battle together with you, and I shall not abdicate.' The King then read to him a memoir, which discussed details of business and included proposed concessions to the liberals, behind which Bismarck suspected the influence of Queen Augusta. Bismarck refused to allow his hands to be tied by this. He gives as his own answer : ' It is a question now, not of conservative versus liberal, but of royal versus parliamentary government. Even if your Majesty were to give me commands which I held to be not justified, I should rather go down with the King than desert your Majesty in the fight against parliamentary government.' Bismarck intended thus to realize in fact the thesis in the ' Booklet ' of March 1858 to the effect that the Prussian government may without danger ' allow parliament more elbow-room even in purely political questions than before '. Instead, Bismarck thereby put his hand to the throat of the constitutional state which among the Germans was to grow out of the development of individual liberty and threatened to choke it to death.

There followed on the 24th of September 1862 the royal decree countersigned by Roon : ' I have nominated my privy councillor Otto von Bismarck-Schönhausen minister of state and given him for the time being the presidency of the Cabinet.' To his wife Bismarck wrote : ' I have been appointed minister. All this is not agreeable, and I am afraid every time I wake up in the morning. But it must be.' A few days after the issue of the decree the King travelled to Baden-Baden, where the Queen was staying. Schleinitz had to accompany him, ' in order to mollify the Queen concerning the nomination of Bismarck '. The moderate section of the Opposition, looking at the matter with reserve, saw in the ' yokel ' ' no incompetent, but still less a safe, man '. The extremists cried out : ' Herr von Bismarck ! That is the *coup d' état.*'

CHAPTER XV

The Government without a Budget

The atmosphere in which Bismarck took up office was truly that of a *coup d'état*. He knew that he had no friend among politically influential people, except Roon and, if necessary, also the King. Men saw in him ' the type of a prime minister who concealed a uniform under his frock-coat ' or ' the last and sharpest arrow of " Reaction by the Grace of God " '. Those who did not hate him as their opponent saw in him, as Napoléon had done, ' not a serious man '. The reserve of the moderate liberal Press was in contrast to the lust for battle of the progressive newspapers. In these the hope was expressed ' soon to see him spinning wool for the benefit of the state ' (as prisoners did). Here originated the proposal which at the beginning of 1863 was adopted in the House of Deputies by a large majority, that ' cabinet ministers should be liable in person and property for expenses contrary to the constitution '. Bismarck consequently thought of ' handing over his landed property to his brother in order to save it '. He only refrained from taking this measure because ' his seat in the Upper House was bound up with the land he owned ' and because the transfer of the property ' would have given an impression of nervousness and anxiety about money matters which was obnoxious to me '. That he did not regard this step as either intrinsically unacceptable or as uncalled for by the situation shows in what a serious light he regarded the position. His belief in God came again more strongly into the foreground. ' My faith remains firm that God will not allow me to fall into disgrace in this position.' But his old friend, the strong believer Ludwig von Gerlach, who had once welcomed Bismarck into the Pomeranian circle of Pietists, had now lost something of his trust in the genuineness of Bismarck's religion. ' May God protect him against himself,' he writes in his *Memoirs*, ' and let him learn in time that the Short Catechism is valid also for statesmen.' He added with a sigh, two months later, ' Bismarck's energy gives little or rather no guarantee.'

This energy was at first directed, as on previous occasions, to preventing the conflict with the Chamber from coming to an open breach, and instead to manipulating the House. Efforts were made to employ the means of warfare used by him on other occasions both as party politician in parliament and as diplomat in settling the external issue with Austria, namely he tried to put his opponent in the wrong as aggressor and represent his own cause as that of injured innocence. On the 29th of September he attended for the first time in his new dignity a sitting of the budget commission of the House of Deputies. Here he announced in the name of the government the withdrawal of the budget for 1863, which had already been accepted by the Chamber, from further parliamentary discussion. He gave for this the very conciliatory sounding excuse that a new budget bill was intended 'for the beginning of the next session', after the hoped for 'understanding concerning a fresh bill about liability to military service' had been reached. The Chamber, however, saw in this withdrawal not a sign of an inclination to meet them in the matter of army reorganization, but rather the threat of a fresh interference with their budgetary rights, an attitude not altogether unexpected by Bismarck. It was expressed by the deputy who had to report on the budget the following day when he proposed 'to ask the government to lay the budget for 1863 before the House of Deputies promptly enough for its confirmation to be possible before the 1st of January 1863'.

Bismarck accepted the challenge the next day and took up position for battle, entrenching himself behind his legal rights. He declared that the Chamber had exceeded its legal power in deleting from the budget the charge for the army reorganization. Already ten years before he had supported the view that the right to refuse taxes was 'destroying the independence of the crown'. Now he declared positively his conviction that the budget was legally made valid by an agreement between the King and the two Chambers and that this implicit contract was the basis of its efficacy, as was the case with every law according to the nature of the constitution. So his former assertion that the budget of the previous year was automatically made valid for the next found its interpretation in the fact that the agreement of the previous year about the taxes to be levied remained in force 'till it was replaced by another agreement'. There was in fact a provision in the constitution by which the application of the last budget could be prolonged for a precisely defined period in the event of the new one not being presented in time. To this Bismarck now gave an extension which radically altered its purport, making the budgetary rights of the Chamber in fact subject to the whim of the crown. Starting from the proposition that in Prussia the constitution is a gift by the crown to the people, he did not indeed go so far as Roon, who made the keeping of the constitution dependent on 'further free royal decisions'. But he did assert, 'what in the constitution is not expressly handed over to other legislative bodies remains the right of the Throne'. By means of such 'devilish sophistries' (R. Morier) Bismarck arrived at the so-called 'theory of gaps', according to which 'the government has to jump in if the state is not to stand still '. But whither was he thus steering ? To no goal save what he himself had called the ' perilous ' enterprise of an absolutism ' supported by pliable parliaments ', an absolutism ' which requires no further justification but the reference to the approval of the majority '. It is obvious that in this he was encouraged by the pattern set up by Napoléon.

But as on former occasions Bismarck's theorizing was only the prelude ; soon the theoretical garment is shed and before us stands the man of brute force. He advocates indeed an ' understanding ' with the Chamber, and asks for ' confidence '. But it was impossible to ignore his threat that ' the question of right could easily become a question of might '. Once more he used ' public opinion ' and ' the Catilinarian beings who take a great interest in revolutions ' to add fuel to his boiling wrath. ' Public opinion changes ', he exclaims, ' the Press is not public opinion. We know how the Press originates. The deputies have the higher task, to direct the mind of the public so as to stand above it.' Then the ' red reactionary who smells blood ' breaks out in the explosive words :

We prefer to carry a weight of armour which is too great for our frail body. Now we shall also use it to the full. Germany does not look to the liberalism of Prussia, but to the might of Prussia. Prussia must concentrate her forces and hold them together for the favourable moment which has already several times been missed. The boundaries of Prussia according to the Treaty of Vienna (1815) are not favourable to a healthy state life. The great questions of the time are not decided by speeches and majority decisions—that was the great mistake of 1848 and 1849—but by blood and iron.

In his *Reflections and Reminiscences* he supplements this, saying : ' The Gordian knot in German affairs is not to be untied by the agreement of both parties [Austria and Prussia] in love, but only to be hacked to pieces by military force.' These clear words are the expression of an excitement which, as so often with Bismarck, did not arise without some conscious whetting of himself to fury so as to enhance the effect. The words ' *ferro et igni* ' are to be found already in the memoir of May 1859, and his ' reputation of frivolous proneness to violence ' had been offered to the King by Bismarck already three months before this speech as a means of warfare, Bismarck's words before the Chamber may be opposed to the King's speech from the throne about the desire of Prussia for ' moral conquest in Germany ' and his will to ' defend the right '. But the same King had also, although in private, said : ' Who wants to rule Germany must conquer her for himself.' Roon, however, according to Bismarck's account, ' on our way home, expressed his dissatisfaction with my speech and said among other things that he did not consider such " brilliant digressions " advantageous to our cause '.

So Bismarck had, immediately after taking over responsibility for the government, clearly declared what issue he regarded as the main subject of his future activities—'the German material question', as he had earlier called it, the 'knot in German affairs', as he says now, the question of the national unification of Germany, as it was called by the supporters of the programme. Bismarck at the same time had put in opposition to each other two ways of solving the question. Against the solution by blood and iron chosen by himself he set a policy in which 'love' plays a rôle. We know what significance attaches to the relation of love to others, not only in Bismarck's private life, but also in his public activities. He regards the relation of husband and wife and the foundation of a family as a part of the process by which the state is built up and as itself mirroring the latter's development. He alleges that the relation to the state has its culmination in the patriarchal loyalty to the person and institution of the monarch, a loyalty based on the position of feudal vassal and officer. Connected with it is the personal relation to the fellow-members of his class, the 'nobility', 'kindness' towards the 'common people', and the preference for 'the men with the nature of soldiers who have warm Prussian blood in their bodies', as well as the attachment to the soil of one's estate and of the fatherland. To this is added a very strong emphasis on his own person with his great self-assurance and self-righteousness confirmed by his connexion with state service, becoming ever more deeply rooted and ever more the focal point of his public activities. All this together made up for Bismarck the living content of his feeling for the 'Prussian clan' (*Stamm*) and for the dynasty, which constitute the basis of his political efforts. This 'Prussian clan' was 'his' German clan.

This clan, however, was only a fraction of the 'German nation'. Besides it there were other German clans, the Bavarians, the Saxons, the Hessians, and, last of all, the Austrians. And Bismarck did not stand in this same relation of love to them all. To his monarch he indeed declared himself 'true to the bitter end', but to all the others he felt 'no trace of obligation'. The threat of blood and iron was in the first place directed only against Austria, which was capable of any 'perfidy' against Prussia, and therefore had in Bismarck's plan to stay outside the national union of Germany. But are Bismarck's feelings really more friendly towards wide circles of the 'clans' which are to belong to this unified Germany? As a basis of their relation to Prussia he had emphasized and enhanced ever more the motive of 'fear' as an antidote to their inclinations towards the 'Rhine League'. The particularly influential liberal and democratical bourgeoisie in their midst with their 'parliamentary celebrities' could for him be nothing but the partner in a 'shameful alliance'; the 'rotten fermentation of south German indiscipline' must be kept from harming Prussia. Against the 'catholicizing opponents of Prussia' with their 'mind bent on conquest' now as before 'open war' is the order of the day. The non-Prussian 'cancerous bureaucracy' is not any less deserving of hate than the Prussian. Political expediency might recommend 'voluntary agreements subject to notice' with the governments of these states. But how was there to be a link possible with them which could lead Bismarck from the unity of the Prussian clan to the national unity of Germany?

In Bismarck's emotional world there was no basis to be found for any voluntary concessions to the other German clans and their states, which had been the object of the Nationalverein with its demand for sacrifices. Bismarck was the defender of 'state egoism' as 'the only sound foundation of a great state'. His 'specifically Prussian patriotism' speaks quite clearly out of the words 'the two ends coincide': 'the leadership of Prussia from the Prussian standpoint' and 'the unification of Germany from the national standpoint'. This kind of patriotism was already indicated in his own somewhat tortuous words: 'I should have had no weapon against the Brandenburg ruling House, if I had had to realize my German national feeling by a breach with it and a rising against it.' The application of a policy of blood and iron, not only against Austria, but also within the German nation which was to be united, was suggested by the national struggle for the unification of Italy, the first phase of which had just been completed. To this application also pointed the words of Napoléon to Bismarck, that Prussia should 'consolidate herself by the addition of Hanover and Schleswig-Holstein' and the latter's own alleged disclosure to Disraeli about his plans once he became prime minister. The same was expressed very unambiguously in the words of Bismarck just pronounced in public about the too 'frail body' of Prussia, her 'not favourable boundaries' and the rejection of 'majority decisions' concerning 'the great questions of the time'.

But was it really the case that 'the concentration of Prussia's forces' in a battle of 'blood and iron' was the only way which could lead from the unity of the different clans as shown by history to the national unity of Germany which was to be created? Was there not besides and in opposition to this division among the German clans within Germany a tendency of a spiritual, not physical nature, an element making for unity which had been there for long but had so far only played a hesitating and uncertain part? An affirmative answer to this question constituted the central content of German Liberalism, not only since '1848 and 1849' but ever since the idea of the *Kulturstaat* as the 'adequate expression of a national entity founded upon the equality of all human beings and grown out of the development of individual liberty ' had gained a footing in the minds of the classical German thinkers and poets. This idea was again and again impressed upon Bismarck by the traditions of his mother's family, influenced as it was by the spirit of the French Revolution and the aims of the volunteers of the Wars of Liberation, by the tendencies in the Grammar School and the students' fraternities. This thought Bismarck encountered in the work of the German universities and of the Prussian bureaucracy, in the parliamentary life which surrounded him and the parliamentary battles in which he was engaged, in persons such as Schleiermacher, Dahlmann, Georg von Vincke, Bethmann-Hollweg, and finally Bonin, as also in Radowitz and even in Frederick William IV, in Queen Augusta and the tradition of the Weimar court.

Bismarck might well object to the spiritual heritage of the German classical thinkers and poets and their followers, saying that by itself it was too indefinite and unpractical to form the basis of the state. But had he for this reason to undertake against them the war of annihilation which he had commenced as soon as he came into power ? Was his idea of *Realpolitik*, and ' political relations of power ', based on the ' serried ranks of our troops ' and directed towards ' attaining the position of a European Great Power ' really sufficient as the basic idea behind a newly created state ? Was it not rather the case that the power principle determined only the relations of the state and its subjects to the surrounding states ? Did it not rather urgently require supplementation by the idea of a union among these very subjects which would, overcoming all oppositions of race, religion and social differences, give to their common life a common meaning ? Was it not possible and indeed a matter of duty to adopt the German classical idea of the worth and freedom of personality as an ' inner decoration ' within that state building whose walls of defence Bismarck was now about to erect ? When Bismarck told his sovereign that the essence of the actual constitutional conflict lay in the settlement of the issue of ' royal versus parliamentary government ', he thought that he had thereby expressed the full nature of the question. In reality, his exclusive point of view had led to his ignoring one decisive aspect of the problem, namely that a state structure based on blood and iron without a real community among its inhabitants would become a prison, against whose wardens the captives would rise one day. Bismarck believed that he could settle his struggle in home politics in the same way as Napoléon did his, without considering that the latter had only to erect the fabric of a modern state for a nation which had been unified for centuries, while he himself had first to seek for this foundation of German national unity.

It was not only with Roon and within the parliament but also among the wider public that Bismarck's blood-and-iron-speech encountered the sharpest opposition. The liberal newspapers made it known to the public with comments calculated to increase its strange and threatening effect. The King in Baden-Baden heard of the speech only indirectly, through the Press. Bismarck was well aware what the reaction of the sovereign would be and how it would be intensified by the representations of the Queen. Having obtained leave he journeyed to meet the King on the 4th of October on the latter's way back to Berlin, and about 40 miles away from the terminus he entered the carriage in which the King was sitting alone. Bismarck found him, as he had anticipated, in a ' depressed mood '. To his request that he should be allowed ' to explain what has happened in your absence ' the monarch replied : ' I foresee exactly how all this will end. There in the Opera Square, in front of my windows, they will cut off your head, and mine somewhat later.' Bismarck :—' *Et après*, Sire ? '—The King : ' Yes, *après*, then we shall be dead.'—Bismarck : ' Yes, then we shall be dead, but we must die sooner or later and could we come to our end in a more worthy fashion ? I should die fighting for the cause of my King. And your Majesty would seal with your own blood the rights of the monarch based on God's Grace. Will Charles I not always remain famous in history because he drew the sword on behalf of his rights, lost the battle, and unswervingly confirmed his royal conviction with his blood. Your Majesty must fight. You cannot capitulate. You must oppose the violation of your rights, even if it involved danger to life and limb.'

Bismarck had earlier asserted that he knew how to deal with the King. The appeal to the providence of God must not be forgotten. ' May God give me as much power as I have goodwill,' he says in his next New Year's congratulation to the King, although he calls himself in a contemporary private letter ' the helpless plaything of the times ', as he did in his godless bachelor days. The appeal to the King in his capacity as officer also always has a good effect. But it is remarkable how Bismarck characterizes the quality of military leadership in his ' all-gracious Majesty '. He calls him

the ideal type of Prussian officer who will fearlessly go to meet a certain death on the call of duty with the simple words ' At your order ', but who, where it is a question of acting on his own responsibility, fears so much the criticism of his superior that the energy of his decision is impaired by the fear of blame.

This is a strange ideal, this officer afraid of responsibility. He would hardly be admitted to a Prussian military college and would certainly not be qualified for the post of a general, but would have to remain a subaltern. Still more remarkable in Bismarck's mouth is the personification as the King's 'superior officer' of those who exercise 'criticism'. This figure personifies, besides history, public opinion and the Queen. Now, public opinion, according to Bismarck, is the 'clamour of unreason', and the Queen is trying to influence the King with *aide-memoires* 'drawn up for the purpose'.

The result of Bismarck's exhortation on the journey to Berlin was, according to him, that the King, inspired by the consciousness of being 'the first officer of the Prussian monarchy', arrived 'in a joyful and warlike mood', and that this 'was made clear in the most unambiguous fashion to the Cabinet ministers and officials who were receiving him' at the station. Thus Bismarck's move to depict the situation to the King, for whom he 'cherished strong feelings of attachment and devotion', ended with a dramatic picture of unity with the King ostentatiously displayed to an entourage, few of whom approved Bismarck's policy and considered its maintenance possible. Before these he showed himself now complete master of the situation in unqualified unity with his monarch. This unity received a further confirmation when in the course of the next few days his 'temporary appointment' was converted into a definite nomination as prime minister and foreign minister.

For Bismarck this meant an extraordinary increase in the security of his position over and against the Chamber. He did not altogether abandon the idea of a voluntary surrender on the part of Parliament as the result of his skilful manipulation of the conflict. But when the Chamber, in accordance with the proposal of the member who had to give the report on the budget, resolved: 'The further collection in the budgetary year 1863 of the non-recurrent expenditure for military preparations authorized for the years 1860 and 1861 constitutes a violation of the budget law', Bismarck launched a new counter-attack. He continued to play the rôle of defender of injured innocence and to emphasize the conciliatory attitude of the government. But he said of the resolution of the Chamber: 'This rejects our proffered hand; it answers the proposal for an armistice with a challenge to continue the fight at once. The government takes cognizance of this fact.'

The mode of this cognizance is extraordinarily characteristic of Bismarck. He undertook the task of drawing into the fight the third body which had a share in legislation, the Upper House, as an ally against the Lower House. He brought it about that the former, as it was competent to do, rejected on the 10th of October the budget which the Lower House had mutilated on the 23rd of September. He brought it about further that the Upper House, exceeding its legal competence and, defying the constitution, accepted in full the budget originally proposed by the government, including the items struck out by the Lower House. The Upper House thereby did

Bismarck the service of challenging on its own account the other House and thus removing from his shoulders at least a part of the load of responsibility in the struggle. The Lower House, however, followed up without long deliberation the direction in which the conflict had now been turned, and resolved three days later : ' The decision of the Upper House is null and void. The government of the state can derive no rights from this resolution.' These words meant the doom of this parliament. The government took immediate steps to deprive the Lower House of the power to utter any more words. Bismarck read out a royal message, according to which the sittings of Parliament were declared closed, and delivered in the afternoon a speech winding up the session for both Houses. The government would, he said, ' be guilty of a grave violation of duty ' if it ' were willing to cancel the reorganization of the army which had been carried out up to the present '. Therefore it was necessary ' to carry on the management of the state without the basis provided in the constitution '. Among the ' duties of the government towards the country is included the defraying of all expenses which are required for the maintenance of the existing state institutions, till the budget has been legally ratified '.

Therewith, ten days after the return of the King from Baden-Baden to Berlin, his government began to handle the finances of state in defiance of the constitution. The flirtation with the thesis that the Prussian ' government may without danger allow parliament more elbow-room even in purely political questions than before ' was at an end. Once more, as in earlier times, the watchword was : ' The struggle ' between the ' sovereignty by God's Grace set in power by God ' and the ' rights nominally based on the will of the people, really on the club-law of the barricades, is one that permits of no mediation '. The tension which prevailed in the whole country surrounded also the King. It was not only that the popular expressions of opinion affected him, but that he had to hear the same views from the liberal circle of his own court, and especially from the members of his family with whom inclination to liberal ideas was combined with anxiety for the continuance of the dynasty. But the King who was certainly not unaffected by this anxiety continued to maintain his ' warlike ' attitude, even allowing himself to be convinced of the ' rightness ' of the procedure of his government. Bismarck quotes a New Year's message from an East Prussian aristocrat to the King, which says : ' The people remain loyal to your Majesty, but they also hold fast to the rights which the constitution unambiguously grants ', and also the answer of the King, according to which ' since the Deputies have used their right for the destruction of the army and the country ', he was ' bound, as a good father of the house, to carry on the household and later to render account for it '. ' Who then ', he adds, ' has made the constitution impossible ? Certainly not I.' The letter corresponds exactly to the purpose of Bismarck, but it was written without his intervention and even without his knowledge, for the King had given him a copy a week after its dispatch with the request ' to communicate it also to the other Cabinet ministers '. The King also gave his prime minister for a public occasion the instructions : ' Only make quite clear how the Lower House has abused its rights and contributed to the ruin of the land, and how the Upper House has also made use of its rights and put itself on the side of the government.'

Bismarck, now, on assuming office, took two steps which were bound to exercise a tranquillizing influence on his royal master. He forced himself to send Herr von Beust, the stubborn reformer of the German Confederation, whom he so much disliked, a letter expressing his intentions. In it he gave voice to the conviction that he could ' protect the power of the Throne against the increasing pressure of the House of Deputies, without violating anything positively laid down in the constitution '. Further, he assured him in quite general terms that he ' was far from all adventurous plans which have been ascribed to me in the Press by political children and opponents '. That this letter would become known to wider circles followed from the position and the person of the recipient. About the same time Bismarck made use of the constitutional dispute in Kur-Hesse in order to make quite clear that, if he was to allow himself to violate the constitution, this was by no means allowed to others. By the Prussian memoir to the Federal Diet of 1859 this dispute had been deferred but had not been settled. In October 1862 the Prince Elector of Hesse again tried to force a reactionary constitution on his Parliament, and the latter turned to Prussia for help. Only a few weeks after his own violation of the constitution, Bismarck sent an official note to the Elector, very seriously warning him. He was told that Prussia could not allow such a grave political confusion to break out again in her neighbourhood. Were the Elector to continue in his resolve, Prussia would immediately enter into the necessary negotiations with his possible heirs for his deposition.

An important task for which Bismarck was responsible at this time was the completion of the list of his colleagues in the Cabinet. It was not easy to find suitable men to be in charge of the particular departments of the 'Cabinet of Conflict'. For this purpose only reactionary Junkers could be considered, and among these a high degree of intelligence was even then not all too common, while several who were in themselves qualified for such a post would not join in a ministry which they anticipated would be very short-lived. The composition of the Cabinet gives us an opportunity of coming to know Bismarck in a new capacity, namely as holding the position of chief in a circle of semi-independent colleagues. He has not made it at all difficult for us to do this. We have already come to know Bismarck as an enemy and political opponent inexorable in his hate, and as a rebellious self-willed subordinate. Now, when he comes on the scene as leader of the bureaucracy whom he had always despised, and has to apply to others the ' strict concepts of subordination and duty of service ' which he had taken none too seriously for himself, he shows no trace of kindness or good-will but very much of the harshest, thoroughly scornful criticism. It is as if he wished to justify the words which he a little while before had written to a friend : ' It is a fault of my eye that it is keener for seeing weaknesses than for seeing good qualities.' ' The conviction that the other person ' with whom he had to deal ' in everything that he undertakes is at best limited but probably also evil-intentioned and unscrupulous ', was now no longer restricted to political opponents. That Bismarck does not hesitate to entertain this view even about his ' colleagues of his own class, the nobility ' is the result of his extreme self-assurance and self-righteousness which, once combined with the highest office of the Prussian state, had lost all restraint.

Among Bismarck's colleagues in the Cabinet his old friend von Roon comes off the best, his moral and intellectual qualities receiving express recognition. But even he does not escape adverse criticism altogether. Roon's ' hot temper ' is mentioned, and it is alleged that one ' missed in him the politeness which was expected in intercourse with a colleague '. Above all, however, it is objected against him that when he had to deputize for Bismarck as prime minister owing to an illness of the latter ' he did not oppose the lies and slanders about me, which have been systematically spread, with the decisiveness I should have shown if the case had been reversed '. The second-best place is given to the minister of the interior, Count Eulenburg, who is described as a ' subtle mind ' and as ' clever and ready-witted '. But he is accused of ' aversion to work, love of pleasure, lack of sense of duty, touchiness even towards me '. After him comes the minister of justice, Count zur Lippe, who ' by his scornful expression of superiority put parliament and his colleagues in a bad mood '. Next in the list is the minister of ecclesiastical affairs, von Mühler. He is very much under the influence of his wife and consequently ' not firm enough in his convictions to avoid making concessions at the expense of the policy of the state for the sake of peace at home '. The minister of agriculture, von Selchow, ' was not possessed of gifts which corresponded to the reputation which had gone before him '. The minister, von Jagow ' through his excited manner of speaking, his garrulousness, and the disputatious tone he assumed in debates soon excited the aversion of his colleagues in such a degree that he had to be dismissed '. Finally, as regards the finance minister, von Bodelschwingh, and the minister of commerce, Count Itzenplitz, 'it was clear that they were not capable of managing their departments; they confined themselves to affixing their signatures to the decisions of their advisers '. ' Support of my policy I personally could not expect from these two colleagues in view of their lack of understanding for it and the small amount of goodwill which they had for me as a president younger than they were.' Here Bismarck had also the opportunity of dealing a blow at the subordinate ranks of the bureaucracy, who ' were biased partly by liberal ideas, partly by a narrow departmental point of view, and the majority of whom belonged at heart to the Opposition against the " Ministry of Conflict " and expressed this by '' passive resistance " '. However, he expressly recognized ' the competent management in technical questions of the adviser in the ministry of commerce, Delbrück ', who was to become one of his closest collaborators. For the rest, in his reference to the activity of the lower ranks of the bureaucracy Bismarck made the minister of finance particularly ridiculous, in that he ' according to his personal views constituted the extreme Right among us ministers, but usually in voting (under the influence of his advisory council) took the position on the extreme Left '.

For Bismarck himself personal relations in his professional activity were made extraordinarily easy. People were willing to stand a surprising amount from him. The politician of the Right, Hans Blum, the son of the Robert Blum who had been court-martialled and shot in 1848, reports full of pride in his biography of Bismarck the latter's remark to him : ' I also should have had your father shot. But to-day, I should judge more justly. Your father was liberal—very liberal, but also a good patriot.' In order to win men for himself personally Bismarck needed to pay very little in the shape of courtesy. A member of the parliament of Kur-Hesse, who paid Bismarck a visit in connexion with the constitutional conflict there, makes the following report on this call : ' Servile Junker, inveterate aristocrat, hunting maniac, light-hearted gambler —those were the descriptions with which men referred to the prime minister of Prussia.' But he himself had encountered ' no trace of aristocratic arrogance, limited Junkerdom, feudal one-sidedness '. The minister ' kindly came to meet me at the door, reached me his hand, offered me a chair and turned to me with a winning smile '. These trite civilities apparently filled the visitor with pride and astonishment.

The first development in foreign affairs which affected the new ministry of Bismarck was favourable to it. This was the confirmation of the Franco-Prussian commercial treaty of March 1862 by the Customs Union. Austria had opposed the agreement on the ground that it was incompatible with the 'fiscal unification' which she herself had in view, and had found support for this policy in south Germany. But Prussia made up her mind to carry out her threat not to renew the Customs Union treaty, and the confirmation which she demanded followed at Munich in October. This increased the efforts of Bismarck to bring the Customs Union more under Prussian control and to develop it into a kind of Federal Union not including Austria, in order to undermine the German Confederation from within. When at the end of October Bismarck went to Paris in order to say good-bye to Napoléon in his capacity as former ambassador, he was in a position to refer to this confirmation as a circumstance favourable to the relations between the two countries at the cost of Prussian relations with Austria. The confidential discussions in a private audience also seem to have taken this line. Napoléon again expressed decided opposition to the idea of a power of seventy millions on his eastern frontiers, the 'Prusso-Austro-German bloc of states', and seems to have welcomed Bismarck's intimation that he intended to solve the question of the reform of the German Confederation not with but against Austria.

In fact, Prussia had not renounced her interest in such a reform, although her proposal for an improvement in the Confederate military organization had been rejected. There was under consideration in Berlin a *kleindeutsche* reform of the Confederation, namely, the constitution of a narrower Confederation (i.e., without Austria) within the wider one and of an elected German parliament by the side of the Federal Diet. The Grand-Duke of Baden was a supporter of this scheme. But before it reached the Federal Diet, in October 1861, a (*grossdeutsche*) counter move was advanced by Herr von Beust, who asked for a directorial committee, in which the smaller states should participate, and for periodical conferences of the ministers of the single states. To this Prussia replied in December, sending to the different courts notes in which her (*kleindeutsche*) proposal was elaborated. Three months later there came in reply a series of notes from Austria and some of the smaller states, all sharply rejecting the proposal in similar language. The next move came from Austria, who in the summer of 1862 suggested an extension of the powers of the Confederation and the establishment of an assembly of delegates of the single parliaments as a further Confederate organ besides the Federal Diet. For the liberally minded persons in important posts in Berlin, and in particular for the Crown Prince, the Austrian proposal constituted yet another reason in favour of avoiding any internal constitutional conflict by meeting the liberal wishes. But the King would not consider the

Austrian desire. He was at that time interested only in the military reform of the Confederation. Consequently the relations between Prussia and Austria became more delicate again. In the smaller states men already said that the Prussian policy was leading to a war with Austria.

Now Bismarck entered the stage in his capacity as leader of the Prussian government. He was thus in the position to carry into practice on his own responsibility the ideas and experience he had accumulated in years of work and thought in Frankfurt about the German Confederation and its significance for Prussia. His watchword in doing this he had formulated three years before: ' I see in our relation to the Confederation an infirmity of Prussia which sooner or later we will have to heal.' As the medicine that would cure this infirmity Bismarck had so far in view either the undermining of the Confederation from within through ' voluntary agreements subject to notice ' with the single states or the sheer annihilation of the Confederation—but in any case a policy directed not in conjunction with, but against Austria. At first Bismarck decided to impart his views in person to the Austrian ambassador in Berlin, Count Aloys Karolyi. This was done in two interviews, which took place in the first half of December 1862. It is easy to imagine Bismarck's state of mind at these interviews. He had for years in Frankfurt been obliged to subordinate himself to the representative of Austria as the presiding Power, was exposed to his moods, had to consider his wishes, and to treat what he said with respect. Now he encountered as himself superior the representative of the same Austria, now he was the head of the government of the Power to which the latter was accredited, and could at any time make his will felt by communicating over the other's head with the minister under whom the latter worked. Bismarck revealed to the ambassador the decision of the Prussian government to reject the Austrian proposal for reform of the Confederation, and ' to consider any extension of the powers of the Confederation by a majority vote as a breach of the confederating treaty, and to recall their ambassador from the Diet without appointing a substitute '. Bismarck quotes the following words of his: ' You will have to deal with us as a European Great Power. The paragraphs of the Act of the Congress of Vienna have not the power to stop the development of German history.' Yes, Bismarck actually gave Austria the advice ' to move her centre of gravity to Budapest '.

Still the open conflict with Austria, towards which Prussian policy seemed to be leading, did not come yet. Bismarck had the satisfaction of receiving after this conversation with Count Karolyi a visit from Count Thun, who had treated him with such rudeness and arrogance at the beginning of his Frankfurt activity.

Thun's visit to Berlin was paid in the course of his journey from Vienna to his St. Petersburg post and was intended to second the endeavour of Count Karolyi. It confirmed Bismarck in his conviction that Austria was in need 'of winning and keeping our support'. Then the Federal Diet did Bismarck the favour of postponing for a month the decision on the Austrian proposal for reform and later even of rejecting it by a small majority. In giving reasons for the negative vote of Prussia Bismarck for the first time made clear to a wide public his idea of 'the German people as the ally of Prussia'. He overtrumped the Austrian demand for a Second House comprising delegates of the state parliaments, by declaring,

only in a representation which by direct election proceeds from each state in proportion to its population can the German nation find the proper organ with which to work for the common good. Direct voting and universal suffrage I take to be securities for a conservative attitude [so he continued]; experience has shown us that the masses are honestly concerned with the maintenance of good order in the state. In a country with a monarchical tradition and a loyal frame of mind universal suffrage will lead to monarchical elections. And in Prussia nine-tenths of the people are loyal to the King.

So Bismarck began to carry out the enterprise announced in the 'Booklet' of 'depriving Austria of her dominating influence' in the Confederation and winning for Prussia the leadership as soon as he was in office. He, who in Prussia felt himself called to power under the watchword 'royal versus parliamentary government', began at the same time to realize the 'German mission of Prussia' under the watchword 'German Parliament versus Austrian rule'. So, in fact, he appeared as the man who 'is prepared to represent himself as a revolutionary in foreign affairs, so that he might be a conservative in internal affairs'.

All the same Bismarck was neither able nor willing, under the given circumstances, to display his hostility to Parliament too sharply within Prussia. As he wrote about this time to one of his subordinates, he decided to 'treat the Chamber leniently'. He had always been one who affirmed the advantages of 'an inexpensive friendship' and of 'showing goodwill'. So he was ready to try this policy once more with parliament. He decided to respect its formal rights and invited the Chamber to a new sitting starting in the middle of January 1863 in accordance with the law of constitution. In his opening speech Bismarck pointed out that the 'fixing of the budget was the principal business of the session'. The budget for the year 1863 was again to be brought before Parliament. Single items in it were amended. The budget for 1864 was likewise to be brought by the government before the Chamber for discussion 'after being completed shortly'. The government was 'to be guided by the earnest endeavour to attain harmonious co-operation with the two Houses of Parliament '. So Bismarck had made no use of the suggestion of his more simple-minded lord that he should sting the House to anger by the complaint that ' it is misusing its rights '. On the contrary, in the rôle of protector of injured innocence he spoke in the most alluring and melodious tones of peace and reconciliation.

But as regards one special charm to bewitch the House, Bismarck was in agreement with his lord. That was the charm which Napoléon had recommended to him a little while before, when he suggested that he might ' further the patriotic parties ', in order to secure his power over the Chamber. So Bismarck struck the full and sonorous chord of Prussian patriotism in its most militaristic and at the same time its most popular form. Two weeks after the opening of parliament Bismarck announced as a ' message from the all-Highest ' that the fiftieth anniversary of the 17th of March 1813, the day on which as a result of the appeal of the King *An Mein Volk* there began the Prussian rising which led to the Wars of Liberation against Napoléon I, should be celebrated by a great popular holiday and an increase in the pensions of invalided veterans—hardly a numerous class after fifty years. This was to be done in order ' to honour the memory of such an unprecedented rising and the example thereby given to all succeeding generations of loyalty and patriotism '. Was the government not aware that it had by its action towards the Landwehr, the permanent expression of this movement, just sinned in the gravest fashion against that pattern of loyalty and patriotism ? Had Bismarck himself forgotten that at the beginning of his own parliamentary career he had misrepresented the spirit of this ' unprecedented rising ' in the most one-sided and distorting fashion ?

The House showed itself quite unsusceptible to the siren song of Bismarck. In Prussian patriotism, indeed, and loyalty to the King, even the progressives and liberals of the Second Chamber would not allow anyone to outbid them. But they were just as little ready to give up in any way their constitutional conception of the state. So they evaded the issue by saying that the King had not wanted the conflict and that the Cabinet had conjured it up without the knowledge or desire of the King. The draft of the address of the Chamber to the government declared : ' The constitution has been violated by the Cabinet. The grave evil of a government without a budget has fallen on the land.' It then expressed the hope that the King ' will distinguish the honourable voice of his lawful representatives from the advice of those who, in the strife of parties, try to cover and support their own, in themselves feeble, efforts, by the exalted name of his Majesty '. Bismarck's reply was of trenchant sharpness :

The address presupposes a distinction and division between the King and the government, as if the King had been prevented by sickness or absence from taking cognizance of the actions of the government and of the country. This is not the case. The address is directed against the King; a distinction is not to be made.

With all emphasis Bismarck referred to what for him was the real issue :

Through this address the royal House of the Hohenzollern is required to surrender its constitutional rights to rule, in order to hand them over to the majority of this House. I reject the separation between the Cabinet and the Crown because it conceals the fact that you find yourselves at war with the Crown for the dominion of this land.

But ' the Prussian Monarchy has not yet fulfilled its mission, it is not yet ripe to become an ornamental adornment of your constitutional fabric. It is not yet ripe to be fitted as a dead cog into the machine of parliamentary government '. Therewith he entered on the theme of Prussian power politics. In the following debate Bismarck uttered these characteristic words : ' Since the life of the state cannot stand still even for a moment, he who is in possession of the power is compelled to use it.' Thus we see now fully effected the transition in Bismarck's mind from the ' question of right ' to the ' question of might '. The prime minister of 1863 is in no wise more moderate than the representative of the Junkers in 1847, but the elementary emotions of anger, pride and contempt are now intermingled with feelings which are controlled and excited with an eye to tactics as means to political success.

Naturally a reply on the part of the Opposition in the Chamber was not lacking. A leader of the progressives in this struggle was the great scientist and keen experimenter, Rudolf von Virchow, an ardent fighter for human freedom and opponent of the omnipotence of the state. Himself a fully conscious Prussian he called to Bismarck in Parliament : ' There is a Prussian way of speaking which nobody in the whole world understands, the way that the gentlemen of the Cabinet table are now using.' This led to the reply : ' I am proud to have a Prussian way of speaking and you will hear me using it very often.' The great historian of this period, Heinrich von Sybel, expresses himself in Parliament against this Prussian way of speech in still more definite terms :

The treasures of our past are being falsified in our hands. A Prussian government which is to be qualified for the tasks which rest on the nation in the nineteenth century must understand how to bring together the wishes of the people under her own banner by setting up great ideal aims. We can demand that it should not be exactly the opposite tendencies to this which occupy our government.

One of his party colleagues described the ministry as one ' which counts only the newly created battalions and not the hearts of the people '. Bismarck's support at the same time of the parliamentary principle in the Confederation gained him no approval in the Prussian Parliament. ' Let us postpone the solution of this question ', he was told, ' to a time when the good genius of Prussia reveals itself not in blood and iron and not in thunder and lightning, but in the peaceful sunshine of a government true to the constitution founded on freedom and right.'

But these times were farther off than ever. The draft of the address of parliament denouncing the government for having violated the constitution was carried by an overwhelming majority. The King, however, refused to receive the deputation appointed to hand in the address.

The tension between government and parliament was to be still further increased. This was due to matters of foreign policy connected with events in Poland. Following the bloody suppression by Nicolas I in 1832 of the Polish revolt, which through the complications affecting Prussian Poland had elicited Bismarck's fierce attack against the friends of the Poles in parliament in April 1848, Polish movements against the oppressive Russian system had never quite come to an end. In recent years they had indeed been considerably stimulated by the increasing practice of buying out the peasants. Tsar Alexander II, famed as a friend of the peasants, had only after long inquiries based on statistical material quite gradually made up his mind to take real steps for their liberation. These had at first produced more discontent than reconciliation among those intended to be benefited. Their mood became one of excitement. The whole of the poorer classes showed active sympathy. Then the Russian government decided to paralyse the revolutionary Polish youth by compulsory recruitments for military service. For the revolutionary organizations this was a signal to take up arms. From the end of January 1863 there occurred a series of acts of arson, sanguinary excesses, and conflicts with the organs of public security.

Since 1848 Bismarck had lost none of his hostility towards the Poles and those who favoured them. But while at that time their supporters were despised democrats of Berlin with their ' lachrymose sympathy ', now this rôle was played by a far more important personality. The Emperor Napoléon thought that he could find in the support of the revolutionary Poles an opportunity ostentatiously to intervene on behalf of the principle of nationalism, and used the occasion in order to obtain a base for French interests in the east of Europe. But in Bismarck the desire for an understanding with Napoléon was opposed not only by his aversion to the Poles but also by his strong sympathy for Russia. While good relations with France always meant for him only a temporary help in difficulties, friendship with Russia was becoming in ever-increasing measure a fundamental pillar of his foreign policy. This friendship he thought might be threatened by the presence in St. Petersburg of influential circles who strove for a 'pan-Slav, anti-German brotherhood between Russians and Poles' and who had access even to the person of the Tsar. With them were associated persons who had a liking for the ideas and institutions of the Western Powers, especially the Russian prime minister, Prince Gortschakoff. Bismarck's always lively talent for thinking out combinations in foreign politics now turned to the idea that the westernizing and pan-Slav circles in Russia might come to an agreement with France, not only about Poland, but also abôut general questions, so that Prussia was not only pushed to the side but put between two fires.

Thus, on the 1st of February 1863, a few days after the outbreak of the Polish revolt and before it was possible to see what its influence would be on the existing Russian order, the Prussian government sent a general to St. Petersburg as plenipotentiary. He had to tell the Tsar that Prussia 'in face of the Polish rising set herself as an ally on the side of the Empire of the Tsar, which is threatened by a common foe'. The step was intended, so Bismarck said, to have above all a diplomatic significance, namely to drive the Tsar in a direction hostile to the Poles and to fix his course there. In fact, it produced an altogether agreeable effect on the Tsar, who could hardly count on very much European sympathy in the strife which had broken out, and had indeed to face opposition in his own country. Two days afterwards Prussia massed four army corps on the Polish border, and on the 8th of February there were drawn up in St. Petersburg minutes of an agreement between the two governments, which committed Prussia to co-operate with Russia in suppressing the Polish rising. Bismarck himself described this agreement as 'the successful move which decided the game, playing off against each other within the Russian Cabinet the influence of the "anti-Polish monarchist" and the "polonizing pan-Slavist"', as he called them. In fact, this rather ingenious lightning-like seizure of the position of fulcrum in this balance of power meant a diplomatic victory for Bismarck over Gortschakoff as well as over Napoléon, which made them both sit up and take notice. The impression of it was not easily overcome by Napoléon and was in Bismarck's opinion never forgiven by Gortschakoff.

Although those who had concluded the negotiations were agreed on secrecy, Gortschakoff at once communicated the terms to France in order to prevent himself being made an object of Napoléon's anger. Bismarck had no qualm in speaking about them to the

English ambassador, appending the remark: 'The suppression of the revolt is for us a matter of life and death.' The agreement was not carried out, owing to the pressure of the Western Powers and of Austria. However, Bismarck intimated that Prussia was thinking of attacking the Poles on her own initiative if Russia were to discontinue the campaign. It is even said that Bismarck, through an intermediary, came into relation with a Polish Refugee Bureau in Paris, in order to keep Russia loyal to the agreement by further abetting the Poles. He is also reported to have said to a member of the Prussian parliament: 'We must allow the situation to become more aggravated, then take possession of the Polish kingdom on Prussia's account.' These efforts of Bismarck were not without their effect on the Tsar. The relations between him and Napoléon deteriorated, which helped to improve Bismarck's relation to the latter. Austria's rancour against Russia induced her to take up the cause of Napoléon. Bismarck mentions a letter of this time of the Tsar to King William, in which he declares that he is tired of the West European and Austro-Polish chicanery and determined to draw the sword, and asks the King to join him in common action. The King declined, but nevertheless the friendship between Prussia and Russia was strengthened by the Polish episode, thanks, so the King thought, to Bismarck, 'martyr of the idea of old princely authority'.

The Prussian parliament did not feel itself obliged to render such thanks for Bismarck's service of love towards Russia and martyrdom on behalf of princely authority. When, on the receipt of reports about the St. Petersburg agreement, it interpellated the government as to whether it had been drawn up and, if so, what it contained, this was not done with a view to rendering thanks, but because the 'police service' which Prussia gave to Russia 'must make every Prussian blush'. Bismarck, however, announced the decision of the government not to answer the interpellation. When the Chamber none the less decided to discuss it, he expressed his own attitude to the Polish question in an arrogantly mocking way: 'That Russia does not pursue a Prussian policy I know; everyone knows that her duty is to pursue a Russian policy. Whether an independent Poland would pursue a Prussian policy, whether she would try to keep Posen and Danzig in Prussian hands, that I leave to you to judge.' The reproach against the patriotism of the bourgeoisie which he had made fifteen years before, he now repeated: 'The desire to become enthusiastic for national movements abroad, even at the cost of one's own fatherland, is a kind of political disease which is unfortunately confined to Germany.'

The opposition between Bismarck's Cabinet and parliament now spread to the personal field, when the Speaker wished to use his disciplinary powers against the Ministers. ' I am not subordinate to the disciplinary power of the Chamber,' said Bismarck. ' I have as my superior only his Majesty the King ; and I am not aware what article of the Constitution subjects me to the discipline of the Speaker of this House.' The Chamber acquiesced ; but the issue was thereby delayed, not settled. This is clear from a letter of Bismarck of those days written during a sitting of Parliament to his friend Motley :

At this moment as I write to you I am compelled to listen to unusually distasteful speeches from the mouths of unusually childish and excited politicians. I had never thought that in my mature years I should be forced to pursue such an unworthy profession as that of a parliamentary minister. I have come down in the world and myself do not know how.

The debates of the following weeks were concerned with minor matters, such as the salary of some diplomatic officials, a commercial treaty with Belgium, and the regulation of charges for shipping on the Elbe. Neither the budget for 1863, with single items emended already in January, nor the one for 1864, which Bismarck had then promised to be ' completed shortly ', was brought up for discussion. After some time the Chamber itself gave life to the proceedings by proposing a law about Cabinet responsibility, which the Chamber wished to be secured by making ministers subject to the ordinary courts. The proposal was rejected not only by the government, but also by the Upper House. Bismarck justified its rejection by means of one of the most liberal of all liberal principles, Montesquieu's doctrine of the division of powers, saying that the measure ' would entrust to the judge also the function of lawgiver '. During the discussion of this matter Bismarck's colleague and like-thinking friend, Roon, felt insulted by the speech of one of the deputies and wished to put him in his place on his own responsibility. When the Speaker interrupted him, Roon appealed to Bismarck's declaration about the limits of the latter's disciplinary power, but without success. Thereupon Bismarck intervened and brought about a decision of the Cabinet to absent themselves from parliamentary sittings till their views had been accepted by parliament. A week later a ' warning ' from the King reached the Chamber ' to grant to our ministers the recognition required by them of their constitutional rights '. In their reply the Chamber asserted that they ' refused to participate in the present policy of the government ' and in the name of the country ' demanded full respect for their constitutional rights '. Thereupon the King authorized the prime minister to conclude the present sitting of both Houses of parliament, since the Lower House had ' declared their intention of altogether refusing to the government that co-operation which was their duty according to the constitution '.

This happened on the 27th of May 1863, and was followed on the 4th of September by the dissolution of the House. On the 1st of June, Bismarck gave concrete expression to his hostile attitude towards public opinion and towards the ' Catilinarian beings ' in the Press in particular, and issued the notorious Press Decrees, which gave to government officials the power to supervise the newspapers of the progressive party and to prohibit them after warning. The latter power was to be exercised if, either through particular articles, or through their general attitude, the papers showed that they were trying ' to undermine the sense of reverence and loyalty towards the King or to expose to hatred or contempt the institutions of the state, the public officials, and their regulations '. Thus Bismarck satisfied the wish he had had ' ever since 1847 to " secure " the possibility of public criticism of the government ". To achieve his purpose he chose to circumvent the constitution. The latter gave the government the right provisionally to issue decrees with the force of laws between the sessions of parliament without the previous approval of the latter. Bismarck, however, utilized the dissolution of parliament which he had himself brought about in order, only five days later, to work by means of such a decree against the openly expressed wish of the latter for freedom of the Press. But the Press Decrees did not constitute an isolated episode ; they were a particularly conspicuous symptom of the policy which Bismarck turned against the supporters of the Opposition in the country. These were everywhere exposed to pressure, interference and ill-will on the part of the authorities. The public officials among them were threatened in their position and were neglected when it came to promotion and the conferring of distinctions. The trades-men among them were subjected to encroachments or had their applications for concessions and permits rejected. As ordinary citizens they were followed and spied on when they exercised their rights of free speech, free movement and free assembly.

However, Bismarck had in view a measure against the Opposition which was intended to go a good deal further. In one of his speeches in the Chamber at the beginning of the year he insinuated that the Opposition did not represent the majority of the people. Of the adult population only about 27 to 30 per cent had a vote, so that the Opposition had in fact behind it only 20 to 25 per cent of the entire adult population. This could very well be regarded as indicating Bismarck's antagonism to the three-class-system of franchise, on the basis of which the Chamber had been elected. This antagonism had already gone beyond merely verbal expression, for Bismarck, at the beginning of the year, had in the Federal Diet met the Austrian proposal for reform by proposing a confederate parliament based on universal franchise. This was an institution which the liberalism of that day in all its shades from the National-verein up to and including the progressive party altogether rejected. Liberalism was at that time a thoroughly bourgeois movement which based its claims for political rights on the high intellectual and economic level of its members. As regards the strata of society beneath their level, the proletariat, which was now awakening to social self-consciousness, they were indeed ready to win them over as allies by means of economic help and an improvement in their education. But the idea that the proletariat could by attaining the political franchise become an independent political factor contra-dicted not only their principles, but certainly also their class interest.

Bismarck was naturally not unacquainted with these anxieties and wishes of his parliamentary opponents, and they were not without some good use in his proceedings against them. The con-cept of 'people' from which he had started was the ethnological one of the community of 'clans'. But he had too vigorous and adaptable a mind to exclude consideration of the socio-economic concept of the people then gaining ground and thereby also of the proletariat. One of the scholars who knows this period best has said of Bismarck: 'His receptivity for modern ideas was inex-haustible; it was only exceeded by the freedom with which he brushed them aside.' In Bismarck's own circle of friends there were some who viewed the new social problem with a total lack of understanding. Thus Ludwig von Gerlach wrote even later in the *Kreuzzeitung*: 'The factory workers are not a class and have no prospect of becoming one.' On the other hand, Hermann Wagener was a well-informed and open-hearted social reformer. A question which in these years aroused particular public interest was the right of the workers to form unions, which had been abrogated in Prussia, together with the corresponding right of the employers, since 1845. Two proposals of the liberal party in favour of these rights in the Prussian parliament of 1862 and 1863 were not accepted by the government. Wagener was a champion of the right of forming unions. For him, however, social reform was not an end in itself but a means for party political warfare. He desired the government and the conservatives to take the initiative in it in order to win the masses away from democracy.

Bismarck's attitude towards the workers was much influenced by Wagener. His method of approach to the artisans followed the lines which he had learnt in dealing with the workers on the land. Both were for him 'common people' towards whom one must be 'mild', but who could then be easily 'managed'. They were conservative and loyal to the King, and in contrast to the democratic and liberal bourgeoisie, were not so easily 'seduced' by 'revolutionary slogans'. Bismarck, who for a long while had thought that he could repudiate the name 'constitutional renegade' and a few months before had been of the opinion that he could paralyse the existing constitution by clever 'interpretation', changed his opinion very quickly after taking over office. He certainly was not unable to produce an 'interpretation' which contradicted the 'supposed spirit of the constitutional system'. But success was wanting.

Consequently he thought quite seriously of a *coup d'état* by a new kind of compulsory amendment of the constitution, namely one which aimed at limiting the powers of parliament indirectly by extending the franchise. By decreeing universal suffrage he thought he could create a political power which would balance the forces of Progress. This was where the socio-economic concept of the people led Bismarck, now that he encountered it in practical politics for the first time. He did not envisage, as the basis of the national unification of Germany, unity between the different economic strata, the unity of the producing people (*das ' schaffende Volk '*), but only unity between the different racial strata (*Stämme*). For him the economic concept of the people meant not unity, but class war in politics not less than in economics. In dealing with this concept, Bismarck thus for the second time during his short premiership came within sight of applying in relation to the people the idea of a fulcrum in the balance which he had so cultivated in foreign affairs. He entered into personal contact with Ferdinand Lassalle, at that time the most influential leader of the labour movement, and heard his views on the proposal to institute universal franchise in Prussia by decree. The reactionary and the revolutionary found themselves united in order to destroy as a political power the bourgeois party of progress, which they both equally hated and despised. In doing so either strove to misuse the other for his own ends and to guard himself against the same misuse by the other.

But before the idea of solving the constitutional conflict by force exercised within the state had yet taken shape, the solution, much more congenial to Bismarck, by means of force in foreign affairs, began to be realized. The thought that, as soon as he succeeded in ' gaining for the country an independent and respected position in foreign affairs ', the country could count on the ' loyalty and self-sacrifice ' of the citizens, now assumed practical significance for Bismarck. He speaks of the ' means to overcome internal difficulties by wars, as used especially in French policy '; in the case of Germany he does not deny the efficacy of this means ' if the war in question is in line with national development '. Thus the war of which he was thinking was bound to be in this line.

CHAPTER XVI

Towards the Danish Conflict

The issue of the Press Decrees was not only a blow in the face for parliament, as the representative of the constitutional idea in Prussia, it also aroused great excitement in the population as a whole. Festivities were held in honour of the deputies when they came home ; funds were collected for the benefit of those threatened by the measures of the government, addresses and deputations were sent to the King in order to induce him to yield. The monarch himself, now sixty-six years of age, was mentally in the worst condition. One of the people bringing a petition to him in this matter heard him say : ' I never sleep at night.' Bismarck also had to suffer from the hostile attitude of the population. This was forcibly brought home to him by insulting letters and written threats, and he had to have a guard to protect him. His wife, who a little while before had removed from Reinfeld to ' Ministry for Foreign Affairs, 76, Wilhelmstrasse ', wrote to a friend : ' Anxiety about Bismarck and the King never leaves me.' For a long time she had ' only one motto : " If only Bismarck and the children keep well." ' Almost the whole royal family and the entourage of the King were hostile to Bismarck. His action was regarded as a menace to the security and power of the Hohenzollern family. Above all the Crown Prince Frederick William now developed into an active and dangerous opponent of his.

The Prince, more than sixteen years younger than Bismarck, mentally not outstanding and of not too strong a personality, had been regarded by the latter as a person whom he could easily dominate by his influence. Bismarck reports how Prince Frederick William on the occasion of some political discussions between his mother, the then Princess Augusta and Bismarck, in his presence ' let me see where his political sympathies lay by greeting me with a friendly and vigorous handshake in the dark as I got into the carriage to go away in the evening, as if he was not in a position openly to declare his views by daylight '. Bismarck was startled when a few years later the marriage of the Prince with the English Princess Victoria, the daughter of the reigning Queen, carried out in January 1858, was first mooted in court circles. That was in the spring of 1856, when Bismarck was himself still at Frankfurt, but already very inclined ' to exercise influence on the decisions in Berlin ', and this not only with a view to the general political situation, but also to his own present and future position. The ' English marriage ' meant thus for Bismarck the appearance of a new, most important and far-reaching factor to examine in reviewing his own prospects. So he wrote at that time to Gerlach :

As regards the personal qualities of the Princess I have no judgement to make. But the political result can only be to naturalize with us English influence and Anglomania, without bringing us any equivalent gain in England. If our future Queen, when she is on the Prussian throne, remains even in any degree English, I see our court encircled by English efforts to gain influence without our gaining any attention in England except that the Opposition in English Press and Parliament vilifies our royal family and our country.

The man who had accused himself of ' sympathy for England and her inhabitants ' and had complained that ' this people will not let themselves be loved by us ' is also revealed in these words. This disappointment gave him a special incentive to meet the new personality in his circle with mistrust and suspicion. Bismarck always saw—not indeed without some justification—in the wife of Frederick William the true daughter of the proud island-empire with its political tradition which constantly looked on the political problems of Prussia in a critical and coolly reserved spirit.

Before his marriage the Crown Prince had wavered between the liberal-German tendencies of his mother and the wishes of his autocratic Prussian father without coming to a firm decision. His marriage meant for him a strengthening of his liberal constitutional tendencies and above all of his inclination towards British institutions and ideas, all the more so as his wife soon showed herself the stronger-willed of the pair. Thus Bismarck foresaw not only opposition in the entourage of the Crown Prince, but also an alliance in this opposition between this Prince, and Queen Augusta, and further the Grand-Duke of Baden. It was all the more remarkable that it was just Frederick William who, by rejecting the proposal of his father to abdicate, was the involuntary cause of the attainment to power by the anti-liberal policy of Bismarck. Shortly after the summons by his father to Berlin in September 1862, the Prince took a long sea voyage. While away he sent to the new prime minister, obviously as a reply to the notification that he had taken over office, at the end of October a few lines with the wish that Bismarck might succeed ' in bringing about the urgently needed understanding with Parliament '. This was the beginning of a meaningless correspondence. In its course, the Prince, at the end of December, came to speak of the question of his participation in the sittings of the Cabinet, and asked that when important items were under discussion he should have previous notice of the agenda. This was granted as a matter of course.

Shortly before the conclusion of the session of Parliament in May were visible the first signs of a gathering storm in the relations between the Crown Prince and the prime minister. Through a semi-official report by a high civil servant it came to Bismarck's ears that a rumour was being spread by the progressive party that Frederick William was favourably disposed to them and that this was encouraging not only the ' common people ', but also ' educated men ' to keep on good terms with this party in anticipation of a change of monarch. The report ended with the recommendation to induce the Prince ' to express his complete agreement with the political principles of the King in some decided and public fashion '. Bismarck was naturally much too clever to listen to such unpolitic advice. On the other hand, he was not careful enough to prepare the Prince for his move against the Press or if possible even to harness his services in the project, now that Frederick William had expressed a wish to take part in the sittings of the Cabinet. On the day before the decision on the Press Decrees the Prince had gone to Danzig for a military inspection, having just before ' begged the King to avoid any decrees in violation of the constitution '. When a few days later he heard of the issue of those decrees he sent a letter to the King, no doubt composed under the influence of 'his wife, as Bismarck hints. In this he expressed both disapproval of what had been done and annoyance that he had been personally ignored in making the decision.

But above all, the Crown Prince made a public speech on the occasion of his official reception in Danzig on the 5th of June 1863 for which, as Bismarck likewise indicates, the Liberal mayor gave him the cue following a previous understanding. The Prince said that the new '·quarrel between government and people ' had surprised him in the highest degree. ' I have ', he added, ' known nothing of the arrangements which have led up to this. I was absent. I had no part in the decisions.' Immediately afterwards the Crown Prince sent a formal protest to Bismarck against the Press Decrees and demanded that this should be laid before the whole Cabinet. Bismarck, however, obtained from the King not only a ' command ' that this should be omitted, but also ' an earnest answer of his Majesty ' directed immediately to the princely offender. When the latter thereupon gave way and asked for pardon, Bismarck, who did not allow any feeling of his own responsibility for the quarrel to trouble him, took on the rôle of generous mediator ' in the interests of the dynasty '. He gave it out as the result of his efforts that ' the father's anger was softened by reasons of state ' and ' the Crown Prince was not made a martyr '. Of the many activities as mediator between conflicting interests in which we have already found Bismarck involved, the present was certainly the one most intimately connected with his position and career as he was now acting as the leader of Prussian policy in a conflict between his present and his future overlord. This he indicates in saying that his behaviour throughout the episode ' was a telling proof that he had no desire to remain minister after the change of monarch, which might indeed come soon'. In reality this statement is rather a revelation than a justification of himself. It may be that the desire to stick to his post was not the decisive factor in Bismarck's conduct on this occasion, but we cannot avoid the idea that it was included in the considerations which influenced him, or at any rate was not excluded from these *a limine*. But it was not at all in Bismarck's character to indulge in analysing or criticizing his own motives.

With the granting by the King of the pardon for which the son had asked, the opposition between the two fell into the background for the time being. The son could here claim a certain objective token of success. The Press Decrees of the 1st of June 1863 were suspended already on the 25th of November of the same year and other measures against the Opposition which Bismarck desired were rejected by the King. The relations between Bismarck and the Crown Prince, on the other hand, in no wise improved. They were in fact made even worse by the publication of a detailed account of the Danzig episode and its background in the London *Times*. The article dwelt on the ' difficult position of the Prince and his wife ' between ' a self-willed sovereign and a pernicious Cabinet on one side and an excited people on the other '. Bismarck was very much concerned to find who had written the article, but he did not arrive at any adequate proof, only at suspicions. However, he therefore indulged himself all the more in the latter. The Crown Prince himself was not altogether unsuspected of relations with the writer. But Bismarck's misgivings were especially directed against the circle of persons by whom ' according to my conviction, the Crown Prince was induced to take up his attitude '. The advisers he had in mind were ' the Crown Princess and her mother, who strove to have Prussia governed according to the English pattern, through shifting parliamentary groups, and thought that thus only could they save the Prussia of the nineteenth century from the catastrophe of the England of the 17th.'

A further deterioration of relations was brought about by a sharp but in no wise unjustified letter of the Crown Prince to Bismarck, in which he condemned the latter's policy, saying that it denied to a ' willing loyal people ' the proper ' respect and goodwill ', that it told against ' the quietening of men's minds and the establishment of peace ' and always brought ' new insults to their sense of justice '. The sharpness of tone which Bismarck was inclined to regard as his own privilege in dealing with others was here turned against him in full measure.

You will be quibbling about the constitution for so long that it will lose its worth in the eyes of the people. You will thereby on the one hand arouse anarchic movements, and on the other be driven from one risky interpretation to another till ʿyou come to advise an open breach of the constitution. Those who lead the King in such a direction I regard as the most dangerous advisers of all for Throne and Fatherland.

The letter concluded by saying that the writer had asked the King to excuse him from attending cabinet meetings ' during the existence of the present Cabinet '. At the beginning of September the Prince and Princess and Queen Augusta met the Queen of England and others of the Princess' relatives in Coburg. The manner in which Bismarck used his power in Prussia was bitterly criticized in this gathering. The Queen of England held a particularly unfavourable opinion on the subject; she took an even gloomier view of the situation than her son-in-law and was anxious about the position and the fate of her daughter. She turned to the Austrian Emperor to whose government Bismarck stood in opposition, and on the occasion of a visit of his to Coburg besought him with particular urgency to think of the future of her daughter Victoria and her son-in-law. About the same time there occurred in Berlin the dissolution of parliament. The Prince thereupon wrote to the King repeating his decision not to attend the meetings of the Cabinet whose ' decided opponent ' he was.

Bismarck has said in his *Reflections and Reminiscences* that the ' misunderstanding ' with the Crown Prince caused by the ' Danzig Episode ' was only ' temporary ' and that ' lasting misunderstandings ' had not occurred. In fact, the opposition between the Crown Prince and the policy of Bismarck lasted for several years. When the Danish question became acute he condemned in a letter to Bismarck the whole ' Prussian policy of aggrandizement '. He participated in the Danish campaign—quite contrary to the Prussian tradition—not as commander-in-the-field, but as a mere spectator at the base. The reports which Bismarck sent to him there concerning the political situation and political aims he always accepted with great reserve. As late as September 1865 a conversation of Bismarck with the Crown Prince on the future of Schleswig-Holstein ' took on a very heated character '. But when political success came to be ever more clearly on Bismarck's side, the attitude of the Crown Prince towards this policy underwent quite a noticeable change. In the Austrian campaign he undertook to lead an army. His letters show an ever-increasing identification of his own will with Bismarck's political aims, and his intervention gave Bismarck's policy a support which at the decisive point contributed a great deal to its success.

In the Crown Prince Bismarck has again met a representative of the idea of the liberal *Kulturstaat*, who repeatedly and at vital points put himself in opposition to Bismarck's *Realpolitik* based exclusively on the ' serried ranks of our troops '. The support of this cause by such an advocate seemed particularly likely to lead to success, not only in view of his influential position, but because his personal relations might well lead to the lack in definiteness and practical applicability of the German idea of the liberal state being corrected through contact with the realism of English politics. But Bismarck saw in the Crown Prince and his circle only opponents ' at best narrow-minded, probably malicious and unscrupulous ' and so spared himself an objective investigation of the motives and aims of their policy. The Crown Prince, however, was one of the first of those liberals who dropped their original policy owing to the apparent practical success of the new *Realpolitik*. He was pleased to see how with his liberal middle-class friends the ' realpolitical ' attainments in the economic field took a growingly prominent place beside the more ideal political aims of their fathers and so brought them nearer to understanding and approving Bis-marck's *Realpolitik*.

The troubles in relation to his eldest son were not the only ones brought on the King in the summer of 1863 as the result of the efforts of his new political collaborator. After the struggle with Parliament and the dispute with the Crown Prince the King together with Bismarck had gone for the sake of health first to Carlsbad and then, at the end of July, to Bad Gastein. ' The affair of the Crown Prince gnawed at the King's heart ', he was ' absorbed in himself and forced himself to be cheerful ', Bismarck reported from there to his wife. Of himself, who on earlier holidays had so very much delighted in company, now says that he regarded loneliness on his long walks as essential for recreation. Once the wish escaped him ' that some intrigue might induce the King to form another Cabinet, so that I could live quietly in the country '. A few days after the arrival of the King and his entourage in Gastein, the Austrian Emperor Francis Joseph appeared there and at his very first call took up again the thread of the personal discussions about reforms of the Confederation where he had left it off three years ago at Teplitz. Objectively the plan now worked out by the Austrian government did not offer much that was new, but was a kind of combination of the proposal of Beust in 1861 with its directorial committee and the Vienna proposal of 1862 with its assembly of delegates of the parliaments of the single states, both of which Bismarck had already met by his project of a directly elected confederate parliament. The plan was therefore from the beginning unacceptable for him, if he was not prepared to disavow his former attitude. On the other hand, the plan included a particular bait for the Prussian King; namely the body which the Austrian Emperor was first to entrust with the deliberation of his views was to be an assembly of Princes in the German Confederation to be invited to Frankfurt on the 16th of August. This manifestation ' of princely solidarity in the fight against parliamentary absolutism ', as Bismarck characterized it, was not only in accord with the general lofty view taken by the King of monarchy and its divine origin, but was bound to appeal to him especially now when this idea was exposed to such severe attacks by his own parliament. To Bismarck the plan must have seemed a particularly objectionable attempt of Austrian ' perfidy ' to sow dissension between him and his royal lord.

It was for Bismarck no light task to persuade the King to refuse the invitation to Frankfurt ; however, he did not think of inducing the King ' to form another Cabinet ' as a result of this ' intrigue ', but left no stone unturned to carry out his own will in spite of it. While at Gastein, he succeeded in this by persuading the King that the invitation was a trap, and a summons at short notice which thus cast a slight on him. It was decided to propose that, instead of an immediate meeting of the Princes, a preparatory conference of their prime ministers should take place. This proposal was, however, rejected and the Princes met at Frankfurt, the King of Prussia excepted. The Princes then decided that one of them, the King of Saxony, whom the Prussian monarch particularly ' loved and honoured ', should be sent, together with his minister, von Beust, to the royal absentee. The latter and Bismarck had meanwhile changed their spa from Gastein to Baden-Baden, not far from Frankfurt. There the Saxon King appeared in order to repeat the invitation in the name of the assembled Princes with particular solemnity. The ladiès of the royal house pressed King William to accept ; was he, who lived on terms of hardly tolerable tension with his parliament, to reject the support offered by the German Princes or even to let a state of tension arise also with them ? With the King himself the furtherance of the monarchical principle came into the foreground again and with increased emphasis. ' With thirty Princes to send an invitation and a King to act as diplomatic courier, how can one refuse ! ' he is said to have exclaimed after a discussion with Bismarck. The latter, however, set his sober will in opposition to the emotional attitude of the King. The decisive argument was, as always, that here we had a repetition of the Schwarzenberg policy which threatened Prussia with a new Olmütz. The historian Sybel reports Bismarck's over-dramatized account of the issue of the invitation :

After much hesitation and resistance [i.e., by King William] the letter of rejection was written and sealed. When I left my Lord, we were both exhausted to the point of illness by the nervous tension of the situation, and my subsequent oral communication to the Saxon Minister von Beust still bore the stamp of this agitation.

After closing the door behind the departing Saxon, Bismarck broke to pieces a dish and glasses standing on the table. ' I must destroy something,' he said, ' now I can breathe again.'

In Frankfurt the Grand-Duke of Baden took up the cause of Prussia eagerly on his own initiative. The opposition led by him brought it about that the draft constitution under discussion should only be binding after acceptance by Prussia. Bismarck, however, made three fundamental objections. He demanded for Prussia the right to conduct her foreign policy independently of the Confederation, even as regards the issue of peace and war. Secondly, he demanded for Prussia full equality with Austria within the Confederation. Finally, he repeated the demand he had made in the previous year as a ' *conditio sine qua non* of any reform of the Confederation', namely the election of a Confederate parliament on a universal franchise. This was approximately simultaneous with the expression of his contempt for the parliamentary principle by the final dissolution of the Prussian parliament, whose members he had sent home on the 27th of May. It was, moreover, done at a time when Bismarck, diverging ever more from the standpoint of ' constitutional renegade', had in view the forcible solution of the constitutional conflict by a decree as discussed with Lassalle ' if the King had not been too high-minded for that '. This moment Bismarck used publicly to express the idea of ' the German people as the ally of Prussia ' in a very thorough and characteristic way.

My standpoint [he said] does not rest on a political theory, but on material Prussian interests which are identical with those of the majority of the German nation. Not the German governments but the overwhelming majority of the German people have the same interest as we. Prussia needs a counterweight against the dynastic policy of the governments and can only find this in national representation.

So it is neither constitutionalism nor German nationalism which led to Bismarck's support of a Confederate parliament, but now just as before his ' specific Prussian patriotism ' and the transfer to internal affairs of the principle of the balance of power, which he had so often fostered and applied in foreign affairs. In this way ' the undecided conflict for hegemony ', i.e., that between Austria and Prussia was—in Bismarck's remarkable words—' to be of use for reviving our national feelings and developing them rationally '. Eventually the opposition of Bismarck's Prussia frustrated the

Austrian plan of reform brought before the Frankfurt Congress of Princes. The Princes of the rest of Germany—the 'Third Germany' as they were called—were indeed appreciably more in favour of Austria than of Prussia, but yet declined to come to an agreement with Austria which excluded Prussia. The 'undecided conflict for the hegemony' spelled security for the 'Third Germany' and was therefore not only desired by the latter, but even deemed to be altogether indispensable. So again much effort and good will was uselessly spent in order to heal the trouble in the Confederation, this 'infirmity of Prussia'. All that it led to was an increasing estrangement, not so much between Austria and Prussia, but rather, very emphatically, between Austria and the 'Third Germany'. Bismarck, however, after his half-success in relation to Poland, could show his lord a full success in the step in foreign policy which he had taken against the will of the latter. Owing to the absence of Prussia, the Congress of the Princes at Frankfurt had become a fresh factor in the political isolation of Austria. This was the case not only within, but also outside Germany. Russia indeed was anxious that the conflict should not be sharpened and took a diplomatic step in Vienna to bring about an agreement. In Paris, on the other side, there was an inclination to give Prussia a free hand. The latter's co-operation with Russia in the previous year against the Poles, favoured by the Emperor of France, was not yet forgotten. But the Austrian proposal for reform of the Confederation with its intention of creating a 'Power of Seventy Millions', the 'Austro-Prusso-German bloc of states', on the eastern border of France was far more objectionable to Napoléon. For him Bismarck's refusal of the Austrian reform meant turning against this bloc of states and approximating to the policy of France. Prussia was at that time represented in Paris by Count Robert von der Goltz, the former member of the *Wochenblatt* party and personal friend of Bismarck, a clever diplomat, but not very compliant as a subordinate. Napoléon declared to him at the end of August 1863 : ' This unfortunate Polish question has not led to our quarrelling. That has not happened. But our relations have become colder as a result. It is our only point of difference. I should give a great deal if one could rid the world of it.' Bismarck actually replied within a week by expressing his pleasure at the re-establishment of friendly relations. The more the Emperor's dissatisfaction over the Austrian behaviour increased, the more friendly he grew towards Prussia. ' You belonged ', he said to the Prussian ambassador at the beginning of September, ' in the Polish question to my opponents. But your behaviour was clear and open. With you one always knows what to expect ', a view which, though it would be welcome to Bismarck, he could hardly regard as objectively justified.

To approximate to the French policy was a course which was possible to Bismarck, but in no way necessary. Another, certainly surprising possibility was an approximation to Austria, the latter country in her increasing political isolation being particularly open to such an approach. In fact, there was in progress a reversal in the attitude of Vienna to the German question, especially as a result of the failure of the Frankfurt Congress of Princes. The advocates of a solution consisting in a close relation between Austria and the ' Third Germany ' lost ground. The advocates of a solution which handed over to Austria and Prussia equal rights of leadership, the ' dualistic ' solution, with which Bismarck had already flirted during the Crimean War, came into the foreground. At their head stood the then foreign minister of Austria, Count Bernhard von Rechberg. He had already, during the negotiations in Frankfurt, called to the obstinate advocates of the ' Third Germany ' : ' Well, if you insist we can also come to an understanding with Prussia.' Rechberg was an extreme reactionary, and what attracted him above all in that idea was what had appealed to Bismarck also at the time of Olmütz, where he exclaimed : ' Austria and Prussia must unite, in order to rescue Germany from the hand of revolution.' Rechberg had known Bismarck for long. He had been presiding representative in Frankfurt during the last years of Bismarck's activity there. Bismarck described him as ' an angry man but one who loved honour '. There had been one occasion on which a professional difference of opinion had led to a challenge to a duel, but it had been settled without fighting. Bismarck was convinced that he had ' won the confidence and perhaps even the friendship ' of Rechberg, and that he had done this by abstaining from abusing a confidence given in error. In reality, however, Rechberg seems to have formed a much more correct and sober judgement of Bismarck. During the latter's time of office in Paris he said to a French diplomat that Bismarck was ' incapable of sacrificing a preconceived idea, a prejudice, a party view, to any principle of a higher order. He is a party man in the strongest sense of the word. He possesses a winning personality and a powerful influence in affairs, but he is hostile to Austria.' In connexion with the change of Cabinet in Berlin, Rechberg speaks of him as ' the terrible Bismarck, a man who is capable of taking off his coat and himself going up to the barricade '. Only such a blind reactionary as Rechberg could think of coming to a political understanding with such a dangerous and unreliable man.

Altogether different were the motives which suggested to Bismarck an agreement with Austria. They were throughout of such a kind as to presuppose ' state egoism and not romantics as the sole sound basis of a great state '. Behind them was the idea of throwing external political power into the scale of the Prussian internal situation which was ever becoming more difficult. He wished to awaken and strengthen in the subjects of the state 'the readiness to meet the government with confidence' by seeing that 'their country was gaining a worthy position in external affairs'. The understanding with Austria was intended by Bismarck as a means of solving a very delicate question of foreign affairs, the Danish question. The attempt to regulate the relation between Denmark and the duchies of Schleswig and Holstein more in accordance with the interests of Prussia, or indeed Germany, had to reckon with the opposition of the European Great Powers, who in August 1850 and May 1852 had taken over in London the guarantee of the integrity of the whole state of Denmark, including the duchies. Already in the days when he had talked about 'blood and iron' (22nd December, 1862) Bismarck had written down the sentence: 'The Danish question can only be settled in a way favourable to us through war; the occasion for war is to be found at whatever moment our situation in relation to the other Great Powers is most favourable for waging war.' For this reason it seemed to him expedient and perhaps indispensable to base the Danish enterprise on the power of the Prusso-Austro-German bloc of states with a population of seventy millions and 'one million soldiers', as Bismarck wrote to Goltz. Napoléon's very aversion to the idea of this bloc was a proof that this would be most advantageous to Prussia. As long as this situation remained, the 'hacking to pieces of the Gordian knot in German affairs by military force' had to be postponed in favour of 'a dualistic solution in love' with Austria. But at the same time this dualism must be so arranged that any 'Olmütz' was excluded and that Prussia might use Austria without being used by her. Now was a first opportunity for Bismarck to show how he understood the words that 'the two ends coincide: the leadership of Prussia from the Prussian standpoint' and 'the unification of Germany from a national standpoint'.

The Danish question again reached an acute phase in November 1863, the approach of which is already reflected in Bismarck's diplomatic correspondence during the later part of his time in St. Petersburg. Now it occupied the whole focus of political interest within the German Confederation, and even outside it in the general politics of Europe. On the 15th of November 1863 there died the reigning King of Denmark, Frederick VII, who in 1848 had decreed the law concerning the incorporation of Schleswig and Holstein which was to form the starting-point of so many unhealthy complications. He left behind no direct successor to the throne. Consequently, in accordance with the London agreement of May 1852, the succession to the throne for the whole country passed to the head of the House of Sonderburg, Duke Christian, who ascended the throne as King Christian IX. Claims on behalf of the other branch of the family, the House of Augustenburg, to Schleswig and Holstein seemed to be legally excluded, after the head of the latter in an agreement brought about in 1852 by the mediation of Bismarck, had renounced his rights to the throne in exchange for the release of a part of his fortune.

More obscure than the question of the succession in the two duchies was the constitutional question relating to their legal position within the Danish monarchy in view of the death of Frederick VII and of the rights of the German Confederation which had been expressly reserved by the London Treaty. A Danish measure to alter the constitution by instituting a single parliament, the Danish Reichsrat, for the whole kingdom was in October 1855 declared by the Federal Diet to violate the rights reserved for the Confederation. In the course of this quarrel a Danish royal patent on the 30th of March 1863 introduced a separate parliament for Holstein which was a member of the Confederation, but limited its functions most drastically in favour of those of the general Danish Reichsrat. On the 9th of July 1863, the Federal Diet in Frankfurt demanded the withdrawal of this royal patent on the ground that it violated the rights reserved for the Confederation. The King rejected this demand and threatened the complete incorporation of Schleswig, thus violating the indivisibility of Schleswig and Holstein, which the Confederation had guaranteed. Thereupon the Federal Diet decided on 'Federal Execution' in relation to Holstein. The Danish Reichsrat replied by actually decreeing the complete incorporation of Schleswig in Denmark on the 13th of November. When Frederick VII died two days later he had not yet given his signature to this decree.

This was the position in regard to the two duchies which Christian IX found in existence when he came into power. He made the much-disputed constitutional question more acute by signing directly after his succession the Reichsrat decree of the 13th of November. In doing this he must have felt fairly secure as regards the question of his succession. But this security soon showed itself deceptive. There was some quibbling in the camp of Augustenburg about the words—indeed not very precise—in which they had renounced the right to the duchies in 1852 and they now interpreted them as meaning that the head of the House of Augustenburg had not renounced this right as such, but only his own exercise of it against the successor to the throne installed by the Great Powers and that this could not touch the highly personal rights of his son. There appeared a declaration by the very Duke of Augustenburg who had issued this renunciation. In it he once more announced his renunciation of the claims already withdrawn, but this time in favour of his son Frederick. At the same time this son Frederick published a declaration of his own to the effect that he, as Frederick VIII, 'in accordance with the old hereditary succession of our land and by the renunciation by my father entered upon the government of the duchies of Schleswig and Holstein'. So there was now indeed only one King of Denmark, Christian IX but two candidates for the duchies of Schleswig and Holstein, namely this Christian IX of Sonderburg and Frederick VIII of Augustenburg. The Federal Diet, however, which in the constitutional question of the relation between the Danish state and the duchies had been so strict, showed itself quite regardless of the legal doubts about the rights of the family of Augustenburg. It allowed the plenipotentiary of one of the smaller states to present himself shortly after the change of ruler in Denmark as plenipotentiary of the Duke Frederick VIII of Holstein. The Diet also agreed that some smaller states should ask that the Danish ambassador, on account of the lack of justification of Christian IX's claim to the dukedom, be disavowed as a representative of Holstein. Now for the first time the new constellation of powers which was forming in the Federal Diet made its actual appearance in practice. Austria and Prussia co-operated in opposing the demand not to admit the Danish ambassador, and when the group of the smaller states thereupon proposed to suspend the representation of Holstein for the time being, this was carried as the decision of the Federal Diet against the votes of both Austria and Prussia.

Support or opposition to the claim of the House of Augustenburg was thus from the beginning not only a question of law but a question of politics and gained more and more in political significance. The smaller states of the 'Third Germany' not only welcomed the increase in their number through the addition of a new member to their group, but also utilized the event to develop their consciousness of unity as against the two Great Powers, who since the Congress of the Princes had been ever more obviously approaching agreement. For Bismarck, however, the happening in the Federal Diet presented a welcome opportunity of keeping Austria true to the understanding once she had accepted it and to drive her forward in this direction. 'Is it not the most complete victory which we could win', he wrote to Goltz in Paris, 'that Austria two months after the attempt at reform [i.e., by the Congress of Princes] joins with us in telling the child of her bosom, the majority of the Diet, that she will not be dominated by a majority?'

Among the population in general the intervention on behalf of the rights of the Augustenburgs became the watchword for liberalism and German nationalism of all shades in the country, not only in

Press and parliament but also in private conversation in all circles. Already before and during the years 1848 and 1849, the national and liberal popular movement had concerned itself with the political fate of the two duchies and had demanded their separation from Denmark and union with the German Confederation as a decisive step in the direction of solving the question of German unity and of creating a German constitution. Already at that time Bismarck had, in his interpellation in the Prussian parliament, opposed these endeavours, because he saw in them an approach between the dynasty and the barricades. Now these feelings and wishes blazed up anew with great strength. They now served as gathering point and stimulus for all those who saw in Bismarck's anti-parliamentary views and *Realpolitik* based on the Prussian military might a danger to the healthy national unification of Germany. So there now presented itself for all those who saw in the idea of the liberal *Kulturstaat* the sound principle for national unification a never-recurring opportunity to proclaim publicly their views.

The Prussian parliament had returned after the dissolution of the 4th of September with a still stronger opposition of extreme liberals. The opening speech from the Throne in November 1863 suggested the possibility of a ' Federal Execution ' against the King of Denmark, in case he did not give a satisfactory answer to the demand of the Federal Diet in relation to the duchies. Parliament thereupon declared two weeks later : ' The honour and the interest of Germany require all German states to combine in defending the rights of the duchies, in recognizing the Prince of Augustenburg as the Duke of Schleswig and Holstein, and in giving him effective support in the defence of his rights.' This declaration was not intended only as an expression of opinion in favour of the liberal solution of the Danish question, but also as a stumbling-block to trip up Bismarck personally. His parliamentary opponents had not yet forgotten his interpellation of 1849. They had already in the preceding session utilized the issue of the Danish royal patent of the 30th of March 1863 in order to raise difficulties for Bismarck by a reference to that interpellation, but had received the clever answer :

The gentleman who spoke before me, I think, expected me to maintain the cause of the two duchies in my official capacity against Denmark. I can hardly believe that it was his wish to make this task easier for me when he read selections from a speech which I made in this hall fourteen years ago. But this will not deter me in my capacity as foreign minister from exclusively defending the interests of this country as they have developed historically, instead of defending personal opinions which I expressed about fourteen years ago.

Equally clever and non-committal was the manner in which

Bismarck now began his declaration to the Chamber on behalf of the Prussian government on the 1st of December :

Our attitude to the Danish question is conditioned by a past which has imposed on us duties towards the duchies, duties towards Germany, and duties towards the European Powers. For the position of Prussia the London Treaty of 1852 is decisive. It is a command of honour and prudence to leave no doubt attaching to our loyalty in keeping agreements.

This was a clear and unambiguous concession to the European Great Powers who had taken over the guarantee of the integrity of the whole Danish state, including the duchies. Not least was this a concession to Austria whose minister Rechberg was concerned above all with the strict carrying out of the personal union between the monarchy and the duchies. It was at the same time a blow in the face for the Prussian Chamber, which with its altogether predominant liberal majority, had made the cause of the Duke of Augustenburg its own, for this attitude was incompatible with holding fast to that guarantee. But Bismarck did not leave it at that ; immediately after the first concession he made a second one. This was made in all appearance to the Chamber and moreover to liberalism in general, and therewith to the cause of the Augustenburgs. ' While we recognize this command [i.e., to be loyal to treaties], as valid for ourselves ', Bismarck continued, ' we insist that it should also be valid for Denmark.' The duty incumbent on either party of keeping its word is conditional, he said, on the duty of the other to do so, ' so that the two duties stand and fall together '. This statement must have made the liberals and the supporters of Augustenburg prick up their ears ; for Denmark had already violated the London Treaty which reserved the rights of the German Confederation when Christian IX gave his signature to the Reichsrat decree of the 13th of November.

But Bismarck was not at all prepared to draw the practical conclusion from this violation which the liberals and their supporters might have expected. For he had to show his new friend, Austria, and her arch-reactionary foreign minister, Rechberg, that he would do anything rather than himself take up his station ' at the barricades ' as a liberal. So he continued in his speech, making his third concession, this time to Austria : ' The decision whether and when the failure of the Danes to fulfil their obligations puts us in a position to repudiate the London Treaty must be reserved for the royal government itself.' Now, there followed a sentence which was calculated somewhat to lessen the ensuing disappointment among the liberals and the re-assurance of Christian IX and his guarantors, particularly of France, but was also to nail Austria securely to her agreement with Prussia, namely a reference to the power of a bloc of seventy millions with a million soldiers: 'We have come to an understanding with the Austrian government, which secures an agreed policy of the two Powers in this matter, and have taken common steps to carry out immediately the measures required by the Confederation.'

What did this speech mean? In any case its effect was that none of those interested in the Danish question, neither Augustenburg, the liberals of the Nationalverein and the 'Third Germany', nor Christian IX and the guaranteeing Powers, nor Austria and the reactionaries, really knew what Bismarck was after. That was not an object of indifference or displeasure to Bismarck, but the very thing he had wanted to bring about. For his object in the solution of the Danish question was not in accord with the wishes of any of the three groups concerned, neither the liberals, nor the insisters on the importance of keeping the treaty, nor the reactionaries, but was opposed to the views of all of them. As a very reliable historian reports, Bismarck rejected both the point of view of legality and that of liberal nationalism in the solution of the question. Legal principles, like all principles, counted little for him in politics, and in this particular case they were especially confused and unutilizable. Liberalism was his enemy, not only in the Prussian Chamber, but even more if it ventured beyond the Prussian border. Might not the Danish question perhaps even serve to deal the liberals a blow, if possible, one which also affected Austria, Prussia's ally at the time? Bismarck's own project for settling the Danish question was—true to the Maxim: state egoism of a great state—the annexation of the two duchies by Prussia. Full of pride and satisfaction he announced later on: 'I have from the beginning kept annexation in view without swerving.' For, as he wrote to Goltz, he was not concerned 'with the politics of the Chamber and the Press, but only with the politics of Great Powers carried on by arms'. If Bismarck had announced this as his aim or if people had only guessed it, this might have resulted in the three groups of his opponents not only forgetting their aversion to each other, but, if possible, even forming a common front against him and making his plan impracticable. But as long as his purpose was secret he could not only keep back the three groups from taking steps, but also play off one against the other, use one as an ally against the others, and finally, through his understanding with Austria, keep the other two in check. Here it was a particular advantage to him that the question had two sides, the constitutional one and the question of the succession to the throne, and that his opponents were sometimes differently grouped in regard to the two. He understood how in masterly fashion to keep the latter question, which alone interested him in fact, overshadowed and obscured by the former. In this manner of tackling the Danish problem it becomes quite clear for the first time in a practical instance how Bismarck represented to himself the realization of the two aims, which he said 'coincided': 'the leadership of Prussia from the Prussian standpoint' and 'the unification of Germany from the national standpoint'. The latter was for Bismarck only of significance as a means to the former, i.e., Bismarck desired the unification of Germany in the manner and degree in which it accorded best with the position of Prussia as a leading Great Power. All the striving for national unity within the Confederation from the liberalism in the 'Third Germany' to the conservatism of imperial Austria was without distinction valued, recognized and utilized by Bismarck only from this point of view.

Bismarck ventured with all caution on the difficult task set him. His 'loyalty in regard to international agreements' he proved by giving formal recognition on behalf of the Prussian government to the new ruler of Denmark on the very day after he ascended the throne. To liberalism he showed the 'friendship which costs nothing' by combining recognition with the urgent advice to the King to refuse his signature to the decree of the Reichsrat about the incorporation of Schleswig. A few days later the Prince of Augustenburg made a personal appearance in Berlin in search of advice and help. In particular he had a meeting with Bismarck, the result of which the Prince thus laid down in a letter to him : 'You said to me openly that you are indeed personally convinced of my rights and approve my action when I seek to get them acknowledged, but that in view of the obligations into which Prussia had entered as well as the general world situation you could make me no promises.' As regards the 'general world situation' this meant for Bismarck at the moment, thanks to the seventy-million-bloc which had now been realized on the whole, little more than an excuse for not deferring to the wishes of the Augustenburgs and the liberals. Of the guaranteeing Powers of the London Treaty, France, who had the strongest hostility to the bloc, was the first to appear on the scene. In his speech from the throne at the end of November, Napoléon supported his favourite idea of 'an international conference as a means to prevent war'. He proposed a conference as 'highest arbitration court concerning all questions in dispute' and not limited to the Danish question. England, being directly interested in shipping facilities over the North Sea and having a royal family related to that of Denmark, desired a special conference for the Danish question. Napoléon, annoyed by this countermove, gave Bismarck to understand that he held firmly to his former idea, that of letting him have a free hand in Schleswig-Holstein. Bismarck's friend from his St. Petersburg days, Gortschakoff, showed himself ready to help; although the Tsar as a relative of the Danish royal house was inclined to support their cause, his prime minister let Bismarck know that he intended to advise Copenhagen to give way. England also tried direct negotiations, but in particular urged Prussia to give up her opposition to the Danish decision to incorporate Schleswig. Therefore Bismarck regarded England as the most dangerous among the Powers concerned. He complained sharply about the tone of a dispatch from Lord John Russell in which it said : ' It appears to H. M. Government that the safest course for Prussia to pursue is to act with good faith and honour.' But he knew that London was only prepared for active intervention if this could be carried out in combination with Paris, and that was from the French point of view out of the question.

It was more difficult for Bismarck to make a settlement with the forces of the opposition in the entourage of the King. Here he had to fight not only against liberal tendencies but also against the personal friendship of the King, and still more of the Crown Prince, for the Prince of Augustenburg. About this time the Crown Princess wrote to her mother : ' My thoughts and wishes are with Fritz Augustenburg, who has embarked on a difficult course, though it was the right one.' Here Bismarck again had recourse to the means so often adopted by him of saying with startling frankness what he really thought and intended. He reports that in the council of ministers held directly after the death of Frederick VII he had described

the acquisition of the duchies for Prussia as the best solution of the problem. . . . I reminded the King [he adds] that every one of his recent predecessors had won an increase of territory for the state and urged him to do likewise. This assertion of mine was left out of the minutes. The person who drew up the minutes, when questioned by me, said that the King had thought I should be better pleased if my words were not given durable form in minutes. His Majesty seems to have thought that I had spoken under the bacchanalian influences of lunch. I insisted on the insertion being made. While I was speaking, the Crown Prince had raised his hands to heaven as if he had doubts concerning my sanity.

It was in such frivolous fashion that Bismarck warded off moral objections to his first war of aggression. This attitude once elicited from the King the reproachful question : ' Are you then also a German ? ' So even the Prussian King regarded Bismarck as too much of a Pan-Prussian. On the whole Bismarck was not inclined to commit himself unambiguously to annexation in the former's eyes. He therefore also spoke of a project which would have given the duchies a kind of independence under the Augustenburgs, subject to the following conditions : abandonment of sovereignty in military affairs, cession of a naval harbour at Kiel, creation of a canal connecting the North Sea and the Baltic for the benefit of the Prussian navy. However, the objections coming from the liberal side were not disposed of thereby. This induced Bismarck a few weeks later to propose that the King should ' choose another foreign minister ' instead of himself, mentioning expressly in this connexion the name of Robert von der Goltz. Yet soon afterwards he wrote to Goltz at Paris :

As regards the Danish question it is not possible that the King should have two foreign ministers, i.e. that the man who holds the most important post [that of ambassador in Paris] should advocate a policy directly opposed to that of the Cabinet. The function of giving advice to the King I cannot officially share with anyone.

Thereby was meant that share in advising the King which Bismarck in his Frankfurt days had not hesitated to demand of the foreign minister von Manteuffel.

Of all the involuntary and unconscious helpers in his Danish policy, the Austrian Rechberg was the one who was worst fooled and who made it easiest for Bismarck. He said concerning Rechberg to a confidant about this time : ' We are so far of one heart and of one mind. How much longer we shall get on together in this fashion I do not know. But we have made a good beginning.' Occasionally indeed Rechberg seemed inclined to take the lead somewhat, which made Bismarck thoughtful in view of his memories of Olmütz. Thus he reports to the King before the real beginning of the dualistic policy that Austria had acted unilaterally in sending an ' unexpectedly sharp ' note of protest to Denmark which carries in itself the danger ' that Austria should outbid us in regard to the Danish question '. Otherwise Bismarck was very anxious as soon as possible to come to the point of taking decisive common steps in regard to this question in order to make it difficult for Austria to back out, and to nail her down to a policy in the eyes of all the other states concerned. Here he found a true helper and willing mediator in the Austrian ambassador in Berlin, Count Karolyi. It was agreed that Austria and Prussia should jointly propose in the Federal Diet that the ' Federal Execution ' decided on the 1st of October 1863 in regard to Holstein should be carried on as quickly as possible. Thereupon the Federal Diet actually decided on the 7th of December to bring this about as proposed, and to ask its members, Austria, Prussia, Hanover, and Saxony, to take responsibility for doing so, the latter two providing the army of occupation and the former two the reserve army. Bismarck further managed to guide matters so that, in spite of the enthusiasm of the small states for Augustenburg, the Confederation reserved for itself the power to decide in the question of succession. What is still more, Austria, who during the Italian war and the discussions connected with it concerning the military organization of the Confederation, had opposed so uncompromisingly any subjection of the Confederate forces to Prussia, now made an offer before the Diet to place the forces prepared by her for the Execution under the supreme command of Prussia, while the army of occupation was to be led by a Saxon general.

The occupation of Holstein took place without any friction. The Danish troops fell back before the invading army and avoided any armed clash. But all this did not satisfy Bismarck, either as regards its objective effects or as regards promoting his purpose of making Austria toe the line. In two directions he desired an extension, firstly, he wanted to deal a personal blow against Augustenburg, secondly, he wished the 'Federal Execution' to be applied to Schleswig too, because only in this way could he approach his goal, the union of the two duchies with Prussia. The former achievement did not seem so difficult as the latter. Augustenburg had at once followed the army of occupation and had installed himself in Holstein as master of the land. Bismarck induced Rechberg, who hated Augustenburg as a liberal and did not consider the consequences further, to propose in the Federal Diet together with Prussia his expulsion from Holstein. The proposal was rejected, but a first step towards Bismarck's goal was made. It was a still more delicate matter to secure the extension of the 'Federal Execution' to Schleswig. For Schleswig, unlike Holstein, was not Confederate territory, therefore belonged in a closer sense to the Danish kingdom, and so was more unambiguously covered by the London Treaty. None the less, Bismarck immediately prepared Rechberg and the Federal Diet for this extension, alleging again and again as ground of the 'Execution' in defiance of truth the Reichsrat decision of the 13th of November—i.e., six weeks after the ordering of the Execution—concerning the incorporation of Schleswig and its signature by Christian IX.

At the same time, the decision to entrust to Prussia the carrying out of the 'Federal Execution' through the Federal Diet gave Bismarck a welcome opportunity to silence the Prussian parliament during the further development of the Danish question. Two days after this decision, he brought before parliament a bill concerning the granting of 'means for military measures on the occasion of the Danish conflict'. Thereupon the Chamber decided to recommend the immediate recognition of Augustenburg, and even to demand that the London Treaty should be denounced by Prussia, and that this demand be submitted directly to the King. The address stated that the only result of Bismarck's policy would be the return of the duchies to Denmark. In a reply drawn up by Bismarck the King declined to denounce the London Treaty, described the question of the succession as an issue for the Federal Diet, and recommended the Chamber to authorize the provision of means adequate for the military measures required. Bismarck also brought it about that an address of the Upper House described the address of the Lower as an ' infringement on the rights of the Crown ' and that the King openly expressed his unqualified approval of this description of it. Thereupon the proposed bill about means for the Danish conflict was rejected by the Lower House, and a few days later this body was itself prorogued. The government ascribed a ' hostile character ' to the decisions which it had made and declared that ' for the time the hope of an agreement was abandoned ' and that ' the government stood up for the weal and the honour of Prussia in full exercise of the royal rights '. While Bismarck was thus striking a blow against the liberal cause, he himself had to pocket a personal slight inflicted by one of the most distinguished liberal representatives, the famous scientist Rudolf Virchow. When the latter amid the applause of the House declared that Bismarck had ' no idea of a national policy ', Bismarck found only the lame retort to give to the man ' who carries on anatomy as a side-line ', that he had ' said that I am lacking in understanding for national policy. I can do nothing but return the reproach, omitting the adjective '.

But what was meanwhile happening in Denmark, the country against which this storm was gathering ? Denmark looked to the signatories of the London Treaty, above all to England, sure of having the support of the latter. England, however, did not confine herself to energetic efforts to exercise a mediating influence on Prussia, but sought also to induce Denmark to give in to the demands of the Federal Diet, and in particular to those of Austria and Prussia. Bismarck caused England to recognize the moderation of his own attitude, namely that of keeping to the London Treaty on condition that it was also respected by Denmark, and was thereby able to increase his pressure on the latter. Yet when Denmark tolerated without resistance the occupation of Holstein, it seemed as though she were going to give way altogether. This, however, would have made it very difficult and perhaps impossible for Bismarck to annex the duchies. He himself told the Saxon minister von Beust a few years later that this had been his main anxiety and how he had reacted to it. ' I succeeded ', he said to Beust, ' in making sure that the Danes should not give way. I managed to make them think that England would support them in the event of war, though I knew that this was not the case.' The words of the then English Foreign Minister, Lord John Russell : ' We cannot give active support to a government which puts itself so manifestly in the wrong ', express the exact attitude which Bismarck sought to bring about in him.

Even after the occupation of Holstein, Denmark insisted on the full incorporation of Schleswig which had been effected by the Reichsrat decision of the 13th of November. It was now only a question of extending the ' Federal Execution ' to counter this decision and effect the occupation of Schleswig. When this was done, Bismarck could with a calm mind watch the development of affairs in the direction which he desired. He in fact succeeded, on the 16th of January 1864, in inducing Austria to join him in proposing this extension, and when the ' Third Germany ' caused the proposal to be rejected he managed to persuade Austria, angered by this defeat, to come to an agreement according to which both the signatory Powers of the London Treaty, in consequence of its violation by Denmark, were to occupy Schleswig in common.

But a new difficulty now arose on the way to the annexation which Bismarck always had in view. Austria wished to have included in this agreement the clause that the duchies should only be separated from Denmark if both Powers agreed on this. Bismarck, however, showed himself as tough as he was clever. He induced Rechberg to give up his desire to secure the integrity of the joint Danish monarchy and in a secret clause reserved it for a future settlement by the two Powers. But still there was no end of the difficulties, for the occupation of Schleswig had to be preceded by an ultimatum, thereby conjuring up anew the danger that Denmark might give way. In order to eliminate this last risk in case his enterprise should fail, Bismarck knew how to secure himself in a quite original fashion. He demanded in his ultimatum something the achievement of which was from the beginning impossible, the abrogation within forty-eight hours of the decision of the Reichsrat to incorporate Schleswig. The Reichsrat was dissolved and a new one could not be elected within forty-eight hours, still less could it make a decision. Moreover, a new election would have to take place in accordance with the decision of the 13th of November, that is, with Schleswig included, which in itself would confirm its incorporation and thus mean the rejection of the ultimatum.

When this rejection ensued the Austrian and Prussian reserve armies marched through Holstein, where they were treated in a very hostile manner by their brothers of the Confederation, the Saxon and Hanoverian army of occupation. On entering Schleswig they carried the war on to Danish territory which was clearly protected by the London Treaty. Now Bismarck could breathe again : Austria was pinned, the Great Powers had stayed out and the rest could be left to the military. Already in the first days of February there were sanguinary conflicts with the Danish troops ; under the pressure of their assailants they evacuated their first large fortification, the Danewerk, and fell back further into the interior, part of their troops withdrawing behind another great fortification, the Düppel Entrenchments. This expedition meant for Prussia the first opportunity of seeing the practical effects of the army reforms which had been achieved only after such a severe struggle against parliament. Their military effects did not correspond altogether to expectations, although the plan of advance had been worked out strategically and tactically by a man especially highly qualified in the subject, General Helmuth von Moltke ; for the commander-in-chief was a self-willed old man, who disregarded the orders of the Berlin general staff just as much as he did the rules of German grammar.

Bismarck's skill had won him the practical support of his most suspicious and distrustful opponent abroad, Austria. At the same time, his political success was already beginning to weaken the enmity of his most radical and embittered opponents at home, the liberals, though they were still conscious of their spiritual relation with the idea of the *Kulturstaat* handed down by the classical German thinkers and poets. The Nationalverein, the political body which represented most members of this group, knew indeed very well where it had to take its stand on the current subject of controversy. When in these days one of the most honoured among its speakers, the historian Heinrich von Sybel cried out : ' Augustenburg is the living expression of the right and the unity of the duchies,' he spoke out what almost all of them thought. But another, Karl Mathy, a former leader in the Frankfurt parliament, though as convinced as the former that government ' must bring together the wishes of the people by setting up great ideal aims ',

indeed did not approve the tortuous ways adopted by the Foreign Office in Berlin, yet attached more importance to the gains which could accrue to Prussia and Germany from them. When Prussia in bloody battles drove the Danes out of the duchies he said at times ' Herr von Bismarck pleases me more and more '.

The most pre-eminent representative of those who thought that they could meet Bismarck's antithesis of *Grossmacht* and *Kulturstaat* by a kind of synthesis between the two was Heinrich von Treitschke. In the Prussian constitutional conflict he took his stand against Bismarck on the side of liberalism and constitutionalism. He supported Augustenburg in word and deed and described the conduct towards him of the two German Great Powers as ' sheer treachery '. In 1864, however, there appeared his work *The Federal and the Unitary State*, in which he gave the decision in favour of the latter, since German history was not federalist but annexationist.

Prussia must eat up the smaller states in view of her native vitality, Germanism and true statehood. In the second edition, published in 1865, the question of the two duchies, which he had not discussed in the first edition, he now expressly decided in favour of their annexation by Prussia, as ' the first practical demand of *Realpolitik* '.

CHAPTER XVII

Austro-Prussian Friendship

That the expedition of Prussia and Austria against Denmark would lead to a victory of the aggressors was a matter of course, in view of their particularly clever diplomatic preparations and of their immense military superiority, although the resistance of the Danes was brave and stubborn. But while the signatory Powers of the London Treaty failed to prevent the issue being decided by war and could not make up their minds to give Denmark military help, they were by no means ready to watch a struggle between two such unequal Powers without taking any part in it. Also it was a question of the maintenance of an international treaty between Powers to whom the principle of keeping international treaties was by no means a matter of indifference. So they turned their attention to giving diplomatic help with a view to the speediest possible ending of the sanguinary conflict and chose the method of an international conference, which had indeed already been tried at the beginning of the conflict and was particularly zealously advocated by Napoléon. When Denmark saw her hopes of military help from outside disappear, and in consequence had to defend herself on her own soil against the far more powerful foe, she gave in to the English advocacy of such a conference and asked that the London Treaty of 1852, guaranteeing the integrity of Denmark, should be the basis of negotiations. The invitation was issued by England, the place of meeting to be London and the time the middle of April 1864. Russia agreed without further ado, France, who saw herself tricked out of the initiative, only with hesitation. An invitation to the conference was extended not only to Prussia and Austria, but to a representative of the ‘ Third Germany ’, and as representative Herr von Beust was accepted on the suggestion of Bismarck, who now described him as ‘ a distinguished statesman ’.

The more the idea of the conference crystallized and the nearer the intervention of other Great Powers in the conflict with Denmark came, the more difficult became relations between Prussia and Austria. The Danish war had never, become popular in Austria. It was too far from her borders to arouse interest, and there was no popularly comprehensible motive or aim. The relationship of brother-in-arms with Prussia had very few adherents there. Prussia had long been distrusted and despised. The aversion towards Austria which Bismarck had hardly ever suppressed was returned by the Austrians many times over. Now there appeared the danger that Austria in conjunction with this unpopular and doubtful ally would clash with the other Great Powers at the conference table with consequences that could not be foreseen. When Bismarck in the spring of 1864 visited the battlefields of Denmark he said to his companion : ' It is not easy to grasp why the Austrians have really come here where they cannot remain. So far we have drawn our allies on by a thin string. But the string may one day break.' In the Austrian parliament a little while before someone had said from the benches of the deputies :

We go into the war hand in hand with the Cabinet of Prussia which the world has condemned. Why go with Prussia ? Is she in any respect our friend ? Hardly has she digested stolen Silesia when she stretches out her jaws towards the duchies, and we allow our good regimental music to be played and march in to the sound of drums and pipes. And to the accompaniment of what melodies will we march out ?

The position of Bismarck between his Austrian allies, who were coming to suspect more and more that he had kept them in the dark and led them astray, and the Prussian militarists, who, once let loose would ever advance stubbornly and would not allow themselves to be tamed, constantly increased in difficulty in the course of the campaign. The Prussian military caste not only wished to open the attack on the Düppel Entrenchments at once, but also pressed after the Danes who were retreating in a northerly direction, thus crossing the boundary between Schleswig and Denmark proper. In Vienna it was declared that this step was not covered by the agreement of the 16th of January ; a good deal was said about Prussian rapacity, and reference was made to the threat of a quarrel with the other Great Powers. The orders therefore issued by the Prussian government restricting the movement of their troops led to disputes between Bismarck and his old friend Roon, in the course of which Bismarck became excited and had to hear the words : ' Keep cool and stop getting into a temper.' Still sharper was the self-willed commander of the attacking army, a ' popular figure in the streets ' but no general. In a telegram ' not written in cipher to the King full of the worst insults ' against Bismarck, he referred to him as ' a diplomat who will end on the gallows '. On the other hand, Bismarck staked everything ' on persuading the King not to give the impression in Vienna that Austria was carried away by us against her will ', though he did not, and indeed could not, deny that this impression would have been correct. He caused a royal plenipotentiary to be dispatched to Vienna with the task of pointing out that Denmark must be induced to accept an armistice. This would strengthen the position of the two belligerent Powers against the ' Third Germany ', cool the resolve of the other Great Powers to intervene forcibly in the war, and so give Austria and Prussia the required backing in the impending conference in London. But an armistice, he urged, was not attainable unless the Danish will to resist was broken by the occupation of really Danish territory. In fact, Bismarck succeeded at the beginning of March in inducing the Austria of Rechberg to agree to the occupation of further parts of Denmark proper, but only in return for a big concession on his side. He accepted an alteration of the agreement of the 16th of January, securing the integrity of the whole Danish kingdom for the future. This was to be done by giving Schleswig-Holstein an independent government after the war without tearing it away from the Danish King, the duchies and Denmark to be held together by this bond of union in his person. This would imply abandonment of Bismarck's decision to annex the duchies for Prussia. Did he intend to renounce his plan or was he from the beginning prepared not to keep the new agreement?

For the present Bismarck contented himself with a ' perfidy ' of much less extent towards Rechberg, arising out of the wish to stabilize the relations with France which had been made somewhat tense by the emergence of the ' Seventy-million-bloc'. On the other hand Napoléon was quick to realize that the Austro-Prussian dualism was not too solid and did not withdraw his approval of the annexation of the duchies by Prussia. In March he proposed to the two Powers fighting in Schleswig—a tactically very clever step— the method of a plebiscite, which had been repeatedly tried by himself, to solve the disputed question, hoping thus to drive a wedge between the two. That the reactionary Rechberg would be horrified at such a revolutionary proposal was obvious. He at once ' sharply rejected it '. Now Bismarck had concluded his alliance with Rechberg under the watchword, ' against revolution and barricade ' ; he had also opposed with Austria the summoning of the Holstein Diet proposed by the ' Third Germany ' and made the summoning of a Diet for both duchies dependent on the agreement of Rechberg. But in relation to Napoléon the matter was quite different. The Emperor's sympathy was much too valuable for him to jeopardize it by loyalty to Rechberg. It was in any case worth the sacrifice of an ' inexpensive friendliness ', so Bismarck expressed to Napoléon his pleasure at the suggestion of a plebiscite and emphasized the great significance of the idea that people were to be no longer as before ' objects of exchange and mere things ' at the disposal of third parties, implying regret that he could not decide the question at issue ' alone '.

On the 25th of April the international conference met in London. Shortly afterwards Austria and Prussia, who had drawn up in Berlin an agreed memorandum about the proceedings of their plenipotentiaries, were able to communicate to them the news that an armistice of limited duration had been concluded with Denmark, following the storming of the Düppel Entrenchments. But the attitude of the conference was throughout pro-Danish. In England public opinion demanded of Palmerston unlimited support for little Denmark, overwhelmed by superior forces. Napoléon was unable suddenly to drop the rôle which he had taken up of champion of nationalism against reaction and legitimacy. The Tsar defended the conservative principle of royal power against a breach of agreement in a case which came close to him personally. The efforts of the Three Powers were directed to the re-establishment of the personal union between the Danish monarchy and the ducal power in Schleswig and Holstein. This was just what Austria wanted and what Bismarck had promised Rechberg. So Bismarck was in a very cramped position at the conference. He could not oppose too openly the personal union which was demanded on account of opinions at the conference whose end he had formally made his own. But neither could he openly support it, not only because he would have thereby sacrificed his own aims, but because he would have thus come into opposition to political factors which were indispensable to him at the moment. He would have altogether forfeited the sympathy of the adherents of Augustenburg in Press and parliaments; he would have given a slap in the face to his royal master, the Crown Prince, and other members of the royal family, and he would come at the conference into open conflict with the plenipotentiary of the ' Third Germany ', von Beust, Prussia's attitude at the conference being essentially founded on the unity of the ' Seventy-million-bloc ' of German states.

It was in just such situations as this that Bismarck's ingenuity and skill were displayed most signally. He was naturally by no means particular in the choice of his means. For the present he took in his service a tool that was to him one of the most hateful and detestable things, namely public opinion, the ' phantom which stupifies with its clamour the reason of the Princes ' and, indeed, a public opinion which savoured somewhat of ' revolution and barricade '. Bismarck let it come about that at the middle of May the King was presented with an address to which were attached more than 20,000 signatures, especially of those whom Bismarck defined as ' the more sober-minded and respectable ' part of the population of the duchies. This document cautiously suggested as the wish of its signatories what was Bismarck's own goal, the ' complete separation of the duchies from Denmark '. Two alternatives were proposed, one that they should be ' an autonomous state under the protection of Prussia ', the other that they should be ' part of the Prussian state itself '. This step was also a kind of concession to Napoléon's idea of a plebiscite. The King replied in friendly but non-committal fashion. But in the circle of his friends Bismarck made no secret what the purpose of this step was. ' It seems to me expedient ', he said, ' to let loose against the Danes at the conference all the dogs who will bark. The clamour of the whole pack together will result in the subjugation of the duchies to Denmark.'

Austria was naturally especially displeased with this proceeding. Nevertheless Bismarck was able at about the same time to induce the always compliant Rechberg to combine in a joint declaration at the conference about guaranteeing the political future of the duchies by means of their ' complete political independence and union through common institutions '. The obscurity of this declaration was increased by the words : ' We must first find out who is the rightful sovereign.' This might in case of necessity be interpreted merely as defending the personal union of the duchies with Denmark under a common sovereign and it was understood in this sense by Rechberg ; but this was by no means the only possible interpretation. At a future date this ambiguity was to be important for Bismarck. For the present he was contented that the Austrians took this view of it, and all the more so because the same view was taken by Denmark. For the latter was stimulated' by the Austro-Prussian statement to make a counter-declaration in which the idea of personal union, vital to the conference, was radically and for ever rejected. No doubt one of the factors which contributed to her attitude was the ' pack of barking dogs ' let loose in the duchies by Bismarck. The indefatigable efforts of England to induce Denmark to yield by suggesting the division of Schleswig according to the principle of nationality were now doomed to failure, just as were her endeavours to offer her services as arbitrator for a friendly settlement of the dispute. Napoléon was more pleased by Bismarck's semi-acceptance of the idea of a plebiscite than by the obstinacy of the Danes, and the Tsar continued to lend a ready ear to Bismarck's talk about solidarity between the interests of the eastern monarchies.

When Denmark had finally rejected personal union the conference was deprived of that fundamental agreement on presuppositions which was necessary for successful development of the work. After two months' discussions it dissolved without result. There was no doubt at the conference table that the cause of this lay in the unjustifiable stubbornness of Denmark. Bismarck was able to carry with him the consciousness that he had shown up Denmark to the political world as the violator of the London Treaty of 1852. He was not under any need to face opposition when together with Austria he declared on the 23rd of June in a dispatch to the remaining Powers in London : ' The responsibility for the failure of the conference lies wholly with Denmark.' He could be quite sure of their approval when he did not renew the armistice with Denmark which came to an end in these days, and hostilities were resumed. The issue of the conference was a diplomatic success for him, not only over Denmark but also over the conference Powers. Bismarck further emerged from the conference as a politician whose loyalty to international agreements had successfully stood a test by fire ; but, most important of all for him, the dissolution of the conference relieved him of a tiresome organ of control in the handling of the Danish question and with the resumption of hostilities the need of troubling himself with political considerations about Denmark disappeared.

As soon as Bismarck foresaw this outcome of the conference the question of the Danish constitution altogether lost its present practical interest for him. He was now able to turn his attention in increased degree to the question of succession. It was fundamentally his only interest from the beginning. Since Bismarck's conversation in the middle of the previous November with the claimant to the throne, the Prince of Augustenburg, the latter's position in relation to Bismarck had been in no way strengthened. Bismarck had got rid of a number of anxieties as to whether Denmark would give way without war, whether the Great Powers would remain neutral and whether Austria would continue to co-operate. Augustenburg, on the other hand, had lost some of his main supporters. The Prussian parliament, which was so well disposed to him, had been dumb for several months. The address from the duchies to the Prussian King had shown that not all the future subjects of the Prince were in his favour ; the manner in which he played the rôle of sovereign in Holstein caused widespread displeasure. However, the Prussian Crown Prince now directly intervened with Bismarck as a supporter of the Augustenburg cause. Since Bismarck's principal objection on the occasion of the November conversation, Prussia's obligation to the other Great Powers was losing its weight on account of the impending breakdown of the London Conference, Augustenburg thought that the time had come to resume discussions. The Crown Prince had already won him over in favour of the limitations of his sovereignty casually suggested by Bismarck : a Prussian naval station at Kiel, accession to the Customs Union, a canal between the two seas, and a military convention, and had put them in writing. Bismarck had spoken to the Crown Prince during the Danish campaign about the possibility of a plebiscite in the matter of succession.

So Augustenburg looked hopefully forward to the interview fixed for the 1st of June. Now Rechberg, who saw Bismarck's consent in March to the personal union between the duchies and Denmark dissolve into nothing on account of the latter's hostile attitude to personal union, forgot his hatred of the liberal Augustenburg and shortly before the interview offered him recognition by Austria, provided he refused to make any concessions to Prussia. This strengthened the self-confidence of the Prince, but did not strengthen his position in relation to Bismarck. The latter was a man who in business negotiations adapted his attitude towards the person with whom he had to deal to the latter's power without being affected by what he would regard as useless sentimentalism. Therefore, in June there was no courtesy shown by Bismarck, as was in November when he was polite enough to express his belief in the rights of Augustenburg. He now spoke without restraint, and the unfortunate Augustenburg, whose confidence had just been raised to a very high pitch, replied with no more restraint. He backed out of the limitations which he had just conceded to the Crown Prince and let Bismarck know that he had no idea of renouncing his rights as sovereign. Bismarck says in a report which he published a year later about the interview that at the close he had indicated that the zeal of Prussia for the candidature of the Prince depended on the latter's conduct, and received from him the answer, 'that he need feel no anxiety about this matter, since things had already gone too far for it to be possible to reverse them '.

Bismarck did not want to hear any more. This was just what was necessary to lead him to take his final decision. He is said to have told the sister of Augustenburg that he was a Prussian and in politics tried to be as one-sided as possible, purposely ignoring all good points in his opponent for fear of being diverted from this path. We cannot assume however, that, even if the Prince had been more compliant, Bismarck would have been induced to give up his plan for annexation, to which he had devoted so much thought and for which he had played such high stakes. But Augustenburg helped him by unconsciously providing him with the justification for his action. A contemporary description conveys to us Bismarck's behaviour at an interview of this kind :

Silently brooding he sometimes took up his pencil, sometimes his paper-knife, a certain merriment was at times displayed by his mouth, but then again a demoniacal expression would pass over his face, while his bushy eyebrows lowered themselves. Now and then, he cast a strange questioning piercing glance at his interlocutor.

Bismarck now decided to work actively against the candidature of Augustenburg. However, he did not yet oppose it openly, but brought to bear his official and personal influence against it. This he did by means of the Offices subordinated to him, especially in the diplomatic service, and by making use of the Press. In particular, he saw to it that the general discussion turned on rival candidatures and their justification. For instance he mentioned the Russian Tsar and the Duke of Oldenburg, two close relatives of the reigning

Danish family. He was even able to point to the fact that the Tsar had resigned his claims to the inheritance in favour of that Duke and that in consequence Augustenburg was now opposed by ' a German Confederate Prince, whose true German sentiments have never been doubted by anyone '. So he was able to work against Augustenburg without challenging his still not negligible band of supporters. In these were also included wide liberal circles, among whom, as Bismarck says in friendly fashion, ' the machinations of the Press are disturbingly successful, and the public stupidity is as receptive of their influence as it ever was '. Augustenburg's supporters also included the court circles about the Crown Prince which Bismarck had especially to consider and the *Wochenblatt* party who still held fast to the candidature.

A still more important and difficult factor in the way of the annex-ationist policy was for Bismarck the Prussian King himself, not so much now on account of his inclination towards Augustenburg, as on account of his aversion to the seizure of territory by Prussia. ' With-out having investigated the complicated legal questions involved,' Bismarck said about the King, ' he continued to insist : " I have no right to Holstein." ' But Bismarck of course did not even think of considering, let alone acknowledging, this assertion of the King con-cerning a question of ' right and policy '. Such considerations seemed to him so out of the way that he was even doubtful whether they had formed the real motive for the King's decision. He puts aside the possibility of being influenced by such motives not only for himself but for the King too, and makes a discovery which does more honour to ' the keenness of my eye for seeing weaknesses rather than good qualities ', than to his loyalty as a ' Brandenburg feudal vassal '. Stressing his own *Realpolitik*, Bismarck says : ' It would be impossible logically to justify this policy to the King. He had absorbed his politics from the old liberalism of the advisers of the Queen without undertaking a chemical analysis of their contents.'

It would have been hardly possible for Bismarck to oppose his own political aims more sharply and unambiguously to the *Kulturstaat* defended by liberalism. And it would have been hardly possible to dissect in a sharper and more unloving fashion the ' good horse sense ' which he had graciously admitted in the King, who was incap-able of following the artfully woven and mysteriously tortuous paths of Bismarck's policy. But what does he deduce from the King's incapacity for the ' chemical analysis ' of this policy ? ' It was a matter,' Bismarck declared, ' of winning the King of Prussia con-sciously or unconsciously ' in favour of ' cutting with the sword ' the knot in which German conditions were involved. Is there any such thing as winning a person ' unconsciously ', and what does it really mean in relation to the King, supposed incapable of 'conscious' political analysis ? Bismarck does not leave us without an answer. ' The question of Holstein, the Danish war, the breach with Austria, and the decision of the German question on the battle-field, in this whole game the King would never have taken a hand but for the difficult position into which the " New Era " has brought him.' This is then the winning of the King ' unconsciously ', that is the utilization of his ' difficult position ', or to put it more clearly, emergency, in connexion with Bismarck's entry into office, caused by the interlude of the ' New Era '. He acted as a believer in *Realpolitik* not only in politics but also in his relations to the King, his ' all-gracious Lord '. This was why he had been able as Brand-enburg feudal vassal to offer ' his own blood in battle for the cause of the King '. For he knew that the King was in a position of emerg-ency, on account of which he could be sure of winning him without the latter being conscious of it and therefore of the carrying out of his own will. Consequently the moral scruples of the King might well make more difficult the intended elimination of Augustenburg and annexation of the duchies, but that they should prevent it Bismarck was bound to regard as out of the question.

Bismarck had meanwhile been in a position to express himself more clearly towards Austria on the question of the succession, since the obscurity of the joint declaration of the two Powers at the con-ference must have meant a kind of loosening of the soil, and the peremptory rejection by Denmark of the proposal for personal union must have brought near the time when the seed could be sown. So at the end of May Bismarck requested the ambassador in Vienna formally to raise the question of the succession. At the time when Bismarck was going about to put an end to the candidature of Augustenburg he wrote to Vienna saying that this very solution, the succession of Augustenburg, will ' be realized in the natural course of things very easily without any danger of European complications. We are therefore not disinclined to declare ourselves in its favour provided we can hope for the agreement of the imperial [i.e. Austrian] government.' Bismarck clearly regarded Rechberg's decision at that time to give recognition to Augustenburg, the hated liberal, as noth-ing but a weapon directed against Prussia, a weapon which he could easily knock out of the hand of his opponent by making the latter believe it to be not a weapon but a longed-for benefit. In con-clusion he dropped as a casual remark : ' It can hardly be unknown in Vienna that large circles in the duchies and in Prussia itself regard the incorporation of the duchies in Prussia as the simplest and safest solution.' But in order to emphasize the harmlessness of this remark he adds further : ' The King, however, would only care to bring about the realization of such ideas in full understanding with his imperial ally.' In Vienna it was well understood how to analyse diplomatic notes. They were investigated thoroughly and accurately, especially if they came from Prussia, and above all from Bismarck. Bismarck had certainly not expected by his note to Austria to inspire a sudden outburst of enthusiasm in favour of the annexation of the duchies by Prussia. But he had hoped that he could open a discussion with Austria about this question and that in such a discussion he would in the end come out victor in view of his greater strength of will, intelligence, and keen-sightedness. As he said to a representative of the Prussian Crown Prince, he went on the assumption that ' Austria would rather see the duchies in our hands than in the hands of Prince Frederick '.

But in fact the exact opposite was true. Certainly the aversion of Rechberg to liberalism, to the ' Third Germany ', and even to Augustenburg himself, had not really diminished. But Rechberg had, both inside and outside the government, to reckon with a current of opinion which was much more strongly influenced by aversion to a growth in the territory and power of an increasingly overbearing Prussia. To those who felt like this the recognition of Augustenburg seemed the lesser evil. Bismarck was certainly very astonished and disappointed when three days after the despatch of his note to Vienna he received the news that the Austrians had decided in favour of the candidature of Augustenburg. ' The German Powers should make good by the right of conquest what may be lacking in the legal basis of the Prince of Augustenburg's claims. Therewith begins a new period of our policy.' Bismarck was not in the least desirous for such a ' new period ' in the policy of dualism, but for the time being only wished it to continue as before. But in order to attain this end the agreement which now had been in fact reached about the candidature of Augustenburg must be eliminated. That could not be done by merely letting the Austrians forget it. For the Saxon Minister von Beust was already taking care to imprint it in their memory ; he suggested that the matter should be brought by both Powers before the Federal Diet. Bismarck knew in advance quite accurately what the attitude of the Diet would be. He saw that this step would mean that his overhastiness would lead to the obstruction of his plan of annexation. So he thought of a bold way out and of an unusual justification for it. He declared that the appeal to the Diet was a violation of the rights of the London Conference still in session and a grave insult to it. In fact, he not only caused the proposal in favour of Augustenburg to be submitted to the London Conference, but also managed through his clever formulation to get it rejected, all the non-German states voting against, while Prussia was of those who voted in favour.

In relation to Austria Bismarck now resumed the game with concealed cards in the matter of the succession, but did so with increased caution. At the end of June, immediately before the conclusion of the London Conference, the Prussian and Austrian monarchs together with their foreign ministers met in Carlsbad in order to discuss the situation produced by the imminent breakdown of the conference and the termination of the armistice with Denmark. At first Bismarck had to use the threat of continuing the war alone to keep Rechberg in hand, but finally they came to an agreement which involved the rejection of England's arbitration proposal and the division of Schleswig according to nationality. They decided in favour of separating the whole territory of the duchies from Denmark and postponed the question of the succession to a future date. Bismarck was therefore fortunate enough, after taking so many risks and committing himself to so much, to bring back the decisive question of annexation to the situation of the agreement of the 16th of January 1864, i.e., to ' future settlement between the two Powers ', although this arrangement was so contrary to the interests of Austria and had so often been attacked by her. He was still more fortunate in retaining the full support of Austria in a war which was so senseless from the Austrian point of view. He was justified in ascribing the cheap triumphs of the renewed Danish campaign entirely to the credit of Prussia and to write to his wife: ' The draught from the cup of victory suits the King even better than the waters ' at Carlsbad. But the King also let his prime minister take a sip from this cup. He ascribed to him, so Bismarck told his wife, ' all merit for all that God has bestowed on Prussia ; touch wood,' he added, ' may God lead us further into grace and not leave us to our own blindness '. This ' divine guidance ' cannot escape the charge of showing a certain blindness itself in view of the means chosen by the man who was ' guided '.

At the end of July Denmark was ready to give in. The negotiations for peace which followed immediately were to take place in Vienna, whither Bismarck betook himself in person for this end. Now he had not, as on the occasion of his last official visit to Vienna twelve years before, to consider whether he was received with ' sufficient outward honour '. Certainly the Prussians had not become more beloved in general in Vienna, still less he in particular. But Bismarck had achieved what he had set the Prussian policy ten years ago as a goal, namely that it ' will be Austria's affair to gain and keep our support '. The negotiations themselves began with an unexpected happening which Bismarck quickly saw how to use for his own advantage. Beust, who had just returned to Germany from London, was full of pride at having taken part as a full equal in the conference of the Great Powers, and felt himself now to be altogether the chosen champion of the interests of the ' Third Germany '. It had occurred to him that this ' Third Germany '—of course represented by himself—should take part in the peace negotiations in Vienna and exercise immediate influence there on behalf of her interests. In order to give legitimacy to this step he had proposed at the Federal Diet that a formal retrospective declaration of war should be made against Denmark. It required no special eloquence on the part of Bismarck to persuade Rechberg to oppose this desire of Beust. So the real peace negotiations were preceded by a joint step on the part of Austria and Prussia to underline the fact that they had common interests.

This emphasis on community of interests was indeed badly needed, for Prusso-Austrian relations were clouded by a shadow which just now threatened to become a black thundercloud. This was, as at the time of Bismarck's visit to Vienna twelve years ago, connected with the continuance of the Customs Union. The agreement establishing this lapsed in 1865. Negotiations to renew it had been for some time in progress, and by the end of June or the beginning of July had come to a successful conclusion as regards Prussia and the smaller states, though without the transformation in the direction of greater centralization which Bismarck had in view. Now there arose the dangerous question of the formal ' fiscal unification ' between Austria and the rest of Germany. In the commercial treaty of the 19th of February 1853 this had been promised to Austria as soon as six years had elapsed, thus giving an opportunity to test in practice the working of the treaty. On the part of the Austrians this formal unification was repeatedly demanded, but Bismarck had always opposed it. Now that the Customs Union agreement between the other states had just been renewed, the question concerning the ' fiscal unification ' with Austria was bound to be particularly pressing, and could hardly be answered in the negative by a Prussia which had become an ally and a brother-in-arms of Austria. Prussia could certainly not reckon on the common interests between her and Austria in their negotiations with Denmark, if a complete opposition of interests became at the same time manifest in the customs question. Bismarck pursued the tactics of coming to an agreement with the Danes as quickly as possible, but delaying settlement in the matter of customs. When Rechberg, a month after the renewal of the Customs Union, in a very stiff note, demanded the immediate ' fiscal unification ', Bismarck allowed himself over a fortnight to answer. Then pleading correctness as a screen for procrastination, he said that Austria must first come to an understanding with France, who was entitled to consultation in virtue of the commercial treaty of 1862, which she might do either directly or through the mediation of Prussia. In other respects, he added provokingly, everything would be done in order to hurry up the matter.

The armistice granted to the Danes at the end of July was limited to ten days. How Bismarck understood this limitation is clear from a letter to his wife written shortly after its signature. 'Perhaps we shall have peace with the Danes in a week, perhaps the war will still go on into the winter.' Even three days before the expiry of the time limit it was uncertain 'whether there would be peace or war', despite negotiations 'lasting four hours every day with tough Danes'. That the Danes were tough is understandable, for the demands made of them were hard. A fortnight before Bismarck formulated them in the following way in a note to Rechberg: 'In my view King Christian must renounce in favour of the Allied Powers all the rights that he has possessed or claimed south of the Königsau [the boundary between Schleswig and Denmark proper] and recognize as final any decisions which the two allied Powers will take in regard to the duchies.' This was a renewed confirmation of the agreement of January leaving the question of annexation to 'future settlement'. That Rechberg should now be enthusiastic in its favour was not to be expected. Consequently Bismarck's capacity as diplomat was very much in demand, for he had not only to overcome the opposition of the Danes, but also to urge on the reluctant Austrians, so as to bring about the triumph of Prussian interests against the interests of both the other parties. 'If Prussia and Austria are united, so Germany will be,' was his formula in dealing with Austria. He had no scruples about this proceeding, the consciousness of his own superiority and the anticipation of success giving him wings. 'We drank a lot and were very merry,' wrote Bismarck to his wife during the negotiations concerning a visit to his friend Motley, now American ambassador in Vienna, and added in astonishment, 'Which does not often happen with him, because of his grief about the war.'

The preliminary peace of Vienna of the 1st of August put a new strain on the Austro-Prussian friendship, in that the two countries had to undertake the joint administration of the territory of both duchies with their approximately 6,000 square miles and almost one million inhabitants, after the King of Denmark 'had renounced all his rights over them'. The two Powers had already proposed at the beginning of July that the control of Holstein by Hanover and Saxony should come to an end, and now they succeeded in excluding the 'Third Germany' altogether from the control of the combined duchies, on the ground, as Bismarck said, that 'a firm and strong interim government' was necessary in them, 'such as only the two Allied Powers can carry out'. Baden turned out to be a useful advocate of this proposal in the Federal Diet, otherwise the negotiations which were conducted in Vienna with a view to a final peace showed themselves very difficult and tiresome. Bismarck did well to take part in them while living the life of a spa visitor in Gastein, even if he did exclaim : ' I cannot show myself on the promenade, nobody leaves me in peace.' Be that as it may, he no more speaks of ' long walks alone ', his shyness of society in the preceding year had meanwhile been drowned in the ' cup of victory '.

These difficulties induced Bismarck at the end of August to help forward the Vienna negotiations by arranging a personal meeting of the two Allied monarchs and their foreign ministers at Schönbrunn. At this meeting he wished, if possible, to force a decision on the question of annexation. This was a risky step not only because of his Austrian partners, but especially because of the attitude of his own sovereign who, as he knew, had so far not decided either for the exclusion of Augustenburg or for annexation. What Bismarck, according to his account, allowed himself at Schönbrunn in the way of personal effronteries against the other partners is astonishing. He may be called quite witty when he said at a meeting of the four about the existing alliance that it is ' no trading association which divides profits according to a fixed percentage. It resembles ', he said, ' rather an association for hunting in which every member carries home his booty.' But his wit changed to cheek, when he offered to the Austrian Emperor, instead of territory, ' Prussia's gratitude to Austria ', while refusing to give up ' ancient Prussian soil ' as compensation. As such he dared to describe the county of Glatz, where even ' the autochthonous Austrians ' of Glatz, so he said to the Austrians, protested against such a cession. (Glatz in Silesia had been taken from Austria by Frederick the Great as part of his booty in the Seven Years' War.) All the same, he is convinced that his representations had not failed to make an ' impression ' on the Austrian Emperor, as he did not break off the conversation, but said something about ' difficulties connected with the state of public opinion '. Thereupon Bismarck resolved to make the attempt to obtain from his own sovereign the declaration in favour of annexation. He told the Emperor in reference to the King, who seems to have arrived later at this conversation : ' I desire very much that your Majesty should put the question [i.e., of the annexation] forward in the presence of my all-gracious Lord. I hope on this occasion to learn his views.' But even this emergency, intentionally and regardless of respect prepared by Bismarck, could not induce the King to give up his conviction. The results of Bismarck's tactlessness are clear from his own account : ' The King said hesitatingly and with a certain embarrassment that he had no right over the duchies and could therefore make no claim on them.' We hear Bismarck's anger at the failure of his attempt—and this was clearly the only emotion that he felt—unambiguously from his concluding remark : ' As a result of these words, I was of course put in a position in which I could not continue fighting the Emperor.' So Bismarck's venture at Schönbrunn had failed, its only result being a very indefinite formula in a draft of a treaty which was never signed at all, giving Prussia a prospect of obtaining the duchies in the event of the reconquest of Lombardy by Austria. At a farewell dinner in the house of Rechberg near Schönbrunn Bismarck is said to have told the French ambassador, the Duke of Gramont: 'We Berliners do not now look on Vienna as a German city. It is no more difficult to rule Vienna from Berlin, than it is to rule Budapest from Vienna.' That the report should be true, is, in view of his disgruntled mood, not so improbable as some of his admirers think.

Bismarck has described the meeting in Schönbrunn as the culmination and turning-point in the 'attempted dualism' by the two Powers. Before the conference broke up, Rechberg made a confidential communication to Bismarck that 'his position had been undermined', a message which can hardly have created surprise. In order to retain his office, Rechberg attempted, 'in view of the efforts of Austria to be included in the Customs Union, which were the chief concern of the Emperor, at least to obtain the assurance that Prussia would enter upon negotiations within a limited period'. In practice, this 'assurance' would only renew the promise given in the commercial treaty of 1853 which held out the prospect of a 'fiscal unification' under certain conditions. This assurance was therefore only one of those 'inexpensive acts of friendship' which Bismarck had always recommended and had already so often used with success in his negotiations. Final agreement with Denmark was not yet quite secured, and the probability was very great that in the event of the resignation of Rechberg a party less favourable, or even actually opposed, to the alliance with Prussia would come into power in Austria. Thus Bismarck still had every reason to make the friendly gesture for which Rechberg had asked. Bismarck believed now as formerly that the 'fiscal unification' with Austria was an 'unrealizable utopia'. But what did this matter when he was considering whether to give the assurance asked by Rechberg? An answer to this question is to be found in a sentence in Bismarck's *Reflections and Reminiscences*, which puts in the most pointed way the antithesis between his real purpose and the inexpensive friendly gesture: 'Convinced of the impossibility of the "fiscal unification", I had no hesitation in rendering to Count Rechberg the service he desired in order to keep him in power.' It is left to the reader to decide whether the word 'convinced' expresses a motive or a contradiction.

The King, under the influence of departmental ministers, and especially of Delbrück who saw here a danger for the Customs Union, would have nothing to do with any concession to Rechberg. All the same, Bismarck could induce him to agree that the conference to be held in Vienna concerning commercial relations between Prussia and Austria should discuss the assurance for which Rechberg had asked. In the next weeks, however, the negotiations concerning final agreement with Denmark advanced steadily towards a successful end. Therewith the alliance with Austria lost interest for Bismarck. The policy of ' dualism ' showed itself ever more clearly as an ' episode '. The time approached when Bismarck could write to his friend von der Goltz : ' We have got all the good we can from the Austrian alliance.' In a personal correspondence between Bismarck and Rechberg in September we again see emerging that tendency of his to express suspicions to the latter that Austria was effecting a rapprochement with the ' Third Germany ' and to raise doubts as to whether Austria was a ' German Power '. In the conference about the Austro-Prussian trade relations, however, the assurance demanded by Rechberg became more and more prominent as a condition of success. At the beginning of October Bismarck went away in a happy frame of mind to his beloved Biarritz. The hopes which he could carry with him in regard to the Rechberg affair, according to his own words, only amounted to a ' belief that he was certain ' that the King had decided to give the desired assurance. He felt extremely well and happy at Biarritz.

When I think [he wrote to his wife] how yesterday we sat in the moonlight by the sea till ten o'clock, how we to-day lunched out of doors, and how I am now sitting by an open window looking at the sunlit sea, I must say that the southerners enjoy in their climate a wonderful gift from the grace of God.

During the following days, there came disquieting news from Berlin. In a cabinet meeting ' the eventuality of a change of ministry in Vienna was treated as a bagatelle '. When one of the ministers declared that the assurance ' obliges us *finaliter* and *realiter* to nothing, a punishing glance from Delbrück frightened him back to his departmental affairs '. From Baden-Baden came the report that the King had said that the ' assurance would perhaps avert a cabinet crisis in Vienna, but will bring about one in Berlin '. The news from Vienna was that Austria intended to break off the conference if the assurance was not given. Bismarck wired asking that the demand for the assurance should be granted. But otherwise he did not allow his holiday mood to be in the least affected. In these very days he wrote to his sister : ' It is a very long time since I have found myself in such a pleasant situation, both as regards climate and the state of my business affairs,' and to his wife : ' We are leading a thoroughly idle life. The day before yesterday I received a despatch in cypher from the King. Yesterday I dictated the answer. Otherwise I am doing absolutely nothing, except loafing and eating, when I am not asleep.'

His stay at Biarritz was followed at the end of October by a short visit to Paris, where he had an audience with Napoléon and discussions with members of the government, a circumstance the coincidence of which with the loosening relations with Austria can hardly have been merely a matter of chance. On the 27th of October 1864 Bismarck's so compliant friend Rechberg, his subservient helper in the acquisition of Schleswig and Holstein, was dismissed from office, because the assurance for which he had asked was refused. Just about then Bismarck returned to Berlin. From there he told his wife on the 30th of October : ' The peace with Denmark has been signed to-day,' and did not forget to add : ' The people here find me much improved in health, thinner and stronger,' whereas of his friend Rechberg's dismissal not a word was said.

Whether Bismarck had caused the fall of Rechberg through his neglect in dealing with the Customs matter need not be decided by us. That he felt himself guilty is shown by the vague ' belief that he was certain ' of the King's assurance, out of which he construed the unreliability of the latter as responsible for the occurrence. Afterwards, when the episode of ' joint German union on the basis of dualism ' had come to its end, as Bismarck had anticipated that it would from the beginning, he proceeded to finish off this part of his political activity with violent abuse of the policy of Rechberg and in general of Austria. He did this by way of manœuvring himself from the rôle of aggressor into that of the victim of aggression. He blamed Rechberg for ' the suddenness ' with which he had broken with ' the medium states and combined with us and against them ', and referred to ' the possibility of a new change in [Austrian] policy just as unexpected '. He brought up again the ' well-known ingratitude of Schwarzenberg ' and did not either forget the alleged ' incalculable way in which in Austria the influence of father confessors intersects with political decisions '. Worthy of note is Bismarck's view of the matter a few years later, after the Austro-Prussian war. He said at first that it had been a mistake to drive Rechberg from office by not allowing him the assurance for which he asked, for ' he would have done everything to prevent war ', but, he added, ' the war was bound to come some day, and so it was perhaps a stroke of luck that it happened then under relatively favourable circumstances '.

After the dismissal of Rechberg the rulers of Austria and Prussia promised in letters signed by themselves that the alliance between the two states should remain unimpaired by the change. But there was far too much material for conflict about for this to be possible. The new Austrian foreign minister, Count Mensdorff, was a professional soldier and diplomat, but not the right man for this high office. He had a sensible judgement about men and things and a well-equipped understanding; but his will was very much weaker than his intellect. So it came about that under the influence of others he adopted policies which went against his better judgement. Among these influences two were predominant. Through his mother Mensdorff was related to the Queen of England, and from this quarter there blew a wind of liberalism against which his conservative principles did not always hold fast. Among his advisers in the Vienna civil service, of whom a Herr von Biegeleben was the most distinguished, the contempt of Prussia inherited from Schwarzenberg was predominant and this gradually sapped Mensdorff's will for the continuation of the Rechberg policy. From these quarters he had to hear daily that his predecessor had ' altogether bungled ' the Danish and the German questions and had sacrificed the freedom of Austrian policy to Bismarck.

Very soon after Mensdorff took over office quarrels arose. The first question concerned the evacuation from Holstein of the Hanoverian and Saxon troops, who, sent in consequence of the ' Federal Execution ', were still there. Prussia asked the respective governments to withdraw them. Hanover complied, but on behalf of Saxony Beust declared that he would only yield to force. Bismarck was resolved to use this. Mensdorff, on the other hand, asked in astonishment : ' What reason could we have for removing the Confederate troops from Holstein ? ' Bismarck in reply alleged that their presence provided a basis for the intrigues of Augustenburg. But for Mensdorff, the relative of the Queen of England, this was anything but a reason in favour ; he proposed to put the decision as to evacuation in the hands of the Federal Diet. Bismarck, on his part, wished for nothing less than the intervention of the ' Third Germany ' in the treatment of the duchies. But they came to an agreement, and the Diet immediately accepted the common proposal of the two Powers ordering the evacuation. Once the military as well as the political control of the combined duchies had passed into the hands of the two Great Powers, the rôle of Augustenburg as reigning duke became more and more uncomfortable and impossible.

At the middle of November three memoirs were sent off from Mensdorff's chancellery to Berlin, ' the Works of Herr von Biegeleben ', as they were called. The first in accordance with Prussia declared that the competent body to decide the question of succession was not the Federal Diet, which meant the ' Third Germany ', but exclusively the two victorious Powers. But the second expressly and unambiguously opposed the Prussian annexation of the duchies, referring to the ' wise self-control of King William ', and strongly advocated their political independence over against Prussia. The third refused Bismarck's earlier recommendation of the Oldenburg candidate, and supported Augustenburg as having the best claim to the ducal throne. Against Prussian policy there was made the certainly not unjustified reproach that it aimed at delaying the settlement of the question of succession. Herewith the Austrians passed from a game with concealed cards to an open game. That this change was not an expression of confidence but of a considerably increased distrust was not left in doubt.

Bismarck decided to continue his former tactics. In a first letter he complained of the unfriendly tone of the memoirs. This enabled him to postpone for several weeks the making of a real reply, but even when he gave one it was not intended to bring about a decision, but only to delay it further. In dismissing any idea of bringing in the ' Third Germany ' Bismarck could not say enough. ' The medium states are our common opponents, and the Federal institutions are very unreliable ground for our mutual interests.' On the question of succession he said : ' Prussia does not exclude unconditionally either Oldenburg or Augustenburg, but does not wish to expose herself to the reproach of an overhasty decision without legal investigation.' At present the duchies were the legal possessions of both Powers, and the position could not be changed by unilateral action. A change would require military and political guarantees in favour of Prussia. Bismarck's delaying tactics could hardly any longer be misunderstood. So the reply of Austria included a demand for immediate communication of the Prussian conditions for establishing the independence of the duchies. But Bismarck again allowed himself plenty of time for his answer. When at the beginning of February 1865 the Austrian ambassador, Count Karolyi, called on Bismarck in order to inquire about the delay, he received from him the startling answer : ' Austria brings reproaches against us, whilst we make concessions. It is after all already a concession that we are willing to discuss a change in the *status quo* at all. Why could not this be regarded as something fixed definitively ? ' With these words Bismarck had once more manœuvred himself into the rôle of defender of injured innocence. He was now defending the maintenance of the existing legal status, although his real purpose to alter this by annexation was by now clear to his opponent. Just as he had earlier used the state of emergency in which his King was placed in order to win him ' unconsciously ' for his plans, so now he used the emergency into which he had brought Austria through her alliance, which from her point of view was senseless, in order to make her responsible for any breach of this very alliance. Up to the present he had been concerned to ' draw our allies on by a thin string '. Now he conceived the eventuality of the tearing of this string as giving Prussia the opportunity to carry home the whole ' hunting booty '. In the ironical words with which Bismarck concluded his conversation with Count Karolyi :

'Rest assured, we will keep our word, we shall produce our conditions alright,' there spoke his whole pleasure in the humiliation and torment of his opponent, for whom, in spite of the ephemeral alliance, he had not ceased to cherish a deep aversion.

Bismarck's terms were indeed of such a kind as to strike Austria like a blow in the face. In the Prussian statement given at the end of February no account was taken of the Austrian wish for the political independence of the duchies over against Prussia. On the contrary, the terms which had been laid before Augustenburg on the 1st of June 1864, and which Austria had forbidden the latter to accept, were made considerably more severe in these 'February terms'. A demand was brought forward that the forces of the duchies should pass under the direct command of the King of Prussia, render their oath to him, and hand over to him all places of military importance, and that the financial, postal, and railway system should be subordinated to Prussia. That Austria was bound to reject these conditions was a matter of course, and was definitely expected in Berlin. Already Bismarck was playing with the idea of a second war as means of annexation. When the expected refusal promptly arrived, the Cabinet in Berlin asked the general staff on the same day for an expert opinion concerning the armed forces and military strength of Austria. But Bismarck had not yet made up his mind definitely in favour of war.

About this very time he wrote to his friend Goltz in Paris that in Prussia's 'married life with Austria' he wished 'to continue the usual matrimonial quarrels', and not yet to bring about a divorce. This was the answer to a letter from Goltz to the effect that Napoléon was inclined in the event of a war between Austria and Prussia to come to an understanding with King William. Since at the request of Napoléon the difference over Poland between the two Powers had been buried, Napoléon had stayed in readiness to come to the side of Prussia in the event of the expected break-up of the seventy-million-bloc. An alliance between the two Powers was advocated not only by Goltz but also by the French ambassador in Berlin, Count Benedetti. Bismarck, in spite of all his insinuations against the 'Rhine League policy' of the smaller states and of Austria, took all pains to keep and to increase the goodwill of Napoléon, but he shrank back from a formal alliance, since such a step would enable France 'at any time irretrievably to compromise Prussia in the eyes of Austria and Germany'. For the present he wished to keep open the possibility of accepting either the French or the Austrian alternative and to take his position between both as fulcrum in the balance.

In striving after this position Bismarck had to consider the further fact that his designs on Schleswig and Holstein were meeting with the sharpest protest from his liberal opponents in the 'Third Germany'.

Already at the end of October 1864 the Nationalverein, which championed a solution of the German question that excluded Austria, had announced the following decision : 'The National-verein rejects most decisively the annexation of the duchies by Prussia as a serious menace to the Federal unity of the nation.' Bismarck's 'February terms' in relation to the independence of the duchies aroused the greatest consternation, not only in Austria, but in Germany in general. Bismarck was most directly affected by the displeasure which was expressed to him on the part of the Prussian House of Deputies. The latter was again convened in constitutional fashion in the middle of January 1865. It was once more requested in a speech from the throne, which, following on the military and diplomatic victories of the preceding year, sounded somewhat more arrogant and provocative even than before, to support the King 'in the fulfilment of his duty as sovereign'. Bismarck, however, chose not to address the government request directly to the House of Deputies, but only through the Upper House, by letting the latter know that the House of Deputies had not the power 'to utter a *sic volo sic jubeo* to which the other legislative forces had to bow'.

Nevertheless, the Opposition in the House of Deputies decided to reject the 'February terms', but in their turn did not address themselves directly to Bismarck at a sitting in the Chamber, but passed him over when they made a public declaration in March. In this they asserted as 'inviolable' the right of Augustenburg and of the duchies, 'like any other state in the Confederation to manage independently all internal affairs', and declared the military wishes of Prussia towards them to be 'throughout irreconcilable with the independence of the duchies'. It soon came to a direct clash between Bismarck and the Chamber. The Prussian government had, as a counter-move against the Austrian rejection of their 'February terms' and at the same time against the attitude of the Opposition in the Chamber, begun the unilateral execution of these terms. The Prussian fleet had at the end of March been moved from Danzig to Kiel, the chief naval harbour of the duchies, where it was left riding at anchor outside the port, and preparatory measures had been taken to make the port utilizable for Prussia's own naval purposes. To this end a naval bill was brought in the Chamber for discussion at the beginning of June, its main object being the development and fortification of Kiel harbour. Thus the Chamber had its desired opportunity of dealing a direct blow at Bismarck's policy towards the duchies and at the same time of exercising its constitutional right to reject the budget. Bismarck again knew by what trick to make himself out a champion of injured innocence ; he maintained that the object of the Chamber was not to carry out the existing constitution but to change it in favour of a parliamentary system and 'to enforce this change by harming the commonwealth in matters of foreign policy by refusing their co-operation '. But the Chamber, under the watchword 'Not a farthing for this ministry', rejected the naval bill just a fortnight after it had been introduced. Four days later parliament was prorogued. The government emphasized that ' the law relating to the budget has this year again come to grief in face of the refusal of the House to grant what was an indispensable means for the maintenance of our military strength '. Nor was a farcical element absent in all these happenings. The deputy Virchow had accused Bismarck of ' dishonesty ' and therefore received a challenge to a duel from him. Virchow's friends worked to prevent the duel and induced him to refuse the challenge. But the circles who believed in ' blood and iron ' were of the conviction that matters of difference of opinion even in internal politics were best settled by the gun. So Bismarck's friend Hermann Wagener said mockingly about Virchow that he ' applied his opposition to firearms also to his private affairs '.

After the prorogation Bismarck was able to turn his attention to Austria in increased measure. Relations with the latter deteriorated apace. The common administration of the two duchies by the two Powers provided a variety of explosive matter, and the two partners did all they could to keep this matter ready for blowing up. The Austrian commissary in the duchies used his whole authority to further the anti-Prussian agitation of the adherents of Augustenburg, while the Prussian chose to take the direct path of settling down in the country, pushing Austria aside, and making no secret of the intention never to leave it again. Also the relations between the two monarchs, who had shortly before praised each other for keeping loyal to the alliance, now took on a harsher character. Francis Joseph stiffened in his view that a Prussia which was too rashly striving upwards must be reminded of the imperial power. William had taken a very active part in working out the ' February terms ' and was offended by the attempts of Augustenburg to mobilize popular opinion for himself and against Prussia. A report of the Prussian crown jurists issued at this time, deciding—of course— against the right of Augustenburg, impressed the King, while the former accepted addresses demanding his enthronement and official messages of congratulation for his birthday. Now Austria made a move which was bound to annoy King William still more. She allowed some of the smaller states to bring the question of the succession in the duchies before the Federal Diet and then there occurred what had not happened for about two years. When the resolution that ' this House now looks forward confidently to the enthronement of Augustenburg ' was put to the vote, the Prussian and Austrian votes were cast on different sides. By her action Austria had *de facto* violated her agreement with Prussia, that the competent body to decide this question was not the Federal Diet but the two Great Powers. Thus the string by which Bismarck had ' so far drawn Austria on ' now actually began to break.

Bismarck reacted by reverting to an idea which he had used before in his fight against Austria in the Federal Diet : universal suffrage. He proposed in Vienna that parliament should be summoned in the duchies on a basis of universal franchise and that the question of succession should be laid before it. What did Bismarck mean with this proposal, this mobilization of public opinion which could hardly turn out to the advantage of Prussia ? It might perhaps work as an ' inexpensive gesture of friendship ' to Napoléon, but it might also be interpreted as a concession to the German liberals. But above all he must have hoped that reactionary Austria would expose herself by the rejection of his proposal. But he was mistaken, Austria declared herself in agreement with it. Now he could use it as a means of continuing his former tactics of delaying decision, since the preparations for forming this parliament were bound to provide ample means for these tactics. At the same time the pretext of guarding against undue influence on the elections might provide a reason for expelling Augustenburg from the duchies, thus removing the most dangerous competitor to the Prussian annexation.

Bismarck still considered it not impossible that Austria might eventually yield to Prussia's annexation of the duchies. About this time he said : ' If Austria wishes to remain our ally, she must make room for us.' At the end of May there was a cabinet meeting in Berlin to consider whether it was profitable to try to bring about unlimited control over Schleswig and Holstein by war. Bismarck declared that war might be inevitable, but declined to advise it. He found his way out with the words that the decision in favour of war was a matter for the King, but that this decision would be gladly followed by the whole Prussian people. The chief of the general staff, von Moltke, voted for war. The Crown Prince, influenced by the idea that Bismarck was intending to master his difficulties in internal politics by means of experiments in foreign policy, voted against a ' German civil war ' and for the claims of Augustenburg. The King was undecided. But in the course of the next few weeks the behaviour of Augustenburg became ever more provocative and arrogant in the eyes of the Berlin reigning circles. Matters came to such a pass that the King himself asked him to leave Schleswig-Holstein. Backed by Austria, Augustenburg refused to comply. Thereupon the King sent a personal letter to the Emperor Francis Joseph, asking him to intervene in the matter. When this too remained without success, an ultimatum was sent from Berlin to Vienna, declining any further negotiations about the candidature of Augustenburg while proposing to discuss that of the Duke of

Oldenburg. War seemed imminent and King William was already discussing with his ministers about how to raise the necessary funds. But at the last minute Austria gave in.

At the beginning of August an Austrian plenipotentiary visited the King, who had gone together with Bismarck to Bad Gastein. The Prussian and the Austrian statesmen now worked, so Bismarck wrote to his wife, ' for the maintenance of peace and the stopping of the cracks in the building ', with the result that the Gastein agreement of the 14th of August 1865 indeed stopped these cracks, but broke with the principle on account of which the war with Denmark had begun, that of the indivisibility of the two duchies, Austria being given power over Holstein, and Prussia over Schleswig, ' without prejudicing the continuance of the rights of the two Powers over the whole of both duchies '. Prussia's claims to the naval harbour of Kiel were recognized and a small piece of territory out of the whole, the tiny duchy of Lauenburg, was given to Prussia alone, in exchange for a payment of some million talers to Austria. A few days later the two monarchs met at Salzburg and affixed their signatures to the agreement, with the ' pledge of loyal and honest understanding '. The claim of Augustenburg was thus practically excluded by the agreement and waived by Austria. Bismarck wrote to his wife : ' Thank God with me that I can look in spirit from the wilderness of political life to my family hearth, where the wanderer in an evil night sees the light of his refuge shining.' So Bismarck was evidently not quite content with what had been attained, it was ' only a meagre payment by instalment towards the more far-reaching plans '.

Bismarck, however, had achieved something else, an invasion of the field of liberalism, both on the ideological and on the personal side. It is true, the liberal Opposition did not diminish in intensity. Thus he had to hear one of the intellectual leaders of Prussia say in parliament that his policy was ' in essential points unsuccessful, tolerably inconsequent and illogical, intolerably harsh and obscure ', and when another man of no less intellectual stature exclaimed that the policy of the government ' bears Cain's sign of perjury on the forehead,' Roon's answer, ' this assertion bears on the forehead the stamp of arrogance and insolence ', can hardly have been adequate to convince the other's adherents that his statement was false. But on the other hand, the circle who thought they could meet Bismarck's antithesis between *Grossmacht* and *Kulturstaat* with a kind of synthesis of the two now included persons not only of the emotional party-spirited type of Treitschke, but some with a really earnest and objective attitude. At their head stood the liberal historian and politician, Theodor Mommsen. In a pamphlet *The Annexation of Schleswig-Holstein*, published at the beginning of April 1864 and directed to his constituents, Mommsen said :

You have given us the mandate to defend the constitution against Herr von Bismarck and his followers, and we are seeking to be adequate to the task. The government will not listen to the advice of parliament, and parliament does not feel itself called upon to render those who throw its rightful demands in the waste-paper basket, its advice also, so that that may be treated in the same way.

Passing on to the question at issue, the pamphlet says :

In view of the rights ceded to Prussia, is the erection of Schleswig and Holstein as an independent state still in the interest of the country ? The answer legally lies with the representatives of the duchies and with them alone. We shall still respect their rights of self-determination even if what they determine should appear unwise to us, but our wish is that if a decision is demanded of the duchies they will not look at the matter from the legal but from the patriotic point of view, and that if this way of looking at things does not lead them to favour semi-annexation [to which they would be subject under the ' February terms '] they will come before the Prince of Augustenburg and dare to say to him ' High Lord, it cannot be, it is against the welfare of the land,' a pathetic document of how the most respectable liberals prepared and justified in their own eyes the breaking of their backbones.

CHAPTER XVIII
Preparation for War Against Austria

The Gastein agreement was no solution for the opposition between Prussia and Austria. Bismarck only thought of it as ' stopping up the cracks in the building ' and was altogether averse to its being made anything more. He was convinced that with the Gastein agreement Austria had given ' all the good ' which she was able and ready to give. But, further, he was clear that what had been given him was far from being equal to what he desired to win for Prussia. This was much more than the mere acquisition of the two duchies through incorporation in the system of the Prussian state ; it meant a change in the position of Prussia in the political world. Prussia was now indeed to become a ' Great Power ', not by ' acknowledgement of the other Powers ' but by virtue of ' her own conviction and courageous determination to be such '. Since this was not to be achieved by a free gift on the part of Austria, it had to be taken independently of the will of the latter, or even against it in the strength of Prussia's own power. Half a year before he had written to Goltz : ' I am in no wise shy of war, on the contrary ; you will perhaps very soon be convinced for yourself that war is part of my programme.'

While moving towards the annexation of the two duchies Bismarck had so far looked upon the avoidance of a war-like conflict with the Great Powers as a wise course politically. By a clever utilization of the seventy-million-bloc he had till then succeeded in maintaining this policy. But Bismarck was not so narrow-minded as to limit himself to avoiding such a war. Now he had included it in his political programme, he thought it his duty to prepare ' with statesmanlike skill the way to arrive at it '. One thing only did he think it necessary to lay down in justification of this political preparation for war, namely that he ' had never looked on international disputes from the standpoint of Göttingen students and of the code of honour of private duels ', but that he had ' always made it clear to himself beforehand whether the war, if it led to victory, would bring a prize worthy of the sacrifices which every war demands '. Scarcely any rejection by Bismarck of political principles is so repellent as this justification of aggressive war simply by consideration of its expediency for his own nation. The ideas that international peace is a supreme good and that the sacrifices of the opponent one has attacked deserve consideration as much as one's own find no place in this kind of political thought. In

268

his concluding remark Bismarck passes over such ideas with a staggering matter-of-factness, saying that in planning a war the decisive factor for him was 'always only the consideration of its reactions on the claim of the German people to lead an autonomous political life'. That from this point of view the reproach so often brought against him that he kindled 'a fratricidal war' could not strike home is obvious.

Bismarck did not waste an hour before beginning the political preparation for war. Before the ink on the Gastein agreement was quite dry and while the echoes of the 'pledge of loyal and honest understanding' exchanged between the two sovereigns in Salzburg were still ringing in the lovely mountain air, Bismarck was already on the way to the 'sunlit sea' of his 'beloved Biarritz'; but this time not so much to enjoy 'the clear starlit night and the roaring of the waves', but mainly in order to have a meeting with the Emperor Napoléon. No doubt the imperial residence had an incomparable view of the mountains and the blue sea, but the Prussian visitor had to keep a large part of his attention for the conversations which he carried on with his imperial host. The subject matter of these discussions was the attitude of France in the event of an Austro-German war. Just as in 1859 at the beginning of the Italian war Bismarck was concerned about 'the first shot on the Rhine' from a French gun to which Prussia was much more exposed than was Austria. While he kept his aversion against 'committing himself' by an alliance with France, he was as much as ever concerned to secure her benevolent neutrality.

The Gastein agreement had been received in Paris in no friendly spirit. For Napoléon it was a '*pénible* surprise'. Objection was felt to the separation of the duchies after a war undertaken under the watchword of indivisibility, and to the deciding of their political future over the head of the population, after Prussia had first flirted with a plebiscite. But above all, it was suspected that there existed a secret clause by which Prussia as compensation for the advantages she had gained guaranteed Austria the possession of Venice. Bismarck was a master in controlling his face, tone and words in such a way as to remove the sting from such imputations. To forget his half-promise in Schönbrunn about Lombardy was for him a bagatelle. He repeated his assurance that he was determined not to settle the German question with, but against, Austria. Napoléon said about this time to one of his advisers: 'Believe me, the war between Austria and Prussia is one of those unexpected contingencies which it seems should never arise; it is not for us to oppose war-like plans which open up to our policy more than one advantage.' Bismarck had told him: 'It seems to me to be in the interests of French policy to encourage the ambition of Prussia in the fulfilment of national tasks, for an ambitious Prussia will always be able to set high value on the friendship of France, while a discouraged Prussia will seek its protection in defensive alliances against France.' This was certainly no very conclusive and convincing argument, yet Napoléon let Bismarck know that he held fast to his agreement accepting the acquisition of the two duchies by Prussia. What drove him to it was his conviction that Prussia had to face in Austria a militarily at least equal and probably superior foe with whom she was hardly fitted to cope and by whom she might well be defeated, so that it would come to a war of attrition between the two Powers. In that case Napoléon had unlimited possibilities of intervention as a mediator or arbitrator who could decide the issue of the war and fix the reward for his intervention as he pleased. Bismarck did everything to confirm his host in this surmise, for this was bound to diminish the latter's desire for an alliance with Prussia and for an exact determination beforehand of the prize of non-intervention, since he hoped to determine himself what his reward should be at the expense of the exhausted combatants. So the negotiations in Biarritz produced something like the 'hunting party' so beloved by Bismarck, 'in which every member carries home his booty'. Bismarck left Biarritz with the conviction that in the event of a war with Austria he had nothing to fear from France, and he had secured this without committing himself either to an alliance or to any promise of recompense in payment for the neutrality of France.

That the negotiations should conclude in this way was of great importance for Bismarck, especially in relation to his royal master. For the latter the 'pledge of loyal and honest understanding' exchanged with the Austrian Emperor on the 19th of August was no empty way of talk; it would have been quite incompatible with his views that the Prussians should march against their Austrian 'brethren' by the side of the French, their 'hereditary foes', whom he himself had opposed as officer in the field of battle during the Wars of Liberation. There was indeed, as Bismarck reports, 'a psychological change in the attitude of the King after the agreement of Gastein and the seizure of Lauenburg, the first increase of territory of the kingdom during his reign. He began to develop a taste for conquests.' But, as Bismarck added, 'his predominant feeling was satisfaction that this increase had been won in freedom and in friendship with Austria'. So Bismarck sounded every note which might give the King a taste for an Austrian war. His earlier efforts were marked by particular caution; he warned the King against beginning war as a result of circumstances which might be avoided, but utilized this warning as a cloak under the protection of which to suggest a war to the King, into which he ' would enter unburdened by scruples because the necessity for it was based on the nature of things and on his duty as a monarch '. Some time later he brought up the point of view of expediency and assured the King of his conviction that ' if we now succeed in keeping the peace, the danger of war will threaten us later under less favourable circumstances '. For once more he represented Prussia as victim of threats and aggression in order to win the King for war. Bismarck, whose game with Austria we have been able to observe in its different phases, ventured to describe as the result of his ' sixteen years' service ', in which he ' had been so intimately connected with Austrian politics, that in Vienna hostility to Prussia has become the chief and indeed the sole aim of the government '. In April 1866 the Crown Princess of Prussia wrote to her mother, Queen Victoria, concerning Bismarck's conduct towards the King : ' The tissue of untruths is such that one gets quite perplexed with only listening to them, but the net is cleverly woven, and the King, in spite of all his reluctance, gets more and more entangled in it without perceiving it.'

But the opponents of Bismarck's policy at court did not confine themselves to this indirect criticism of their adversary, whom the Crown Princess called ' *the* wicked man ' and of whom she said that he ' counteracts and thwarts with the greatest ability what is good, and drives on towards war, turning and twisting every thing to serve his own purpose '. The Crown Prince did continue in his conviction—or rather the conviction of his advisers—that Bismarck was playing for war in order to enable him to master his internal political difficulties in Prussia, without knowing how little averse Bismarck was to such a war if only it lay ' in the line of national development '. When the Queen of England asked the Crown Prince for mediation in order to induce the Prussian King to press for a European conference as a means against Bismarck's striving for war, he gave her letter to the King behind the back of his prime minister. But, as the Crown Princess wrote to her mother : ' Fritz does not think the King will accept the proposal, and thinks that the congress could only propose solutions which either Prussia or Austria would not agree to.' That Queen Augusta was opposed to a war with Austria cannot surprise us. But it is astonishing how far Bismarck ventured in intruding on the personal relations of the royal couple. He dared to impose on the King an injunction not to tell the Queen about any measure affecting the two duchies, because he was in doubt whether ' the Queen would keep secret what was communicated to her '. He expressed the wish that a letter of the King on this matter to the Queen should be stopped on the way, and the King not only obediently declared his acceptance of this command, but even felt it necessary to excuse himself by saying: 'I only mentioned the matter because I looked upon it as having lost all relevance to our plans,' thus showing how little Bismarck initiated him into these.

Opposition to Bismarck was also expressed in circles less closely connected with the King. The minister of finances, von Bodelschwingh, objected to the manner in which the mobilization of the army was being prepared, step by step, in accordance with Bismarck's will, and advocated a genuine understanding with Austria, offering his resignation. He allowed himself to be persuaded by the King to remain in office, but finally resigned when the conflict was renewed. A stronger impression was certainly produced on the King by a letter from the head of the *Wochenblatt* party, Bethmann-Hollweg, who openly charged Bismarck with the total absence of any principle in his politics. 'His action was', so the letter to the monarch about his omnipotent prime minister runs, 'from the beginning full of contradictions. Though always a decided supporter of an alliance with Russia and France, he connected with the help which he rendered against the Polish revolt political projects that were bound to alienate both states.' On the death of the King of Denmark in 1863,

he did not deign to put Prussia at the head of an unanimous uprising of Germany, but preferred to ally himself with Austria, the opponent on principle of this plan, in order later to become her irreconcilable enemy. These measures seem to many people like those of a gambler who whenever he loses increases the stakes.

There followed words which show with what keensightedness Bethmann-Hollweg saw through Bismarck's 'unconscious winning' of the King by utilizing his 'difficult position', for the reproaches culminate in the charge that 'in his actions Bismarck set himself in opposition to the aims of his King and showed his greatest skill in bringing the latter step by step nearer to the opposite end till a reversal seemed impossible'.

In face of this, Bismarck had recourse to his sharpest tools. He told the King in writing concerning this action against him: 'All this depends on a well-adjusted plan, according to which the open and secret enemies of your Majesty are trying hard to persuade you to give way to Austria and to develop another policy by representing the present Cabinet and myself in particular as the cause of all evil.' When two articles attacking high-placed champions of the pro-Austrian policy appeared in the *Kreuzzeitung*, which the King described to Bismarck as 'articles of abuse', the latter had to admit that he 'himself was in the main responsible for them'. He thereupon broke out in bitterness: 'It would be expecting superhuman qualities from me to suppose that I could watch in cold blood how the exhausting duties for which I am responsible are deliberately made harder by the disfavour of such high-placed persons, to whom the fame of your Majesty should be dearer than anything.' Without sincerity, but with great effect, he represented himself to the King as the one who was attacked and persecuted : ' My fault is that I do not hesitate to obey your Majesty at the risk of drawing on myself the disfavour of those who stand nearest to you.'

In fact, Bismarck won for the time being the battle for the soul of the King. On the 28th of February 1866 an important council of ministers was opened by the King with a speech which clearly showed the effect of the influence of Bismarck. Austria was accused of ill-will towards Prussia and of the determination to hold her down. The hope of an honourable understanding was becoming dimmer and dimmer. The possession of both duchies was the national desire in the whole of Prussia. One seems to hear again Bismarck's earlier formula in the concluding words of the King : ' We will provoke no war, but we must go forward without shrinking back from fear of a war.' Bismarck insisted afterwards with the explicit approval of the King : ' War was not to be kindled for the sake of the duchies alone ; the greater prize, the German question, must be introduced into the issue.' The prevailing attitude in the discussions of the whole meeting was in accord with this. Speaking of their result Bismarck told the French ambassador in Berlin, Count Benedetti, ' that we have not decided on any rule for immediate practical application ', but that there was almost unanimity that ' the honour as well as the most decisive interest of Prussia commanded us to urge Austria to renounce the duchies '. This communication directly to the French is at the same time to be regarded as a confirmation of the will to friendly relations shown in Biarritz. It was a triumph of Bismarck's domination over the King that the latter sent a personal letter to Napoléon which included a reference to a ' more special understanding ' between the two countries and the offer openly to expound his own attitude through the ambassador. So Bismarck had made the King himself a Bonapartist. The reply of the ' parvenu ' was friendly, but did not miss the opportunity to hint at the question of compensation so objectionable to the King, in connexion with which, as well as Belgium and Switzerland, the Prussian Rhineland was mentioned. Napoléon saw that the final settlement of German affairs was now approaching. He did not wish to prevent it, at least if it did not result in the union between Austria and Prussia, but neither did he wish to leave unused the unique opportunity for drawing profit from it himself.

William I remained only intermittently firm in his war-like

attitude. The 'popular agitation against war' now affected him 'unpleasantly'. At the end of April he said : ' If a Prussian now whispered the word " Olmütz " in my ears, I should certainly lay down my rule.' Meanwhile he was very concerned about the strength of the Prussian troops and their deployment according to the plan of campaign. He complained about Austrian armaments and a few weeks afterwards discussed ' whether the mobilization of 40,000 more men justified the charge that " we were negotiating under arms " '. After that he lamented : ' War with France and Austria if we do not cede the Rhine ! '

All the same, Bismarck felt himself safe enough to deal decisively with another factor relevant to his preparations for war. As in former years so also in 1866 the Prussian parliament was called together at the middle of January. Once again the budget was laid before it, but this time a repetition of the proposal for the reorganization of the army was omitted ' after the many years of fruitless negotiations '. The attention of the Chamber was called to the acquired control of Kiel harbour, the acquisition of the duchy of Lauenburg and the still undecided fate of Schleswig-Holstein ; and the hope was expressed ' that a bond of trust would unite monarch and people now and for all time '. But the Chamber was not to be won by such words ; they pointed out the fact that ' the dark picture of the state of internal affairs which was unrolled at the last session has since grown still darker '. Complaint was raised about the ' administration of the state in a way which was completely devoid of progressive principles '. The Schleswig-Holstein question was said to have become even more serious and complicated through the Gastein agreement. A proposal was made to declare the incorporation of Lauenburg illegal without the consent of the Chamber to the change in the boundaries of the state. Although Bismarck in a fairly long speech pointed to the facts that the expense for the acquisition of Lauenburg was paid from the private purse of the King and not by means of the state, that the fate of Lauenburg had already been decided and that only the fate of Schleswig-Holstein was still in the balance, the declaration of illegality was accepted at the beginning of February by an overwhelming majority. The resolution was communicated by the Chamber to the government which declined in writing to 'accept it and prorogued Parliament at the end of February ; it was accused of not longing for peace but for strife and endeavouring to arrogate ' spheres of interest which the constitution had not put at the disposal of parliament '. Two months later this parliament, the last belonging to the period of the constitutional conflict, was dissolved. Bismarck had thus made a stride further in his preparation for war. The Prussian parliament, the essential mouthpiece of Prussian liberalism, was put out of action for the remainder of the period during which this preparation was in progress.

Still more important than this internal aspect of Bismarck's preparation was its external side. The first steps to secure the neutrality of France had been taken. Subsequent events favoured Bismarck's desire to keep France at a distance while he settled with Austria. At the end of the year Napoléon was involved in difficulties with America. Goltz recommended Prussian intervention for the purpose of mediating. Bismarck, however, replied: ' From the general human standpoint it may be a misfortune, but from the political point of view it is not necessarily to be regarded as a disadvantage for Prussia, if the relations of France to the United States should become involved.' But Bismarck wished for a much more decisive strengthening of the political basis for his military action against Austria. He desired an active ally in this enterprise. Already for a fairly long time he had had Italy in view for this. As ally Italy had essential advantages as compared to France. At the head of the country there stood since the death of Cavour no man who in acumen and vision could be compared with Napoléon. In political strength Prussia was always bound to be her superior; there was no common boundary between the two countries, and Italy had no desire for German territory, while on the other hand she was an immediate neighbour of Austria and had a still unsettled account of her own with that country. In the war which Italy had undertaken six years earlier with French help against Austria she had acquired Lombardy with Milan, but not the province of Venetia, which was as essential for the completion of her national unity as the still papal city of Rome. While she looked with longing towards that province, Austria had on her part not got over the loss of Milan. When in August 1864 Bismarck spoke with the Austrians at Schönbrunn about the ' hunting party ', he had in view as Austria's part of the booty the reconquest of Milan. When exactly a year later the two sovereigns had signed the Gastein agreement at Salzburg, Bismarck seems in the immediately following discussions with Napoléon at Biarritz to have spoken of a possible Prusso-Italian alliance against Austria, from which Italy was to gain Venetia. In any case Bismarck on his way back from Biarritz to Berlin had a meeting with the Italian ambassador in Paris and remarked on this occasion that ' it seems as if the policies of Prussia and Italy [i.e., in relation to Austria] should run parallel ', whereupon he received the ' enthusiastic ' answer: ' Ah well, we shall go together.' But the matter was not quite so simple as that. Prussia's attitude of armed neutrality in the Italo-Austrian conflict of 1859 was regarded in Italy as obscure and ambiguous. Napoléon's shrewd diplomacy had brought it about that in Italy Prussia was regarded as bearing the real responsibility for her failure to complete her national unity. Also the present absolutist régime of Prussia was by no means popular in Italy, proud of her constitutional government. So the feelers of Prussia in Italy towards an alliance did not meet by any means everywhere the joyful reception with which they were met by the Paris ambassador. Thus Bismarck was forced to open up the hearts of the Italians by a gift which meant more than ' an inexpensive gesture of friendship '. In doing this he made a clever choice. In the autumn of 1865 he offered Italy a commercial treaty with the states of the Customs Union. The new Italy found herself in crushing financial difficulties and had already taken daring steps in order to improve her position. The commercial treaty therefore meant for her a welcome help. But it was also not without advantage for the German states. Consequently Bismarck succeeded in obtaining their consent in December 1865 after overcoming initial opposition; this was supported by Austria who felt herself slighted by being still left out of the Union and did not like this rapprochement of Prussia to Italy.

In the middle of January 1866 Bismarck sent a letter to the Prussian ambassador in the Italian court, at that time situated in Florence. In this he referred to the Prusso-Austrian relations which were now becoming more strained, and said ' that the degree of security and the extent of help we have to expect from Italy will be of vital importance as affecting our decision whether we are to let the matter come to a crisis or content ourselves with minor advantages '. From the answer of the ambassador it emerged that the Italians were counting on a voluntary offer of Venetia from Austria, but in any case expected more definite proposals from Prussia for an understanding. Bismarck thereupon considered the dispatch of General von Moltke, a particularly strong advocate of the Italian alliance, as negotiator. That Bismarck hoped to deal with this new ally in a similar way as he had done with the one he was just trying to choke off, Austria, is shown by the instructions given to Moltke. He was to work for an alliance on a basis which left Prussia the right to decide when and whether she should strike against Austria and which pledged Italy to attack Austria at the moment of the Prussian declaration of war. Before Moltke departed, however, the news came that an Italian general was on his way to Berlin in order to negotiate there for an alliance. The instructions given to him were very different from those of Moltke. It was now more than before hoped in Italy that Austria would surrender Venetia without a blow in exchange for a Danubian principality which had just lost its ruler. The alliance with Prussia was only intended as a final means of pressure against Austria. But it is worth noting that once the Italians had entered the lion's den the negotiations proceeded in a very different way from that hoped in Florence and quite as they had been planned in Berlin. Bismarck knew how to convince the Italians of the favourable character of his own position, since he need not, like them, go for the whole, but could content himself with a partial gain to be won without war. The principle of using the person with whom he was negotiating without allowing himself to be used by the latter for his ends was even easier for Bismarck to carry through in relation to the Italians than in relation to the Austrians. Napoléon thought it desirable by winning Prussia for the Italian alliance to put the seventy-million-bloc on his eastern border for ever out of the question and therefore worked with the Italians in favour of Prussia. What was lacking for a settlement was provided by Austria, as she refused to cede Venetia peacefully not only under the given circumstances but on principle. So at the beginning of April the alliance for war came into existence ; the secret agreement said that in case Prussia took up arms against Austria, Italy was to declare war. It was, however, limited to three months, a proviso which certainly was in conformity with Napoléon's wish to realize as soon as possible ' the profit from the unexpected contingency '. Another clause laid it down that peace was only to be concluded by mutual agreement and that Italy should be allowed to conclude it as soon as she had acquired Venetia. It is worth noticing that this treaty was a formal and unambiguous break of the German Confederation Act of 1815 which, though giving international independence to the single states, was incompatible with an agreement about war by a Confederate state with a foreign Power against another member of the Confederation.

Bismarck had at that time the pleasant surprise of finding that the government of the two duchies had, despite the separation decided in Gastein, retained its explosive possibilities for the relations of Prussia and Austria. Already towards the end of 1865 differences of opinion arose about the boundary between the territories taken over by the two Powers. Bismarck rejected the wishes expressed by Vienna in this matter. Some days afterwards he sent a complaint to Vienna in which he made a sharp protest against Press excesses ïh the duchies. At the end of the month the two governors met for a discussion about business matters. The Prussian, a Herr von Manteuffel, and the Austrian, a Herr von der Gablenz, governed their territory according to strictly opposite principles. The former was harsh, bureaucratic, and a foe of Augustenburg, the latter was obliging, accommodating and friendly to Augustenburg. When these differences of principles did not come very much into the foreground in the discussion, the Prussian blamed the Austrian for secretiveness and accused him of having received two sets of instructions.

In time the Augustenburg movement spread from Holstein to Schleswig. Manteuffel not only took the strictest measures in his own territory, but addressed a complaint to Gablenz about the hostile tone to Prussia in the Augustenburg Press in Holstein. Gablenz declined to intervene. Austria permitted Augustenburg to be named in Sunday services as sovereign of the country, and his wife as mother of the land ; in Schleswig even to speak of him as Duke of Schleswig-Holstein was forbidden. At the beginning of 1866 Gablenz allowed a mass meeting from both duchies to take place in Altona in Holstein to advocate the convocation of parliament. On the same day Bismarck let some members of the Schleswig-Holstein knighthood hand him over an address which advocated the annexation of the duchies by Prussia. In his reply he described annexation as ' the most profitable form ' for regulating the question. Then he, who a few months before had suggested to Vienna a plebiscite on the question of succession, declared that events like the Altona meeting made Holstein ' the hearth of revolutionary intrigues '. These, he said, prejudiced ' the monarchical principle, the sense for public order and the unity of the two Powers '. In Vienna this ' claim of Prussia that we should render an account to her for an act of government in Holstein, was decisively rejected '. On the 11th of March there was issued a Prussian decree which threatened with penal servitude those who conducted such intrigues in the duchies against the Prusso-Austrian sovereignty, thereby setting the criminal courts on the war-path against the Augustenburgs.

That a particularly important centre for Bismarck's political preparations for war was the Federal Diet at Frankfurt is obvious from the mere fact that the decisive object of dispute was the question of the national unification of Germany. The Gastein agreement had been opposed very sharply by the liberals of the ' Third Germany '. It was regarded as destroying all hope of making Schleswig-Holstein into a member state of the Confederation with Augustenburg as her sovereign. The right of the people to self-determination, it was held, had been violated and the indivisibility of the duchies sacrificed by its guarantors. From Bismarck's Prussia nothing better had been expected. But Austria a few months before had entered into negotiations with the smaller states about the succession and had voted on their side in the Federal Diet ; now, however, she had allowed herself to be tricked by Prussia into becoming her ally against them. Bismarck set himself to deepen this dissatisfaction, this time not in order to win Austria to his side, but in order to isolate her still more. In the annual meeting of liberal deputies in the state parliaments, the so-called Abgeordnetentag at Frankfurt-on-Main, for the discussion of matters of common interest for Germans, the Gastein agreement was a principal issue. It was strongly attacked, especially on the ground that it violated the right of self-determination. Bismarck then induced Austria to take joint steps with Prussia against the Frankfurt Senate (the governing body of the Free Town of Frankfurt) on account of its ' toleration of subversive movements '. When Austria failed to push the matter with the zeal which Bismarck desired, the latter heaped on her bitter reproaches. When a few weeks later the Federal Diet reminded the two Great Powers of their decision about summoning a parliament in the duchies to settle the question of succession, Bismarck again managed to bring about a joint declaration that they were reserving their decision as to the time.

But more detailed information about Bismarck's visit to Biarritz, better knowledge of the Prussian commercial treaty with Italy, the events in the duchies, and gossip about an exchange of visits between Berlin and Florence stiffened the attitude of Vienna. There was still a strong party there, headed by Count Mensdorff, who were opposed to a war with Prussia. But the war party won the upper hand. At the end of 1865 a request from Berlin for the voluntary renunciation of Austrian claims on the duchies in favour of Prussia in exchange for financial compensation was rejected, as was a similar request by Italy in regard to Venetia. However, from the first months of 1866 on Bismarck had no desire either to keep secret from Austria his determination for war or to moderate the bellicose tendencies in Austria. Bismarck's procedure was again marked by a disconcerting frankness which threw his opponent off balance and plunged the latter in obscurity concerning his real plans. At the beginning of March the wife of the Saxon ambassador was to sound Bismarck at a social function in Berlin about his intentions as to war with Austria. But there was no need for diplomatic ' soundings '. Bismarck said far more and spoke far more clearly than his questioner could hope or wish. ' Have no doubt, the moment is approaching, our guns are already cast and you will soon have the opportunity to convince yourselves that our improved artillery is far superior to that of Austria.' In order that people should know about the negotiations for an alliance with Italy it was arranged that the garrulous old general who by his obstinacy had already bungled the Danish campaign, should be made a confidant under a strict seal of secrecy. It was said that the news thus reached Vienna on the same day. Count Karolyi was then told to ask Bismarck directly ' whether the Berlin court was really thinking of tearing the Gastein agreement to pieces by force '. Bismarck replied: ' No ! ' and then after a pause added the words : ' Do you think I should have given a different answer if I had been full of war-like intent ? '

But the policy of the Austrian government was even clumsier

than it seemed to be from this clumsy question. At any rate it was clumsy enough to expose their weak spot to the counter-measures of Bismarck. Austria made military preparations near the boundary between Bohemia and Prussia, advancing her troops in this region. While these measures were inadequate to secure her defences, which was their sole object, yet they were fully adequate to put in the hand of one so unscrupulous as Bismarck material for propaganda about Austria's will to aggression. Moreover, when the quarrel within the duchies was at its height Austria sent a note to the governments of the smaller states announcing the proposal that if Bismarck should give no satisfying answer to the question of Karolyi, the Federal army should say the last word. In Berlin there had been stored up for a long time a plan of Moltke for an aggressive war against Austria, with a lightning attack preceding mobilization; now it was followed by an expert opinion of the same to the effect that the previous measures of Austria were adequate only for very modest defensive requirements. Bismarck therefore omitted for the moment military counter-measures, egged on the Press against Austria as the 'threatener of world peace', and replied to the Austrian note by telling the smaller states that an Austrian army ready to strike was menacing Prussia's borders. He wished to know what the governments of these states intended to do if Austria passed to the offensive, and at the same time he announced a Prussian proposal for a 'reform of the Confederation which would take account of realities', under the watchword that 'the interests of Prussia and Germany are identical; this is to our as well as to Germany's advantage'. It was not the first time that Bismarck had used the idea of Federal reforms for the purpose of dealing Austria a blow, and again as three years before the purpose was to mobilize the German people as allies for the Prussian Crown against Austria.

After Austria had been thus made the aggressor in the public eye Bismarck thought it necessary, since Austria's will to war was not quite certain, to bring inflammable material from the Prussian side in order that the conflagration should not expire from a lack of fuel. On the 28th of March, a few days after Bismarck had sent his note to the smaller states, a Cabinet meeting took place in Berlin. Moltke reported on the military situation. He based his report on calculations which were seen later not to have been justified and came to the conclusion that new Austrian measures made energetic counter-measures necessary, particularly the increase of the manpower of the frontier battalions in order to secure the Prussian border. All agreed to Moltke's proposal, and the decision was immediately carried out by the Cabinet in order to anticipate and prevent an attempt at procrastination which they feared from the King and which he indeed did make.

Shortly afterwards the Prussian alliance with Italy was concluded, and the announced proposal for the reform of the Confederation sent out. This proposal like the one of three years back was intended to supplement the Federal organs by a Federal Parliament, elected on the basis of equal, direct, and universal franchise. Again the proposal was rejected in most quarters. The Nationalverein declared, ' the German people have no confidence in a government which, while despising the constitutional law in their own country, comes forward with plans for reform of the Confederation '. A popular Bavarian daily newspaper spoke of Bismarck's ' rascally proposal ', the Prussian Crown Prince of Bismarck's ' criminal game with the most sacred matters '. Some of Bismarck's conservative friends turned against this ' flirtation with democracy ' which was bound to ' bring Prussia misfortune '. In what way the proposal was intended directly to affect the political preparation for war against Austria is not quite clear. Bismarck himself gave an evasive answer to a question of von der Goltz on this point. Indirectly, however, it was destined to serve both to distract attention from the constitutional conflict in Prussia and to win adherents among the subjects of the smaller German states against Austria. This follows from the context in which the proposal was first brought forward. At the time when it was announced Bismarck approached Bavaria with the suggestion that in the course of reforming the Confederation Austria should be excluded from it, and Bavaria should be made leader in the south to correspond to the leadership of Prussia in the north. Bavaria had been in fact alienated from her Austrian neighbour by the Gastein agreement, but she had not on that account been brought nearer to the curt, arrogant Prussia. She regarded the diplomatic struggle between the two Great Powers as a not unwelcome strengthening of her own position in the Confederation. So when Prussia asked Bavaria to append her signature to the scheme for reform, the latter refused. In the discussion in the Diet only Baden voted for the measure. The most that Prussia could do was to save it from being utterly rejected by being referred for consideration to a special commission. The latter decided to await further instructions and the whole matter disappeared from political life.

Vienna did not wish to leave unanswered Prussia's declaration about the Austrian army ready to strike. In her reply she asserted her loyalty to the Confederation, the personal will to friendship of the Emperor, and the absence of any aggressive intention, and received thereupon from Prussia a communication of similar purport. Now, however, Vienna demanded the cancellation of the measures for mobilization ordered by Prussia, whereupon Berlin demanded that of the Austrian measures as the first step. The unexpected and, for Bismarck, highly undesirable then occurred. In a communication of the 18th of April the Austrian government, who had meanwhile obtained further information about the Prusso-Italian alliance—probably through Paris—notified the Prussian government that they were willing to withdraw on the 25th of April the troops they had moved to the frontier, if Prussia would pledge herself to reduce her battalions to their peacetime strength the day after. This was a formal proposal for demobilization, accompanied by an offer on the part of the proposer to act first. Its rejection was held in Berlin 'impossible in view of European opinion'. The government therefore accepted it and looked forward to 25th of April with very mixed feelings. But the 25th of April came and did not bring the Austrian order for a withdrawal of the troops.

The deliverance for Bismarck had come from Italy. There the acquisition of Venetia was desired as one decisive step towards national unity, and it was wished to attain this by force of arms, especially once Austria had rejected peaceful settlement on principle. The demobilization negotiations between Prussia and Austria had had a disappointing but also a stimulating effect. There were anti-Austrian demonstrations in the north of Italy. A report arrived at Vienna that Garibaldian formations had crossed the border between Italy and Venetia and that regular Italian troops had marched to the frontier in order to cover their movements. In the prevailing atmosphere of nervousness and confusion in Vienna, this report, the lack of foundation of which was recognized too late, proved sufficient to lead to a substitution for demobilization measures of measures to complete armed preparations. On the very day on which Bismarck had half-heartedly sent his acceptance of the demobilization proposal to Vienna, a great council of war was held there. This ordered the mobilization of the Southern Army intended for war against Italy. The letter of acceptance from Bismarck had no effect on the further course of affairs. The anticipated order for the withdrawal of the Austrian troops from the Prussian frontier on the 25th of April was not sent, and on the next day but one orders were issued for the further mobilization of the Northern Army at the Prussian frontier. At the same time Bismarck heard that Italy had replied to the Austrian mobilization of her Southern Army by mobilizing herself. This was for Bismarck highly welcome news, all the more so since neither country could continue mobilized for any considerable period of time on account of her financial position, but would be obliged to strike soon. Now he had good reason to hope that the intended victim, Austria, might be manœuvred into the rôle of aggressor and that Prussia's intended accomplice, Italy, would not refuse the support demanded from her. To Vienna, where in spite of the changed situation the government wished to

resume the negotiations for demobilization, Bismarck, who knew
Moltke's own preparations and plan for a lightning attack, replied :
' For negotiations in which one side is armed and the other is
completely unarmed the Prussian government cannot promise any
success,' and received the longed-for Austrian declaration that she
' regarded the negotiations about the cancellation of military preparations as exhausted '.

This was the watchword whereupon throughout the German
Confederation not only in Austria and Prussia, but also in the
larger states of the ' Third Germany ', the process of arming set
in with full energy. A tremendous excitement about the imminent
' war between the German brethren ', the ' fratricidal war ', pervaded
all circles. In spite of clever diplomatic preparations public opinion
all over Germany including Prussia was united almost without
exception in agreeing that Bismarck was responsible for the situation
which had been created. In Berlin he ' tried hard to extract
demonstrations for war out of the population ' (R. Morier). But
' of any movement in his support there was a total lack. Everyone
set themselves against him,' says one of his eulogists. The Nationalverein declared : ' The moral consciousness of the whole nation
protests up to the last moment against the arbitrary wilfulness
which plays an irresponsible game with the fate of Germany.' They
were seconded by the Abgeordnetentag : ' We condemn the imminent war as a war of the Cabinet in the service of dynastic aims.'
Political meetings in Berlin passed unanimous resolutions to the
effect that ' a war of Prussia against Austria under existing circumstances would be contrary both to the welfare of Germany and to
the cause of right.' In this chorus also joined one of the oldest
personal and political friends of Bismarck, the president Ludwig
von Gerlach, as the representative of the extreme conservatives.
In the *Kreuzzeitung*, still his organ, he raised his aged voice in
favour of ' dualism ' as the ' real basis of the constitution of Germany '. ' Every wound of Austria is a wound of Prussia,' he
exclaimed. The opposition to a war with catholic Austria was
especially emphatic and loud in the catholic parts of the land,
particularly in the Rhine-province. What was most unusual, the
reserves called up did not everywhere follow the call to the colours
gladly and without opposition. In many places the women tried
to prevent their men from boarding the military trains. To the
mass meetings, protesting against the war, were added addresses in
favour of peace and a great multitude of threatening letters. Yet this
time Bismarck's opponents did not stop at written and oral attacks
on him ; he was also the object of an attempted political murder.
The twenty-two-year-old south-German Cohen-Blind fired several
shots at him in Berlin. Bismarck remained unwounded and himself

co-operated in the arrest of his assailant, who in the following night in prison cut the artery of his wrist. Bismarck's escape from the danger and his bravery in it brought him a great number of personal messages of sympathy, especially one by the King, but there was no considerable change in the attitude towards his policy.

That in this tense situation an attempted mediation by a private individual could have no success was obvious from the first. When Bismarck received a request from an Austrian general to make a proposal for mediation at Vienna, he certainly did not comply because he now either wished or expected Austria to yield. His purpose was undoubtedly to obtain a further document to show the world and the King that Austria was ' the threatener of world peace '. The proposal was in fact so worded that the Emperor Francis Joseph declared : ' So much is clear ; this agreement would give Prussia the lion's share.' All the same Bismarck brought his own sovereign to a point at which the latter said : ' I know, they are all against me. But I should rather perish than that Prussia should give way this time.'

More important than this private mediation was the intervention of the European Great Powers. Napoléon did not give up the benevolent neutrality which he had maintained towards Prussia since Biarritz, but he saw no reason why he should not consent to negotiations with the opposite side too. Although he did not wish to commit himself about the prize he would require for mediating, he would still have been glad if Prussia had made a firm offer instead of merely talking of ' a more special understanding '. He therefore had no objection when about the beginning of May Austria approached him with a view to his mediating with Italy, although the Austrians talked of the cession by Prussia of the district of Glatz and even of the whole of Silesia. Napoléon at first showed some reserve, certainly not on account of any obligation he fèlt towards Prussia, but rather for non-political and highly personal reasons, namely an aggravation of his chronic disease which crippled him. On the whole it pleased him that he was thus in practice recognized as arbitrator. Now for the first time he spoke to Goltz about his wishes for recompense in a formula which, while not compromising him too much, was not to be misunderstood in Berlin. ' The eyes of my country are directed on the Rhine.' The only thing that Bismarck could do about it for the moment was not to hear and not to understand. The result was that Napoléon turned his attention with greater interest towards the possibilities of an Italo-Austrian agreement, but not with such zeal as to silence the voices in Italy which demanded war with Austria. All the same in the first half of May, when Italian mobilization was still in progress, there were some days on which Bismarck had to envisage

the secession of Italy from the alliance and the turning of the weight
of all the Austrian forces against Prussia. But in the end he yet
attained his object. At such times of stress to do this required his
full energy, since he also had to fight symptoms of his old malady
which just then assailed him with greater violence. In order to
keep his hand in the Austro-Prusso-Italian game Napoléon also
considered the convocation of a congress of the Great Powers,
which he hoped would lessen his responsibility without lessening
his gain. England supported him out of aversion to, Russia out
of sympathy for, Bismarck. Bismarck had to agree. The Prussian
army, indeed, pressed for an immediate opening of hostilities in
order to exploit the advantage of the well-thought-out measures of
her deployment, speedier and better organized than that of their
opponents. But the King could not be induced to give his permission to start hostilities. In annoyance Bismarck described it as
the King's 'superstition that he ought not to take the responsibility
for a European war'. But fortune was again in Bismarck's favour.
It was Austria who on the 1st of June rejected—at least practically
—the proposal for a congress. 'Long live the King!' Bismarck
called out in joy, when he received this news, hoping that it would
not fail to exercise its influence on the monarch.

Since the beginning of May direct negotiations between Austria
and Prussia had been broken off, and the armies were formed on
both sides of the Prusso-Austrian frontier preparing ever more
intensely for war. The 'Third Germany' had at first met the
mounting peril of war only by mobilizing public opinion and
replenishing her modest officers' cadres. But it became clearer
and clearer that they could not thereby conjure away the threatening
storm, but must rather be its first victim. Then, at the time when
Napoléon considered the convocation of a European congress, the
smaller German states decided to attempt in the Federal Diet what
in April direct conversations between the two Powers had failed
to achieve: general demobilization within the Federal territory.
Austria and Prussia reserved their views on the proposal, but—
strange enough—after Austria had declined to refer the question
at issue to a congress of the Great Powers, advocated by Napoléon,
she decided to refer it to the small Powers of the 'Third Germany'.
The rejection of Napoléon's proposal was followed immediately by
an Austrian declaration in the Federal Diet to the effect that she
was only arming against the threat of attack from a Prussia combined with Italy aiming at the acquisition of Schleswig-Holstein.
She would at once demobilize if this 'state of affairs came to an end,
and for this purpose she left the question of the succession to the
duchies for the German Confederation to decide and had asked her
governor in Holstein to call parliament together there'. By doing

this Austria committed a breach of the secret clause of the treaty of the 16th of January 1864 which she had *de facto* violated in the preceding year, since that clause bound her to settle the question of succession by agreement with Prussia alone. Bismarck had now the chance to represent Austria once for all as the guilty and aggressive party. He was the man to exploit such an opportunity to the utmost.

He was thus able to depict this action of Austria to his sovereign as such a grave violation of the treaty that the latter now gave the consent to immediate war which he had hitherto refused.

At the Federal Diet [so wrote the King] Austria has broken the treaty by unilateral action without the foreknowledge of Prussia, and contrary to our agreement has laid before the Diet the question of the duchies which ought to have been settled between us and not by that body. Thus on the side of Austria there followed unceasingly perfidy, lying, breach of agreement.

Orally he said : ' After the refusal of Austria to send representatives to the congress, after the unworthy violation of the treaty and after the heated language of the Press the whole world knows who is the aggressor.' This was of course Bismarck's thinking uttered by the King as mouthpiece. Bismarck now did what he could in order to spread this knowledge to the ' whole world '. He published the secret clause of the treaty of January 1864 in order to put Austria openly in the wrong. On the 5th of June the parliament of Holstein was summoned by Austria, and two days later Prussian troops marched into Holstein. The Austrians abandoned the latter without a blow. On the 10th of June the Prussian plenipotentiary to the Federal Diet proposed there the exclusion of the territory of Austria from the German Confederation. The matter did not come to a vote, but Austria immediately recalled her ambassador from Berlin and proposed the mobilization of the Confederate army with the exception of the Prussian contingent. When this proposal had been accepted the Prussian representative announced that mobilization against a member of the Confederation was incompatible with Federal law and that thus the Confederation Act of 1815, already broken by the secret treaty with Italy, was ' broken and no longer binding '. The draft of a new Federal constitution drawn up by Bismarck was made known. It excluded Austria but included the south German states and had in view a much firmer union than the former Confederation. Austria, however, at the very time when she was striving to assemble round her the other Confederate states against Prussia concluded an agreement with France which gave the latter the ' lion's share ' in the most emphatic sense of the word. She pledged herself to cede Venetia to Italy whatever the result of the war, and also not to make any territorial alterations in Germany without the consent of France. As compensation for these concessions Austria was granted nothing, not even the neutrality of Italy; a more drastic self-exposure of her inner weakness was hardly conceivable. A leading Austrian historian has called the agreement ' the diplomatic last will of the then Austrian system of government '. Bismarck, however, was entitled to boast that he had made a decided contribution to the pressure applied to Austria to draw up this last will.

Only a few of the smaller north German states declared themselves in favour of Prussia; the most important, including Saxony, Hanover, and Kur-Hesse, rejected the proposal of Prussia to guarantee their sovereignty in return for a pledge of neutrality. On the 15th and 16th of June the Prussian troops marched into these states. A few days later the main Prussian army in three columns, the two chief led by the Crown Prince and another Hohenzollern Prince, crossed the Austrian frontier. From Silesia, Lausitz, and Saxony they entered Bohemian territory. The war with Austria, in regard to which Bismarck had told a member of the liberal Opposition, his friend von Unruh, that ' it was quite inevitable and would have broken out two years earlier if the episode of Schleswig-Holstein had not come between ', had now begun. Bismarck, however, induced the King to make an appeal on the 18th of June to the ' only ally of the Prussian Crown ', the ' German people '. According to this appeal ' the Confederation is torn asunder ', but nothing is said as to who has torn it asunder. It is as if it were a natural phenomenon which the Prussian Government had to accept as sent by the hand of God. But the man who had stood and still stands against the people in the constitutional conflict, who had drawn such a sharp contrast between the Prussian and the other German clans, and had claimed for the former in his ' specific Prussian patriotism ' a leadership ' based on fear ', now cries out that ' the living unity of the German nation has remained ' and that for it we have to find ' a new vital means of expression. May the German people, looking to this high aim, lend their confidence to Prussia.' In conclusion, however, we see the man who, even in situations where he is most flagrantly the aggressor, knows how to take on himself the rôle of the assailed defender of the right.

The guilt is not mine [he lets the King exclaim] if my people have to fight a hard battle. No choice was left us any longer. We must fight for our existence, against those who wish to push the Prussia of Frederick the Great from the rank which she has attained through the strength of her Princes and the courage of her people. May God grant us victory.

To the English ambassador Bismarck said in these days : ' It will be a bloody war, if we are beaten I shall not return here, I will fall in the last attack, one can only die once and it is better to die than to be beaten.' Later he declared : ' The greatest triumph I have achieved is to have wrung from the King of Prussia the declaration of war against Austria.'

CHAPTER XIX
Nikolsburg

The campaign of Prussia against Austria and her allies, who comprised most of the north German and all of the south German states, was a Blitzkrieg in the most exact sense of this word. Bismarck's political preparation had envisaged a campaign of this sort, and it was rendered possible by the organization of the army carried out by the minister of war, von Roon, in particular the equipment of the infantry with the needle-gun and the detailed planning of manœuvres, in march and in battle, by the chief of the general staff, von Moltke. This time there was not, as in the Danish campaign, conflict, but co-operation between the military authorities. Within a few days the Hessian capital, Kassel, was taken, the Prince was made a prisoner of war, and the Hessian army had fled from their country. In Hanover the army capitulated within a fortnight of the Prussian invasion, the King pledged himself to leave the country, and a Prussian civil administration was instituted. In Saxony the King, the government, and the army left their country and fled to Austria. There they fought very bravely by the side of the Austrians in the battles of Bohemia. While the Italians already in the first few days suffered a severe defeat from the Southern Army of the Austrians near Custozza, the Prussians from the very beginning scored a number of successes over the Austrian Northern Army mustered in Bohemia. When the King, together with Bismarck and the military leaders, entered the Bohemian theatre of war on the 1st of July they came just in time to participate in the decisive battle of Königgrätz (Sadowa) on the 3rd of July.

Those were still the days in which battles took the form of an immediate struggle between man and man and the decision came in close combat. Bismarck told his wife how 'the King exposed himself very much on the 3rd. A tangled mass of ten cuirassiers and fifteen horses of the 6th cuirassier regiment wallowed bleeding on the ground beside us and grenades whirred round my lord in the most unpleasant fashion.' However,

he was filled with enthusiasm for his troops, and rightly so, to such an extent that he did not seem even to notice the whistling shells and the explosions. He was always finding fresh battalions whom he had to thank and to whom he had to say 'Good evening, grenadiers,' till we had again drifted back right into the line of fire.

Yet Bismarck not only understood but also shared his sovereign's enthusiasm for war. 'Our soldiers deserve to be kissed,' he wrote to his wife ; ' everyone is so brave to the death, so calm, so obedient, so well-disciplined, with empty stomach, wet clothes, wet beds, little sleep, the soles of their shoes falling to pieces, friendly to all, no plundering and burning.' Yet he exclaimed at the sight of horribly mutilated bodies in the battlefield : ' Now when I think that Herbert [his eldest son] might in the future once lie like this, I do feel bad.' One of his confidants drew the following attractive picture of him in the battlefield : ' Clad in a grey coat, high up on a huge bay horse, his grey eyes gleaming under the steel helmet, he reminded one of the giants of primeval Nordic times.'

But from the beginning the military campaign was for Bismarck only the means to an end. He did not seek decision in battle but in political measures. When on the evening of the battle of Sadowa Moltke said to the King : ' Your Majesty has won not only the battle, but the whole campaign,' Bismarck is said to have added : ' The question in dispute is therefore settled. Now it is for us to regain the old friendship with Austria.' This expression is very revealing. It shows how intense the political zeal in Bismarck was, enabling him, not only to call up, increase and direct his emotions, but also to suppress them. We note, how even on the battlefield, he could in the very opponent, whose ' supreme, nay sole, political object ' he had told his King was ' enmity against Prussia ', already see the future political ally, untroubled by doubts as to whether he would succeed in overcoming the strong aversion which the van-quished feels against the victor, especially if he is a victim of aggres-sion. The remark also throws much light on the fashion in which Bismarck in his relations with Austria sharply separated the internal and the external side of politics, and on how, with all his firm deter-mination not to allow the period of dualism inside Germany to recur, he still kept the seventy-million-bloc with its significance for foreign policy clear before his eye and was unwilling to surrender it for any other advantage in external affairs.

If we are not excessive in our demands [he wrote a few days after the battle to his wife] and do not think that we have conquered the world, we shall have a peace which is worth the trouble. I have the thankless task of insisting that we do not live alone in Europe, but with three other Powers who hate and are jealous of us.

The quick and decisive victory at Sadowa had indeed shocked the whole political world and thrown everybody off his balance. Statesmen had to admit both to themselves and to others that they had erred in their calculations, and had to find a new orientation for the future. This applied specially to the country most immediately interested in the outcome of the war and best equipped to influence it—the France of Napoléon III. The victory of Sadowa had shown

Napoléon wrong in his belief in the superiority of the Austrian army and in the long war of attrition between Austria and Prussia. Napoléon's army which since Solferino had brought home few laurels felt itself put in the shade by the military feats and achievements of Prussia. They looked on Sadowa as on their own defeat and cried out for 'vengeance'. Catholic and democratic France became very much more conscious of their special opposition to the conquering Power, and patriotic France saw on her eastern border, instead of the comfortable weakness of a set of small states opposed to each other, grow up a dangerous and powerful rival. Of these moods and these views Napoléon was determined and compelled to take account.

This situation in France was at once utilized by Austria in order to gain relief in her disastrous plight. In the first place she wished to get rid with this help of her Italian opponent, whom she had indeed beaten but who was still most troublesome. On the day after the battle of Sadowa the Austrian ambassador in Paris visited Napoléon with the news that Austria had now decided in accordance with the treaty concluded with France three weeks before to carry out the evacuation of Venetia if Napoléon would induce Italy to grant an immediate armistice and thus make it possible for Austria to make her Southern Army free for battle against Prussia. This was, however, something quite different from what Napoléon had foreseen as his position in relation to the belligerents. It meant his undisguised active participation in the struggle as ally of Austria, whereas hitherto he had kept up throughout not only in form but also in fact the relation of benevolent neutrality towards Prussia. Yet on the other hand, the Austrian request might serve him as a handle to preserve or to recover the position as mediator and even as arbitrator, which seemed to be vanishing with the departure of his dream of a long war of attrition. He had now to make up his mind to turn the Austrian offer of mediation in peace negotiations not only to the advantage of Italy but at the same time also to the advantage of Prussia. But haste was required so that Austria should not anticipate him there, as she had already on the day after the battle sent a negotiator to the Prussian headquarters in order to ask for an armistice and had renewed this request a few days later.

There were two political pieces of news, which Bismarck received immediately after the battle of Sadowa, the one from Berlin, the other from Paris, the one pleasing, the other of a mixed nature. The first piece of news concerned the elections following on the dissolution of parliament on the 9th of May, the polling day of which happened to be also the date of the battle of Sadowa. Bismarck had started working for the issue of these elections before the outbreak of war. In the first half of June, in the very days in which he dealt his last blows at the 'Gordian knot of the German problem', finally cutting it to pieces, Bismarck had a series of discussions with leaders of the liberal opposition in parliament, among others with Unruh, about an understanding. The negotiations were successful in so far as the liberals came to give their approval to the foreign policy of Bismarck, which they had a little while before described as 'intolerably harsh and obscure', while in return Bismarck recognized the right of the representatives of the people to control the budget. Thus even while Bismarck was pushing power politics to its height in foreign affairs, he made an attempt to come to terms with liberal ideas at home, thereby slapping in the face his own thesis of the priority of foreign politics. But in fact Bismarck went a step further. The King, he knew, would have nothing to do with an understanding with the Chamber, thinking that if he agreed, parliament might again at the end of the war take away some of the new battalions. Now Bismarck, who a few years ago had fiercely opposed the assumption of the Chamber that there was 'a distinction and division between King and government', committed himself before the liberal negotiators by asserting this division. He even cast an aspersion on the King to extricate himself. He insinuated that his position in relation to a sovereign averse to modern ideas was an extremely difficult one, the King being on account of his advanced age little capable of changing his mind. Here, too, Bismarck succeeded. These negotiations, added to the initial military successes in Bohemia, were an essential factor in causing the elections of 3rd of July to show a substantial trend to the Right, weakening the progressives and putting the moderate liberals in a friendly attitude to the government.

The letter from Paris which Bismarck received came from the French government. It brought the news of the offer of Austria to cede Venetia and of her request for mediation through the French sovereign, 'in order to put an end to the conflict', and not only between Austria and Italy but with the inclusion of Prussia. Napoléon expressed the expectation that the King would 'greet with satisfaction the steps which I shall take in order to help restore to your state as well as to Europe the blessing of peace', and proposed an armistice 'immediately to open the way to negotiations'. A corresponding telegram was sent to the Italian King, and a notice in the French government organ, the *Moniteur* of the 5th of July, was meant to bring before the eyes of the world and the French people the splendour of Napoléon's position. The King of Prussia, who a little while before had lamented 'war with France and Austria if we do not abandon the Rhine', was now enraged because an attempt was being made to take out of his hands the fruits of the victory which had been won with so much uncertainty and diffidence on his part. While the King raged, Bismarck thought about the problem. The King wished to reply with a precise list of armistice terms that would carry with them a complete transformation of the German Confederation and Prussia's position in it. To this Bismarck was opposed. He deliberated : European intervention in the reform of the German Confederation was to be expected, since all those who counted politically wished to avoid the recurrence of the seventy-million-bloc. But Napoléon was no longer Europe, and it was to be expected that the other Powers, above all Russia and England, would be made by the vainglorious intervention of the French Emperor to keep back rather than to take part in his activity, as at the time of the Danish war, On the other hand, Italy had shown herself a reliable, but by no means efficient, ally. The Prussian army had not exploited the victory of Sadowa in such a way as to destroy the opposing army or occupy an important part of the hostile territory as pawn. The south German states, for whom the watchword was : ' Rather French than Prussian ', were as yet unconquered. A French army of observation on the Rhine would form for them a strong support even if it was confined to mere observation. The idea of an alliance with Austria against France was considered to some extent, but soon rejected. Be that as it may, Bismarck was determined in the event of a war on two fronts to grasp at ' every weapon that was provided us by the unchained national movement, not only in Germany, but also in Hungary and Bohemia '. He was prepared in that case, in the words of his former friend Rechberg, ' to take off his coat and himself go up to the barricade '. He had, in fact, already entered into negotiations with a group of Hungarian refugees to arrange for a rising in Hungary. But it seemed better to him not to let things go so far, but to recognize Napoléon as arbitrator, without, however, committing himself, and thus gain time. So on the 5th of July the following telegram was despatched from the Prussian headquarters to Napoléon :

I accept the proposal made by your Majesty and am ready to come to an understanding with you about the means to re-establish peace. I shall tell your Majesty the conditions under which the military situation and my obligations to the King of Italy would allow me to conclude an armistice.

In the following days the Prussian troops advanced further in the direction of Vienna. The Austrians put up no organized resistance and repeated their request for an armistice. The Italians, in spite of their reverse, showed themselves loyal to their alliance, if not very active, and still preferred to acquire Venetia by force of arms rather than as a present through the mediation of Napoléon. Also England and Russia showed the hoped-for reserve. It was not till the 9th of July that the list of the armistice terms which they had in view left the Prussian headquarters to go to von der Goltz in Paris that he might submit them to Napoléon. We might in fact describe them as the proposal of ' a peace which is worth the trouble '. In addition to the annexation of Schleswig-Holstein that of Sáxony, Hanover, and Kur-Hesse was mentioned on the ground that it was demanded by ' public opinion '. It was this ' clamour of unreason ', which Bismarck here invoked as his accomplice. But he added generously that ' the power in some form or other to dispose of the forces of north Germany ' was sufficient for Prussia's ' political needs ' and the question of annexation not important enough ' for us to stake on it again the fate of the monarchy '. Bismarck did not forget to say that he proposed to ' treat the details as a matter to be discussed with parliament ', words which would sound well in the ears of Napoléon, the friend of plebiscites, and which were uttered with a view to cooling Napoléon's desire to intervene, as they served to make the matter an ' internal ' one, secure against international intervention. Instead of ' the disposition of the forces of north Germany ' the expression ' North German Confederacy ' was also used. Its legal content was as yet left undefined, but it was limited by mention of the ' impossibility at the time of drawing in south Germany—" the south German-Catholic-Bavarian element " '. The consolidation of the military and political situation in the last days in favour of Prussia found expression in the instruction to von der Goltz that ' without threatening he should still let it be seen that we are firmly resolved not to accept a peace which would be dishonourable in view of our successes '. We also find a casual suggestion of lesser annexations, namely, besides the duchies, of only a part of Saxony, Hanover, and Kur-Hesse, and certain rights in Brunswick. But in a short telegram which followed next day it says : ' Any full annexation is better than a semi-annexation by means of reform.' As regards the reward to Napoléon for his mediation, mention was made of ' compensation for France outside Germany ' in the exposé of the 9th of July, but the nature of the compensation was not more precisely defined. The words ' outside Germany ' were here expressly introduced for the first time, while on the previous day Bismarck thought of giving up the ' Palatinate ' and ' Hesse-Darmstadt ' (west of the Rhine). In fact, he had four weeks before told the Italian ambassador : ' I am much less a German than a Prussian and would have no hesitation in agreeing to the cession to France of the whole territory between the Rhine and the Moselle. The King, however, would have the gravest scruples about this.' The then following limitation to compensations outside Germany is said to be due to the intervention of the Crown Prince who advised him against ' giving German land to France, since Prussia would thereby injure herself for ever '. This was the time when the relations between the two men began to improve. Bismarck had revealed his political aims to the Crown Prince in an interview immediately after the battle of Sadowa. By this frankness, according to one in the know, 'differences which had lasted for many years were smoothed out'. However, the influence of the Crown Prince did not amount to very much. So in the short telegram of the 10th of July, which has just been mentioned, von der Goltz is told 'no cession of *Prussian* territory'.

These statements are Bismarck's first utterances relating to the unification of Germany ever since that had become an object of practical policy. The decisive point is that they do not show any distinction in attitude from that of four years before, when at the beginning of Bismarck's premiership this project was still regarded as belonging merely to the realm of wishes. Then we saw the same refusal to find a common basis on the same level with the other German states in the sense of the Nationalverein, the same hostility towards the 'rotten fermentation of indiscipline' in the south, and the 'catholicizing opponents of Prussia', the same will, if not to annexation, at any rate to the right to dispose of the forces of the neighbouring states, if necessary by application of the policy of 'blood and iron', the same 'specific Prussian patriotism' based on 'the claim to leadership by the vigorous Prussian military power'. Now as little as then do we find any traces of the liberal *Kulturstaat* with its postulates of 'the equality of all human beings' and 'the development of individual liberty', for all the political haggling with the liberals about budgetary rights.

In the days between the Prussian offer to negotiate of the 5th of July and the final despatch of their armistice terms von der Goltz had to pass through a difficult time in Paris, which made great demands on his diplomatic skill. The Austrian ambassador and his wife, who were personally very much favoured at the Paris court, worked with their combined forces to win for their Emperor the understanding and the help of Napoléon. The French foreign minister, Drouyn de Lhuys, worked in favour of setting up on the Rhine the army of observation which was so much feared by Bismarck. The French Empress combined with her hostility against protestant Prussia a personal aversion towards its diplomatic representative whom she disliked both for his sagacity and his ugliness. Bismarck knew very well what dangers were threatening him from the direction of Paris and how much hung on Napoléon's personal attitude. He delayed the despatch of the terms but insisted all the more on the military position being strengthened. He opposed the desires of the military for further enterprises, which would lengthen the period of instability and thus 'dangerously increase the weight behind the French arbitration'. Now when on the 13th of

July von der Goltz appeared with the Prussian terms before the French Emperor he found a reception kind beyond expectation. The exhaustion of Napoléon as a result of physical illness weakened his power of decision and hindered him from vigorous intervention. But he needed a counterweight against the pressure of his court. He could not make up his mind to set up the army of observation, since it would have meant to him too great a risk in view of the reserved attitude of England and Russia, the continuance of the fight by Italy, and the doubts about his own country's readiness for battle. Already two days before von der Goltz's visit Napoléon had let Vienna know that he had decided ' in the present crisis not to plunge the French nation into a war '. Now he declared himself in agreement with the Prussian conditions, in particular with the creation of a North German Confederacy separated from an internationally independent southern Confederacy. He further declared that ' the inner constitution of this Confederacy was indifferent to him '. The territorial integrity of Austria and her departure from the German Confederation were agreed upon, but the only annexation mentioned specifically was that of Schleswig-Holstein. In the other territories of the North German Confederacy the only right that was expressly cited was the Prussian ' command of the military '. There are various causes which may have led von der Goltz to abstain from pressing the question of annexation further. Certainly of primary importance was the lack of interest shown by Bismarck in this. Perhaps the indifference displayed by Napoléon is also part of the cause, and perhaps Goltz saw in such a proposal a danger for an agreement. Otherwise Napoléon thought it important to give proof that he was really acting as arbitrator ; so he expressed a wish about the division of the costs between the belligerents and he himself sent to Vienna the draft of the Prussian proposals. As regards Napoléon's own reward the conversations were not very fruitful. He indicated to Goltz that he desired at least to win the fortress of Landau in the Palatinate, but without asking for an answer.

Meanwhile the direct negotiations which Austria had started with Prussia on the day after the battle of Sadowa had continued. Bismarck attached value to these direct relations not being broken off. He found in the territory occupied by Prussia Austrians who were suited to act as advocates of the Prussian cause in Vienna and took all pains to keep Napoléon and his representative away from these negotiations. The conditions offered by Bismarck in this fashion were more favourable than those sent to Napoléon through Goltz. There was here no talk of annexations by Prussia, only of ' Prussian aspirations north of the Main ', neither was anything said of a demand for the payment of an indemnity, and the southern Confederacy was not to be closed to Austria.

On the 15th of July, while the direct negotiations were still pending, the armistice terms, drawn up by Napoléon in conjunction with von der Goltz, arrived in Vienna. About the same time Benedetti, after an unsuccessful visit to Bismarck's headquarters, arrived there in order to exercise his influence in Austria in favour of the acceptance of the armistice terms. The French ambassador in Vienna, Gramont, who before had worked on his own initiative to harden Austria's attitude to Prussia, was now forced to alter his point of view and let himself also be harnessed to the work of seriously bringing about this acceptance. The two French diplomats pointed especially to the fact that the acceptance of a direct Prussian offer would be an insult to Napoléon who had been asked by Austria to act as mediator, and might thus endanger relations between France and Austria. But the Austrian government did not wish at once to abandon the opportunity of choosing between two possibilities. Gradually the two French plenipotentiaries became very uncomfortable, they felt themselves practically superfluous in Vienna, and Gramont in particular urged Napoléon to fall back on the idea of the army of observation. The situation became still more complicated because Bismarck's Austrian supporters were not in a position to appear as his official plenipotentiaries; thus it was impossible in the first days to obtain in Vienna an authentic account of Prussia's attitude, so that everybody concerned remained in the dark about the really decisive factor.

The terms discussed between Napoléon and von der Goltz reached the Prussian headquarters in the shape of a telegram only on 17th of July, two days after their arrival in Vienna, and there met with an unexpected opponent in the person of King William. It seems that Bismarck had not unambiguously communicated to him the exact terms of his letter of the 9th of July. In particular, he may not have informed the King that he was leaving vague the question of annexation by using the expression ' the power to dispose of the forces of north Germany ', and that he had abstained from demanding the annexation of any portion of south Germany. The King, however, who hardly two years earlier had refused to take the opportunity to acquire Schleswig and Holstein because he was in doubt concerning his ' right ' to them, and who had striven with all his power to avoid ' taking on the responsibility for a European war ', now as a result of his first taste of conquest allowed himself to entertain fantastic ideas of increasing Prussian power and territory. His demands were now that Austria should cede to Prussia parts of Silesia and of Bohemia, and that Saxony, Hanover, and Kur-Hesse should equally cede considerable stretches of territory, and finally that Bavaria should be stripped of Ansbach and Bayreuth as former Hohenzollern possessions. He also demanded that the German states which had opposed Prussia in the war should lose a substantial part of their sovereignty. The King was supported in his wishes by the military. Indeed, the latter in ' their aversion to breaking off the sequence of victories which they had hitherto enjoyed ', as Bismarck says, went in some respects beyond him.

Bismarck had throughout an understanding for the ' strong dynastic family sense ' which induced the King to make these demands. Nor was there anything more remote from his mind than to revive once more on his own account the legal point of view which the King was just abandoning. Finally, he seems to have had no trouble about the question whether the restriction or even annihilation of the rights of a number of legitimate sovereigns would not endanger the dynastic principle or even to surrender it to its alternative, ' revolution and barricade ', though he was the very man who shortly before had feared such a surrender in any concession to the budgetary rights of parliament. But to the political considerations which told against the King's love of conquest Bismarck could not be blind. That the European Great Powers would quietly accept such an increase in power on the part of Prussia was as little to be hoped as that the states chosen to play the rôle of victims would endure this without resistance. Also the assimilation of the new subjects and the defence of the new borders would have meant a heavy political burden.

So Bismarck was indeed confronted with ' the thankless task of making it clear that we do not live alone in Europe ' to one to whom he had so often emphasized his loyalty as a ' Brandenburg feudal vassal ' and whose at least ' unconscious ' support it had always seemed indispensable to win. He himself describes in his *Reflections and Reminiscences* the difficulty of his position ' as being that of the ' only person at headquarters who bore political responsibility as a minister and who had to make decisions without being able to appeal to a higher command '. Now, the decision which Bismarck, faced by this responsibility, held to be the right one, he had bluntly communicated to von der Goltz on the 9th of July, saying that ' annexations are not important enough to stake on them again the fate of the monarchy '. This responsible decision not only did not correspond to the King's wish, but undoubtedly also went against Bismarck's own inner desires. This is made quite plain by the telegram which he sent the next day to Goltz : ' Any full annexation is better than a semi-annexation by way of reform.' However, this assertion is and remains the expression of a desire and in no wise represents a change in his responsible decision that annexations were not important enough for him to risk anything for their sake, on the contrary it indirectly confirms the latter. The telegram from Goltz concerning the terms discussed with Napoléon, which passed over the 'inner organization' of the North German Confederacy as an 'indifferent' matter and did not expressly mention the annexations, therefore corresponded throughout to Bismarck's orders. Bismarck, thus confronted with the necessity of deciding whether he would keep to the responsible decision which he had already made, or whether he would give way to his and the King's desire for annexation, excused himself ' the thankless task ' of carrying out his previous decision and chose the apparently more comfortable way to which his desire pointed. Already on 17th of July, the very day on which the telegram from Goltz about the terms reached the Prussian headquarters, Bismarck sent out the following telegram in reply : ' As basis for peace the content of your telegram of the 14th (containing the terms) is not adequate. The annexations mentioned earlier have become a necessity.' To this, however, Bismarck decided to add the following conditional clause : ' if the Prussian people are to be satisfied '. When and how had this ' people ', this ' random mob of individuals whom somebody succeeded in winning for his views ', this bearer of the ' popular will, but in fact of the club-law of the barricade ', meanwhile come into play ? Was it really necessary to conceal the King and his responsible minister behind this obedient ' ally of the Prussian Crown ' ?

On the 18th of July Bismarck had a further discussion with the King about annexations in which Moltke and Roon also took part. As its result another letter was sent to Goltz. In this it was stated more precisely and emphatically than before that ' the principal thing for us at the present moment is the annexation of 3 to 4 million inhabitants of north Germany '. To appreciate the importance of this we must remember that the whole population of Prussia at the time was only 19 million. Bismarck also repeated the instruction of the 9th of July : ' The rest is to be achieved by parliamentary means and is as a whole more an internal matter of Germany's.' One finds also in the letter a sentence which, in strict opposition to William I's former wish for annexation in south Germany, repeats and underlines Bismarck's refusal ' to bring in south Germany at present '. This letter offers ' altogether to break off the relation with south Germany ' and ' to give a binding assurance of non-intervention in regard to south Germany '. When Bismarck later said, that Benedetti ' hoped to build up a South German Confederacy as a kind of branch Office of France ', he obviously tried by these words to conceal his own unambiguous connivance in this question. Bismarck describes himself as having shown a ' forceful, almost threatening attitude so as to induce the King to yield on this and some further points, including the territorial integrity of Austria ' which Goltz had already acknowledged towards Napoléon. Indeed, Bismarck's view : ' A further weakening of Austria by annexation of her territory, must not take place, for we shall need her power later for ourselves,' won the day. Yet the King, according to Bismarck, maintained that ' he would rather abdicate than return home without a considerable gain of territory for Prussia as the rightful prize of victory '.

Bismarck was therefore in a by no means enviable position. He had to reckon with the possibility that Austria might accept the terms sent her by Napoleon on the 15th of July which did not involve annexation and that Napoléon might refuse to amend them in the sense Bismarck now wished ; or that even the terms still less favourable to Prussia, offered by his Austrian agents in Vienna, might be accepted by Austria. If then the King insisted on his annexationist demands he had to envisage the continuation of the war, the victory of the war party under Druyn de Lhuys in Paris, and the appearance of the French army of observation on the Rhine. In fact the war party in Paris staked everything on the advantage they thought they would gain as a result of the recent annexationist demands of Bismarck, but the untiring efforts of Goltz with his inexhaustible cunning and courage, his vigour in taking action and his skill in giving way where necessary, prevailed. He actually succeeded not only in retaining the goodwill of Napoléon, in the state of weakness and indecision to which his illness had reduced him, but even in further consolidating it. Bismarck, however, to serve his purposes in Paris brought up, no longer the Prussian people, but the King himself. ' The King ', he wrote to Goltz, ' attaches especial value to annexation,' and referring to the King's mention of his abdieation, he continued : ' I entreat your Excellency to take account of this attitude of the King.' The whole episode in Paris, however, seems to have passed off with such little notice that no news of it reached Vienna. There the negotiations between the French and the Austrians continued and ended with the acceptance of the terms by the Austrians on the 19th of July.

When on this day Benedetti proceeded from Vienna with the news to the Prussian headquarters, which had been removed to Nikolsburg, there was already present a message from Count von der Goltz that Napoléon had described expressly the annexations as details in the internal organization of Germany ïndifferent to himself. The King thought that his wishes for an annexationist peace were realized, and sanctioned the signing of the armistice. Bismarck, however, signed in the expectation that in the subsequent course of negotiations the annexations could be freed from any danger they might involve for ' the fate of the monarchy '. Soon afterwards Bismarck's Austrian agents arrived with the news that Austria was ready for direct negotiations and received from him the answer : ' You have come an hour too late, we have just accepted the mediation of France.' On the 22nd of July the armistice came into force and a day later, at Nikolsburg, negotiations about the preliminary peace between Bismarck and the Austrian delegation, headed by Count Karolyi, began. France took no direct part in those negotiations. Benedetti and Gramont were present as observers in Nikolsburg, but Druyn de Lhuys induced Napoléon to declare at the beginning that the French rôle as a mediator was now at an end. He wished to bring it about that France should not insist on exacting the reward for her mediation at an unsuitable time and should not take on any responsibility for the peace terms. Italy was not invited to partake in the negotiations. Her military position had indeed somewhat improved since Custozza, though not as a result of any considerable activity on her part, but because Austrian troops had been withdrawn to join the Northern Army. This improvement, however, could have hardly survived the return of the Austrian troops whom the armistice rendered superfluous in the north. So in Italy Prussia's conduct was regarded as a violation of the treaty of alliance concluded in April. Bismarck received a report from Florence to the effect that the King of Italy showed ' great dismay at our willingness to conclude an armistice ' without consulting him ; but Bismarck cared little for the now useless ally. Let Italy send an observer to Nikolsburg to report on the proceedings there. But we no longer hear Bismarck say : ' My obligations to the King of Italy do not allow me to conclude an armistice of my own accord ' ; on the contrary, the observer could not do anything more than communicate to his sovereign the desire of Bismarck that Italy should also make peace, since Venetia was now secured. With Bismarck and Karolyi left alone and undisturbed at the conference table, any important hindrance to a speedy settlement seemed to have been removed.

While the hostilities between the former belligerents began to give way to a peaceful attitude, there was a new explosion of great violence within the Prussian headquarters. The annexationist fever of the King, which had been earlier fostered by Bismarck and by high military quarters, had somewhat cooled down by the time of the conclusion of the armistice, but had been by no means extinguished. Soon afterwards it broke out again in full fury. At the very time when the detailed conditions of peace were being discussed and formulated at the conference table between the belligerent Powers, in the neighbouring rooms of Prussian headquarters under the same roof a council of war took place ' under the presidency of the King, intended to decide whether peace should be made on the proposed terms or the war should be continued '. The decisive point at issue was, afterwards as before, the question of the annexations. To this was now added the demand of the military for a triumphant entry of the Prussian army into the capital of the enemy, Vienna. The earlier conflict between the obligations which had been incurred towards Napoléon and the wishes of the King, now that the negotiations for peace were far advanced, came to the front again for Bismarck in a still more painful fashion. 'I gave expression to my conviction', he reported, 'that peace must be concluded in accordance with the Austrian conditions, but nobody joined me in this; the King joined the military majority.' He continued in his graphic, though somewhat coloured fashion : 'My nerves could not resist the impressions which catch hold of me by day and by night. I stood up in silence, went into my neighbouring bedroom and was there seized by violent fits of weeping. Meanwhile, I heard how the council of war in the next room had broken up.'

The next step which Bismarck said he undertook was to set on paper the arguments in support of the acceptance of the terms. If the King was prepared to continue the war against his responsible advice, then, Bismarck declared, he must ask for leave to resign his offices as minister. In the discussion which followed the presentation of Bismarck's memoir the latter yielded to the King's annexationist wishes to a degree which is hardly to be reconciled with the state of the peace negotiations. He proposed besides the 'exclusion of Austria from the Confederation' a 'convention with Saxony to place the whole force of the land at the disposal of your Majesty', and added 'the annexation of Schleswig, Holstein, Hanover, Kur-Hesse, part of Hesse-Darmstadt and Nassau'. Only the military entry into Vienna was to be omitted. But even this was not enough for the King, who had become obstinate, certainly not least through Bismarck's compliancy. The 'standpoint of right' for which he had earlier contended had meanwhile undergone a remarkable change, which made it now a basis for violent extension of power and territory. The King declared that he was called to 'punish' his external foes, among whom he distinguished 'those mainly guilty' from those who were misled. The punishment of the first should consist in the 'loss of territory'. This was, as Bismarck says, 'the principle of retribution' to which the King herewith gave validity as a rightful maxim in foreign politics. But what interested the King perhaps still more was the military aspect of the matter, the wish 'to exploit the military success and to continue the victorious course'. On this account the King fell into 'so violent a state of excitement that a prolongation of the discussion was impossible and I left the room'. For the second time in perhaps twenty-four hours Bismarck and the King separated in this abrupt fashion. Herewith the decision seemed to have gone against Bismarck and the acceptance of peace terms, and in favour of the continuation of the war.

But at the last moment, so Bismarck reports, there appeared a deliverer in the shape of the man from whom perhaps this help was least to be expected, the Crown Prince. When Bismarck, having returned to his room, stood at the open window in a ' mood which brought me near to thinking whether it would not be better to fall out of the window four storeys high ', he felt a hand on his shoulder from behind ; it was the hand of the Crown Prince. Now it was to be seen of how much value the recent rapprochement of the two was in practice. ' You know ', said the Prince, ' that I have been against war. You held it necessary and bear the responsibility for it. If you are now convinced that the end is attained and that peace must be concluded, I am ready to back you and to advocate your views to my father.' Half an hour later, so Bismarck says, the Prince came back with the agreement of the King to accept the peace terms in his pocket. The King's agreement was expressed in a remark written in pencil in the margin on one of my latest memoirs with approximately this content : ' Since my prime minister leaves me in the lurch in face of the enemy and I am not in a position to replace him, I have discussed the question with my son, and since the latter has accepted the view of the prime minister, I see myself to my grief forced after such brilliant victories of my army to accept so shameful a peace. I see myself forced as victor before the gates of Vienna to yield, and leave the judgement to posterity.'

It was as if the personal reproaches were specially devised to wound the ' Brandenburg vassal and Prussian officer ' at his most sensitive point. But Bismarck speaks only of ' the sharpness of the expressions ' and ' their impolite form ', which did not prevent him from ' gladly accepting the royal agreement to what I knew to be politically necessary '. Yet his personal feelings were not altogether untouched. Bismarck emphasized ' the tension intolerable for me ' which the episode brought to him. He also described as particularly painful the circumstance ' that I have been forced so to offend a sovereign whom I loved personally as I did him '.

So at the next sitting of the peace conference the negotiations could be continued without one of the other negotiators suspecting by what dangers they had been threatened since the last meeting. They came to a conclusion on the 25th of July after a good deal of haggling. The fiercest struggle concerned the territorial integrity of Saxony, for which Austria contended energetically under the pretext that Saxon troops had fought at the side of the Austrian to the end. In regard to this question Bismarck fell back step by step and finally gave way altogether, since even so the annexations which he achieved in north Germany corresponded to his highest hopes. Austria gave her consent to the annexation by Prussia of the following north German territories : the Kingdom of Hanover, the Electorate of Hesse, the Dukedom of Nassau, the Free Town of Frankfurt, as well as Schleswig and Holstein, comprising altogether about four and a half million inhabitants, spread over about 25,000 square miles, i.e., an increase of about 25 per cent in population and territory. Austria pledged herself to surrender Venetia and gave ' her consent to a new constitution of Germany in which Austria was not to participate '. Prussia was to form a Northern Confederacy which was to include Saxony ; she had to surrender to Denmark the part of Schleswig in which Danish was spoken. On 26th of July the preliminary treaty of peace was signed at Nikolsburg. It provided new and impressive evidence of Bismarck's view on the ' coincidence of the two ends ' : ' the leadership of Prussia from the Prussian standpoint ' and ' the unification of Germany from the national standpoint '.

Bismarck was in a hurry to obtain Austria's signature. Perhaps he was afraid that his annexationist monarch might again come forward with an extension of his demands. But the most important thing for him was to be prepared for the possibility that the European Great Powers would not take quietly the extraordinary increase in the might of Prussia. Even during the negotiations he received news from St. Petersburg that in Russia the existence of the German Confederation was regarded as guaranteed by the Powers of the Vienna Congress (1814–15) and that only a congress consisting of the same Powers had the right to come to a decision as to its termination. The idea of a congress was bound to bring Russia near to the France of Napoléon. Such a combination Bismarck had to prevent. So in Nikolsburg, while the peace negotiations and the disagreement between him and the King were still hanging in the balance, he took for the first time the step which he had so far always avoided, he spoke openly and unambiguously with Count Benedetti, then at Nikolsburg, about the payment due to France for her activity as mediator. This unambiguous frankness, however, concerned only the question of principle admitting that the French demand for payment was at bottom fully justified. But when they came to discuss the practical carrying out of this principle, Bismarck expanded himself in a multitude of possibilities : naturally the victorious Prussia could not surrender anything of her own ; perhaps France might be compensated by means of the Bavarian Palatinate ; the easiest course would be if she seized Belgium ; on this last point agreement could certainly be brought about ; only just now his attention must not be occupied with questions of detail. Benedetti reported Bismarck's agreement on the question of principle to Paris as a great diplomatic success. Bismarck, however, brought it about thereby not only that he could avoid for the time being committing himself on the questions of detail, postpone a renewed request by

Benedetti, but that Napoléon too recognized the Prussian annexations, which were now taken for granted, and thus made an understanding between himself and Russia more difficult.

When at the beginning of August Bismarck arrived in Berlin, the conversion of the preliminary peace of Nikolsburg into a final peace treaty was entrusted to a conference to be held at Prague. Bismarck took very easily the settlement with the south German allies of Austria : Bavaria, Württemberg, Baden, Hesse-Darmstadt. In order to check these states Prussia had set up a special army. It was not till after the battle of Sadowa that the first armed conflicts occurred in this theatre of war. The engagements, in which the south German troops displayed very little fighting spirit and which without exception ended in victory for Prussia, continued right up to the time of the Nikolsburg negotiations. In these Austria showed interest only in the territorial integrity of Bavaria. But Bismarck had not forgotten the refusal of this very state to support his proposal of April of the same year for the reform of the Confederation. When the Bavarian Premier appeared in Nikolsburg in order to ask for an armistice on behalf of his country, Bismarck snapped at him : ' Do you know that I could have you arrested as prisoner of war ? ' Bismarck's main efforts, however, were now directed towards separating the south German states from Austria and winning them for Prussia, although a little while before he had offered Napoléon ' a binding assurance of non-intervention in regard to south Germany ' and had informed Austria that ' the Southern Confederacy was not to be closed to her '. After his victory Bismarck found in south Germany a quite different response to any he had encountered in the days of the old Confederation. When he spoke to Bavaria of the cession of territory to Prussia, she was at once ready to comply in return for the acquisition of Austrian territory. In fact, Bavaria came very close to a loss of territory, not only on account of the territorial desires of the Prussian King, but also because her dear neighbour and ally, Baden, suggested to Bismarck that in order to ' set up a more equal balance of power in south Germany ' some of the Bavarian territory should be given to herself. Eventually all the south German states, whose representatives appeared one after the other in Nikolsburg, were referred to negotiations to be held after the conclusion of the peace conference. These led to an armistice on the 2nd of August.

The idea of a congress of the Great Powers soon had its edge taken off. St. Petersburg indeed upheld the official view that a conference should settle the questions at issue between Prussia, Austria, and the ' Third Germany ', and communicated this desire to Paris and London. But in London the idea found no response. The new Cabinet under Lord Derby did not wish to get in the way of Prussia. Bismarck was indeed not contented with this English reserve. He blamed England because he could only ' reckon on platonic goodwill and instructive newspaper articles from her ', and he made the remarkable objection that ' this theoretical sympathy would hardly be intensified to the point of providing active support by land and sea '. In fact, without, however, mentioning the reason for such an intensified sympathy, England's attitude meant an extraordinary improvement in Prussia's international position when at the end of July the news came from London that England accepted the strengthening of Prussia with lively satisfaction, had no wish for a congress and would be glad if Prussia refused it. Russia also associated with the congress very different aims from those which France, concerned with her power position, had in mind. Alexander II did not mind the increase in Prussia's power ; he had indeed been very well disposed to Bismarck ever since the latter's stay at St. Petersburg, and the inveterate hate of the Russians for Austria led them to gloat over her defeat. What concerned the Tsar was his aversion to the deposition of whole dynasties, thus threatening the principles of dynastic rights and legitimacy. We might in fact have expected Bismarck to share this aversion, but it apparently exercised no particular influence on him. In order to build a bridge for the Tsar which would enable him to make an honourable retreat from the congress proposal Bismarck had had despatched to him a Prussian plenipotentiary with the special confidence of the King. To this messenger the Tsar expressed the conviction that, as long as the Prussian King found himself in agreement with Old Europe in sparing the hereditary rights of the dynasties, he would be immune from the revolutionary principle represented by France. However, when the Tsar found Bismarck inexorable in regard to the question of annexation, he wrote a long memoir to the Prussian King and then gave up his idea of a congress. That in doing so he had been influenced by the thought that Russia ' could not tolerate the neighbourhood to her Polish border of a Franco-Austrian coalition ', as Bismarck assumes, may be correct in view of her memories of the Polish rising of 1863.

So Napoléon was again stripped of the protection which a congress of the Great Powers would have provided, and was obliged to continue alone his efforts to secure a reward for his work as mediator. He did this unceasingly. Shortly after the conclusion of the preliminary peace treaty von der Goltz reported from Paris that Napoléon had asked him in confidence whether in the final settlement of German affairs France might not acquire Saarbrücken, Landau, and Luxemburg. When the Prussian consent, for which he can hardly have hoped, did not follow, the anti-Prussian group of advisers, under Drouyn de Lhuys, once more gained the upper hand with the indecisive Emperor. In the last days of July they induced him to give his signature to a proposal for a treaty by which Prussia would restore the territory taken from France in 1815, i.e., the region of the Saar, would induce Bavaria and Hesse-Darmstadt to cede their possessions on the left of the Rhine, and would give up her right to occupy Luxemburg. So Bismarck found himself confronted with the fact that the demand for compensation, the rightness of which he had recognized in principle, was to be applied in actual practice. He was now without any ground for evading this practical application.. So instead of evading it he launched a direct attack on it, utilizing the handle which was given him by the excessive character of the French demand. He described this as an ultimatum to Benedetti, who when handing it in had concealed his lack of confidence behind an outward appearance of great firmness, and told him that they might take the rejection of the proposal to constitute a *casus belli*. Prussia would then wage war, and for this purpose seek to win Austria as an ally by surrendering all the conquests she had just won. As usual Bismarck's threats did not fail in their object. Benedetti made himself very small, hurried back to Paris at once, and on his return ten days later he brought with him a declaration of his government that the proposed treaty was now to be regarded as not having been put forward. Drouyn de Lhuys had to leave office. A fortnight later, however, Napoléon came forward with a fresh, more moderate request, limited in the main to Belgium and Luxemburg, apparently as the result of Bismarck's expostulations. This request the latter now met by applying the method of procrastination. He concealed himself behind the negative attitude of his King, with the result that France finally put before him a formal written proposal for a treaty involving the express offer of an alliance and the annexation of Belgium and Luxemburg. The acceptance of this proposal was delayed by Bismarck till it died of neglect, while Napoléon gave up his demands for a time. He did this in formal fashion, namely in a document addressed to the French ambassadors abroad, in which he said that France ought not to take offence at the new independence of Germany. If the national aspirations of the German people were fulfilled, their warlike attitude would cease. Germany, he said, was following the pattern of France and consequently she was brought nearer to her by her action, not further away.

Bismarck was little interested in the conclusion of the Italo-Austrian war after the cession of Venetia had been settled in Nikolsburg. His services were called upon only when the question was to find a formula for this cession which would at the same time involve the recognition by Austria of the new Kingdom of Italy. Here also Napoléon thought it important that his activity as mediator should find expression in the formula. So with Bismarck's agreement a statement was drawn up according to which ' Venetia was passed to Napoléon and acquired by him for Italy, Austria accepted this declaration and gave her agreement to the union of Venetia with the Kingdom of Italy '. Italy was now politically unified, with the exception of Rome, which remained a papal state and for the time had a French garrison. Of greater interest for Bismarck was the conversion of the provisional agreements with south Germany and Austria into a final peace. The first final treaty was concluded in the middle of August with Württemberg, whose representative Bismarck had at first refused to receive at all ' since hostile feelings against him are with us particularly strong '. This treaty with Württemberg Bismarck shamefacedly called ' a treaty of alliance of the well-known type '. It included not only some clauses about economic questions and the mutual guarantee of possessions, but also a secret article which established a defensive and offensive alliance, according to which in the event of a war Württemberg troops should be under the supreme command of Prussia. This was the beginning of the drive intended to bring over to the side of Prussia the sympathies of south Germany which had cooled towards Austria in view of the latter's lack of interest in their affairs. But why was the article made secret ? Bismarck had made the offer to Napoléon on the 18th of July ' altogether to break off the relation with south Germany ' and ' to give a binding assurance of non-intervention in regard to it '. There can hardly be any doubt that France was the enemy threatened by the new treaty and that the extension to Württemberg of the military control of Prussia was not regarded by any of those concerned, least of all by Bismarck, as reconcilable with the promised non-intervention. Bismarck had just shown in the constitutional conflict and in his demands on Augustenburg what decisive significance he attached to the command over the military forces in relation to the sovereignty of the state. But what about Württemberg's inclination towards France, the Rhine League policy ? To combat this Bismarck had at his disposal an effective weapon in the terms of the treaty offered him by France at the end of July, which contemplated the territorial mutilation of south Germany. And of this weapon he at once made the most extensive use. Very soon Baden and Bavaria followed the example of Württemberg in concluding a defensive and offensive alliance with Prussia. Hesse-Darmstadt was in part, Saxony after some opposition, wholly incorporated in the Northern Confederacy, though only after the fall of her prime minister, von Beust, since Bismarck declined to negotiate with him. Thus the ' internationally independent Southern Confederacy ' received its mortal blow before it had come into existence. France for her part was exposed to the utmost distrust by the misuse of the proposal for a treaty which had been more or less elicited from her at the end of July, and done out of the last meagre portion of her reward for mediation, the securing of her eastern border against the revival of the seventy-million-bloc. As if in order to make it still more obvious how she had been cheated, in the very days when the defensive and offensive alliances between the German states were being concluded there was inserted in the final treaty of Prague with Austria, as a concession to the renewed pressure of France, a clause stipulating that a Southern Confederacy should be recognized, which ' will enjoy international independence '. In other respects the treaty of Prague made no innovations on that of Nikolsburg, except for the definite assertion ' that the inhabitants of the northern districts of Schleswig, if they by free vote express the wish to be united with Denmark, shall be allowed to do so '.

With the treaty of Prague Bismarck had dealt a death blow at the German Confederation, which he himself fifteen years before had described as the bearer of ' the highest diplomatic German authority since the times of the Hohenstaufen '. With it there fell in ruins a Germany whose life had lasted more than fifty years. No one guessed that the Germany that was to replace it would not have a much longer life. In ruins there fell also the last remains of a liberal will and a liberal disposition which had still found a refuge in the fabric of that Confederation. This ruin, in which Bismarck had a decisive part to play, was accompanied by a suicidal act of liberalism itself, the self-dissolution or rather self-laceration of its thought. The most impressive evidence of this suicidal act is the writing of Hermann Baumgarten, *German Liberalism, a Self-Criticism* published in 1866, after Sadowa. Baumgarten begins with a criticism of the classical German thinkers and poets who created the intellectual and moral outlook of liberalism.

The literature of the classical period [he says] has ascribed an exaggerated significance to intellectual cultivation, to knowing and feeling, and has neglected the side of our nature concerned with action. Poets and thinkers of that glorious circle had a thoroughly distorted view of the material basis of all human development.

It is not the emphasis on human dignity and freedom, but the refusal to give its rightful place to human efficiency and will to power, which is thus declared to be the hallmark of the birth of liberalism. The Wars of Liberation and the preparations for them reveal this weakness : ' We urgently needed a chastisement to teach our people by blows of the hard fist that the revival of our state is not an affair of the songs of poets but of the saving deeds of statesmen and generals and the blows of peasants used to devotion.'

Then there follows quite logically from a liberal mouth the anti-liberal cry for the status of a Great Power : ' For men to work in the state they must above all have a state ; all those small states to which liberalism saw itself limited by the resignation of Prussia [from the position as constitutional state] were no states.' The attempt of 1848 failed owing to uncertainty about ' the real power of the decisive factors '. But now Prussia arises ' through a bold offensive. This offensive constituted in all relations the law of her life.' Her neighbours who are ' intriguing ' against her, are to be made to ' tremble before her might '. In the constitutional conflict ' the acceptance of the military budget was inevitable '. Since the liberals failed to recognize this, ' the liberal concept has shown itself incapable of ruling Prussia '. That is why we have lived through the time in which ' Herr von Bismarck showed to the House of Deputies the most extreme contempt that has ever been encountered in parliamentary battles. Would he have dared this without knowing by experience that words were the most which he had to expect ? ' The issue of the conflict about Schleswig and Holstein, this ' considerable reverse ' for liberalism, is described as a ' victory of the German nation, rich with consequences '. The words ' right must remain right ' are a ' banal phrase ' ; what is at stake is ' the right of Germany when at last a power arose in her which knew how to act and to win victories. A man of singular power showed it the right way ; opponents waited with trembling knees '. That ' my liberal fellow party members ' had not declared themselves sooner for Bismarck's policy ' is already a death sentence on German liberalism '. The liberal slogan : ' Through freedom to unity ', was according to Baumgarten ' an obvious chimera ', a ' claim of undisciplined individualism ', for ' Germany needs the important elements which Prussia has to contribute of state power, stern discipline, military bearing, an aristocratic foundation '. When these forces had ' within a week smashed to pieces boastful Austria ', the rest of the world recognized that Prussia ' in a nonce had advanced to one of the highest positions in the circle of the Powers ', but in Germany herself ' the realization of the extraordinary magnitude of the good fortune she had experienced had to fight its way slowly to consciousness '. Only if liberalism becomes aware of this, will ' the next decade bring us the German state which is just as necessary for our learning, art, and morals as for our political development and national position of power '. ' Liberalism must become capable of ruling ' ; it must ' become a force capable of carrying out its principles ' (with or against Bismarck ?). These ideas the liberal Baumgarten declares to be the expression not of ' treachery ', but of ' devotion ' to the liberal aim.

If before the war Bismarck had described it as his ' greatest triumph ' to have wrested from the King the declaration of war, he was entitled to count as no less a triumph after its victorious conclusion his success in persuading liberalism to be untrue to itself and fall under the dominion of its most dangerous and merciless opponent.

CHAPTER XX

The Foundation of the North German Confederacy

When at the beginning of August 1866 Bismarck returned to Berlin from the Austrian theatre of war his unpopularity had changed to its opposite. To the man who had earned new laurels of victory for Prussia, increased her territory to an extraordinary degree and raised her to a high rank in power was now given the full favour of the people with the same zest as they had formerly shown against him. His government, which ' had won for the country an independent and respected position in its external relations ', might now well expect to find the people ' willing to meet it with loyalty and self-sacrifice '. The benefit which resulted from this state of public opinion, this popularity which Bismarck twenty years before held ' worthless in the absence of the contentment of your Majesty ', now appeared when he looked to the tasks ahead as really useful or rather indispensable. After the conclusion of the final peace treaties two such tasks were prominent, the establishment of internal peace within Prussia and the establishment of a new state organization in place of the old German Confederation.

Bismarck, who had once spoken of the ' people ' as the ' ally ' of the Prussian dynasty, had in the meantime through his political activity made the constitutional representative of this ally, the Prussian parliament, into the embittered enemy of the very dynasty to help which he had thought fit to call it up. To put an end to this internal Prussian conflict was the most urgent need at home. Now, the attitude towards each other of the two opponents in this conflict had changed essentially since they had stood face to face for the last time at the beginning of the year. The strength of the government in relation to parliament had been enormously increased by military victory. The earlier will to battle of parliament had given place to an inclination to yield and to come to an understanding. The government had now to choose between ending the conflict by unilateral exercise of their power or by meeting the will of the Chamber to an understanding. The first possibility, which Bismarck described as a ' return to absolutism ' or ' a restoration in the sense of caste government ', was one that had been suggested to him in the earlier phases of the constitutional conflict. He had, however, always declined it, not on grounds of principle, but because he at that time did not regard the power of the dynasty as great enough for it to be able to stand an intensification of the internal crisis in addition to the burdens arising from foreign politics. Now, however, such reactionary efforts had a hope of success 'in view of the mood of enthusiasm prevailing in the country'. This hope was 'in the background of the efforts of the extreme Right' who had sent representatives to the theatre of war in order to win the approval of the King. On earlier occasions—as in connexion with the strengthened friendship between Russia and Prussia during the Polish revolt, and at the time of the Congress of Princes at Frankfurt—which suggested a closer collaboration of these monarchs, William I had, according to Bismarck, rejected without hesitation to effect such a violent change. Now, however, so Bismarck reports, 'the King could not so quickly make up his mind concerning the question whether he should break the resistance of parliament by his own force'. The already observed change of his view concerning his right to territorial conquest was accompanied by an analogous change in his views as to the right of the Crown over and against the constitution. The sentence earlier asserted by him 'where constitutions exist we must keep them', now lost gradually its best support, namely the influence exercised on the King by his liberal environment. 'The inner conflict', as Bismarck reports with self-satisfaction, 'lost a good deal of its might to influence the King's decisions, once he had found ministers who were ready openly to support his policy. The alarms raised by the Queen and the ministers of the "New Era" had lost their power.'

Bismarck himself, who three years before had earnestly considered enforcing a constitution which extended the franchise, was now in no wise disposed to reject outright the idea of decreeing a reactionary constitution. He did not say this in so many words, but it is clear from the way in which he speaks of points of view which could be adduced in its favour. The oft-proved interpreter and misinterpreter of legal formulae considered that 'through the extension of the kingdom' we have 'now a basis for the suspension and revision of the Prussian constitution. This constitution was not devised for the enlarged Prussia, still less for her inclusion in the future constitution' of the North German Confederacy. 'We were thus given', Bismarck continues, 'an opportunity, with a certain varnish of legality, to unhinge the constitution and the attempts at parliamentary rule of the Opposition majority.' But the grounds against such an enforced constitution showed themselves much stronger than the grounds in its favour. In the first place Bismarck could not now put aside the last remains of constitutionalism without contradicting himself in the grossest fashion, since even in July he had declared himself in favour of a reform of the Confederation with a parliament based on universal franchise as *conditio sine quâ non*. Then there were considerations of foreign politics, the 'need to let foreign nations see no trace of present or future impediments arising from our internal condition, but only the unified national will'.

But clearly still more important for Bismarck was the viewpoint of internal German politics, at present considered with particular care by him. He thought that 'this suspension of the constitution and humiliation of the Opposition in parliament would give everyone in Germany and Austria who was dissatisfied with the successes of 1866 a useful weapon against Prussia for future conflicts', and that 'Austria and south Germany would for the time being have got their revenge by taking over the leadership in the field of liberalism and nationalism which had been abandoned by Prussia. The national party in Prussia herself would have sympathized with the opponents of the government.' The conclusion, however, which Bismarck drew from these considerations runs thus : ' In that case we should have conducted a Prussian war of conquest. But the sinews of the national policy of Prussia would have been severed, and a most powerful argument for justifying the German " fratricidal war " would have lost its force.' The idea to which Bismarck is evidently alluding here is his watchword of 'two coinciding ends : the "leadership of Prussia " and the "unification of Germany " '. How this apparent coincidence could be affected by the substitution of open absolutism for sham-liberalism is hard to see. It is, however, correct to say that the introduction of open absolutism would have made the liberals, whom Bismarck here practically identified with the nationalists, into open enemies of Prussia, who could only have been brought to obey the Prussian government by open violence. Now, open violence on the part of an absolutist Prussia must in practice have replaced the ' national unity of Germany ' by the open discord between oppressor and oppressed within it. It is true, indeed, that this unity might be loosened by the concealed force of sham-liberalism, i.e., by instilling fear without actual violence, but it was not necessary that it should turn into open discord. Consequently, so long as the ' leadership of Prussia ' was not enforced by open violence, though not coinciding with the ' unity of Germany ', at any rate the discord between the oppressor, Prussia, and the other, oppressed, Germans did not become obvious. This was, in fact, what Bismarck wanted. The consequence of open absolutism of Prussia would not be that 'a Prussian war of conquest' pushed aside the 'national policy of Prussia', but that what appeared as national policy turned out to be a war of conquest. This was the feature about open Prussian absolutism which really alarmed Bismarck and which he wanted to conceal from others, perhaps even from himself, by the alleged ' coincidence of the two ends '. From his own words we may gather that this was the reason why he did not finish up the constitutional conflict by a unilateral use of the power of the government, but wished to see it ended by appealing to the will of the Chamber for an understanding.

In order to come to such an understanding only a small step was needed on the side of the dynasty to span the gulf between it and parliament, and the embittered foe of the government returned in due form to the rôle which the elections of the 3rd of July had in practice already prescribed, that of an ' ally easy to handle '. This step was taken when the government made a formal request for indemnity for the violation of the parliamentary rights over the budget. Bismarck had already in June declared himself ready for this step when speaking with the leaders of the Opposition. He continued willing, for this step fell for him within the class of ' friendliness which costs nothing '. ' *In verbis simus faciles,*' he declared expressly not without a touch of frivolity. The question was taken much more seriously by a part of the Cabinet, by the conservative party, and, above all, by the King. In these quarters the proposal to ask for an act of indemnity was rejected because it was regarded as an ' admission that wrong had been done '. Bismarck retorted with the very clever pettifogging excuse that ' the grant of the indemnity [which he expected for certain] means nothing more than the recognition of the fact that the government and its royal master have acted rightly *rebus sic stantibus* '. For him the whole business was not much more than a game with the House of Deputies, to whom he had just ' shown the most extreme contempt '. About this time he said to a confidant : ' Courage on the battlefield is with us a common possession,' but one will not seldom find ' that quite respectable people are lacking in civil courage '. In regard to the Opposition in the Chamber he expressed himself kindly, saying that among them ' only those at most who later formed the progressive party are malicious, the others are just obstinate '. In the numerous discussions with the King about the indemnity question the Crown Prince also often took part in support of Bismarck as in Nikolsburg, not now by words, but in that he ' with his easy changes of countenance at least strengthened me over against his father by showing me his complete understanding '.

On the 15th of August 1866 a new Parliament was opened. For the first time during Bismarck's premiership the King read his speech from the throne in person. One of the first sentences of the speech ran : ' In harmonious co-operation the government and the representatives of the people will allow the crops to mature which must grow up from the bloody seeds (of war).' Was this a new note on Bismarck's lyre ? Was this an announcement that after their exploits in war the people were to cease to be the pliable, easily handled ally and to find acceptance as partner by the dynasty with equal rights ? Bismarck asserted this in connexion with his description of the opening of parliament : ' Absolutism on the part of the Crown is just as little defensible as absolutism on the part of parliamentary majorities. The demand for understanding between the two is a fair one.' Yet it is remarkable that the above sentence from the speech from the throne sounds almost verbally the same as that which in January 1863 had introduced the acute phase of the constitutional conflict, when mention was made of the ' earnest efforts ' of the government ' to attain harmonious co-operation with the two Houses of Parliament '. It may perhaps be objected that on the former occasion the words were followed by open conflict, while on the latter they were connected with the government's outstretched hand of peace.

The expenses of state which had been incurred in the last years [so the King says now] are lacking in legal basis. I cherish the confidence that my government will be willingly given the indemnity for the administration which is being conducted without a budget for which parliament is to be asked, and that thereby the conflict which has hitherto prevailed will be put to an end for all time.

So it might be said that Bismarck's action now went further than his words had done in that he laid the basis of an understanding on equal terms with the representatives of the people. Unfortunately, Bismarck himself with complete openness and without any ambiguity makes this conclusion impossible. He says : ' Before our victory I should never have spoken of indemnity. Now, after the victory, the King was in a position generously to grant it.' But ' generous granting ' is something different from coming to an ' understanding on equal terms '; it is, on the contrary, the unilateral act of the superior towards a compliant ally who has to let himself be treated in this way by the other. Based on the same attitude towards parliament as shown by the memoir of March 1858, which proposed the granting of ' more elbow-room ' to the latter, Bismarck's new step expresses most emphatically the self-assertion and arrogance of the victor in a decisive political campaign.

The new Chamber, well disposed as it was to the government, had obviously at first not the impression that the latter was inclined to make important changes in their relative power. For, in the address intended to answer the speech from the throne a fortnight later, though the words of the King about ' co-operation between government and parliament ' are taken up sympathetically, yet a demand is made for the ' development of the constitutional rights of the people '. In relation to the proposed indemnity confidence is expressed ' that in future through the due fixing of the budget before the beginning of the financial year any further conflict will be avoided '. The King is also instructed concerning the

significance of ' Prussian history ', which teaches that ' to the will
to power òf her Princes is joined that of the people to sacrifice and
devotion '. Bismarck, however, who in his *Reflections and Reminiscences* in this very same context spoke of the 'just division of
legislative power ' between ' three factors, the King and two Houses ',
was certainly as little prepared as three years before to remain
impartial in the playing out of one factor against the other. The
King indeed ' graciously accepted ' the address of the House of
Deputies, but the contrast between it and the simultaneous address
of the Upper House can hardly have escaped his notice, much less
displeased him or pleased the Lower House. For in this address
nothing is said about the ' people ' as such and its ' constitutional
rights ', but only about the ' Prussian people in arms ', who have
stood ' the test to which their Lord and King has called them '. In
particular the statement is made that ' the knowledge of your Majesty
as to what the Prussian fatherland needs is to be in no wise fore-
stalled by parliament '. Now, the ' civil courage ' of the ' respectable people ' of the House of Deputies did not in this hour of
the highest power of the Prussian dynasty go beyond cautious and
gentle advice. Bismarck again applied the mixture of menace and
enticement which he had so often used. ' We wish for peace ', he
roared, 'not because we are incapable of fighting in this internal
battle. Many reproaches have been brought against the Cabinet,
but they do not include that of timidity. We seek peace because
the fatherland needs it.' Then followed the soothing side : ' Our
task is not yet fulfilled, it requires the unity of the whole country.
If we have often heard it said that what the sword has won the
pen had destroyed, I have full confidence that we shall not hear
that what sword and pen have won has been destroyed by this
platform.' The Chamber could not withstand this combination of
methods. It passed the act of indemnity by a majority of three
to one and also granted a credit for the financial year 1866 in lieu
of the budget for this year, which the government alleged it could
not now draw up. A few weeks later a large gift was pressed on
Bismarck by parliament with which he later bought the estate of
Varzin. On the 18th of December the budget laid before parliament for 1867 was adopted almost unanimously without amendment after a merely formal discussion of the specific headings.
Thus the Prussian constitutional conflict after lasting four years
reached its end, now that the will of the Chamber to reconciliation
had become more or less a will to subjection. The progressive
Virchow was right in uttering these words in accompaniment to the
act : ' Let us beware of making an idol of success.'

But while one of the ' malicious people ' in this fashion made
known unambiguously his attitude of aloofness towards Bismarck,

the 'merely obstinate' were all the more ready to give themselves to him body and soul. In these days a new party was formed out of the ranks of the moderate liberals, called the national liberal party. They declared: 'The most sacred duty of those who represent the people in parliament is to manifest in the eyes of the whole world the assistance on which every government in Prussia may reckon as long as it is prepared to further German unity and increase the power of Germany as a whole.' Thus we see that this party advocated the kind of liberalism championed by Baumgarten: 'Liberalism must be capable of rule.' This capacity for rule in national liberalism meant in fact less the capacity to rule than the willingness to be ruled in the very sense in which Bismarck had always represented the rôle of the people when he looked upon them as compliant allies of the Crown, easy to be handled. But alliance with the national liberals did not at first mean for Bismarck abandoning his traditional alliance with the reactionaries, but its strengthening through fresh reinforcements; these had to labour under the disadvantage of the later arrival for whom there were left over not many important posts in the Cabinet or the administration. This was how Bismarck viewed his relationship to them:

> I held the distinction of party doctrines to be of subordinate importance in comparison with the necessity for political protection from external dangers by means of the closest possible unity of the nation. In this consideration my first question was not whether a man was liberal or conservative but concerned the free self-determination of the nation and its Princes.

National liberalism could only become the political body-guard of Bismarck by carrying out in practice the 'treachery' to liberalism of which Baumgarten had spoken. Bismarck, however, was not acting without skill when he included among his followers a body-guard of political renegades, doubly zealous against the adherents of their former faith. National liberalism was the political heir and successor of the Nationalverein founded seven years before. But it was at the same time the destroyer of their ideals. It was no longer a question of the 'sacrifices which the state governments had to make' being devoted to an 'imaginary whole'. These sacrifices were now demanded by the 'real' power of Prussia and not denied her. The old liberal idea of the *Kulturstaat* was changed into the national liberal state which, as Baumgarten interpreted it, being necessary for 'our learning, art, and morals', was so by realizing 'our political development and national position of power'. There were indeed among the national liberals still representatives of the cultural side of social life. However, the newly arising class of leaders of industry gained for themselves a larger and larger share of control in the party. The liberalism of political economy determined ever more clearly the direction in which the developing industrial state should proceed. *Realpolitik* in economics became within liberalism ever more decidedly the ally which offered itself to Bismarck's *Realpolitik* in state affairs, and was accepted and fostered by him. The political and spiritual ideals of original liberalism constituted the sacrifice which was offered up to this alliance. Thus one year of political activity of national liberalism stirred up the almost forgotten liberalism of the Crown Prince so strongly that he wrote reproachfully to Bismarck : ' According to everything that I read and hear it becomes ever clearer to me that we are losing the confidence of the " original liberals " and that this is specially so in the incorporated territories, and that south Germany is less capable than ever of feeling sympathy with us.'

A little time before the conclusion of the discussions on the budget, a draft of a law concerning the union of Hanover, Kur-Hesse, Nassau, and Frankfurt with Prussia was laid before parliament. A message from the King declared that these states had rejected the Prussian offer of neutrality with guarantees, had allied themselves with Austria, and thereby ' made themselves subject to the arbitrament of war '. This arbitrament had ' in accordance with the divine will ' gone against them. If their independence were retained they would constitute ' a danger for Prussia, the character of which had already been experienced '—a particularly remarkable statement in view of the total failure of their intervention in the war. We have ' no desire to acquire new territories ', so continued this signal example of devotion to veracity in politics, ' but it is our duty to protect our hereditary territories from the recurrence of danger '. Therefore it had been decided ' to unite these territories for ever with our monarchy '. Also the annexation ' should provide the national reconstruction of Germany with a broader and firmer basis '. What this ' national basis ' was to be like was clear from the fact that the man who, when concerned with the political fate of Schleswig and Holstein, had appealed against Austria to a decision by universal suffrage in the summer of 1863, now declined the popular vote. He did so expressly on the ground that ' we know that only a part of the population of those states shares with us the conviction of this necessity '. When Bismarck was challenged on the matter in a Committee of the House, and it was said that thus the annexation depended solely on the so-called ' right of conquest ' and that without a plebiscite this was ' open violence ', he replied : ' In this case the right of conquest rests on the right of the German nation to exist, to breathe, to unite itself.' In saying this he made the boldest of efforts to read into the open violence of a war of conquest ' the national policy ' of men ' uniting themselves '. He then continues : ' As long as wars are waged it is unreasonable to deny the right of conquest ; the lauded plebiscites are matters rather of appearance than of reality '. With these words Bismarck made an interesting, but for him quite irrelevant, distinction, irrelevant because according to the very words of the King's message it was the reality and not the appearance of a plebiscite, which turned him against it, for it was the real ' conviction of the people ' of which he was afraid.

The law authorizing the annexations was then accepted by parliament almost unanimously. Excited disputes were, however, caused by the treatment of the separate law concerning the incorporation of Schleswig-Holstein and the discussion of the situation of the Danes living in the north of Schleswig. Once more Bismarck proved his capacity to interpret and misinterpret the text of laws in accordance with his wishes. He had no intention of carrying out the free plebiscite promised by the treaty of Prague to enable those Danes to determine by their free vote to which state they should belong. He refused this plebiscite on the ground that only the partners in the treaty, Prussia and Austria, could derive rights from it. In the course of the debate Bismarck declared : ' I deem a rule ', then, correcting himself, ' a living together of Germans in the same community with opposed nationalities as not useful, but sometimes necessary.' Evidently in this connexion he did not think of transfer of populations as he did later.

In September 1866 Bismarck, maybe in consequence of the severe intellectual and emotional strain of the preceding months, had another, particularly severe, attack of that ' rheumatic-digestive-nervous disease ', which had first tormented him in the autumn of 1859. As a convalescent he spent two months in a very charming estate of a member of the nobility on the island of Rügen. This time his wife and also his daughter Marie were allowed to be with him. The former showed herself a particularly self-sacrificing and conscientious nurse. She was concerned not only with the re-establishment of Bismarck's physical health, but also with the care of his mental equanimity. ' So far ', he writes during these weeks, ' I have only been allowed to read letters the contents of which were agreeable. My wife acts as censor.' When after some time he wrote his first letter, he did this ' in the absence of my wife who watches me with Argus eyes '. While he was still in Rügen, however, he began to occupy himself with his next great task, the construction of the North German Confederacy which the negotiations for peace had brought in view. The first ideas on the subject he dictated to his wife as amanuensis.

The basis of this Confederacy was constituted by the treaties of alliance which were concluded by Prussia with most of the north

German states, on the 18th of August 1866 and with a few laggards in the following days. Even in the case of these treaties the union was not thoroughly voluntary and was not effected without concealed or even open violence. The Princess-Regent of one of the smallest of the future members of the Confederacy, the principality of Reuss, was forced to sign it by the Prussians who occupied her capital with two companies of infantry. In a slightly larger one, the duchy of Meiningen, military intervention was necessary to compel the ruler to abdicate and leave it to his successor to sign the treaty. All these treaties refer to the draft of a constitution drawn up by Bismarck and made known to the former Federal Diet at the middle of June, before Sadowa. This was the constitutional basis for the Confederacy which was now to be produced with ' the co-operation of a parliament to be summoned for all the states together '. Up to then there was to be between the states concerned a ' defensive and offensive alliance in order to preserve their independence and integrity ' and all the troops were at once to pass ' under Prussian command '.

On his return from Rügen to Berlin Bismarck at once set to work on the projected constitution. After discussion with the expert advisers of the different ministries he pretends to have dictated the whole draft in a single afternoon to one of his councillors. He referred it to the Prussian Crown Council on one of the following days and then sent it to the representatives of the remaining states of the would-be Confederacy for their consideration. There was no question of invoking the people at this stage of the proceedings. The people had had to see the treaties of alliance concluded over their heads and the same applied to the first and decisive steps in settling the constitution. The draft constitution was a complete expression of Bismarck's personal relation to the state and to state action. This relation was now not one to a state which Bismarck had found fashioned by tradition, as was the Prussian state based on personal ties of loyalty and the *esprit de corps* of the ruling caste. The relation was one to a state which sprang from Bismarck's own head and in which therefore only one personal tie was of decisive importance, namely that to himself as the self-assured and self-righteous creator of the state. Accordingly this draft was throughout directed with a view to utility and to making it a suitable instrument for a strong directing will accompanied by high intelligence and comprehensive experience. All considerations of principle were banished ; during the negotiations concerning it Bismarck turns again and again to combat what he calls ' stubborn fighters on behalf of principles '. Everything which political theory in struggles lasting for centuries had developed in the way of fundamental concepts of the state, such as indivisibility of sovereignty, threefold division of powers, rights of citizens, the antithesis of absolutism and popular sovereignty, was passed over and apparently put aside without heed.

Bismarck in private expressed himself quite clearly as to what his main object was in the conversion of the treaties with the north German states into an objectively binding constitution. 'The strength of treaties alone, without an adequate power derived from the dynastic background (*Hausmacht*) of the leading monarch, has never been sufficient to secure to the German nation freedom and unity in the Reich.' In public, however, he said during the negotiations on the subject: 'I do not regard it as our task to appeal to the power and superior might of Prussia in order to force a concession. The basis of this relation should not be force, but trust in the loyalty of Prussia to her agreements.' Yet in fact, power remained the watchword of Prussia in the new Confederacy as it had been in the looser, old Confederation. The force involved had only to be more closely concealed under the confidence in 'Prussia's loyalty'. The thesis maintained by Bismarck as a basis for the Confederacy was therefore that one 'should find the minimum concessions which the states existing separately in German territory had to make for the Whole, if this Whole is to be capable of life'. He declined the proposal of his advisers that the new state should be given a very centralized constitution with a Federal Cabinet and parliament with two Chambers, an Upper House consisting of the Princes of the Federated States, and a Lower House elected by their subjects, one of the liberal demands of 1848 which Bismarck suspected and disliked already for that reason. At the same time he threw overboard the main liberal demand, that for a 'constitutionally responsible Cabinet'. As if no such principle existed Bismarck asked: 'Who is to appoint this Cabinet?' This could only be done, he answered in a thoroughly unconvincing manner, 'by a single head with monarchical character', contending that in that case 'one would have no longer a federation but the subjection of the Princes to the King of Prussia'. This, however, was 'neither approved by our Confederates nor the object of our efforts'. So Bismarck advanced to the solution that the totality of the Federated states, united in the Federal Council, should constitute the sovereign of the new Confederacy. Every one, even the smallest, should have a share in this sovereignty, none, not even Prussia, though it far exceeded all others together in size, should be the sole sovereign Power in this new state. As sovereign the Federal Council had a share in every function of the state, legislative, executive, and judiciary.

At the time of these discussions Bismarck wrote to his trusted friend Roon: 'The form in which the King exercises power in

Germany has never had particular importance for me. To secure that in fact he exercises this power, I have devoted all the strength that God has given me.' How is this requirement, so intimately bound up with Bismarck's political purposes, to be reconciled with the new idea of the ' minimum concessions ' to be made by the single states and the consequent view of these states as bearers of sovereignty in the Confederacy ? In a speech in parliament by Bismarck in the middle of August 1866 we find a distinction hitherto unknown in German political theory and practice between different kinds of sovereignty in the state, namely that of the military and that of the civil ruler. He explains there that he had earlier entertained ' a lively inclination in favour of this system ', i.e., the distinction between military and civil sovereignty, but had now lost that inclination and, among other objections, regarded the distinction ' as a lasting source of misunderstandings '.

However, it is a remarkable fact that Bismarck about the very same time as he expressed this view was just bringing such a system into existence. In the middle of August there came into being the first of the defensive and offensive alliances with the north and the south German states ; civil sovereignty was left to them, military sovereignty—though not completely except in case of war—was transferred to the King of Prussia. We may also recall that two years before Bismarck had tried to compel Augustenburg to adopt such a system for Schleswig and Holstein. One only need look quite cursorily at Bismarck's political plans and ideas throughout his whole political activity to see by whom he thinks, in the event of a separation between military and civil sovereignty, supreme power in Germany would actually be exercised. Bismarck could also count on full understanding from his King just on this question. Already in 1860 William I had in the presence of the great German historian Leopold von Ranke expressed the intention ' to spare the German Princes in their sovereignty, but to bring about unity in military matters '. He had, as the historian appreciatively recognizes, ' a perfect idea of how the military power includes in itself the sovereignty '. It was just this kind of separation between military and civil sovereignty which Bismarck had in view for the new constitution of the Confederacy. The sovereignty of the Federal Council was the authority of the merely civil sovereign. In military and naval matters this body could only form a ' permanent committee '' without any constitutional power except that of making reports to the Federal Council. Prussia, on the other hand, who as regards civil sovereignty was only distinguished from the others by being president of the Federal Council, had military sovereignty thrown into her lap,—not indeed in the main fabric of the constitution but in a subsidiary article, so to speak by the way. A few

superficial concessions made to Saxony were of no practical importance. This mode of investing Prussia with military sovereignty
derives directly from Bismarck's character as is shown by a remark
of his to Roon : ' *In verbis simus faciles*, in fact it does not matter
whether our navy is called Prussian, German, or north German.
It is the navy of our King.' Bismarck also shows a deep contempt
for the states other than Prussia when he entrusts them with civil
sovereignty only, for, according to him, ' every state to whom her
honour and her independence are dear must be conscious that her
peace and her independence rest on her own sword '.

But this distinction was not enough. Bismarck made still
another one within the sovereignty of the Confederacy, that between
internal and external sovereignty. He had always, but particularly
in the ' booklet ' of March 1858, decisively championed the priority
of foreign over against internal politics. He had demanded that
internal politics should be subordinated to the aim of giving Prussia
' once more the leading position ' in Europe and that therefore
' the united power of Prussia was not to be broken through internal
friction '. Despite occasional concessions to make his internal
policy seem liberal, he held the conviction that the natural point of
gravity of politics lay in foreign policy and that internal politics
could not be separated from this. Now again he asserts : ' I said to
myself that the first main object is independence and security abroad
and that we might postpone all internal questions till our national
aims abroad are secured.' But he held the further conviction that
it was foreign policy to which the attention of the people was directed
and that success there would make the people into a unity by making
it ready to ' meet the government with loyalty and self-sacrifice '.
Or, as he now expressed himself : ' Independence, freedom for the
state, national honour concern a people like ours more than anything else does.' In comparison with this the significance attached
to internal politics ranked second, though it could not be altogether
disregarded as a means of influencing the people in view of the many
amenities it gave. It was the sovereign in external affairs who ' in
fact exercised power in Germany ', even if he had only a very
modest share in the sovereignty in internal affairs. But it was not
necessary to express this explicitly. One might say that it was the
task of the King of Prussia as president of the Federal Council
' to represent the Confederacy among nations, declare war and
conclude peace in the name of the same, enter into alliances and
other conventions with foreign countries, accredit ambassadors and
receive them ', and yet one could still go on describing the Federal
Council as bearer of sovereignty. Yes, the constitution could even
allow the single states the right of international representation and
make the agreement of the Federal Diet necessary for the declaration

of war, ' except in case of an attack upon the territory of the Confederacy '. For that every war which Bismarck waged was a war of self-defence was certain from the beginning. This was the fact to which Bismarck pointed sneeringly, when, dealing with the question of military service, he said in parliament: ' That we do not proceed rashly in these matters, experience has proved.'

So it was the totality of the Federated states represented by the Federal Council which remained the sovereign of the North German Confederacy, apart from the trifling circumstance that the sovereignty in military matters and foreign affairs belonged to the King of Prussia. Bismarck tried, however, by all means to emphasize how small were the ' minimum concessions ' to be made by the single states. It is true, indeed, that in relation to all the possible tasks of the state the powers of the Federal Council were by no means too extensive, since it had to share its powers in internal affairs with those reserved for the single states as such. In return for that the powers were enumerated at full length. We found among them some of those which Bismarck as ambassador once in the ill-considered frankness of his Frankfurt days had described as ' trifles '. On the other hand, the position of Prussia within the Federal Council was—though not by law, but as a matter of fact—very strong. Did not she in size, population, and resources surpass many times over all the others combined ? Had not Prussia waged a successful war in which she had shown an overwhelming superiority over her opponents ? Was not she the initiator of the new political creation, the content and aim of which she was therefore bound to determine ? Consequently she was also able within the Federal Council ' to exercise the power in practice ' and in doing this content herself with a ' minimum of concessions ' by the others. So it was provoking rather than reassuring when Prussia was satisfied in the Federal Council with only 17 out of 43 votes, not much more than a third of the whole.

This was the way in which Bismarck fashioned the relation between the members of the new Confederacy and he was able to carry his proposals through after agreeing to certain changes. There was, however, within the Confederacy which Bismarck was about to create, a further factor besides the princely members, namely the people. Bismarck had not only theoretically described the German people as the natural ' ally ' of Prussia, but had also in practice repeatedly stood for the demand that a parliament resting on universal suffrage should take part in future German politics. The treaties with the north German states had indeed cursorily referred to the people by alleging ' the co-operation of a parliament ' in producing the new constitution. Bismarck actually anticipated in his draft a parliament elected by universal suffrage, the

'Reichstag', not only in the creation of the constitution but also for its maintenance. He thus introduced in his Confederacy the socio-economic concept of the people, with its antithesis between the haves and the have-nots. Therefore, when he spoke in the Prussian parliament on the franchise for the election of the constituent Reichstag, the extreme liberals, the representatives of the bourgeoisie, objected to it that Bismarck wanted to adopt the system of Napoléon III and let the voters be driven like sheep to the poll by prefects and clergy. Indeed, when he now decided in favour of an equal universal franchise, he was no longer motived by the idea of the cohesion between the various peoples and their dynasties, based on the ethnological concept of the nation. It no longer seemed to him that 'the conservative attitude of the masses concerned with the preservation of order with their monarchical tradition' was a sufficient guarantee of 'monarchical elections'. So Bismarck sought for another 'counter-poise' against the equality of franchise and found it in the abolition of the secret ballot which excluded 'the influence of the educated'. This abolition was indeed to be disguised by a poetic vesture, it being stated that 'secrecy contradicted the best qualities of German blood'. In reality, however, the 'counter-poise' is a straightforward'consequence of his socio-economic concept of the people. For the 'educated' are 'the class whose prudence has as its material basis the preservation of property'. Certainly, says Bismarck, 'the striving to earn an income is not less justified, but for the security and development of the state it is more expedient that those who possess property should preponderate'. This represents an essential change of view since the time when Bismarck thought that he could and ought to mobilize politically the have-nots against the purse-proud progressives. However, by now many of this purse-proud bourgeoisie had become as national liberals Bismarck's special political bodyguard.

But these considerations did not issue in practical results. For in the course of the discussions in the constituent Reichstag, public voting was replaced by secret. Thereby the universal franchise had lost its original value as 'a principle justified not only theoretically but also in practice', since now 'the influences and dependencies which the practical life of man brings with it, the god-given realities', as Bismarck viewed them, were ignored. Now, however, universal suffrage received a meaning for Bismarck far more important than before, namely that of a weapon in war.

In view of the necessity [he said] under which we are in war to grasp in the last extreme even at revolutionary means in face of a superior foreign Power, I had no hesitation in throwing into the frying-pan even what was at that time the strongest of the tricks of freedom-lovers, universal suffrage, in order to frighten away monarchical foreign lands from the attempt to stick their fingers into our national omelette.

Thus by universal suffrage ' a national popular movement must be cultivated and preserved ', so that in the event of a coalition attacking the North German Confederacy ' it could be launched into action as a last resort '.

It was now for Bismarck to draw the conclusions from this view of the right of the people to share in government by determining the functions of their representatives within the fabric of the state in peace time. A few years before he had said to parliament : ' The Prussian monarchy has not yet fulfilled its mission, it is not yet ripe to become an ornamental adornment of your constitutional fabric ' ; now his endeavours were concerned with making the Reichstag in practice just such an ' ornamental adornment '. His action in refusing to allow ministerial responsibility to parliament in the new Confederacy any more than in Prussia was nothing else than a first step to this end. ' The possibility of lifting into the saddle cabinet ministers who possess the required qualifications must be allowed in the life of a constitution ' (i.e., the King must have the power to do this), but the constitution must also make it possible ' to keep in power those who satisfy these requirements despite occasional majority votes against them '. The Reichstag was a purely legislative organ ; not only all control of the executive but also all influence on the latter was denied it. Indeed, the executive, as carrying out the will of the sovereign, had a decisive preponderance over the Reichstag, which limited this will. Bismarck now insisted that, while even ' the most ideal monarch needs the criticism ' which is exercised ' through parliaments in the modern sense ', this criticism must not ' pass into dominion ' and that the Reichstag must in turn subject itself ' with political tact and discretion ' to the decision of the person criticized. It was in accordance with the preponderance of the executive that the initiative of the Reichstag in legislation was without significance in practice over against that of the Federal Council, which was also endowed with executive powers. The activity of Bismarck in the formation of coalitions, first between national liberals and conservatives, and then between other parties in the Reichstag, hindered the emergence of a political will of its own in the latter body. The facts that the members of the Reichstag were preponderantly Prussian and that no salary was paid them for political activities—the raising of funds for payment being actually forbidden—also tended in the same direction. The practical influence of the Reichstag was so limited that unprejudiced foreign observers described it as a ' debating society '.

This limitation was the subject of a fierce controversy in the constituent Reichstag, which met on 24th of February 1867. Before its convocation Bismarck had induced the governments of the other states in the Confederacy to take a step which makes clear in a particularly drastic way his attitude to the people and to popular representation. He suggested to them that in case the Reichstag rejected or mutilated the proposed constitution they should come to a secret agreement to the effect that the constitution should be imposed by force without ' the co-operation of the parliament summoned for all the states together '. He had apparently forgotten that secrecy was ' in contradiction to the best qualities of the German blood '. There actually seemed to be a danger of such a move when the constituent Reichstag wished to extend its competence to a sphere from which Bismarck had not only excluded Federal competence altogether, but in regard to which he was quite especially sensitive to intervention, namely the military budget. In order to secure Prussian military sovereignty over against the budgetary rights of parliament without expressly denying the latter, Bismarck had in his draft constitution recourse to the following device : the Reichstag was once for all to make the definite annual grant of a lump sum for each soldier serving with the colours and a fixed percentage of the population was always to be retained with the colours. But nobody in the constituent Reichstag was in agreement with such a permanent arrangement, not even the national liberal party which had so unreservedly committed itself to Bismarck. The task of setting up a constitution seemed incapable of being brought to a conclusion in a manner envisaged by the laws. But before Bismarck actually took the step of imposing one by force he made a last attempt to come to an agreement. On the 11th of March 1867 he used these words in one of his most characteristic speeches :

What answer would you give to a man invalided home from Sadowa, if he asked what the fruits were of the mighty efforts of 1866 ? You would say to him ' Well, again nothing has come of German unity; this we shall achieve some day or other. But we have won the right of putting in question every year the existence of the Prussian army, a right of which we as good patriots should never make use. That is the reason why we fought against the Emperor of Austria under the walls of Pressburg.' Gentlemen, this situation is impossible.

Bismarck concluded this speech with the words which have become famous : ' Let us work quickly. Let us set Germany in the saddle. She will be able to ride all right.' Who else is this invalid of Sadowa whom Bismarck allows to speak for him, but the young Bismarck himself, who in his first address before the Prussian parliament twenty years before spoke in exactly the same way as champion of ' national honour ' against the champion of an ' intimate understanding between government and people '. If at that time he had seen his vocation in being a ' supporter of the throne ' over against the 'random mob of individuals called people', it is incomprehensible that he could expect that the very same attitude would now lead to the 'people' being set in the political saddle as rider. But nevertheless his audience in the Reichstag seemed to have this expectation. The liberals of 1847 had turned into the adherents of the Great Power of 1866 for whom military obedience was sufficient to set them in the political saddle. A compromise was concluded by which the unlimited military sovereignty of Prussia was *de facto* extended to budget matters. The Reichstag agreed to the payment of the lump sum suggested and to the proposal to fix the number of people subject to service in the way asked, these laws to hold—though not for ever—in any case up to 31st of December 1871. On 16th of April 1867 Bismarck's proposed constitution of the North German Confederacy was accepted by a majority of almost 4 to 1 and was ratified a few weeks later by a specially summoned meeting of the Prussian parliament.

Thus the 'constitution of the new Confederacy realized almost completely the wishes and aims of Bismarck, for it set up a structure giving nearly complete power to the Prussian King with his absolute military sovereignty, his almost absolute sovereignty in foreign affairs, and the not too stringent limitations to his political sovereignty in internal affairs. This was done in a fashion which justified Bismarck's long-cherished expectation that 'the men with the nature of soldiers who have warm Prussian blood in their bodies', through their devotion to the supreme war lord would indeed be willing to unite in a spirit of 'loyalty and self-sacrifice'. This would be especially so in circumstances in which this loyalty and self-sacrifice was demanded on the largest scale, namely in war. The sovereign power of the new Confederation thus was to find its most exacting test and its highest confirmation in war. It was so constituted that it could face any war. Was it to make use of this capacity? The state is not a mere tool set in motion by man, but a machine working on its own power. He who builds it up must know that he is necessarily at the same time both its master and its servant and that the tendencies which he puts into it will display themselves as autonomous powers in it. Let us now reconsider the main features of the new Confederacy : the military and external sovereignty of the Prussian King, in these domains inaccessible to any parliamentary criticism or control, the preponderance of the executive over the legislative, and the ever-ready unity of the 'people in arms' with the 'national popular movement to be launched into action as a last resort'—and we cannot avoid the conclusion that the new Confederacy is not only capable of facing any war, but is in itself a step in the direction of war, or, to be more exact, a very preparation for war. The aim of this preparation for war was bound to be the extension of the North German Confederacy into a union comprising the whole German nation. In this aim, as Bismarck says, two ends coincided : ' the Prussian leadership from the Prussian standpoint and the unification of Germany from the national standpoint '. Yet that leadership was now changing its meaning. The unification of the whole German nation was to bring about more or less that seventy-million-bloc on the eastern frontier of France which Napoléon had always opposed and which no doubt he would now too try to prevent from coming about even at the risk of war. Now, the issue of this war was nothing else than the decision between Prussia and France about the leadership not of a united Germany but of the whole of Europe. This was the coincidence of ends which Bismarck then had to envisage : leadership of Europe and unification of Germany. Would this coincidence stand the final test ?

After this view of the sovereign power of the new Confederacy we turn now to the cohesion within it, to be constituted between one citizen and another. As we know, Bismarck had always rejected the conception of national unity as a unity directly of man to man among the people. He had always and everywhere opposed and suppressed the idea on which liberalism was based, namely the idea of the *Kulturstaat* which saw this unity in a common spirit founded upon the equality of all human beings and growing out of the development of human liberty. Against it he had always held as the factor on which national unity should be based the idea of a firm link between everyone and the powerful head of the state, this link being con- stituted by loyalty and obedience towards the person and institution of the monarch. But meanwhile, he had admitted into his state the institution in which, according to the conviction of the original liberals, that immediate unity within the people came most strongly to the fore, namely the parliament founded on universal and equal suffrage. For the liberal movement had in the work of co-operation in building up the state on the basis of equality found the strongest stimulus for rendering the members of the nation conscious of themselves as immediately bound together and taking this union as the basis of their activity. Now, Bismarck had done everything to deprive the Reichstag of its significance for the unity of the nation. To the people as represented in the Reichstag he had opposed and preferred the people as represented in the army, a body none of whose regular members had the right to vote. He had not only allowed the parliament of the particular states to continue their existence beside the Reichstag, but had actually shown favour to them and had spoken not without pleasure of the ' new particularism, the parliamentary type, "here the Landtag and there the Reichstag " '. However, still more important than the opposition between the two kinds of parliaments was the opposition between the two aspects of the people which they represented. In the state parliaments there spoke the people of the state as a clan (*Stamm*) united by their relation to the state dynasty, the people in an ethnological sense. In the Reichstag, on the other hand, Bismarck sought to express in legal form the antithesis between haves and have-nots which was included in the socio-economic conception of the people. Thus he planted the seed of class strife in the Reichstag. The religious conflict, too, which was so deeply ingrained in the German people, found before long, owing to Bismarck's inveterate hate of the catholics, a battlefield in parliamentary life. So Bismarck allowed the German parliamentary system to become the centre of the clashes and struggles of the living forces which combated with each other among the people, and thus brought it about that the great task of self-government set to parliament failed to make the citizens conscious of their immediate unity. By reducing the Reichstag to a distortion of the original nature of parliament, he did everything conceivable which made for a splitting up of the people—outside its unity in military life—into groups representing different powers or interests, and for the exclusion of anything that could lead to a deepened unity founded in the people themselves. Parliamentary life became for him a mere means to enable him to rule more firmly the German people, ' this easily manageable ally of the dynasty ', according to the principle of *divide et impera*. The manner in which Bismarck managed the civil life of the people under the new constitution thus led in the very same direction which he had taken often and with such success, first in foreign policy and then also in the internal policy of Prussia, the playing against each other of different social forces in relation to which he could act as fulcrum in the balance. So the people stood between military and civil life, between the single state and the Confederacy, between executive and legislative powers, between Princes and parliament kept in disunion by racial, economic, and religious differences, with their longing for unity wholly and exclusively directed towards the military sovereign, ready for loyalty and self-sacrifice towards the omnipotent rule of the Prussian commander-in-chief and waiting for the moment when they could put these feelings to the most exacting test and give them the highest confirmation in war.

But what in time of peace or rather preparation of war within this complicated system with its division between military, external, and internal sovereignty and this manifold interplay of political forces was the position of the man who built all this up, the position of Bismarck himself? Bismarck was, afterwards as well as before, Prussian prime minister and foreign minister and was as such chief adviser of the person who was the sovereign of the Confederacy in military and foreign affairs. That Bismarck's manner of influence on military strategy was complicated had already been proved by the preceding campaigns, but his position in these matters was strengthened by the fact that he had a determining share in the decisions of peace and war. In regard to the other political tasks of the Confederacy Bismarck had created for himself a unique position, that of Chancellor of the Confederacy ; this position indeed turned out to be virtually that of the prime minister of the entire Confederacy. The post was adapted to the character of the man, for Bismarck being exceptionally self-confident and self-righteous desired a position in which he was conscious that he was the only person responsible for decisions and also appeared in this guise externally. ' Real responsibility in big politics ', thus he justified the post he had created, ' can only be held by a single directing minister, never by an anonymous Cabinet dependent on a majority vote.' He goes so far as to say that it may happen that ' the conflict between one's own feeling of honour and the complications of the relations between departments leads to a fatal nervous fever or to symptoms of mental derangement '.

As his chief assistant, as head of the office of the Chancellery, Bismarck chose a man whom he had formerly repeatedly and violently attacked as the prototype of the hated liberal bureaucracy, Rudolf Delbrück, thus giving to his official surroundings a pronouncedly bureaucratic character. The post of Chancellor of the Confederacy was also specially adapted to another distinctive feature of Bismarck's character ; he had indeed already as Prussian prime minister given a free run to the ' defect of his eye in being keener for weaknesses than for good qualities ', especially at the expense of his then colleagues in the Cabinet. So he wished for a place in the Confederacy in which he would neither be president of a board nor *primus inter pares*. The post of representative of the presiding Power, Prussia, in the Federal Council, which was bound up with that of Chancellor, was also adapted to Bismarck's character. He made everything depend on his receiving his instructions in this capacity, not from the Prussian Cabinet, but from the Prussian foreign minister, who was himself. But perhaps more important than all this was the fact that Bismarck as Chancellor—and as time went on ever more also as prime minister—stood over against the King as man to man. Now no longer had he to speak to the King ' in the name of the Cabinet ', he could on the contrary use the undisguised ' I ' in his main official capacity. The ' sovereignty of the great man ' now looked immediately into the eyes of the ' royal sovereignty '. The relation between King and Chancellor was thus more and more determined by the power of personality. The right of the former to decide upon the latter's resignation was kept in check by the threat of the latter to offer it. Bismarck himself

gives a cautious hint as to the exceptional character of his position :
' Relations such as I had with King William are not exclusively of a
constitutional or a feudal nature, rather are they personal relations.'

Bismarck's position within the Confederacy which he had
created thus presents a remarkable contradiction in itself. It is easy
to understand that a man with exceptional gifts of statesmanship
should mark out for himself a body of tasks to be carried out by him
in a dictatorial fashion, a body which would begin with the beginning
of his activity and end with its end. The reverse is also thinkable :
a great statesman might be so patriotic and so ready to deny
himself that he would exercise his talents and gifts on behalf of the
state as holder of an office for which a niche had been left in ' the
latter's fabric but which was not beyond the capacity of a less distinguished man. But if an office is introduced into the structure
of the state as an organic part of the latter—and still more as the key
position—which can only be filled by one man with quite unusual
gifts of will and intellect, then at the same time a fatal germ is
implanted in that state by the very person who built it up.

This becomes clearer still if we consider how Bismarck in his garb
as Chancellor, now no longer the Junker but already the dictator in
the guise of bureaucrat, developed his activities within the framework
of the new state. He did not come to this point as herald and path-
finder of a unity residing within the people now to be realized and
developed. Without principles and ideas such a unity was not to
be built up. Principles and ideas, however—and this was not
limited to liberal ideas—were to be rejected in political life as
' romanticism '. ' As minister in a constitutional state ', Bismarck
said at this time, ' I am under an obligation to give up convictions
the abandonment of which I do not fear will have disadvantage for
the common weal.' He therefore excluded from his constitution
the enumeration of the rights of man and citizen which is to be found
in almost all modern constitutions as the sign that the unity of the
state is based on an idea. The unity of the new Confederacy was
based on Prussia as its centre and Prussia herself found her unity
in increased measure in the person of her ruler with his new powers.
Bismarck regarded it as his task to focus the political aspirations
of the new members of the Confederacy on the head of the Prussian
state as symbol of the Confederate power, and to strengthen them
in this direction as well as to make the Prussian King and the
Prussian people aware that there were also other peoples in the
Confederacy. The political forces and counter-forces, invoking
the antitheses of the Prussian King versus the Princes of the Confederacy, of the Reichstag versus the state parliaments, of the executive
versus the legislative powers, of the army versus the civil government,
of conservatism versus liberalism, were not to be removed as

antitheses but to be balanced against each other ; not to be brought to an end but to be bridged over. This was Bismarck's task in the new Confederacy which he had covered with the formula of the ' two coinciding ends '. It was a task which involved discussion and mediation, in which all means of negotiation ranging from convincing speeches to concealed—verging on open—force were at his disposal and could be brought into play. It was his task not so much to bring those concerned to an understanding, but to keep them from coming to too close an understanding, to play them off and egg them on against each other, and to ally himself with one in this rivalry. Bismarck's special gifts lay in this direction ; he was qualified for this task by the compelling and overwhelming nature of his presence, by his inner security and unerring purpose, by his capacity to read the motives and aims of his fellow-men, by his readiness to exploit the fact that attachment is created more by favours rendered than by favours received, by his, contempt for mankind concealed under a watertight polish, by his enjoyment of politics as a game, by his power quickly to grasp and adapt himself to changes in the situation by his unscrupulousness ·in the choice of means. Thus Bismarck in building up his North German Confederacy employed the very weapons by which he had won his successes in external affairs and had made his conquests in war. In internal politics he aimed at acquiring the same position which he had always sought and continued to seek in foreign affairs, that of fulcrum in the balance between opposed social forces. What he could and wished to achieve there as here was the suppression and smoothing down of opposition, not the construction of a national unity founded in the people itself. His work was the work of a politician, not that of the founder of a state.

The means, however, which Bismarck had always looked upon as decisive in holding together the people by their common subjection to the head of the state, namely the increase of the latter's power by successes in external affairs, it was now for him to bring into play in increased measure, since it was now a matter not only of maintaining an existing state but of bringing into action for the first time a new state system. It was success in external affairs which must guarantee ' the independence, political freedom, and national honour which for a people like ours exceed everything else in importance ', and which make it ready ' to trust its rulers and sacrifice itself for them '. This success, however, had first to be made sure by preparing in advance men and arms for what was to give the final decision in external affairs, namely, war.

CHAPTER XXI

The Working of the North German Confederacy

Bismarck had now to develop his own political activity within the constitution of the North German Confederacy which he had created. He had to continue his own march forward in the direction which he had mapped out for himself in this constitution, and he was concerned with making it work in a way corresponding to his own aims.

The first task that fell to his lot had to do with the powers with which he had endowed the head of the new state. It concerned the financial compensation to be paid to the rulers of the states incorporated in Prussia. The Elector of Hesse had already in the course of the year 1866 released his subjects from their oath of allegiance in return for the restoration of his private estate which had been seized by Prussia. The negotiations about compensations with the King of Hanover and the Duke of Nassau, however, did not come to a conclusion until 1867, and ended with the authorization of the payment of a sum of several million talers to each of them. While Bismarck in all his numerous transactions of this kind had thrown into the scales the weight of his strong-willed personality, the keenness of his dialectic, and the power with which his external position provided him, he now also brought the might of the state immediately into play. When the ratification of these agreements was discussed in the Prussian parliament, Bismarck said that he was thinking of not paying the capital to the King of Hanover, as he had raised troops for a ' legion under French protection ' with a view to a future war against Prussia and had collected about 1,400 men. The measures taken to seize this capital were, in the spring of 1868, extended also to cover the interest, after the former King of Hanover had at a family feast ' openly associated himself with the hostile endeavours of his retinue against the Prussian state and had encouraged them to continue these endeavours '. This money, the so-called Guelphic Fund, was spent for ' particular purposes ' of the Prussian state, e.g., in order to provide a subsidy for the newspapers which were or were to be made friendly to the government, but also, as we shall see, for still more disreputable purposes. The above-mentioned legion played no part in the Franco-Prussian war, since, as Bismarck reported, ' people initiated in the movement were found who informed me of the preparations and offered to frustrate the whole plot, on condition that the emoluments which they enjoyed formerly from Hanover were secured for them '. Bismarck proceeded in the same manner in regard to the property of the Elector of Hesse which he had restored to him, because he found the Elector to be guilty of machinations against the Prussian state, in particular of the dispatch of a memoir concerning ' the dissolution of the German Confederation and the usurpation of the electorate by the Prussian Crown '. When in parliament remarks were made about this ' act of violence, perhaps also of revenge, and certainly of a revolutionary character ', Bismarck in his reply spoke of ' legal cobwebs ' over which ' a government must trip up in the exercise of its duty ', and obtained the consent of parliament which he had sought.

If Bismarck thus in the exercise of his abundant power in his relation to the deposed ruling houses crossed the boundary which divides the open from the concealed exercise of force, it is also true that in relation to many sections of the population he did not stop far from this boundary. In the annexed territories it was just the conservative element, particularly the nobility and the clergy, which clung to the floundering state, the princely residences of Hanover and Kassel being incapable of easily forgetting their former glory. While the debate concerning the constitution of the Confederacy was still going on, the objection was raised in the Reichstag by these elements that in Hanover Prussia was conducting the government ' against the supporters of the traditional dynasty with absolute lawlessness and that private persons were being taken off to the fortress without any proper legal procedure '. Bismarck was not concerned with the objective issue at stake but with the question of who was the stronger. ' I advise you and your friends most urgently ', he exclaimed, ' not to challenge us. You will encounter an energy which you are not fitted to face.' At this time the clever and learned English diplomatist, R. Morier, said about Bismarck : ' The political arena is to him, in a very literal sense, a prize-ring, in which the bigger man knocks down the lesser man and pockets the stakes.' But for his former friends, the extreme conservatives, even this energy of Bismarck was not enough. They felt themselves always threatened in their Old-Prussian feelings or, at any rate, not adequately supported. When Bismarck wished to leave to Hanover, now only a Prussian ' province ', a definite sum, provided from the coffers of the former state, in order to cover the cost of a part of the public services, his old opponent Georg von Vincke, who had now gone over to the conservatives, accused him of wanting to buy the patriotism of the Hanoverians with gold, and the *Kreuzzeitung* saw already in the powers given to the Confederacy ' the sacrifice of one piece of Prussia after another '. The King, too, had similar doubts about the ' German policy ' of his chancellor. At the beginning of 1869 matters came to a dispute between the two on the occasion of the regulation of a subordinate financial question concerning the annexed city of Frankfurt on Main. Bismarck brought forward a long list of complaints and grievances and offered his resignation. The re-establishment of the former harmony between King and Chancellor was then by no means a simple matter. Bismarck was also suspected by the extremists because he insisted on the continuance in the Confederacy of the small states which had been introduced into it. ' The nature of things tends to make the existence of the small states impossible and will do so more and more,' was said in the Prussian parliament. To this Bismarck's answer was : ' I must reject the insinuation in the name of the Federal constitution ; we have guaranteed the existence of these small states. Therefore their existence *is* possible.' He was concerned above all things to avoid giving the impression in the south that north Germany had become merely a ' Greater Prussia '.

An ingrained aversion increased the severity with which the power of the state was displayed in threatening some sections of the population. A Polish deputy protested ' in the name of the Polish people against the incorporation of formerly Polish lands of the Prussian monarchy in the Confederacy '. To his description of the partition of Poland as a ' crime ', Bismarck replied : ' Look into your own heart and tell yourself that you have committed the crime of conquest a hundred times over when you were powerful enough to do so,' forgetting indeed that on the occasion of the above-mentioned partition there had been no need for ' conquest ' of the then almost completely defenceless Poland. At the same time Bismarck showed no false modesty in singing the praises of what Prussia had done for Poland : ' The Prussian part of the former republic of Poland rejoices in a degree of prosperity, security of rights, and a devotion of her inhabitants to their government, such as was never known in the whole circumference of the republic of Poland so long as there was a Polish history.' He shows bitterness not only against the Poles, but also against the catholics, the ' catholicizing opponents of Prussia ', to whom he ascribed without hesitation opposition to the new Confederacy. As chief official in the province of Posen (Poznan) Bismarck proposed to the King ' one of the catholics on whose loyalty your Majesty can count, so that the machinations to which the otherwise loyal Polish peasant is subject in the religious field are counteracted '. However, in the newly-created Reichstag the political representatives of the catholics as the ultramontane party became stronger. Already during the discussions in the constituent Reichstag Bismarck attacked them. He spoke of the ' six hundred years long history of Germany's woes ', and to an objection made by the opposition to this expression he replied that these woes had begun with ' the decay of the German Empire during the Interregnum. Whence came this decay ? ' he asked, ' from the secession of the Guelphs and the victory of the ultramontane party.' Bismarck went carefully into a question which concerned not only the German ultramontanes but all Roman catholics, namely that raised by the proclamation of papal infallibility which was expected to result from the Council which opened in Rome in December 1869. He described this movement as ' the absolutist *coup d'état* with which the Pope is threatening to break the organization of the Church '; however, he declined to take the initiative against the measure on behalf of the North German Confederacy, since the latter ' is in the eyes of Rome preponderantly a protestant Power '. Sometimes he wished to leave this to the ' catholic courts ', sometimes he described ' the battle against the absolutism of the Curia as a matter for the bishops '. He also would not commit himself to the proposal to have ' a permanent conference of ambassadors in Rome as a sort of counter-Curia '. When he then was about to proceed against the Council and its decision in conjunction with the catholic Powers, Austria, France, and Bavaria, all declined to co-operate and so no official step was taken at the time in this matter by Bismarck's government.

Particularly unexpected for Bismarck must have been the experience he had with the ' common people ' to whom he had opened the doors of the Reichstag by the grant of universal suffrage. The expectation that universal suffrage would be a ' security for a conservative attitude ' and the belief based on his ' experience that the masses are honestly concerned with the maintenance of good order in the state ' were to be shown false by the first appearance of their representatives in parliament. In the elections to the constituent Reichstag the ' class-conscious proletariat ', which had set up a number of candidates of its own, was beaten everywhere, the progressive party in particular having shown itself as an embittered opponent. But in the first Reichstag elected on the basis of the new constitution there were two representatives of the working-class movement. Of these one in the debate on the law regulating compulsory military service held forth about the violence on which the North German Confederacy was based, described the Reichstag as the mere fig-leaf to cover absolutism, and the standing army as a tool of the policy of violence carried on by Bismarck while the other directed his attacks against conditions within the Confederacy.

Bismarck's desire for as powerful a head of the new state as possible was also responsible for his attitude to a particular question, which had at the same time an important bearing on the controversies of party-politics. In the discussions concerning a penal code for the whole Confederate territory the decision about the death penalty was the subject of a very violent dispute. A great number of the deputies were against it, including many members of the national liberal party. But Bismarck supported it in a very decided fashion and sharply opposed ' the over-estimate of the value attached to life in the world and of the significance ascribed to death '. This was one of the occasions, becoming ever rarer, on which he laid emphasis on his own religious belief. ' I can well think ', he said, speaking in a very pharisaical fashion, ' that to one who does not believe in a continuation of individual life after bodily death, the death penalty will seem severer than to one who believes in the immortality of the soul bestowed on him by God.' Then, however, he turned to what was his real concern, the state as supreme judge, and said : ' I have further the impression that the view of the Opposition is due to a certain morbid desire to devote more attention to sparing criminals and protecting them from injustice than they devote to the protection of their victims.' This desire is ' one of the diseases of our time, the fear of responsibility, of passing a judgement of life and death on the strength of one's own conviction '. Finally, to the delight of Bismarck's conservative friends, altar and throne were united in the concluding words : ' A human power which has no sense of justification from above in itself is certainly not strong enough to wield the sword of justice.' Despite these words the Opposition in parliament against the death penalty remained strong. Only after lengthy discussions was a narrow majority obtained in favour of capital punishment, thus removing the obstacle to the acceptance of the whole penal code.

While the constitution of the Confederacy provided a basis for subordinating the inhabitants of its territory to its head, corresponding measures had not been taken for dealing with the finances of the new state. Bismarck had declared in the constituent Reichstag that legislation about taxes was ' to be a matter for the future, and for laws to be made after we have been constituted a state'. So the constitution included no final decisions about the revenues of the Confederacy as such, but only laid it down that any lack in these was to be covered by contributions of the member states. This side of the constitution, too, had its cause not in contingent external matters, but throughout in Bismarck's own nature. He showed no active interest in these financial affairs ; talent for state finance was, as his admirers admit, just the talent which was least developed in him, despite his versatility. He felt, in his own words ' neither obliged by my office nor possessed of the calling to carry on the politics of finance '. ' If I have not myself gone further ', he said later in the Reichstag, ' in facing the task of financial reform, I can defend myself on the ground that I did not regard the introduction of financial reforms as a task incumbent in the first instance on the prime minister.' The consequence was that the contributions from the member states formed an ever-increasing part of the income of the

Confederacy; still Bismarck disliked them because they made the latter a 'dependent on the states', and thereby introduced an 'element of decomposition'. All the same he put up with this till the financial difficulties of the chief contributor, Prussia, caused by a bad harvest and a slump, necessitated a change. The Prussian minister of finance proposed the raising of a state loan and the parliamentary Opposition supported it. Bismarck wished to strike at both, when in the spring of 1869 he said in the Chamber : ' That the Opposition is bent on the diminution of the wealth of the state and on preventing us from sanctioning a permanent income for it, does not surprise me in view of their lack of political instinct.' He himself is neither in favour of direct taxes ' which with a certain angular brutality lay a weight on those subject to them ', nor for those indirect taxes ' levied on the primary needs of life, such as bread and salt '. He described as ' the basis of taxation which suggests itself in the present times those luxuries that are enjoyed by enough people to provide a revenue which will exceed that of the tax on so-called pure luxuries '. As luxuries of the former kind he mentioned ' beer, brandy, wine, tobacco, tea, coffee ', all things which ' it is desirable that man should have ', while he ' remains capable of living even if he does not have them '. Finally, Bismarck touched on the question of reducing expenses. ' Naturally ', he added, ' this reduction cannot affect the army, the sole secure guarantee of peace and independence.' In this his Majesty agreed completely with him, as the former assured him in writing.

Bismarck's quarrel with the minister of finance which has already been mentioned burst into open flame when the former proposed to introduce percentage increases in indirect taxation in order to alleviate the financial crisis, ' without having the least doubt as to the unpopularity of this measure '. The minister of finance, however, had not only the majority of his colleagues in the Cabinet, but also the King himself on his side. In the years after the Austrian war, when his nervous disease was frequently giving him trouble, Bismarck often withdrew to his new Varzin estate in order to recover, sometimes for a long period. He also looked forward from there to the result of the present conflict about the increases in taxation and left the actual settlement of the dispute to his friend Roon, who was joined by the King ' in a state of uncommon anxiety about the financial situation '. The conflict was settled, then blazed up again and finally led to the dismissal of the minister of finance. The King himself, however, informed Bismarck that the ' general view ' was that the ' Chamber will not grant an increase in indirect taxation to any minister, because that would make the re-election of those who voted for it impossible '. The new minister of finance too declined in a letter to Bismarck to start his tenure of office with such ' a hopeless début'. He also made a number of positive proposals, such as the conversion of state loans, which won Bismarck's approval. They passed parliament, yet the public financial crisis was not healed thereby, either in Prussia or in the Confederacy as a whole, but was only temporarily patched up.

It was in the domain of economics where Bismarck met half-way the wishes and principles of his new allies in internal politics, the national liberals. They had Delbrück as a liaison officer and a decisive co-operator. Freedom to set up a business and to change one's place of residence were introduced, a bill was passed giving a right of support to the destitute, the commercial laws were unified, common weights and measures and a common postal system were introduced. Bismarck did not, however, forget the interests of the landowning conservatives—which were indeed his own. He took part in agricultural discussions initiated in Berlin and promised ' to make an effort to cure our system of mortgage law of its defect '. However, he interested himself in economic policy mostly from the standpoint of military matters and foreign affairs. He took the initiative in developing the railway system, not least in Pomerania, and concerned himself with developing the militarily so important canal connecting the North Sea and the Baltic. But he was especially interested in the tariff policy towards south Germany. The German Customs Union was regarded as put on one side by the declarations of war in 1866. Within the North German Confederacy it was replaced by this new political body which implicitly took over all its functions, while the Customs Union with the south German states had to be renewed. This renewal was used by Bismarck in order to carry on the effort which he had been making since 1862 for the centralization of the Customs Union and its development into a single Confederacy for commercial purposes. While the Customs Union had already before been of great significance for him from the general political point of view, he now declared expressly ' Customs Union goes hand in hand with military union '. The Customs Union formed for him an additional means, over and above the defensive and offensive alliances, to destroy the international independence of south Germany recognized by the treaty of Prague. At the same time it gave Bismarck the opportunity to introduce into south Germany institutions belonging to the new north German political body. All this had to be done cautiously, since the south Germans for fear of France and Austria desired ' to avoid at this stage of Germany's development a discussion about the political relations between the south and the north '.

Legislation about customs and the carrying out of the laws in regard to south Germany was now to be the function of the Federal Council with the addition of some members from south Germany,

as Federal Customs Council and of the Reichstag, likewise extended
so as to form a ' Customs Parliament '. So Bismarçk had now, as
he expressed it, a 'third parliamentary battleground', besides Prussia
and the Confederacy. The south German states accepted willingly
or unwillingly—Bavaria in the main unwillingly—the new organization of the Customs Union demanded by Bismarck. In the
spring of 1868 the first elections for the new Customs Parliament
took place in south Germany. They gave a picture of the attitude
of the south German population to Bismarck's reorganization of
Germany. The result was that everywhere with the exception of
Baden the opponents outweighed the friends of Prussia. Thus
Bismarck held it necessary that very cautious language should be
used both about internal and external affairs in the opening speech
from the throne of April 1868.

Keep firmly in view the common interests of Germany [he let the
King declare] ; the friendly relations which the German governments
maintain with all foreign Powers justify us in being confident that the
blessings of peace, for the defence of which the German states have allied
themselves, remain secure.

As reply to the speech an address was suggested which expressed
the conviction that ' the power of the national idea will bring about
the complete unification of the whole German fatherland in a peaceful
and prosperous fashion '. But this address did not win the assent
of the majority ; against it voted not only the ' south German party '
which was hostile to Prussia, but also a considerable number of
north Germans. It shows how little the ' coincidence of the two
ends : Prussian leadership and German unification ' corresponded
at this time to reality, and how little foundation there was for
speaking of ' a right of the German nation to unify itself '. ' Why
will the south Germans not come to us ? ' Bismarck asked in
parliament and gave the astonishing answer : ' Not because we are
not liberal enough for them, but because we are too liberal.' Otherwise the Customs Parliament did quite good work in its three sessions.
It produced a new tariff law, it worked in bringing to their conclusion
a series of commercial treaties and took a share in bringing about
reforms which ' simplified the tariffs and made easier the production
of objects of immediate utility, of tools for work and raw material for
industry '.

The Confederacy which Bismarck had created in order to prepare war had of course its main weight not in internal but in external
politics and in military force ; so the consideration of its working
in internal politics can only give a subordinate partial aspect of it as
a whole. Now when Bismarck speaking of the function of this
Confederacy in foreign politics had just said that the German states

have combined in order to 'defend the blessings of peace', this is contradicted by the very structure of the Confederacy, the kernel of which was preparation of war, of the war against the old 'hereditary enemy of Germany, France'. Napoléon, for his part, had at the middle of September 1866 in his circular letter to the French foreign embassies sanctioned the Prussian conquests. But this did not mean that he thereby had buried for ever his wishes for compensation for France. He was convinced that he could not bury them without weakening his position inside France in a menacing fashion. Yet he came gradually to realize that he had already let the right moment for dealing with Bismarck pass, that the latter had in the meantime become much too powerful and independent to let himself be used as a tool for French desires. Napoléon consequently decided to adapt his wishes for compensation to the actual situation.

The object which he now had in view in the spring of 1867 was the duchy of Luxemburg. This used to belong to the German Confederation and the capital as a Federal fortress had been occupied by a Prussian garrison since 1815. It had not joined the North German Confederacy and had the King of Holland as its ruling Prince. The decision of Napoléon to ask for this country as compensation was noteworthy in two respects. The small state of Luxemburg was only a meagre fragment of what had formerly been the goal of his desires, and the acquisition of it was to be by purchase, one monarch buying from the other. In this the champion of nationality and plebiscite assigned to the latter a very subordinate significance. The King of Holland was quite ready to enter into the transaction provided that Prussia, who was much feared in Holland, gave her consent. King William had, so Bismarck told Benedetti, dropped his original objections. Bismarck himself spoke in a benevolent fashion about the project to the French ambassador. This friendly attitude in Berlin to his proposal induced Napoléon to enter upon official negotiations with the Dutch government, and the latter to take the necessary preparatory steps for a formal inquiry in Berlin about the Prussian assent. Then Bismarck suddenly decided to publish in the official gazette the defensive and offensive alliances with the south German states which he had so far kept secret and to make them the object of a thorough discussion in the Reichstag. The moment for their publication was selected with extraordinary skill, since Napoléon had rather exposed himself by his approaches to Holland and would probably be reluctant at the same time to pick a quarrel with Prussia about the interpretation of the treaty of Prague. Perhaps Bismarck's friendly attitude to the French undertaking was devised for this purpose, which is indeed a probable explanation. For, when on the following day Benedetti had an interview with him in order to notify him of the imminent request of Holland, Bismarck received the ambassador in a ' cold and rigid ' fashion and asked him ' in the interest of his own country to keep Holland from submitting that request to Prussia '. But the warning came too late : the Dutch government had already proceeded formally to raise the question in Berlin before the order was countermanded and were told that Prussia refused an answer. Napoléon on top of his defeat had now to endure the humiliation of being disavowed before the Dutch, who of their own accord withdrew the transaction. Bismarck, however, raised a storm of indignation in the north German Press and in popular meetings on account of Napoléon's threat to alienate a territory with German inhabitants.

But the excitement which arose on the other side of the Rhine was even greater. The French felt that a slight had been cast on their national honour and saw clearly that Bismarck had lured their Emperor into a trap (*piège*). "Bismarck ', Napoléon exclaimed, ' has striven to dupe me ; an Emperor of the French must not let himself be duped.' Count von der Goltz reported from Paris that military preparations were being made. But now Bismarck adopted a more conciliatory tone ; he did not want a war yet, since Prussia had not quite recovered in a military sense from the Austrian war and had not yet had time to apply the lessons learnt from it. Also the military incorporation of south Germany was only at its beginning. Furthermore, if it was to come to war, France must be shown up as the unmistakable aggressor and guilty party. So Bismarck told Benedetti that Prussia could indeed accept the alienation of Luxemburg but could not agree to it in advance. A few days later, on the 1st of April, he expressed his conviction in the Reichstag ' that no foreign Power would interfere with the indisputable rights of German states and German population ' ; in the same context, however, he emphasized his peaceable intentions, saying that he would ' protect these rights by means of peaceful negotiations and without endangering the friendly relations of Germany with her neighbours '. He concluded with the statement that the psychological mobilization had succeeded, in that ' we have confirmed by our debates the unshakable confidence and the inseparable cohesion of the German nation with its governments and among these governments '. In relation to foreign Powers Bismarck utilized the episode for representing Napoléon as a disturber of international peace. He tried to mobilize public opinion against him in England and Russia, and opened an extensive propaganda campaign in Austria. In the south German states also the episode was widely used by him for purposes of propaganda. To the prime minister of Bavaria Bismarck spoke bluntly about the common ' utilization of the episode ' for the purpose of the 'consolidation of the national cause'. Some years later Bismarck explained the considerations which directed his policy in connection with the Luxemburg affair. It is not advisable, he said, 'to wage a war at once just because it is probable that one's opponent would soon begin it; but it is also not expedient to let him count on our awaiting his attack in any case'. Nor did he forget to refer here to 'the ways of Divine Providence' which one can 'never know in advance with sufficient certainty'.

It is a clear sign of the increasing power wielded by Bismarck beyond the Prussian frontiers and particularly with the French government that his speech in the Reichstag with its orchestra of war trumpets and harps of peace had a cooling effect on the French war fever. In the French parliament the foreign minister announced that the negotiations with Holland about the acquisition of Luxemburg had never had an official character, but constituted merely an exchange of ideas. He further gave the explanation, no doubt congenial to Napoléon, that he had only thought of the possibility of its acquisition conditionally on the agreement of the King of Holland and 'on the interests of the Great Powers and the wish of the population expressed by a plebiscite with universal suffrage being fully considered'. Austria had indeed not been won over by Prussia's wooing, but had kept herself during the period of general tension very non-committal and unbiased in relation to Prussia. Now Austria proposed a conference of the Great Powers in order to facilitate an honourable retreat for Napoléon. This conference declared Luxemburg neutral for all future time, Bismarck bringing as his contribution Prussia's voluntary renunciation of her right to keep a garrison in the capital. In fact, this was one of the 'inexpensive acts of friendship' of which he was so fond. For Prussia's right to keep the garrison was after the end of the German Confederation legally very dubious and after the defensive and offensive alliances with the south German states without practical significance for Prussia. Napoléon, on the other hand, was not satisfied after all with this neutralization of Luxemburg. Benedetti had to visit Bismarck once more and offer him among other things the recognition of the south German alliances on condition that he allowed Luxemburg to be joined to France. Bismarck's only answer was to ask that the proposal should be put in writing. He then had this document published in the London *Times* at the beginning of the Franco-Prussian war in order to expose Napoléon.

The Luxemburg affair was for the relations between Prussia and France more than a mere diplomatic episode. It provided the first opportunity for Bismarck after his triumph over his Austrian opponent to look his next victim straight in the eye and to take his measure. Bismarck could now tell himself that his survey of the resources on either side had turned out in his favour. Thus he could set about employing his strength against the other, the hereditary enemy, in a game which, as either knew, was a matter of life and death for both of them and for many of their fellow-countrymen, while the prize of the contest was the hegemony of Europe. Now Bismarck could recall how thirteen years earlier, when he was an unknown diplomatic official of the King of Prussia, he for the first time had met in Paris the Emperor of the French on whom all eyes in Europe were turned with fear and admiration. He saw him then at the zenith of his power and success and noted how his activity was based on a far-reaching, well-thought-out, and well-balanced view of political, economic, and social life. Such an unusual personality in so high a position and with such far-flung aims in just the domain of politics in which Bismarck himself sought entry was something new for the latter. He had met no one like him, either among the Pomeranian Junkers, or in the Prussian court, or among his Frankfurt colleagues. He had gone to Paris inspired by an inherited hate and contempt for the French and determined not to give this up but on the contrary to cultivate it. Yet all the same he was unable to avoid recognizing and indeed admiring the great work of the Frenchman. Although he had a particularly keen eye for any weakness and defect in other people, he began, where he expected to have only to reject and to despise, actually to learn to give up some of his views and even to imitate what he saw.

But there was one point where the eye of Bismarck greedily searching for weaknesses and faults' gradually found its object. That was the inharmonious and self-contradictory aspect of the personality of the French ruler. He succeeded not only in taking the confidence of the latter by storm but even in overwhelming him by the vitality of his own untamed will. This personal relation developed the more as the Prussian gained in experience and security in his own environment and the Frenchman, mainly through physical exhaustion, suffered a decline in the force of his intellect and will. The relative power at the disposal of the two men had also been altered. Bismarck had now come to the head of his state which he had formerly represented in more or less secondary posts and was on the way to making this state equal or rather superior in power to France. He was just putting one of the coping stones to his enterprise by assimilating the south German army organization to that of Prussia and by making arrangements for joint mobilization. ' It was decided ', reports the Chief of the Prussian General Staff himself, ' that the best way of protecting south Germany would be by an incursion into Alsace across the central part of the Rhine.' The Napoléonic system, on the other hand, had not only suffered in external prestige, but was also at this very time on the way to losing its internal popularity. The parliamentary Opposition, originally consisting of five members, had in 1863 risen to thirty-five, and the two million votes cast against the government in 1863 had increased in 1869 to nearly three and a half million. The moment was approaching when Bismarck could claim for his state a place in Europe which would leave no room for the France of Napoléon. He had to reckon with the likelihood that France would not voluntarily fall behind him in the race. Nor did he wish that France should fall back voluntarily, for it was part of the instinct of the hunting animal in him first to chase his prey half in play but then not to rest till he had fallen upon it and seen it come to an end beneath his blows. What made this war particularly fascinating for Bismarck was the vast gallery in view of which it was played, comprising the whole political system of Europe, not like spectators but like very active participants in the sport. It was a game which kept many balls in play at once, and thus gave the highest development to Bismarck's incomparable skill.

The next step in this war game was a courtesy visit of Bismarck to his prospective victim in the latter's dwelling-place in Paris in the summer of 1867 just after he had inflicted on him a very painful wound in the Luxemburg affair. The occasion for this visit was provided by the International Industrial Exhibition of this year to which Napoléon had invited all the crowned heads of Europe. Bismarck may have been influenced by various motives when he decided to accompany his King on this visit. Certainly the continuation of discussions which had just been begun in Berlin with the Tsar, who was expected to arrive at the same time in Paris, and his Chancellor Gortschakoff, was not without interest for Bismarck. Also the tourist in him may have influenced his decision. But his personal relationship as guest to his host Napoléon was just now so delicate that he could not fail to take it into account. It seems that he in several direct political conversations let fall some words of justification for his conduct of the Luxemburg affair and in relation to the treaties with south Germany. But we cannot altogether reject offhand the supposition that the inexorable hunter wished to see with his own eyes the wounds inflicted on his victim and to explore on the spot how to deal further blows. The French Press described Bismarck's visit as a piece of ' audace '. A person in Napoléon's entourage when asked by Bismarck : ' Now, have I followed your teaching ? ' gave the answer : ' I must admit that the pupil has incomparably surpassed his teacher.' Napoléon, however, insisted on telling Bismarck about the reforms in internal politics which he had in view and asking for his advice. Shortly afterwards, Bismarck gave the answer to this confidence. When

Napoléon came forward with the project of preparing the way for the domination of Belgium by acquiring possession of the Belgian railways for the French state, Bismarck had a good share in causing the failure of this project.

In the end therefore Napoléon was forced to the conclusion that he could not avert the doom threatening him from Bismarck's quarter by demonstrations of friendship only. Without counter-measures there was no restraining of Bismarck's determination to dominate. Now, the obvious counter-measure to take was to come to an understanding with Austria as the victim who·had already succumbed to the same ruthless will. The French Empress succeeded in making Napoléon receptive to this idea. In Vienna the former Saxon prime minister, Beust, had become the leading minister. Formerly an eager champion of the ' Third Germany ', he had been obliged to give up his former office because in the autumn of 1866 Bismarck had refused to conduct peace negotiations with him. That he now took a reserved attitude towards a Prussia ruled by Bismarck was easy to comprehend, though, as the Luxemburg affair had shown, he was by no means mastered by hate. Yet that Beust welcomed an approach to France was the result not only of his personal inclination, but above all of the situation of the country for whose foreign politics he was responsible. So in August 1867, under the pretext of a visit of condolence for the Austrian Archduke Maximilian, who had been executed in Mexico by the revolutionary party, it was arranged that the French Emperor and his wife should visit their Austrian counterparts in Salzburg. Each ruler was accompanied by his adviser in foreign politics. The common interest of both states was concerned in preventing Prussia from further intervention in the affairs of the south German states which were to be regarded as internationally independent. Beust wished to do this indirectly by luring Prussia into a Balkan adventure, Napoléon by his immediate influence on the south German states. They nearly came to the point of a written treaty of alliance. But Napoléon rejected this for fear of irritating Bismarck. They contented themselves with laying down their agreement on all essential questions of foreign politics on the basis of a memoir drawn up by Beust. Bismarck, however, knew how by means of the north German Press to throw out the suggestion that in Salzburg a conspiracy had been hatched against German national unity, and so succeeded in making the feeble attempt of his opponents to brew poison into an effective means to enable him to spread poison on his own account.

The alliance of Italy with Prussia in the spring of 1866 had not brought her the full national unity towards which she strove. Rome, her natural capital, still stood outside the newly created

Kingdom. The French garrison had indeed left the city, but the papal sovereignty continued. Prussia, on the other hand, as a result of the war with Austria, was now only regarded by Italy as a half-friend. A change of Cabinet in the spring of 1867 seemed to indicate a more decisive turn in Italian foreign policy, away from Prussia to her former patron Napoléon and therewith to Austria. In the autumn of this year Bismarck wrote to the Prussian ambassador in Florence that the European Press described the change of Cabinet as the beginning of a policy based on a Franco-Austrian alliance against Prussia and added that ' a Power like Prussia can in the present situation only found her policy on a basis which is completely secure '. However, a few weeks later, lack of skill in the French policy threw—at least for the time being—this ' secure basis ' into the lap of Prussia without her doing anything in the matter. For some time Garibaldi with the half-approval of the Italian government had been planning and preparing a *coup d'état* against Rome. In the end Napoléon could not any longer resist clerical influence. He declared that by these preparations the agreement concerning the withdrawal of the French garrison from Rome had been broken and issued an order for the renewal of the occupation, a measure which the Italians hated above everything. When the followers of Garibaldi attempted their *coup d'état* on Rome, in November, the French garrison with their new *chassepot* gun supported the papal troops so effectively that there were several hundred deaths among the ill-armed assailants. In the French parliament a representative of the government declared : ' Italy will never acquire possession of Rome, never.' Bismarck put his seal on the consequent change in Italian foreign policy by sending the Prussian Crown Prince on a visit of courtesy to Florence. The welcome extended corresponded to Bismarck's expectations. ' The reception accorded to the Crown Prince ', Bismarck wrote, ' has surprised nobody but the Crown Prince himself. The King has sent him because he knew that he would be received enthusiastically. A Cabinet hostile to us is now not possible.' With this favourable sentiment towards Prussia, Bismarck was able to utilize the French proposal for the settlement of the question of Rome by a European congress so as to give himself the pleasure of meeting a French desire with the usual rejection.

Even after the beginning of this tension with Italy Napoléon continued his efforts to win her as an ally. Now they were undertaken with the help of Austria. On one occasion Bismarck described their success as not ' outside the realm of probability '. From them there resulted in 1868 a request emanating from Beust, but through the intermediacy of England, that the Powers should disarm. This Bismarck rejected, describing it as a ' proposal of the wolves for the abolition of sheepdogs '. Later, plenipotentiaries of the three Powers, Italy, France, and Austria, came together in order to work out a joint plan in case of a military campaign against Prussia. But the result of their endeavours only showed how far the three Powers were removed from a real understanding. The desire of Napoléon to secure himself without angering Bismarck was everywhere in evidence and the results corresponded to this ambivalent attitude. However, we have not yet completed our account of the background of the coming war between Bismarck and Napoléon. In particular England and Russia belonged equally to this background and needed to be watched. England stood at the zenith of her power and prosperity; her trade encircled the globe; she desired the maintenance of peace, every threat to which was a burden to her. Napoléon's vacillating foreign policy she looked upon as a source of continued unrest, and Bismarck knew very well how always to supply fresh provender for this attitude. Russia's inclination was and remained pro-Prussian, this feeling being actually stronger with the Tsar than with his Chancellor, Gortschakoff. The French sympathy for Poland and the French desire to act as protector towards the Turkish Sultan annoyed the Russians, the lack of interest shown by Prussia in Russian ambitions in the Balkans was a great advantage. In April 1868, Bismarck thus described to a south German politician the position of the North German Confederacy as to foreign affairs :

I am not afraid of France. We are far superior to the French. If God is not unfavourable to us and favourable to the French we shall repel the French attack and march to Paris after our victory. Napoléon knows that we are so strong. Austria will under all circumstances remain neutral. Even apart from her financial position she cannot wage war. All her interests are against it. In case of need we shall with the help of Russia hold Austria completely in check. We do not need to give the Russians anything even if we make an alliance with them in a war against France. Their weak side is Poland. A single French battalion would bring Poland into a state of revolt. With England we are on excellent terms. The English had formerly relied on Austria. Since the war of 1866 they have like practical people put their stake on another card. They have no objection to a national reorganization of Germany.

At the same time Napoléon had to listen to his clever and circumspect ambassador in Berlin, Benedetti : ' German national unity goes without check towards its realization. France has only to choose between friendly relations with Prussia involving the renunciation of any attempt to interfere in German affairs and a violent war.'

In fact it was no longer within France's power to make such a choice, since Bismarck had already made his decision in favour of the ' violent war '. Certainly there were times in which he entertained the possibility of avoiding this war and of attaining his goal by a further weakening of the French Emperor in the power of his government, but the main line of Bismarck's foreign policy was undoubtedly directed towards a settlement with France by war. Now it was for him to find the politically right moment and the adequate excuse for beginning this war. Once again luck placed the ball in Bismarck's hand and he did not fail in catching it adroitly when it came. About this time he wrote to his friend Motley: ' My intimate enemies call me the " diplomat with the wooden shoes ".' But his procedure on this occasion was such as to be anything but a justification of this title.

In September 1868 a military rising in Spain resulted in the expulsion of the Queen, Isabella II, after thirty-five years of misgovernment. She took refuge in Paris, and the Spanish parliament declared the throne vacant. At first they looked about for a successor within Spain, then they entrusted the prime minister and *de facto* regent, Marshal Prim, with the selection of one of the ruling houses of Europe. After a few unsuccessful approaches he turned his eyes, towards the end of 1868, to one of the sons of Prince Carl Anton von Hohenzollern, who had been a predecessor of Bismarck as Prussian prime minister. This family was distantly related to the Prussian ruling House ; it had its seat in south Germany, was only moderately endowed with wealth, and remained loyal to Roman catholicism. In 1849 the reigning Prince, Carl Anton, had renounced his sovereignty over his small principality in favour of the King of Prussia. Thereby he surrendered to the King the power which, according to traditional German institutions, was possessed in very great degree by reigning Princes over the members of their families. The presumptive candidate to the Spanish throne was also related to Napoléon III, being a descendant of Murat, brother-in-law of Napoléon I. Napoléon III had positively co-operated in securing the throne of Roumania for another member of that family. So the candidature seemed acceptable to two of the most powerful states, Prussia and France, and thus guaranteed against international repercussions.

However, perhaps because the intrigues of the dethroned Queen now living in Paris were feared, the first unofficial negotiations with the candidate, Prince Leopold, were conducted in secret. The person in charge was a Spanish diplomat well-acquainted with German affairs. The prospective candidate, who led the pleasant and carefree life of an officer of the guards in Berlin, was decidedly against the offer. In the spring of 1869, Bismarck was directly approached by Marshal Prim in the matter. His attitude is not accurately known ; perhaps the matter interested him as a countermove against the Franco-Austro-Italian negotiations which were then pending. But it is quite certain that the approach took place. Nor did the visit by a Spanish representative escape the attentive eye of the French ambassador Benedetti. He gave it at once the correct interpretation, asked for information from the Berlin foreign office, but failed to obtain a satisfactory reply owing to the absence of Bismarck, and reported to Paris. From there he was directed to get further information, but to avoid anything that might give the appearance of trying to pick a quarrel. A few weeks later the ambassador called on Bismarck in person. Bismarck replied that he knew nothing of the affair, that the Prince could not accept such an offer without the permission of the King, and that the King would probably, in view of the complete uncertainty of the conditions in Spain, advise him not to accept it. However, Benedetti noted that Bismarck carefully ' avoided saying that the King would in no circumstances allow the Prince to accept the crown '. In the autumn of the same year another Spaniard came to Germany, Salazar, a member of the Spanish State Council, also without a public mission, but probably on an understanding with Marshal Prim. He made use of the mediation of a German friend, the Prussian ambassador in Vienna, a friend of Bismarck of long standing, and a person directly under the latter's authority, who certainly would not have meddled in such a business without the approval of his superior. He introduced Salazar to Prince Carl Anton in the latter's south German estate with an exaggerated display of secrecy. In the course of a discussion with Prince Leopold in the presence of his father, acceptance was made conditional on the Spanish government obtaining the consent of Napoléon and of King William. The German intermediary seems to have interested himself in inducing Prince Leopold to accept, for he took on his side further steps in order to achieve this.

In February 1870 there followed the first official move of the Spanish government in the question of the succession. The above-mentioned Salazar now came with a mission entrusted to him by Marshal Prim to secure the express consent of Prince Leopold and brought for this purpose letters from the Marshal to the King of Prussia and to Bismarck. The King declined to receive the representative ; Prince Leopold maintained his negative attitude. But Bismarck now supported the candidature with all his energy. When he had received the Spaniard, he handed to the King a memoir in which he laid down that it would be of inestimable value politically to have a friendly country in the rear of France under Hohenzollern rule, and that it was economically of no less value to have the great natural resources of Spain at the disposal of Prussia, and to acquire a secure export market for Prussia's own products. Bismarck was opposed to involving the Cabinet in this matter and recommended that it should be only brought to the knowledge of specially selected confidential agents. Thereupon there was held on the 15th of March in Berlin a conference presided over by the King in which the Crown Prince, Prince Carl Anton, Prince Leopold, and also Bismarck, Roon, Moltke and three other high state officials, among them Delbrück, took part. Under the influence of Bismarck all the ministers and officials became convinced that it was the Prince's patriotic duty to accept the candidature. The Crown Prince and Prince Carl Anton referred to possible international complications ; the King, on the other hand, refused to bind Prince Leopold by a definite command, and the latter in consequence persisted in his refusal.

But Bismarck did not give way : he sought, though in vain, to induce the younger brother of the Prince to come forward as a candidate. He encouraged the Spanish ambassador to pursue the matter further and to approach Prince Leopold personally. He wrote to Marshal Prim describing the plan as an ' excellent matter ', and sent one of his closest collaborators to Spain in order to explore the territory there. He also secretly remitted, so Lord Acton relates, to Spain a sum of money to the value of £50,000 from the Guelphic Fund to be used for furthering the Hohenzollern candidature. When the King expressed to Bismarck disapproval of his eager activities, Bismarck replied that the stimulus had come from Spain and that the King had nothing to do with the matter as sovereign, while as head of the family he could only advise but not make the decision. Finally, however, Prince Leopold gave way to the pressure of his relatives and above all of Bismarck who had just been complaining about ' the poor progress of the Spanish affair ', and at the middle of June consented that his name should be brought before the Cortes as that of an official candidate. At the same time he asked King William, as supreme head of the family, for his agreement, and in fact received this, though, it is said, ' with reluctance and displeasure '. The Cortes happened to be just sitting. The plan was that Salazar should return immediately to Madrid and that the election, for which a majority had been secured, should be carried through before the Cortes were dissolved. The secret had been kept up to the present, so that it was possible to hope that Napoléon could be confronted with the *fait accompli* of an election to the throne based on a popular vote. By thus taking Napoléon by surprise Bismarck wished to bring it about that the candidature, when it did come to the former's notice, should have already acquired ' the form of a specifically Spanish question '. ' I regarded it ', he said, ' as a Spanish, and not as a German, matter.' In this way, he went on, ' the intervention of France will be from the beginning an interference in Spanish, not in Prussian, affairs '.

But events did not actually take the course envisaged in Bismarck's plan. The Cortes—apparently in consequence of a mistake in the deciphering of a dispatch in code—had been prorogued two days before Salazar arrived in Madrid. To summon them back was a matter of weeks, and Marshal Prim did not dare to keep the plan secret from Napoléon all that time. Within a few days (the 3rd of July) he had it communicated to the French ambassador in Madrid. The latter protested at once in the name of his country against the proposal to let the Spanish crown fall into the hands of a Prussian and reported to Paris. Herewith, Bismarck's ' Spanish bomb ' was exploded before it had reached its victim and in such a way as to threaten the assailant more than the former. Napoléon was enraged, which is not to be wondered at when we consider what a great significance in his lifework was attached to combating the menace of a seventy-million-bloc on the French eastern frontier. For he had recently learned that a bloc of this type was threatening afresh by the breach of the Prague treaty ; now his morbid anxiety made him foresee its spreading to the French western frontier to include the Spanish people. The Paris Press raised loud protests against what it called the ' Prusso-Spanish conspiracy '. In the Chamber the foreign minister, Duke of Gramont, the former ambassador in Vienna, used hard words about the injury to the honour of France and the disturbance of the European balance of power. Bismarck was particularly offended by the words :

We do not believe that respect for the rights of a neighbouring people obliges us to allow a foreign Power to set one of her Princes on the throne of Charles V. This will not happen ; of that we are quite sure. But, should it be otherwise we should know how to do our duty without hesitation and without weakness.

The French government did not, as Bismarck had expected, turn against Spain but decided that this would put her in the wrong from the beginning. So the ambassador in Berlin was asked to approach Prince Leopold in this matter either directly or through the King of Prussia. As Benedetti was absent on his summer holidays, his deputy visited the Prussian foreign office, but found Bismarck away and the officials who acted for him quite without knowledge of the matter. Bismarck had gone first with the King to Bad Ems and then to Varzin where he deliberately gave orders that nobody should approach him for weeks.

Since Bismarck's plan to keep the candidature for the Spanish throne a ' specifically Spanish affair ' and not a matter for his own government had failed through the premature disclosure of the plot and the immediate understanding which France had shown for the position, he had to try another trick in order to save the diplomatic situation. This trick Bismarck had had in view and prepared from the beginning of his whole treatment of the matter. It was a remarkable and indeed dangerous operation which he had for this purpose to undertake on himself and his King. He had to divide both persons into two parts which were completely separated from each other and had nothing in common with each other, especially in respect of knowledge and will. The one part was Bismarck the Prussian minister, the other Bismarck the Brandenburg vassal; the one part was William the monarch of Prussia, the other William the head of the Hohenzollern family. Bismarck had already made use of such a division, as where he disguised the Junker or the dictator in himself as the bureaucrat or when he wrote to a political friend : ' My criticism is not intended in my capacity as minister, but in my capacity as friend and member of the party.' But now this division was a matter of bitter earnest. The very question of the French ambassador about the candidature for the Spanish throne was rejected by the minister Bismarck with great indignation as ' unjustified ', and was answered, ' in accordance with truth by saying in evasive fashion that the Cabinet knew nothing of the matter '. For ' the acceptance of the election by Prince Leopold had been treated by his Majesty as a mere family matter, which had nothing to do with either Prussia or the North German Confederacy and which concerned merely the personal relation of the head of the Hohenzollern family to those who bore the name of Hohenzollern '. There had not been ' a council of ministers ' at Berlin on March the 15th ; Prince Carl Anton had only invited to dinner the head of the Hohenzollern family and some of the latter's trusted advisers. Bismarck's letter to Marshal Prim, the exact words of which the writer ' no longer remembered ', had sprung from the idea that a descendant of Murat as a popular figure in the French court would win for Spain the goodwill of France. Bismarck had indeed in the memoir preparing the conference of March the 15th declared the question of the succession to be a decidedly Prussian one and made clear its great political and economic importance for Prussia. But this was only intended for use at home. Abroad, the matter looked different, very different. The non-recognition by France of Bismarck's operation on himself and the King was a ' falsification by the Napoléonic policy ' by means of which the question ' was to become a Prussian one '. This proceeding on the part of France was ' internationally unjustified and a provocation, and it proved that the time had come when France sought a quarrel with us and was ready to grasp at any pretext for this which seemed utilizable '.

The course of events had indeed made it impossible to let the question of the succession appear in the eyes of the world as a 'specific Spanish question' and so to make ready for Prussia the position of fulcrum in the balance between France and Spain which Bismarck had had in view for her. But therefore Spain need not be left out of account altogether. She was of value at least as a menace in the rear of France 'in case of the outbreak of the Franco-German war which is to be anticipated sooner or later'. For this purpose Bismarck declared that France was looking for 'a pretext in international law to intervene at the expense of the freedom of Spain to select her King'. He looked upon 'the French intervention as an injury and therefore also as an insult to Spain'. Although Bismarck did not expect 'of the Spanish nation that she would attack a Power like France out of love for us', yet he entertained the thought that 'a Spain which loves honour could not bear to look on quietly and see how the Germans fought against France as a matter of life and death for the independence of Spain and her right freely to choose a King'. So after the speech of Gramont Bismarck warned the German Press not to discuss the Spanish question; the Prussian government respected the independence of Spain; the harsh words of Gramont against Spain were an insult to the rightful pride of the latter; the personal rule of Napoléon III was revealed as a dangerous disturbance of European order, he was steering towards a new war of the Spanish Succession. An instruction sent to the Prussian embassies abroad was similar in tone. According to this, Prussia had nothing to do with the negotiations about the candidature for the Spanish throne, which had been carried on without the knowledge of the King. The government was on principle ready for negotiations, but Gramont's words in the French Chamber had closed their mouth. They would not begin any quarrels. But if the French attacked they would defend themselves with all their might.

The initiative which was thus put by Bismarck in the hands of the French was at once taken up by the latter. But they did not deal with Bismarck immediately. He was now in Varzin, having left the King behind at Bad Ems. The Chancellor was lying in ambush, inaccessible to anybody. He was observing how the poison concerning the 'destruction by Napoléon of the European order' which he had spread abroad was working. He noticed how in Paris his attempt to keep the Prussian government out of the dispute, especially his dissecting operation on himself and his King, was condemned as hypocritical and mendacious, and how it thus strained the situation. The next step taken by France was a measure which she had already considered before, namely that the ambassador in Berlin should approach the Prussian King and ask him to intervene in the matter. So Count Benedetti sought an interview with the King, who had been left at Bad Ems, and obtained one on the 9th of July. In accordance with the instructions given him from Paris he had to induce the King to withdraw his agreement to the candidature of Prince Leopold. The King was asked to declare that the Prussian government did not approve of the acceptance of the Spanish throne by the Prince and order him to take back his decision. The King refused, saying that he had given his agreement to the action of the Prince in accepting the throne, though this had not been known to him beforehand, and that he had to adhere to it. But he gave the ambassador to understand that he had entered into negotiations on the subject with Prince Carl Anton, that he would impart his answer to the ambassador and that, if Prince Leopold decided to withdraw, he would approve this step. While King William took this rational and conciliatory attitude towards the French ambassador, a similar step, independently of it, was being taken by the French Emperor. The latter had so far left the task of dealing with the question more or less to his foreign minister, Gramont, who was inclined to war, though he himself had, as Bismarck expressly testified, no such inclination. Now the Emperor intervened in the matter on his own account in the interest of the preservation of peace. He let Prince Carl Anton know through the King of Belgium that the rejection of the Spanish Crown was the means necessary to keep peace in Europe. On the 11th of July a second interview took place at Ems between the Prussian King and Benedetti, and in the course of it the latter guessed from an assertion of the King that the withdrawal of the Prince's candidature was imminent. On the following day Prince Carl Anton decided to issue a statement in the name of Prince Leopold, who was not accessible at the time, that in view of the present complications the vote of the Spanish people could not take place with the freedom and publicity on which his son had counted in accepting the candidature. On his son's behalf he withdrew. Herewith the episode seemed to be liquidated in accordance with the wishes of the two monarchs and the whole complication brought to an end. Napoléon, in particular, regarded the declaration of Prince Carl Anton and the consequent solution of the crisis as his own work and spoke with great satisfaction to the English and Italian ambassadors about the settlement of the difficulties.

But the two monarchs had reckoned without their foreign ministers. In the meantime Bismarck, in the course of his solitary stay at Varzin, had arrived at the conviction that now the moment had come for the warlike settlement with France which he had long contemplated and that it would not be too difficult to make the latter appear as aggressor. One thing only did not please him, the *casus belli*.

In France an attempt was made [he wrote later] to find a pretext for war against Prussia which should be as far as possible free from national German colouring, and it was believed that they had found such a one in the dynastic field, in the appearance of a pretender to the Spanish throne who bore the name of Hohenzollern.

Bismarck, however, needed a *casus belli*, which was not free from such a ' colouring ', not only on account of his Prussians, but chiefly in order to bring into action the south German alliances. So, already after the first interview between the King and Benedetti, he telegraphed to Ems : ' Politically our situation would be very favourable in the event of a French attack,' and offered to go to Ems. However, he did not leave Varzin until two days later, and then only went as far as Berlin. There he learnt more precisely what had happened in the meantime. The news that the conversations with the French ambassador had been continued by the King on the 11th of July ' after the French threats and insults in parliament ', made him very angry, and he was still more depressed by the news of the withdrawal of the candidature of Prince Leopold. ' The sense of the blow to our national honour ', he declared, ' through the forced withdrawal dominated me so much that I had already made up my mind to announce my resignation in Ems.' Yet the man who complained that the King had not ' referred the Frenchman with cool reserve to his minister ' and saw the Queen at work in Ems ' with her cowardice and her lack of national feeling ', did not now stake everything on hastening to the side of his harrassed sovereign as loyal ' Brandenburg vassal ', but spent the night of the twelfth in Berlin and went on the next morning to his Berlin office. There he uttered to Roon : ' We have received a box on the ear from the French and have been brought by the compliance [i.e., of the King] into such a position as to appear to be looking for a quarrel if we want to go to war and thus employ the only means by which we can remove the stain.' He spent the rest of the day conferring with his advisers and with the ambassadors of Russia and England in an unsuccessful search for a chance of going to war without appearing to be ' looking for a quarrel '.

It was his French counterpart, Gramont, who freed him from this difficulty, not only taking away any need to think of resignation, but also giving a *casus belli* with a ' national German colouring ', indeed he forced it on him. While Bismarck now as ever remained true to his maxim : ' The only sound foundation of a great state is the state's egoism, and not romantic ideals ', Gramont had a certain dash of this romanticism. That kind of diplomat was very well known to Bismarck, who had always had an excellent understanding of how to make use of their weaknesses. Already after the first interview between the King of Prussia and Benedetti,

Gramont had telegraphed to the latter that the point to be attained was not so much that the Prince's candidature should be withdrawn as that the King should bring it about that it was. Gramont thus adopted the very course which Bismarck wished French policy to adopt. A personal insult to the Prussian King, who according to Bismarck's dissecting operation knew nothing at all of the whole business, could, if skilfully elaborated and handled, not only justify Bismarck's charge against France ' of seeking a quarrel under any pretext ', but also provide the desired ' colouring ' of the *casus belli*. Gramont was indeed obliging enough to Bismarck to go a few steps further still on the way entered by him. On the afternoon of the 12th of July he was received in audience by Napoléon, and although the Emperor was now rejoicing in the solution of the crisis as the result of his own action, he succeeded, by working on the weak will of an invalid, in winning Napoléon for his point of view. This was that the dispute was only half-settled by Prince Leopold's withdrawal and that in order fully to atone for the implied insult to France there was required further a declaration by the Prussian King that the resumption of the candidature was ruled out for *all future times*. On the same afternoon Gramont suggested to the Prussian ambassador that the King should write a letter of apology to Napoléon. In the evening he, with an express order from the Emperor, wired to Benedetti asking him to approach the Prussian King at once with the demand for the guarantee for the future. It was only the following morning that Gramont formally carried his point in a Cabinet meeting under the presidency of the Emperor in face of a numerous opposition among the other ministers.

The occasion on which this Cabinet met, namely the morning of the 13th of July, was just the time when Bismarck was sitting in his Berlin office and considered the possibility of going to war without appearing to be looking for a quarrel. Then he received the first news of Gramont's request for a letter of apology ; he pounced on it as providing the first chance of kindling some fire again in the dispute which had almost died out. The acceptance of the request by the Prussian ambassador, he decided, was incompatible with the dignity of the King ; this gave Bismarck the opportunity to recall the ambassador, so that henceforward Prussia was no longer formally represented in Paris. For the second and decisive chance, which was to come from Ems, Bismarck had had to wait the whole day. In Ems, on the morning of this date, King William was taking his constitutional with the telegram received shortly before and announcing the decision of Prince Carl Anton in his hand. He met Benedetti and showed him the telegram with the words : ' You see here a good piece of news. With this all our troubles and anxieties are ended.' But the answer he received was quite contrary to his expectations. Benedetti informed the King of the desire of the French government for a guarantee for the future. The King at once declined. The ambassador repeated the request, the King his refusal, and the latter concluded by declining to speak to the ambassador again on the matter. Yet the same afternoon he sent an adjutant to Benedetti bringing the confirmation of the telegram shown him in the morning. The King did not think of the possibility that Benedetti's move might have put into question the whole settlement, and still less had he the wish to revive the quarrel. In the evening he received news of Gramont's request for a letter of apology, and this gravely displeased him. But it had no influence on the course of events, as he had already sent to Bismarck a telegram about the event of the morning, the famous ' Ems telegram '. In this it says with reference to the request for a promise that the candidature should never be renewed :

I rejected this proposal at the end in somewhat grave tones, since one neither ought nor can undertake such an engagement *à tout jamais.* Naturally I told him that I had not yet had any news (i.e., as to Spain's attitude to the step) and that, since he gets earlier news from Paris or Madrid than I do, he could see well that my government has again not interfered.

This makes it clear that there is no trace of indignation, sharpness, or any rupture in personal relations, but only the desire to make intelligible his own attitude, and indeed to excuse it. The dispatch of an adjutant to Benedetti in the afternoon is also mentioned and it is added that the ambassador's personal reception had been omitted on account of the demand of the morning. In conclusion, it is left to Bismarck to decide ' whether the new demand of Benedetti and our rejection of it should be at once communicated to the Press '.

On the evening of 13th of July, a day which had not so far brought much comfort to Bismarck, he was sitting with the minister of war, Roon, and the chief of the General Staff, Moltke, and discussed with them the state of readiness of the Prussian army and its strength in the event of a war against the French. Here he received the telegram from Ems. His first impression was no doubt that of indignation at the episode which he must have felt as a renewed ' box on the ear ' from the French. Then, however, he turned his attention to the question, which was left to his decision, of communicating the telegram to the Press. Publication in the way which the King had in mind could only be regarded as a confirmation of the willingness of Prussia to end the quarrel, thus stressing her peaceableness. But was it not possible to read into

the telegram the *casus belli* with 'national German colouring' and
to interpret it as meaning that 'we are the victims of aggression,
and that French arrogance and irascibility have put us into this
position'? If the French foreign minister had again fanned the
flames of strife, acting over the head of his sovereign, why should
not Bismarck in the same fashion make the flames blaze up by
adding his own faggots to the fire? What was required was only
that the conciliatory and almost apologetic words of the King which
have just been cited should be omitted and replaced by the bare
statement that 'the King refused to receive the ambassador again',
and that the report sent through the adjutant to Benedetti should
be represented as being that 'the King has nothing more to communicate to the ambassador'. Bismarck knew that to publish the
news in this way meant war and that the King did not want war.
But 'we must strike if we are not to take upon ourselves the rôle
of those vanquished without battle'. After the reading of the new
version, the three conspirators were unanimously of the opinion
that 'by omissions' and without 'adding or altering a word' what
was the 'signal for a retreat' had been made into 'a trumpet-call
in answer to a challenge'. Without asking the King's permission
to publish his call for retreat as such a 'trumpet-call', Bismarck
was careful when communicating the matter to the Press to see
that the telegram 'not only on account of its content, but also
on account of the manner in which it was published would necessarily make the impression of a red rag on the French bull'. At
the same time, in these very days, Bismarck read again with particular zeal the Bible and the 'Words of the Day' of the Pietist
Brotherhood before going to bed, underlining passages and adding
notes, particularly on passages concerning war and peace.

Napoléon, after letting himself be taken in tow on the 12th and
13th by the warlike disposition of his foreign minister, resumed the
peaceful line which he had adopted earlier. He occupied himself
with the thought so very familiar to him of an international conference to settle the questions still left open in the present dispute.
If such a conference were to sanction the exclusion of Princes of
the Great Powers from foreign thrones for all future time, then the
statement demanded from the King of Prussia had become superfluous. Gramont did not contradict him. In the French Cabinet
meeting of this day the mood was also more peaceable than in that
of the preceding day, although the negative attitude of the Prussian
King towards Benedetti, which had in the meantime become known,
did not remain unnoticed. On the report of the minister of war
that the army was 'arch-ready', it was decided indeed to mobilize,
but the carrying out of this decision was postponed. In the evening, however, the news of Bismarck's publication of the Ems

Telegram—in a distorted form—arrived from Munich. Bismarck's calculations as to its effect in Paris were confirmed throughout. Gramont declared almost in the words used by Bismarck to Roon two days before : 'This is a slap in the face for France. I shall lay down my office rather than endure such an insult.' His entreaties carried the Emperor with him ; already on the evening of the 15th the Cabinet decreed that mobilization should be carried out, and the following day the Chamber after stormy scenes—for there was opposition—and a passionate appeal on the part of the Cabinet voted credits for war.

When on this morning King William in Bad Ems learned through published news what Bismarck had made of his telegram of the preceding day, he was 'surprised and taken aback'. He had on the advice of Bismarck fixed his return to Berlin for this day, and everywhere on his way he encountered manifestations of a warlike mood among the population, but the thought of war he kept far from him, now as earlier. He was very astonished to find in a station some distance before reaching Berlin Bismarck waiting for him with Roon, Moltke, and the Crown Prince. During the journey to the Berlin terminus Bismarck expounded to him his views on the necessity for immediate mobilization. But the King showed himself impervious to these views and expressed a firm hope that the country could be spared a war and that the French excitement would calm down. Yet when he arrived in Berlin itself, Bismarck could bring him the news of the French mobilization and authorization of war credits. Thereupon the King said to him : 'This looks very warlike, we shall have to mobilize three army corps at once.' Bismarck replied : 'Your Majesty, that is not enough. The French are already mobilizing the whole army.' The King then ordered the Paris dispatches to be read again. 'But this is the declaration of war,' he exclaimed in a state of deep emotion, 'so we must really again have such a war. It is true,' he added, 'it is war. Well then, so be it in the name of God.' 'The Crown Prince, however,' so reports an eyewitness, carried away by enthusiasm, 'stood by the King like a flaming God of war, the prototype of Teutonic rage, with head thrown back, and right arm threateningly raised.' A Council of war during the following night decided : 'The army is to be mobilized in accordance with our plans.' As regards the carrying out of this mobilization order the chief of the General Staff reports :

The means of mobilizing the army had been reviewed year by year, in view of any changes in the military or political situation. The orders for marching and travelling by rail or boat were worked out for each division of the army, together with the most minute directions as to their different starting-points, the day and hour of departure, the duration of the journey, the refreshment stations, and the places of destination. At the meeting-points cantonments were assigned to each corps and division, stores and magazines were established ; and thus it needed only the royal signature to set the entire apparatus in motion with undisturbed precision. There was nothing to be changed in the directions originally given ; it sufficed to carry out the plans prearranged and prepared.

Of the mobilization of France, the ' dangerous disturber of European order steering towards a new war of the Spanish Succession ', the same source reports :

The regiments had marched out of quarters incomplete as to numbers and insufficiently equipped. The progress to their destination was delayed, for it was often unknown at the railway stations where they were to be encamped. The corps and divisions had no artillery or baggage, no ambulance, and only a very insufficient number of officers. No magazines had been established beforehand.

CHAPTER XXII
The Franco-Prussian War

That in north Germany mobilization proceeded without friction was, at least indirect, evidence that the North German constitution was capable of proving its worth as an instrument of preparation for war. But the direct signs were no less impressive. It was a convincing proof of the absolutism of the sovereignty of Prussia in military matters and foreign affairs that Bismarck did not report to the sovereign in internal affairs, the Federal Council, till the 16th of July, when ' he made his first statement in the Federal Council about the political situation and the development of events up to the 15th of July ', as an eye-witness tells us. For, once the general mobilization order had been issued, there was in practice for Prussia no way back, and the right of the Federal Council to insist on its consent before war was made, except in case of invasion, was thus rendered of no effect. But the Council did not take any offence at this apparent violation of its rights. When Bismarck announced : ' There remains no other choice but either war, or a guarantee from the French government against the recurrence of similar menaces,' the representative of Saxony, in the name of all the confederated states, communicated to him ' their agreement with all the steps hitherto taken by the President of the Confederacy and the view of the situation expounded by Prussia '. He added : ' France wants war. May the war then be waged with as great rapidity and force as possible.'

The Reichstag with no less emphasis proved its capacity as factor in the preparation of war. It was summoned for the 19th of July, but even before it had received from the government any authentic communication about political events, it had already been decided by the single parties on the day before the meeting that ' all parties would accept all proposals of the government without debate '. In the speech from the throne Bismarck let the King say :

The federated governments are conscious that they have done all that honour and dignity allowed in order to preserve for Europe the blessings of peace ; it is unambiguously clear to our eyes that the sword has been forced into our hand. In this fight, in which we seek no other goal but permanently to secure the peace of Europe, God will be with us.

Following immediately on this speech Bismarck was able to announce: ' I have to inform the House that the French plenipotentiary has to-day handed to me France's declaration of war.' After the words

364

'declaration of war', as an eye-witness reports, 'any further words were drowned in the cheers of hundreds of voices in indescribable enthusiasm. Applause, claps, shouts of "hurrah" resounded for minutes at a time, and arose again and again in the hall and the galleries. Everyone had risen from his seat at once.' Yet none of those who were applauding had authentic knowledge of what had really happened. For Bismarck had heard the applause of the Federal Council for the war against the hereditary foe only after he had made his official statement on the political situation. Yet the analogous report to the Reichstag followed only on the day after the enthusiastic approbation of that body and after the latter's address with the peroration 'the German people will find on the battlefield the place of union'. And the report when it came was meagre enough. In substance it consisted in little more than the reading out of some documents relating to the outbreak of war and announcing that 'we have during the whole episode received from the French government only a single official message; that was yesterday's declaration of war'.

In connexion with this Bismarck brought forward once more his theory about the dissection of the King into two parts. For all the conversations of Count Benedetti with the King in Bad Ems were 'conversations of a personal and private nature which have no significance for international relations'. That the content of the 'Ems Telegram', the real occasion of the war, thus lost its 'international significance' too was not noticed in the general war fever, and the war credits demanded by the government were granted almost unanimously without a debate. Thereupon Bismarck was able to give a good mark in the name of the King to the nation represented in the Reichstag, now that it had fulfilled the expectations set on it as 'an ally of the throne easy to handle'. In the name of his sovereign he thanked 'the Reichstag for the speed and unanimity with which it for its own part had come to the help of the fatherland in need'. The president of the Reichstag concluded: 'The work of representing the people is for this time brought to a conclusion. Now the work of arms will take its course. May the blessing of the Almighty God rest on our people also in this holy war.' The last cheer of this strange champion of the constitutional idea in Prussia was given not for his King by the constitution, but for the 'Commander-in-Chief of the German army'.

In fact, the parliament had almost done its work for the duration of the war; during the whole course of the latter it was only summoned once for a few days in order to give its assent to the constitutional changes rendered necessary by the conversion of the Confederacy into the Reich. But when it came to the formal act of solemnly founding this Reich the presence of the Reichstag was undesired, and it was not invited. In any case the constitution of the North German Confederacy had passed its test as an instrument for preparing war ; so had the real driving force in the centre of the Confederacy, the Chancellor, in his political war preparation.

The defensive and offensive treaties of alliance which he had concluded against the hereditary enemy were fulfilled by the south German states. That Baden, which for several years had been trying, altogether against Bismarck's wishes, to secure admission to the North German Confederacy, should fulfil its obligation without delay was to be expected, and the same applies to Hesse-Darmstadt, half of which already belonged to the Confederacy. But it was impressive that Bavaria, which had always taken a very reserved attitude towards Prussia, mobilized almost simultaneously with the latter and—against the votes of the ultramontanes—authorized the war credits in parliament, and that Württemberg followed immediately.

Spain disappointed Bismarck's expectations and remained neutral. But he had every reason to be content with the declaration of neutrality by England on 19th of July, after the attempts of mediation initiated by England on 14th of July had come to grief, not least as a result of Bismarck's opposition, and although Prussia had not yet confirmed the guaranteed integrity of Belgium. Bismarck had to thank above all the change in the English foreign office, owing to the death of the former Minister, Lord Clarendon, who for his part a few years before had acted as mediator in the demands of Austria and Italy that Prussia should disarm. Bismarck's sentiments on this death are said to have been expressed to the Earl's daughter in the words : ' Never had the news of a death rejoiced me more than the news of your father's death.' At the same time Bismarck brought the following remarkable charge against the English government : ' With a readiness offensive to us the government in London took on the representation of France in north Germany, and during the whole war they never compromised themselves so much in our favour as to prevent their friendship with France being preserved.' These words were hardly to be explained as an expression of ' sympathy for the people who will not let themselves be loved by us '. Such a phrase the Bismarck of these days would no longer have uttered, indeed he would not have understood it.

Russia also decided to keep neutral in the war. Her neutrality was the subject of special negotiations between her and Prussia, originating in a meeting of the two monarchs and their Chancellors, Bismarck and Gortschakoff, in June 1870 in Bad Ems at the time when Bismarck was staying there before his departure for Varzin. The treaty of Paris of 1856, which had brought the Crimean War to an end, had subjected Russia to severe limitations in her utilization of the Black Sea and its coasts. Bismarck now described these as 'the least wise conditions in the Paris treaty'. 'To a nation of a hundred millions', he continued, 'the exercise of her natural rights of sovereignty on her coast cannot be permanently denied.' All the same Russia had in Paris bound herself by signing these 'least wise conditions', and Prussia had as guarantor appended her signature to the treaty. But this did not prevent Bismarck from using his gift of persuasion in Ems to induce Russia to renounce her treaty obligation and from promising the support of Prussia in this. Bismarck called this utilizing 'the possibility of rendering a service not only to the Russian dynasty but to the Russian Empire' and 'of employing this as a handle in order to cultivate our relations with Russia'. His real purpose was to induce the Russians to send an army, 300,000 strong, to the Austrian border in order to prevent Austria's entry into the war, and also to throw an apple of discord among the neutrals, especially between Russia and England, who were, respectively, the would-be breaker and the guarantor of the Paris treaty, so as to distract their attention from the Prussian War.

Bismarck declared expressly that in relation to Gortschakoff he had taken the 'initiative' in suggesting to him a breach of the treaty by 'sounding him in this direction'. He was angered because Gortschakoff 'only reluctantly accepted the proposal'. What could have made the latter take this attitude? Loyalty to a treaty is not mentioned, nor is political foresight. On the contrary, Bismarck says : 'His personal malice was stronger than his Russian sense of duty. He did not wish to receive any kindnesses from us.' So it required special encouragement from Bismarck before Russia at the end of October 1870 unilaterally denounced the clause about the Black Sea coast by a circular note addressed to the signatory Powers. The latter were choked by this step ; but for Bismarck it meant a great asset, since it eased a situation in foreign affairs which was just then particularly tense. But when the English ambassador spoke to Bismarck about the Russian note the latter washed his hands of it and said 'that it had taken him by surprise, that while he had always held that the treaty of 1856 pressed with undue severity upon Russia, he entirely disapproved of the method adopted by the Russian government to force the revision of the treaty'. Unfortunately this statement was communicated to Gortschakoff and Bismarck had to make a feeble apology. The question was settled by a congress in London at the beginning of 1871, which in general condemned breaches of international treaties and at the same time legitimized the Russian breach. Russia's benevolent neutrality at any rate was secured for the whole course of the war.

This attitude of Russia was not without influence on that of Austria for whom now the hour of revenge seemed really to have come. As a matter of fact, Napoléon pressed for the conclusion of an alliance against Prussia, but this was opposed even by the minister von Beust, whom Bismarck had treated so insultingly and suspected as friend of the Rhine League policy. Beust advocated the adoption of a waiting policy, but a Crown Council went beyond this proposal and three days after the war began it declared the neutrality of Austria. Now Beust took one further step for the benefit of France: he let it be known in Paris that Austrian neutrality would be one of benevolence towards France. Thereupon he was personally attacked by Bismarck on every possible and impossible occasion as the ' hindrance to an approach of Prussia to Austria '. Beust, however, remained concerned with ' sweetening for France the bitter pill of the rejection of her alliance '. He recommended her to bring ' the Italians straightforwardly to our side ' by ' pulling the Roman thorn out of their foot '. ' On the same day ', he added, ' on which the French leave Rome the Italians must march in there with the agreement of France and Austria. Through such a generous policy ' one would ' oppose a dam to the surging flood of Teutonism which the protestant Prussians have produced in Germany '. As a matter of fact, for all Powers concerned the attitude of Italy on the question of neutrality was most doubtful, and for it the development of the Roman question was decisive. The French garrison in Rome was as much hated by the Italians as ever, and the blood bath it had produced among the followers of Garibaldi had been as well remembered as the statement in the French Chamber that ' Italy will never seize possession of Rome, never '. Now the clerical watchword in the Tuileries was : ' Rather the Prussians in Paris than the Italians in Rome.' Napoléon, in accordance with the habit of his later years, could not bring himself to the radical decision advocated by Beust, and in a personal letter to King Victor Emmanuel proposed that the French as well as the Italian troops should keep out of Rome.

Victor Emmanuel was ready to seek an understanding with France on this basis. But disorders broke out in the big Italian towns, the mob shouting : ' Death to the French, long live Prussia.' In the Chamber a deputy declared : ' Now it is a question of taking Rome by an independent resolve without regard to France ; if the Monarchy does not do it, the Revolution will.' This made the King of Italy change his mind. On the 23rd of July a royal manifesto announced the neutrality of Italy in the war and the Chamber passed a vote of confidence in the government by a majority of more than four to one. At the beginning of September the French evacuated Rome, too late to gain the friendship of Italy, and on the 20th of September Italian troops occupied the city. Certainly Bismarck was justified in doubting ' what conclusions would have been reached in Vienna and Florence if in Wörth, Spichern, Mars-la-Tour success had been scored on the side of the French, or had been less dazzlingly on our side '.

Bismarck viewed it as his task not only to prepare for the war by his internal and external policy, but also to make sure of its issue by the means of diplomacy. From the beginning of August he undertook this task from the military headquarters in France, to which he had proceeded in the company of the King. Here he witnessed the extraordinary train of victories of the Prussian army in these weeks. While the Prussian deployment was successful, the French was ' tactically as well as strategically ' a failure, and the first skirmishes between the two armies went against the French. They retired to Metz and after several battles in which they suffered heavy losses were cut off in this fortress by the end of August and subjected to a siege. A new army, made up of the remainder of the forces of the French Emperor, who was himself present with them, was intended to relieve the troops shut up in Metz. But before they arrived there, they were attacked by the Prussians on the 1st of September at Sédan, surrounded and driven into the town. Their surrender and the capture of the Emperor followed on the next day. Then the Prussians marched against Paris, in which city were crowded together all available mobilized and mobilizable French troops. The siege of Paris began on the 19th of September, one and a half months after the outbreak of hostilities. The swift and successful course of the campaign was of decisive significance for the direction of the political activity with which Bismarck accompanied the war. First he had to find out the military objectives of the enemy and to ' determine and define ' his own, to come to an understanding with the King about these, to work on the public by propaganda, and to influence his south German allies in such a way as to lead them to intensify their co-operation in the war. He spread reports about French violations of international law alleging that they had fired on men sent to negotiate under the white flag and had allowed the employment of *francs-tireurs*. He tried to refute stories of German atrocities, and reported English deliveries of arms to France. He had also to keep an eye on the neutral Powers and to find out whether they intended ' to support the enemy in the first place by diplomatic and then by military means', and whether there was a danger that there might develop ' a wider war from the intervention of neutrals and especially to judge when the right time has come to initiate the transition from war to peace '. Bismarck insisted very emphatically that for this task ' knowledge of the European situation is required ' which only a specialized study of it could give. All this called for a continued collaboration between Bismarck and the military authorities, which at the beginning proceeded quite without friction.

On the evening of the 1st of September 1870, the day of the

battle of Sédan, Napoléon addressed the following letter to King William in the Prussian headquarters : ' Sire, my brother, since it has not been granted to me to die in the midst of my troops, there is nothing left to me but to lay my sword in the hands of your Majesty.' Bismarck in the reply drafted by him at once referred to the ambivalence of Napoléon's words : ' Sire, my brother, I accept the sword of your Majesty [that was taken by Bismarck to mean the declaration of subjection to the Prussian will] and am ready to discuss the surrender of your army ' [i.e., the military consequences of the victory]. The change in the political situation in France and the military capitulation of the French army were thus united in a single act. So Bismarck in the letter to Napoléon also specified the person who had to discuss the surrender of the army, he having appointed for this task general von Moltke. This did not, however, mean a division of labour between Bismarck and Moltke, but rather the reverse. The terms of surrender were discussed by the two men in common and fixed with a view to seeing whether it was possible to make concessions ' to the sense of military honour of the beaten army without injuring German interests '. On the occasion of the first, purely military, negotiations which were conducted with the French military commanders, Bismarck was present and spoke a decisive word in support of the Prussian standpoint, emphasizing that Prussia had been attacked and that France must be chastised ' for her arrogance and her eternal love of aggression threatening peace, and must be made incapable of resisting us, if permanent peace is to be obtained '. In the course of the same negotiations Bismarck also came to grips on political matters and asked whether the sword of Napoléon which had been handed over was also ' the sword of France '. When a negative answer was given, he showed himself astonished and displeased and let it be understood that for him the kernel of the negotiations lay here. These were then brought to an end without any practical result either military or political, since the French were not willing to surrender on the terms demanded by Moltke.

Napoléon attended a second discussion in person. The French Emperor thus as a prisoner of war put himself into the power of Bismarck and the Prussian government represented by him. Their meeting on the 2nd of September 1870, at Domchéry, a little town in the neighbourhood of Sédan, marks historically and politically a decisive event, namely the transference from France to Prussia of the hegemony of the European continent.

We sat for an hour [Bismarck tells his wife] in a room ten foot square, with a deal table and two wicker-chairs. It was a striking contrast with our last meeting in '67 in the Tuileries. Discussion was difficult if I was to avoid touching on matters which were bound to affect painfully one who had been cast down by the mighty hand of God.

The tact which Bismarck, according to his account, showed in this conversation with Napoléon, stands in remarkable contrast to the manner in which he had behaved towards the Emperor in the last years before the latter's defeat. Yet the miserable situation, in which he who had once been the most powerful man in Europe now confronted Bismarck in the little room in Domchéry, was nothing else than the desired result of that course of behaviour. Certainly there was a contrast between this little room and the luxurious halls of the Tuileries which on the occasion of the International Industrial Exhibition of the summer of 1867 saw almost all the crowned heads of Europe round the French Emperor. But was this ' striking contrast ' not simply a contrast in the surroundings for Bismarck ? Was there not a direct and necessary connexion between his earliest plans and decisions and this meeting in Domchéry ? Why conceal this even from one's own wife ? Why not simply say : ' We have opposed each other in a struggle to the death, I have shown myself the stronger, the prize of the victory is mine.' Perhaps Bismarck was prevented by a generosity unusual for him from meeting his vanquished foe with this attitude ; but his wife had a right not to be excluded from knowledge of the true feelings of her husband. Certainly we can understand that he felt bound in writing to her to bring the victory which he himself had won in connexion with the providential help of God, not only on account of her own religious beliefs, but also because the thought of his wife, of his solidly founded private life, and the success of his life work, must have brought to his mind particularly vividly the disaster which he had consciously brought on his opponent in both respects. But was it therefore necessary to conceal his own achievement altogether by a reference to ' the mighty hand of God ' ? Was this real humility and piety, was it scepticism about human values and successes in general, and so even about his own, or was it a trace of that fear of responsibility which Bismarck himself had so severely blamed in others ?

The event meant the end of a chapter in European history. Bismarck described it as the settling of the account for ' two centuries of twenty French wars of aggression '. But the politician looks into the future and looks on the future as providing his task. In the case of most of Bismarck's objective aims personal hostility constituted an important factor, and his hostility towards Napoléon had been of greater significance than any. For the man whom he represented to his fellow-countrymen as the prototype of the ' hereditary national foe ' was for him personally the rival in a race towards the goal whose attainment constituted the central point of his life work, namely the making of Prussia into the greatest Power in Europe, with himself the mightiest man in it. This competition won, there was nothing else in Bismarck's life to fill completely its place. To do without it meant for Bismarck that the policy of preparation for war, as he had hitherto pursued it, had lost its point. When he saw with his mind's eye that he was now confronted with the task of giving a new content to the policy of the state which he had created and which was now expanding so vigorously, he might well be driven to call on the help of ' the mighty hand of God ' not less for the victor than for the vanquished.

On the military and the political aspect of the event Bismarck wrote to his wife: ' Yesterday and the day before yesterday cost France 100,000 men and an Emperor. It is an event of world historical importance, a victory which decides the war.' However, the conversations between Napoléon and Bismarck did not take colouring congruous with their historical background, they were rather like a mere business discussion. As Bismarck reported to the King, he declined ' from the beginning to negotiate with the Emperor about the capitulation of the army ' and stated as his reason that this question was ' one to be settled between General von Moltke and the French military authorities '. In the political field, Napoléon now showed the dignity and self-control which he had not always displayed in former years. Bismarck told King William that the starting-point of the negotiations was for him the desire for ' information ' about the point which he insisted had not been made clear when Napoléon handed over the sword. ' I asked the Emperor ', so he told his sovereign, ' whether his Majesty was inclined to negotiate for peace.' The reader will ask what value peace negotiations could have with one who, though not yet deprived of his throne, was as prisoner of war completely without power. But Bismarck had not addressed this question without having a particular purpose in view. Though he could not count on Napoléon's answer leading to peace, he might use it to bring pressure in negotiations with other French authorities. Yet the Emperor declined briefly to enter into the question because ' he was as prisoner of war not now in a position to do so '. But Bismarck did not desist so quickly from squeezing the other. He now asked ' by whom in Napoléon's opinion the supreme power of France was represented at present '. The obviously weary and disgusted Emperor gave the answer: ' By the government in Paris.' This Napoléon himself had set up before his departure for the battlefield, putting at its head the Empress. Thus the political discussion between the two men came to a close, the remainder of it having no political importance. One has the impression that Napoléon felt it as a cruel torture and that Bismarck could not have failed to notice this. It in no wise followed the line which one would expect in view of Bismarck's alleged former tact. A little while after the end of the conversation, the negotiations between Moltke and the French officers concerning the fate of the army shut up in Sédan were resumed and very soon brought to a close by unconditional surrender. There followed a meeting between Napoléon and King William. The first question of the former when he met Bismarck had, as the latter himself reports, concerned the possibility of such an interview. But Bismarck, in agreement with Moltke, had postponed it under some pretext till the military capitulation had been signed. He wished to prevent an earlier meeting of the two monarchs, since he feared that this would lead to terms of capitulation more favourable to France.

The siege of Paris, which had begun on the 19th of September, now came more and more into the forefront of events. There, the government of the Empress had already come to an end on the 4th of September. Napoléon was declared to have lost his throne, and the second French Empire had ceased to exist. In its place there arose a bourgeois republic, with a 'Provisional Government of National Defence' at the head and the military governor of Paris as president. Its foreign minister, Jules Favre, had on the 6th of September in a circular note to the diplomatic representatives of France announced its aims : 'We surrender to the enemy not a finger's breadth of earth, not a stone of our fortresses.' From the fall of Napoléon on, Bismarck's diplomatic activity to make victory secure lost more and more of its identity of aims with military action. He himself expressed his new purpose in the following words :

> The task of those who command the army is to destroy the forces of the enemy ; the object of the war is to win peace on terms which are in accordance with the policy pursued by the state. The ways and means of waging war are always dependent on whether policy has been directed by the desire to attain the end finally won.

This indicated a reversal of Bismarck's former policy of preparing war almost into its opposite, the preparation for peace, while the military forces were still in the midst of war, thus retaining their former objective and perhaps devoting themselves to it even more vigorously than before. In this reversal of his aims Bismarck had on the occasion of the conversations at Domchéry failed to obtain any support from Napoléon. Later on he lost also the support of the Prussian military authorities and experienced their violent opposition. Napoléon had declined to let himself be moved about as a willing pawn in Bismarck's political game of chess, as he had done so often before. The new French government, however, had clamorously vowed war to the knife and seemed to have killed in the bud any movement towards peace.

So Bismarck officially took the standpoint that ' the German governments in France have up to the present not recognized any government save that of the Emperor Napoléon' and do not look upon any other ' as competent for international negotiations '. He had in this way to seek of his own accord his manner of working for peace within the framework of the war of expansion planned by him under the guise of a war of defence. A hint was given of his own views by a pamphlet unofficially circulated in Germany about the end of August with his consent. This demanded a ' single Reich and secure frontiers '. In the next weeks, in consequence of the victories which had been won, the idea of securing the frontiers was clarified—we should not say changed—into that of extending them, by the acquisition of the French fortresses of Strassburg and Metz with the border territories of Alsace and Lorraine. This meant, as had Bismarck's attitude in the Polish and Danish questions, the refusal of boundaries based on nationality, and in this instance the refusal was made in the interest of strategic frontiers. The method now adopted by Bismarck in order officially to open his campaign for the establishment of such a peace was the same as that adopted by the new French government, that of sending a circular note to the diplomatic representatives abroad. Indeed, two such notes were sent out in rapid succession a few days after the French one. Bismarck took up a word which Napoléon had let fall to the effect that the latter had been forced to make war by the pressure of public opinion and that, when peace had been made after the present defeats, the French nation would only wait for the day on which they could ' successfully realize in action their desire to avenge the wounds dealt to their vanity and their ambition '. Prussia, Bismarck says, had been ' forced into the war which she had tried to avoid '. She must therefore have guarantees ' against the next attack ', and she ' must demand them not from a temporary government of France but from the French nation '. They were to be found by ' moving further back the hitherto defenceless south German frontier, the starting point of French attacks ' and by bringing ' the fortresses with which France threatened her under the power of Germany as a defensive bulwark '. This Bismarck describes as ' the unanimous voice of the German governments and the German people '. In the second, supplementary, document Bismarck goes on, becoming clearer :

Our terms of peace are dictated to us by the law of self-defence against a violent and unpeaceable neighbour people. As long as France remains in the possession of Strassburg and Metz, her offensive is strategically stronger than our defensive as regards the whole of south Germany. In German possession Strassburg and Metz acquire a defensive character. In more than twenty wars we have never been the aggressor against France. From Germany no disturbance of European peace is to be feared.

The first effect of these circular notes was remarkable enough. The new French government had, in spite of the intransigent standpoint which it had publicly taken up, promptly sent out feelers through London to the Prussian headquarters and had made contact with them by this underground communication. Although Bismarck's circular notes indicated an almost unbridgeable gap between the aims of the two parties and therefore were bound to have the tendency to frighten off the French, Jules Favre decided to make a direct approach to Bismarck with a view to an armistice. The negotiations between the two statesmen took place on the 19th and 20th of September in the neighbourhood of the Prussian headquarters. They remained, as was indeed to have been expected, without any objective result. This did not prevent the great historian and politician, Adolphe Thiers, the most representative person of the France of that day, from renewing the attempt, with the same negative result. From Favre we have a picturesque description of Bismarck as his opponent in the negotiations.

His great height, his mighty head, his impressive features, gave him a presence at once commanding and hard yet softened by a natural simplicity. I was struck by the clarity of his thoughts, the keenness of his understanding, the originality of his mental make-up. As a man of business in politics he seemed to me superior to anything one can imagine. He is a man who only takes account of what is a 'fact and is only concerned with positive and practical solutions.

Bismarck, however, is even better characterized by the characterization which he gives himself of the other French negotiator, Thiers :

He is an able and likeable man, but with hardly a trace of diplomatic quality, he is not fit to make a bargain about an armistice, hardly fit, indeed, to buy or sell a horse, he betrays his feelings and lets himself be pumped. I got all sorts of things out of him ; for instance, that they have only three or four weeks' provision left inside.

In what a practical fashion Bismarck tackled the problem of making peace is shown by the fact that he repeatedly considered, publicly announced, and in fact prepared the way for the opening of negotiations with Napoléon and even with the Empress, then living in England. He went so far as to think of restoring freedom to the Emperor and his armies and even of giving him a free hand in Belgium in order to play out in France one political force against the other, as he had so often successfully done in his political activities.

For, just because of his ' practical ' attitude, the complete failure of the attempts he had hitherto made for peace was not quite indifferent to Bismarck. His remark, ' He [i.e., Favre] seems to be in a hurry, but we are not,' was not entirely straightforward. For, in fact, there were reasons too why he should think a certain haste required. In the first place, following the commencement of the siege of Paris there began under Gambetta the people's war of the republican government. It was conducted with flamboyant *élan* and such fanatical fury as to make it formidable even for the well-organized German army with its habit of victory. The latter had now to face the desperate efforts of the French people to save their capital from investment by the invaders. Further, Bismarck's attempts at peace were complicated by the danger of the intervention of neutral Powers. This followed immediately on the great military victories, since these gave grounds to fear a radical change in the balance of power which could not leave neutral Powers unaffected. Already soon after the battle of Sédan, Beust proposed in London that a ' common movement for the re-establishment of peace ' should be undertaken, so as to ' see Europe emerge from the kind of stupor in which she has fallen in face of the great revolution '. Bismarck opposed the carrying out of such joint efforts in his circular notes of the middle of September, in which he said that it would be ' a cruel act of the neutrals if they allowed the Paris government to foster unrealizable hopes of intervention and thereby prolong the war '. But he himself assisted these efforts by making known his terms of peace with their demand for the alteration of frontiers which was everywhere received with indignation. A circular tour by the venerable Adolphe Thiers, who with devoted zeal visited the courts of London, St. Petersburg, Vienna, and Florence, worked in the same direction. But the only result was an exchange of opinions among the neutrals, not joint action. At the beginning of October Beust made use of the siege of Paris which was just beginning and the consequent menace to the food supplies of its two million inhabitants in order to repeat the reference to collective action. This time it was accompanied by the argument that ' in the judgement of history part of the responsibility will fall on the neutrals if they in dumb indifference let the menace of unheard-of wrong be placed before their eyes '. The Austrian government held it to be ' their duty to declare that they still believed in common European interests and that they would prefer a peace brought by the unbiased work of neutrals to the annihilation of more hundreds of thousands '. ' If there was no Europe left to seek this end ', Beust wrote later, ' that was Bismarck's work.' In fact, Bismarck was just engaged in dealing a very serious blow at the idea of European community by considering the bombardment of Paris. He had also prepared diplomatically for this blow with his characteristic circumspection and expertness. For the two Powers, England and Russia, whom Beust had begged to intervene on behalf of this idea were just the two Powers whom Bismarck had managed to bring into opposition to each other by his offer to support Russia if she should denounce the clause about the Black Sea coast.

So, although the danger of 'an understanding between the neutral Powers about their measures to influence the peace' was not very immediate, Bismarck, according to his own account, was very much afraid of intervention from these quarters, since it 'could only have the tendency to curtail the prize of victory for us Germans by means of a congress'. Therefore he was 'in a state of uneasiness by day and by night' considering how to 'hurry up the conclusion of peace as effectively as possible'. But this pre-supposed the possession of Paris. Thus Paris which for the neutrals symbolized 'the belief in common European interests', had for him now nothing to do with this 'discovery of Europe', but grew to be of major political and military significance.

That the conclusion of peace would not have been practicable before the taking of Paris [he argued] was to be foreseen in view of the traditional predominance of the capital in France. As long as Paris held out, it was not to be expected from the provinces that they would give up hope of a change in fortune.

Thus it was important not only to take Paris, but to take it quickly. The method, however, by which Bismarck wished to bring about the quick capture of Paris was to bombard the city with heavy guns. But, when he made known this intention, he aroused a fresh storm of indignation, not only among the neutrals but this time even among his own ranks. Bismarck asserted that these objections 'had come from England to our camp by devious routes through Berlin'. He spoke of the 'slogan of the "Mecca of Civilization"' and of other 'useful applications of English cant'. He accused England of 'expecting other Powers to behave humanely, but of not always showing humanity to her own opponents'. In Berlin these humanitarian objections against the bombardment of Paris were suspected by Bismarck to have the support of a number of influential ladies of English descent, and especially of the Crown Princess. The Crown Prince noted at this time in his diary : 'It is now the order of the day to vilify my wife as being mainly responsible for the postponement of the bombardment of Paris and to accuse her of acting under the direction of the Queen of England, all this exasperates me beyond measure.' But Bismarck also brought reproaches of this kind against Queen Augusta even in the presence of the King. Once again he did not shrink from allowing his political designs to affect the most personal and intimate relationship of his royal master. He reports himself that he had hinted to the King about the rumours which 'ascribed to Queen Augusta the exercise of an influence in the direction of humanity on her exalted husband by means of her letters'.

This communication, however, produced 'a sharp outbreak of anger' on the part of the King. But, in his anger, he did not imply 'that the rumour was unfounded, yet only uttered severe threats against any expression of such a suspicion against the Queen'.

In his efforts to pave the way for peace and to hasten this by the bombardment of Paris, Bismarck encountered a new opponent, in relation to whom the opposition of views took on a particularly far-reaching and fundamental character. This antagonism was to be found in the leaders of the Prussian army, headed by the high authority of the Prussian General Staff. Since Bismarck's former policy of preparing war had changed into its opposite, the preparation for peace, whereas the military command were still in the middle of their former task, that of making war, this discrepancy in goal had the most harmful effect on the collaboration between the two authorities. On the 9th of August Bismarck had apologized on behalf of the army for inadequacies in the communication of military reports to the political government, and on the 20th of September he still invited the generals to a discussion in which he reported to them the negotiations with Jules Favre. But there is no doubt that already at this time the military authorities held the view which Bismarck formulates in the following way : 'The foreign minister can speak again only when the commanders of the army find that the time has come to close the temple of Janus.' The dispute now took a personal colouring and so fitted in with Bismarck's custom of using his personal antagonisms to gain a new zest in his struggle for objective aims. The dispute also gave Bismarck the opportunity to live himself into the rôle of a victim of aggression in order thereby to strengthen his own will to aggression. He professed that he had 'brought home from the Austrian war the ill will of the higher military circles' and was not surprised when this 'continued during the French war'. He points out that 'the competent minister can only give the King adequately informed advice if he has knowledge of the present position and the plans for conducting the war'. Bismarck complains that the military authorities had decided not only 'to exclude him from military discussions', but even 'to keep all military measures and plans as a rule in strict secrecy as far as he was concerned'. As to the position of the King, Bismarck reported the latter's own statement, quoting what he described as '*ipsissima verba regis*'. According to these, he, Bismarck,

in the Bohemian [i.e., Austrian] war had as a rule been included in the Council of war, and it had happened there that, in opposition to the majority, he had hit the nail on the head; that this had annoyed the generals and that they wished to deliberate about their department alone was, not surprising.

Bismarck asserts that in the French war he had sometimes to depend for his knowledge of military events on the communications of some Princes who accompanied headquarters as sightseers, and that also the English correspondent, Russell of the *Times*, had been a useful source of his informations.

As regards the speeding-up of the siege of Paris now under discussion, it was supported not only by the political grounds brought forward by Bismarck, but doubtless also by military considerations. It was obviously desirable to bring the siege to an end before the French people's army could become a source of danger for the besiegers. Also, as the siege drew on, they would have to reckon with epidemics among the investing forces. But the military authorities gave a different answer to the question whether the hurrying on of the siege would be effected by the bombardment of the city with heavy artillery. On this question the smouldering glow of opposition between Bismarck and the military broke into open flame. ' War was declared within the headquarters ', writes one of the best authorities on Bismarck's life work. It was doubtless an overstepping of the limits of his department for Bismarck now to demand that bombardment should be used to hurry on the siege, for this was clearly a technical question of military tactics. However, there was among the generals one who was of Bismarck's opinion, the war minister, von Roon. This fact sufficed to make Bismarck not only condemn the opposite view, but also look for discreditable motives behind it.

If we ask what can have led other generals to oppose the view of Roon it will be hard to find objective grounds for the delay [i.e., of the bombardment]. From the military as well as from the political point of view the hesitating policy seems senseless and dangerous; and that the grounds for it are not to be sought in the indecision of our military commanders we may conclude from the swift and decisive conduct of the war up to the gates of Paris.

That the motives of the opponents of the bombardment were to be condemned Bismarck was the more ready to suspect because a leading position among them was occupied by the Crown Prince who was the commander of the besieging army, and also by the latter's chief of staff. However, the principal opponent of Bismarck was the highest strategic authority in the whole Prussian army, von Moltke.

Already at the beginning of the siege of Paris the military command had arranged for the supply of heavy guns from Germany together with the requisite ammunition. But since these guns could not move on their own wheels transport difficulties arose. The latter could be used as pretext by those who were opposed to the whole scheme. The Crown Prince and his entourage held the reduction of the city by starvation to be the preferable course. On the 22nd of October there is the following entry in the diary of the Crown Prince :

> To-day the first works began for building the siege batteries. Though I have ordered the preparations for a siege to be carried out with the greatest energy and all possible judgement, I am still in hope that Paris will be forced simply and solely by hunger to open her gates to us, and that many lives will thus be spared to us.

To this Bismarck later on made the noteworthy reply :

> Whether the method of bringing about the surrender of Paris by means of hunger was the more humane may be disputed. It also may be disputed whether the horrors of the commune would have broken out if the period of hunger had not prepared the way for the unshackling of savagery.

In the case of Moltke the motives for his attitude were no doubt of a military character. In particular he was concerned whether the heavy siege artillery would have an effect worth the trouble of bringing it up and would not perhaps involve very costly attempts to storm the town. But even in the case of Moltke Bismarck imputes in a veiled manner some improper motive, combining with the reference to the English wife of the Crown Prince the statement that the ' deceased wife ' of Moltke was an Englishwoman. Bismarck now again says of the King that he had been on the side of the military and against himself, not indeed as the driving force, but as the driven, who where possible was led into error. ' The initiative in bringing about any change in the conduct of the war ', so he reports in connexion with the bombardment, ' did not as a rule come from the King, but from the General Staff of the army or the highest commander on the spot, the Crown Prince.'

So the two sides had closed their ranks for the ' war at headquarters ', when in November Bismarck came to the conclusion that if the siege would continue in the present way the daily reports " Nothing new in the Paris sector " must last for ever and the town could not be taken at all. Consequently the military situation in front of Paris had ceased to be a help and became a hindrance for the policy of preparing the way to peace. The heavy siege artillery did indeed gradually arrive and was mounted at the prearranged points. But progress could not be made with the provision of munitions. The sight of the guns, from which Bismarck had expected the greatest success, still standing idle raised his impatience to the utmost extreme.

> Everyone here complains about hindrance of an anonymous character [he writes to his wife] ; one man says that the artillery transports are kept back on the railways, so that they do not arrive ; another lays the

blame on the neglect of earlier preparations; a third says there is still not enough ammunition, a fourth that the gun emplacements are not completed.

At the same time Bismarck was himself soldier enough to recognize that ' the bombardment could not be begun till the requisite quantity of ammunition for carrying it through effectively without interruption was available '. One reason for delay stuck especially in his memory, namely that there were about 600 trucks laden with provisions for the Parisians in order to give them swift help if they surrendered, and these 600 trucks were therefore not available for the transport of ammunition. Bismarck suspected the ' influential ladies of English descent ' to be behind this arrangement and fell into a stormy and bitter mood. He spoke of his ' midnight anger ' against Princes and General Staff, ' attacks of undermining distrust and hot rage ' mastered him. He did indeed succeed in winning to his side the King ' who in his heart was always on the side of the " shooters " ', but the ' good and clever old Moltke ' held fast to his views. For him an open battle in the field was always the decisive measure in war. Moltke has ' become old and lets things take care of themselves ', Bismarck thought. But the real fury of Bismarck's hate was directed against the Crown Prince and the military ' demigods' of the General Staff, with whom 'success has gone to their heads and produced emperor-madness'. Again as formerly in similar situations Bismarck's homelife and wife come to the forefront. The anxiety about his two sons who both belonged to the fighting forces and of whom the elder had been wounded; sometimes also the interest in his own estate, which shows itself in detailed directions to his bailiff, served to cover the irritation aroused by the disappointment in his professional activities. Bismarck sought out solitude, he went for lonely rides at Versailles ' in the clear autumnal air of the wide plains through Louis XIV's long straight drives, through rustling leaves and trimmed hedges by quiet ponds and gods sculptured in marble ', and ' gave myself up to the nostalgia which the fall of the leaves and the solitude in a foreign land bring, with childhood memories of clipped hedges that are no more '. He felt himself ' politically and emotionally alone without anybody with whom to exchange views ', and described how, after eight years of office and success, ' the cold swamp of envy and hate gradually rose higher and higher till it reached my heart. In short, I spiritually shiver and long to be with you '.

However, the increasing depression of Bismarck did not diminish but rather augmented the energy which he threw into the pursuit of his goal. It meant for him a decided step forward towards this goal when one day Roon told him ' that he had now been personally given responsibility by being asked whether he was ready to bring up the munitions in a foreseeable time. But he was in doubt as regards the possibility of doing this'. It appeared that in consequence of the lack of rail transport a large number of horses were needed thus involving an expense of millions of marks. Bismarck replied in grandiloquent style : ' I cannot understand what doubts there could be about whether these millions of marks were available, as soon as they were needed for military purposes.' According to his account he asked Roon ' to take on at once the task which had been set him ', adding : ' I declared myself ready to debit the Federal Treasury with any sum that was needed for this, if Roon would buy the 4000 horses or so, which he had described as his approximate requirement, and set them to bring up the munitions.' Yet a little while later he again wrote to his wife : ' Our guns are still silent, about three times as many have arrived as are needed for the moment. It seems as though they are going to let the 400 heavy barkers and the 100 thousands of hundredweights of shells remain there till the peace and then take them back to Berlin.' On Christmas Eve there appeared a first gleam of light, though it certainly did not come from the Star of Bethlehem. ' At last there is a prospect of firing against Paris, I hope before New Year's Eve,' is Bismarck's Christmas greeting to his wife. ' At last, at last ', we read in the diary of one of Bismarck's assistants, ' on December 27th the long-desired bombardment of Paris began on the east side of the city.' Many years later Bismarck spoke of the ' bombardment of Mont Avron, long awaited with painful impatience and greeted with joy ' as ' a result of the turn in affairs which we owe mainly to Roon '. But much of his ' soldier-worship ' he thought he had lost in the course of this winter.

But a still keener and more embittered struggle between the Chancellor and the military lay ahead. The bombardment of Paris by heavy guns had its effect. ' The former opponents of the attack have been converted ', Bismarck wrote already at the beginning of 1871, ' and almost all former opponents have sour looks at the swift successes of the artillery. For everyone says in secret that we could have done this two months ago.' Speaking of January 1871 Moltke said in retrospect : ' The effect of six days' bombardment was decisive.' In Paris the lack of food increased, and political disturbances broke out among the population. Sorties by the Paris garrison ended in complete failure ; the people's army fighting in the south of France sustained one defeat after another and approached a state of dissolution. In the first weeks of 1871 it was a question of discussing in the Prussian headquarters the terms for the capitulation of Paris and the armistice with France, and so of preparing the basis for negotiations with the representatives of the enemy. Now again Moltke became an opponent of Bismarck, and was now himself guilty of passing beyond the bounds of his department and entering the foreign territory of politics. The peace terms approved by Bismarck were themselves by no means modest; he did not object to the acquisition of Strassburg and Metz with considerable parts of Alsace and Lorraine, and a high war indemnity. These terms were intended to make possible a speedy peace without the intervention of the neutrals. Yet to these terms Moltke opposed the absolute will to annihilation characteristic of the military. In the event of the capitulation of Paris he demanded that the war should be carried on in the south of France till the enemy was completely destroyed. This time the opposition between the two men quite openly took on a personal character. After they had kept away from each other for weeks the Crown Prince invited them both to a meal. But instead of the reconciliation for which he had hoped, the gulf between them was only widened. Moltke was more caustic than the hot-tempered Bismarck, and the definite stand taken by each showed clearly how great the difference is between the military and the political view of the conduct of the state and how irreconcilable they may be. Now Bismarck turned to the King and asked him to decide the dispute. The King decided in favour of Bismarck and admonished Moltke to abandon his objections to Bismarck's proposed terms for the capitulation and armistice. In great excitement Moltke had worked out a sharp reply to the request of his lord, but replaced it by a milder one, and finally by one milder still. He first put forward the alternative : ' He or I ', but later he confined himself to a counter-complaint, though still a violent one, with the request of equal and fair treatment. Finally, Moltke restrained himself altogether, pigeonholed all the three drafts, and subjected himself to the will of the King. Bismarck remained both objectively and personally the victor ; as always, the element of personal opposition had contributed to his energy in pursuing the objective goal. In the end he could not restrain himself from complaining that the King had intervened in too mild a way. Yet Bismarck's greatest admirer is convinced that the opposition could not have been removed if the King had not intervened ' with an authority which gave way, avoided complications, smoothed things over, and yet remained authority'.

On the basis of the agreement which had been reached among the parties within the Prussian headquarters and the military successes achieved before Paris, Bismarck now devoted his energies to keeping the European Powers neutral and making France comply with the conditions of peace to be imposed on her. Since Italy's attention was fully occupied and her desire satisfied by the occupation and incorporation in her territory of Rome, and England and Russia were more interested in the political and military arrangements relating to the Black Sea coast than in the Franco-Prussian war, the only serious threat could come from Austria. But Beust, despite all his sympathy with ' the idea of European community ', had neither the power nor the will to expose Austria to a new struggle with victorious Prussia. So, in fact, Bismarck had in the main, while negotiating armistice and peace terms, to deal with the French alone. Among the latter there was a division between those willing to come to terms, headed by Thiers and Favre, and the intransigents under Gambetta. Once again Bismarck considered starting negotiations with Napoléon or even with the Empress and proposed this to his sovereign. Making himself the fulcrum in the balance in a conflict between the French political forces, however, proved to be superfluous this time. His former adversary in negotiations, Favre, appeared again, now ready to go very far to meet him. On the 28th of January there was concluded the Convention of Versailles, which involved, as regards Paris, capitulation, and, as regards France as a whole, a three weeks' armistice to allow elections to determine a new government. Gambetta yielded on the 6th of February after an unsuccessful attempt at obstruction. The elections took place two days later. As a result of them Thiers, now chief of the French executive, and Favre became plenipotentiaries of France in the peace negotiations. Once again Bismarck brought all his capacities as a negotiator and mediator into play. Certain concessions were made to the military, others to neutrals and to the south German states. The strategic frontier, adopted by Bismarck from the beginning, was conceded by the French with a further extension, beyond what Bismarck had before wanted, near Metz. The victorious army was allowed to march into Paris, though there was no prolonged occupation. On the other hand the demand of Belfort, pressed by the Prussian General Staff, was dropped, and the war indemnity originally demanded was reduced. The result was that in all quarters, among the military, in the neutral states, among the south German Cabinet ministers whose opinion had been asked, even among the French negotiators and their compatriots, men were to be found who looked upon the terms of the preliminary peace, concluded on the 26th of February, as at least in part their own work, and yet these terms exactly corresponded to what Bismarck had originally set as his goal.

There followed at Frankfurt-on-Main discussions about particulars of the new frontier and the mode of payment of the indemnity, till at last the final peace was signed on the 10th of May 1871.

CHAPTER XXIII

The New Reich

Bismarck's task of diplomatically accompanying the course and securing the issue of the war made great demands on his diplomacy and resolution, but this was not the only task which occupied him in these days, and not even the most important. The negotiations which Bismarck conducted with Napoléon in the 'room ten foot square' in Domchéry determined the birth of a new state, which extended the North German Confederacy into a union comprising the whole of the German nation. This union was destined now to take over from France the leadership of Europe as a Great Power at the head of the Great Powers. It was thus for Bismarck to give to the state for which he had striven the form which made it secure and strong in its position as a Great Power and at the same time gave it the necessary inner cohesion as a Confederacy. The account due for 'two centuries of twenty French wars of aggression' meant for Bismarck not only the dethronement of France from her position at the head of all continental Powers, but also the enthronement of Prussia in the same exalted position, the claim to succession being made as victor by 'right of conquest'. While Bismarck had formerly spoken of Prussia's 'preference for carrying armour too large for our frail body', now it was his aim to give to the small body of Prussia the increased size and weight to enable her not only to occupy this high seat among the other Powers, but to fill it and to make it inaccessible for others.

The way to this extension seemed to Bismarck to be unambiguously prescribed by his words of the 'coincidence of the two ends: leadership of Prussia from the Prussian point of view and unification of Germany from the national point of view'. But also the deeds which Bismarck had undertaken hitherto, the defensive and offensive alliances with the south German states, the development of the Customs Union into a Customs Confederacy with a Customs parliament, the realization of the alliances by persuading the states concerned to take an active part as Prussian allies under Prussian command in the sanguinary settlement with France, all made in this direction. It was only a logical step and not a very large one, to make a formal change in the 'international independence' of the southern states, which now only existed on paper, by incorporating them legally in the North German Confederacy.

Bismarck did not use this incorporation as the only means of attaining a Great Power status for Prussia, but employed another method too, the annexation of Alsace and Lorraine. Thus, he went on to give to the new state an extension of its domain which had nothing to do with the national unification of Germany, being merely able to secure and fortify Prussia's position as a Great Power. Bismarck did not seek this extension where it could have been most easily understood and justified from a national point of view, in the German part of Austria. At this time he did not support any policy which had the least smattering of the 'Dualism' which had influenced his own policy between Olmütz (1850) and Schönbrunn (1864) so many times and so decisively. On the contrary the annexation of Alsace and Lorraine involved the extension of Prussia's own territory at the direct expense of her beaten rival in the struggle for hegemony in Europe. Alsace and Lorraine had by no means been a really decisive factor in the liberal German movement for unity. Bismarck as a young politician had, more than twenty years earlier, brought against this movement as a reproach that it had not turned 'the first élan of German strength and unity to demanding that France should surrender Alsace and to hoisting the German flag on the tower of Strassburg cathedral'. Alsace, and still more Lorraine with Metz, regarded Paris and not Berlin as their cultural and political centre. The demand for the incorporation of Alsace and above all of Lorraine meant the rejection of an ethnological in favour of a strategic frontier. Still, Bismarck had objected to the incorporation of Austria into the German Reich on the ground that she was not throughout the German nationality, and had said in discussing the Danish question: 'I deem a living together of Germans in the same community with opposed nationalities as not useful.' The question of a plebiscite in the annexed districts he never raised, for it would have been all too rash to maintain that 'even a part of the population' had the wish to be united with German territory. As for the claim that the two fortresses served an offensive strategy in French hands and a defensive in German, on the ground that the south German frontier was defenceless, it is an altogether transparent screen. For the Rhine flowing between these fortresses and south Germany, though no doubt strong as a means of offensive warfare, was, combined with the Black Forest, not at all to be despised as a defensive line in the then state of military means. The objection to the existing frontier might perhaps be not that it provided no good defence for Germany, but that it provided too good a defence for France. In fact, the fortresses of Strassburg and Metz were of decisive importance in the German scheme for an offensive in 1914; besides serving as immediate bases for offensive operations, they kept very large enemy forces pinned down, and thus, though not necessary to make possible offensive operations farther north, at any rate made these very much easier than they would otherwise have been.

This suggests a new answer to the question how Bismarck understood the coincidence of the two ends : Prussian leadership and unification of Germany. Already at the end of the Danish and still more at that of the Austrian war he had shown that for him the leadership of Prussia was an end in itself and the unification of Germany not much more than a means to this end. What he then did was decided by the desire for that leadership and as regards manner and extent the unification had to be adapted to this. But now, it was not only that the unification of Germany was a mere means, but that it was only one means among others, and had to be linked with other means, which in content and significance stood in contradiction to it and could signify for it a source of dangers. For this other means to Prussian leadership, the annexation of Alsace and Lorraine, was alien to the original German nationalism, and was the mere expression of military power politics, of what Bismarck had called earlier the ' real relations of power ' based on the ' serried ranks of our troops '. Thus Bismarck's solution of the German question is not only anti-liberal, but at the same time also anti-national. In Bismarck's hand it was expressly a solution by open force. Thus he was false to the task which events had set him and which he had set himself.

The annexation of French territory was bound to be regarded by the French people, whose watchword had been : ' We surrender to the enemy not a finger's breadth of earth, not a stone of our fortresses,' as an ever-open wound to their national pride. It was bound to be an unquenchable source of desire for military revenge and therefore impose on the victor the task of a protracted preparation for war. As is shown by his speech in the Reichstag of the 2nd of May 1871, Bismarck knew perfectly well what incorporation of foreign territory meant for the political attitude of the state which had been robbed. He had considered this question very carefully during the Austro-Prussian war and on that occasion, on account of the danger of continued political enmity being aroused by annexations, had decided to dispense with these, despite strong opposition in his own camp. Such recollections can hardly have failed to be present in his mind when he thought of annexing Alsace and Lorraine, and must have led to doubts as to the wisdom of annexing any territory and the extent of such annexations. But these doubts did not determine Bismarck's decision. He repudiated the idea of merely dismantling the two fortresses or of incorporating them into a new buffer state. He even considered and rejected the creation of a twenty-mile zone from which the French population was to be evacuated to make room for German settlers. We also have good reason to deny that the decision of annexation was forced on Bismarck as a second best, as a last resort in relation to the completion of national unity by extending it to south Germany. Both aims were revealed to the world at about the same time independently of each 'other. At the end of July 1870, Bismarck had allowed mention in the Reichstag of ' the battlefield as the place of union for the German people '. At the end of August there appeared a leaflet not opposed by him which alluded in the same breath to the two ideas of ' a united Reich and secured frontiers ', and then there came, in the middle of September, the official circular notes which expressly defined the way in which the securing of the frontier was to be effected, namely by the annexation of Strassburg and Metz. But, while in justifying his action he did not forget to refer to ' the united voice of the German governments and the German people ', nothing was said of the voice of the people of Alsace-Lorraine. Within the German people none sought their voice ; as outsiders their voice was drowned.

Both the strategical and the national extensions of the territory of the victor were the subject of controversy within its own borders. As regards Alsace-Lorraine doubts were at first brought forward as to whether annexation ought to take place at all, and there was a more marked division as to whether the extent of the annexation should be determined purely by military or also by cultural and racial considerations. But the most disputed topic was to which of the German states this prize of victory should fall. The south German states were all mentioned as candidates, at least by themselves. Baden was the immediate neighbour along almost the whole eastern border of Alsace ; Bavaria, the strongest south German Power, possessed the Palatinate bordering Alsace in the north; Württemberg and Hesse-Darmstadt also had territorial ambitions in the interest of which this new conquest could serve at least as an object of exchange. Treitschke spoke on behalf of Prussia ; he wished to bring Prussia into south Germany and to trust the defence of the frontier to Prussia alone. Bismarck did not agree with any of these proposals. He chose a compromise solution, which was to turn out badly. He did not wish to give Alsace-Lorraine to south Germany, because it would strengthen the political power of the latter. Prussia received the military sovereignty and therefore the function of protecting the frontiers of the newly acquired land. To give her also the civil sovereignty would have aroused the envy and dislike of the other, particularly the south German, states. Bismarck also knew that ' the Alsatians would rather resign themselves to becoming Germans than " Prussians " '. So he took civil sovereignty only indirectly for Prussia, namely in her capacity as president of the Confederacy. Alsace-Lorraine was declared a ' Reichsland ', thus placing it directly under the sovereignty of the Reich as a whole. Having no immediate connexion with any of the single states and being itself no single state, it therefore necessarily came to be dependent on the strongest state—Prussia. Since the population was not related to the population of any of the victor states, but was entirely isolated, the wound which severance from France had left behind remained unhealed, not only in France but in the severed territories too. The feeling of being a stranger and of distrust towards the victorious states constituted a wall of division, perpetually increasing and strengthening itself; the lamentation of France for the ' daughter' who was snatched away from her found an echo that became ever deeper and more sincere.

Objectively of greater importance than the extension of power by annexation of conquered territory was that through the expansion of national unity to cover the south. While in the former case open force was employed without a cloak, here the way of voluntary union by agreement was chosen, here any talk of open force should be impossible and the disguise cloaking the force behind it impenetrable. Bismarck was indeed a master not only in pulling all the strings for impressing his will on another in the guise of winning his reason by convincing arguments, but also in utilizing such almost imperceptible gradations that the other party was hardly conscious how the screw was being turned. Now, he had also put in far-reaching and far-sighted preliminary work for the winning of the south German states, so that, as one of his admirers says : ' The compulsion of things-to-be of itself already drove these lands forwards.' However, his project was very differently received in the different states. In Baden, where the son-in-law of King William was the ruler, there was hardly any resistance ; government and country alike were prepared to accept almost without limitation anything which was asked of them. The northern part of Hesse-Darmstadt already belonged to the North German Confederacy, and for the southern part resistance hardly came in question. In Württemberg the opposition to the unification of Germany under Prussia was considerable ; the sovereign and his wife were not in favour, and the population, looking back to a democratic tradition, resisted it. To give the advocates of unification the upper hand, the military victories in France and the dissolution of parliament followed by fresh elections under the influence of strong propaganda were necessary. The representative of Württemberg, sent to Versailles, was very cautious in the negotiations and not easily accessible to influences on his will. Not till the end of November did Bismarck succeed in coming to an agreement with him after the concession of certain privileges similar to those granted to Saxony.

The most difficult partner was Bavaria. Bismarck had prejudiced himself with regard to her. For he had in the days before the outbreak of the Austrian war proposed a reform in the Confederation which would not only exclude Austria from the latter, but also allow Bavaria as leading state in the South an analogous position to Prussia as leading state in the North. Certainly, Bavaria had not then accepted the proposal, because she was at that time unwilling to share anything with arrogant Prussia. But this did not do away with the proposal altogether, for its basis remained, namely the fact that Bavaria was the only important state besides Prussia in the territory which it was proposed to take over. It was also of significance that there sat in these years on the throne of Bavaria a personality who was not without active influence on the political fortune of his land, a man of an original and self-willed stamp. Of the persons with whom Bismarck had so far had to do, King Ludwig II of Bavaria reminds us most of King Frederick William IV. Like the latter he was incoherent in thought and very ready to jump to conclusions; and the same applied to his will. He had the gifts of an artist and was many-sided in his interests, shut up in a world of imagination and unwilling to enter reality. He was filled with a consciousness of the high dignity of his royal vocation, yet always on the look-out for purely earthly values and interests, a true Bavarian and self-conscious member of the serene family of the Wittelsbach, but yet open to a gleam of national German patriotism. So the King was an adversary in negotiations of whom it was hard to get hold and still harder to keep hold. He was certainly not an equal match for Bismarck and not comparable in personal significance to some of the men with whom Bismarck had had a reckoning before, but still he was a person who had to be approached with caution and could only be kept to the point with skill.

Already at the middle of September several national liberal party-leaders from Berlin arrived in Munich in order to open negotiations with their party friends there and the Bavarian ministers about the question of unification. At the end of the month Delbrück followed them in accordance with the direct orders of Bismarck. What Delbrück was to carry out, namely the extension of the constitution of the Confederacy to include Bavaria, went much beyond what the Bavarians were willing to grant, which was only a treaty of alliance between the two states. After prolonged efforts Delbrück, acting under Bismarck's instructions from Versailles and carefully pushing forward, succeeded in inducing Bavaria to accept the constitution of the Confederacy at least as a basis for negotiations and to formulate her wishes for special privileges within this constitution. The demand for such privileges went so far as to affect not only the civil sovereignty of the Confederacy, especially in legislation, finance, and economic life, but even to threaten very considerably the military sovereignty, which had been hardly challenged by

Saxony and Württemberg, and the sovereignty in foreign affairs. These negotiations in Munich cleared the field, but did not achieve any substantial result. The discussions were then transferred to Versailles and directly taken in hand by Bismarck. The personality of the strange Bavarian King became less, that of the strong Prussian minister, more prominent. The negotiations with the four south German states thus were centred in Versailles, yet they were not carried out in common but separately, in order to exclude the possibility of joint opposition and to make it possible to play out the concessions of the one against the resistance of another. Bismarck retained his reserve, the Bavarians their suspicion. Bavaria again started the negotiations with the wish to remain outside the Confederacy and only bind herself by treaty. After a fortnight the Bavarian plenipotentiary, driven into a corner by Bismarck, suddenly abandoned the idea of a mere treaty. The incorporation of Bavaria into the Confederacy was secured. Now Bavaria shifted the main point of the negotiations to the demand for special privileges and, since the Achilles heel of their opponents was naturally known to the Bavarians, to special privileges in military matters. They demanded a far-reaching military independence, a separate army organization, even a separate military budget of their own. The picture was also spoiled by the wishes expressed by Bavaria in foreign politics; but after ten days there was found here and in internal politics a tolerable solution. The military organization remained the apple of discord which apparently could not be made palatable. Even after it had been divided it was hardly tasty to either party. In place of the separate Bavarian military budget proposed, it was agreed that the whole cost of the Bavarian army should be authorized by the Reich and the Reichstag, but that the detailed expenditure of this sum should be left to the Bavarian parliament. A Bavarian army was retained with the Bavarian King as commander in peace time, but it was made subject to Prussian supreme command in war, this being expressed in a special formulation of the oath to the colours. The Bavarians were given independence as regards the arming and training of their forces, but the uniformity of this with that of Prussia was to be secured by inspections in time of peace. A number of difficult compromises were also necessary in not altogether insignificant questions of form and externals in military matters. On the evening of the 23rd of November Bismarck joined his assistants in Versailles with the words: ' Well now, the Bavarian agreement is made and signed. German unity is complete.'

However, he had in fact not advanced as far as he thought; for also from the Prussian side there came complaints against Bismarck's extension of the national unity to south Germany. The conservatives objected in one breath to the preference given to the national liberals and to the ' submergence of Prussia in Germany '. Bismarck's old friend, Moritz von Blanckenburg, wrote after a visit to Bismarck at Versailles at the end of 1870 : ' I think of the political future with sorrow ' ; he was

terrified by the rash entry of Hesse, Württemberg, and Baden into the Confederacy, and I look upon it as a settled matter [he said] that the majority of the new Reichstag must become national liberal, since it is impossible to obtain other elements from such quarters. The aim of all liberals remains to economize in military matters. Yes, an inner necessity drives them ; they are bound to devote all their efforts to disarming the forces after the peace.

Roon also, to whom this letter was directed, feared that a ' " liberal development " is bound to start in which the old flags will mean no more than an historic memory '.

However, these Prussian objections against the new Reich were not the really decisive ones. The most important objections from Prussia came from the royal house itself. The Reichstag during the session lasting from the 24th of November to the 10th of December 1870 had to express its views on the treaties concluded with the south German states. In these discussions the Reichstag—on hints coming from Versailles—took the view that in place of the expression ' Confederacy ' there should be substituted ' German Reich ' and for the expression ' Presidency of the Confederacy ' there should be substituted ' German Kaiser '. The Crown Prince, who since the beginning of the war had occupied himself with the extension of German national unity to south Germany, had directed special attention to the position and title of the head of the extended unity and had handed a memoir to Bismarck on the subject. When he discussed it with a confidant, the latter made the remark : ' The Prussians do not desire for their King a new name, but only new power.' ' Thereupon ', so the confidant reports, ' the Crown Prince burst forth with shining eyes, " No, he must become Kaiser." '

To the objection [so the report continues] that the south German Kings would hardly be content with such an arrangement, the Prince answered with the assumption that the power was now at our disposal to compel those who resisted. He admitted that the title Kaiser had in recent years depreciated in value and prestige, but he said ' This, however, is to be altered ' ; out of his princely pride there grew up in the soul of the Crown Prince the idea of the German Reich [so the report concludes].

However, this ' pride in the soul ' of the Prince was founded on that desire for open force, which Bismarck wished to avoid with all means at his disposal. To Bismarck's requirement that ' the basis of the relation which constituted the Confederacy should be trust in the loyalty of Prussia to her agreements ', the Prince opposed a quite open and unadulterated profession of violence. That Bismarck was annoyed by these wishes is intelligible. His comment on them was that the Prince 'lends his ear to political dreamers'. Also when the Crown Prince in direct conversation with him spoke in favour of the title 'King of the Germans', and maintained the view 'that the dynasties of Bavaria, Saxony and Württemberg would have to stop bearing the title of kings and revert to that of dukes', Bismarck naturally opposed this. It is noteworthy how much in earnest he was in opposing the proposal. He was clearly quite sincere in his dread that the forcible carrying through of this demand 'would not be forgotten for centuries and would scatter the seed of distrust and hate'. So Bismarck, too, had reckoned on a Reich lasting centuries and ascribed to his monarchical idea a validity that would satisfy ages to come.

Also King William had objections against Bismarck's new political creation. The latter asserts that the King in August 1870 on his way to joining his army in Mayence had spoken of the deposition of the King of Bavaria as a step towards German unification. Later on, however, his objections on the question of the title of Kaiser seemed to have stood very much in the foreground. In Bismarck's opinion he was dominated by ' the need to secure recognition for the superior prestige of the ancestral Prussian Crown rather than for that connected with the title of Kaiser'. His inclination was, by emphasizing the dignity of the Prussian kingship as a feature of his position in the Reich, ' to bring the superiority of our dynasty to the eyes of the other dynasties'. Bismarck met this petty-minded attitude to the decision to be taken with a counter-stroke of equal level. In the Prussian headquarters he met the Master of the Horse of the Bavarian King as personal liaison officer. The attitude of this King, in view of his power in the new Reich territory, was bound to be of special significance for the position and title of the future head of the Reich. Bismarck won the liaison officer for his own views :

> Prussian authority exercised within the bounds of Bavaria would hurt Bavarian feelings. Yet a German Kaiser would not be the neighbour but the compatriot of Bavaria. King Ludwig could more easily authorize the concessions which had been made [i.e., in the agreement of 23rd of November] if they were made to a German Kaiser rather than to a King of Prussia.

Bismarck induced the man to defend this view before his King Ludwig and eventually to go to the latter's residence with a document in his hand drawn up by Bismarck himself for the Bavarian King to copy, to sign, and to send as his own letter to the King of Prussia. The content of this letter was constituted by the

Bismarckian argument for the title Kaiser which has just been expounded. The argument was, however, strengthened, as Bismarck himself reports, by the 'forceful implication that Bavaria could make the granted but not yet ratified concessions *only* to the German Kaiser, not to the King of Prussia'. Bismarck added to this account the words : ' I had expressly chosen this turn of the argument in order to exercise pressure to overcome the aversion of my gracious sovereign to the title of Kaiser.' The method of 'winning unawares' was thus still in full use as a means to enable Bismarck to achieve his ends, and it was once again successful, and indeed with both Kings, since King Ludwig signed, and King William accepted the argument of the letter. The Prussian King now dropped his objection on principle to the title of Kaiser.

Yet there was still another demand put forward by Bismarck to the Bavarian King. The latter should ' propose the erection of the German Empire' to his fellow Princes in Germany. Here the method of 'winning unawares' does not seem to have been successful, for, as Lord Acton relates, the King of Bavaria agreed to this proposal only on the condition that ' in return £15,000 a year should be paid to him secretly out of the Guelphic Fund and that his Master of the Horse was handsomely rewarded out of the same purse'.

But a new difficulty arose. The Prussian King wished to be called ' Kaiser of Germany' not ' German Kaiser', Bismarck was against this title. He objected to the King that it 'involved the claim of sovereignty over the non-Prussian territory, a claim which the Princes would not be inclined to grant'. When this objection did not prevail, he abandoned the path of persuasion and attempted once more to win over the King 'unawares'. By the time of the solemn ' proclamation' of the newly created dignity of Kaiser in the palace of the French Kings at Versailles on the 18th of January 1871, the opposition had not yet been overcome. On the very evening before, the King had said that he ' would be Kaiser of Germany or not Kaiser at all'. How then was the new Kaiser to be addressed by the Princes when they gave him the acclamation which was to ratify the institution of the ' Kaiser' title ? The Grand Duke of Baden was to speak for the Princes on this occasion. He was determined to acclaim King William under the title of ' Kaiser of Germany', but Bismarck succeeded in inducing him to evade the difficulty by acclaiming him just as ' Kaiser William'. This time, however, the new Kaiser took badly this ' winning of him unawares'. Bismarck reports that after the solemn ceremony the Kaiser ' on stepping down from his dais ignored me, as I stood by myself in a free space, and passed by me in order to shake hands with the generals standing behind me'.

Why did Bismarck take so much trouble about the title ' Kaiser ' ? In his *Reflections and Reminiscences* he mentions in favour of its introduction the '·political need' of establishing 'a factor which would make for unity and centralization' and says that in the ' word " Kaiser " there lay a great stimulus'. But. Bismarck expresses himself more clearly in the draft of a letter of acceptance which the Prussian King had dispatched to the Princes four days before his proclamation as Kaiser. In it the significance of this dignity is described as lying in the fact that it represents ' claims to power for the realizatión of which the might of Germany has been staked in the most glorious times of our history'. The best-informed interpreter of Bismarck's policy, however, adds that he desired the institution of the title ' Kaiser '. as the sole possible expression of a monarchical power standing above all other powers and exceeding them. As he says : ' The title gave to the great realist the highest imponderable with all its irradiations of power into the future.' One may understand from these words alone what the title meant to Bismarck. It was for him the precise, sharply accentuated expression of what had been the centre of his whole political working and striving from the time of his activity in the Prussian parliament up to his chancellorship in the Confederacy and the Reich, namely the formation of Prussia into a real political power, a Great Power, and, finally, the leading continental Great Power. The dignity of Kaiser was for him the announcement of the fact that ' Prussia had now found the conviction and the courage necessary for her to be called to the position of Great Power in virtue of her own strength '. It meant a formal declaration to the European Great Powers, to this effect : We also are concerned in all events of international politics, we wish to be asked for our opinion wherever political questions of general interest arise and shall stake everything on making our will count in such matters. This is the idea of imperialism which Bismarck thus set before the political world as the goal and task of the Reich which he had created. It was symbolized by the public bestowal on the King of the dignity of ' Kaiser ' on conquered soil and in the very residence hallowed by tradition of the most powerful ruler of Prussia's hereditary enemy.

Bismarck has expressly designated the ' German Reich ' as an ' extension ' of the North German Confederacy. This no doubt applies as regards spatial extent. This Confederacy had been extended to south Germany, had there gained ground step by step, thus securing an ever firmer hold and so winning the extended territory which had to form the essential basis of the Reich. The Reich certainly also constituted an extension of the Confederacy in regard to the actual articles of the constitution. The constitution of the Confederacy was by no means put aside when the Reich was founded and replaced by a Reich constitution. On the contrary, the constitution of the North German Confederacy was designed from the beginning to serve as the constitution of a far more extensive state, a Confederacy for the whole of Germany. The object of the Reich constitution was to realize this plan. There were in the first place a number of purely mechanical extensions to effect, such as the completion of the number of Confederated states by the addition of some more, the increase of votes in the Federal Council by adding those of the south German states, the fixing of the number of the deputies to the Reichstag in accordance with the addition to the population. Further, in some cases deviations were necessary from the line originally intended, especially in view of the many special privileges of Bavaria and the far fewer privileges of Saxony and Württemberg. Further changes resulted from the introduction of the dignity of ' Kaiser ' and the annexation of Alsace-Lorraine, the latter point being settled by a special law. There were also slight extensions of the central government's powers, e.g., in relation to political clubs and to the Press. The decisive point, however, is that all this does not supersede the constitution of the North German Confederacy as a whole, but is incorporated in the form of this constitution as part of it.

The German Reich, moreover, is an extension of the North German Confederacy also in its inner significance. The inner significance of that Confederacy we have found to consist in the preparation for war. This was shown by the sovereignty in military matters and foreign affairs of a monarch who in these questions was inaccessible to any control from outside, to any parliamentary criticism and opposition. It was also shown in the strong preponderance of the executive over the legislative, thus giving preference to the need for ready action rather than to that for quiet deliberation. It was further shown in the ever mobile unity of the ' people in arms ' with its strong orientation towards its culminating point in a supreme commander who was honoured because of his power and therefore emphasized power most strongly, and in its ' unchained national people's movement ', cultivated by Bismarck as *ultima ratio*. Finally, and most significantly for Bismarck, it allowed the whole apparatus of state power to be, in practice, set and kept moving by the dictatorial will of one man, who as Chancellor of the Reich was able to mobilize in all branches of the state's life forces that lead up to war and were intended to guarantee the successful outcome of the latter. Yet, not only did the new Reich include as strong and significant provisions making for the preparation of war as did the Confederacy; it also included two new measures of no little importance which increased and strengthened the same tendency.

The annexation of Alsace-Lorraine carried with it the necessity of preparing for war, even if it was not in any way taken as the overture to new annexations. For the Reich was now bound always to keep ready to repel any attempt at military revenge by her beaten and robbed adversary. Secondly, the introduction of the idea of German imperialism also made it more necessary to prepare for war. The intervention in world affairs herewith foreshadowed could not fail to force the Reich to give her policy a stronger support, not only by arguments to appeal to the understanding, but primarily by those measures which appeal to the will, even a hostile will. A factor in this appeal might be constituted by a strengthened policy of alliances, but this did not make superfluous strong military preparations of war. It rather made them doubly necessary, since it was a question now of Prussia having her way not only as against her enemies but sometimes even against her very allies.

There can therefore be no doubt that the constitution of 1871 was inspired by the same directing idea as that of 1867, namely the idea of preparation for war. Indeed, this found here a deeper and stronger expression. But there is a fundamental difference between the two. The aim of the preparation for war dating from 1867 had been the extension of the North German Confederacy into a union comprising the whole of Germany and also winning from France the leadership of the whole of the Continent. Whether we admit that this union was only the means to the decision between France and Prussia or whether we dispute this, in either case the fact remains that with the coming into force of the Reich constitution the two aims of the military preparation were achieved. The whole of Germany was united and the hegemony of Europe was also torn from France and passed into the hands of Prussia. What was then the aim of the preparation for war in the new Reich? To answer this question we have to turn to the man who, as creator of the constitutions of the Confederacy and of the Reich, not only gave them their outer form and their inner significance, but also as dictator in the guise of bureaucrat determined their course and decided their fate. Bismarck has, in fact, expressed his position in regard to this question most definitely and unambiguously. In the letter in which William I accepted the title of 'Kaiser', while allusion is made to the historical 'claims to power' of this office, in referring to its present restoration he gave emphatic expression also to the 'firm resolve to be the guardian of all rights and to wield the sword of Germany only in their protection'. Four days later, in proclaiming himself Kaiser, William I still more clearly and definitely laid it down as the task of the new Kaiser 'to be augmenter of the German Reich not in warlike conquests, but in the goods and gifts of peace'. Needless to say, the text of these utterances was drafted by Bismarck. So it was not preparation for war but the preservation of the achieved power position, and thus the preservation of peace, which was proclaimed as the idea of the new Reich constitution by the man who was first called to expound and interpret its purpose.

Now, one who has followed the course of Bismarck's life and work and then hears the words of this proclamation and knows nothing more than what had been uttered, may be pardoned if he surmises that we have here only another instance of the method so often and so skilfully employed by Bismarck in his political activity when he tried to deceive and lead astray actual or possible opponents or even his own allies. But this in itself not unjustified supposition is in this case refuted by facts. The twenty years or so of Bismarck's dictatorship which followed 1871 are years of peace without any military enterprises by Prussia. If we consider the power actually possessed by Bismarck within the Reich he had created and his repeatedly proved capacity to bring about a war when he wanted one, we can say quite definitely, without going into details, that the peace of these twenty years was preserved not against Bismarck's will, but in accordance with it, and that this preservation was indeed his very own work. Bismarck, looking back to these last twenty years of his activity, says:

I was so far from intending to attack France in 1875 or later that I should rather have resigned than lent my support to picking a quarrel which led to war. Europe would have seen in our action an abuse of the strength we had won, and everybody's hand, including the centrifugal forces in the Reich itself, would have been permanently raised against Germany. It is just the peaceful character of German policy, coming after the surprising proofs of her military strength, that has made an essential contribution towards reconciling foreign Powers and internal opponents to the new German development.

Summing up, Bismarck described it as his 'ideal aim, once we had brought about our unity, to win men's confidence that German policy, after having repaired the dismemberment of the nation, will be peaceable and just'. To his successors in office also he directed the warning

to try by the honourable and peaceful use of our superior power to diminish the ill-will which has been evoked by our rise to the rank of a real Great Power, so as to convince the world that a German hegemony in Europe is useful and unbiased, and works harmlessly for the freedom of others.

So Bismarck himself approaches the Reich, which he had created with a view to the policy of preparation for war, with the demand expressed in the most emphatic fashion that it should champion the course of preserving the peace. Was it within the capacity of this will to peace of Bismarck to remove the prevailing tendency to war which had grown up with the growth of the state or even to reduce it to a standstill ? We have already indicated that with a great state such an enterprise far exceeds the power of a single man, even the strongest and most determined. The state is not a mere tool but a machine working on its own power. He who builds it up is necessarily at the same time both its master and its servant, and the tendencies which he puts into it will display themselves as autonomous power in it. Now, Bismarck had in fact when he founded the state introduced into it forces which were bound to hinder and disorganize this process of preparation for war. The ' internal opponents ', the ' centrifugal forces in the Reich itself ', of whose action he speaks as working against a German will to war, were to a very large extent due to his own action. There was the annexed Alsace-Lorraine which was bound always to constitute a strong force making against any united will to war ; there was Bavaria with her special military privileges, who must have seemed to him a possible danger for this united will ; and there were the further centrifugal forces mentioned earlier, such as political catholicism and the rising social democratic party as representative of the class-conscious proletariat. But did the presence of these internal opponents constitute a factor which pointed unambiguously to the preservation of peace and against the inclination to war ? On the contrary, it might very well be that the intolerable internal situation produced by them would form the stimulus to a warlike venture. The Crown Prince had indeed accused Bismarck of showing such a tendency before the Austrian war.

The decisive point, however, is that Bismarck had not at all the intention of sacrificing to the preservation of peace the measures of preparation for war. That would have contradicted most sharply his very nature. Certainly he wished to stand on a peaceful footing with the other European Powers. He also spoke of the ' confidence ' that he wished to ' win ' from them, just as he had formerly spoken of ' confidence ' as the basis of relations with the Princes within the Confederacy. But Bismarck was not the man to be ready to build up peaceful relations to others merely on their goodwill and readiness to meet him half-way. His nature required that he should at least be always in a position in which he could force his decisions on others and that he should occasionally translate this possibility into action. For this reason he had demanded on behalf of Prussia's relations with the Princes the ' security provided by an adequate power derived from the dynastic background ' (*Hausmacht*). And for this reason also he emphasized now, as an indispensable factor, if the new Reich was to keep the peace, the presence of a strong army ready to strike. On this he spoke with great emphasis in all

publicity. For instance, in the year 1887 he said in the Reichstag:
'Our efforts to establish an epoch of peace lasting more than thirty
years are sincere, but above all we need for this a strong army,
an army which is strong enough to secure our independence.' He
spoke even more decidedly a year later in the same body:

In these days we must be as strong [i.e., militarily] as we can possibly
be, and we have the power to be stronger than any other nation in the
world with the same population. It would be a crime if we did not
make use of this possibility. In courage all civilized nations are equal,
but our people, our 700,000 men, are veterans in war, *rompus au métier*,
proven soldiers, who have not forgotten what they had learned, and, a
point where no people in the world can vie with us, we have the material
in commissioned and noncommissioned officers to command this immense
army.

So Bismarck could well claim for himself that he had been no
'enemy of the army', and it is only logical that he should publish
in a prominent place a letter from his supreme military lord, the
King, of this very year 1888, in which the latter tells him 'that
where it was a question of perfecting the welfare of the army, its
power of defence and its readiness to strike, you never failed to
fight the battle to its end'. These were only the remains of Bismarck's hereditary 'soldier-worship'.

Bismarck had introduced the preservation of peace as part
of the inner significance of the new constitution, but had neither
the capacity nor the will to exclude from this constitution the
purpose of preparation for war. The one tendency as well as the
other was therefore side by side to constitute the meaning of the
new Reich. Now the principle of war and its preparation is that
of open force, the principle of preserving peace is that of negotiation
and coming to an understanding. The latter culminates indeed in
persuasion and conviction and under certain circumstances may
make use of concealed force. But as soon as open force plays a
part, peace is no longer maintained, but replaced by war. Therefore
it is impossible that preservation of peace and preparation for war
should constitute on the same level of importance the policy of one
and the same state. It is necessary that either the one or the other
should acquire the upper hand and subordinate the second to itself
as a means to an end. There is no other choice. We may assume
that Bismarck had the honourable intention of subordinating the
preparation for war to the preservation of peace as the end. This
he had at the time when this alternative came before his mind with
special force, immediately after the destruction of the Napoléonic
Empire. He expressed this quite unequivocally, when he said:

The task of those who command the army is to destroy the forces
of the enemy; the object of the war is to win peace on terms which are

in accordance with the policy pursued by the state. The ways and means of waging war are always dependent on whether policy has been directed by the desire to attain the end finally won.

Bismarck, however, had then also to learn that the subordination of the making or preparing of war to the winning or preserving of peace is not something which is given without further ado but has to be led up to and carried through. He at that time accounted for his difficulties solely on personal grounds, namely that the General Staff, being opposed to himself, demanded out of self-will that 'the foreign minister should speak again only when the commanders of the army find that the time has come to close the temple of Janus'. In reality, however, the difficulty lay in the objective problem itself. In social and also in individual life the relation of end and means is almost always exposed to sudden and rapid interchanges, so that what is to-day an end may to-morrow become a means and vice versa. This Bismarck had experienced very clearly to his own advantage, when he juggled so cleverly with the 'coinciding ends : Prussian leadership and national unification of Germany'. The relationship is especially liable to be interchanged when preparation for war is the means and preservation of peace the end, because the former may preserve but also destroy the peace. Whether it has the one or the other effect depends not only and indeed not predominantly on the conscious will of the men who have the decisive position or on objective data, such as the magnitude of the military preparations. A decisive rôle is played in this relation rather by imponderables, such as public opinion in one's own country and the degree in which foreign countries fear or will war. These factors are obscurely conditioned by changes in economic relationship and nationalistic currents. But most important of all perhaps is the prestige and personal influence of the men who stand for peace on the one hand and war on the other, and especially whether they are regarded at home and abroad as men with a sense of responsibility. A hardly noticeable change at any point in this connexion of circumstances may be sufficient to convert the preparation for war from the servant of peace into its destroyer.

This shows clearly enough that Bismarck in basing his new Reich on the policy of the preservation of peace by preparing for war had given it a very weak and unstable foundation. The man who despised principle in politics thereby gave the final seal to his negative attitude towards them. But the instability of this foundation was increased still further by the conduct both of those who stood for the preparation for war and of those who stood for peace. In itself it was bound to be difficult to induce the General Staff, proud of its technical proficiency and its practical success in the use of armed force, to accept the opposed unattractive principle of peaceful influence as the chief end and aim of their activities. What was bound to make them still less inclined to subject their efforts to the principle of preserving peace was that the Prussian army looked back on a tradition as ' creator of the greatness of Prussia ' reaching to the time of Frederick the Great and even earlier, a tradition which was regarded as most glorious by the Prussian King and people just because it was not bound by the principle of peace, but could realize itself freely and without hindrance. The Prussian General Staff had just now proved in three successful wars what extraordinary significance for the expansion and the might of the state attached to its activity. Bismarck himself had emphasized the ' loyalty and self-sacrifice ' of the ' people in arms ' as the essence of unity and cohesion in the state which he had built up. This essential nucleus was now hampered by him, by a civilian, that is, by a man who, according to the military, could not be supposed to have any real knowledge and understanding of the difficult tasks and problems concerned with war and could still less be expected to have sympathetically entered into and lived through the hardships and needs connected with such problems. The head of the Prussian army, however, was his sacred Majesty, the Prussian King, and the army was immediately under him without the intervention of any civil authorities. It was undoubtedly a grave violation of the King's basic rights if his unqualified relationship to the most important instrument of his power was confined and limited by rules of peace and not of war.

What had Bismarck to set against this exaltation of the principle of preparation for war in order to support the counter-principle of preservation of peace ? During the war he had found himself powerless against the secretiveness of the military. It was of little use to him then that he had been concerned in military matters from youth on and that he had felt happy in them. That he had done everything to serve the military, from the pushing through of the army reform to the granting of a strategic frontier in Alsace-Lorraine, was easily forgotten. As we have said, the strength of Bismarck's position as Chancellor over against the General Staff lay in the fact that he had an important share in deciding between peace and war. This influence of Bismarck had remained constitutionally the same after the founding of the Reich in 1871 as it had been at the time of the North German Confederacy. But it did not retain the same practical significance as before. In regard to his own future policy Bismarck had decided the question whether it should be war or peace, which had been hitherto in the balance, once for all in favour of peace. So there remained hardly any chance that the General Staff should induce him to decide for war. The power which he could exercise in this question had therefore become practically a dead, instead of a living issue, and could no longer serve as a factor in his actual influence.

Also in regard to his political work in general, Bismarck's activity as preserver of the peace was bound to fall into ill repute. People had in Prussia always been accustomed, and had accustomed themselves still more after three successful wars, to find in the military the factor which really gave the state its security and strength. It was now Bismarck's task to impose checks and limitations on this factor. We have seen that it was contrary to the prestige of the Reichstag that its work among the people was regarded not really as constructive but very markedly as merely that of controlling and criticizing the executive, culminating in the monarch. Now Bismarck as the preserver of the peace had a similar task in dealing with the military. Consequently, influential circles among the people were inclined on the occasion of a difference of opinion between Bismarck and the military to set themselves *a limine* on the side of the latter. Moritz von Blanckenburg's letter during the war is typical of this. From the beginning of his policy of peace Bismarck saw himself again and again induced to make concessions to the General Staff. The series of these concessions began with the sacrifice of the ethnological in favour of the strategical frontier when Alsace-Lorraine was annexed, and was never completely brought to an end.

Could and ought Bismarck to have been contented with such a basis for his policy of preserving peace ? Must he not have told himself that, if already while he was in power the preservation of peace required the fullest exploitation of his personal influence, will-power, experience and skill, this task would prove too much for his successors who had not these properties in equal measure ? Was he justified in making the preservation of peace dependent to a large extent on his own continuance in office, leaving it in doubt after the end of this ? Was he not bound, if there was any possibility at all of strengthening in respect of intensity and duration the personal basis for the preservation of peace, at least to make an attempt to strengthen it so ? There was in fact such a possibility : he might have accepted to a greater degree the co-operation between people and government by strengthening the position of the Reichstag. One cannot object that Bismarck could not be expected to make such an attempt because, if he had done so, he would have contradicted altogether his own nature and that of the state built up by him, and had ceased to be Bismarck. For he had, after all, repeatedly proposed to the German Confederation a parliament based on universal suffrage as a political factor side by side with the Federal Diet, and he had indeed introduced such a parliament in the Federal state created by himself. If it be retorted that the former proposal was only a tactical move in the political campaign against Austria and the latter not much more than a dummy, there are various utterances which show that this was not the last word of Bismarck in the matter. On the contrary, he declared : ' Ever since 1847 I have been in favour of striving to secure the possibility of public criticism of the government in parliament.' Moreover, in his important memoir of March 1858 he said : ' The security that the King of Prussia will still remain master in the land ' is unique on the continent. Therefore the Prussian ' government may without danger allow parliament more elbow-room even in purely political questions than before '. But when could the position of this King in his country ever be stronger in the eyes of the man who had carried through the indemnity law as the ' generous grant ' of a victorious King than it was now after three victorious wars ? When could it have been more apposite to allow of elbow-room to parliament than now when it was a question of strengthening the highly insecure basis for the preservation of the peace at which the government aimed ?

What might have been expected from Bismarck in this connexion was not a complete change of course, such as he had at the very time carried through with regard to war and preparing war. It was not a question of ' the Prussian Monarchy not yet being ripe to be fitted as a dead cog into the machine of parliamentary government '. It was not a case of an absolute alternative, but merely of what Bismarck had himself from his opportunist point of view contemplated, namely giving ' more elbow-room '. Now who would have been more qualified to decide about this question of more or less and to carry out the decision than the all-powerful dictator Bismarck himself ? And what time could have been more suitable than that of his greatest power after overwhelming military victory ? There was no immediate question of the much discussed and demanded ministerial responsibility to parliament, but there was of what Bismarck himself called a Cabinet *à la Gladstone*, that is, a ministry which was constituted in conformity with the party majority in the Reichstag by politicians, not by constitutional right but by the good grace of the King. Such an institution was favoured by Queen Augusta, the Crown Prince, and other liberals of the Court. Another point that came in question was the recognition of the right of the Reichstag to a certain say in the fixing of the military budget, so much disputed since 1862. While it was difficult to bring direct pressure to bear on the General Staff after the great victories, and the indirect pressure by Bismarck through his influence on the decision of war had lost much of its weight, a certain control of the military budget by the Reichstag would have exercised an indirect pressure in matters relating to the military preparation for war. Other points were the strengthening of the right of initiative of the

Reichstag in legislation and further extensions of its competence. These concessions would have not upset but realized the 'equal rights of the Crown and Parliament' so often demanded by Bismarck. Through the great task of self-government set to parliament the people would have become conscious that they directly belonged together. The political unification of Germany might have been followed by a unification in spirit. To the unity of the 'people in arms' based on the might of a supreme commander would have been added the unity of political citizens, based on the great task of political self-government. The prevalence of 'dynastic interests' would have been 'reduced to the right measure' demanded by Bismarck himself. However bellicose one may think the German people, the policy of preserving peace would have been rendered easier especially for Bismarck's successors in relation to the General Staff, if such a task of practical political education had been undertaken. At any rate a Prussian war of conquest motived by dynastic interests could then hardly have been represented as a 'struggle for existence'. The introduction of the people into politics would have given to the official peace policy an invaluable imponderable in the shape of the approval and goodwill of foreign states and spared the Chancellor many a 'nightmare of coalitions'. Above all, it would have based the peace policy, not on the skill and readiness of an individual, limited in his political activity in respect of time, but on the co-operation of a people whose life would last as long as that of the state.

Moreover, from the point of view of the people there was a particular inducement to extend and deepen their share in the activity of the state. Had not the three last wars and above all the third of them, according to Bismarck's repeated statement, served to contribute to the national unification of this people? Had not this unification been completed just by the sacrifice of this very people in military service, a sacrifice which Bismarck in his letters to his wife could not recognize too much? If the national unification of the German people played any part in the creation, even only as a means to an end, it was almost logically required that this element should be somehow expressed in the shape of the new Reich. Was not a state which had been created with a view to unify the people bound to be made also in some degree a matter for this people? But Bismarck in the moment of victory refused to turn his own attention to the people and ask after their political wishes. For him the people, this 'easily manageable ally of the Crown', remained even after victory a 'people in arms'. In so far as it deserved attention at all as a people of voters, it had to his mind been adequately satisfied by general suffrage, this 'strongest of the arts of freedom'. Bismarck did not make the least further attempt at fulfilling the political wishes of the liberals. Even after the attainment of the national aims the adjournment of internal questions remained in force. But when a few years after the conclusion of peace the representatives of the people wished to intervene in settling the issue between preparation for war and preservation of peace by trying to secure the right to influence the military budget, Bismarck sharply and ruthlessly turned against their endeavour, and in this matter showed himself completely at one with those who advocated preparation for war. After the war of 1866, Bismarck had made against a proposal to alter the constitution in a reactionary sense the objection : ' We should then have carried out a Prussian war of conquest.' To this very objection he had rendered himself liable in regard to the Franco-Prussian war which after all began in connexion with a dynastic question of the Hohenzollern family, when he refused to make it a starting-point for a policy of peace, guaranteed by the active participation of the people.

The people, however, made hardly any opposition to this policy of Bismarck. The liberalism, which had been developed by the classical thinkers and poets of Germany in connexion with the idea of the *Kulturstaat* and had passed its first test in the movement of 1813, had in the following decades substantially lost in force. In the decade during which he was Chancellor Bismarck had dealt it a mortal wound. It must not be denied that Bismarck felt himself an educator of his people. His words ' Let us put Germany in the saddle ' indicate that he meant to be a teacher of Germany. But he was a peculiar kind of teacher for a nation, and what he had to teach had a strange content. He called it unity of the people, but it was not a unity based on the development of their own inner consciousness and of a corresponding ideal arising from this. It was rather the teaching of a common subjection to the will of a strong state power irresistible both at home and abroad. Bismarck, however, had put forward his teaching in an only too impressive and forceful fashion, and the people had accepted it only too willingly and without restraint. For, when this irresistible state power had been established in Germany in the year 1871 with the support of the people's own strength, the nation had completely forgotten that they had once, in 1848 and 1849, themselves been concerned with the realization of the liberal idea of national unity and liberty, and that they had then claimed the power of the state only as a means for the attainment of this end. Enthusiasm about the military victory had damped and quenched whatever was left in the people of a desire for a unity founded on their own freedom. When later they approached Bismarck in order to persuade him cautiously to prepare the way for ministerial responsibility by a ' Cabinet *à la Gladstone* ', the enthusiasm which the founding of the Reich had brought with it was already exhausted and the workaday mood of cool calculation had returned again, a mood which did not allow of generous concessions. So in the years of peace which followed the people were denied the political platform from which the demand, so congenial to the common man, for the maintenance of peace could have been made with emphasis and effective power in opposition to those who supported the cause of preparation for war. Thus the victory celebration of 1871 turned out to be a fatal hour for the German nation, since this victory had a share in causing the ills which, a few decades after Bismarck's departure, were to come on Germany.

Bismarck retained his dictatorial position in the new Reich even when the end of the war and the cessation of the necessity for preparing war had removed any excuse for its retention. The German people had thus entrusted the power over their fate, not only to Bismarck personally, but also to his successors in office, though the people had legally not the least influence on their selection. They thereby displayed that lack of ' civil courage ' for which Bismarck himself had blamed them. They deprived themselves of the opportunity of acquiring the political education which was necessary to set them really in the saddle and to enable them to discover and satisfy their true political needs. Because they did not take into their hands the task of preserving peace, they became partly responsible for the failure to carry out this task adequately and must bear their share of blame for the final breakdown of peace. Bismarck, however, who after 1871 was certainly in earnest about the keeping of peace, did not draw the final conclusion from the policy which he had herewith introduced. He was unwilling to make up his mind to let the people, the natural guarantor of, and interested party in, the preservation of peace, take a genuine share in his peace policy. He would not bring himself to this because he hated sharing ' responsibility in big politics ' out of distrust and contempt of his fellow-men. His self-confidence and his self-righteousness made it distasteful to him to share his power with anybody, least of all with the people, this ' easily manageable ally of the Crown '. He had opposed the first attempt in this direction, the ' Cabinet *à la Gladstone*,' because ' its main object was a negative one, to get rid of me '—of course an ungrounded supposition of his. In this conflict between Bismarck's exaggerated self-will and the unmistakable needs of the state, the former won and frustrated any attempt at providing a really sound basis to this policy of peace through calling in the people to take a greater part in governing the state. In the refusal to try this course lies Bismarck's guilt and his responsibility for the catastrophe which a quarter of a century after he had laid down office befell the German nation and the whole civilized world.

BIBLIOGRAPHY
(Selection)

I. WORKS, SPEECHES, LETTERS, ETC.

Bismarck, Die Gesammelten Werke, 2nd ed., Berlin, 1924–32, 15 vols. in 19.

Hahn, Ludwig, *Fürst Bismarck, sein politisches Leben und Wirken*, Berlin, 1878–91, 5 vols.

Fürst Bismarck, Gedanken und Erinnerungen, ed. by Horst Kohl, Stuttgart, 1898–1919, 5 vols.
> (*Bismarck, the Man and the Statesman :* being the Reflections and Reminiscences of Otto Prince von Bismarck, transl. from the German, London, 1898, 2 vols.)

Preussen im Bundestag, 1851–9, Dokumente der kgl. preuss. Bundesgesandtschaft (i.e., Bismarck's reports), ed. by Heinrich von Poschinger, Berlin, 1882, 3 vols.

Die politischen Berichte des Fürsten Bismarck aus Petersburg und Paris, 1859–1862, ed. by L. Raschdau, Berlin, 1920, 2 vols.

Bismarck-Briefe, 1836–1873, ed. by Horst Kohl, 7th ed., Bielefeld, 1898.

Politische Briefe Bismarcks aus den Jahren 1849–1889, Berlin, 1889–93, 4 vols.

Kaiser- und Kanzler-Briefe. Briefwechsel zwischen Wilhelm I. und Fürst von Bismarck, Leipzig, 1900.

Bismarcks Briefe an den General Leopold von Gerlach, ed. by Horst Kohl, Berlin, 1896.

Bismarcks Briefwechsel mit dem Minister Frhr. von Schleinitz, 1858–1861, Stuttgart-Berlin, 1905.

Bismarck-Briefe, 1844–1870, Originalbriefe an seine Gemahlin, seine Schwester und andere, Bielefeld-Leipzig, 1876.
> (*Prince Bismarck's Letters to his Wife, his Sister and Others from 1844 to 1870*, transl. from the German, London, 1878.)

Fürst Bismarcks Briefe an seine Braut und Gattin, ed. by Fürst Herbert Bismarck, 2nd ed., Stuttgart-Berlin, 1906.
> (*The Love Letters of Prince Bismarck*, transl. from the German, London, 1901, 2 vols.)

Bismarcks Briefe an seine Gattin aus dem Kriege 1870–1871, Stuttgart-Berlin, 1903.
> (*Bismarck's Letters to his Wife from the Seat of War, 1870–1871*, transl. into English, London, 1915.)

Bismarcks Briefe an Schwester und Schwager, ed. by Horst Kohl, Leipzig, 1915.

Vom jungen Bismarck. Briefwechsel Otto von Bismarcks mit Gustav Scharlach, Weimar, 1912.

Bismarck-Portefeuille, ed. by Heinrich von Poschinger, Stuttgart 1898–1900, 5 vols.

Bausteine zur Bismarck-Pyramide. Neue Briefe und Konversationen, ed. by Heinrich von Poschinger, Berlin, 1904.

Fürst Bismarck als Redner. Vollständige Sammlung der parlamentarischen Reden Bismarcks seit dem Jahre 1847, ed. by Wilhelm Böhm, Berlin-Stuttgart, 1890, 16 vols.

Die politischen Reden des Fürsten Bismarck. Historisch-kritische Gesamtausgabe, ed. by Horst Kohl, Stuttgart, 1892–1905, 14 vols.

Die Reden des Abgeordneten von Bismarck-Schönhausen in den Parlamenten 1847–1851, ed. by Th. Riedel, Berlin, 1881.

Ausgewählte Reden des Fürsten von Bismarck, mit einer biographischen Skizze, etc., Berlin-Cöthen, 1877–88, 6 vols.

Fürst Bismarcks gesammelte Reden, Berlin, 1894, 3 vols.

Die Ansprachen des Fürsten Bismarck 1848–1894, ed. by Heinrich von Poschinger, Stuttgart, 1895–1900, 2 vols.

Fürst Bismarck. Neue Tischgespräche und Interviews, ed. by Heinrich von Poschinger, 2nd ed., Stuttgart-Leipzig, 1895–9, 2 vols.

(*Conversations with Prince Bismarck*, collected by H. von Poschinger, English edition, London-New York, 1900.)

Poschinger Heinrich von, *Also sprach Bismarck*, 3 vols., Wien, 1910–11.

Bismarck's Table Talk, ed. by C. Lowe, London, 1895.

II. BIOGRAPHIES

Fürst Bismarck, Regesten zu einer wissenschaftlichen Biographie des ersten Reichskanzlers; Stuttgart, 1891–2, 2 vols.

Hagen, Maximilian von, *Das Bismarckbild in der Literatur der Gegenwart*, Berlin, 1929.

Bamberger, Ludwig, *Herr von Bismarck*, Breslau, 1868.

(Bamberger, Ludwig, *Count Bismarck, a Political Biography*, London, 1869.)

Hesekiel, J. G. L., *Das Buch des Grafen Bismarck*, Berlin, 1869.

(Hesekiel, J. G. L., *The Life of Bismarck, Private and Political*, London, 1870.)

Lowe, Charles, *Prince Bismarck, an Historical Biography*, London, 1885, 2 vols.

Blum, Hans, *Fürst Bismarck und seine Zeit, Eine Biographie*, München, 1894, 6 vols.

Lowe, Charles, *Prince Bismarck, an Historical Biography*, London, 1898 (in one volume reduced and continued).

Stearns, Frank Preston, *The Life of Prince Bismarck*, Philadelphia-New York, 1899.

Benoist, Charles, *Le Prince de Bismarck, psychologie de l'homme fort*, Paris, 1900.

Lenz, M., *Geschichte Bismarcks*, Leipzig, 1902.

Klein-Hattingen, Otto, *Bismarck und seine Welt*, Berlin, 1902–4, 3 vols.

Heyck, C., *Bismarck*, Bielefeld, 1905.

Matter, Paul, *Bismarck et son temps*, Paris, 1905–8, 3 vols.

Egelhaaf, G., *Bismarck, Sein Leben und sein Werk*, Stuttgart, 1911.

Eigenbrodt, August, *Bismarck und seine Zeit*, Leipzig, 1912.

Headlam, James W., *Bismarck and the Foundation of the German Reich*, New York-London, 1914.

Spahn, Martin, *Bismarck*, 2nd ed., München-Gladbach, 1915.
Marcks, Erich, *Bismarck, eine Biographie*, 1st vol., Stuttgart-Berlin, 1915.
——, *Otto von Bismarck, ein Lebensbild*, 2nd ed., Stuttgart-Berlin, 1915.
Du Moulin Eckart, Richard Graf, *Bismarck, der Mann und das Werk*, Stuttgart, 1915.
Liman, Paul, *Bismarck in Geschichte, Karikatur und Anekdote*, Stuttgart, 1915.
Matthias, A., *Bismarck, sein Leben und sein Werk*, München, 1915.
Schäfer, Dietrich, *Bismarck*, Berlin, 1917, 2 vols.
Valentin, Veit, *Bismarck und seine Zeit*, 4th ed., Leipzig, 1918.
Robertson, Charles Grant, *Bismarck*, London, 1918.
Ludwig, Emil, *Bismarck, Geschichte eines Kämpfers*, Berlin, 1927.
 (Ludwig, Emil, *Bismarck, The Story of a Fighter*, London, 1927.)
Zechlin, Egmont, *Bismarck und die Grundlegung der deutschen Grossmacht*, Stuttgart, 1930.
Beumelburg, W., *Bismarck gründet das Reich*, Oldenburg, 1932.
Eyck, Erich, *Bismarck (Leben und Wirken)*, Erlenbach-Zürich, 1941-4, 3 vols.

III. ESSAYS

Bismarck-Jahrbuch, ed. by Horst Kohl, Stuttgart, 1894-9, 6 vols.
Vilbort, J., *L'œuvre de M. de Bismarck, 1863-1866*, Paris, 1869.
Frantz, Constantin, *Die Religion des Nationalliberalismus*, Leipzig, 1872.
Klaczko, Jul. Zwei Kanzler. *Fürst Gortschakoff und Fürst Bismarck*, Basel, 1877.
Dawson, W. H., *Bismarck and State Socialism*, London, 1890.
Smith, Munroe, *Bismarck and German Unity*, New York, 1898.
Marcks, Erich, *Fürst Bismarcks Gedanken und Erinnerungen, Versuch einer kritischen Würdigung*, Berlin, 1899.
Blume, W. von, *Die Beschiessung von Paris und die Ursachen ihrer Verzögerung*, Berlin, 1899.
Schmoller, Gustav, Lenz, Max, und Marcks, Erich, *Zu Bismarcks Gedächtnis*, Leipzig, 1899.
Kobell, L. von, *König Ludwig II. und Fürst Bismarck, 1870*, Leipzig, 1899.
Anschutz, Gerhard, *Bismarck und die Reichsverfassung*, Berlin, 1899.
Prutz, H. G., *Bismarcks Bildung, ihre Quellen und ihre Äusserungen*, Berlin, 1904.
Eigenbrodt, A., *Bismarck und der Kronprinz in der Kaiserfrage*, Cassel, 1901.
Schultze, W., *Die Tronkandidatur Hohenzollern und Graf Bismarck*, Halle, 1902.
Rathlef, Geo., *Zur Frage nach Bismarcks Verhalten in der Vorgeschichte des deutsch-französischen Krieges*, Dorpat, 1903.
Küntzel, G., *Thiers und Bismarck. Kardinal Bernis*, Bonn, 1905.
Jakob, K., *Bismarck und die Erwerbung von Elsass-Lothringen, 1870-1871*, Strassburg, 1905.
Wolf, Gustav, *Bismarcks Lehrjahre*, Leipzig, 1907.

Geschichte des Fürsten Bismarck in Einzeldarstellungen, ed. by Johannes Penzler.

   (*a*) Penzler, Johannes, *Jugendgeschichte des Fürsten Bismarck*, Berlin, 1907.

   (*b*) Schmidt, Geo., *Das Geschlecht von Bismarck*, Berlin, 1908.

Promnitz, Kurt, *Bismarcks Eintritt in das Ministerium*, Berlin, 1908.

Nirrnheim, Otto, *Das erste Jahr des Ministeriums Bismarck und die öffentliche Meinung*, Heidelberg, 1908.

Ruville, A. von, *Bayern und die Wiederaufrichtung des deutschen Reiches*, Berlin, 1909.

Müller, Conrad, *Bismarcks Mutter und ihre Ahnen*, 1st vol., Berlin, 1909.

Brandenburg, Erich, *Der Eintritt der süddeutschen Staaten in den Norddeutschen Bund*, Berlin, 1910.

Küntzel, G., *Bismarck und Bayern in der Zeit der Reichsgründung*, Frankfurt a.M., 1910.

Marx, Ernst, *Bismarck und die Hohenzollernkandidatur in Spanien*, Stuttgart, 1911.

Ritter, Gerhard, *Die preussischen Konservativen und Bismarcks deutsche Politik, 1858–1876*, Heidelberg, 1913.

Baumgarten, Otto, *Bismarcks Glaube*, Tübingen, 1915.

Augst, Richard, *Bismarcks Stellung zum parlamentarischen Wahlrecht*, Leipzig, 1917.

Jöhlinger, Otto, *Bismarck und die Juden*, Berlin, 1921.

Grundmann, Gerhard, *Der gegenwärtige Stand der historischen Kritik an Bismarcks 'Gedanken und Erinnerungen'*, 1st vol., Berlin, 1925.

Franz, Günther, *Bismarcks Nationalgefühl*, Leipzig, 1926.

Wolff, Hellmuth, *Geschichtsauffassung und Politik in Bismarcks Bewusstsein*, München, 1926.

Meyer, Arnold O., *Bismarcks Kampf mit Österreich am Bundestag zu Frankfurt a.M.*, Berlin-Leipzig, 1927.

Roloff, G., *Bismarck and German Unity*, Cambridge, 1928 (Cambridge Modern History, 11th vol.).

Stolberg-Wernigerode, Albrecht Graf zu, *Bismarck und die schleswig-holsteinische Frage*, Kiel, 1928.

——, *Bismarck und die Verständigungspolitik, 1864–1866*, Berlin, 1929.

Schüssler, Wilhelm, *Bismarcks Kampf um Süddeutschland*, 1867, Berlin, 1929.

Reiche, Friedrich, *Bismarck und Italien, ein Beitrag zur Vorgeschichte des Krieges 1866*, Berlin, 1931.

Stadelmann, Rudolf, *Das Jahr 1865 und das Problem von Bismarcks deutscher Politik*, Oldenburg, 1933.

Clark, Chester Wells, *Franz Josef and Bismarck*, Oxford, 1934.

Richter, Adolf, *Bismarck und die Arbeiterfrage im preussischen Verfassungskonflikt*, Stuttgart, 1935.

Mombauer, Hans, *Bismarcks Realpolitik als Ausdruck seiner Weltanschauung, die Auseinandersetzung mit Leopold von Gerlach, 1851–1859*, Berlin, 1936.

Nolde, Boris E. Baron von, *Die Petersburger Mission Bismarcks*, Leipzig, 1936.
Valentin, Veit, *Bismarcks Reichsgründung im Urteil englischer Diplomaten*, Amsterdam, 1937.

IV. REMINISCENCES

Bunsen, Christian von, *Memoirs by F. Baroness Bunsen*, London, 1868, 2 vols.
 (Ch. v. Bunsen, *Aus seinen Briefen und nach eigener Erinnerung geschildert von seiner Witwe*, Leipzig, 1868–71, 3 vols.)
Benedetti, Comte V., *Ma mission en Prusse*, Paris, 1871.
Gramont, Duc de, *La France et la Prusse avant la guerre*, Paris, 1872.
Lamarmora, Alfonso, *Un po' piu' di luce sugli eventi politici e militari dell' anno 1866*, Firenze, 1873.
Busch, Moritz, *Graf Bismarck und seine Leute während des Krieges mit Frankreich*, 2nd ed., Leipzig, 1878, 2 vols.
 (Busch, Moritz, *Bismarck in the Franco-German War, 1870–1871*, London, 1878, 2 vols.)
Treitschke, Heinrich von, *Zehn Jahre deutscher Kämpfe*, 2nd ed., Berlin, 1879.
Wagener, Hermann, *Erlebtes*, Berlin, 1884.
Busch, Moritz, *Unser Reichskanzler*, Leipzig, 1884, 2 vols.
 (Busch, Moritz, *Our Chancellor*, London, 1884, 2 vols.)
Robolski, Hermann, *Bismarck in Versailles, Erinnerungen an Versailles 1870–1871*, Leipzig, 1886.
Beust, Friedrich von, *Aus drei Viertel-Jahrhunderten, 1809–1885*, Stuttgart, 1887, 2 vols.
 (*Memoirs of Count von Beust*, transl. by Baron H. de Worms, London, 1887, 2 vols.)
Vitzthum von Eckstädt, Graf C. F., *London, Gastein und Sadowa, 1864–1866*, Stuttgart, 1889.
Curtis, G. W., *The Correspondence of John Lothrop Motley*, London, 1889, 2 vols.
Bismarck Intime, by a fellow-student, transl. by Henry Haywood, London, 1890.
Gerlach, Leopold von, *Denkwürdigkeiten aus seinem Leben*, ed. by his daughter, Berlin, 1891–2, 2 vols.
Bernhardi, Felix Theodor von, *Aus dem Leben Theodor von Bernhardis*, Leipzig, 1893–1906, 9 vols.
Loftus, Lord A., *Diplomatic Reminiscences*, two series, 1862–79, London, 1894, 2 vols.
Poschinger, Heinrich von, *Fürst Bismarck und die Parlamentarier*, Breslau, 1894–5, 3 vols.
Roon, Graf Albrecht von, *Denkwürdigkeiten aus dem Leben des General-Feldmarschalls Grafen Albrecht von Roon*, 4th ed., Breslau, 1897, 3 vols.

Abeken, H., *Ein schlichtes Leben in bewegter Zeit*, Berlin, 1898.

Bamberger, Ludwig, *Erinnerungen*, ed. by P. Nathan, Berlin, 1899.

Freytag, Gustav, *Erinnerungen aus meinem Leben*, 11th and 12th ed., Leipzig, 1899.

(Freytag, Gustav, *Reminiscences of my Life*, transl., London, 1890, 2 vols.)

Busch, Moritz, *Tagebuchblätter*, Leipzig, 1899, 3 vols.

(Busch, Moritz, *Bismarck : Some Secret Pages of his History*, London, 1898, 3 vols.)

Poschinger Heinrich von, *Fürst Bismarck und die Diplomaten*, Hamburg, 1900.

Gustav Freytag und Heinrich von Treitschke, im Briefwechsel, Leipzig, 1900.

Simson, Bernhard von, *Eduard von Simson, Erinnerungen aus seinem Leben*, Leipzig, 1900.

Manteuffel, Frhr. Otto von, *Unter Friedrich Wilhelm IV. (1848–1858)*, ed. by Heinrich von Poschinger, Berlin, 1900–1, 3 vols.

Blumenthal, Leonhard Graf von, *Tagebücher aus den Jahren 1866 und 1870–1871*, Stuttgart, 1902.

(Blumenthal, Leonhard Graf von, *Journals of Field-Marshal Count von Blumenthal for 1866 and 1870–1871*, London, 1903.)

Keudell, F. von, *Fürst und Fürstin Bismarck, Erinnerungen aus den Jahren 1846–1872*, Stuttgart-Berlin, 1902.

Delbrück, Rudolf von, *Lebenserinnerungen, 1817–1867*, Berlin, 1905, 2 vols.

Poschinger, Heinrich von, *Aus grosser Zeit. Erinnerungen an den Fursten Bismarck*, Berlin, 1905.

Hohenlohe-Schillingsfürst, Fürst Chlodwig zu, *Denkwürdigkeiten*, Stuttgart, 1906–7, 2 vols.

(Hohenlohe-Schillingsfürst, Prince Chlodwig, *Reminiscences*, transl. London, 1907, 2 vols.)

The Letters of Queen Victoria, A Selection between the Years 1837 and 1861, London, 1907, 3 vols.

Poschinger, Heinrich von, *Stunden bei Bismarck*, Wien, 1910.

Memoirs and Letters of Sir Robert Morier, from 1826 to 1876, ed. by his daughter, London, 1911, 2 vols.

Johanna von Bismarck, ein Lebensbild in Briefen, 1844–1894, ed. by Eduard Heyck, 3rd ed., Stuttgart-Berlin, 1915.

Thiers, Louis Adolphe, *Memoirs*, transl. by F. M. Atkinson, London, 1915.

(Thiers, Louis Adolphe, *Notes et Souvenirs, 1870–1873*, Paris, 1904.)

Schlözer, Kurd von, *Petersburger Briefe*, Stuttgart, 1921.

Ponsonby, Sir Frederick, *Victoria, Consort of Frederick III, German Emperor, Letters*, London, 1928.

(*Deutsche Ausgabe*, Berlin, 1929 introd. by William II.)

Die Brautbriefe der Fürstin Johanna von Bismarck, ed. by Fürst Herbert von Bismarck, Stuttgart-Berlin, 1931.

Orloff, Nicolaus, *Bismarck und die Fürstin Orloff*, München, 1936.

V. HISTORY OF THE TIME

Die Auswärtige Politik Preussens 1858–1871. Diplomatische Aktenstücke ed., by the Historische Reichskommission, Berlin, 1930 and later, 12 vols.

Kohl, Horst, *Dreissig Jahre preussisch-deutscher Geschichte, 1858–1888, in amtlichen Kundgebungen,* Giessen 1888.

Hahn, Ludwig, *Der Krieg Deutschlands gegen Frankreich und die Gründung des deutschen Kaiserreiches. Die deutsche Politik, 1867–1871.* In Aktenstücken, amtlichen und halbamtlichen Äusserungen, Berlin, 1871.

Les origines diplomatiques de la guerre de 1870–1871. Recueil de documents publié par le Ministère des Affaires Etrangères, Paris, 1909 and later, 29 vols.

Treitschke, Heinrich von, *Deutsche Geschichte im 19. Jahrh.,* Leipzig, 1879 and later, 5 vols.

Kaufmann, Georg, *Politische Geschichte Deutschlands im 19. Jahrh.,* Berlin, 1900.

Zwiedeneck-Sudenhorst, F. von, *Deutsche Geschichte von der Auflösung des alten bis zur Gründung des neuen Reichs,* Stuttgart, 1897–1905, 3 vols.

Schnabel, Franz, *Deutsche Geschichte im 19. Jahrh.,* Freiburg i. B., 1929–36, 4 vols.

Mommsen, Wilhelm, *Politische Geschichte von Bismarck bis zur Gegenwart, 1850–1933,* Frankfurt a.M., 1935.

Ward, A. W., *Germany 1815–1890,* Cambridge, 1916–18, 3 vols.

Marriott, J. A. R., and Robertson, C. Grant, *The Evolution of Prussia,* Oxford, 1917.

Dawson, W. H., *The German Empire 1867–1914,* London, 1919, 2 vols.

Gooch, G. P., *Germany,* London, 1925.

Sybel, Heinrich von, *Die Begründung des deutschen Reiches durch Wilhelm I.,* 5th ed., München-Leipzig, 1889–94, 7 vols.

Marcks, Erich, *Der Aufstieg des Reiches, deutsche Geschichte von 1807–1871/78,* Stuttgart, 1936, 2 vols.

Brandenburg, Erich, *Die Reichsgründung,* Leipzig, 1916, 2 vols.

Srbik, Heinrich von, *Deutsche Einheit,* München, 1935, 2 vols.

Ziekursch, Johannes, *Politische Geschichte des neuen deutschen Kaiserreichs,* Frankfurt a.M., 1927, 2 vols.

Maurenbrecher, W., *Gründung des deutschen Reichs, 1859–1871,* Leipzig, 1892.

Biedermann, K., *Dreissig Jahre deutscher Geschichte, 1840–1870,* Breslau, 1896.

Lorenz, Ottokar, *Kaiser Wilhelm I. und die Begründung des Reichs,* Jena, 1902.

Friedjung, Heinrich, *Der Kampf um die Vorherrschaft in Deutschland, 1859–1866,* Stuttgart, 1897–8, 2 vols.

Mehring, Franz, *Geschichte der deutschen Sozialdemokratie,* 11th ed., Stuttgart-Berlin, 1921, 2 vols.

Bernstein, A., *Revolutions- und Reaktionsgeschichte Preussens und Deutschlands von den Märztagen bis zur neuesten Zeit,* Berlin, 1882–4, 3 vols.

Brück, H., *Geschichte der katholischen Kirche im 19. Jahrh.*, Mainz, 1887–1900, 4 vols.

Friedjung, Heinrich, *Österreich von 1848–1860*, Stuttgart-Berlin, 1908, 2 vols.

Favre, Jules, *Gouvernment de la défense nationale*, Paris, 1871–5, 3 vols.

Meinecke, Friedrich, *Weltbürgertum und Nationalstaat*, Stuttgart-Berlin, 1928.

Baumgarten, Hermann, *Historische und politische Aufsätze und Reden*, Strassburg, 1894.

Acton, John Emerich Edward, *Historical Essays and Studies*, London, 1907.

Busch, Wilhelm, *Die Kämpfe um Reichsverfassung und Kaisertum*, Tübingen, 1906.

Binding, Karl, *Die Gründung des Norddeutschen Bundes*, Leipzig, 1889.

Bergsträsser, Ludwig, *Geschichte der Reichsverfassung*, Tubingen, 1914.

Haym, R., *Reden und Redner des ersten preussischen Vereinigten Landtages*, Berlin, 1847.

Heyderhoff, J., and Wenzke, P., *Deutscher Liberalismus im Zeitalter Bismarcks*, Berlin, 1925.

Borries, Kurt, *Preussen im Krimkrieg*, Stuttgart, 1930.

Lettow-Vorbeck, O. von, *Geschichte des Krieges von 1866*, Berlin, 1896–1902, 3 vols.

Moltke, Hellmuth von, *Geschichte des deutsch-französischen Krieges von 1870–1871*, Berlin, 1891.

(Moltke, Hellmuth von, *The Franco-German War of 1870–1871*, London, 1891, 2 vols.)

Jansen, K., *Schleswig-Holsteins Befreiung*, ed. by K. Samwer, Wiesbaden, 1897.

Matschoss, A., *Die Luxemburger Frage*, Breslau, 1902.

Oncken, Hermann, *Die Rheinpolitik Kaiser Napoléons III. von 1863–1870 und der Ursprung des Krieges von 1870–1871*, Berlin-Leipzig, 1926.

Sybel, Heinrich von, *Les droits de l'Allemagne sur l'Alsace et la Lorraine*, Bruxelles, 1871.

Solling, Gustave, *L'Alsace et la Lorraine*, Berlin, 1871.

Michiels, Alfred, *Les droits de la France sur l'Alsace et la Lorraine*, 3rd ed., Bruxelles, 1871.

VI. CONTEMPORARIES

Marcks, Erich, *Kaiser Wilhelm I.*, Leipzig, 1897.

Kaiser und König Wilhelm I., Reden, Proklamationen, Kriegsberichte, etc., von Übernahme der Regentschaft bis zur Eröffnung des ersten deutschen Reichstags, Berlin, 1879.

Wilhelms des Grossen Briefe, Reden und Schriften, ed. by E. Berner, Berlin, 1900.

Ranke, Leopold von, *Friedrich Wilhelm IV.*, Leipzig, 1874 and later (*Sämtliche Werke*, vol. 51, 52.)

Petersdorff, H. von, *Kaiserin Augusta*, Leipzig, 1900.

Poschinger, M. von, *Kaiser Friedrich*, Berlin, 1898–1900, 2 vols.

Philippson, M., *Das Leben Kaiser Friedrichs III.*, Wiesbaden, 1900.

Freytag, Gustav, *Der Kronprinz und die deutsche Kaiserkrone*, 9th ed., Leipzig, 1889.
  (Freytag, Gustav, *The Crown Prince and the German Imperial Crown*, transl., London, 1890.)
Oncken, Hermann, *Grossherzog Friedrich I. von Baden und die deutsche Politik von 1854–1871*, Berlin-Leipzig, 1927.
Srbik, Heinrich von, *Metternich, der Staatsmann und Mensch*, Munchen, 1925, 2 vols.
Bigge, W., *Feldmarschall Graf Moltke*, München, 1900, 2 vols.
Moltke, Hellmuth von, *Gesammelte Schriften und Denkwürdigkeiten*, Berlin, 1891–3, 8 vols.
Elster, Hans Martin, *Graf Albrecht von Roon, sein Leben und Wirken*, Berlin, 1938.
Meinecke, Friedrich, *Radowitz und die deutsche Revolution*, Stuttgart-Berlin, 1913.
Ackermann, E. W., *Georg Frhr. von Vincke und die innere preussische Politik in den Jahren 1845–1849*, Marburg, 1917.
Oncken, Hermann, *Rudolf von Bennigsen, ein deutscher liberaler Politiker*, Stuttgart-Leipzig, 1910, 2 vols.
Freytag, Gustav, *Karl Mathy*, Leipzig, 1870.
Eickhoff, Richard, *Rudolf Virchow*, in *Politische Profile*, Dresden, 1927.
Poschinger, H. von, *Ein Achtundvierziger, Lothar Buchers Leben und Wirken*, Berlin, 1890–4, 3 vols.
Oncken, Hermann, *Ferdinand Lassalle*, 4th ed., Stuttgart-Berlin, 1923.
Sybel, Heinrich von, *Napoléon III.*, Bonn, 1873.
Simpson, Frederick, *Louis Napoléon and the Recovery of France, 1848–56*, 2nd ed., London, 1930.
Guérard, Albert, *Napoléon III*, London, 1945.
Wertheimer, Eduard von, *Graf Julius Andrassy, sein Leben und seine Zeit*, Stuttgart, 1910–13, 3 vols.
Ashley, Evelyn, *Viscount Palmerston*, London, 1879, 2 vols.
Walpole, Spencer, *Lord John Russell*, London, 1889, 2 vols.
Maxwell, Herbert, *The Life and Letters of George, Earl of Clarendon*, Edinburgh, 1893, 2 vols.
Morley, John, *William Ewart Gladstone*, London, 1903, 3 vols.
Monypenny, W. F., and Buckle, G. E., *The Life of Benjamin D'Israeli, Earl of Beaconsfield*, London, 1910–20, 6 vols.

INDEX